Drug Delivery: Principles and Applications

Drug Delivery: Principles and Applications

Edited by Brendon Krauss

hayle medical

New York

Hayle Medical,
750 Third Avenue, 9th Floor,
New York, NY 10017, USA

Visit us on the World Wide Web at:
www.haylemedical.com

ISBN: 978-1-63241-527-1

Cataloging-in-Publication Data

Drug delivery : principles and applications / edited by Brendon Krauss.
p. cm.
Includes bibliographical references and index.
ISBN 978-1-63241-527-1
1. Drug delivery systems. 2. Pharmaceutical technology. I. Krauss, Brendon.
RS199.5 .D78 2018
615.6--dc23

Table of Contents

Preface IX

Chapter 1 **Peptide Carrier-Mediated Non-Covalent Delivery of Unmodified Cisplatin, Methotrexate and other Agents via Intravenous Route to the Brain** 1
Gobinda Sarkar, Geoffry L. Curran, Jann N. Sarkaria, Val J. Lowe, Robert B. Jenkins

Chapter 2 **Pharmacokinetic Changes Induced by Focused Ultrasound in Glioma-Bearing Rats as Measured by Dynamic Contrast-Enhanced MRI** 11
Feng-Yi Yang, Chia-En Ko, Sheng-Yao Huang, I-Fang Chung, Gin-Shin Chen

Chapter 3 **Periadventitial Application of Rapamycin-Loaded Nanoparticles Produces Sustained Inhibition of Vascular Restenosis** 19
Xudong Shi, Guojun Chen, Lian-Wang Guo, Yi Si, Men Zhu, Srikanth Pilla, Bo Liu, Shaoqin Gong, K. Craig Kent

Chapter 4 **Controlled Delivery of Zoledronate Improved Bone Formation Locally *In Vivo*** 31
Wenlong Gou, Xin Wang, Jiang Peng, Qiang Lu, Yu Wang, Aiyuan Wang, Quanyi Guo, Xupeng Gao, Wenjing Xu, Shibi Lu

Chapter 5 **Dual-Layered Nanogel-Coated Hollow Lipid/Polypeptide Conjugate Assemblies for Potential pH-Triggered Intracellular Drug Release** 40
Wen-Hsuan Chiang, Wen-Chia Huang, Ming-Yin Shen, Che-Hsu Wang, Yi-Fong Huang, Sung-Chyr Lin, Chorng-Shyan Chern, Hsin-Cheng Chiu

Chapter 6 **Ergocalciferol and Microcirculatory Function in Chronic Kidney Disease and Concomitant Vitamin D Deficiency: An Exploratory, Double Blind, Randomised Controlled Trial** 51
Gavin Dreyer, Arthur T. Tucker, Steven M. Harwood, Rupert M. Pearse, Martin J. Raftery, Muhammad M. Yaqoob

Chapter 7 **Microfluidic-Enabled Liposomes Elucidate Size-Dependent Transdermal Transport** 62
Renee R. Hood, Eric L. Kendall, Mariana Junqueira, Wyatt N. Vreeland, Zenaide Quezado, Julia C. Finkel, Don L. DeVoe

Chapter 8 **Intracellular Gold Nanoparticles Increase Neuronal Excitability and Aggravate Seizure Activity in the Mouse Brain** 69
Seungmoon Jung, Minji Bang, Byung Sun Kim, Sungmun Lee, Nicholas A. Kotov Bongsoo Kim, Daejong Jeon

Chapter 9 **Effect of Needle Insertion Speed on Tissue Injury, Stress, and Backflow Distribution for Convection-Enhanced Delivery in the Rat Brain** 77
Fernando Casanova, Paul R. Carney, Malisa Sarntinoranont

Chapter 10 **MRI-Based Computational Model of Heterogeneous Tracer Transport following Local Infusion into a Mouse Hind Limb Tumor**...... 92
Kulam Najmudeen Magdoom, Gregory L. Pishko, Lori Rice, Chris Pampo, Dietmar W. Siemann, Malisa Sarntinoranont

Chapter 11 **Novel Epigenetic Target Therapy for Prostate Cancer**...... 103
Ilaria Naldi, Monia Taranta, Lisa Gherardini, Gualtiero Pelosi, Federica Viglione, Settimio Grimaldi, Luca Pani, Caterina Cinti

Chapter 12 **Analysis of Vaginal Microbicide Film Hydration Kinetics by Quantitative Imaging Refractometry**...... 116
Matthew Rinehart, Sheila Grab, Lisa Rohan, David Katz, Adam Wax

Chapter 13 **Autonomous Device for Application in Late-Phase Hemorrhagic Shock Prevention**...... 125
Vlad Oncescu, Seoho Lee, Abdurrahman Gumus, Kolbeinn Karlsson, David Erickson

Chapter 14 **ICAM-1 Targeted Nanogels Loaded with Dexamethasone Alleviate Pulmonary Inflammation**...... 132
M. Carme Coll Ferrer, Vladimir V. Shuvaev, Blaine J. Zern, Russell J. Composto, Vladimir R. Muzykantov, David M. Eckmann

Chapter 15 **Therapeutic Efficacy of Combining PEGylated Liposomal Doxorubicin and Radiofrequency (RF) Ablation: Comparison between Slow-Drug-Releasing, Non-Thermosensitive and Fast-Drug-Releasing, Thermosensitive Nano-Liposomes**...... 139
Alexander V. Andriyanov, Erez Koren, Yechezkel Barenholz, S. Nahum Goldberg

Chapter 16 **Engineering a Segmented Dual-Reservoir Polyurethane Intravaginal Ring for Simultaneous Prevention of HIV Transmission and Unwanted Pregnancy**...... 151
Justin T. Clark, Meredith R. Clark, Namdev B. Shelke, Todd J. Johnson, Eric M. Smith, Andrew K. Andreasen, Joel S. Nebeker, Judit Fabian, David R. Friend, Patrick F. Kiser

Chapter 17 **Bimatoprost-Loaded Ocular Inserts as Sustained Release Drug Delivery Systems for Glaucoma Treatment: *In Vitro* and *In Vivo* Evaluation**...... 165
Juçara Ribeiro Franca, Giselle Foureaux, Leonardo Lima Fuscaldi, Tatiana Gomes Ribeiro, Lívia Bomfim Rodrigues, Renata Bravo, Rachel Oliveira Castilho, Maria Irene Yoshida, Valbert Nascimento Cardoso, Simone Odília Fernandes, Sebastião Cronemberger, Anderson José Ferreira, André Augusto Gomes Faraco

Chapter 18 **Cellular Uptake and Antitumor Activity of DOX-hyd-PEG-FA Nanoparticles**...... 176
Wei-liang Ye, Jiang-bo Du, Bang-le Zhang, Ren Na, Yan-feng Song, Qi-bing Mei, Ming-gao Zhao, Si-yuan Zhou

Chapter 19 **Submicron-Bubble-Enhanced Focused Ultrasound for Blood–Brain Barrier Disruption and Improved CNS Drug Delivery** 192
Ching-Hsiang Fan, Hao-Li Liu, Chien-Yu Ting, Ya-Hsuan Lee, Chih-Ying Huang, Yan-Jung Ma, Kuo-Chen Wei, Tzu-Chen Yen, Chih-Kuang Yeh

Chapter 20 **Efficacy of a Metalloproteinase Inhibitor in Spinal Cord Injured Dogs** 205
Jonathan M. Levine, Noah D. Cohen, Michael Heller, Virginia R. Fajt, Gwendolyn J. Levine, Sharon C. Kerwin, Alpa A. Trivedi, Thomas M. Fandel, Zena Werb, Augusta Modestino, Linda J. Noble-Haeusslein

Permissions

List of Contributors

Index

Preface

Drug delivery is the technique of delivering drugs in the body for the desired results. The goal of drug delivery is to achieve a therapeutic outcome. Pharmaceutical drugs may either be consumed orally or injected into the living organism. This book discusses the fundamentals as well as modern approaches of drug delivery. The objective of the book is to give a general view of the different areas of drug delivery and its applications. As this field is emerging at a rapid pace, the contents of this book will help the readers understand the modern concepts of the subject.

Various studies have approached the subject by analyzing it with a single perspective, but the present book provides diverse methodologies and techniques to address this field. This book contains theories and applications needed for understanding the subject from different perspectives. The aim is to keep the readers informed about the progresses in the field; therefore, the contributions were carefully examined to compile novel researches by specialists from across the globe.

Indeed, the job of the editor is the most crucial and challenging in compiling all chapters into a single book. In the end, I would extend my sincere thanks to the chapter authors for their profound work. I am also thankful for the support provided by my family and colleagues during the compilation of this book.

Editor

1

Peptide Carrier-Mediated Non-Covalent Delivery of Unmodified Cisplatin, Methotrexate and Other Agents via Intravenous Route to the Brain

Gobinda Sarkar[1]*, Geoffry L. Curran[2], Jann N. Sarkaria[3], Val J. Lowe[4], Robert B. Jenkins[1]*

1 Department of Experimental Pathology, Mayo Clinic and Foundation, Rochester, Minnesota, United States of America, **2** Department of Neurology, Mayo Clinic and Foundation, Rochester, Minnesota, United States of America, **3** Department of Radiation Oncology, Mayo Clinic and Foundation, Rochester, Minnesota, United States of America, **4** Department of Nuclear Medicine, Mayo Clinic and Foundation, Rochester, Minnesota, United States of America

Abstract

Background: Rapid pre-clinical evaluation of chemotherapeutic agents against brain cancers and other neurological disorders remains largely unattained due to the presence of the blood-brain barrier (BBB), which limits transport of most therapeutic compounds to the brain. A synthetic peptide carrier, K16ApoE, was previously developed that enabled transport of target proteins to the brain by mimicking a ligand-receptor system. The peptide carrier was found to generate transient BBB permeability, which was utilized for non-covalent delivery of cisplatin, methotrexate and other compounds to the brain.

Approach: Brain delivery of the chemotherapeutics and other agents was achieved either by injecting the carrier peptide and the drugs separately or as a mixture, to the femoral vein. A modification of the method comprised injection of K16ApoE pre-mixed with cetuximab, followed by injection of a 'small-molecule' drug.

Principal findings: Seven-of-seven different small molecules were successfully delivered to the brain via K16ApoE. Depending on the method, brain uptake with K16ApoE was 0.72–1.1% for cisplatin and 0.58–0.92% for methotrexate (34-50-fold and 54–92 fold greater for cisplatin and methotrexate, respectively, with K16ApoE than without). Visually intense brain-uptake of Evans Blue, Light Green SF and Crocein scarlet was also achieved. Direct intracranial injection of EB show locally restricted distribution of the dye in the brain, whereas K16ApoE-mediated intravenous injection of EB resulted in the distribution of the dye throughout the brain. Experiments with insulin suggest that ligand-receptor signaling intrinsic to the BBB provides a natural means for passive transport of some molecules across the BBB.

Significance: The results suggest that the carrier peptide can non-covalently transport various chemotherapeutic agents to the brain. Thus, the method offers an avenue for pre-clinical evaluation of various small and large therapeutic molecules against brain tumors and other neurological disorders.

Editor: Marta M. Alonso, University Hospital of Navarra, Spain

Funding: This work has been funded by the Mayo Clinic and by Bernie and Edith Waterman and the Ting Tsung and Wei Fong Chao Family Foundation. The funders had no role in study design, data collection and analysis, decision to publish, or preparation of the manuscript.

Competing Interests: The authors have declared that no competing interests exist.

* E-mail: sarkar.gobinda@mayo.edu (GS); rjenkins@mayo.edu (RJ)

Introduction

The blood-brain barrier (BBB) severely inhibits the ability to deliver therapeutics to the brain. Indeed, it has been reported that >98% of potential drugs having molecular weights of even <500 Daltons cannot reach the brain because of the BBB [1,2]. Existing methods for delivering drugs to the brain (e.g. convection-enhanced delivery (CED) [3,4], ultrasound-mediated delivery [5]) suffer from several limitations: they can be very invasive, they can compromise drug efficacy; and/or they can cause irreversible damage to the brain [6–8]. Thus, there is a great need for methods that can deliver drugs to the brain while reducing or eliminating these limitations.

Since the BBB poses a serious obstacle to delivering therapeutics to the brain, a damaged BBB associated with brain tumors provides a common avenue for delivering chemotherapeutics. However, the BBB is only marginally disrupted in grade 2 and 3 gliomas. Furthermore, in grade 4 gliomas the BBB damage is limited to the area of vascular damage. In all gliomas neoplastic tumor cells have widely invaded well beyond the region of obvious radiologic involvement. Thus it has been argued that novel methods are urgently needed that can enhance drug delivery throughout the brain beyond the level obtained via a damaged BBB [9].

The BBB harbors receptors that allow transport of cognate protein ligands from the vasculature to the brain through transcytosis [10,11]. Several investigators have utilized such ligand-receptor systems to develop strategies for delivering various proteins to the brain. However, all these methods employ *covalent linking* of the target proteins to a peptide carrier comprised of the receptor-binding domain of a ligand [12,13], an antibody against a receptor [14–16] or to other peptides and proteins deemed to have BBB transport activity [17,18]. Covalent linking of a carrier entity to a protein 'load' involves complex issues such as expertise in linkage chemistry, necessity of purification after linkage, evaluation of functionality after purification etc. Incorporating a given drug into BBB-penetrating nanoparticles also requires considerable efforts to formulate the nanoparticles harboring the drug of choice and a separate method such as CED to deliver the nanoparticles across the BBB [19,20]. Consequently, we sought to develop non-covalent brain delivery methods of therapeutic agents that would avoid these limitations. We have recently reported creation of a carrier peptide (termed K16ApoE) that transported various proteins and immunoglobulins across the BBB in a non-covalent manner [21]. Since cancer therapeutics comprise both large and small-molecule agents, we explored if the carrier peptide would also enable non-covalent delivery of 'small molecules' to the brain.

Based on our previous work [21] we hypothesized that the ApoE-like protein-K16ApoE complex causes conformational change of LDLR-expressing cells at the BBB creating transient pores through which passive transport of other (non-ligand) molecules to the brain can take place. We extend our hypothesis to include the possibility that normal ligand-receptor interactions at the BBB also create transient pores that allow some non-ligand molecules to passively cross the barrier. We have tested these hypotheses in the context of delivering methotrexate (MW 454.4), cisplatin (MW 300.06), Evans Blue (MW960.81), Crocein Scarlet (MW 584.54), Light green SF (MW 792.88), a synthetic 8-amino acid peptide, Y8 (MW 1323) and I-125 to the brain. Our results appear to support the above hypotheses, and illustrate a novel approach to modulate the BBB for systemic delivery of 'drug-size' chemotherapeutics and radioisotopes to the brain in a non-covalent manner.

Materials and Methods

Materials

Ethics Statement: This study was carried out in strict accordance with the recommendations in the Guide for the Care and Use of Laboratory Animals of the National Institutes of Health. The protocol was approved by the Institutional Animal Care and Use Committee (IACUC) of the Mayo Clinic (Protocol number A55911)). All surgery was performed under sodium pentobarbital anesthesia, and all efforts were made to minimize suffering.

Only female mice (B6SJLF1) purchased from the Jackson Laboratories were used. Evans Blue was obtained from Fisher Scientific (catalog# E515),Crocein Scarlet was from Bio Rad (catalog # 161-0417) and Light Green SF was obtained from Sigma-Aldrich (catalog # L1886).

Synthesis of the peptides used was carried out at the Mayo Proteomic Core Facility. The transporter peptide K16ApoE, has the following amino acid sequence (in single-letter code): KKKK KKKK KKKK KKKK LRVR LASH LRKL RKRL LRDA, this peptide had NH2 group at both ends.

Delivery of Various Dyes and other Molecules to the Brain

The femoral vein was catheterized as follows: the medial surface of the left hind limb was first shaved and sterilized with Betadine. A 2-cm incision was made along the mid line of the medial surface of the limb. The skin and muscles were retracted to expose the femoral vein. The vein was catheterized with PE50 polyethylene catheter heat tapered to PE10. The femoral vein was secured with three ligatures as follows: one ligature supported the catheter with attachment to muscle tissue laterally, a second ligature supported the catheter with the femoral vein, and the third ligature was placed medially at the point where the venous catheter was introduced into the femoral vein. The carrier peptide (or other peptides) was first injected through the catheter, the dyes and other small molecules were injected through the same catheter ten minutes after injecting the carrier peptide. In some experiments, the carrier peptide and other molecules such as cisplatin and methotrexate were first mixed and then injected. At the completion of the experiment, the animal was sacrificed with an overdose of sodium pentobarbital (200 mg/Kg, IP). Each animal was then transcardially perfused with PBS followed by perfusion with 10% neutral buffered formalin, and half the brain was processed for analysis.

Brain Imaging by Micro Single Photon Emission Computed Tomography (microSPECT)

Imaging by micro SPECT was conducted on a Gamma Medica X SPECT System (GE Healthcare) [22]. Radiolabeled $^{I-125}$peptide (Y8) or free I-125 was injected 10 minute after injection of the carrier peptide alone or after injection of the carrier peptide mixed with cetuximab or after injection of insulin through the use of a catheter in the femoral vein. After 1 h, each mouse was euthanized and the systemic blood supply was transcardially perfused with 10 ml of phosphate buffered saline, followed by imaging.

Quantification of Cisplatin in Brain

Fresh or frozen brain hemispheres were weighed and then placed in 10 ml glass vials. 2 ml of 70% nitric acid was then added and heated at 120°C to dryness; the process taking ~2 h. This step was repeated once. One ml of 30% hydrogen peroxide was then added, followed by heating at 120°C to dryness; the process taking ~1 h. This step was also repeated once. Finally, the digested product was dissolved in 1 ml of 1% nitric acid. Brain specimens digested this way were sent to the Mayo Clinic Metals Laboratory for quantification of cisplatin by Atomic Absorption Spectrometry.

Quantification of Methotrexate in the Brain

Fresh or frozen brain specimens were sent to the Mayo Clinic Drug and Toxicology laboratory which offers quantification of methotrexate for clinical specimens. Briefly, the method involves weighing the brain followed by homogenization in water. A fixed amount of an internal methotrexate standard is then added to an aliquot of the brain homogenate, and the total amount of methotrexate is then extracted and reconstituted in a reconstitution solution. An aliquot of the reconstituted methotrexate is then analyzed and quantified through LC-MS/MS.

Evaluation of Permeabilization of the BBB by Insulin

Various amounts of insulin (Humulin) were injected into the femoral vein through catheter placed as described earlier. I-125 or other molecules were then injected 10 min after injecting insulin. MicroSPECT imaging was done on post-perfused mice brain as described earlier to quantify amount of I-125 uptake by the brain.

Intracranial Injection of Evans Blue

A Stoelting stereotaxic frame fitted with a custom fit anesthesia inhalation system was devised to deliver 1.5–2% isoflurane with 2 L/min oxygen through the custom fit nose cover. Hair was clipped from the head and the skin was decontaminated with betadine. Ocular lubricant (Artificial Tears) was applied to prevent drying of the eyes. The mouse head was stabilized in the frame using ear bars. A 6 mm midsagittal incision was completed. The following coordinates were located: 1) 2.0 mm posterior to

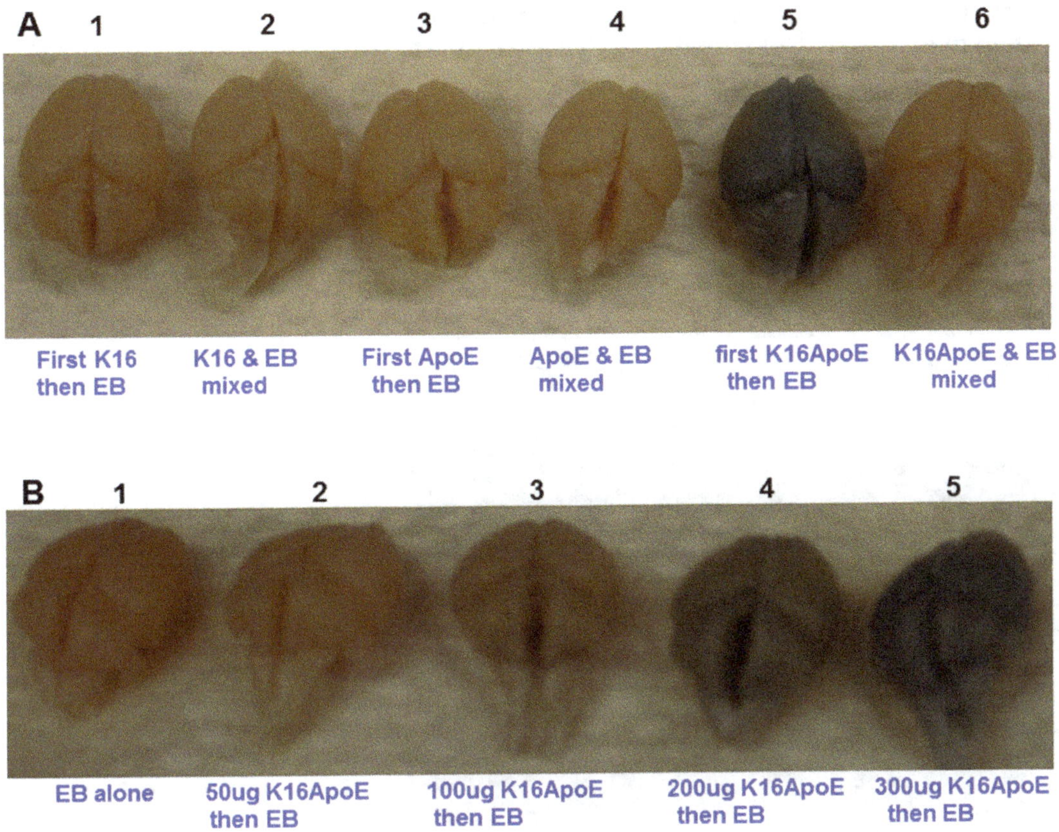

Figure 1. Evaluation of brain delivery of Evans Blue (EB) by various peptides (A) and by different concentration of peptide K16ApoE (B). 67.5 picomoles of each of the peptides (K16, ApoE and K16ApoE) was either injected first followed in 10 min by injection of EB (40 ul of a 2% solution) or the dye and the peptides were mixed together and then injected. Mice were perfused with saline 2 h after injection and then brains were collected for visualization.

bregma, 2) 2.0 mm lateral to midline, 3) 3.0 mm ventral to the surface of the skull. A hole was drilled into the skull using a frame attached Series SR Foredom drill, but did not penetrate the dura. Delivery of Evans Blue was accomplished by using a pre-loaded microinjection syringe (fitted with a 30-gauge needle) attached to the microinjection device holder on the frame. The 30-gauge needle was slowly lowered to 3 mm and the predetermined volume of Evans Blue was injected over 3 min. After injection the needle remained at the predetermined depth for 2 min and then subsequently removed slowly. The skin incision was closed with 3-0 vicryl suture. Each mouse was euthanized at 1 hr post-surgery. The mouse was transcardially perfused with 10 ml phosphate buffered saline pH 7.4.

Results

The Peptide Transporter K16ApoE, can Transport Evans Blue Non-covalently in a Dose-dependent Manner

We previously observed that intra-venous injection of free K16ApoE resulted in transient delivery of beta-galactosidase across the BBB [21]. This observation led us to hypothesize that such transient permeabilization of the BBB by the carrier peptide K16ApoE should allow passive transport of other molecules to the brain. We also hypothesized that molecules smaller in size than beta-galactosidase delivered in this manner would have enhanced passive transport to the brain. To test these hypotheses, we have first evaluated passive non-covalent transport of Evans Blue (EB, MW 960.81) to the brain with prior injection of free K16ApoE or other control peptides. In this experiment, EB was injected after injection of either K16 (a peptide consisting of 16 lysine residues only), ApoE (a 20-aa peptide consisting of the LDLR-binding domain of ApoE), K16ApoE (a 36-aa peptide consisting of the K16 and ApoE peptides) or mixed with each of these peptides and then injected. Visual inspection of the results presented in Figure 1A show that a visible amount of the dye crossed the BBB when the dye was injected after K16ApoE. It is interesting to note that there was no brain-uptake of the dye when K16ApoE and the dye were injected together. Results presented in Figure 1B show that increasing amounts of the dye was transported to the brain with increasing amounts of K16ApoE. These results provide strong evidence that by itself K16ApoE can allow passive delivery of EB to the brain in a non-covalent manner.

K16ApoE Allows other Dye Molecules to be Transported to the Brain Besides Evans Blue

To evaluate if K16ApoE would enable delivery of other molecules to the brain besides EB, we attempted to deliver Crocein Scarlet (MW 584.54) and Light Green SF (MW 792.88) to the brain. In addition to using K16ApoE alone, an alternative strategy was also employed that took advantage of the protein carrying ability of the peptide. This strategy involved mixing K16ApoE with a therapeutic protein (in this instance cetuximab - a monoclonal antibody against EGFR), injecting this mixture, and then injecting the dyes. (Figure S1 demonstrates that K16ApoE

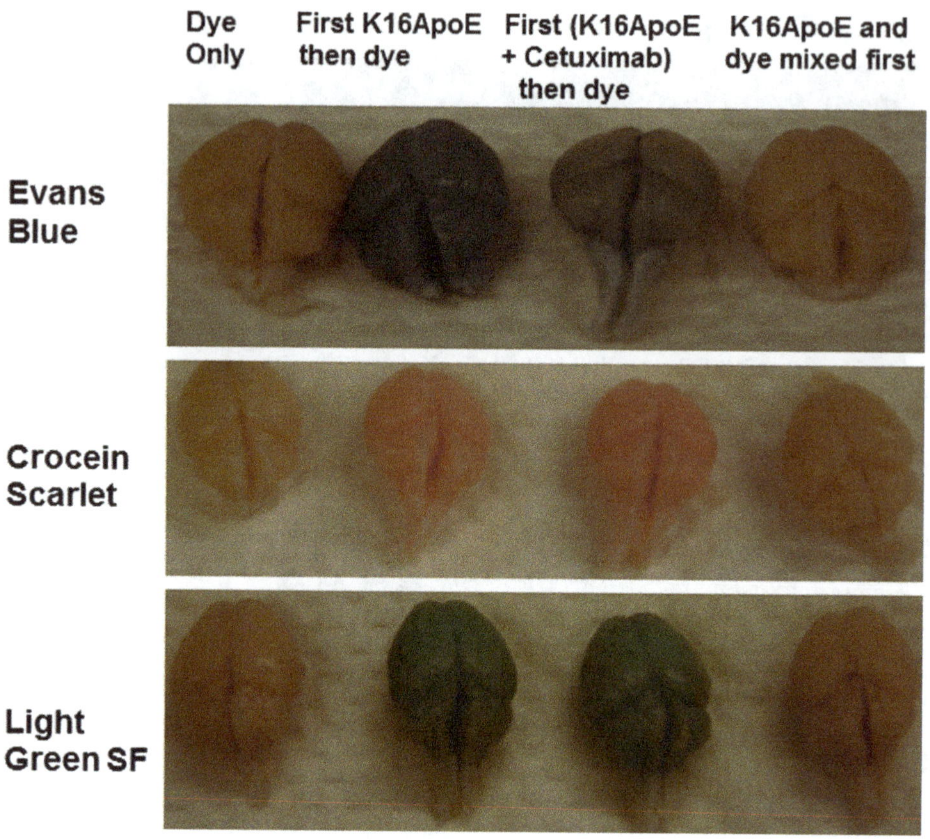

Figure 2. K16ApoE-mediated brain delivery of blue (EB), red (Crocein Scarlet) and green (Light Green SF) dyes to the brain. Three different approaches were assessed for dye delivery: 1. K16ApoE was injected first then a given dye was injected 10 min after (second columns of brain specimens); 2. K16ApoE was mixed with 300 ug of cetuximab and injected followed by injection of a given dye 10 min after 3rd column of brain specimens), and 3. K16ApoE and the dyes were mixed and injected (fourth column of brain specimens). The first column of brain specimens represents animals receiving injection of a given dye alone. Mice were perfused with saline 2 h after injection and then brains were collected for visualization. 67.5 picomole of K16ApoE was used in each experiment. 40 ul of a 2% solution of each of the dyes were used for injection into a 20 g mouse (amount of dye injected varied accordingly with weight of mice).

mediates brain uptake of cetuximab when the two were first mixed and then injected). Results presented in Figure 2 demonstrate that both the original and the alternative strategies can successfully deliver the dye molecules to the brain. Collectively, these results provide strong evidence for the generality of our method for delivering various 'drug-size' molecules to the brain in a non-covalent manner. Brain-uptake of radiolabeled cetuximab was evaluated by microSPECT (Figure S1).

Opening of the BBB by K16ApoE is Transient but EB Delivered via the Peptide Remains in the Brain for a Long Time

Transient opening of the BBB is required for all approaches that attempt to deliver therapeutic agents to the brain. However, to minimize potential toxicity, the duration of BBB permeability must be limited. Limiting the duration of permeability should also facilitate retention of the agent(s). Thus we investigated the duration of permeability and how long molecules remained in the brain.

To ascertain the length of time the BBB remains open after IV administration of K16ApoE, we injected EB from five minutes to 4 h after the injection of the peptide. The intensity of the staining of the brain specimens indicates that the BBB remains permeable for up to 30 min, after which it gradually reverts to normal (Figure 3A). The length of time the BBB remains open after administration of K16ApoE allows an appropriate time-frame for administration of a given drug after injection of the peptide.

To assess the length of time the dye remains within the brain after being delivered by our K16ApoE-mediated method, we injected the peptide followed by EB 10 min later. Brain specimens were collected at different times from 15 min to 24 h after injection of the dye. Visual inspection of the results presented in Figure 3B indicate that a considerable amount of EB delivered in this manner remains in the brain for up to 4 h and lesser amount for up to 24 h. These results imply that a potential drug molecule the size of EB (MW 960.81) delivered to the brain via our method will have a reasonable time-frame to exert its clinical effect.

Delivery and Quantification of Cisplatin, Methotrexate and a Synthetic Peptide Y8 to the Brain via K16ApoE

We explored the delivery of cisplatin (MW 300.06) and methotrexate (MW 454.06) to the brain via K16ApoE for three reasons: First, they are well-established chemotherapeutic agents [23,24]; second, they have in vitro efficacy against glioma [25,26]; and third these drugs poorly cross the BBB [27,28].

We explored three different but related methods to accomplish K16ApoE-mediated brain uptake of cisplatin and methotrexate. In the first, K16ApoE was injected first and then cisplatin or methotrexate was injected 10 min later (method 1). In the second,

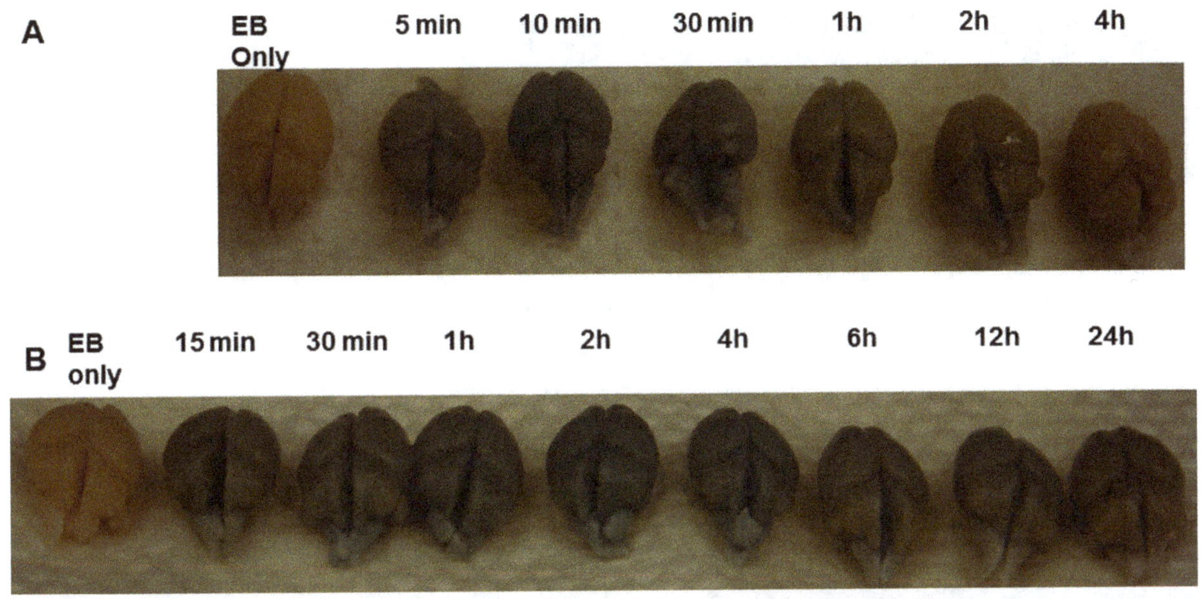

Figure 3. Evaluation of time-frame of BBB permeabilization by K16ApoE and retention-time of EB in the brain delivered by K16ApoE. A- Stains of EB from brain specimens from mice in which K16ApoE was injected first and then EB was injected 5 min, 10 min, 30 min, 1 h, 2 h and 4 h after. Cardiac perfusion was done 1 h after injection of the dye followed by collection of brains. B - Stains of EB from brain specimens from mice in which K16ApoE was injected first and then EB was injected 10 min after. Perfusion was done at indicated times followed by collection of brains.

a mixture of K16ApoE and cetuximab were mixed and injected followed by cisplatin or methotrexate 10 min later (method 2). The third involved one injection of a mixture of K16ApoE with cisplatin or methotrexate (method 3).

Results presented in Table 1 show that all three K16ApoE-mediated approaches allow transport of both cisplatin and methotrexate to the brain. Uptake of cisplatin to the brain appears to be about 0.72–1.14% of the injected dose depending on the method, which is 34-53-fold greater with K16ApoE compared to brain-uptake of cisplatin injected alone. Interestingly, the results also show that comparable brain-uptake of cisplatin occurs irrespective of whether the drug is administered separately (39-fold over cisplatin alone) from K16ApoE or mixed with it (33-fold over cisplatin alone). K16ApoE-mediated brain uptake of methotrexate was 0.54 to 0.92% of the injected dose, which was 54 to 92-fold greater with the carrier peptide than without. Thus,

Table 1. Quantification of K16ApoE-mediated brain-uptake of cisplatin (Cp) and methotrexate (MTX).

Brain uptake of cisplatin (Cp)			
Experimental group	**Brain Cp level (Mean ± SD)**	**Fold change**	**% delivery**
Group 1	64.66±19.21 ng		0.02
Group 2	2557±421.4 ng	39	0.86
Group 3	3417.66±843.01 ng	53	1.14
Group 4	2178±1789.95 ng	34	0.72
Brain uptake of methotrexate (MTX)			
Experimental group	**Brain MTX level (Mean ± SD)**	**Fold change**	**% delivery**
Group 1	22.42±2.26 ng		0.01
Group 2	2745.01±2070.91 ng	92	0.92
Group 3	1618.65±1037.77 ng	54	0.54
Group 4	1735.43±2007.19 ng	58	0.58

300 ug of the carrier peptide K16ApoE, 300 ug of cetuximab and 300 ug of cisplatin (Cp) were used in this experiment. Group 1- these animals received only Cp or MTX. Group 2- these animals received injection of K16ApoE then injection of either Cp or MTX. Group 3- these animals received an injection of K16ApoE mixed with cetuximab, followed by an injection of Cp or MTX. Group 4- these animals received an injection of K16ApoE mixed with Cp or MTX. Post-perfused brains were collected after 1 h of final injection and processed for respective assays. Fold change for Group 2 has been obtained by dividing the mean value for Group 2 by the mean value for group 1; fold change for Group 3 has been obtained by dividing the mean value for this group by the mean value of Group 1, and so on. '% delivery' indicates the fraction of Cp or MTX in brain compared to the injected dose. Six animals in each group have been used.

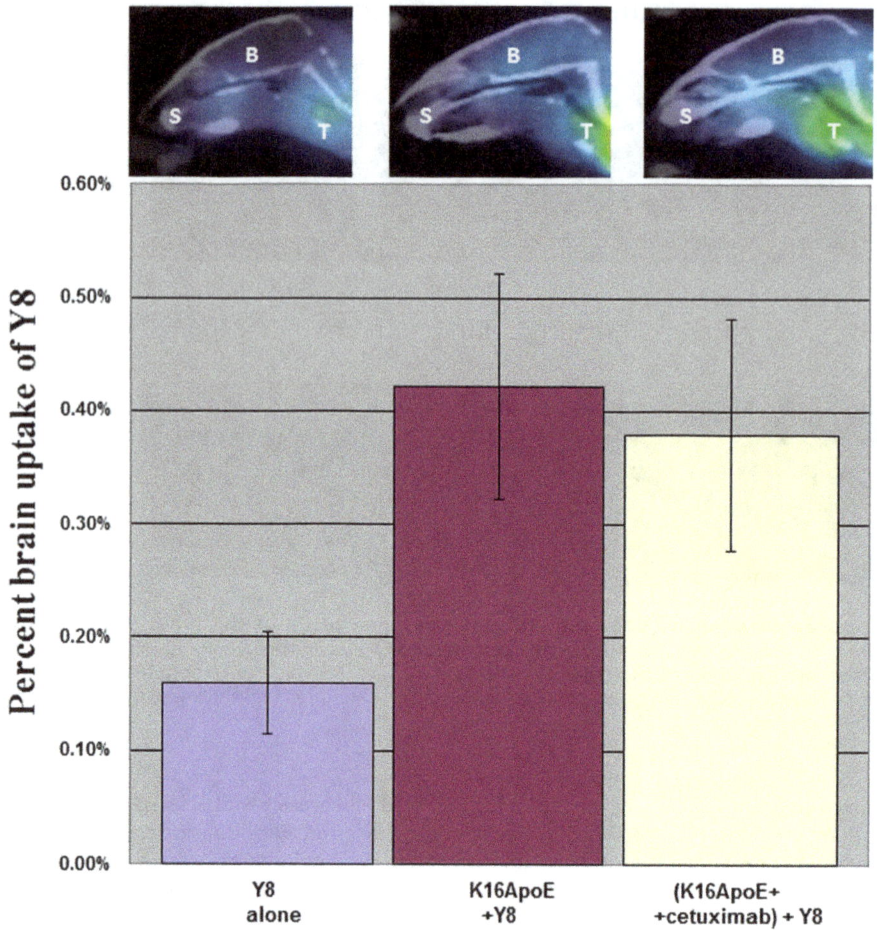

Figure 4. Brain imaging and quantification (via microSPECT) of brain-uptake of Y8 delivered via K16ApoE. $^{I-125}$labeled Y8 was delivered to the brain by first injecting K16ApoE then injecting Y8 as described earlier. Brain delivery of Y8 was also assessed after injection of a mixture of K16ApoE and cetuximab (300 ug of each). A. The bars represent brain uptake of $^{I-125}$labeled Y8 when injected by itself (blue), injected after injection of K16ApoE (majenta) or injected after injection of a mixture of K16ApoE and cetuximab (yellow). Six mice were evaluated for each group. Images of brains by microSPECT representing delivery of $^{I-125}$labeled Y8 at different conditions are presented on top of the bars. Brain images were taken after cardiac perfusion with saline. T- thyroid gland; S – salivary gland; B- brain.

K16ApoE-mediated brain uptake of cisplatin and methotrexate appears to be comparable.

We also quantified brain uptake of a short synthetic peptide consisting of eight tyrosine residues (Y8, MW 1323). Y8 was radio-labeled and uptake quantitated by micro-single photon emission computed tomography (micro-SPECT). Brain-uptake of $^{I-125}$Y8 was measured after prior injection of either K16ApoE or a mixture of K16ApoE and cetuximab. Figure 4A shows that >2.5-fold of Y8 was transported to the brain by either method compared to transport of Y8 by itself. MicroSPECT images of brain specimens presented in Figure 4B provide additional evidence of enhanced brain-uptake of Y8 by K16ApoE.

Administration of Insulin Enhances Brain-uptake of I-125

One conceptual extrapolation of the preceding results is that normal ligand-receptor interactions intrinsic to the BBB may routinely allow passage of additional non-ligand molecules across the barrier. To test this hypothesis, we evaluated BBB permeability after administration of insulin, a ligand having cognate receptors/ transporters on the BBB [29]. Experiments to visually assess brain-uptake of EB via administration of insulin did not show any transport of the dye to the brain. Assuming there is a size limitation of molecules permitted to cross the BBB through transient pores created by a particular ligand-receptor interaction, we decided to assess the permeability of cisplatin, a molecule smaller in size than EB. Three different concentrations of insulin were used: 250 ug, 500 ug and 1000 ug. No increase in brain-uptake of cisplatin was observed at 250 and 500 ug insulin administration. However, ~18% more cisplatin in brain was observed at 1000 ug of insulin compared to administration of cisplatin alone, but the result was not statistically significant (data not shown).

Next, we evaluated if administration of insulin modulates brain-uptake of I-125, a molecule much smaller than either EB or cisplatin. There was no significant increase in the uptake of I-125 after administration of 250 ug and 500 ug of insulin (Figure 5). However, there was 61% more brain-uptake of I-125 when I-125 was injected after administration of 1000 ug of insulin; this increase in brain-uptake of I-125 appeared to be statistically significant ($p<0.05$). It is noteworthy that brain-uptake of I-125 was ~400% greater when injected with K16ApoE compared to administration of I-125 alone ($p<0.00002$).

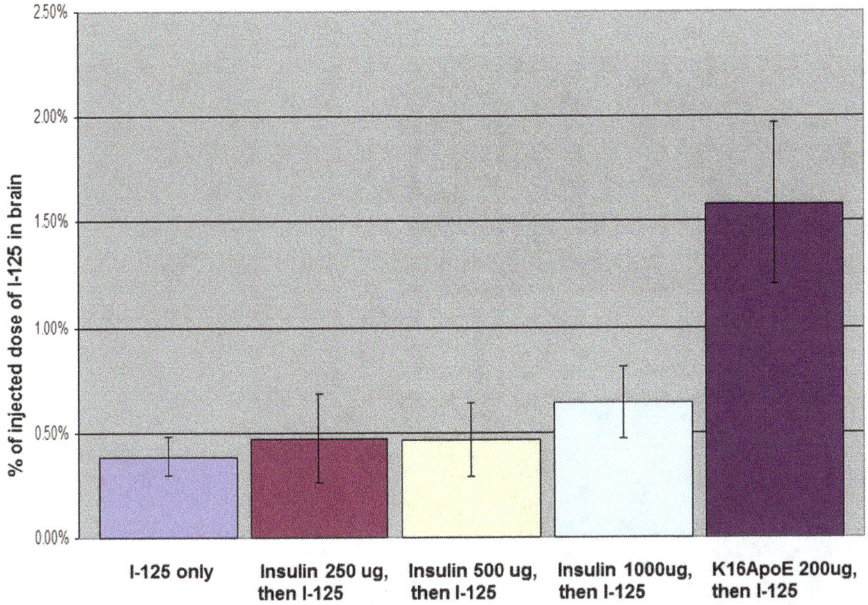

Figure 5. Brain imaging and quantification (via microSPECT) of brain-uptake of I-125 via insulin injection. I-125 was injected 10 min after injection of 250 ug, 500 ug and 1000 ug of insulin, respectively, and 200 ug of K16ApoE. Quantification of I-125 in the brain was done after cardiac perfusion. Six mice were evaluated for each group.

Brain Distribution of Evans Blue (EB) via K16ApoE-mediated Intravenous Injection is Global but is Localized via Intracranial Injection

In many situations, intracranial injection is employed to administer various drugs into the brain. To be acceptable as a realistic drug-delivery method, brain distribution of a drug delivered via K16ApoE-mediated intravenous route should be comparable to that obtained by intracranial injection. To explore a visual comparison of brain distribution of Evans Blue (EB) by direct intracranial injection and by K16ApoE-mediated intravenous injection into the femoral vein, EB was delivered to the brain by both methods. Brains were collected after cardiac perfusion with saline. Photographs of whole brains and half-brains obtained after coronal sections were taken. The results presented in Figure 6, especially after coronal section, clearly show that whereas brain distribution of the dye remain localized after intracranial delivery, it is distributed throughout the brain when delivered via K16ApoE-mediated femoral vein injection.

Discussion

Currently, several strategies have been developed that overcome the restriction imposed by the BBB for delivering therapeutic agents to the brain. In general, these methods rely on physical and/or chemical means to disrupt the BBB transiently for subsequent passage of therapeutics (especially small molecules) across the barrier [30–36]. These methods, however, have several limitations. For example, convection-enhanced delivery requires invasive procedures and can result in ineffective tissue distribution of the drugs injected. Intra-arterial injection of hyperosmolar agents such as mannitol causes reversible disruption of the BBB but the strategy is believed to cause lengthy disruption of the BBB and is also believed to cause significant expansion of the vascular volume. Drug delivery across the BBB by ultrasound generation of microbubbles is currently being investigated in several laboratories. Limitations of this method include controlling the size of the microbubbles, and preventing irreversible damage to blood vessels and endothelial cells [6–8]. Since lipid solubility enhances passive diffusion of a molecule across the BBB, several investigators have pursued such chemical modification (lipidization) to deliver drugs to the brain. However, lipidization is an expensive and time-consuming process, and the process itself may alter the pharmacokinetic properties of the drug [37,38].

In this paper we demonstrate the ability of a synthetic peptide carrier, K16ApoE, to deliver eight different molecules (cisplatin, methotrexate, cetuximab, three different dyes, a synthetic peptide (Y8) and I-125) to the brain without requiring any chemical modification of the molecules. Brain delivery of the molecules is based on the premise that upon injection into the vasculature, K16ApoE binds to proteins in the blood creating apolipoprotein E (ApoE)-like entities. These entities are recognized by LDLR on the endothelial cell surface at the BBB as near-normal ligands and transcytosis is initiated. We further speculate that during ligand-receptor-mediated transcytosis transient pores are formed, which passively allow transport of other molecules to the brain. Since interaction of ApoE-like molecules with LDLR is an active process and since this interaction is speculated to create transient pores across the BBB that allow passive transport of non-ligand molecules, we use the term 'actively-passive transport (APT)' to describe this phenomenon. Conceptually and mechanistically, APT is likely an integral part of the BBB. Indeed, the brain-uptake of I-125 by insulin provides evidence of transient BBB permeability associated with ligand-receptor-based signaling intrinsic to the BBB. Similar data have been reported by Carman et al [39] that demonstrate BBB permeability as a consequence of AR signaling. Thus, APT is a two-step process: transcytosis of a ligand (or a ligand-like molecule such as K16ApoE-bound proteins) through interaction with its receptor at the BBB followed by transient permeabilization of the BBB as a result of transcytosis. We further speculate that most, if not all, ligand-receptor interactions that occur on the cell surface elicit APT probably even at non-BBB locations. At this time, we do not know if APT allows one-way

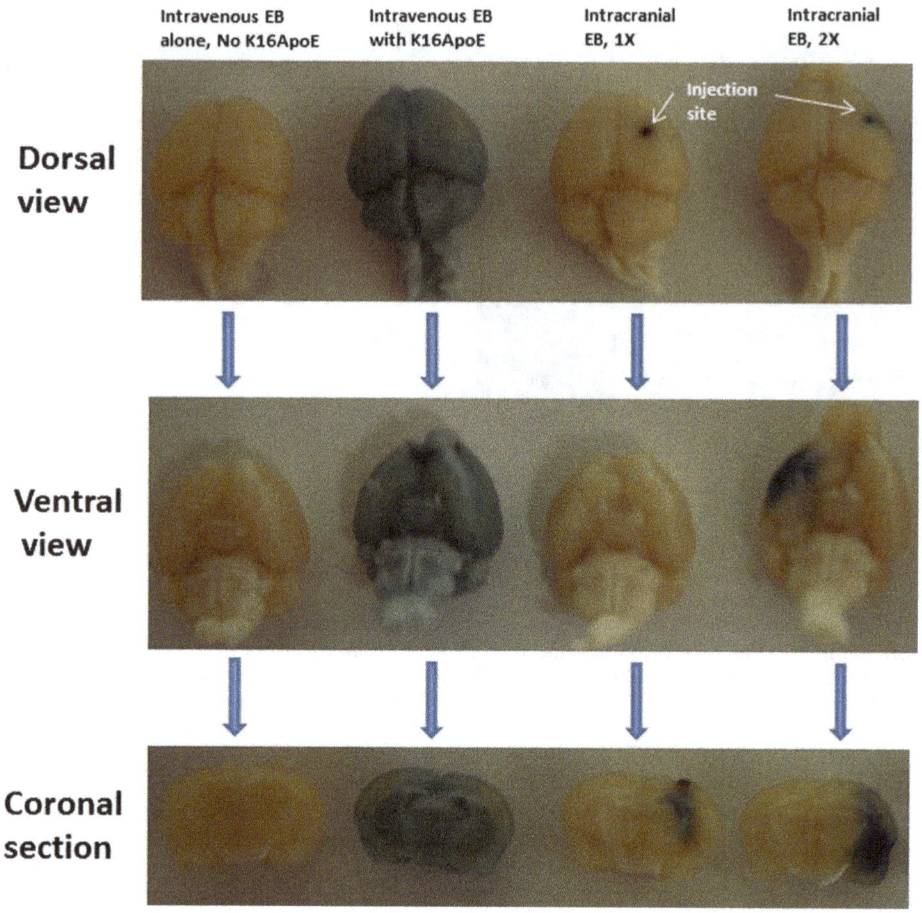

Figure 6. Qualitative comparison of brain uptake of Evans Blue (EB) via direct intracranial and K16ApoE-mediated intravenous injections. Intravenous injection through femoral vein involved delivery of 1mg of EB with or without K16ApoE. Assuming (based on several experiments and results from delivery of cisplatin and methotrexate presented in this paper) 1% of the intravenously-injected molecules reaches into the brain (when delivered via K16ApoE), 10 ug (1X in the Figure) and 20 ug (2X in the Figure) of EB were used for intracranial injection. All animals used in the experiment underwent cardiac perfusion 1 h after delivery of the dye by either method, after which brains were collected and photographed before and after coronal sections were made.

(only to the brain) or two-way (to and from the brain) passage of molecules.

Before proceeding to explore delivery of cisplatin and methotrexate via K16ApoE, we tested K16ApoE-mediated brain-uptake with three dye molecules. No brain-uptake of the dyes was observed when the dyes were first mixed with K16ApoE and then injected. This result may be explained by the possibility that dye binding to K16ApoE blocked the ApoE moiety of the peptide. Thus the complex may have become inaccessible to the LDLR preventing transient opening of the BBB. Indeed, all the three dyes we have used are known to bind to proteins [40–42]. However, the fact that the dyes crossed the BBB when administered separately from the peptide illustrates a practical means to deliver such small molecules to the brain.

We have essentially developed three different APT approaches to delivering various potential drugs to the brain assisted by K16ApoE. In the first, agents that might bind to the transporter peptide and mask its ApoE moiety are delivered to the brain by separate injections of the drug and the peptide. In the second, agents that do not bind to the peptide can be delivered by mixing the two molecules and injecting only once. The third approach may be the most practical – this approach considers the likelihood that K16ApoE injected alone binds proteins (and other entities) in the blood, all of which could transcytose to the brain. This may be undesirable. To minimize such a possibility, K16ApoE can be premixed with any desired protein (human serum albumin, for example) and used as the transporter. We mixed K16ApoE with cetuximab to illustrate that this approach can be adopted to deliver two anti-cancer drugs (such as cetuximab and cisplatin) simultaneously to the brain.

Direct intracranial delivery of a drug is routinely practiced in certain clinical situations. To be effective and acceptable as an alternative and relatively non-invasive means to deliver a drug to the brain, a method in question should allow comparable distribution of the drug in the brain to that obtained by intracranial injection. This premise was explored by delivering Evans Blue by both intracranial and K16ApoE-mediated methods. The results obtained provide a striking contrast in favor of the K16ApoE-mediated approach such that whereas EB was localized in a small area of the brain after intracranial delivery, the dye appeared to have a homogeneous distribution *throughout* the brain when delivered via K16ApoE, suggesting that the K16ApoE-based method is not only able to deliver a molecule to the brain, the method may be preferable over other options since it enables distribution of the molecule throughout the brain, which may be particularly desirable in the treatment of certain brain-associated disorders.

The BBB is practically a 'closed door' in the context of delivering therapeutics to the brain. It is known that receptors at the BBB provide a normal means for the transport of cognate ligands to the brain. Based on the results presented herein, coupled with the reports that the BBB can be transiently opened by activation of the adenosine receptor and endothelial cell B2 receptors by bradykinin [39,43,44], we propose that routine ligand/receptor binding also permits various other molecules to passively cross the barrier. Data presented in Table S1 suggest effective K16ApoE-mediated brain-delivery depends upon size. The effective brain-uptake by this method probably is also influenced by structure of a 'cargo' and other parameters implying that there could be certain molecules which will be resistant to brain-uptake by our method. Consequently, brain-uptake of a given molecule by our method must first be empirically determined before attempting to address its functional relevance to brain-associated parameter. In the future, molecules with defined structural variation without significantly changing molecular weight will need to be systematically created to adequately evaluate structure-activity relationship (SAR) relevant to the method to determine structural parameters of molecules that may have either positive or negative effect on the utility of the delivery method presented herein.

Our approach, in effect, mimics a normal physiological process, which might affect the BBB less than methods which utilize physical or chemical means to open the barrier. Since multiple ligand-receptor based systems are operational at the BBB, it is possible that many of them can be modeled to mimic our strategy. Thus, various combinations of such strategies may be employed to deliver a 'larger' amount of therapeutics, whenever necessary. It may also be possible to deliver a relatively greater amount of a drug to cross the BBB by employing a combination of our approach and inhibitor of efflux pumps [45,46]. In addition, these methods may also be used to lower the conventional dose of BBB-penetrating therapeutics by enhancing their brain-uptake. Very recently, Siegal [47] has put forward five requirements that a chemotherapeutic or a brain-delivery strategy must fulfill to establish its potential to change clinical practice. As such, our method presented herein appears to fulfill three of the five requirements (feasibility of repeated or continuous administration, easy introduction into clinical practice and usefulness irrespective of size and location of a tumor in the brain). Whether our method fulfills the other two requirements (effectiveness and favorable adverse effects profile) will need to be investigated. Thus, future investigation will need to focus on evaluating clinical efficacy of the K16ApoE-mediated brain uptake of therapeutics in the management of patients with brain cancer and other brain-associated disorders. In this context, it is important to note that we have very recently demonstrated near-complete recovery of disease symptoms in a mouse model of Batten disease by K16ApoE-mediated delivery of recombinant tripeptidyl peptidase 1(TPP1) in TPP1 knockout mice [48,49].

Supporting Information

Figure S1 Brain uptake of cetuximab with and without K16ApoE. Different ratios of cetuximab and K16ApoE were used. One animal was evaluated for a given amount of cetuximab and K16ApoE.

Table S1 Relationship between K16ApoE-mediated brain uptake of molecules and their size. Extent of brain uptake of four different molecules with molecular weights ranging from 125 to 1323 daltons are shown.

Acknowledgments

This work was supported by the Mayo Clinic and by Bernie and Edith Waterman and the Ting Tsung and Wei Fong Chao Family Foundation.

Author Contributions

Conceived and designed the experiments: GS GC JS VL RJ. Performed the experiments: GC GS. Analyzed the data: GS GC JS VL RJ. Contributed reagents/materials/analysis tools: RJ VL. Wrote the paper: GS GC JS VL RJ.

References

1. Banks WA (1999) Physiology and pathology of the blood-brain barrier: implications for microbial pathogenesis, drug delivery and neurodegenerative disorders. J Neurovirol 5: 538–555.
2. Lee J-H, Hua Lu H (2011) Chimeric p53 as an alternative therapy for hypoxic tumors. Cancer Biol Ther. 11: 108–110.
3. Hdeib A, Sloan AE (2011) Convection-enhanced delivery of 131I-chTNT-1/B mAB for treatment of high-grade adult gliomas. Expert Opin Biol Ther. 11: 799–806.
4. Kioi M, Husain SR, Croteau D, Kunwar S, Puri RK (2006) Convection-enhanced delivery of interleukin-13 receptor-directed cytotoxin for malignant glioma therapy. Technol Cancer Res Treat.; 5: 239–50.
5. Choi JJ, Feshitan JA, Baseri B, Wang S, Tung YS, et al. (2010) Microbubble-size dependence of focused ultrasound-induced blood-brain barrier opening in mice in vivo. IEEE Trans Biomed Eng. 57: 145–54.
6. Groothuis DR (2000) The blood-brain and blood-tumor barriers: a review of strategies for increasing drug delivery. Neuro Oncol. 2: 45–59.
7. Siegal T, Zylber-Katz E (2002) Strategies for increasing drug delivery to the brain: focus on brain lymphoma. Clin Pharmacokinet. 41: 171–86.
8. Bellavance MA, Blanchette M, Fortin D (2008) Recent advances in blood-brain barrier disruption as a CNS delivery strategy. AAPS J.; 10: 166–77.
9. Steeg PS, Camphausen KA (2011) Smith QR. Brain metastases as preventive and therapeutic targets. Nat Rev Cancer. 11: 352–63.
10. Jefferies WA, Brandon MR, Hunt SV, Williams AF, Gatter KC, et al. (1984) Transferrin receptor on endothelium of brain capillaries. Nature; 312: 162–163.
11. Zlokovic BV, Jovanovic S, Miao W, Samara S, Verma S, et al. (2000) Differential regulation of leptin transport by the choroid plexus and blood-brain barrier and high affinity transport systems for entry into hypothalamus and across the blood-cerebrospinal fluid barrier. Endocrinology. 141: 1434–1441.
12. Spencer BJ, Verma IM (2007) Targeted delivery of proteins across the blood-brain barrier. Proc Natl Acad Sci U S A. 104: 7594–7599.
13. Wang D, El-Amouri SS, Dai M, Kuan C-Y, Hui DY, et al. (2013) Engineering a lysosomal enzyme with a derivative of receptor-binding domain of apoE enables delivery across the blood–brain barrier. PNAS 110: 2999–3004.
14. Boado RJ, Hui EK, Lu JZ, Pardridge WM (2010) Drug targeting of erythropoietin across the primate blood-brain barrier with an IgG molecular Trojan horse. J Pharmacol Exp Ther. 333: 961–969.
15. Deeken JF, Löscher W (2007) The blood-brain barrier and cancer: transporters, treatment, and Trojan horses. Clin Cancer Res. 13: 1663–1674.
16. Dietz GP, Bähr M (2004) Delivery of bioactive molecules into the cell: the Trojan horse approach. Mol Cell Neurosci. 27: 85–131.
17. Karkan D, Pfeifer C, Vitalis TZ, Arthur G, Ujiie M, et al. (2008) A unique carrier for delivery of therapeutic compounds beyond the blood-brain barrier. PLoS One. 3: e2469.
18. Schwarze SR, Ho A, Vocero-Akbani A, Dowdy SF (1999) In vivo protein transduction: delivery of a biologically active protein into the mouse. Science 285: 1569–1572.
19. Zhou J, Patel TR, Sirianni RW, Strohbehn G, Zheng MQ, et al. (2013) Highly penetrative, drug-loaded nanocarriers improve treatment of glioblastoma. Proc Natl Acad Sci U S A. 110: 11751–6.
20. Allard E, Passirani C, Benoit JP (2009) Convection-enhanced delivery of nanocarriers for the treatment of brain tumors. Biomaterials 30: 2302–18.
21. Sarkar G, Curran GL, Mahlum E, Decklever T, Wengenack TM, et al. (2011) A carrier for non-covalent delivery of functional beta-galactosidase and antibodies against amyloid plaques and IgM to the brain. PLoS One. 6(12): e28881.
22. Carlson SK, Classic KL, Hadac EM, Bender CE, Kemp BJ, et al. (2006) In vivo quantitation of intratumoral radioisotope uptake using micro-single photon

emission computed tomography/computed tomography. Mol Imaging Biol. 8: 324–32.
23. Mouzon A, Kerger J, D'Hondt L, Spinewine A (2013) Potential Interactions with Anticancer Agents: A Cross-Sectional Study. Chemotherapy. 59: 85–92.
24. Kudawara I, Aoki Y, Ueda T, Araki N, Naka N, et al. (2013) Neoadjuvant and adjuvant chemotherapy with high-dose ifosfamide, doxorubicin, cisplatin and high-dose methotrexate in non-metastatic osteosarcoma of the extremities: a phase II trial in Japan. J Chemother.; 25: 41–8.
25. Lillehei KO, Kong Q, Withrow SJ, Kleinschmdt-DeMasters B (1996) Efficacy of intralesionally administered cisplatin-impregnated biodegradable polymer for the treatment of 9L gliosarcoma in the rat. Neurosurgery. 39: 1191–7.
26. Dhanikula RS, Argaw A, Bouchard JF, Hildgren P (2008) Methotrexate loaded polyether-copolyester dendrimers for the treatment of gliomas: enhanced efficacy and intratumoral transport capability. Mol Pharm. 5: 105–16.
27. Minami T, Okazaki J, Kawabata A, Kuroda R, Okazaki Y (1998) Penetration of cisplatin into mouse brain by lipopolysaccharide. Toxicology. 130: 107–13.
28. Angelov L, Doolittle ND, Kraemer DF, Siegal T, Barnett GH, et al. (2009) Blood-brain barrier disruption and intra-arterial methotrexate-based therapy for newly diagnosed primary CNS lymphoma: a multi-institutional experience. J Clin Oncol. 27: 3503–9.
29. Banks WA, Owen JB, Erickson MA (2012) Insulin in the brain: there and back again. Pharmacol Ther. 136: 82–93.
30. Marquet F, Tung YS, Teichert T, Ferrera VP, Konofagou EE (2011) Noninvasive, transient and selective blood-brain barrier opening in non-human primates in vivo. PLoS One; 6: e22598.
31. Blanchette M, Fortin D (2011) Blood-brain barrier disruption in the treatment of brain tumors. Methods Mol Biol. 686: 447–63.
32. Cosolo WC, Martinello P, Louis WJ, Christophidis N (1989) Blood-brain barrier disruption using mannitol: time course and electron microscopy studies. Am J Physiol. 256: R443–7.
33. Deng CX (2010) Targeted drug delivery across the blood-brain barrier using ultrasound technique.Ther Deliv. 1: 819–848
34. Mesiwala AH, Farrell L, Wenzel HJ, Silbergeld DL, Crum LA, et al. (2002) High-intensity focused ultrasound selectively disrupts the blood-brain barrier in vivo. Ultrasound Med Biol. 28: 389–400.
35. Sheikov N, McDannold N, Vykhodtseva N, Jolesz F, Hynynen K (2004) Cellular mechanisms of the blood-brain barrier opening induced by ultrasound in presence of microbubbles. Ultrasound Med Biol. 30: 979–89.
36. Hynynen K, McDannold N, Vykhodtseva N, Raymond S, Weissleder R, et al. (2006) Focal disruption of the blood-brain barrier due to 260-kHz ultrasound bursts: a method for molecular imaging and targeted drug delivery. J Neurosurg. 105: 445–54.
37. Waterhouse RN (2003) Determination of lipophilicity and its use as a predictor of bloodbrainbarrier penetration of molecular imaging agents. Mol Imaging Biol. 5: 376–89.
38. Greig NH, Daly EM, Sweeney DJ, Rapoport SI (1990) Pharmacokinetics of chlorambuciltertiarybutyl ester, a lipophilic chlorambucil derivative that achieves and maintains highconcentrations in brain. Cancer Chemother Pharmacol.; 25: 320–5.
39. Carman AJ, Mills JH, Krenz A, Kim DG, Bynoe MS (2011) Adenosine receptor signaling modulates permeability of the blood-brain barrier.J Neurosci.; 31: 13272–80.
40. Stopa B, Rybarska J, Drozd A, Konieczny L, Król M, et al. (2006) Albumin binds self-assembling dyes as specific polymolecular ligands. Int J Biol Macromol. 40: 1–8.
41. Crowle AJ, Cline LJ (1977) An improved stain for immunodiffusion tests. J Immunol Methods 17: 379–81.
42. Mittal A, Kaur D, Mittal J (2009) Batch and bulk removal of a triarylmethane dye, Fast Green FCF, from wastewater by adsorption over waste materials. J Hazard Mater 163: 568–77.
43. Côté J, Savard M, Bovenzi V, Dubuc C, Tremblay L, et al. (2010) Selective tumor blood-brain barrier opening with the kinin B2 receptor agonist [Phe(8)psi(CH(2)NH)Arg(9)]-BK in a F98 glioma rat model: an MRI study. Neuropeptides.; 177–85.
44. Bartus RT, Elliott PJ, Dean RL, Hayward NJ, Nagle TL, et al. (1996) Controlled modulation of BBB permeability using the bradykinin agonist, RMP-7. Exp Neurol. 142: 14–28.
45. Lagas JS, van Waterschoot RA, Sparidans RW, Wagenaar E, Beijnen JH, et al. (2010) Breast cancer resistance protein and P-glycoprotein limit sorafenib brain accumulation. Mol Cancer Ther. 9: 319–26.
46. Agarwal S, Sane R, Gallardo JL, Ohlfest JR, Elmquist WF (2010) Distribution of gefitinib to the brain is limited by P-glycoprotein (ABCB1) and breast cancer resistance protein (ABCG2)-mediated active efflux. J Pharmacol Exp Ther. 334: 147–55.
47. Siegal T (2013) Which drug or drug delivery system can change clinical practice for brain tumor therapy? Neuro Oncol. 6: 656–69. Epub 2013 Mar 15.
48. Meng Y, Sohar I, Sleat DE, Richardson JR, Reuhl KR, et al.(2014) Effective intravenous therapy for neurodegenerative disease with a therapeutic enzyme and a Peptide that mediates delivery to the brain. Mol Ther. 22: 547–53. doi: 10.1038/mt.2013.267. Epub 2013 Dec 26.
49. Sands MS (2014) A hitchhiker's guide to the blood-brain barrier: *In Trans* delivery of a therapeutic enzyme. Mol Ther. 22: 483–484.

2

Pharmacokinetic Changes Induced by Focused Ultrasound in Glioma-Bearing Rats as Measured by Dynamic Contrast-Enhanced MRI

Feng-Yi Yang[1,2]*, Chia-En Ko[1], Sheng-Yao Huang[3], I-Fang Chung[3], Gin-Shin Chen[4]

1 Department of Biomedical Imaging and Radiological Sciences, National Yang-Ming University, Taipei, Taiwan, 2 Biophotonics and Molecular Imaging Research Center, National Yang-Ming University, Taipei, Taiwan, 3 Institute of Biomedical Informatics, National Yang-Ming University, Taipei, Taiwan, 4 Division of Medical Engineering Research, National Health Research Institutes, Miaoli County, Taiwan

Abstract

Focused ultrasound (FUS) combined with microbubbles has been shown to be a noninvasive and targeted drug delivery technique for brain tumor treatment. The purpose of this study was to measure the kinetics of Gadolinium diethylenetriamine pentaacetic acid (Gd-DTPA) in glioma-bearing rats in the presence of FUS-induced blood-brain barrier disruption (BBB-D) by magnetic resonance imaging (MRI). A total of ten glioma-bearing rats (9–12 weeks, 290–340 g) were used in this study. Using dynamic contrast-enhanced (DCE)-MRI, the spatial permeability of FUS-induced BBB-D was evaluated and the kinetic parameters were calculated by a general kinetic model (GKM). The results demonstrate that the mean K_{trans} of the sonicated tumor (0.128±0.019 at 20 min and 0.103±0.023 at 24 h after sonication, respectively) was significantly higher than (2.46-fold at 20 min and 1.78-fold at 24 h) that of the contralateral (non-sonicated) tumor (0.052±0.019 at 20 min and 0.058±0.012 at 24 h after sonication, respectively). In addition, the transfer constant K_{trans} in the sonicated tumor correlated strongly with tissue EB extravasation ($R = 0.95$), which suggests that DCE-MRI may reflect drug accumulation in the brain. Histological observations showed no macroscopic damage except for a few small erythrocyte extravasations. The current study demonstrates that DCE-MRI can monitor the dynamics of the FUS-induced BBB-D process and constitutes a useful tool for quantifying BBB permeability in tumors.

Editor: James Bradley Elder, The Ohio State University Medical Center, United States of America

Funding: The authors have no support or funding to report.

Competing Interests: The authors have declared that no competing interests exist.

* E-mail: fyyang@ ym.edu.tw

Introduction

The blood-brain barrier (BBB) blocks molecules with a molecular weight higher than 180 Dalton due to its physiological and anatomic properties [1,2]. Hence, most potent therapeutic agents might be ineffective if they cannot reach tumor cells lying beyond the BBB. Despite the fact that the integrity of the BBB is often reduced somewhat near a brain tumor, therapeutic agents are rarely effective in patients with brain tumors because the selective permeability of the BBB still limits the agent reaching the target [3]. Recently, the permeability of the BBB can be temporarily increased by focused ultrasound (FUS) in the presence of an ultrasound contrast agent (UCA) [4,5]. This effect is reversible, allowing for a time window during which the chemotherapy must be administered to maximize delivery to the target site of the brain tumor. Previous studies have reported that FUS increases the tumor-to-normal tissue ratio for drugs and increases treatment efficacy in the brain tumor [6–8]. Additionally, repeated use of FUS may be effective for achieving planed high-dose chemotherapy for brain diseases with minimal systemic toxicity [9,10].

Dynamic contrast-enhanced MRI (DCE-MRI) is a noninvasive method for calculating the pharmacokinetic parameters of contrast agent distribution within tissues. DCE-MRI has been widely employed in past research to assess kinetics in tumor-bearing rats [11,12]. The chemical structure, paramagnetic properties, and pharmacokinetics of Gd-DTPA have been described previously [13]. The kinetic models should be adjustable to the properties of the disease to be optimally implemented. In the general kinetic model (GKM), the transfer constant and rate constant between blood plasma and extracellular extravascular space (EES) are defined by K_{trans} and K_{ep}, respectively [14]. When using this modeling approach, a reliable arterial input function (AIF) must be identified to define the concentration of contrast agent in the plasma. Accordingly, vascular permeability can be analyzed quantitatively by DCE-MRI.

FUS-mediated drug delivery requires more information of the mechanism for delivery and models for the transport of drugs across the BBB. The real mechanisms of BBB-D induced by FUS are still unclear. Previous studies have shown that MR imaging signal-intensity changes can be used to determine BBB-D during sonication [15–17]. Furthermore, nuclear imaging can be used to quantify the amount of radiotracer extravasation following FUS-induced BBB-D [18,19]. Dynamic PET imaging was shown to be capable of evaluating lipid materials deposited as the result of sonication [20]. Another study demonstrated that PET scans provide a useful tool for estimating the pharmacokinetics of drugs after administering BBB-D and the optimal therapeutic window for effective radiotherapy [21].

Recently, several studies have characterized the kinetics of the BBB permeability of normal brains after FUS exposure using DCE-MRI [22–24]. However, more information is needed to create an optimum theoretical model for various conditions. Evaluations of brain tumor models are also necessary for investigating whether kinetic models can be translated to situations wherein the vasculature is abnormal. Therefore, in this study, F98 glioma-bearing rats were sonicated and DCE-MRI was used to characterize permeability changes as a function of time after BBB-D. Moreover, the correlation between the transfer constant K_{trans} and tissue EB extravasation in the sonicated tumor was calculated for further confirmation.

Results

BBB permeability dynamics in tumors were assessed for a period of approximately 1 h using serial DCE-MRI after Gd-DTPA administration. Figure 1 shows examples of the two glioma-bearing rats 20 min and 24 h after FUS sonication, respectively. Prior to the Gd-DTPA injection, no enhancement was found in the T1-weighted MR images (Fig. 1, left column). Compared to the control tumor, the increased BBB permeability in the right sonicated tumor was evident from a higher signal enhancement in the MR images, especially 20 min after sonication. This finding confirms that BBB permeability decreased over time following FUS-induced BBB-D.

The middle cerebral artery (MCA) was selected for determining Gd-DTPA concentration in the blood plasma and, subsequently, the parameters of AIF. The AIF was accurately fitted to the bi-exponential equation to yield the mean values of the amplitude constants and decay rates: $(A_1, m_1, A_2, m_2) = (0.168, 0.011, 0, -0.521)$, which were used for the EES concentration fits. Four groups of brain tumors were divided based on FUS sonication and the duration after FUS treatment: 20-min FUS Tumor, 24-h FUS Tumor, 20-min Tumor, and 24-h Tumor. The 20-min FUS Tumor and 24-hr FUS Tumor groups were the tumors sonicated at 20 min and 24 hr, respectively. The groups of 20-min Tumor and 24-h Tumor were the corresponding contralateral control tumors. Figure 2 shows an estimation of the mean changes in Gd-DTPA concentration in the sonicated tumor, contralateral tumor, and the ipsilateral brain. The 20-min FUS Tumor group had the highest concentration of Gd-DTPA in the tumor site. The estimated curves for the changes in Gd-DTPA concentration for the 20-min FUS Tumor group and the 24-hr FUS Tumor group could also be seen to be higher than those of the contralateral tumor for the 20-min Tumor and the 24-h Tumor. The data point groups in Fig. 2 with the lowest Gd-DTPA concentrations are the mean changes in Gd-DTPA concentration in the left contralateral brain and the ipsilateral brain for the 20-min FUS Tumor and the 24-hr FUS Tumor. No significant differences were found among them.

As shown in Fig. 3, EB enters the brain tumors regardless of whether the tumor is sonicated or the control. The representative brain sections indicate that both the size and color intensity of EB in the right sonicated tumors were significantly greater than those in the left control tumors (Fig. 3A). Figure 3B shows the average extravasation of EB (in μg/g of tissue) in the tumor-bearing brains injected intravenously with EB 3 h and 27 h after sonication. In both cases, the degree of EB extravasation in the sonicated tumors was significantly greater than in the unsonicated control tumor. Compared to the tumors injected with EB 3 h after sonication, BBB integrity appeared to have been partially re-established at 27 h, based on the fact that EB administration at this time resulted in a significant difference between the two groups of sonicated tumors.

The mean K_{trans}, and K_{ep} values were derived from DCE-MRIs in the ROI of the sonicated tumor, contralateral tumor, and the ipsilateral brain. Table 1 shows the mean permeability coefficients K_{trans} and K_{ep} using the GKM as well as $v_e = K_{trans}/K_{ep}$ and the corresponding correlation coefficient related to EB extravasation. As expected, the mean K_{trans} in the 20-min FUS Tumor (0.128 ± 0.019) was significantly higher than in the contralateral tumor (0.052 ± 0.019). However, no significant difference was found for the mean K_{trans} between 24-hr FUS Tumor (0.103 ± 0.023) and the contralateral tumor (0.058 ± 0.012) because BBB had been partially recovered at 24 h after FUS exposure. Furthermore, the mean K_{trans} in the contralateral 20-min Tumor and the 24-h Tumor were significantly higher than in the

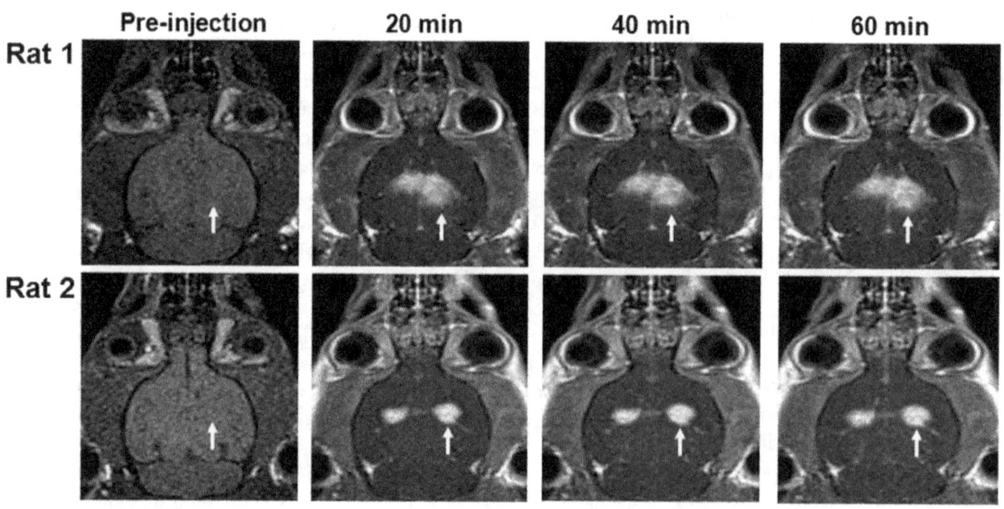

Figure 1. Time series of axial DCE-MRI for FUS-induced BBB-D in brain tumors before and after Gd-DTPA administration. Relative to the control tumor in the left hemispheres, rat 1 and rat 2 show serial contrast changes in the right sonicated brain tumors (arrows) 20 min and 24 h after sonication, respectively.

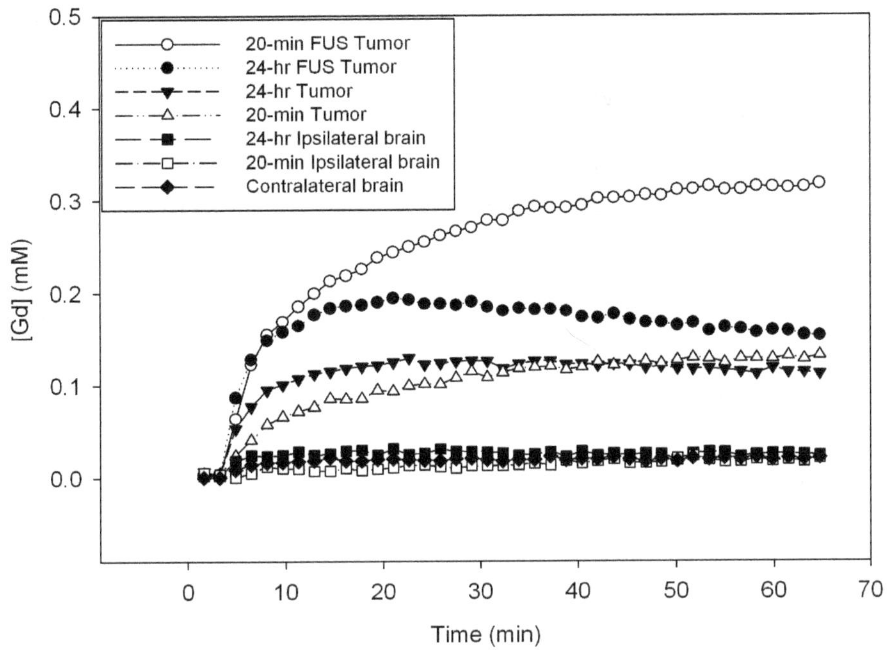

Figure 2. Gd-DTPA concentration as estimated from the ROI in the brain tumor 20 min and 24 h after sonication, ipsilateral brain, and contralateral normal brain.

respective ipsilateral brains. In addition, there was a higher correlation coefficient (0.95) in the brain tumors between the mean K_{trans} and EB extravasation compared with the mean V_e (0.85).

MR images were taken to monitor tumor growth noninvasively as a function of time for tumor-bearing rats 20 min and 24 h after sonication (Fig. 4, left column). Histological observation of the brains obtained from tumors 20 min and 24 h after sonication showed mild extravasation of red blood cells in the sonicated tumor tissues in and around the focal region (Fig. 4, middle and right column).

Discussion

Previous studies have shown that DCE-MRI can be a useful tool for evaluating microvascular permeability and thus drug delivery efficiency through FUS-induced BBB-D in normal brains [22,24]. This study quantified the permeability of the brain tumor to Gd-DTPA after BBB-D was induced by FUS in the presence of microbubbles. Moreover, EB extravasation was used to assess drug accumulation in the brain tumor after DCE-MRI scanning. These two molecules can be used as a surrogate marker for drug delivery because they normally do not enter the brain tissue from blood capillaries. The results reveal that the transfer constant K_{trans} of Gd-DTPA analyzed by DCE-MRI correlated highly with EB extravasation in the brain tumor ($r^2 = 0.95$), suggesting that the kinetics of Gd-DTPA by DCE-MRI can potentially estimate the permeability of the BBB and the accumulation of drugs in the brain tumor after FUS exposure.

Leakage of Gd-DTPA through a defective BBB can be measured quantitatively using DCE-MRI [25]. This technology can characterize the permeability of the BBB in the normal brain after FUS exposure. In this study, the transfer constant K_{trans} in the brain tumor increased significantly after sonication (Table 1). The ability of sonication to increase BBB permeability for the brain tumor is consistent with the findings of earlier studies, which assessed BBB permeability in the normal brain [24,26]. However, the rate constant K_{ep} showed a mild increase but with no significant differences. It has been proposed that there is a direct relationship between the $V_e = K_{trans}/K_{ep}$ value and the quantity of materials in the blood vessel that penetrate into the brain tissue due to BBB disruption. The data indicate that FUS exposure mainly increased Gd-DTPA leakage from the systemic circulation to the EES as well as the value of V_e.

Figure 2 shows the Gd-DTPA concentration in the sonicated tumor, contralateral tumor, and the normal brain during a one-hour MRI scan. After Gd-DTPA administration, the concentration in the sonicated tumor and the contralateral tumor showed a rapid increase during approximately the first 15 min and 10 min, respectively. A longer duration was noted for Gd-DTPA delivery into the sonicated tumor than for delivery into the contralateral tumor. While the effectiveness of the BBB may be partially reduced in the area of a brain tumor, Gd-DTPA uptake was nonetheless significantly impeded by the blood-tumor barrier, compared with the sonicated tumor. Quantitative estimation provided numerical permeability values of the BBB, as shown in Table 1. The permeability value K_{trans} was higher in the 24-h Tumor than in the 20-min Tumor. This was probably due to the fact that the 24-h Tumor group had an additional day for tumor and vascular growth, relative to the 20-min Tumor group. With the ultrasound parameters used in this study, we did find a few minor erythrocyte extravasation in the sonicated tumor from H&E examination (Fig. 4). Future investigation is necessary for understanding whether any side effects are induced from this minor damage.

Despite the growing number of studies, the mechanism of barrier recovery after FUS-induced BBB-D is still unknown. In particular, the duration of BBB-D has been investigated inadequately. Measuring the therapeutic window during which a drug may entered across the BBB is crucial for estimating the accumulation of drugs released in the target region and to optimize dosage. Recently, one study demonstrated a theroretical model to fit DCE-MRI data and derive a calibration curve to

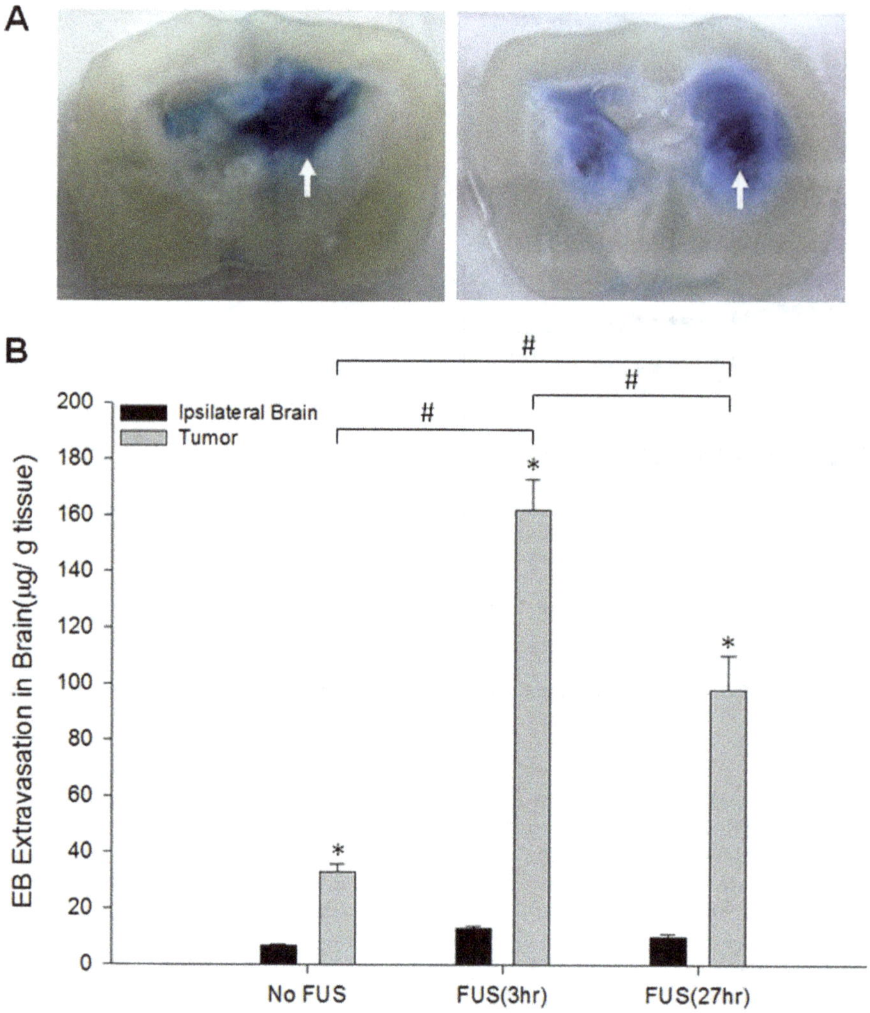

Figure 3. EB extravasation for brain tumors with and without sonication. (A) Distribution of BBB-D in the right brain tumor at 3 h (left column) and at 27 h (right column) after sonication (arrows). Left brain tumor received no sonication as the control tumor. (B) Amount of EB in the control tumor and the sonicated tumor at 3 h and 27 h after FUS exposure. * and # denote significant differences compared with the ipsilateral brain and the tumor, respectively ($^{*,\#}P<0.05$; n = 3).

predict the duration of BBB-D in the normal brain [26]. Investigations in brain tumor models are need to confirm whether this methodology used for normal brains can be translated to tumors wherein vasculature growth is abnormal.

Table 1. Quantitative kinetic parameters estimated from DCE-MRI.

DCE-MRI	Parameters	n	K_{trans}	K_{ep}	V_e
FUS	20 min	5	$0.128 \pm 0.019^{*}$	0.032 ± 0.009	4
Tumor	24 hr	5	0.103 ± 0.023	0.092 ± 0.02	1.12
Contralateral	20 min	5	$0.052 \pm 0.019^{\#}$	0.026 ± 0.013	2
Tumor	24 hr	5	$0.058 \pm 0.012^{\#\#}$	0.077 ± 0.016	0.75
Ipsilateral	20 min	5	0.008 ± 0.003	0.049 ± 0.036	0.16
Brain	24 hr	5	0.017 ± 0.004	0.099 ± 0.018	0.17
EB	R		0.95		0.85

R: Correlation coefficient between the parameter and EB extravasation.
* and #/## denote significant differences compared with the contralateral tumor and ipsilateral brain, respectively ($^{*,\#}P<0.05$, $^{\#\#}P<0.01$).

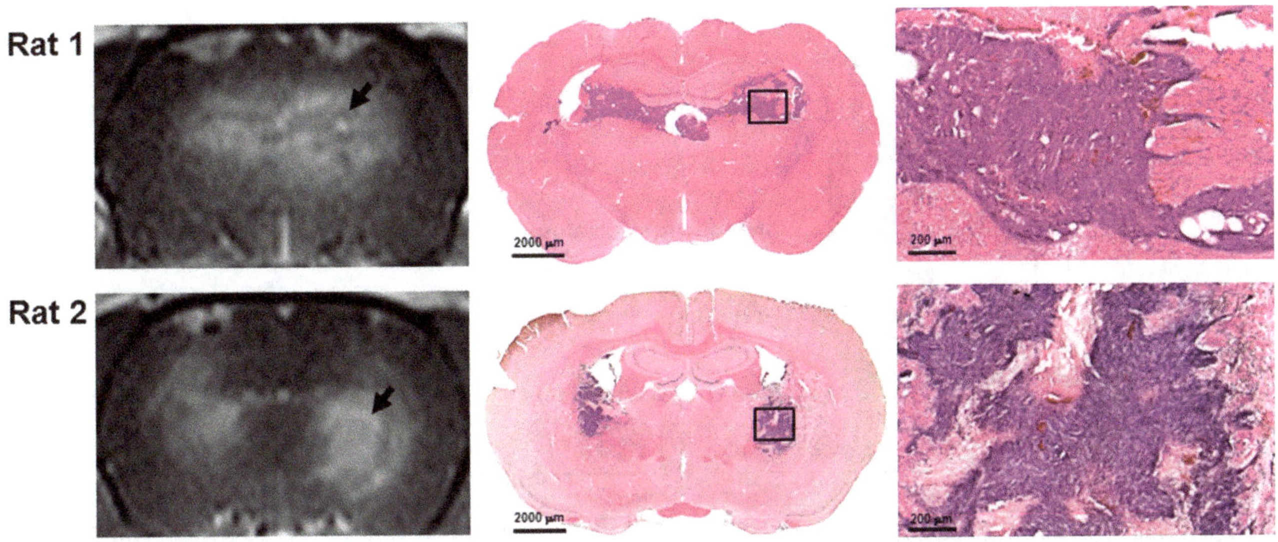

Figure 4. Representative sample of tumors with and without FUS exposure by T1-weighted MR images and hematoxylin-eosin-stained sections on day 8 after implantation. Rat 1 and rat 2 show contrast changes and histology in the right sonicated brain tumors 20 min and 24 h after sonication, respectively. Right column shows the amplification of the rectangular regions in the H&E staining for the whole brain slices. Arrows indicate the brain tumor regions.

In short, this study characterized the kinetics of BBB permeability in the brain tumor model using DCE-MRI and correlated them with measured tissue accumulations of EB in sonicated tumors. The transfer constant K_{trans} and the EB accumulations showed a good linear correlation in the brain tumor. To our knowledge, this is the first ever demonstration of the usefulness of DCE-MRI in the quantitative assessment of BBB in brain tumors after sonication. More research is needed to create a pharmacokinetic model for evaluating the permeability of the capillary, thereby optimizing drug delivery through FUS-induced BBB-D.

Materials and Methods

Brain Tumor Model

A total of ten Fischer 344 rats (9–12 weeks, 290–340 g) were used in this study. Male Fischer 344 rats (11–13 weeks, 250–280 g) were anesthetized with an intraperitoneal administration of pentobarbital at a dose of 40 mg/kg of body weight. Then, 1×10^5 F98 rat glioma cells (a generous gift from Dr. Rolf F. Barth, Ohio State University) in 10 μL Hanks' balanced salt solution without Mg^{2+} and Ca^{2+} were injected into the rats' brains. The tumor cells were stereotactically injected into a single location in each hemisphere (5.0 mm posterior and 3.0 mm lateral to the bregma) of the rat's brain at a depth of 5.0 mm from the brain surface. Finally, the holes in the skull were sealed with bone wax, and the wound was flushed with iodinated alcohol. All glioma-bearing rats were treated with sonication in the right brain hemisphere on day 8 after tumor cell implantation. All procedures were performed according to guidelines and approved by the Animal Care and Use Committee of the National Yang-Ming University.

Focused Ultrasound Setup and Sonication

Ultrasound sonication was generated by a 1.04-MHz, single-element focused transducer (H101MR, Sonic Concepts, Bothell, WA, USA) with a diameter of 64 mm and a curvature radius of 62.64 mm. The half-maximum pressure amplitude diameter and length of the focal zone were 1.5 mm and 8 mm, respectively. The transducer was mounted on a removable cone filled with degassed water, and its tip were sealed with a polyurethane membrane. The experimental ultrasound setup was the same as the one used in our previous study [27]. The rats were anesthetized intraperitoneally with urethane (1.2 g/kg) prior to the experiments. UCA (SonoVue, Bracco International, Amsterdam, the Netherlands) was injected into the femoral vein of the rats approximately 15 s before each sonication. The UCA used in this procedure contained phospholipid-coated microbubbles with a mean diameter of 2.5 μm, at a concentration of 1×10^8 to 5×10^8 bubbles/ml. The transducer was applied with a burst length of 50 ms at a 5% duty cycle and a repetition frequency of 1 Hz. The duration of the sonication time was 60 s at an acoustic power of 4.1 W and a UCA dose of 150 μL/kg. The ultrasound beam was targeted precisely using a stereotaxic apparatus that used the bregma of the skull as an anatomical landmark. Ultrasound exposure was delivered to one location in the right brain hemisphere, centered on the tumor injection site. The schematic diagram of the FUS system for sonication is shown in Fig. 5.

MRI Protocol and Signal Analysis

Each glioma-bearing rat was treated with sonication at the tumor site in the right brain. Immediately or 24 h after sonication, five rats from each group were moved to a 3T MRI system (TRIO 3-T MRI, Siemens MAGNETOM, Germany) for image data acquisition (Fig. 6). A loop coil (Loop Flex Coil, approximately 4 cm in diameter) for RF reception was placed symmetrically under the brain. To detect the position of the MCA for determining the AIF, a set of 3D TOF-MRA (Time-of-Flight magnetic resonance angiography) images was first obtained [28].

Subsequently, 40 sets of T_1-weighted DCE-MRI images were captured to evaluate the permeability of the BBB in the brain tumor before and after FUS exposure. These 40 sets of DCE-MRI images consisted of the two sets of MRI images taken prior to the Gadolinium diethylenetriamine pentaacetic acid (Gd-DTPA, Omniscan, GE Healthcare, Cork, Ireland) injection (1 mmol/kg), referred to as the initial condition of the brain image, and a

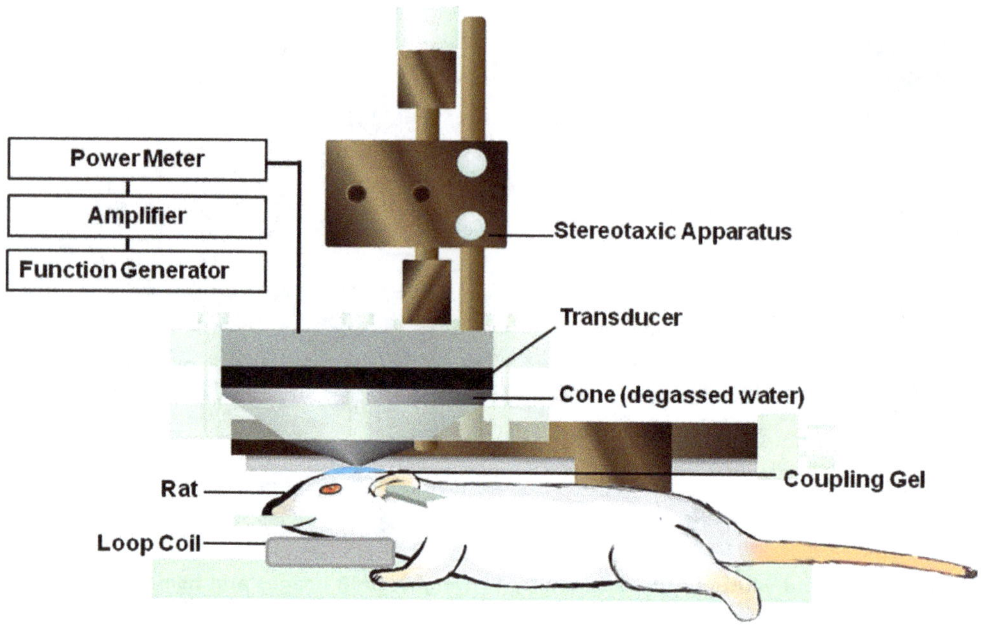

Figure 5. Schematic of the FUS system setup for BBB disruption in rats.

total of 38 sets of DCE-MRI images acquired continuously approximately 1 h after Gd-DTPA injection. The parameters of the images for TOF-MRA and T_1-weighted DCE-MRI are listed in Table 2.

The following procedures were performed for estimating the Gd-DTPA concentration in the sonicated brain region. First, 3 consecutive slices from a set of DCE-MRI images were selected to monitor the sonicated area of the right brain tumor. Then, each of the 3 consecutive DCE-MRI images was set to the region of interest (ROI) of 25 pixels at brighter portions of the sonicated brain tumor. After determining the average strength of the image signals at each of the three ROI, the mean strength of the three averages taken together was calculated to represent the status of the sonicated region in the brain tumor at which point in time the Gd-DTPA penetrated into the tissues due to FUS-induced BBB-D. Finally, the respective mean values from the corresponding DCE-MRI image signals of the 40 points in time were obtained through these two steps, and then a transformation was used to represent the changes in Gd-DTPA concentration in the sonicated brain tumor. Similarly, three ROI of the same size were selected at each point in time in regions of the contralateral brain tumor. The mean value of the signal intensities of the three ROI was calculated for the control tumor group.

Kinetic Model and Data Analysis

The DCE-MRI images were processed by a GKM, which was a generalized form of the Tofts-Kermode model [25]. Several studies have demonstrated the practicability of the GKM in quantitatively assessing the permeability of FUS-induced BBB-D [22–24]. This model is described by the following equation.

$$C_p(t) = A_1 e^{-m_1 t} + A_2 e^{-m_2 t} \quad (1)$$

$$dC_t(t)/dt = K_{trans} C_p(t) - K_{ep} C_t(t) \quad (2)$$

where A_1 and A_2 are amplitude constants, m_1 and m_2 are decay rates, and C_p and $C_t(t)$ are the Gd-DTPA concentrations at time t in the blood plasma and the EES, respectively. The expression of $C_t(t)$ can be obtained by substituting equation (1) into (2):

$$C_t(t) = \frac{K_{trans} A_1}{m_1 - K_{ep}} \left(e^{-K_{ep} t} - e^{-m_1 t}\right) \quad (3)$$

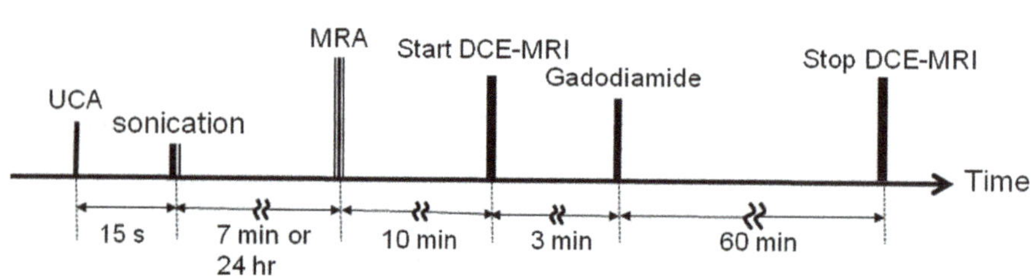

Figure 6. Experimental time line for FUS exposure and the MRI procedure. Fifteen seconds after UCA administration, the sonication was performed before MRA and DCE-MRI scanning.

Table 2. MRI parameters used in this study.

Sequence	Purpose	FOV(mm)	RT(ms)	ET(ms)	Matrix	FA(°)	SL(mm)	No. of slices	ST
GE	3D TOF-MRA	85×85	14	5.42	256×256	20	0.3	108	10 min 27 s
SE T1-W	DCE	47×80	500	13	152×256	-	1.5	22	64 min 40 s

GE: gradient echo, SE T1-W: spin echo T1-weighted sequence, FOV: field of view, RT: Repetition time, ET: Echo time, FA: Flip angle, SL: Slice thickness, ST: Scan time.

The values of the four constants in Eq. (1) can be estimated by using data regarding the Gd-DTPA concentration of the cerebral artery from 40 points over time. K_{trans} and K_{ep} values can be calculated from the data regarding Gd-DTPA concentration in the brain tissue region from the same 40 points over time. The Levenberg-Marquardt fitting algorithm in Matlab was used to estimate those variable values for a selected ROI. The Gd-DTPA concentration in tissues can be calculated from the transformation of DCE-MRI signal intensities using the formula:

$$C_{Gd} = \frac{S_{post} - S_{pre}}{S_{pre} \times T_{10} \times r_1} \tag{4}$$

Here, T_{10} is the T_1 relaxation time of the arterial blood or the brain tissue before Gd-DTPA administration. The values of T_{10} for the brain tissue and arterial blood were 0.9 and 1.5, respectively [29]. r_1 The DCE-MRI relaxivity of the contrast agent r_1 was found to be 4.62 $mM^{-1}s^{-1}$ in the 3T MRI system [30]. $S_{pre}$and S_{post} denote the image signal intensities before and after Gd-DTPA injection, respectively [31]. Furthermore, plasma concentration can be calculated as a fraction of 55% blood concentration, $C_p(t) = 0.55C_b(t)$.

Delivery of Evans Blue

BBB permeability can be quantified based on the extravasation of Evans blue (EB), which acts as a marker for albumin extravasation [18,27]. Here, we used EB to investigate the relationship between the kinetic parameters and the concentration of EB delivered to the sonicated brain tumor. After MRI scanning, EB (Sigma, St. Louis, MO, USA) (100 mg/kg) was injected intravenously 3 h and 27 h following FUS exposure. The rats were sacrificed approximately 4 h after the EB injection. These rats were then perfused with saline through the left ventricle until colorless perfusion fluid appeared from the right atrium. After perfusion and brain removal, the brain was sectioned into three slices (6 mm posterior to the bregma) and mounted on glass slides. The left unsonicated brain tumors acted as the controls. Samples were weighed and then soaked in 50% trichloroacetic acid solution. After homogenization and centrifugation, the extracted dye was diluted with ethanol (1:3), and the amount of dye present was measured using a spectrophotometer (PowerWave 340, BioTek, USA) at 620 nm. The EB present in the tissue samples was quantified using a linear regression standard curve derived from seven concentrations of the dye; the amount of dye is denoted as the absorbance per gram of tissue.

Histology

After MRI scanning, two rats from each group were prepared for histological examination. The rats were perfused with saline and 10% neutral buffered formalin. The brains were removed, embedded in paraffin, and then serially sectioned into 30 μm-thick slices. The slices were stained with hematoxylin and eosin (H&E, Thermo-Scientific, Waltham, MA, USA) to visualize their general cellular structure. Photomicrographs of 5 μm-thickness of the H&E staining tissues were obtained using a Mirax Scan digital microscope slide scanner (Carl Zeiss, Mirax 3D Histech) with a Plan-Apochromatic 20/0.8 objective lens.

Statistical Analysis

The relationship between kinetic parameters (K_{trans} and V_e) and EB extravasation was analyzed by calculating correlation coefficients. All values are shown as means ± SEM. Data analysis was performed using an unpaired Student t test. Values of $p \leq 0.05$ were regarded as statistically significant.

Author Contributions

Conceived and designed the experiments: F-YY. Performed the experiments: F-YY C-EK. Analyzed the data: F-YY C-EK S-YH I-FC. Contributed reagents/materials/analysis tools: F-YY S-YH I-FC G-SC. Wrote the paper: F-YY.

References

1. Kroll RA, Neuwelt EA (1998) Outwitting the blood-brain barrier for therapeutic purposes: osmotic opening and other means. Neurosurgery 42: 1083–1099; discussion 1099–1100.
2. Neuwelt EA, Abbott NJ, Drewes L, Smith QR, Couraud PO, et al. (1999) Cerebrovascular Biology and the various neural barriers: challenges and future directions. Neurosurgery 44: 604–608; discussion 608–609.
3. Black KL, Ningaraj NS (2004) Modulation of brain tumor capillaries for enhanced drug delivery selectively to brain tumor. Cancer Control 11: 165–173.
4. Hynynen K (2008) Ultrasound for drug and gene delivery to the brain. Adv Drug Deliv Rev 60: 1209–1217.
5. Liu Y, Miyoshi H, Nakamura M (2006) Encapsulated ultrasound microbubbles: therapeutic application in drug/gene delivery. J Control Release 114: 89–99.
6. Yang FY, Teng MC, Lu M, Liang HF, Lee YR, et al. (2012) Treating glioblastoma multiforme with selective high-dose liposomal doxorubicin chemotherapy induced by repeated focused ultrasound. Int J Nanomedicine 7: 965–974.
7. Yang FY, Wang HE, Lin GL, Lin HH, Wong TT (2012) Evaluation of the increase in permeability of the blood-brain barrier during tumor progression after pulsed focused ultrasound. Int J Nanomedicine 7: 723–730.
8. Yang FY, Wong TT, Teng MC, Liu RS, Lu M, et al. (2012) Focused ultrasound and interleukin-4 receptor-targeted liposomal doxorubicin for enhanced targeted drug delivery and antitumor effect in glioblastoma multiforme. J Control Release 160: 652–658.
9. Yang FY, Lin YS, Kang KH, Chao TK (2011) Reversible blood-brain barrier disruption by repeated transcranial focused ultrasound allows enhanced extravasation. J Control Release 150: 111–116.
10. Yang FY, Chen CC, Kao YH, Chen CL, Ko CE, et al. (2013) Evaluation of dose distribution of molecular delivery after blood-brain barrier disruption by focused ultrasound with treatment planning. Ultrasound Med Biol 39: 620–627.
11. Su MY, Wang Z, Roth GM, Lao X, Samoszuk MK, et al. (1996) Pharmacokinetic changes induced by vasomodulators in kidneys, livers, muscles, and implanted tumors in rats as measured by dynamic Gd-DTPA-enhanced MRI. Magn Reson Med 36: 868–877.
12. Su MY, Muhler A, Lao X, Nalcioglu O (1998) Tumor characterization with dynamic contrast-enhanced MRI using MR contrast agents of various molecular weights. Magn Reson Med 39: 259–269.
13. Goldstein EJ, Burnett KR, Hansell JR, Casaia J, Dizon J, et al. (1984) Gadolinium DTPA (an NMR proton imaging contrast agent): chemical structure, paramagnetic properties and pharmacokinetics. Physiol Chem Phys Med NMR 16: 97–104.
14. Tofts PS, Brix G, Buckley DL, Evelhoch JL, Henderson E, et al. (1999) Estimating kinetic parameters from dynamic contrast-enhanced T(1)-weighted MRI of a diffusable tracer: standardized quantities and symbols. J Magn Reson Imaging 10: 223–232.
15. Choi JJ, Pernot M, Brown TR, Small SA, Konofagou EE (2007) Spatio-temporal analysis of molecular delivery through the blood-brain barrier using focused ultrasound. Phys Med Biol 52: 5509–5530.
16. Yang FY, Horng SC, Lin YS, Kao YH (2010) Association between contrast-enhanced MR images and blood-brain barrier disruption following transcranial focused ultrasound. J Magn Reson Imaging 32: 593–599.
17. Hynynen K, McDannold N, Vykhodtseva N, Jolesz FA (2001) Noninvasive MR imaging-guided focal opening of the blood-brain barrier in rabbits. Radiology 220: 640–646.
18. Yang FY, Wang HE, Lin GL, Teng MC, Lin HH, et al. (2011) Micro-SPECT/CT-based pharmacokinetic analysis of 99mTc-diethylenetriaminepentaacetic acid in rats with blood-brain barrier disruption induced by focused ultrasound. J Nucl Med 52: 478–484.
19. Yang FY, Wang HE, Liu RS, Teng MC, Li JJ, et al. (2012) Pharmacokinetic analysis of 111 in-labeled liposomal Doxorubicin in murine glioblastoma after blood-brain barrier disruption by focused ultrasound. PLoS One 7: e45468.
20. Tartis MS, Kruse DE, Zheng H, Zhang H, Kheirolomoom A, et al. (2008) Dynamic microPET imaging of ultrasound contrast agents and lipid delivery. J Control Release 131: 160–166.
21. Hsieh CH, Chen YF, Chen FD, Hwang JJ, Chen JC, et al. (2005) Evaluation of pharmacokinetics of 4-borono-2-(18)F-fluoro-L-phenylalanine for boron neutron capture therapy in a glioma-bearing rat model with hyperosmolar blood-brain barrier disruption. J Nucl Med 46: 1858–1865.
22. Park J, Zhang Y, Vykhodtseva N, Jolesz FA, McDannold NJ (2012) The kinetics of blood brain barrier permeability and targeted doxorubicin delivery into brain induced by focused ultrasound. J Control Release 162: 134–142.
23. Vlachos F, Tung YS, Konofagou EE (2010) Permeability assessment of the focused ultrasound-induced blood-brain barrier opening using dynamic contrast-enhanced MRI. Phys Med Biol 55: 5451–5466.
24. Vlachos F, Tung YS, Konofagou E (2011) Permeability dependence study of the focused ultrasound-induced blood-brain barrier opening at distinct pressures and microbubble diameters using DCE-MRI. Magn Reson Med 66: 821–830.
25. Tofts PS, Kermode AG (1991) Measurement of the blood-brain barrier permeability and leakage space using dynamic MR imaging. 1. Fundamental concepts. Magn Reson Med 17: 357–367.
26. Marty B, Larrat B, Van Landeghem M, Robic C, Robert P, et al. (2012) Dynamic study of blood-brain barrier closure after its disruption using ultrasound: a quantitative analysis. J Cereb Blood Flow Metab 32: 1948–1958.
27. Yang FY, Lin GL, Horng SC, Chang TK, Wu SY, et al. (2011) Pulsed high-intensity focused ultrasound enhances the relative permeability of the blood-tumor barrier in a glioma-bearing rat model. IEEE Trans Ultrason Ferroelectr Freq Control 58: 964–970.
28. Peruzzo D, Bertoldo A, Zanderigo F, Cobelli C (2011) Automatic selection of arterial input function on dynamic contrast-enhanced MR images. Comput Methods Prog Biomed 104: e148–e157.
29. Thomas DL, Lythgoe MF, Gadian DG, Ordidge RJ (2006) In vivo measurement of the longitudinal relaxation time of arterial blood (T1a) in the mouse using a pulsed arterial spin labeling approach. Magn Reson Med 55: 943–947.
30. Bilgen M, Narayana PA (2001) A pharmacokinetic model for quantitative evaluation of spinal cord injury with dynamic contrast-enhanced magnetic resonance imaging. Magn Reson Med 46: 1099–1106.
31. Simpson NE, Evelhoch JL (1999) Deuterium NMR tissue perfusion measurements using the tracer uptake approach: II. Comparison with microspheres in tumors. Magn Reson Med 42: 240–247.

3

Periadventitial Application of Rapamycin-Loaded Nanoparticles Produces Sustained Inhibition of Vascular Restenosis

Xudong Shi[1]⁹, Guojun Chen[2,3]⁹, Lian-Wang Guo[1], Yi Si[1], Men Zhu[2,3], Srikanth Pilla[2], Bo Liu[1], Shaoqin Gong[2,3,4]*, K. Craig Kent[1]*

1 Department of Surgery, University of Wisconsin Hospital and Clinics, Madison, Wisconsin, United States of America, **2** Wisconsin Institutes for Discovery, University of Wisconsin, Madison, Wisconsin, United States of America, **3** Materials Science Program, University of Wisconsin, Madison, Wisconsin, United States of America, **4** Department of Biomedical Engineering, University of Wisconsin, Madison, Wisconsin, United States of America

Abstract

Open vascular reconstructions frequently fail due to the development of recurrent disease or intimal hyperplasia (IH). This paper reports a novel drug delivery method using a rapamycin-loaded poly(lactide-co-glycolide) (PLGA) nanoparticles (NPs)/pluronic gel system that can be applied periadventitially around the carotid artery immediately following the open surgery. *In vitro* studies revealed that rapamycin dispersed in pluronic gel was rapidly released over 3 days whereas release of rapamycin from rapamycin-loaded PLGA NPs embedded in pluronic gel was more gradual over 4 weeks. In cultured rat vascular smooth muscle cells (SMCs), rapamycin-loaded NPs produced durable (14 days versus 3 days for free rapamycin) inhibition of phosphorylation of S6 kinase (S6K1), a downstream target in the mTOR pathway. In a rat balloon injury model, periadventitial delivery of rapamycin-loaded NPs produced inhibition of phospho-S6K1 14 days after balloon injury. Immunostaining revealed that rapamycin-loaded NPs reduced SMC proliferation at both 14 and 28 days whereas rapamycin alone suppressed proliferation at day 14 only. Moreover, rapamycin-loaded NPs sustainably suppressed IH for at least 28 days following treatment, whereas rapamycin alone produced suppression on day 14 with rebound of IH by day 28. Since rapamycin, PLGA, and pluronic gel have all been approved by the FDA for other human therapies, this drug delivery method could potentially be translated into human use quickly to prevent failure of open vascular reconstructions.

Editor: Xiaoming He, The Ohio State University, United States of America

Funding: This work was supported by National Heart, Lung, Blood Institute Grant R01-HL-068673 (to KCK) and a grant from National Science Foundation (DMR 1032187 to SG). The funders had no role in study design, data collection and analysis, decision to publish, or preparation of the manuscript.

Competing Interests: The authors have declared that no competing interests exist.

* E-mail: kent@surgery.wisc.edu (KCK); sgong@engr.wisc.edu (SG)

⁹ These authors contributed equally to this work.

Introduction

Over a million vascular reconstructions including more than 300,000 conventional open surgical interventions are performed in the USA each year to treat cardiovascular disease. Unfortunately a large number of these eventually fail due to the development of restenosis or intimal hyperplasia (IH). Despite our in depth understanding of this process and the development of inhibitors, treatments have lagged behind because of the lack of an effective method of drug delivery; this is particularly true for open vascular surgery where there are currently no clinically available methods to prevent recurrent vascular disease. Although systemic drug delivery has been attempted, toxicity has limited its success [1]. In addition systematic therapy cannot provide sufficient therapeutic drug levels at the target artery for a long time. To maintain effective drug concentrations without toxicity, local application is the optimal approach.

Advances in local drug delivery have been made for percutaneous vascular interventions. Both paclitaxel and rapamycin have advanced to clinical use and are currently applied *via* stents or balloons following percutaneous angioplasty. Although this approach has limitations including an increased risk of thrombosis, with the use of these stents, the rate of restenosis has diminished by at least 50% [2]. However, drug-eluting stents are not applicable in the case of open surgical procedures such as bypass, endarterectomy or dialysis access. For these procedures there currently are no viable clinical options for the prevention of restenosis. The result is an unmet clinical need for an effective method of drug delivery following open surgical revascularization. The absence of a technique for drug delivery following open surgery is surprising since the challenges of remote drug delivery following percutaneous angioplasty would seem more formidable than those for open surgery. At the time of open vascular reconstruction, the treated vessel is readily accessible making application of drug more direct and easily achievable. Periadventitial drug delivery has additional advantages, including minimized effect of the drugs on luminal endothelial cell growth due to the creation of a gradient resulting in diminished luminal drug concentrations.

Rapid progress in the field of nanomedicine in recent years offers new promising approaches to diagnose and treat many major diseases including cancers, vascular diseases, infections (*e.g.*,

HIV, malaria, tuberculosis), metabolic disease (*e.g.*, diabetes and osteoporosis), and autoimmune diseases (*e.g.*, glaucoma) [3–5]. Nanoparticles (NPs) encompass a variety of submicron colloidal nanosystems that may be inorganic, liposome-based, or polymer-based. Poly(lactic-co-glycolic acid) (PLGA) NPs are likely the most widely studied drug delivery NPs for the treatment of a broad range of diseases [4,6,7]. The popularity of PLGA NPs can be attributed to a number of factors. (1) PLGA has excellent biocompatibility and has been approved by FDA. (2) The biodegradability of PLGA and similarly, the drug release profiles of PLGA NPs can be conveniently engineered from weeks to months by controlling the chemical structure of PLGA (LA/GA ratio), its molecular weight, and the size of the NPs *etc* [8]. PLGA NPs can be used to encapsulate either hydrophobic drugs or hydrophilic drugs (*e.g.*, nucleic acids and proteins) using well-established emulsion processes. (4) PLGA NPs can provide local, site-specific, and sustained and controlled drug release. (5) PLGA NPs can enhance the cellular uptake of drug *via* endocytosis and may deliver drug to the target tissue/cell much more specifically *via* receptor-medicated endocytosis [6].

Originally used as an anti-fungal agent, rapamycin has been shown to be a potent anti-proliferative and anti-inflammatory drug which inhibits the mTOR-S6 Kinase 1 (S6K1) pathway [9]. Rapamycin also inhibits cell proliferation and inflammatory responses after angioplasty which are contributors to IH [10–12]. Intraluminal rapamycin-eluting stents are effective in suppressing IH, but detrimental late thrombosis develops due to the fact that locally released rapamycin also inhibits endothelial cells [13–15]. Moreover, patients treated with rapamycin-eluting stents still develop IH although to a lesser degree than bare metal stents. The potential use of NPs for the perivascular delivery of rapamycin to treat IH has not been fully explored. Rapamycin-loaded PLGA NPs (hereafter denoted as rapamycin-loaded NPs or rapamycin-NPs) may be potentially an ideal tool to provide sustained drug release to inhibit this process. Although several studies using animal models indicate that periadventitial application of rapamycin is a promising approach, currently there is no established method to provide sustained drug delivery after surgical procedures. Both rapamycin and PLGA are FDA approved, so it is relatively easy to translate these methods to clinical applications [12,14].

Using rapamycin as a model drug and PLGA NPs as the drug carrier, we have developed a drug delivery system that provides combined benefits of periadventitial local drug administration (convenient for application at the time of open surgery) and prolonged drug release resulting in improved efficacy. We found *in vitro*, that NPs were readily taken up by SMCs, allowing for more sustained release of rapamycin, and that rapamycin-loaded NPs produced a more sustained inhibition of S6 kinase than rapamycin alone. *In vivo*, in a rat carotid injury model, rapamycin-loaded NPs led to a more sustained inhibition of S6K1, SMC proliferation, IH and restenosis compared to rapamycin alone. Importantly, treatment with rapamycin-loaded NPs did not affect reendothelialization. Our studies thus suggest that periadventitial application of rapamycin-loaded NPs has a potential to develop into an improved therapeutic strategy for treating restenosis at the time of open vascular reconstructions.

Materials and Methods

Ethics Statement

The experiments involving animal use were carried out in strict accordance with the recommendations in the Guide for the Care and Use of Laboratory Animals of the National Institutes of Health. The protocol (Permit Number: M02273) was approved by the Institutional Animal Care and Use Committee (IACUC) of the University of Wisconsin-Madison. All surgery was performed under isoflurane anesthesia (through inhaling, flow rate 2 ml/min), and all efforts were made to minimize suffering. Animals were euthanized in a chamber gradually filled with CO_2.

Materials

Rapamycin was purchased from LC Laboratories (Woburn, MA). Chloroform (HPLC grade) was from Acros Organics (Fair Lawn, NJ). DMEM and fetal bovine serum (FBS) were from Invitrogen (Calsbad, CA). Poly(D,L-lactide-co-glycolide) (PLGA, 50:50, MW 40 to 75 kDa), poly (vinyl alcohol) (PVA, 95%, hydrolyzed, average MW 95 kDa), dimethyl sulfoxide (DMSO), Tween 80, paraformaldehyde, and FITC were from Sigma-Aldrich (St. Louis, MO). SDS gels (10% acrylamide) were from Bio-Rad (Hercules, CA). The FITC loaded NPs were a product from Phosphorex (Hopkinton, MA). The diameter of FITC-NPs is 220±30 nm; the PLA:PGA ratio of NPs is 50:50. Kolliphor P407 (Poloxamer 407, a poly(ethylene oxide)-poly(propylene oxide)-poly(ethylene oxide) triblock copolymer) was kindly provided by BASF Corporation (Tarrytown, NY) and was used to prepare pluronic gel. Other reagents were purchased from Thermo Fisher Scientific (Fitchburg, WI) unless otherwise stated. TEM grids were purchased from Electron Microscopy Science (Hatfield, PA). The HPLC system is a product of Hitach High Technologies American, Inc. (Dallas, TX).

Rabbit anti-Ki67 antibody was from Abcam (Cambridge, MA); Rat anti-CD31 was from R&D Systems (Minneapolis, MN), antibodies to mTOR, phospho-S6 kinase-1 and S6 kinase-1 were from Cell Signaling Technologies (Danvers, MA); Alexa-468 conjugated secondary antibody was from Invitrogen (Carlsbad, CA). Fluorescence and bright field images were acquired using a Nikon Ti-U Eclipse microscope equipped with the Nikon Elements software packages. Microscopic images were processed and analyzed using the Image J software (NIH).

Preparation of Rapamycin-loaded NPs

Rapamycin-loaded NPs were prepared using a single emulsion (w/o) method as previously described [16,17]. Briefly, 12 mg of rapamycin and 65 mg of PLGA were added into a 100 ml flask. Subsequently, 6.5 ml of chloroform was added to the flask and stirred at 500 rpm at 40°C for 5 h. Thereafter, 26 ml of PVA water solution (3%) was added to the rapamycin/PLGA/chloroform solution followed by sonication using a probe sonicator (UP 100H from Hielscher) at 65% amplitude for 15 min. The resulting solution was stirred vigorously at room temperature for 6 days to evaporate the chloroform. Rapamycin-loaded NPs were collected *via* centrifugation at 22,800×*g* for 20 min at 4°C, and then freeze-dried and stored at −80°C in a desiccator. These rapamycin-NPs were found to be stable at least within a year. Blank PLGA NPs were prepared using a similar procedure without rapamycin.

Characterization of the PLGA NPs

The size distribution of the PLGA NPs dispersed in deionized water was measured using dynamic light scattering (DLS) (Malvern Zetasizer Nano-ZS90, 633 nm laser) at 25.0°C in triplicates. The morphology of the PLGA NPs was studied using transmission electron microscopy (TEM, Tecnai T12 G2) at 120 kV. The PLGA NPs were diluted with deionized water and then deposited on a copper grid coated with carbon. The NPs were negatively stained with 1% phosphotungstic acid solution and dried at room temperature.

Rapamycin loading level and its release rate from the rapamycin-NPs were measured by a high-performance liquid chromatography (HPLC) using ultraviolet (UV) detection at 278 nm. Rapamycin concentration in solution was quantified according to a standard curve established with known concentrations of rapamycin.

Localization of PLGA Nanoparticles in Cultured Vascular SMCs and in Injured Rat Carotid Arteries

Vascular smooth muscle cells (SMCs) were isolated from the thoracoabdominal aorta of male Sprague-Dawley rats based on a protocol described previously [18]. Cells were seeded in 4-well chamber slides with a density of 1×10^4 cells/well in DMEM containing 10% FBS and cultured at 37°C overnight with 5% CO_2 supplied. Then the culture media were changed to DMEM containing 2% FBS with 10 μg/ml fluorescein isothiocyanate (FITC)-loaded nanoparticles (FITC-NPs; 2% FITC loaded). The cells were then fixed by 4% paraformaldehyde at the indicated time points and imaged using fluorescence microscopy. For *in vivo* experiments, 1 mg of FITC-NPs was applied to the outside of the balloon-injured rat carotid artery as we have previously reported [19]. Carotid arteries were retrieved at the indicated time points and embedded in optimal cutting temperature compound (OCT); 5 μm frozen sections were prepared and imaged using a fluorescence microscope (200×).

In Vitro Rapamycin Release Study

To prepare 30% pluronic gel, 3 grams of Poloxamer 407 were dissolved in 10 ml PBS buffer by stirring overnight in the cold room. The *in vitro* rapamycin release profiles from either rapamycin-loaded NPs dispersed in pluronic gel (rapamycin-loaded NPs) or free rapamycin directly dispersed in pluronic gel (rapamycin) were determined in PBS (pH 7.4) containing 0.2% Tween 80 as described [20]. Three mg of rapamycin-loaded NPs or 300 μg of rapamycin in 15 μl DMSO/H_2O (v/v = 9/1) were dispersed in 300 μl of 30% pluronic solution contained in a microfuge tube on ice. The tube was then transferred to a 37°C incubator. After pluronic gel solidified at 37°C, 1 ml of PBS was added. At the indicated time points, microfuge tubes were spun at 22,800×*g* for 5 min to separate the supernatant from the PLGA NPs/gel mixture (recovery rate 99.6%); the supernatant was collected and replaced with fresh PBS buffer. The supernatant was filtered (membrane pore size 200 nm) to remove any uncollected NPs. The rapamycin concentration in the supernatant was then analyzed by HPLC. The drug release tests were conducted four times.

Western Blot

Rapamycin or rapamycin-loaded NPs (15 μg rapamycin for both) dispersed in 100 μl pluronic gel were placed in dialysis tubes with a molecular weight cut off (MWCO) of 10,000 Daltons (Thermo Fisher Scientific; Davenport, IL) that was capable of retaining NPs but not rapamycin. Dialysis tubes were then incubated with cultured smooth muscle cells. Cell culture media were replaced with fresh media every 24 h. Cells were retrieved at the indicated time points and lysed in RIPA buffer (50 mM Tris-HCl, 150 mM NaCl, 1% Nonidet P-40, 0.1% sodium dodecyl sulfate, and 10 μg/ml aprotinin). For *in vivo* experiments, carotid arteries were collected 14 days after surgery and treatment, and homogenized in RIPA buffer. Thirty micrograms of proteins from each sample were separated by SDS-PAGE on 10% gels and then transferred to nitrocellulose membranes. Protein expression was assessed by immunoblotting with rabbit anti-phospho-S6K1 or anti-S6K1 antibodies (Cell Signaling, Boston, MA). After incubation with horseradish peroxidase-conjugated secondary antibodies, specific proteins bands on the membranes were visualized by using enhanced chemiluminescence reagents (Pierce, Davenport, IL).

Cell Viability and Proliferation Assay

Cell proliferation was determined by modified 3-[4,5-dimethylthiazol-2-yl]-2,5-diphenyltetrazolium bromide (MTT) assay (Thermo Fisher Scientific; Davenport, IL). Rapamycin or rapamycin-loaded NPs (both 15 μg rapamycin) was mixed with 100 μl pluronic gel on ice, and then transferred into a microdialysis tube with a molecular weight cut off of 10,000 Dalton (Thermo Fisher Scientific; Davenport, IL). The dialysis media (1.5 ml) was collected (and stored) and replaced with fresh PBS buffer every day. Prior to rapamycin treatment, rat vascular SMCs were plated at 30–40% confluence on a 96-well plate and incubated overnight with 100 μl DMEM containing 10% FBS. Then 30 μl of the dialysis media collected at each time point was added to SMCs and cultured for 96 h. MTT solution (10 μl; 12 mM) in phenol red-free culture medium was added to each well and incubated at 37°C for 4 h followed by addition of 100 μl of the SDS-HCL solution. After incubation of the plate at 37°C for 4 h, absorbance was measured at 570 nm.

Rat Carotid Artery Balloon Injury and in vivo Drug Delivery

Male Sprague-Dawley rats (~350 g) underwent carotid artery balloon injury. Briefly, after induction of anesthesia with isofluorane, a longitudinal incision was made in the neck. A 2-F balloon catheter (Edwards Lifesciences, Irvine, CA) was inserted through the left external carotid artery and inflated to a pressure of 2 atm to simulate the angioplasty procedure. Blood flow was re-established after injury. Rapamycin or rapamycin-NPs (100 μg rapamycin per 100 g body weight) was dissolved in 300 μl of 30% pluronic gel which remained as liquid on ice. The pluronic gel solution was then applied around the outside of the injured segment of carotid artery [19]. The gel solidified immediately after exposure to body temperature.

Tissue Processing

Animals were sacrificed and perfused with 4% paraformaldehyde at the pressure of 100 mmHg on day 14 or day 28 after surgery; then the carotid arteries were retrieved and processed for embedding and sectioning. Serial cross-sections were made at 50 μm intervals and used for histological analysis and immunostaining.

Immunohistochemistry (IHC)

Paraffin-embedded artery sections were immunostained with rabbit anti-Ki67 antibody (Cambridge, MA) and detected using goat anti-rabbit HRP conjugate IgG, developed in 3,3′ diaminobenzidine (DAB) solution, and followed by a counterstain of hematoxylin.

Immunofluorescent staining was performed on paraffin-embedded sections with rat anti- CD31antibpody (R&D Systems, MN; 1:400), signals were detected using donkey anti-rat Alexa Fluor 546 antibody (Invitrogen; Carlsbad, CA). DAPI was used to identify nuclei. Antibody controls included species-matched normal rabbit IgG antibodies.

Quantification of IHC Results

Five stained tissue sections from each animal were used. On each section images were taken from six different fields (magnification 200×). The Ki67 positive cells were manually counted. The number of Ki67 positive cells in each 200× image was defined as Ki67 positive (cells) per high power field (HPF). The data were pooled to generate the mean and standard deviation for each animal. The means from each of 5 animals were averaged, and the standard error of the mean (SEM) was calculated for each group.

For quantification of reendothelialization, previously published methods were used with minor modifications [21,22]. Briefly, the luminal perimeter and the percentage of this perimeter that stained for CD31 on serial sections (n = 5) were measured using NIH Image J. The percentage of reendothelialization was then scored from 1 to 5 (1: <20%; 2:20 to 40%; 3:40 to 60%; 4:60 to 80%; 5:80%–100%) and the scores were averaged.

Morphometric Analysis

Morphometric study was performed using H&E-stained paraffin sections of the carotid arteries. The areas enclosed by the external elastic lamina (EEL), the internal elastic lamina (IEL), and the luminal area were measured using the NIH Image J software as previously described [23]. Intimal area (IEL area minus luminal area) and medial area (EEL area minus IEL area) and their ratio (I/M ratio) were then calculated. Five sections per animal were used and a mean ± SEM was derived from at least three independent experiments. Data were analyzed by one-way analysis of variance (ANOVA). If significant, the ANOVA was followed by Turkeys multiple comparison test. P values less than 0.05 are considered statistically significant.

Results

Preparation and Characterization of Rapamycin-loaded NPs

Rapamycin was encapsulated in PLGA NPs *via* a single emulsion method. PVA was coated on the surface of PLGA NPs to enhance their solubility/dispensability in aqueous solutions. The rapamycin encapsulation efficiency and loading level in the PLGA NPs were of 69.1% and 11.6%, respectively. Figure 1A shows a representative transmission electron microscopy (TEM) image of the rapamycin-loaded NPs. The average diameter of the NPs was around 250 nm. The size distribution of the rapamycin-loaded NPs measured by DLS (Figure 1B) ranged from 220 to 350 nm with an average diameter around 265 nm, which was in agreement with the TEM analysis.

To evaluate the comparative release of rapamycin or rapamycin-loaded NPs *in vitro,* both were dispersed in pluronic gel to mimic our *in vivo* model. The amount of released rapamycin was determined by HPLC. For rapamycin dispersed directly in pluronic gel, the amount of drug released after 2, 4, and 5 days was 50.0%, 78.4% and 86.4%, respectively. In contrast, sustained drug release was observed for 28 days from the rapamycin-loaded NPs dispersed in pluronic gel (Figure 1C). In both studies, pluronic gel dissolved after 3–4 days. The release of rapamycin from the rapamycin-NPs-Gel system exhibited a well-defined tri-phasic profile [20]. The initial burst of release of rapamycin during the first 4 days is likely attributed to the release of rapamycin near the surface of the PLGA NPs (Figure 1C). During the second phase of rapamycin release (5 to 15 days), rapamycin was released slowly from the PLGA NPs *via* a diffusion-controlled process [24,25]. During the third phase (16 to 28 days), there was relatively rapid release of rapamycin again (16 to 21 days) likely attributable to the degradation and erosion of PLGA NPs [6,26,27], and then there was very minimal release of rapamycin after 21 days. These results demonstrate that rapamycin-loaded NPs dispersed in pluronic gel provide drug release in a more sustainable manner than rapamycin directly contained in a pluronic gel.

Uptake of NPs by SMCs *in vitro* and After Periadventitial Application Around Injured Rat Carotid Arteries

To evaluate the cellular absorption and distribution of NPs *in vitro,* FITC-loaded PLGA NPs (FITC-NPs) were applied to cultured vascular SMCs as described in Methods. As is evident in Figure 2A, FITC-NPs were readily taken up by SMCs as early as 2 hours and NPs accumulated primarily in the cytoplasm. Punctate collections of nanoparticles were observed by 24 hours. We then investigated whether PLGA NPs could be readily dispersed into the arterial wall. FITC-NPs in pluronic gel were applied to the adventitia of rat carotid arteries immediately after balloon injury. We found at 24 h, FITC-NPs were localized around and within the adventitia of the injured carotid arteries (Figure 2B). At 72 h, after dissolution of the pluronic gel, FITC-NPs had migrated into the arterial wall as well as into the loose connective tissues that surround the artery (Figure 2B). Only a small portion of FITC-NPs was located in the arterial wall compared to the total applied amount, probably because of fast dissolution of pluronic gel, emphasizing the need to develop long-lasting gels in the future for *in vivo* applications.

Rapamycin-loaded NPs Produce Sustained Drug Release *in vitro* and *in vivo* in Balloon-injured Rat Carotid Arteries

After confirming uptake of NPs by SMCs *in vitro* and distribution into the arterial wall *in vivo,* we next examined the functional effect of drug release from rapamycin-loaded NPs on SMCs *in vitro* and on cells of the arterial wall. Previous studies have shown that rapamycin halts cell cycle progression by specifically targeting the mTOR pathway and inhibiting the phosphorylation of downstream S6K1 [9,28]. We first compared the inhibitory effect of rapamycin-loaded NPs with that of free rapamycin on S6K1 phosphorylation in cultured SMCs. Rapamycin or rapamycin-loaded NPs dispersed in pluronic gel were placed in a dialysis tube, capable of retaining NPs but allowing the release of rapamycin into the culture dish. Cells were seeded with a low density to allow their long term viability. Cell culture media were replaced with fresh media every 24 h. SMCs were then collected at the specified time points, and S6K1 phosphorylation was evaluated by Western blotting. Whereas free rapamycin inhibited S6K1 phosphorylation for only 3 days following treatment, rapamycin-loaded NPs significantly suppressed S6K1 phosphorylation for up to 14 days (Figure 3A, panels a and b). A similar pattern was observed regarding the effect of rapamycin-loaded NPs and rapamycin on SMC proliferation (Figure 3A, panels c and d). These results suggest that rapamycin-loaded NPs facilitated prolonged drug release which produced a sustained inhibitory effect on SMC function as evidenced by S6K phosphorylation.

Since the *in vitro* data indicated that on day 14 rapamycin-loaded NPs but not free rapamycin suppressed S6K1 phosphorylation (Figure 3A), we then assessed using that same time point whether perivascular application of rapamycin-loaded NPs provided prolonged drug release into the arterial wall compared to rapamycin alone (Figure 3B). We again used S6K1 phosphorylation as a surrogate for measuring rapamycin's functional effect. We placed rapamycin-loaded NPs or rapamycin alone in pluronic gel, which was then applied to the outside of balloon-injured rat carotid arteries. Arteries were retrieved 14 days after balloon injury and drug application. Proteins were then extracted and Western blotting was performed to examine S6K1 phosphorylation. Consistent with our *in vitro* findings, S6K1 phosphorylation

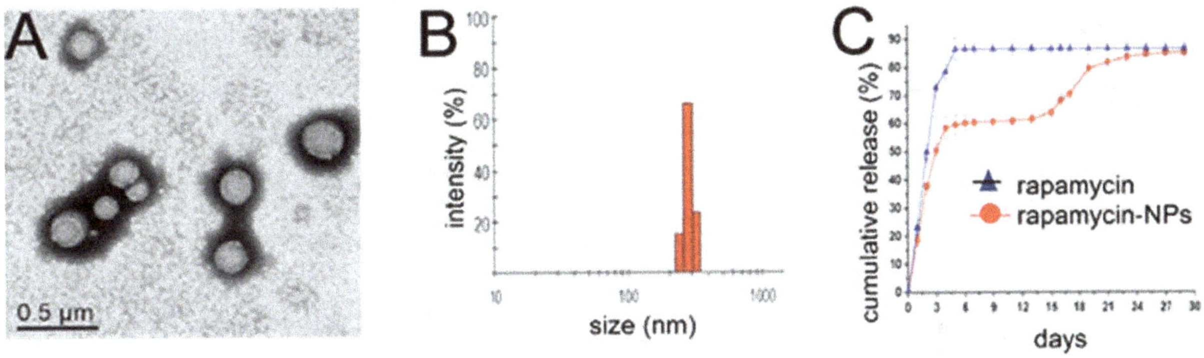

Figure 1. Characterization of rapamycin-loaded PLGA NPs (rapamycin-NPs) *in vitro.* (A). Transmission electron microscopy (TEM) image of rapamycin-NPs. (B). Size distribution of the rapamycin-NPs measured by dynamic light scattering analysis (DLS). (C). *In vitro* cumulative rapamycin release profiles from rapamycin-NPs (●, red) or free rapamycin (▲, blue), both encapsulated in pluronic gel immersed in PBS buffer. Data are presented as mean as mean). (C). ing analysis (DLS). (C.

on day 14 following treatment was reduced by ~70% in the rapamycin-NPs-treated group, however no significant effect was observed in the group treated with rapamycin alone (Figure 3B). Together, our data demonstrate that rapamycin-loaded NPs versus free rapamycin, provide sustained inhibition of S6K1 phosphorylation in SMCs both *in vitro* and *in vivo*. These findings suggest that a drug delivery strategy employing NPs can provide prolonged drug release with more sustained functional effects.

Periadventitial Administration of Rapamycin-loaded NPs Produces Sustained Inhibition of Intimal Hyperplasia (IH)

Encouraged by the observed sustained functional effect of rapamycin-loaded NPs compared to free rapamycin, we evaluated the comparative ability of both approaches to inhibit intimal hyperplasia in a rat carotid artery injury model. Rapamycin-loaded NPs or free rapamycin were placed in pluronic gel and applied around the carotid artery immediately following balloon injury. For controls, we applied the solvent for rapamycin (DMSO) or unloaded NPs in pluronic gel. Arteries were retrieved 14 days or 28 days following treatment. As shown in Figure 4A at 14 days compared to both controls, intimal hyperplasia (measured by the I/M ratio) was markedly reduced and the arterial lumen was significantly greater in arteries treated with either rapamycin alone or rapamycin-loaded NPs. Thus, at 14 days both treatments were equally effective. Twenty-eight days after treatment there was sustained inhibition of IH and maintenance of lumen size in animals treated with rapamycin-loaded NPs. However, in animals treated with free rapamycin in pluronic gel, IH returned to a level similar to untreated controls with a corresponding diminution in lumen diameter (Figure 4B). These results suggest that sustained drug release from rapamycin-loaded NPs prolonged the inhibitory effect of rapamycin on IH leading to a durably patent vessel following arterial injury.

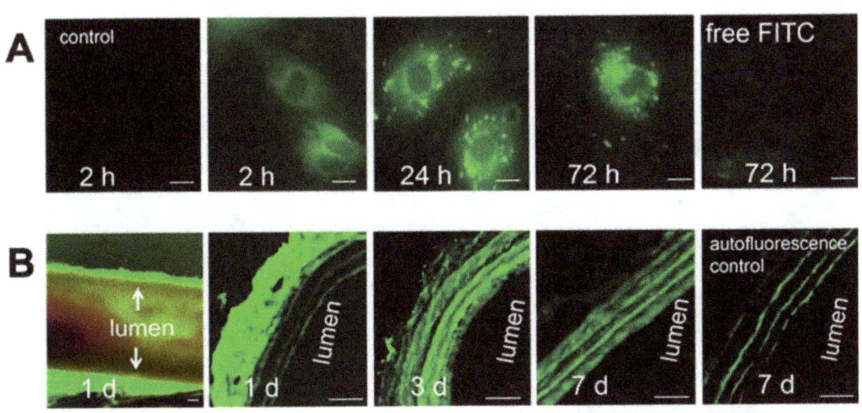

Figure 2. Accumulation of FITC-loaded NPs in cultured smooth muscle cells and in the arterial wall of the injured rat carotid artery after periadventitial application. (A). Representative fluorescence microscopic images demonstrate timein the arterial wall of the injured rat carotid arteμg FITC/ml) by cultured rat vascular smooth muscle cells (SMCs) (n = 3). Scale bar represents 10 μm. (B). FITC-NPs were applied around the rat carotid artery immediately after injury (see methods). Representative fluorescence microscopic images of carotid arteries demonstrate the in vivo distribution of FITC-NPs *(n = 3)* (1 mg FITC-NPs in 300 μl pluronic gel/artery). The first panel of B is a low-magnification longitudinal image of the artery showing perivascular application of NPs. Panels 2–4 are images of cross sections. The last panel shows the auto-fluorescence background of laminas. Scale bar represents 120 μm.

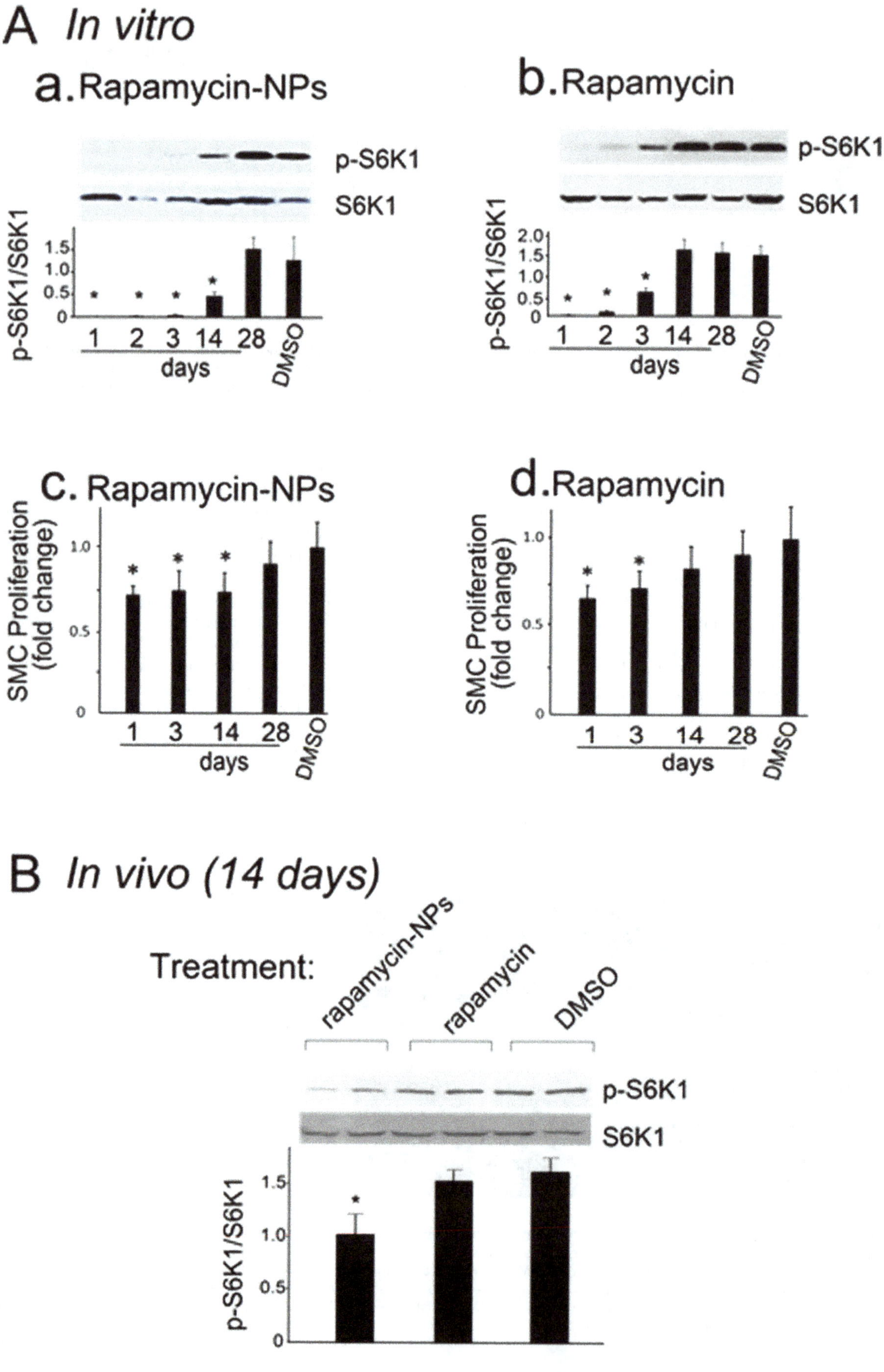
A In vitro
a. Rapamycin-NPs
p-S6K1
S6K1
p-S6K1/S6K1
0
0.5
1.0
1.5
1 2 3 14 28
days
DMSO
b. Rapamycin
p-S6K1
S6K1
p-S6K1/S6K1
0
0.5
1.0
1.5
2.0
1 2 3 14 28
days
DMSO
c. Rapamycin-NPs
SMC Proliferation (fold change)
0
0.5
1.0
1 3 14 28
days
DMSO
d. Rapamycin
SMC Proliferation (fold change)
0
0.5
1.0
1 3 14 28
days
DMSO
B In vivo (14 days)
Treatment:
rapamycin-NPs
rapamycin
DMSO
p-S6K1
S6K1
p-S6K1/S6K1
0
0.5
1.0
1.5

Figure 3. Prolonged inhibitory effects of rapamycin-loaded NPs on S6K1 phosphorylation *in vitro* and *in vivo*. (A). *In vitro experiments.* Treatment of SMCs with Rapamycin or rapamycin-NPs (15 µg rapamycin for both) is described in detail in Materials and Methods. Panels a and b show the effect of rapamycin-NPs and rapamycin on p-S6K, respectively. Proteins were extracted from SMCs at the indicated time points, and phosphorylated S6K1 (p-S6K1) and S6K1 were measured by Western blot analysis. Panels c and d show the effect of rapamycin-NPs and rapamycin on SMC proliferation (measured by MTT assay), respectively. Quantified data are presented as mean MC proliferation (measured by MTT (* $P<0.05$). (B). *In vivo experiments.* Following balloon angioplasty in rat carotid arteries, rapamycin or rapamycin-NPs (300 µg rapamycin for both) were dispersed in 300 µl pluronic gel and applied periadventitially to injured carotid arteries, as described in Methods. Carotid arteries were retrieved 14 days after surgery. Proteins extracted from carotid arteries were subjected to Western blot analysis for phosphorylated S6K1 (p-S6K1) and S6K1. Quantified data are presented as mean njured carotid arteries, as descri (* $P<0.05$).

Rapamycin-loaded NPs Provide Prolonged Inhibition of Cellular Proliferation in Media and Subintima of Injured Rat Carotid Arteries

Previous studies have indicated that rapamycin impedes IH at least in part by effectively inhibiting SMC proliferation [29]. In these studies we investigate the mechanism underlying the attenuation of IH by rapamycin-NPs. Using histological sections from the animals treated in the foregoing experiments, immunostaining for Ki67 was performed to evaluate cell proliferation. Our data reveal that the proliferation or Ki67 index was substantially decreased (by ~50%) in both the free rapamycin and rapamycin-NPs treated groups compared to controls at 14 days following treatment (Figure 5, A and B). However 28 days after treatment, whereas the Ki67 index remained suppressed in the rapamycin-NPs treated group, the Ki67 index in the free rapamycin-treated group returned to the level of control (Figure 5, C and D). These results demonstrate that compared to rapamycin alone, the use of NPs to locally deliver rapamycin produced a prolonged inhibitory effect on cell proliferation in balloon-injured arteries likely accounting for the sustained inhibition of IH (Figure 4).

Rapamycin-loaded NPs Have no Effect on Reendothelialization of Injured Rat Carotid Arteries

It has been well demonstrated that rapamycin-eluting stents inhibit endothelial cell proliferation and thus delay reendothelialization, producing the adverse side effect of acute vascular thrombosis [30]. To evaluate the potential for periadventially applied rapamycin-loaded NPs to inhibit reendothelialization, we performed immunostaining for CD31 (a marker for endothelial cells) on carotid sections derived from animals treated with rapamycin-NPs, free rapamycin or controls. We found equivalent rates of reendothelialization in animals treated with rapamycin-NPs compared to controls (Figure 6). Moreover, the rate of reendothelialization was also not diminished in arteries treated with free rapamycin in pluronic gel. These findings were verified at both 14 and 28 days after injury. Thus rapamycin when applied to the arterial adventitia does not affect the regrowth rate of the endothelial layer.

Finally, we evaluated whether rapamycin-loaded NPs provide systemic toxicity to treated animals. We found that periadventitial application of either rapamycin alone or rapamycin-loaded NPs had no effect on weight gain (Supplemental Figure 1) or blood cell counts (Supplemental Tables 1 and 2) during the course of these experiments. Thus, local application of rapamycin externally to the artery wall, is a safe method for sustained drug release without systemic effects.

Discussion

Through periadventitial application of rapamycin-loaded NPs, we have achieved prolonged attenuation of intimal hyperplasia (IH) for at least 4 weeks while avoiding impairment of endothelialization. Our *in vitro* and *in vivo* experiments together indicate that NPs facilitate prolonged release of rapamycin. Persuasive evidence can be summarized as follows. Rapamycin-loaded NPs produce sustained drug release for up to 28 days compared to 3–5 days with free rapamycin. Rapamycin-loaded NPs produce prolonged inhibition of S6K1 phosphorylation (14 days) in cultured SMCs compared to rapamycin alone (3 days). It is well established that rapamycin inhibits mTOR leading to decreased downstream S6K1 phosphorylation, which is required for cell cycle progression and cell proliferation [10,31]. Thus, phospho-S6K1 is widely used as a valid functional marker for rapamycin bioavailability. Using phospho-S6K1 inhibition as an indicator, we found that rapamycin-loaded NPs applied periadventitially promoted prolonged release of rapamycin into the vessel wall compared to rapamycin alone. Finally, rapamycin-loaded NPs applied around the injured artery greatly outperformed rapamycin alone in durable inhibition of SMC proliferation and IH. These lines of evidence clearly show that NPs improve the durability of drug release and prolong the effect of rapamycin in impeding IH.

Currently the only clinically applied methods for treating IH are stents or balloons that release anti-proliferative drugs such as rapamycin or paclitaxel [1,32]. Drug-eluting stents have been successful in reducing the incidence of IH in patients treated with coronary artery angioplasty although there are limitations including the need for chronic platelet inhibition, the potential for stent thrombosis related to delayed endothelialization, as well as cost. Despite advances made over the past two decades in percutaneous angioplasty, thousands of patients each year are still treated with traditional open surgery. These procedures include lower extremity bypass both vein and prosthetic, coronary artery bypass and carotid endarterectomy (total up to 270 thousand cases per year) and vascular grafts placed for dialysis (~50 thousand cases per year) [33]. Unfortunately drug-eluting stents or balloons used following percutaneous angioplasty are not applicable for the patients undergoing open surgical procedures. There are currently no available measures to prevent the development of IH in these patients where the incidence ranges from 20–80%. Thus, there is a tremendous unmet clinical need for a clinically applicable technique to prevent IH in patients undergoing open vascular reconstructive surgery.

Since angioplasty is performed remotely, intraluminal drugs applied to the site of angioplasty must also be delivered remotely. Thus the challenges of drug delivery following a percutaneous intervention are substantial. Alternatively, drugs that inhibit IH can be directly applied to bypass grafts, anastomoses, prosthetic grafts, or endarterectomized arteries. The task of drug delivery following open surgery is conceptually less challenging since drugs can be directly applied to the arterial wall. In addition to the accessibility of the vessel at the time of surgery there are other distinct advantages of applying drugs to the arterial adventitia. Inhibitors of SMC proliferation also inhibit endothelial cell proliferation. Interestingly, rapamycin inhibits endothelial cells to a much greater extent than SMCs. Thus, rapamycin when applied intraluminally *via* a stent

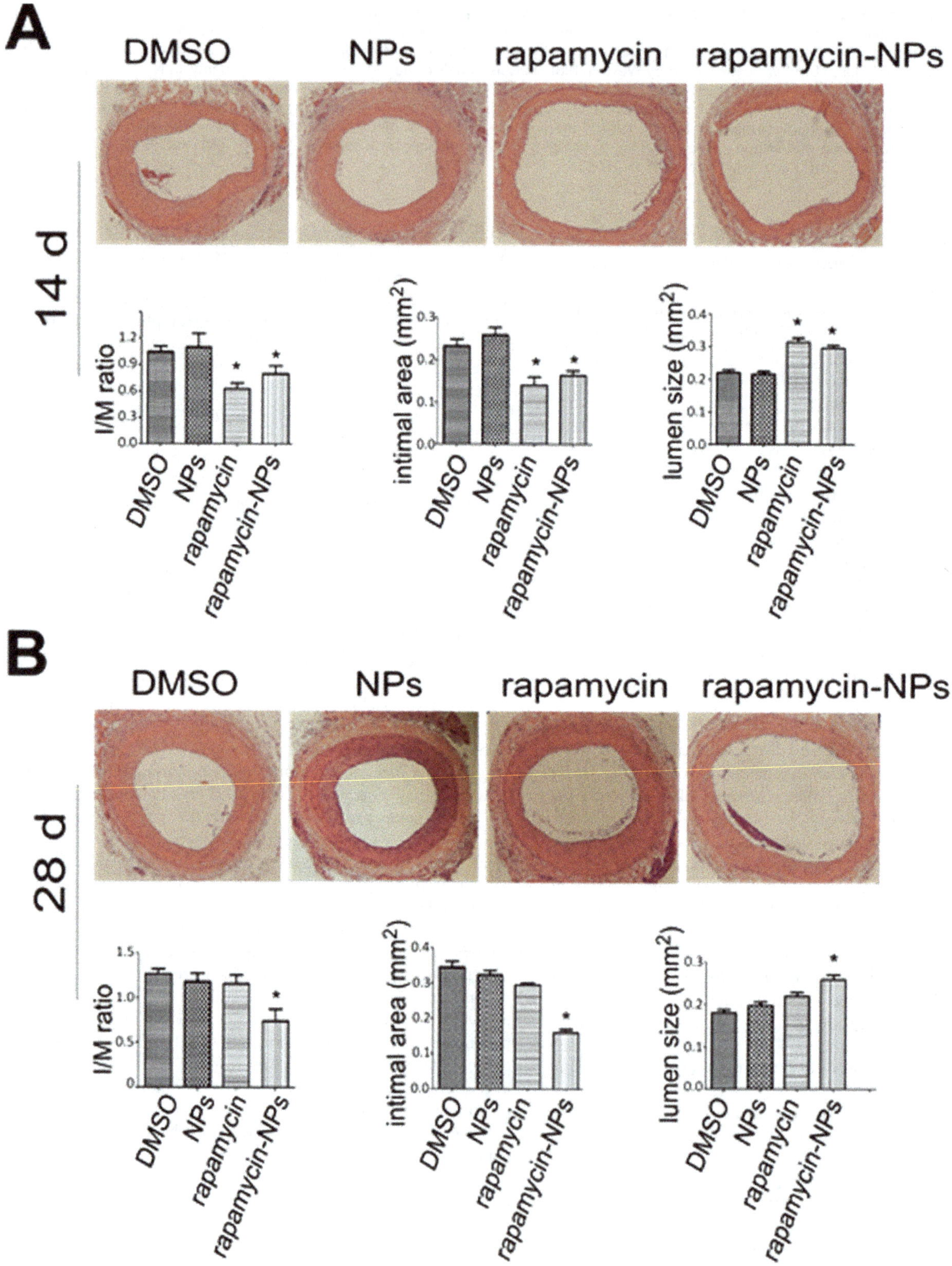

Figure 4. Sustained inhibitory effects of rapamycin-loaded NPs on intimal hyperplasia in balloon-injured rat carotid arteries. Balloon injury of rat carotid arteries was performed and rapamycin or rapamycin loaded NPs (300 μg rapamycin for both) dispersed in 300 μl pluronic gel was applied periadventitially immediately after vascular injury, as described in Methods. Solvent (DMSO) and NPs alone dispersed in pluronic gel were used as controls. Carotid arteries were retrieved 14 (A) or 28 days (B) after surgery. Sections were then prepared and H&E stained. Top panel shows representative microscopic images of carotid cross-sections from the indicated treatment groups. Bottom panel shows quantification of lumen size, intimal area, and intimal to media ratio (I/M). Data are presented as mean ± SEM from 5 animals in each group (*$P<0.05$ compared to DMSO control).

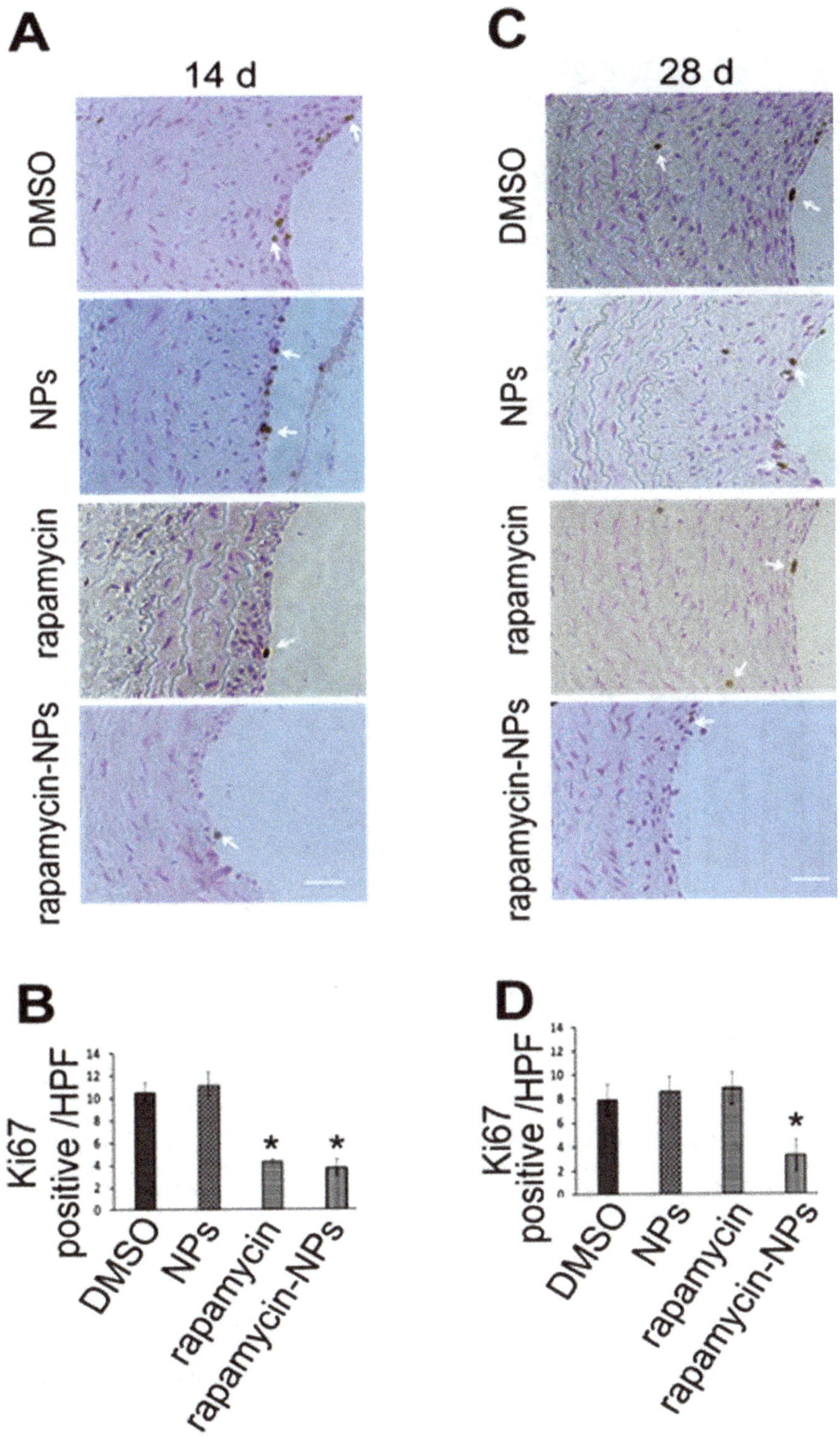

Figure 5. Sustained inhibitory effect of rapamycin-NPs on cell proliferation in balloon-injured rat carotid arteries. Rat carotid cross-sections were obtained from the same experiments as in Figure 4. Sections were immunostained for Ki67 as described in Methods. Representative microscopic images of Ki67 staining on arteries retrieved 14 days (A) and 28 days (C) after surgery. Arrows point to Ki67 positive cells. Quantification of Ki67 positive cell number per high power field (HPF) on sections retrieved 14 (B) and 28 days (D) after surgery (magnification is 200X). Each bar represents a mean ±SEM of 5 animals (* $P<0.05$ compared to DMSO control).

markedly inhibits endothelial cell proliferation leading to loss of the endothelial lining, the potential for acute vessel thrombosis and the need for prolonged platelet inhibition [1,34]. Periadventitial application of rapamycin has the potential of creating a gradient so that the greatest concentrations of rapamycin influence the adventitia followed by the media and the

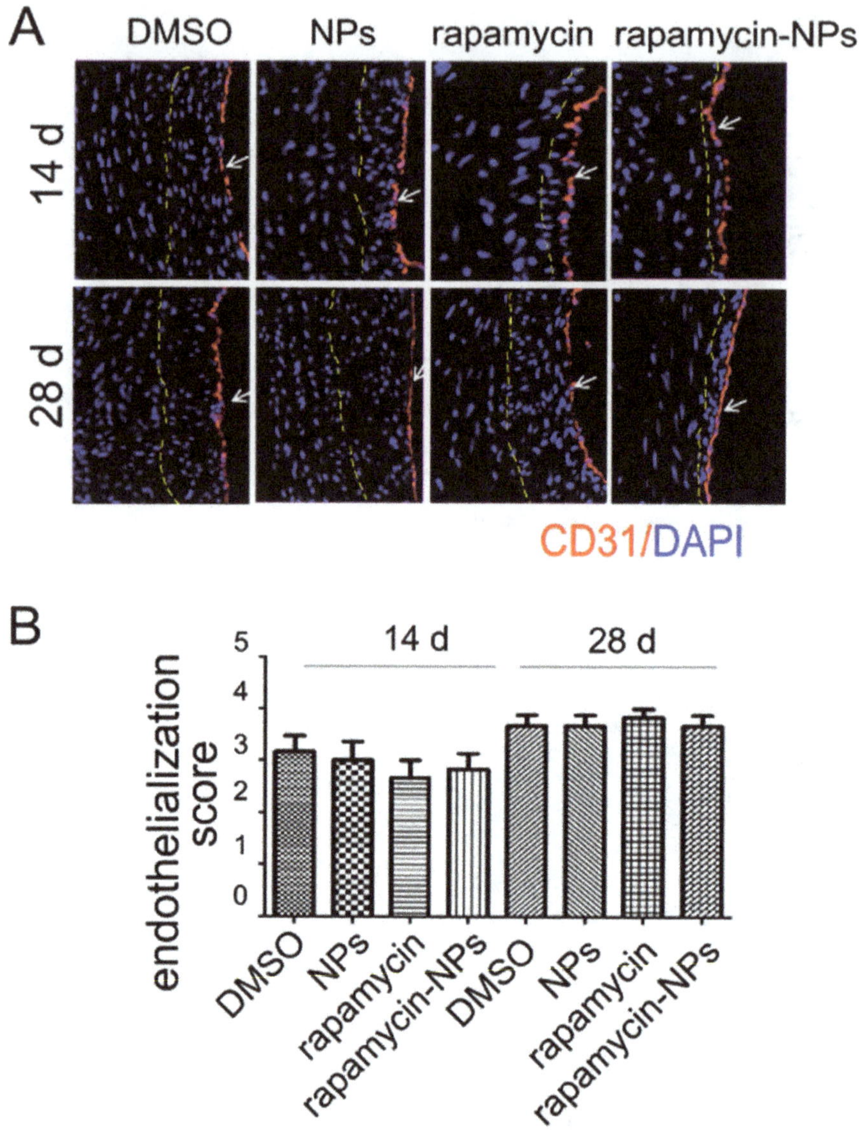

Figure 6. Periadventitial application of rapamycin-loaded NPs does not affect carotid artery reendothelialization after angioplasty. Rat carotid cross-sections were obtained from the same experiments as in Figure 4. (A) Representative fluorescence microscopic images of CD-31staining (red, marked by arrows) of arteries retrieved 14 or 28 days after surgery. Blue dots are DAPI-stained nuclei. Dashed lines define internal elastic lamina (IEL). (B) Quantification of reendothelialization (CD-31 positive versus total perimeter) on sections retrieved 14 or 28 days after surgery. Each bar represents a mean ±SEM of 5 animals.

subintima with intimal endothelial cells exposed to the lowest concentration of drugs. To this end we studied reendothelialization in our model and found that when rapamycin was applied to the periadventitial tissue there was rapid endothelial regeneration without rapamycin's usual inhibitory effect. An additional theoretical advantage of periadventitial application of drugs that inhibit cellular proliferation is the ability of these drugs to influence cells in the adventitia. Myofibroblasts in the adventitia significantly contribute to neointimal hyperplasia. There is extensive data demonstrating that adventitial myofibroblasts migrate to the subintima and contribute to the formation of plaque [35,36]. Thus inhibition of adventitial myofibroblast proliferation may enhance the ability of drugs such as rapamycin to protect against IH. With an effective method of drug delivery, the potential to reduce morbidity and mortality associated with recurrent disease, graft failure and vascular occlusion is substantial.

There is mounting evidence that prolonged drug delivery may be advantageous. There are various stimuli after vascular reconstruction that lead to the development of IH. Inclusive is vessel wall damage that accompanies manipulation and suture of a graft to the vessel wall. Veins used for bypass during harvest are exposed to trauma, desiccation, over-distention and *ex vivo* preservation. Endarterectomy produces direct trauma to the arterial media. Although these events are transient, the degree of injury can be profound leading to a protracted course of healing. A short burst of drug may be inadequate to completely block the maladaptive healing response that leads to IH. Moreover, some vascular reconstruction procedures are associated with an ongoing stimulus for IH. Following the creation of a bypass, "low pressure" veins are subject to arterial pressure, which provides a persistent (for the life of the bypass) stimulus for arterial remodeling that can lead to IH. Altered flow dynamics at the site of an anastomosis are persistent and likewise provide an ongoing hyperplastic stimulus. Grafts for bypass eventually reach a steady state of adaptive healing; however, this is likely not to be achieved for at least 3 to 6 months following the initial reconstruction. Thus prolonged delivery of drug over a several months period of time would seem advantageous.

Many of the pharmacological properties of conventional or "free" drugs can be improved through the use of NP drug delivery systems. First, NP drug delivery systems can significantly enhance the solubility of hydrophobic drugs in aqueous solutions. Encapsulating rapamycin in the PLGA NPs can significantly enhance its concentration in an aqueous solution [6]. Second, NPs provide controlled and sustained drug release profiles. Our *in vitro* data revealed that free rapamycin in pluronic gel was released over a period of 3 to 5 days whereas rapamycin in PLGA NPs was released over 3–4 weeks. Moreover, S6K1 phosphorylation and cell proliferation were effectively suppressed for at least 28 days in animals treated with rapamycin-loaded nanoparticles. It is likely that sustained release of rapamycin was a major factor that led to more durable inhibition of IH in our model. Another mechanism through which NPs can promote drug delivery is by enhancing the accumulation and absorption of drug by target cells or tissues. NPs can release rapamycin into the extracellular space and then free rapamycin can diffuse into cells of the arterial wall. NPs can also be taken up readily by cells *via* endocytosis, due to their relatively small size (~200 nm *vs.* SMCs being ~20 micrometers in size) [6]. In our *in vitro* system we observed that NPs were internalized by SMCs *via* endocytosis within two hours. The relative cellular uptake of free drug versus NPs varies and depends on the cell type, the nature of the drug, as well as the chemical, physical, and surface properties of the NPs (*e.g.,* specific ligand-receptor interaction) [37]. In our system it is clear that rapamycin is able to enter the cell *via* both mechanisms. It is worth noting that once NPs are exposed to cell culture medium, proteins/peptides present in cell culture may coat the surface of the NPs, which later serve as a targeting ligand promoting cellular uptake of NPs [37]. Lastly, NPs prevent drug from premature enzymatic degradation *in vivo.* The *in vivo* half-life of free rapamycin is much shorter than *in vitro.* However, rapamycin encapsulated in NPs is protected from any enzymatic degradation until it is released from the NPs.

While many strategies involving NPs have been designed for the luminal treatment of restenosis, intraluminal approaches have the potential to cause undesirable inhibition of the inner endothelial protective lining [1]. A number of approaches for perivascular drug delivery of rapamycin have been employed but with varying success. These approaches include rapamycin-loaded microbeads, PLGA membranes, synthetic meshes, and non-constrictive cuffs [7,38,39]. Recently, periadventitial application of rapamycin-eluting microbeads (200 μm) was evaluated in a pig vein graft model. Low concentrations of rapamycin only partially inhibited IH whereas higher concentrations produced anastamotic disruption related to absent healing [40]. NPs have the advantage over these other approaches in penetrating the arterial wall allowing more direct cellular delivery.

Although our study has clearly demonstrated that perivascular application of rapamycin-loaded PLGA NPs is effective in the inhibition of IH, further research is needed to optimize this drug delivery system. For example, we were not able to evaluate whether rapamycin-loaded NPs might affect IH beyond 4 weeks. A longer-term model of IH will be necessary to accomplish this evaluation. The current NP drug delivery system can also be improved through a number of manipulations. Pluronic gel was used to immobilize NPs in the periadventitial space. However, pluronic gel dissolves within 3–4 days after *in vivo* application. Using a long-lasting yet biodegradable temperature-responsive polymer gel to replace pluronic gel will further extend *in vivo* drug release from NPs. Moreover, NPs can be modified to meet specific needs for optimal drug release. Polymer chemistry and size of NPs can be altered to vary NP durability, and drug release profile. In addition, various ligands can be conjugated to the surface of the NPs to target specific cell populations overexpressing corresponding receptors in the hyperplastic vessel wall. Lastly, NPs are capable of encapsulating a mixture of drugs with complementary functions, which may further enhance the efficacy of drug-releasing NPs for treating restenosis. Further studies with new polymer gels, drug nanocarriers, animal models, and multi-drug administration regimens should be able to further improve the efficacy of drug delivery.

Conclusion

Our study shows that periadventitial delivery of rapamycin-loaded NPs is a promising approach for the development of a safer, more efficacious drug delivery system to treat IH. Using rapamycin as a model drug we have demonstrated that NPs extend drug release *in vitro* and *in vivo.* When applied outside the arterial wall, rapamycin-loaded NPs compared to rapamycin alone substantially prolonged inhibition of IH and maintained lumen patency in balloon-injured rat carotid arteries. Thus local drug delivery with NPs provides a useful template approach for future development of safe and efficacious drug delivery methods to treat IH and restenosis, particularly for patients undergoing open vascular reconstruction.

Supporting Information

Figure S1 Periadventitial application of rapamycin-loaded NPs does not affect body weight. Animal body weights were measured at the indicated time points after surgery. Data are presented as mean sents a mean ±SEM of 5 animals.CD-31s.

Table S1 Periadventitial application of rapamycin-loaded nanoparticles does not affect blood cell counts (14 days after Surgery). Hematological analysis from Sprague Dawley Rats 14 d after surgery. Results are expressed as mean ± SD, n = 5. RBC, red blood cells; WBC, white blood cells.

Table S2 Periadventitial application of rapamycin-loaded nanoparticles does not affect blood cell counts (28 days after Surgery). Hematological analysis from Sprague Dawley Rats 14 d after surgery. Results are expressed as mean ± SD, n = 5. RBC, red blood cells; WBC, white blood cells.

Author Contributions

Conceived and designed the experiments: XS GC LWG SG KCK. Performed the experiments: XS GC YS MZ SP. Analyzed the data: XS GC LWG SG KCK BL. Wrote the paper: XS GC LWG SG KCK.

References

1. Seedial SM, Ghosh S, Saunders RS, Suwanabol P, Shi X, et al. (2013) Local drug delivery to prevent restenosis. J Vasc Surg 57: 1403–1414.
2. Curcio A, Torella D, Indolfi C (2011) Mechanisms of smooth muscle cell proliferation and endothelial regeneration after vascular injury and stenting: approach to therapy. Circ J 75: 1287–1296.
3. Acharya S, Sahoo SK (2011) PLGA nanoparticles containing various anticancer agents and tumour delivery by EPR effect. Adv Drug Deliv Rev 63: 170–183.
4. Lü J-M, Wang X, Marin-Muller C, Wang H, Lin PH, et al. (2009) Current advances in research and clinical applications of PLGA-based nanotechnology. Expert Rev Mol Diagn 9: 325–341.
5. Martin-Banderas L, Durán-Lobato M, Muñoz-Rubio I, Alvarez-Fuentes J, Fernández-Arevalo M, et al. (2013) Functional PLGA NPs for oral drug delivery: recent strategies and developments. Mini Rev Med Chem 13: 58–69.
6. Danhier F, Ansorena E, Silva JM, Coco R, Le Breton A, Preat V (2012) PLGA-based nanoparticles: an overview of biomedical applications. J Control Release 161: 502–522.
7. Semete B, Booysen L, Lemmer Y, Kalombo L, Katata L, et al. (2010) In vivo evaluation of the biodistribution and safety of PLGA nanoparticles as drug delivery systems. Nanomedicine 6: 662–671.
8. Panyam J, Labhasetwar V (2003) Biodegradable nanoparticles for drug and gene delivery to cells and tissue. Adv Drug Deliv Rev 55: 329–347.
9. Fingar DC, Richardson CJ, Tee AR, Cheatham L, Tsou C, et al. (2004) mTOR Controls Cell Cycle Progression through Its Cell Growth Effectors S6K1 and 4E-BP1/Eukaryotic Translation Initiation Factor 4E. Mol Cell Biol 24: 200–216.
10. Zohlnhofer D, Nuhrenberg TG, Neumann F-JJ, Richter T, May AE, et al. (2004) Rapamycin effects transcriptional programs in smooth muscle cells controlling proliferative and inflammatory properties. Mol Pharmacol 65: 880–889.
11. Reddy MK, Vasir JK, Sahoo SK, Jain TK, Yallapu MM, et al. (2008) Inhibition of apoptosis through localized delivery of rapamycin-loaded nanoparticles prevented neointimal hyperplasia and reendothelialized injured artery. Circ Cardiovasc Interv 1: 209–216.
12. Daemen J, Kukreja N, van Twisk PH, Onuma Y, de Jaegere PP, et al. (2008) Four-year clinical follow-up of the rapamycin-eluting stent evaluated at Rotterdam Cardiology Hospital registry. Am J Cardiol 101: 1105–1111.
13. Abizaid A Costa JR (2010) New drug-eluting stents: an overview on biodegradable and polymer-free next-generation stent systems. Circ Cardiovasc Interv 3: 384–393.
14. Virmani R, Farb A, Guagliumi G Kolodgie FD (2004) Drug-eluting stents: caution and concerns for long-term outcome. Coron Artery Dis 15: 313–318.
15. Siqueira DA, Abizaid AA, Costa J de R, Feres F, Mattos LA, et al. (2007) Late incomplete apposition after drug-eluting stent implantation: incidence and potential for adverse clinical outcomes. Eur Heart J 28: 1304–1309.
16. Guzman LA, Labhasetwar V, Song C, Jang Y, Lincoff AM, et al. (1996) Local intraluminal infusion of biodegradable polymeric nanoparticles. A novel approach for prolonged drug delivery after balloon angioplasty. Circulation 94: 1441–1448.
17. Lutsiak MEC, Robinson DR, Coester C, Kwon GS, Samuel J (2002) Analysis of poly(D,L-lactic-co-glycolic acid) nanosphere uptake by human dendritic cells and macrophages in vitro. Pharm Res 19: 1480–1487.
18. Clowes MM, Lynch CM, Miller a D, Miller DG, Osborne WR, et al. (1994) Long-term biological response of injured rat carotid artery seeded with smooth muscle cells expressing retrovirally introduced human genes. J Clin Invest 93: 644–651.
19. Kundi R, Hollenbeck ST, Yamanouchi D, Herman BC, Edlin R, et al. (2009) Arterial gene transfer of the TGF-beta signalling protein Smad3 induces adaptive remodelling following angioplasty: a role for CTGF. Cardiovasc Res 84: 326–335.
20. Jhunjhunwala S, Raimondi G, Thomson a W, Little SR (2009) Delivery of rapamycin to dendritic cells using degradable microparticles. J Control Release 133: 191–197.
21. Brown MA, Zhang L, Levering VW, Wu J, Satterwhite LL, et al. (2010) Human Umbilical Cord Blood – Derived Endothelial Cells Reendothelialize Vein Grafts and Prevent Thrombosis. Arterioscler Thromb Vasc Biol 30: 2150–2155.
22. Tian W, Kuhlmann MT, Pelisek J, Scobioala S, Quang TH, et al. (2006) Paclitaxel delivered to adventitia attenuates neointima formation without compromising re-endothelialization after angioplasty in a porcine restenosis model. J Endovasc Ther 13: 616–629.
23. Tsai S, Hollenbeck ST, Ryer EJ, Edlin R, Yamanouchi D, et al. (2009) TGF-beta through Smad3 signaling stimulates vascular smooth muscle cell proliferation and neointimal formation. Am J Physiol Heart Circ Physiol 297: H540–H549.
24. Zhu W, Masaki T, Bae YH, Rathi R, Cheung AK, et al. (2006) Development of a sustained-release system for perivascular delivery of dipyridamole. J Biomed Mater Res B Appl Biomater 77: 135–143.
25. Kawatsu S, Oda K, Saiki Y, Tabata Y, Tabayashi K (2007) External application of rapamycin-eluting film at anastomotic sites inhibits neointimal hyperplasia in a canine model. Ann Thorac Surg 84: 560–567.
26. Makadia HK, Siegel SJ (2011) Poly Lactic-co-Glycolic Acid (PLGA) as Biodegradable Controlled Drug Delivery Carrier. Polymers (Basel) 3: 1377–1397.
27. Avgoustakis K, Beletsi a, Panagi Z, Klepetsanis P, Karydas a G, et al. (2002) PLGA-mPEG nanoparticles of cisplatin: in vitro nanoparticle degradation, in vitro drug release and in vivo drug residence in blood properties. J Control Release 79: 123–135.
28. Ding M, Xie Y, Wagner RJ, Jin Y, Carrao AC, et al. (2011) Adiponectin induces vascular smooth muscle cell differentiation via repression of mammalian target of rapamycin complex 1 and FoxO4. Arter Thromb Vasc Biol 31: 1403–1410.
29. Liuzzo JP, Ambrose JA Coppola JT (2005) Sirolimus- and taxol-eluting stents differ towards intimal hyperplasia and re-endothelialization. J Invasive Cardiol 17: 497–502.
30. Lüscher TF, Steffel J, Eberli FR, Joner M, Nakazawa G, et al. (2007) Drug-eluting stent and coronary thrombosis: biological mechanisms and clinical implications. Circulation 115: 1051–1058.
31. Rosner D, McCarthy N, Bennett M (2005) Rapamycin inhibits human in stent restenosis vascular smooth muscle cells independently of pRB phosphorylation and p53. Cardiovasc Res 66: 601–610.
32. Yang J, Zeng Y, Zhang C, Chen Y-X, Yang Z, et al. (2013) The prevention of restenosis in vivo with a VEGF gene and paclitaxel co-eluting stent. Biomaterials 34: 1635–1643.
33. Jim J, Owens PL, Sanchez LA, Rubin BG (2012) Population-based analysis of inpatient vascular procedures and predicting future workload and implications for training. J Vasc Surg 55: 1394–1399.
34. Inoue T, Croce K, Morooka T, Sakuma M, Node K, Simon DI (2011) Vascular inflammation and repair: implications for re-endothelialization, restenosis, and stent thrombosis. JACC Cardiovasc Interv 4: 1057–1066.
35. Si Y, Ren J, Wang P, Rateri DL, Daugherty A, et al. (2012) Protein kinase C-delta mediates adventitial cell migration through regulation of monocyte chemoattractant protein-1 expression in a rat angioplasty model. Arterioscler Thromb Vasc Biol 32: 943–954.
36. Siow RCM, Mallawaarachchi CM, Weissberg PL (2003) Migration of adventitial myofibroblasts following vascular balloon injury: Insights from in vivo gene transfer to rat carotid arteries. Cardiovasc Res 59: 212–221.
37. Cartiera MS, Johnson KM, Rajendran V, Caplan MJ SW, Cartiera MS, Johnson KM, Rajendran V, Caplan MJ, et al. (2009) The uptake and intracellular fate of PLGA nanoparticles in epithelial cells. Biomaterials 30: 2790–2798.
38. Pires NMM, van der Hoeven BL, de Vries MR, Havekes LM, van Vlijmen BJ, et al. (2005) Local perivascular delivery of anti-restenotic agents from a drug-eluting poly(epsilon-caprolactone) stent cuff. Biomaterials 26: 5386–5394.
39. Chorny M, Fishbein I, Golomb G (2000) Drug delivery systems for the treatment of restenosis. Crit Rev Ther Drug Carrier Syst 17: 249–284.
40. Rajathurai T, Rizvi SI, Lin H, Angelini GD, Newby AC, Murphy GJ. (2010). Periadventitial rapamycin-eluting microbeads promote vein graft disease in long-term pig vein-into-artery interposition grafts. Circ Cardiovasc Interv. 3(2): 157–65.

4

Controlled Delivery of Zoledronate Improved Bone Formation Locally *In Vivo*

Wenlong Gou[9], **Xin Wang**[9], **Jiang Peng***, **Qiang Lu, Yu Wang, Aiyuan Wang, Quanyi Guo, Xupeng Gao, Wenjing Xu, Shibi Lu**

Institute of Orthopaedics, Chinese PLA General Hospital, Haidian District, Beijing, P.R. China

Abstract

Bisphosphonates (BPs) have been widely used in clinical treatment of bone diseases with increased bone resorption because of their strong affinity for bone and their inhibition of bone resorption. Recently, there has been growing interest in their improvement of bone formation. However, the effect of local controlled delivery of BPs is unclear. We used polylactide acid-glycolic acid copolymer (PLGA) as a drug carrier to deliver various doses of the bisphosphonate zoledronate (Zol) into the distal femur of 8-week-old Sprague-Dawley rats. After 6 weeks, samples were harvested and analyzed by micro-CT and histology. The average bone mineral density and mineralized bone volume fraction were higher with medium- and high-dose PLGA-Zol (30 and 300 μg Zol, respectively) than control and low-dose Zol (3 μg PLGA-Zol; $p<0.05$). Local controlled delivery of Zol decreased the numbers of osteoclast and increased the numbers of osteoblast. Moreover, local controlled delivery of medium- and high-dose Zol accelerated the expression of bone-formation markers. PLGA used as a drug carrier for controlled delivery of Zol may promote local bone formation.

Editor: Luc Malaval, INSERM U1059/LBTO, Université Jean Monnet, France

Funding: This work was funded by a grant from the National Technology Research and Development Program of China (2012AA020502, 2012CB518106) and the National Science Foundation of China (30930092, 30973047, 31240048), and BWS11J025. The funders had no role in study design, data collection and analysis, decision to publish, or preparation of the manuscript.

Competing Interests: The authors have declared that no competing interests exist.

* E-mail: pengjiang301@126.com

[9] These authors contributed equally to this work.

Introduction

The skeletal system functions and is maintained on the basis of the balance between osteoclast-mediated bone resorption and osteoblast-mediated bone formation. Bone fragility leading to fracture and disability is implicated in the pathogenesis of various bone resorption diseases. Preservation of bone strength, mainly determined by the amount of minerals, is key to the management of these conditions [1].

Bisphosphonates (BPs) are synthetic analogs of naturally occurring pyrophosphate (P-O-P) in which a carbon atom replaced the oxygen atom connecting the two phosphates (P-C-P) [2]. Because of their strong affinity for bone and their inhibition of bone resorption, BPs have been widely used in clinical treatment of bone diseases with increased bone resorption, including Paget's disease, hypercalcemia of malignancy, fibrous dysplasia, and inflammation-related bone loss [3–7]. Recent studies indicated that BPs not only inhibit bone resorption induced by osteoclasts but also accelerate bone formation induced by osteoblasts, albeit with varying or conflicting effects, in relation to the concentration of BPs [1,8–11]. In most studies, BPs were administered intravenously or orally. However, systemic administration of BPs, especially in high doses and over the long term, increased the risk of osteonecrosis of the jaw [12,13]. Local administration, such as local injection and implanting allografts soaked with BPs solution, has been used in animal research for the treatment of ischemic osteonecrosis of the femoral head and protecting newly formed bone against resorption [14,15]. However, to this day, controlled local delivery of BPs has rarely been reported.

Polylactide acid-glycolic acid copolymer (PLGA) is a poly (α-hydroxy-ester) that is depolymerized in the presence of water. Because of biodegradable and bioabsorbable qualities that allow for the passive degradation of the polymer in aqueous environments [16], PLGA has been widely used in the research into controlled release drug delivery [17–19]. Previous studies have successfully conjugated alendronate sodium to PLGA [20].

In this study, we used PLGA as a drug carrier to deliver the BP zoledronate (Zol) and investigated whether the PLGA-Zol composite could deliver the Zol gradually, inhibit bone resorption, and promote local bone formation.

Materials and Methods

Preparation of PLGA-Zol composite cylinders

PLGA (D,L-lactide 75: glycolide 25) with average molecular weight 10,000 was purchased from the Shandong Institute of Medical Instruments (Jinan, Shandong, China). Zol was purchased from Sigma (SML0223, St. Louis, MO, USA). Details on the synthesis of the polymer conjugate have been reported elsewhere [20]. In brief, various weights of Zol were dissolved in 10% aqueous acetic acid and lyophilized to obtain the free acid form (Edward Modulyo freeze-dryer). The free acid form was dissolved in dimethyl sulphoxide (DMSO) and added to a certain amount of

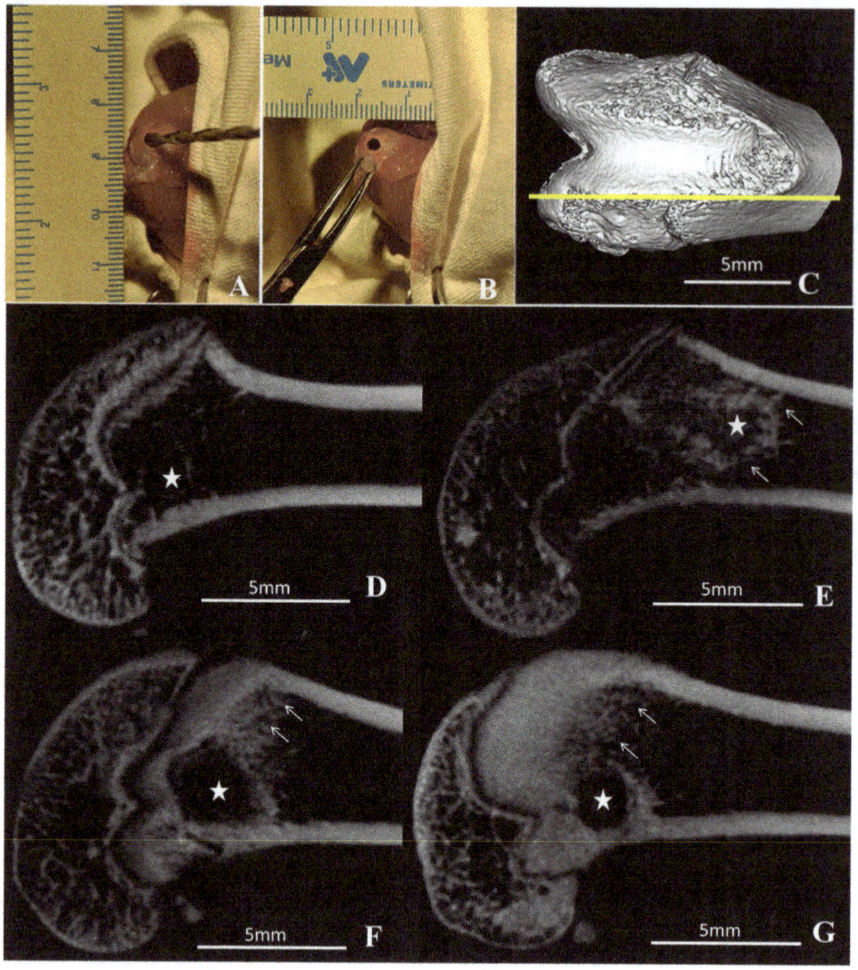

Figure 1. Intraoperative photographs and two-dimensional slices of micro-CT images representing the distal femur. (A) drilling a tunnel (2×4 mm diameter) in the medial femoral condyle along the transepicondylar axis; (B) implantation the PLGA-Zol cylinder; (C) orientation of two-dimensional slice indicated by the yellow line; (D) polylactide acid-glycolic acid copolymer (PLGA) implantation, 0 μg Zol; (E) PLGA-zoledronate (PLGA-Zol), 3 μg Zol; (F) PLGA-Zol, 30 μg Zol; and (G) PLGA-Zol, 300 μg Zol. Stars indicated the site of implantation and arrows indicated where the significant changes happened.

PLGA, previously activated by N′-(3-dimethylaminopropyl)-N-ethyl carbodiimide hydrochloride (EDAC). After the completion of the conjugation reaction, the reaction solution was purified by dialysis against 3×1l water (CelluSep H1 MWCO 2000; M-Medical s.r.l., Cornaredo, Italy) and the dialyzed sample was frozen in liquid nitrogen and lyophilized. The composite was melted at 85°C and processed into cylinders (2×4 mm diameter) under the closed condition. The content of Zol in the cylinders was designated as 0, 3, 30 and 300 μg per each sample.

Ethics statement

This study was carried out in strict accordance with the recommendations in the Guide for the Care and Use of Laboratory Animals of the National Institutes of Health (NIH publication No. 85–23, revised 1985). The protocol was approved by the Animal Care and Use Committee of the Chinese People's Liberation Army General Hospital (Permit Number: 2013-35). All surgery was performed under chloral hydrate anesthesia, and all efforts were made to minimize suffering.

Animal care and surgery

We purchased 40 male Sprague-Dawley rats 8 weeks old (200±25 g) from the Animal Resources Centre (Chinese People's Liberation Army General Hospital, Beijing). Rats were allowed to acclimatize for 1 week to local vivarium conditions before surgery. Animals were housed in a light- and temperature-controlled environment and given food and water ad libitum. Rats were anesthetized with an intraperitoneal injection of 10% chloral hydrate (3.0 ml/kg, Drug Manufacturing Room of CPLA, Beijing), then injected with a preoperative dose of benzyl penicillin (4×10^5 IU/kg; North China Pharmaceutical Co., Shi Jiazhuang, China) for infection prophylaxis. Under aseptic conditions, a longitudinal incision was made over the anteromedial aspect of the right knee to expose the vertex of the medial femoral condyle. A tunnel (2×4 mm diameter) was made with a drill along the transepicondylar axis, and the PLGA-Zol cylinder (2×4 mm diameter) was implanted into the tunnel (Figure 1A and Figure 1B). After the procedure, rats were given an intramuscular injection of an analgesic (0.05 mg/kg buprenorphine) and allowed unrestricted cage activity.

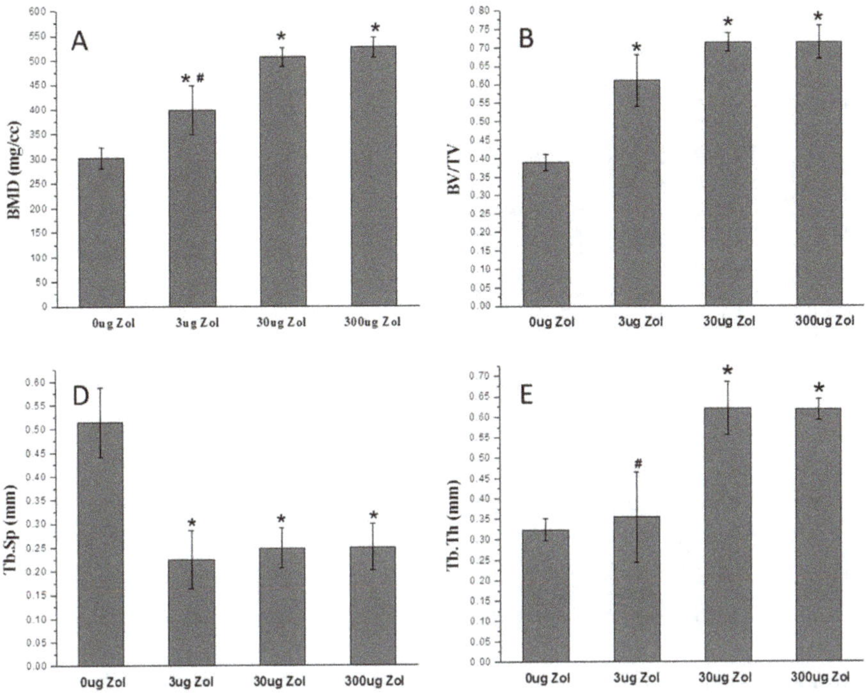

Figure 2. Quantitative micro-CT measurements of (A) bone mineral density (BMD), (B) bone volume fraction (BV/TV), (C) trabecula number (Tb. N.), (D) trabecula thickness (Tb. Th.) and (E) trabecula space (Tb. Sp.). *P<0.05 compared with control group; #P<0.05 compared with PLGA-30 μg Zol and PLGA-300 μg Zol.

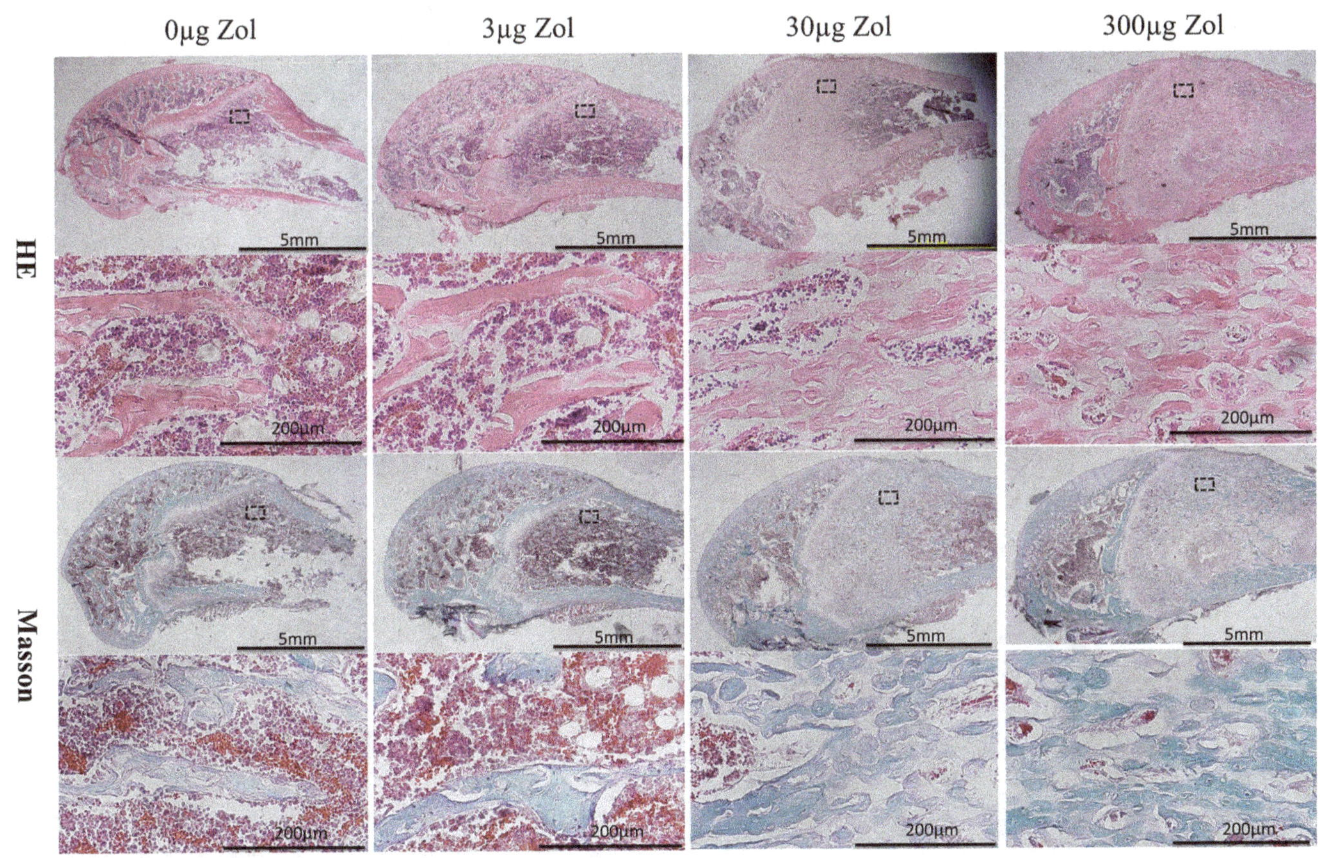

Figure 3. Histology of hematoxylin and eosin (HE) and Masson trichrome staining in epiphysis to metaphysis regions of specimens with PLGA-Zol and control treatment.

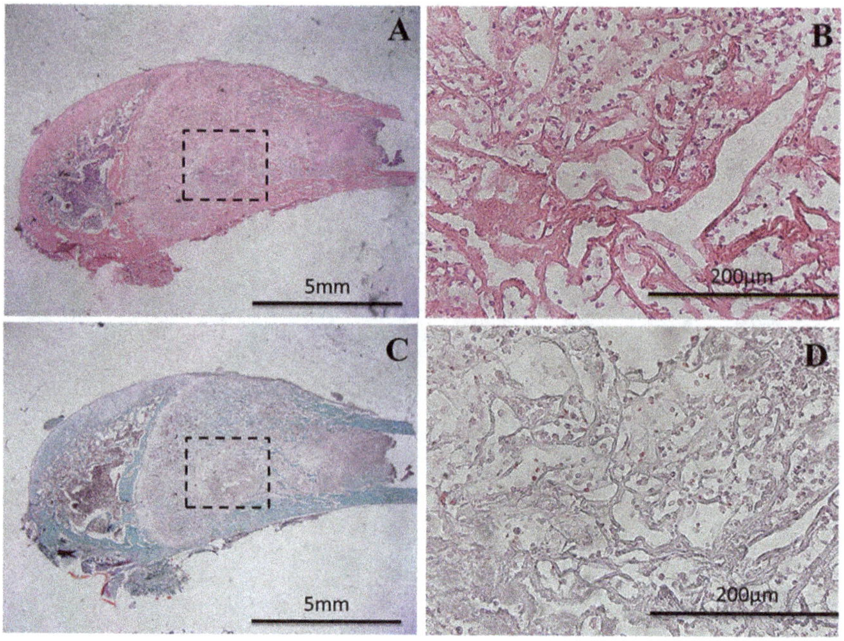

Figure 4. Histology of the implantation site with PLGA-30 μg Zol treatment. (A, B) Hematoxylin and eosin (HE) staining; (C, D) Masson trichrome staining.

Rats were randomly divided into 4 groups (10 rats per group) for treatment: 1)control (PLGA cylinder without Zol); 2)low-dose PLGA-Zol (3 μg Zol); 3)medium-dose PLGA-Zol (30 μg Zol); 4)high-dose PLGA-Zol (300 μg Zol).

Micro-CT evaluation

At 6 weeks, rats were killed by CO_2 asphyxiation unless otherwise noted. The distal femur was harvested and fixed in 4% formaldehyde. The specimens were scanned by micro-CT (system: RS-9, software: MicroView2.1, GE Healthcare, London, ON, Canada) at 27 μm resolution. The scanning protocol was 80 kV and 450 μA, with an isotopic resolution of 20.589×20.589×20.589 μm voxel size and an integration time of 88 ms. A standardized region of interest (ROI) covering an 8-mm region from the epiphysis to the metaphysis was defined in specimens. Bone mineral density (BMD), mineralized volume fraction (BV/TV), trabecula number (Tb.N), trabecula thickness (Tb.Th.), and trabecula space (Tb.Sp.) were calculated as previously reported [21].

Histological and histomorphometric analyses

After micro-CT scanning, specimens were decalcified, dehydrated, embedded in paraffin and cut parallel to the long axis of the femur with use of a microtome. Sections from the middle of

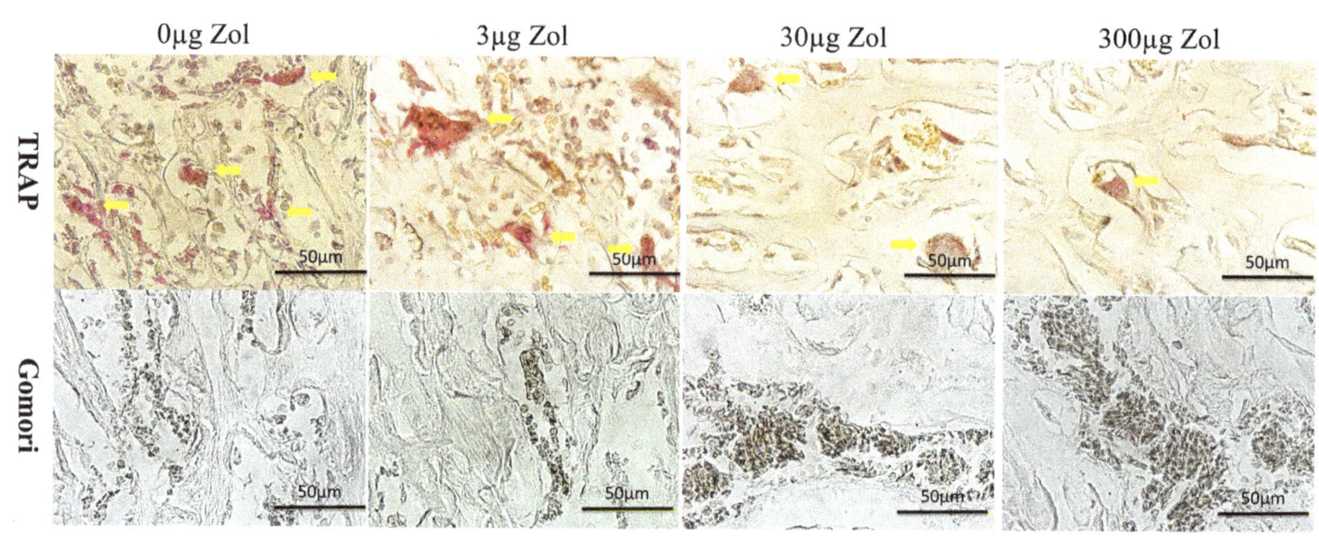

Figure 5. Histology of tartrate resistant acid phosphatase staining (TRAP) and alkaline phosphatase staining (ALP). Yellow arrows indicated the TRAP-positive cells in the row above and ALP-positive cells showed brown in the row below.

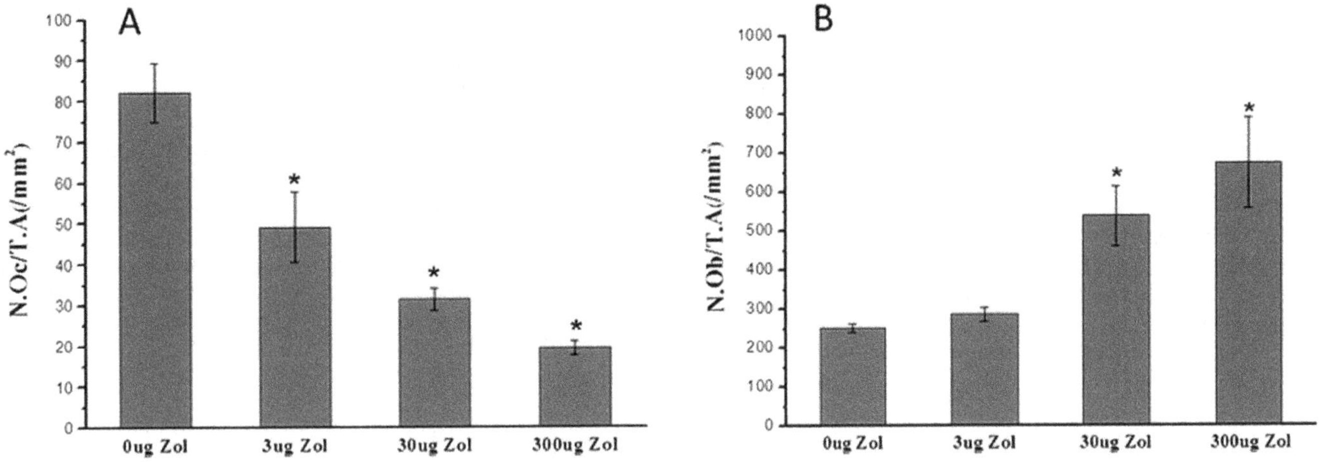

Figure 6. Quantitative analysis of the number of osteoclasts and osteoblasts. (A) number of osteoclasts per unit tissue area, N.Oc/T.A(/mm^2); (B) number of osteoblasts per unit tissue area, N.Ob/T.A(/mm^2) *P<0.05 compared with control group.

specimens, each cut at 5-μm intervals, were stained with hematoxylin and eosin (H&E) and Masson trichrome. Osteoclasts and osteoblasts were identified based on both morphology and staining with tartrate resistant acid phosphatase (TRAP) (Sigma, St. Louis, MO, USA)or alkaline phosphatase (modified Gormori staining). Osteoclast and osteoblast numbers were quantitated in the entire area of the bone marrow cavity 1–2 mm from the growth plates and expressed as numbers per square millimeter. Values were calculated from at least five nonconsecutive sections per rat.

Immunohistochemistry

For immunostaining, commercially available antibodies were used with paraffin-embedded sections for detecting osteocalcin (OCN), bone morphogenetic protein 2 (BMP2), bone morphogenetic protein 7 (BMP7), type I collagen (Col I) and Runt-related transcription factor 2 (RUNX2). The OCN antibody was from Santa Cruz Biotechnology (Santa Cruz. Europe) and others were from Abcam (Hong Kong). Sections were incubated with primary antibodies at a dilution recommended by the manufacturer in a humidified chamber at 4°C overnight, then with 50 μl secondary antibody (Maxim Ltd., Fuzhou, China) for 15 min followed by DAB development. Finally, sections were counterstained with Mayer's hematoxylin for identifying nuclei and mounted with Permount. The negative control was with the same procedure but omitting the primary antibody. Photomicrographs were taken with use of a BX51 Olympus microscope coupled to a DP71 camera (Olympus, Tokyo, Japan) and Picture Frame software. Analysis of images involved ImagePro Plus 5.02 (Media Cybernetics). The special macro for optical density analysis of immunohistochemical staining was acquired at the official web address of the Media Cybernetics Corporation. Using the special macro, the average optical density (AOD) of positive staining area per specimen point in the microarray was calculated as a protein. To eliminate variation, the microscope light source intensity used during image capture was kept constant for all tissue points stained on a given day [22].

Statistics

All data are presented as mean±standard deviation. Statistical differences among groups were evaluated by Student-Newman-Keuls test (SNK-q) or Mann-Whitney U-test if necessary. Statistical analysis involved use of SPSS 16.0 for Windows (SPSS Inc., Chicago, IL). P<0.05 was considered statistically significant.

Results

No wound infections occurred in rats. A femoral condyle fracture occurred in a control-group rat during surgery, and it was excluded from the analysis.

Mineralized tissue formation with PLGA-Zol

Micro-CT revealed a large amount of mineralized tissue, mainly near the distal femoral epiphyseal plate, with medium- and high-dose PLGA-Zol at 6 weeks after surgery (Figure 1F, G), with little mineralized tissue formed around implantation tunnel with low-dose PLGA-Zol and hardly any with PLGA alone (Figure 1E, D). At week 6, average BMD and BV/TV in the metaphyseal region of femurs was higher with low-, medium- and high-dose PLGA-Zol than PLGA alone (P<0.05; Figure 2A, B). Additionally, the mean BMD was higher with both medium- and high-dose than low-dose PLGA-Zol (P<0.05; Figure 2A), with no difference between medium- and high-dose PLGA-Zol. Local controlled delivery of various doses of Zol ameliorated the pathological changes in the microstructure of bone, including increased average thickness of trabecula (P<0.05; Figure 2E) and reduced trabecular space as compared with the control (P<0.05; Figure 2D). Furthermore, trabecular thickness was greater with both medium- and high-dose than low-dose PLGA-Zol (P<0.05; Figure 2E). The trabecula number with low-dose PLGA-Zol was significantly greater than the control, medium- and high-dose PLGA-Zol treatment (P<0.05; Figure 2C).

Medium- and high-dose PLGA-Zol improved the immature bone formation as revealed by histology

At 6 weeks, histology revealed a large amount of new bone formed in the region near the distal femoral epiphyseal plate with medium- and high-dose PLGA-Zol; however, unlike the trabecula in the control and low-dose groups, the structure of the new bone was irregular, defined as woven, immature bone (Figure 3). The thickness of trabecula was greater and the trabecular space was reduced with medium- and high-dose than low-dose PLGA-Zol and control treatment (Figure 3).

All the PLGA and PLGA-Zol cylinders were degraded and absorbed completely, and the site of implantation was filled with a large number of bone-marrow cells and inflammatory cells. Of note, no bone formed in the centre of the implantation site in all groups (Figure 4). In addition, the length of every implanted leg is equal to the control side in all groups.

Decreased numbers of osteoclast and increased numbers of osteoblast with PLGA-Zol delivery

As shown in Figure 5, local controlled delivery of various doses of Zol decreased the numbers of osteoclast (TRAP-positive cells) as compared with the control. The average number of osteoclast was lower with low-, medium- and high-dose PLGA-Zol than PLGA alone ($P<0.05$; Figure 6A). On the other hand, medium- and high-dose PLGA-Zol increased the numbers of osteoblast (ALP-positive cells) as compared with control and low-dose PLGA-Zol. The average number of osteoblast was higher with medium- and high-dose PLGA-Zol than PLGA alone and low-dose PLGA-Zol ($P<0.05$; Figure 6B). However, the low-dose PLGA-Zol did not change the number of osteoblast as compared with control.

Increased expression of bone-formation markers with PLGA-Zol delivery.

To evaluate the expression of the bone-formation markers Runx2, BMP2, BMP7, OCN and Col I at 6 weeks after surgery, we used immunohistochemistry of positive stained areas (Figure 7). The AOD of BMP2, OCN, Col I and RUNX2 positive staining

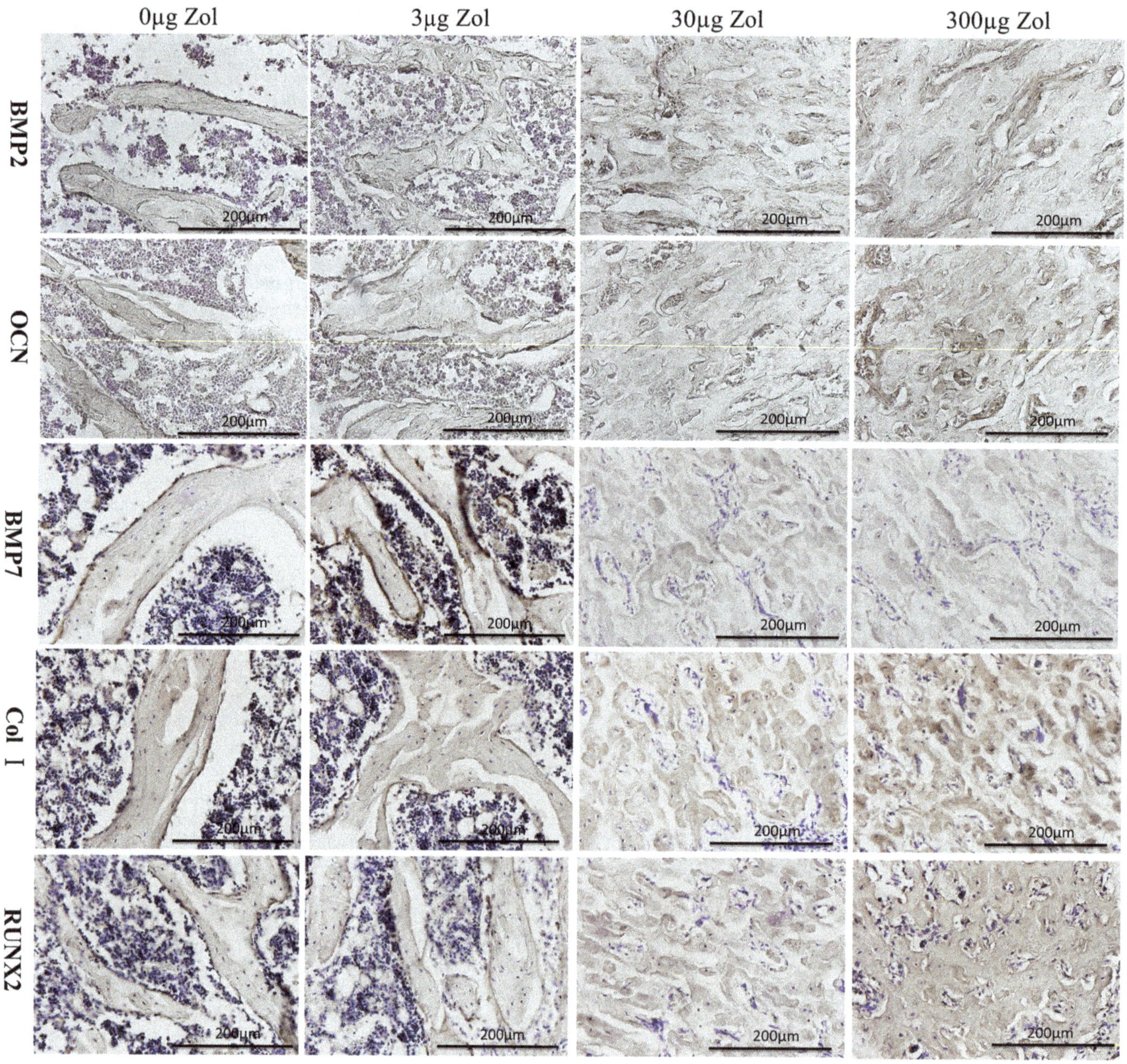

Figure 7. Immunohistochemistry of bone trabecular near the distal femoral epiphyseal plate. BMP2, OCN, BMP7, Col I and RUNX2 were expression in the bone matrix of newly formed trabecula. Osteocalcin (OCN), bone morphogenetic protein 2 (BMP2), bone morphogenetic protein 7 (BMP7), Type I collagen (Col I) and Runt-related transcription factor 2 (RUNX2).

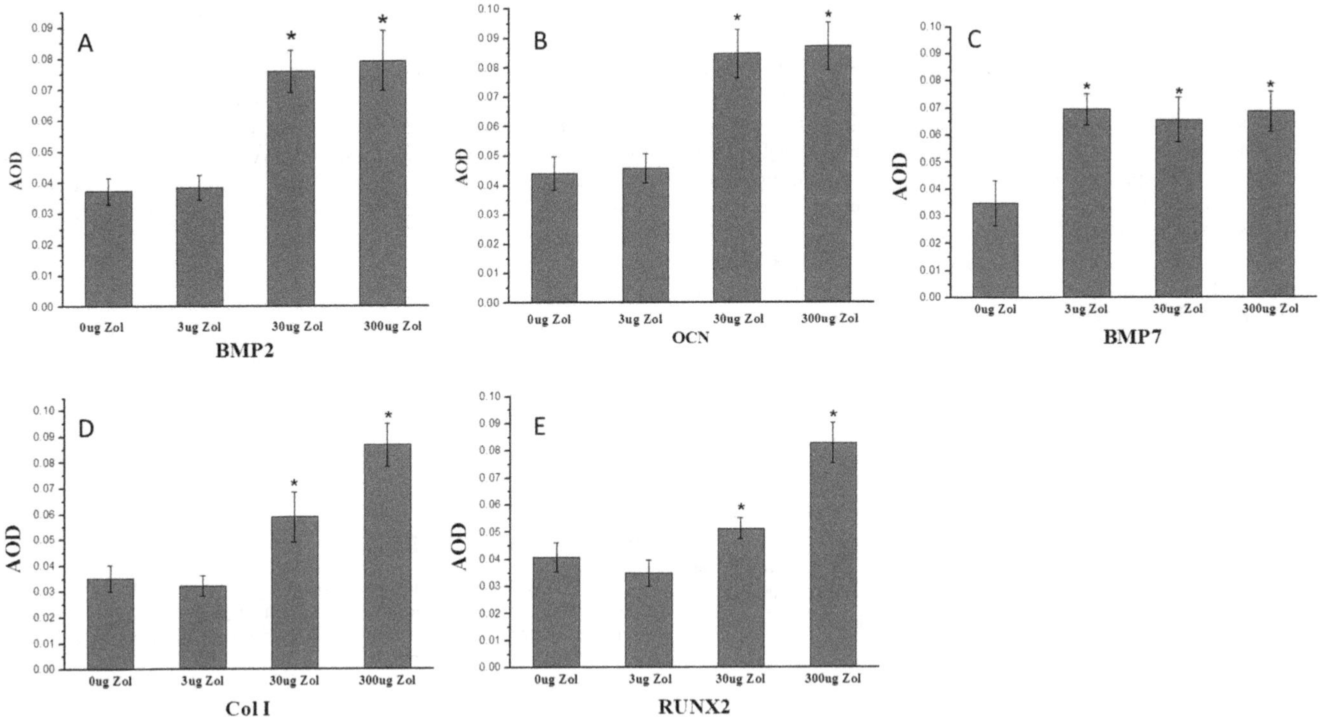

Figure 8. Quantitative results of immunohistochemistry staining for the expression of BMP2, OCN, BMP7, Col I and RUNX2. Osteocalcin (OCN), bone morphogenetic protein 2 (BMP2), bone morphogenetic protein 7 (BMP7), Type I collagen (Col I) and Runt-related transcription factor 2 (RUNX2). *P<0.05 compared with control group. AOD, average optical density.

area was higher with medium- and high-dose PLGA-Zol than control and low-dose treatment respectively (P<0.05; Figures 8A, 8B, 8D and 8E). Furthermore, AOD of BMP7 positive staining area was higher with various doses of PLGA-Zol than PLGA alone (P<0.05; Figure 8C).

Discussion

Our study has shown that a large amount of new bone formed near the distal femoral epiphyseal plate in rats with medium- and high-dose PLGA-Zol treatment. Controlled delivery of medium- and high-dose Zol enhanced mineralized tissue formation via decreasing the osteoclast number and in the meanwhile increasing the osteoblast number. Furthermore, medium- and high-dose PLGA-Zol accelerated the expression of bone-formation markers such as BMP2, OCN, BMP7, Col I and RUNX2 at the site of implantation.

Therapeutic approaches with BPs represent a convenient and effective mode of treating bone-related cancers, Paget's disease, and especially osteoporosis [23]. Intravenous Zol within 90 days after repair of low-trauma hip fracture was associated with the reduced rate of new clinical fractures and improved survival [24]. However, BPs inhibiting bone resorption cannot completely explain the reduction in fracture incidence. Most research has focused on inhibiting bone resorption by targeting the end effector cell, the osteoclast. Recently, some *in vitro* and *in vivo* evidence indicated that BPs may promote osteoblastic bone formation [9,11,25]. On the contrary, others suggested that BPs could decrease the proliferation of and inhibit osteoblast differentiation and mineralization [26–28]. Some researchers suggested that growth and prodifferentiation effects are exerted at low concentrations of BPs, with the inhibitory effects exerted at high concentrations [1]. Additionally, the effects of BPs may be time-dependent [29]. Thus, in this study, we used PLGA as a drug carrier to deliver the BP Zol and investigated the effect on local bone formation in rat. Controlled delivery of medium- and high-dose Zol enhanced bone formation at the site of implantation. In our study, the average BMD and BV/TV of the femoral metaphysis were greater with medium- and high-dose than low-dose PLGA-Zol and control treatment. The trabecular thickness was greater and the trabecular space was reduced with medium- and high-dose than low-dose PLGA-Zol and control treatment. However, the structure of the new bone was irregular. Using PLGA as a drug carrier for controlled delivery of Zol may promote local bone formation.

Some researchers investigated the effect of local delivery of BPs from screw or titanium implants *in vivo* and also found that locally delivered BPs could improve the bone density around the implant. However, biomechanical analysis showed that the maximal pullout force of the implant was associated with BPs concentration and treatment time [30,31].

The mechanism by which BPs increase bone mineral density and enhance bone formation is not completely understood. In the cellular level, many studies have shown that BPs can affect osteoclast recruitment, differentiation, and resorptive activity, and some may induce apoptosis [32]. On the other hand, BPs are able to prevent osteoblast apoptosis and have an anabolic effect on osteoblasts, which is an important role in enhancing bone formation [10,33]. The decreased osteoclast number and increased osteoblast number in our study also demonstrated this point. Someone suggested that the anti-apoptotic effects of BPs do not depend on inhibitory effects on osteoclasts because analogs that lack anti-resorptive activity could still inhibit apoptosis in osteoblasts without decreasing osteoclast viability [34,35]. BPs' anabolic effect on osteoblast might be via upregulation of BMP2, which is well recognized for stimulating proliferation and differentiation of mesenchymal progenitor cells.Thus resulting in the production of bone tissue [36]. It has been demonstrated that BMP2 is a necessary component of the signaling cascade that governs fracture repair [37]. In our study, immunohistochemistry revealed greater expression of BMP2 with medium- and high-dose than low-dose PLGA-Zol and control treatment. This result is consistent with the mass of newly formed bone. Other studies indicated that the anabolic effect of BPs on osteoblasts was possibly mediated by Cx43 hemichannel opening, thus leading to activation of Src/ERK [35,38,39]. Also, the combined use of BMP2 and Zol could enhance bone fracture healing in a mouse model of neurofibromatosis type 1 deficiency [40].

OCN is described as a necessary protein for bone mineralization. Our results show that local controlled delivery of low-dose Zol did not affect its expression, whereas medium- and high-dose PLGA-Zol increased its expression. In agreement with our results, Ponader et al. found a positive differentiation stimulus on osteoblast differentiation with quantification of alkaline phosphatase and OCN gene expression [41]. Koch et al. found that Zol at high concentrations enhanced the gene expression of OCN, whereas lower concentrations led to decreased gene expression [42].

The present study is potentially limited by the fact that detecting the distribution of local controlled delivery of Zol *in vivo* is difficult. The exact drug concentration on the site of implantation at different times is not clear and the mechanism of local action at various concentrations is not completely understood. In addition, the end time of this experiment was 6 weeks after surgery, which may be not the best observation period for new bone formation induced by BPs, because some investigators suggested that BPs could reduce bone turnover rate [43,44].

Conclusions

Our study supports that using PLGA as a drug carrier to deliver the BP Zol could promote local bone formation in rat. This method could be used for promoting local bone formation in the femoral head of osteonecrosis. However, this hypothesis needs further testing before clinical validation and further well-designed studies.

Author Contributions

Conceived and designed the experiments: JP SL. Performed the experiments: WG XW. Analyzed the data: QL YW AW. Contributed reagents/materials/analysis tools: QG XG WX. Wrote the paper: WG.

References

1. Bellido T, Plotkin LI (2011) Novel actions of bisphosphonates in bone: preservation of osteoblast and osteocyte viability. Bone 49: 50–55.
2. Green JR (2003) Antitumor effects of bisphosphonates. Cancer 97: 840–847.
3. Rodan GA, Martin TJ (2000) Therapeutic approaches to bone diseases. Science 289: 1508–1514.
4. Liberman UA, Weiss SR, Broll J, Minne HW, Quan H, et al. (1995) Effect of oral alendronate on bone mineral density and the incidence of fractures in postmenopausal osteoporosis. The Alendronate Phase III Osteoporosis Treatment Study Group. N Engl J Med 333: 1437–1443.
5. Eggelmeijer F, Papapoulos SE, van Paassen HC, Dijkmans BA, Breedveld FC (1994) Clinical and biochemical response to single infusion of pamidronate in patients with active rheumatoid arthritis: a double blind placebo controlled study. J Rheumatol 21: 2016–2020.
6. Lala R, Matarazzo P, Bertelloni S, Buzi F, Rigon F, et al. (2000) Pamidronate treatment of bone fibrous dysplasia in nine children with McCune-Albright syndrome. Acta Paediatr 89: 188–193.
7. Bembi B, Parma A, Bottega M, Ceschel S, Zanatta M, et al. (1997) Intravenous pamidronate treatment in osteogenesis imperfecta. Journal of Pediatrics 131: 622–625.
8. Tenenbaum HC, Torontali M, Sukhu B (1992) Effects of bisphosphonates and inorganic pyrophosphate on osteogenesis in vitro. Bone 13: 249–255.
9. Xiong Y, Yang HJ, Feng J, Shi ZL, Wu LD (2009) Effects of alendronate on the proliferation and osteogenic differentiation of MG-63 cells. J Int Med Res 37: 407–416.
10. Im GI, Qureshi SA, Kenney J, Rubash HE, Shanbhag AS (2004) Osteoblast proliferation and maturation by bisphosphonates. Biomaterials 25: 4105–4115.
11. Kim HK, Kim JH, Abbas AA, Yoon TR (2009) Alendronate enhances osteogenic differentiation of bone marrow stromal cells: a preliminary study. Clin Orthop Relat Res 467: 3121–3128.
12. Ruggiero SL, Dodson TB, Assael LA, Landesberg R, Marx RE, et al. (2009) American Association of Oral and Maxillofacial Surgeons position paper on bisphosphonate-related osteonecrosis of the jaw - 2009 update. Aust Endod J 35: 119–130.
13. Sharma D, Ivanovski S, Slevin M, Hamlet S, Pop TS, et al. (2013) Bisphosphonate-related osteonecrosis of jaw (BRONJ): diagnostic criteria and possible pathogenic mechanisms of an unexpected anti-angiogenic side effect. Vasc Cell 5: 1.
14. Aya-ay J, Athavale S, Morgan-Bagley S, Bian H, Bauss F, et al. (2007) Retention, distribution, and effects of intraosseously administered ibandronate in the infarcted femoral head. J Bone Miner Res 22: 93–100.
15. Belfrage O, Flivik G, Sundberg M, Kesteris U, Tagil M (2011) Local treatment of cancellous bone grafts with BMP-7 and zoledronate increases both the bone formation rate and bone density: a bone chamber study in rats. Acta Orthop 82: 228–233.
16. Gopferich A (1996) Mechanisms of polymer degradation and erosion. Biomaterials 17: 103–114.
17. Sinha VR, Trehan A (2003) Biodegradable microspheres for protein delivery. J Control Release 90: 261–280.
18. Freiberg S, Zhu XX (2004) Polymer microspheres for controlled drug release. Int J Pharm 282: 1–18.
19. Kost J, Langer R (1992) Responsive polymer systems for controlled delivery of therapeutics. Trends Biotechnol 10: 127–131.
20. Cenni E, Granchi D, Avnet S, Fotia C, Salerno M, et al. (2008) Biocompatibility of poly(D,L-lactide-co-glycolide) nanoparticles conjugated with alendronate. Biomaterials 29: 1400–1411.
21. Dai R, Ma Y, Sheng Z, Jin Y, Zhang Y, et al. (2008) Effects of genistein on vertebral trabecular bone microstructure, bone mineral density, microcracks, osteocyte density, and bone strength in ovariectomized rats. J Bone Miner Metab 26: 342–349.
22. Lu JG, Li Y, Li L, Kan X (2011) Overexpression of osteopontin and integrin alphav in laryngeal and hypopharyngeal carcinomas associated with differentiation and metastasis. J Cancer Res Clin Oncol 137: 1613–1618.
23. Russell RG, Watts NB, Ebetino FH, Rogers MJ (2008) Mechanisms of action of bisphosphonates: similarities and differences and their potential influence on clinical efficacy. Osteoporos Int 19: 733–759.
24. Lyles KW, Colon-Emeric CS, Magaziner JS, Adachi JD, Pieper CF, et al. (2007) Zoledronic Acid in Reducing Clinical Fracture and Mortality after Hip Fracture. N Engl J Med 357: nihpa40967.
25. Pan B, To LB, Farrugia AN, Findlay DM, Green J, et al. (2004) The nitrogen-containing bisphosphonate, zoledronic acid, increases mineralisation of human bone-derived cells in vitro. Bone 34: 112–123.
26. Idris AI, Rojas J, Greig IR, Van't Hof RJ, Ralston SH (2008) Aminobisphosphonates cause osteoblast apoptosis and inhibit bone nodule formation in vitro. Calcif Tissue Int 82: 191–201.
27. Pozzi S, Vallet S, Mukherjee S, Cirstea D, Vaghela N, et al. (2009) High-dose zoledronic acid impacts bone remodeling with effects on osteoblastic lineage and bone mechanical properties. Clin Cancer Res 15: 5829–5839.
28. Greiner S, Kadow-Romacker A, Lubberstedt M, Schmidmaier G, Wildemann B (2007) The effect of zoledronic acid incorporated in a poly(D,L-lactide) implant coating on osteoblasts in vitro. J Biomed Mater Res A 80: 769–775.
29. Wang CZ, Chen SM, Chen CH, Wang CK, Wang GJ, et al. (2010) The effect of the local delivery of alendronate on human adipose-derived stem cell-based bone regeneration. Biomaterials 31: 8674–8683.
30. Peter B, Pioletti DP, Laib S, Bujoli B, Pilet P, et al. (2005) Calcium phosphate drug delivery system: influence of local zoledronate release on bone implant osteointegration. Bone 36: 52–60.
31. Roshan-Ghias A, Arnoldi J, Procter P, Pioletti DP (2011) In vivo assessment of local effects after application of bone screws delivering bisphosphonates into a compromised cancellous bone site. Clin Biomech (Bristol, Avon) 26: 1039–1043.
32. Russell RG (2011) Bisphosphonates: the first 40 years. Bone 49: 2–19.
33. Plotkin LI, Weinstein RS, Parfitt AM, Roberson PK, Manolagas SC, et al. (1999) Prevention of osteocyte and osteoblast apoptosis by bisphosphonates and calcitonin. J Clin Invest 104: 1363–1374.
34. Xu XL, Gou WL, Wang AY, Wang Y, Guo QY, et al. (2013) Basic research and clinical applications of bisphosphonates in bone disease: what have we learned over the last 40 years? J Transl Med 11: 303.

35. Plotkin LI, Bivi N, Bellido T (2011) A bisphosphonate that does not affect osteoclasts prevents osteoblast and osteocyte apoptosis and the loss of bone strength induced by glucocorticoids in mice. Bone 49: 122–127.
36. Mundy G, Garrett R, Harris S, Chan J, Chen D, et al. (1999) Stimulation of bone formation in vitro and in rodents by statins. Science 286: 1946–1949.
37. Tsuji K, Bandyopadhyay A, Harfe BD, Cox K, Kakar S, et al. (2006) BMP2 activity, although dispensable for bone formation, is required for the initiation of fracture healing. Nature Genetics 38: 1424–1429.
38. Plotkin LI, Lezcano V, Thostenson J, Weinstein RS, Manolagas SC, et al. (2008) Connexin 43 is required for the anti-apoptotic effect of bisphosphonates on osteocytes and osteoblasts in vivo. J Bone Miner Res 23: 1712–1721.
39. Jeong HM, Jin YH, Choi YH, Chung JO, Cho DH, et al. (2013) Risedronate increases osteoblastic differentiation and function through connexin43. Biochem Biophys Res Commun 432: 152–156.
40. Schindeler A, Birke O, Yu NY, Morse A, Ruys A, et al. (2011) Distal tibial fracture repair in a neurofibromatosis type 1-deficient mouse treated with recombinant bone morphogenetic protein and a bisphosphonate. J Bone Joint Surg Br 93: 1134–1139.
41. Ponader S, Brandt H, Vairaktaris E, von Wilmowsky C, Nkenke E, et al. (2008) In vitro response of hFOB cells to pamidronate modified sodium silicate coated cellulose scaffolds. Colloids Surf B Biointerfaces 64: 275–283.
42. Koch FP, Merkel C, Al-Nawas B, Smeets R, Ziebart T, et al. (2011) Zoledronate, ibandronate and clodronate enhance osteoblast differentiation in a dose dependent manner–a quantitative in vitro gene expression analysis of Dlx5, Runx2, OCN, MSX1 and MSX2. J Craniomaxillofac Surg 39: 562–569.
43. Gourion-Arsiquaud S, Allen MR, Burr DB, Vashishth D, Tang SY, et al. (2010) Bisphosphonate treatment modifies canine bone mineral and matrix properties and their heterogeneity. Bone 46: 666–672.
44. Paccou J, Confavreux CB, David C, Leboime A, Mehsen N, et al. (2010) Stabilized severe osteoporosis: should the treatment be stopped? Joint Bone Spine 77 Suppl 2: S120–127.

5

Dual-Layered Nanogel-Coated Hollow Lipid/Polypeptide Conjugate Assemblies for Potential pH-Triggered Intracellular Drug Release

Wen-Hsuan Chiang[1], Wen-Chia Huang[1], Ming-Yin Shen[1,2], Che-Hsu Wang[1], Yi-Fong Huang[3], Sung-Chyr Lin[3], Chorng-Shyan Chern[4], Hsin-Cheng Chiu[1]*

1 Department of Biomedical Engineering and Environmental Sciences, National Tsing Hua University, Hsinchu, Taiwan, **2** Department of Surgery, National Taiwan University Hospital-Hsinchu Branch, Hsinchu, Taiwan, **3** Department of Chemical Engineering, National Chung Hsing University, Taichung, Taiwan, **4** Department of Chemical Engineering, National Taiwan University of Science and Technology, Taipei, Taiwan

Abstract

To achieve effective intracellular anticancer drug delivery, the polymeric vesicles supplemented with the pH-responsive outlayered gels as a delivery system of doxorubicin (DOX) were developed from self-assembly of the lipid/polypeptide adduct, distearin grafted poly(γ-glutamic acid) (poly(γ-GA)), followed by sequential deposition of chitosan and poly(γ-GA-co-γ-glutamyl oxysuccinimide)-g-monomethoxy poly(ethylene glycol) in combination with in situ covalent cross-linking on assembly surfaces. The resultant gel-caged polymeric vesicles (GCPVs) showed superior performance in regulating drug release in response to the external pH change. Under typical physiological conditions (pH 7.4 and 37°C) at which the γ-GA/DOX ionic pairings remained mostly undisturbed, the dense outlayered gels of GCPVs significantly reduced the premature leakage of the uncomplexed payload. With the environmental pH being reduced from pH 7.4 to 4.7, the drug liberation was appreciably promoted by the massive disruption of the ionic γ-GA/DOX complexes along with the significant swelling of nanogel layers upon the increased protonation of chitosan chain segments. After being internalized by HeLa cells via endocytosis, GCPVs exhibited cytotoxic effect comparable to free DOX achieved by rapidly releasing the payload in intracellular acidic endosomes and lysosomes. This strongly implies the great promise of such unique GCPVs as an intracellular drug delivery carrier for potential anticancer treatment.

Editor: Xiaoming He, The Ohio State University, United States of America

Funding: This work is financially supported by the National Tsing Hua University (102N2733E1 and 101N2716E1) and National Taiwan Hospital-Hsinchu Branch (HCH-101-17 and NTHU-HCH100-03). The funders had no role in study design, data collection and analysis, decision to publish, or preparation of the manuscript.

Competing Interests: The authors have declared that no competing interests exist.

* E-mail: hscchiu@mx.nthu.edu.tw

Introduction

Over the past decades, various nanoassemblies such as liposomes, polymeric micelles and polymeric vesicles (polymersomes) have been exploited extensively as anticancer drug transport vehicles due to their great capability of delivering payloads to tumor regions achieved primarily by the enhanced permeability and retention effects [1,2,3,4,5,6]. Although these nanovehicles show promise in selective delivery of therapeutic agents to target sites, several intractable problems (e.g., the premature drug leakage from carriers and poor intracellular drug-release property that lead to an insufficient drug bioavailability for killing cancer cells and undesired side effects) have not been completely overcome yet [7,8,9]. In this regard, substantial efforts have been devoted to the development of stimuli-responsive devices as novel drug delivery systems capable of controlling payload release in response to biological stimuli such as temperature [10,11], pH [12,13,14,15], and redox potential [16,17,18]. The stimuli-triggered drug liberation could significantly promote therapeutic efficacy and minimize side effects. Among these stimuli, acidic pH has been frequently adopted as an optimal internal trigger due to the mildly acidic pH existing in tumor tissues and in the intracellular organelles including both endosomes and lysosomes [13,14]. To achieve the pH-triggered intracellular drug release, various nanovehicles functionalized with pH-responsive structural characteristics have been developed. By contrast, in order to meet the basic requirement of the assembly stability in practical drug delivery application without impairing or even with promoting the stimuli-triggered characteristics, several approaches such as covalent crosslinking [19,20,21], mineralization [22,23,24], and surface modification [25,26,27] of nanoparticles have been supplemented to enhance their structural integrity under varying conditions.

As described by Shuai and co-workers [20], through the formation of disulfide cross-links inside the intermediate layer of polymeric micelles assembled from a triblock copolymer composed of monomethoxy poly(ethylene glycol) (mPEG), 2-mercaptoethylamine-grafted poly(L-aspartic acid) and 2-(diisopropylamino)ethylamine-grafted poly(L-aspartic acid) (PAsp(DIP)) in aqueous solution of pH 10.0, dual pH- and redox-responsive cross-linked micelles were developed as carriers for intracellular delivery of anticancer drug (doxorubicin (DOX)). With being internalized into cancer cells and localized within glutathione-rich acidic lysosomes (ca. pH 5.0), DOX-loaded micelles showed a prompt payload release as a result of both cleavage of the disulfide crosslinks of intermediate gel layers and disintegration of PAsp(DIP) cores. Han et al. [23] reported that the hyaluronic acid-based nanoparticles after being mineralized by calcium phosphate exhibited a rather robust structure at pH 7.4 and were utilized as a pH-responsive DOX delivery vehicle. While the solution pH being adjusted from 7.4 to 5.0, the DOX release from the mineralized nanoparticles was significantly promoted by the dissolution of calcium phosphate in weak acidic environment. On the other hand, Nguyen and co-workers [27] developed the polymer-derived nanocages as a potential molecular drug delivery platform by the insertion of the cholesterol-modified poly(acrylic acid) into lipid membranes of liposomes and subsequent covalent crosslinking with alkyne-functionalized diamine linker. These gel-caged liposomes exhibited pH-responsive characteristics capable of triggering the DOX release from the liposomes under mild acidic conditions upon the formation of temporary pores throughout liposomal membranes as a result of the structural variation of gel-like polymer cages.

Distinct from these pioneered studies, a step-by-step polyelectrolyte deposition technique in combination with in situ covalent crosslinking was used in this work to endow polymeric vesicles with highly biocompatible, robust and pH-responsive outlayered gels for improved intracellular DOX delivery efficiency. The proposed approach involves the synthesis of the lipid/polypeptide conjugate, poly(γ-glutamic acid-co-γ-distearin glutamate) (poly(γ-GA-co-γ-DSGA)), followed by the self-assembly of the resultant conjugate into polymeric vesicles in aqueous solution of DOX. Through the sequential deposition of chitosan and poly(γ-GA-co-γ-glutamyl oxysuccinimide)-g-mPEG (poly(γ-GA-co-γ-GAOSu)-g-mPEG) on the outer surfaces of DOX-encapsulated lipid/polypeptide conjugate vesicles upon paired electrostatic attraction and then covalent crosslinking via aminolysis of γ-GAOSu moieties with primary amines of chitosan, drug-loaded gel-caged polymeric vesicles (GCPVs) were thus attained. The physicochemical properties of these unique drug-loaded GCPVs were then characterized in detail. The effects of the dual-layered gels of GCPVs on the in vitro drug release performance were also explored. In addition, the cell uptake of the DOX-loaded GCPVs and their cytotoxicity against human cervical tumor cell line, HeLa cell, were evaluated to demonstrate the GCPVs developed in this study as a rather potential intracellular drug delivery carrier.

Materials and Methods

Materials

1,2-Distearoyl-rac-glycerol (distearin) was purchased from Bachem and DOX (in the hydrochloride salt form) obtained from Seedchem. Poly(γ-GA) (M_n > 100 kDa) was purchased from Vedan. *N*-Hydroxysuccinimide (NHS) and *N,N'*-dicyclohexylcarbodiimide (DCC) were obtained from Aldrich and Acros, respectively. Chitosan was purchased from Fluka. Synthesis and characterization of mPEG-NH_2 (5000 g/mol) was described in our previous studies [28,29]. HeLa cells were purchased from Food Industry Research and Development Institute of Taiwan. Dulbecco's modified Eagle medium (DMEM) and Hoechst 33258 were purchased from Invitrogen. The reagent 3-(4,5-dimethylthiazol-2yl)-2,5-diphenyltetrazolium bromide) (MTT) was purchased from TCI. Deionized water was produced from Milli-Q Synthesis (18 MΩ, Millipore). All other chemicals were reagent grade and used as received.

Fractionation of Poly(γ-GA)

Poly(γ-GA) (1.0 g) was dissolved in aqueous solution of $NaHCO_3$ (67.6 M)/NaOH (5.0 M) (9/1 (v/v)) with a total volume of ca. 10 mL and the treatment was carried out at 90°C for 3 h. Subsequently, HCl solution (with a concentration equivalent to NaOH) was added into the above polymer solution. This was followed by dialysis (Cellu Sep MWCO 3500) against deionized water for 7 days. The poly(γ-GA) product was then collected by lyophilization. The molecular weight and polydispersity of the resultant poly(γ-GA) were determined by size exclusion chromatography (SEC) (Agilent 1100, PL Aquagel-OH columns in series GF083: separation range 100-30K; GF084: 10K-200K and GF086: 200K-10M, calibrated with poly(sodium acrylate) standards of known molecular weights with narrow molecular weight distributions (eluent: tris buffer 0.01 M, pH 7.4; flow rate: 1.0 mL/min; RI detector (Aglient 1100)).

Synthesis of Lipid/Polypeptide Adduct

The synthetic route of poly(γ-GA-co-γ-DSGA) is illustrated in Figure 1a. To partially activate the γ-GA residues of poly(γ-GA) into the reactive γ-GAOSu moieties, NHS (50 mol % with respect to the γ-GA residues) and DCC (equal to molar concentration of NHS) used as the coupling agent were added to the solution of poly(γ-GA) in DMSO/pyridine (3/1 (v/v)). The reaction was carried out at 4°C for 48 h. The undesired product, *N,N'*-dicyclohexylurea (DCU), was then removed by the repeated filtration of the concentrated polymer solution. The partial transesterification of poly(γ-GA-co-γ-GAOSu) with distearin (25 mol% with respect to the original γ-GA residues in poly(γ-GA)) was then conducted at 60°C for 7 days, using 4-dimethylaminopyridine as the catalyst. This was followed by the dialysis (Cellu Sep MWCO 12000~14000) against DMSO/THF (3/1 (v/v) solution) to eliminate the unreacted lipid species. Afterward, full hydrolysis of the remaining γ-GAOSu into the γ-GA residues was achieved by the addition of pH 7.4 tris buffer. The solution was then dialyzed (Cellu Sep MWCO 12000~14000) against deionized water to remove NHS, DMSO and THF. Finally, the purified lipid/polypeptide conjugate was collected by lyophilization. The chemical composition was determined by ^{1}H-NMR (Varian Unityinova 500 NMR Spectrometer) using DMSO-d_6 as the solvent.

Synthesis of Poly(γ-GA-co-γ-GAOSu)-g-mPEG

Coupling poly(γ-GA-co-γ-GAOSu) with mPEG-NH_2 grafts (M_w 5000 g/mol) (10 mol% with respect to the original γ-GA residues in poly(γ-GA)) was conducted at 25°C for 96 h under stirring. The polymer solution was dialyzed (Cellu Sep MWCO 12000~14000) against DMSO/ethanol (1/1 (v/v)) for 5 days to remove NHS and unreacted mPEG-NH_2. The final product was collected by precipitation from ether/ethanol solution. The grafting reaction is illustrated in Figure 1b. The purity was confirmed by SEC. The chemical composition was determined by ^{1}H-NMR using DMSO-d_6 as the solvent at the ambient temperature.

Preparation of DOX-Loaded Lipid/Polypeptide Vesicles

The lipid modified polypeptide (1.0 mg) was first dispersed in 1.0 mL phosphate buffer (pH 7.4, I 0.01 M) containing DOX (0.125 mg/mL) and then stirred for 12 h. The above dispersion was then subjected to ultrasonication with cooling in an ice-water bath for 5 min (VCX750Vibra-Cell Ultra Sonics Processor, a probe-type ultrasonicator) to produce the vesicle suspension. Afterward, the aqueous solution of the DOX-loaded vesicles was

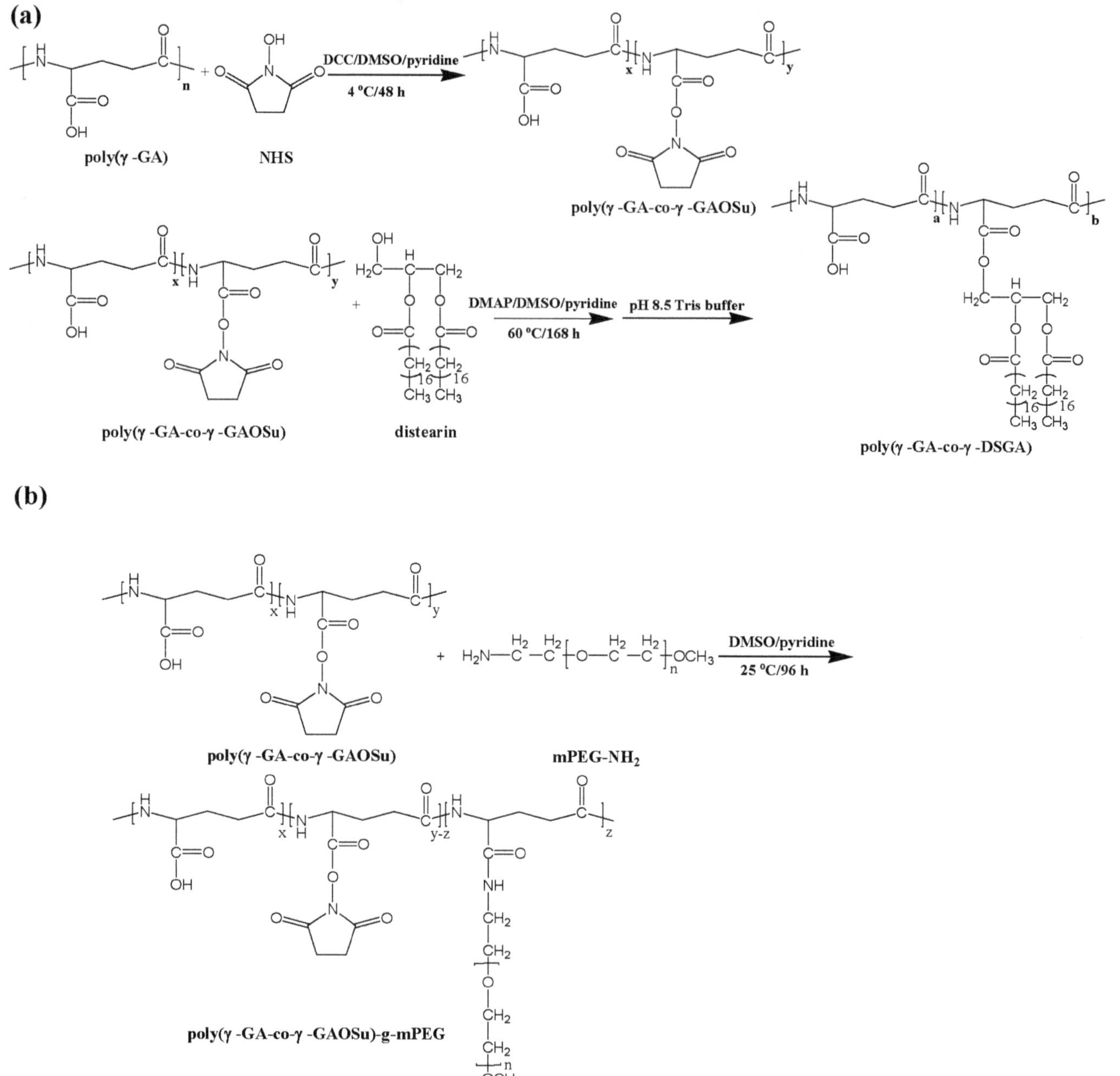

Figure 1. Synthetic route of (a) poly(γ-GA-co-γ-DSGA) and (b) poly(γ-GA-co-γ-GAOSu)-g-mPEG.

dialyzed (Cellu Sep MWCO 12000~14000) against phosphate buffer (pH 7.4, I 0.01 M) for 12 h to remove unloaded DOX species. The DOX-loaded vesicles were dissolved completely by the addition of DMSO at a volume ratio of $DMSO/H_2O$ = 9/1 and the amount of DOX was quantitatively determined by fluorescence measurements on a Hitachi F-7500 fluorescence spectrometer. The excitation was performed at 480 nm and the emission spectra were recorded in the range 500–700 nm. The calibration curve was established by standard DOX solutions of seven concentrations in the $DMSO/H_2O$ (9/1 (v/v)) solution. Drug loading efficiency (DLE) was calculated as follows:

$$DLE(\%) = W_L / W_F$$

where W_L and W_F represent the weights of loaded DOX and DOX in feed, respectively.

Preparation of DOX-Loaded GCPVs

Coating dual-layered nanogels on the DOX-loaded polymeric vesicles was achieved by depositing chitosan and poly(γ-GA-co-γ-GAOSu)-g-mPEG in sequence onto the vesicle surface via the complementary electrostatic attraction. The aqueous solution of chitosan (5.0 mg/mL, 4.0 mL, pH 5.0) was directly added into the

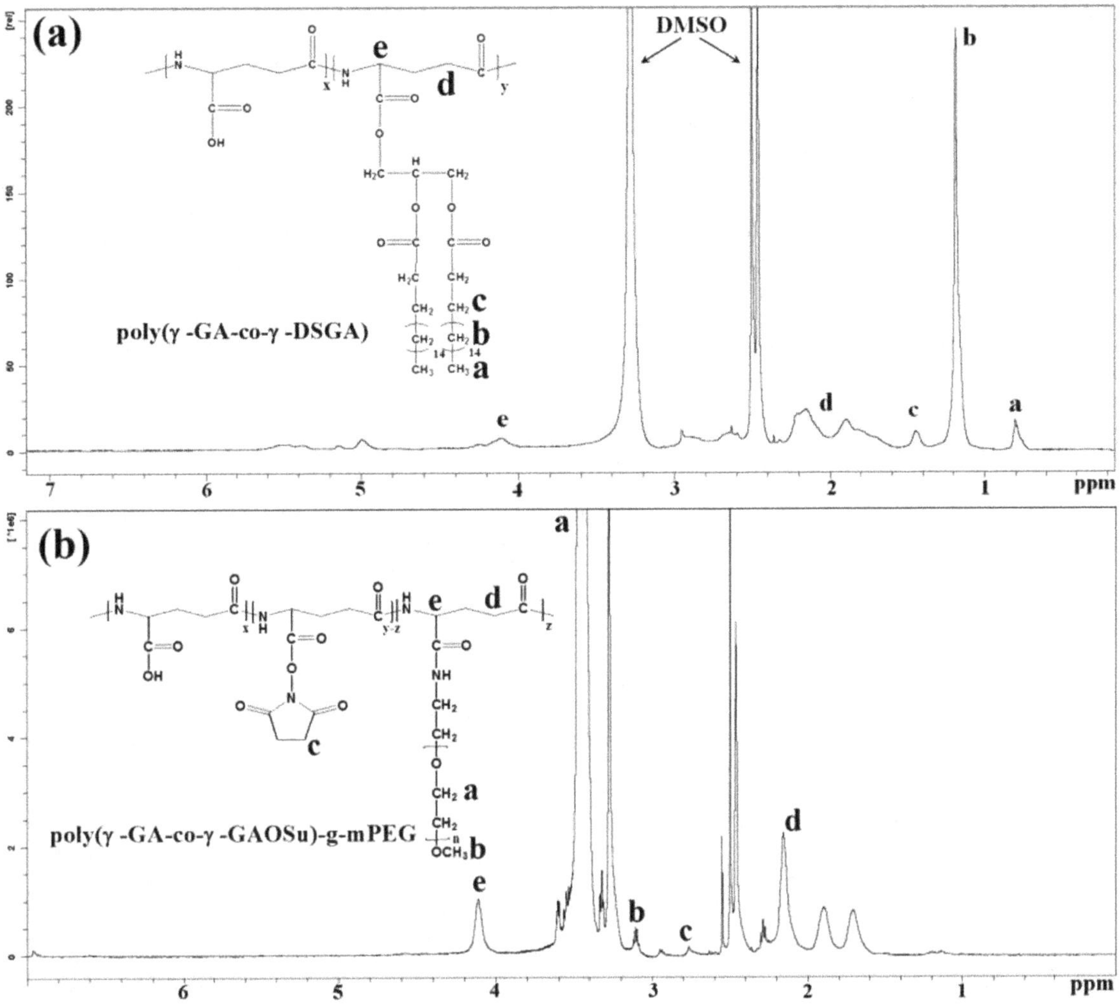

Figure 2. ^{1}**H-NMR spectra of (a) poly(γ-GA-co-γ-DSGA) and (b) poly(γ-GA-co-γ-GAOSu)-g-mPEG in DMSO-d_6 at 25°C.**

above DOX-loaded vesicle suspension of pH 7.4 (6.0 mL) and the mixture was then stirred for 8 h. This was followed by the addition of the DOX-loaded chitosan-coated vesicle dispersion (1.0 mL) to the aqueous solution of poly(γ-GA-co-γ-GAOSu)-g-mPEG (3.5 mg/mL, pH 7.4). The resultant dispersion was then stirred at ambient temperature for 12 h to achieve the ionic polyelectrolyte complex formation and in situ covalent crosslinking via aminolysis of primary amines from chitosan with reactive γ-GAOSu residues. The aqueous dispersion of the DOX-loaded GCPVs was subjected to ultrafiltration (Amicon 8200 with a Millipore PBMK membrane, MCWO 300000) in phosphate buffer (pH 7.4, I 0.01 M) to eliminate the coating materials that were not cross-linked.

Table 1. Recipes, compositions and average molecular weights of the derived polypeptide adducts.

sample	reaction feed (mol %)	composition ratio[a] (mol %)	M_w ($\times 10^{-4}$ g/mol)
poly(γ-GA-co-γ-DSGA)	γ-GA/NHS/distearin	γ-GA/DSGA	
	100/50/25	82/18	2.81[b]
poly(γ-GA-co-γ-GAOSu)-g-mPEG	γ-GA/NHS/mPEG	γ-GA/γ-GAOSu/mPEG	
	100/30/10	76/20/4	4.09[c]

[a]Determined by ^{1}H-NMR in DMSO-d_6 at 20°C.
[b]Obtained by theoretical calculation as follows: poly(γ-GA) M_w 15600 (g/mol) + number of conjugated distearin moieties × 625 (M_w of distearin)
[c]Obtained by theoretical calculation as follows: poly(γ-GA) M_w 15600 (g/mol) + number of conjugated Osu moieties ×114 (M_w of OSu) + number of mPEG grafts ×5000 (M_w of mPEG).

Structural Characterization

The mean hydrodynamic diameter (D_h), particle size distribution (PSD) and zeta potential of the pristine polymeric vesicles, the DOX-loaded vesicles and GCPVs in aqueous solutions were determined by a Malvern Zetasizer Nano-ZS instrument at a scattering angle of 173° equipped with a 4 mW He-Ne laser operating at λ = 632.8 nm. Prior to measurement, the sample was equilibrated at 25°C for 20 min. The data reported herein represent an average of at least triplicate measurements. To identify the morphology of polymeric assemblies, the ratio of the root-mean-square radius of gyration (R_g) to hydrodynamic radius (R_h) of particles was obtained by dynamic and static light scattering (DLS/SLS) measurements. Herein, R_h was determined by a Brookhaven BI-200SM goniometer equipped with a BI-9000 AT digital correlator using a solid-state laser (35 mW, λ = 637 nm) at a scattering angle of 90°. The CONTIN algorithm method was employed for DLS data analysis in order to confirm the absence of bimodal particle size distribution of the polymeric assemblies with greatly enhanced reliability. As to R_g, it was obtained from the angle-dependent measurement of the light scattering intensity. A Berry plot of the scattering intensity ($I_{ex}^{1/2}$) versus the square of scattering vector (q^2) was used for quantitative determination of R_g [30]. In addition, the angular dependence of the autocorrelation functions was assessed using the same instrument as described above. Correlation functions were analyzed by the cumulant method at different angles.

Transmission Electron Microscopy (TEM) Examination

The sample was prepared by placing a few drops of aqueous dispersion of the lipid/polypeptide conjugate assemblies on a 300-mesh copper grid covered with carbon and allowed to stand at 25°C for 20 s. Excess solution on the grid was gently removed with absorbent paper. This was followed by negative staining of the sample for 20 s using a uranyl acetate solution (2.0 wt %). The sample was then dried at 25°C for 2 days. The TEM image was acquired on a JEOL JEM-1200 CXII microscope operating at an accelerating voltage of 120 kV.

In vitro Drug Release

The in vitro DOX release from the drug-loaded polymeric vesicles was assessed in buffer solutions. The phosphate buffer saline (PBS) of pH 7.4 (or the succinate buffer of 4.7) was used as the release medium in this study. The DOX-loaded polymeric vesicles (or GCPVs) dispersed in phosphate buffer (pH 7.4, 2.0 mL) was transferred to a cellulose membrane tube (Cellu Sep MWCO 12000–14000). The dialysis tube was then placed in the release medium (100 mL) and gently shaken (100 rpm) in a water bath at 37°C. At the preset time intervals, 1.0 mL of external buffer solution (either PBS or succinate buffer) was withdrawn and replaced with an equal volume of fresh medium. The concentration of DOX was determined by fluorescence measurements using the pertinent calibration curve of DOX with various concentrations in aqueous solution of either pH 7.4 or 4.7.

Cellular Uptake Study

HeLa cells (1.0×10^5 cells/well) were incubated in culture medium for 24 h and then treated with free DOX and the DOX-loaded vesicles and GCPVs, respectively, at a DOX concentration of 10 μM at 37°C for either 1 or 2 h. After being washed twice with PBS, cells were detached by trypsin-EDTA solution and dispersed in 0.5 mL of PBS. The cellular uptake of DOX was examined by a FACSCalibur flow cytometer (BD Bioscience). For confocal laser scanning microscopy (CLSM) studies, HeLa cells (1×10^5 cells/mL) were cultured in DMEM in glass bottom culture dishes at 37 °C for 24 h. The medium was then removed and the cells were washed twice with PBS. Cells were treated with free DOX and the DOX-loaded GCPVs, respectively, at a DOX concentration of 10 μM at 37°C for 2 h. Cells were washed with PBS, fixed with 4% formaldehyde and then stained with Hoechst 33258 for 10 min. The cellular uptake of DOX was visualized by OLYMPUS FV1000 confocal imaging system (Olympus, Japan) at the excitation and emission wavelength of 488 and 590 nm, respectively.

In vitro Cytotoxicity Evaluation

The in vitro cytotoxicity of the DOX-loaded GCPVs and DOX-free GCPVs was evaluated by MTT assay with HeLa cells. For comparison, free DOX was used as a positive control. HeLa cells were seeded in 96-well plates (1×10^4 cells/well) and incubated at 37°C for 24 h. The medium was then replaced with 100 μL of fresh medium containing free DOX or the DOX-loaded GCPVs at an equivalent DOX concentration ranging from 0.01 to 10 μM or the DOX-free GCPVs, and cells were incubated for additional 48 h. Afterward, 10 μL of MTT (5.0 mg/mL) was added into each well, followed by incubation at 37°C for 4 h. Following the removal of the supernatant, 100 μL of DMSO was added into each well to dissolve the precipitate. The optical density (OD) at 570 nm was measured with a SpectraMax M5 microplate reader.

Results and Discussion

Synthesis and Characterization of Poly(γ-GA-co-γ-DSGA) and Poly(γ-GA-co-γ-GAOSu)-g-mPEG

The relative molecular weight and polydispersity of the fractionated poly(γ-GA) were determined by SEC to be ca. 15600 g/mol and 1.46, respectively. Through partial transesterification of poly(γ-GA-co-γ-GAOSu) with distearin and subsequent full hydrolysis of the residual γ-GAOSu moieties into γ-GA residues in tris buffer of pH 7.4, the lipid/polypeptide conjugate,

Table 2. D_h, PSD and zeta potential of the polymeric vesicles, DOX-loaded vesicles, DOX-loaded chitosan-caged vesicles and DOX-loaded GCPVs in aqueous solutions at 25°C.

Sample	D_h (nm)[a]	PSD	Zeta potential (mV)
Pristine vesicles at pH 7.4	150±7	0.24	-24±4
DOX-loaded vesicles at pH 7.4	142±4	0.25	-18±4
DOX-loaded chitosan-caged vesicles at pH 6.0	149±5	0.20	+26±3
DOX-loaded GCPVs at pH 7.4	168±5	0.17	-5±1

[a]Determined by DLS (Malvern Zetasizer Nano-ZS instrument) at a scattering angle of 173°, using the cumulant analysis method.

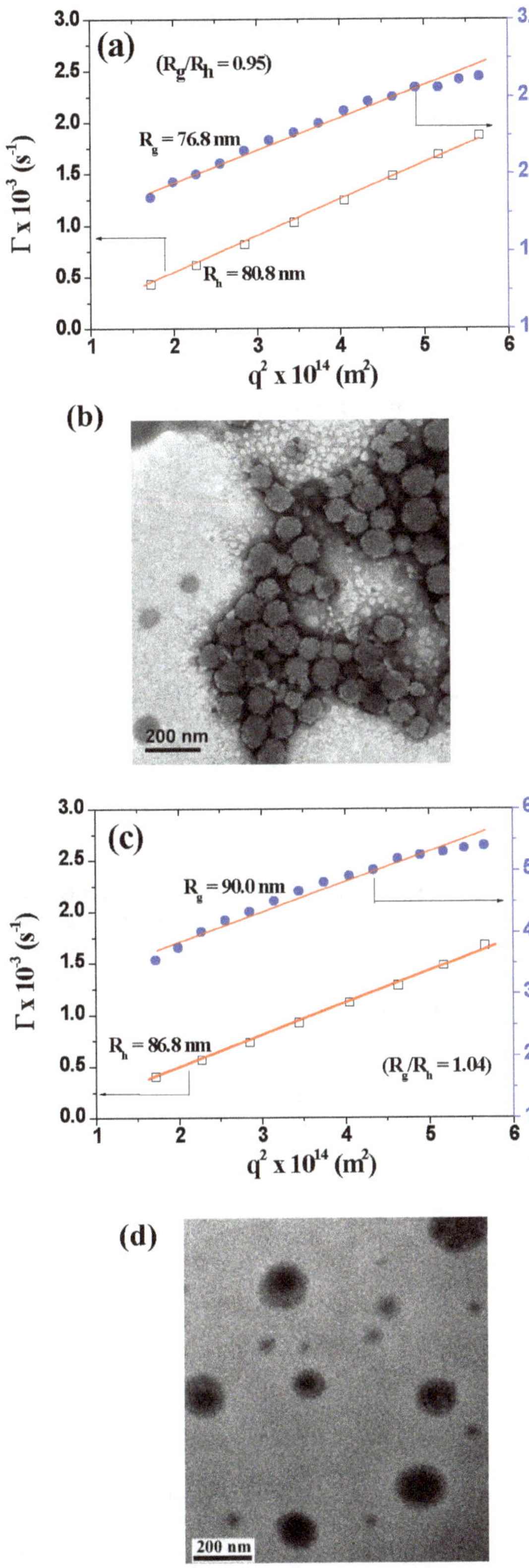

Figure 3. Angle-dependent DLS/SLS data and TEM images of lipid/polypeptide conjugate vesicles (a, b) and DOX-loaded GCPVs (c, d).

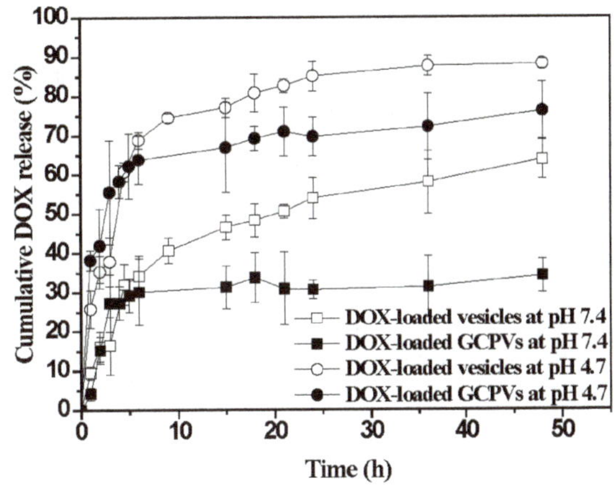

Figure 4. Cumulative drug release profiles of DOX-loaded vesicles and DOX-loaded GCPVs in aqueous solutions of pH 7.4 and 4.7, respectively, at 37°C.

poly(γ-GA-co-γ-DSGA), was successfully attained. The ^{1}H-NMR spectrum of this distearin-grafted polypeptide in DMSO-d_6 is shown in Figure 2a. Based on the integral ratio of the feature signals of glutamic α proton of γ-GA at δ 4.1 ppm and methyl protons of distearin grafts at δ 0.81 ppm, the lipid content was estimated to be ca. 18.0 mol% with respect to the initial γ-GA residues. On the other hand, the mPEG-grafted polypeptide, poly(γ-GA-co-γ-GAOSu)-g-mPEG, was synthesized by the partial aminolysis of reactive γ-GAOSu moieties (24.0 mol% obtained from ^{1}H-NMR analysis) of poly(γ-GA-co-γ-GAOSu) with mPEG-NH_2. Figure 2b shows the ^{1}H-NMR spectrum of poly(γ-GA-co-γ-GAOSu)-g-mPEG in DMSO-d_6. Based on the signal integral ratio of glutamic α proton of γ-GA at δ 4.1 ppm to ethylene protons of mPEG at δ 3.5 ppm, the mPEG content amounting to ca. 4.0 mol% in the graft copolymer was attained. The recipes, compositions and average molecular weights of these two derived polypeptide adducts are summarized in Table 1.

Preparation and Characterization of DOX-Loaded Polymeric Vesicles

By virtue of the inherent hydrophobic nature of distearin covalently conjugated to a significant extent with the hydrophilic polypeptide segments, it is anticipated that such a lipid/polypeptide adduct exhibits strong amphiphilic characteristic in aqueous phase. This distearin grafted polypeptide (1.0 mg/mL) subjected to the probe-type sonication in phosphate buffer of pH 7.4 underwent hydrophobic association of γ-DSGA residues into supramolecular packing assemblies with particle size of ca. 150 nm in D_h and PSD of ca. 0.24 (Table 2). Notably, a linear relationship between the relaxation frequency (Γ) and the square of the scattering vector (q^2) in the angle-dependent DLS data (Figure 3a) demonstrates the assembly morphology in a spherical particle form [10,15,30]. This was further confirmed by the TEM examination, as shown in Figure 3b. In addition, the mean particle size of lipid/polypeptide conjugate assemblies examined by TEM is slightly smaller than those measured by DLS. This discrepancy is because of the transition of assemblies from the swollen (DLS) to dried state (TEM). In order to gain a fundamental insight into the molecular packing architecture of colloidal assemblies in aqueous solution (pH 7.4), their R_g and R_h were evaluated by SLS and DLS measurements, respectively. R_g is intimately associated with the mean spatial distance from the mass center of the target assembly to individual atoms (groups) that constitute the assembly, whereas R_h represents the radius of a hypothetical hard sphere that diffuses with the same speed as the target under examination. It is therefore readily understood that the R_g/R_h ratio is susceptible to the assembly topology and this parameter can be employed for the structure assessment [10,15,31,32]. As revealed in Figure 3a, the R_g/R_h ratio (ca. 0.95) of the lipid/polypeptide conjugate assemblies in aqueous solution that is quite close to the theoretical value (1.0) for thin-layer hollow spheres [31,32] distinctly demonstrates the structure in a vesicle-like morphology. Compared to the γ-GA residues, the γ-DSGA moieties are obviously more hydrophobic, thus being prone to self-assemble into the non-polar internal membrane layer structure during the molecular packing process of the lipid-derived polypeptide adduct. It was reported that polymer vesicles attained from amphiphilic block copolymers were generally characterized in membrane morphology by continuous hydrophobic internal layers surrounded by hydrophilic coronae, while graft copolymers very often undergo the vesicle formation with the membrane structure comprising discrete nonpolar islets embedded within the hydrophilic matrix [13,33]. This difference is primarily due to the configurational dissimilarity between these two types of amphiphilic copolymers. In spite of more resembling the latter, the objective of this work was not to study the detailed vesicle structure, but to develop functional drug-loaded nanovehicles for effective intracellular payload release instead. Nevertheless, a relatively high negative zeta potential of the polymeric hollow colloids at pH 7.4 was detected (Table 2). This implies that the vesicle surfaces are abundant in the negatively charged γ-GA residues that can serve as facile binding sites for the oppositely charged anticancer agents.

To encapsulate DOX molecules into the biomacromolecular conjugate vesicles, the phosphate buffer containing DOX (0.125 mg/mL, pH 7.4) was employed instead of the drug-free phosphate buffer used in the procedure for preparing polymeric vesicles described above. As shown in Table 2, both particle size and particle size distribution of the drug-loaded vesicles are comparable to those of the pristine counterpart. This indicates that encapsulation of DOX does not significantly interfere the development of polymeric vesicles under the conditions adopted in this study. The polymeric vesicles exhibit an appreciable reduction in the zeta potential after drug loading. This indicates that the positively charged DOX species are not only confined within the inner aqueous chamber of polymeric vesicles but also partly bound with the ionized γ-GA residues via the cooperative electrostatic attraction [34,35]. Hence, such a high drug loading efficiency amounting to ca. 80% corresponding to a payload quantity of 10.0 wt % was achieved by the approach proposed in this work.

In vitro Drug Release of DOX-Loaded Polymeric Vesicles

To assess the drug release performance, the aqueous suspension of the DOX-loaded assemblies placed in the dialysis tubes was immersed into the buffer solution of pH 7.4 or 4.7 (ionic strength of 0.15 M) at 37°C. As shown in Figure 4, the DOX-loaded vesicles at pH 4.7 over a period of 10 h exhibit a significantly higher cumulative drug release (ca. 75%) than those at pH 7.4 (40%). This is because, in addition to the increased aqueous solubility of DOX with the medium pH being reduced from 7.4 to 4.7, an appreciable reduction in the ionization extent of γ-GA residues leads to the massive disruption of the original electrostatic interaction between γ-GA residues and DOX species and, thus, accelerates drug liberation. Although the DOX-loaded polymeric vesicles show a prominent pH-responsive drug release behavior, more than 60% of the payload is released at pH 7.4 within 48 h.

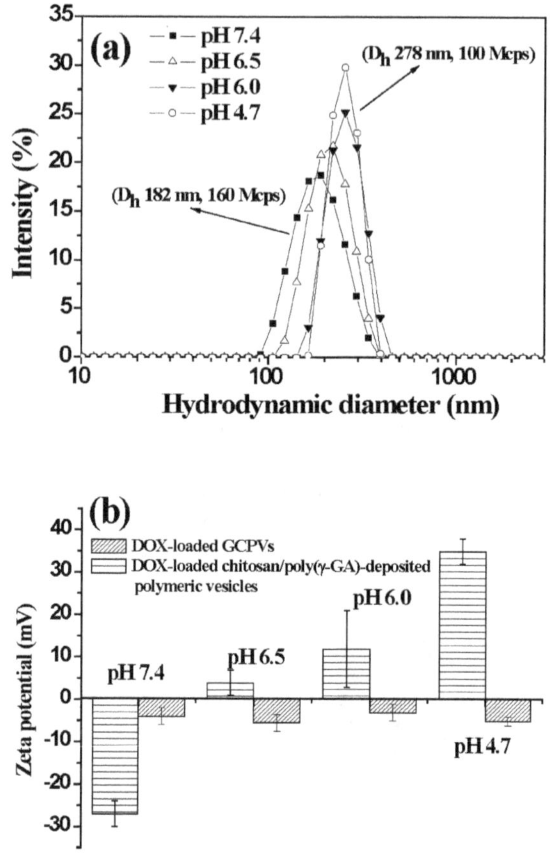

Figure 5. pH-dependent characteristics of DOX-loaded GCPVs and DOX-loaded chitosan/ poly(γ-GA)-deposited polymeric vesicles. (a) DLS colloidal particle size distribution profiles of DOX-loaded GCPVs in aqueous media of various pH. (b) Zeta potentials of DOX-loaded GCPVs and DOX-loaded chitosan/ poly(γ-GA)-deposited polymeric vesicles in different pH aqueous media.

Such a substantial level of drug liberation at pH 7.4 implies severe impairment of the lipid/polypeptide conjugate vesicles in drug delivery application. This is attributed to the premature drug leakage in the blood stream prior to arrival at the target tumors, which obviously may cause undesired side effect and reduce therapeutic efficacy.

Development of DOX-Loaded GCPVs and Their in vitro Drug Release

In order to overcome the aforementioned drawback, the DOX-loaded lipid/polypeptide vesicles were further functionalized with the pH-responsive dual-layered gels acting as a spatial valve-like controller with capability to retard drug release at pH 7.4 (e.g. in blood circulation system), but allow cargo release in weak acidic media (e.g. intracellular endosomal/lysosomal compartments). To achieve this goal, chitosan and poly(γ-GA-co-γ-GAOSu)-g-mPEG were sequentially layered onto the outer surfaces of the drug-loaded vesicles to form polyelectrolyte complexes via the cooperative electrostatic interaction at pH 7.4. The in situ covalent cross-linking was simultaneously achieved upon the aminolysis of γ-GAOSu moieties with primary amines from chitosan. The step-by-step polyelectrolyte deposition on the outer surfaces of polymeric vesicle was monitored by DLS and zeta potential measurements. As shown in Table 2, incorporation of the

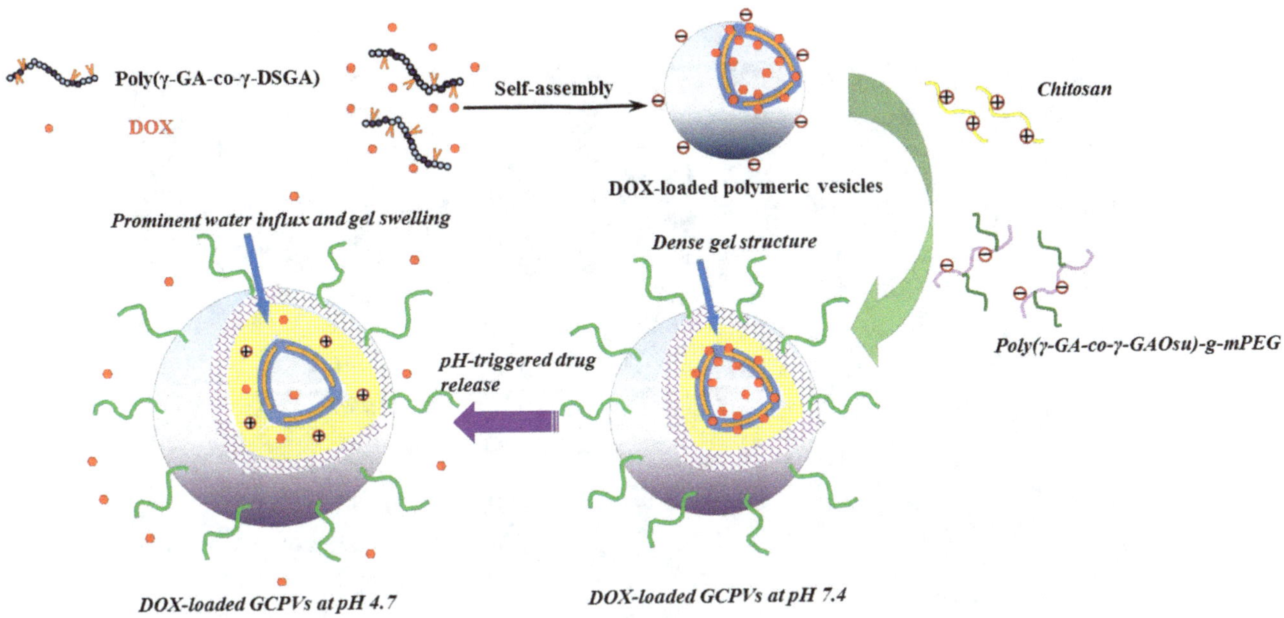

Figure 6. Schematic illustration of the development of DOX-loaded GCPVs and their pH-triggered drug release.

outlayered polyelectrolyte gels increases the particle size from 142 to 168 nm in D_h. The zeta potential of the DOX-loaded polymeric vesicles with the intermediate deposition of chitosan is shifted from ca. −19 to +26 mV. Furthermore, after being combined with poly(γ-GA-co-γ-GAOSu)-g-mPEG, the zeta potential of the chitosan-coated DOX-loaded polymeric vesicles then changes from +26 to ca. −5 mV. Similar results with the development of the layer-by-layer structure on nanoparticle surfaces via the electrostatic interaction that gave rise to the increase of particle size and the inversion of nanoparticle surface charges were also reported elsewhere [36,37]. Herein, it should be mentioned that the spatial barrier of intermediate chitosan-based layers and the stable pairing of DOX with γ-GA residues of vesicles at pH 7.4 could efficiently inhibit the covalent conjugation of γ-GAOSu moieties with loaded DOX during the polyelectrolyte deposition process. The linear relationship of the Γ versus q^2 data (Figure 3c) and the TEM image (Figure 3d) of the drug-loaded GCPVs clearly demonstrate that the resultant complex assemblies still possess a spherical shape after being decorated with the dual-layered gels. Moreover, the TEM imaging contrast of drug-loaded GCPVs was significantly amplified compared to that of polymeric vesicles. In addition to the staining difference, it is also attributed to that the encapsulated DOX molecules in the interior of the drug-loaded GCPVs increase the electron scattering level of nanoparticles, thus promoting TEM imaging contrast. Note that the R_g/R_h value (1.04) of the DOX-loaded GCPVs in aqueous solution of pH 7.4 (Figure 3c) illustrates that the polymer complexes with supplemented layered gels retain the original hollow sphere architecture. Importantly, the DOX-free and DOX-loaded GCPVs after being subjected to large-volume dilution with FBS-containing (10%) PBS at 37°C still retain unchanged in particle size for at least ten days. This strongly indicates that the amide linkage-containing outlayered gels and the outmost hydrophilic PEG chain segments endow the GCPVs with better colloidal stability and serum protein-repellent property. In this regard, it is expected that the DOX-loaded GCPVs have a prolonged blood circulation time,

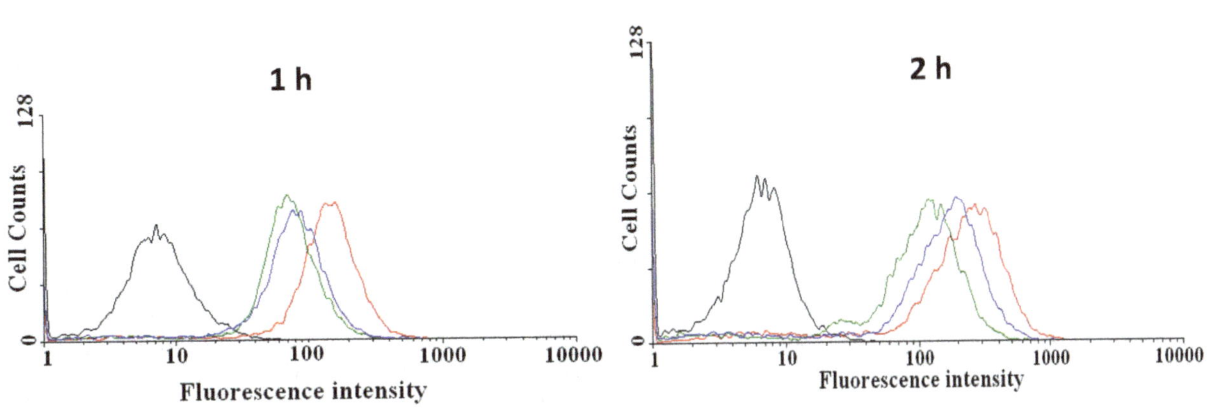

Figure 7. Flow cytometric histogram profiles of HeLa cells incubated with free DOX, DOX-loaded vesicles and DOX-loaded GCPV. DOX fluorescence intensity of HeLa cells incubated with free DOX (red), DOX-loaded vesicles (green) and DOX-loaded GCPV (blue) at 37°C for 1 and 2 h, respectively. Untreated cells (black) were used as a control.

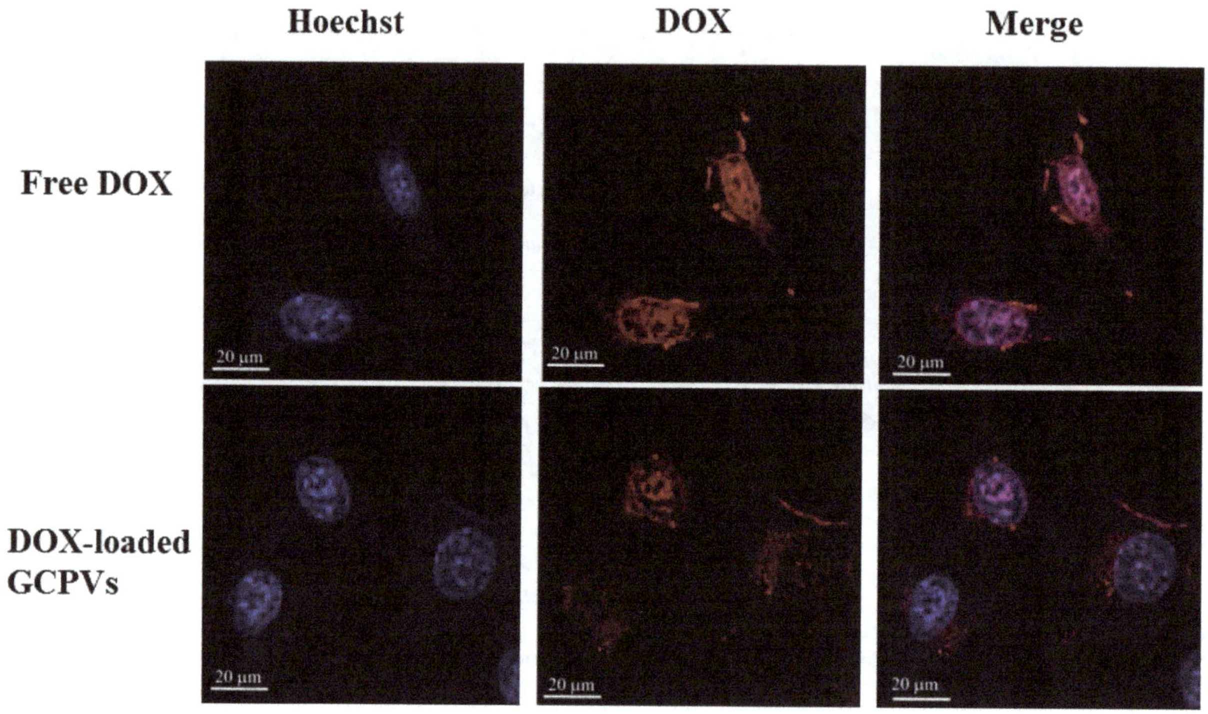

Figure 8. CLSM images of HeLa cells incubated with free DOX and DOX-loaded GCPVs at 37°C for 2 h (DOX concentration = 10 μM). Cell nuclei were stained with Hoechst 33258.

enabling to promote the therapeutic efficacy of cancer treatment by enhanced permeability and retention effect.

Figure 4 shows the effect of the dual-layered gels of the DOX-loaded GCPVs on the in vitro pH-involved drug liberation. The cumulative drug release (ca. 28%) of the DOX-loaded GCPVs at pH 7.4 over a period of 48 h is much lower than that (ca. 60%) of the DOX-loaded vesicles under exactly the same conditions. Furthermore, at pH 4.7, the DOX-loaded GCPVs exhibit a prompt drug release profile comparable to the DOX-loaded polymeric vesicles prior to the nanogel coating. These results manifest that the dual-layered gels indeed play a vital role in fine tuning the drug release in response to the external pH change. The

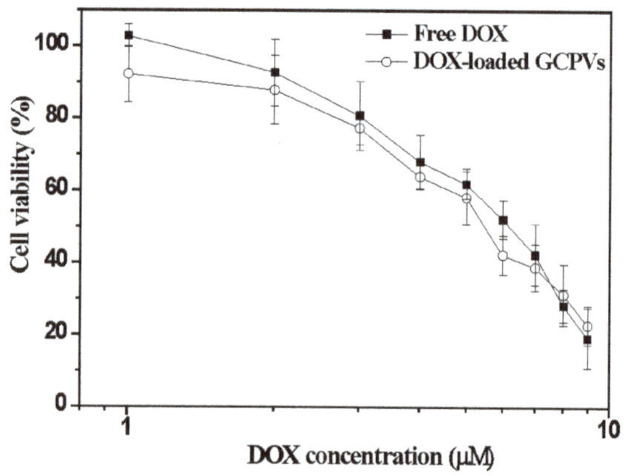

Figure 9. In vitro cytotoxicity of free DOX and DOX-loaded GCPVs against HeLa cells with an incubation time of 48 h. The data presented herein represent an average of at least triplicate experiments.

γ-GA/DOX ionic complexes remained to some extent within either polymeric vesicles or GCPVs at pH 4.7, thus giving rise to an incomplete unloading of DOX species from these nanovehicles. Figure 5a shows that, with the external pH being decreased from pH 7.4 to 4.7 (ionic strength 0.15 M), the particle size of the DOX-loaded GCPVs is remarkably enlarged from 182 to 278 nm along with the light scattering intensity being appreciably reduced from 160 to 100 Mcps. By contrast, only slight variations in the particle size and light scattering intensity of the DOX-loaded vesicles without the outlayered gels were observed when the pH decreased from pH 7.4 to 4.7 (data not shown here). This result clearly confirms the swelling of the outlayered gels of GCPVs in weak acidic environment. With the medium pH being switched from 7.4 to 4.7, the massive disruption of the chitosan/poly(γ-GA) complexes and the ionic osmotic pressure gradient developed within the interfacial polysaccharide layers occur primarily due to the increased protonation of both the γ-GA residues and the primary amino groups from chitosan chain segments, thereby rendering the outlayered gels themselves more hydrated and swollen. Furthermore, the zeta potential of the DOX-loaded GCPVs in response to the pH change remained in the range 0~–10 mV (Figure 5b). This signifies that despite the significant disruption of the polyelectrolyte complexes, the outlayered gel structure still can be preserved without dissociation into individual macromolecular unimers, even at low pH. Under the circumstance, the charge-shielding effect of the outmost mPEG chain segments is maintained. By contrast, in the absence of both mPEG chain segments and covalent crosslinking between the two external layers, the chitosan/poly(γ-GA)-deposited polymeric vesicles became unstable with the pH being adjusted from 7.4 to 4.7 as evidenced by showing the dramatic change in zeta potential from ca –27 (pH 7.4) to 35 mV (4.7) owing to large disruption of the non-crosslinked chitosan/poly(γ-GA) complexes and detachment of the poly(γ-GA) layer from the particle surfaces (Figure 5b). Based on the above results, we have demonstrated that coating these robust pH-responsive dual-layered gels onto the DOX-loaded polymeric vesicles not only prevents the payload from premature leakage at pH 7.4 by their effectively protective dense structure but also retains the passage for drug release at pH 4.7 by the pertinent gel swelling (Figure 6).

Cellular Uptake

To gain a better insight into the cellular uptake of the DOX-loaded GCPVs, the flow cytometry and CLSM measurements were conducted, using HeLa cells as a cancer cell model. Figure 7 shows the flow cytometric histograms of the DOX fluorescence of HeLa cells incubated with free DOX and the DOX-loaded vesicles and GCPVs at 37°C for 1 and 2 h, respectively. Cells alone without any DOX treatment were used as a negative control. With the same incubation time, appreciably higher cellular uptake of free DOX compared to the DOX-loaded vesicles and GCPVs is ascribed to two distinct internalization pathways. Free DOX is well known to be transported into cells via passive diffusion [10,38], whereas the DOX-loaded vesicles and GCPVs are predominantly internalized by cells through an energy-dependent endocytic process. Moreover, with the incubation time being prolonged from 1 to 2 h, the cellular uptake of the DOX-loaded GCPVs was appreciably enhanced compared to that of the DOX-loaded vesicles. This could be ascribed to the different surface features of nanoparticles. For the DOX-loaded polymeric vesicles, the ionized γ-GA-rich surfaces partially reduce the cellular uptake by the electrostatic repulsion against the negatively charged membranes of cells [39]. By contrast, the DOX-loaded GCPVs exhibit a relatively neutral surfaces that certainly diminish the electrostatic repulsion with cell membranes, in addition to the inherent amphiphilic nature of the attached PEG coronae enhancing the particle surface contact with cell membrane [40]. On the other hand, the CLSM images (Figure 8) illustrate that the DOX fluorescence intensity within HeLa cells treated with drug-loaded GCPVs (for a time period of 2 h) was somewhat lower than that of cells incubated with free DOX. In addition, being distinct from the profound accumulation of free DOX molecules within the nuclei of HeLa cells by passive diffusion, the appreciable depositions of the drug species transported by GCPVs in both cytoplasm and nucleus regions were observed as a result of the acid-triggered drug release of the endocytosed GCPVs within acidic endosomes and lysosomes. These results are in well agreement with the flow cytometry measurements of intracellular DOX fluorescence intensity as shown in Figure 7.

In vitro Cytotoxicity

The cytotoxicity of free DOX and the DOX-loaded GCPVs against HeLa cells evaluated by MTT assay is presented in Figure 9. As a crucial control, the high viability of HeLa cells incubated with drug-free GCPVs even at high concentrations was observed (data not shown here). This implies that the pristine GCPVs be virtually nontoxic to HeLa cells. The drug doses for 50% cellular proliferation inhibition (IC_{50}) of free DOX and the DOX-loaded GCPVs were observed to be ca. 0.63 and 0.45 μM, respectively. In comparison with other DOX vehicles that exhibited lower cytotoxicity than free DOX due to slow drug liberation from carriers and delayed nuclear uptake in HeLa cells [41,42], the DOX-loaded GCPVs showed the capability of efficiently inhibiting cell proliferation comparable to free DOX. Based on the results of the in vitro drug release (Figure 4) and cellular uptake (Figure 7), it is expected that a high intracellular drug concentration can be attained by virtue of the pH-triggered prompt DOX release from GCPVs while residing within intracellular acidic endosomes and lysosomes, thereby maximizing the therapeutic efficiency [43].

Conclusion

In this study, the drug-loaded lipid/polypeptide conjugate vesicles were further augmented with the pH-responsive dual-layered gels for highly efficient intracellular drug delivery. Through the sequential deposition of chitosan and poly(γ-GA-co-γ-GAOSu)-g-mPEG in combination with in situ covalent cross-linking on the outer surfaces of the DOX-loaded vesicles, the drug-loaded GCPVs were successfully attained. The GCPVs exhibited superior capability of controlling drug release in response to the external pH change. The additional pH-responsive dual-layered gels not only effectively prevent the drug payload from premature leakage at pH 7.4 by the dense gel structure but also retain facile passage of DOX release at pH 4.7 due to the pertinent gel swelling. The GCPVs after being internalized by HeLa cells via endocytosis showed prominent antitumor ability comparable to free DOX by rapidly releasing payload in intracellular acidic organelles. This work demonstrates the great potential of GCPVs as an intracellular drug delivery nanovehicle for improved anticancer treatment.

Author Contributions

Conceived and designed the experiments: HCC WHC SCL CSC. Performed the experiments: WCH CHW YFH. Analyzed the data: WHC MYS CHW WCH SCL. Wrote the paper: WHC HCC CSC.

References

1. Samad A, Sultana Y, Aqil M (2007) Liposomal drug delivery systems: an update review. Curr Drug Deliv 4: 297–305.
2. Elbayoumi TA, Torchilin VP (2010) Current trends in liposome research. Methods Mol Biol 605: 1–27.
3. Park JH, Lee S, Kim JH, Park K, Kim K, et al. (2008) Polymeric nanomedicine for cancer therapy. Prog Polym Sci 33: 113–137.
4. Miyata K, Christie RJ, Kataoka K (2011) Polymeric micelles for nano-scale drug delivery. React Funct Polym 71: 227–234.
5. Broz P, Driamov S, Ziegler J, Ben-Haim N, Marsch S, et al. (2006) Toward intelligent nanosize bioreactors: a pH-switchable, channel-equipped, functional polymer nanocontainer. Nano Lett 6: 2349–2353
6. Blanazs A, Armes SP, Ryan AJ (2009) Self-assembled block copolymer aggregates: from micelles to vesicles and their biological applications. Macromol Rapid Commun 30: 267–277.
7. Wang W, Cheng D, Gong F, Miao X, Shuai X (2012) Design of multifunctional micelle for tumor-targeted intracellular drug release and fluorescent imaging. Adv Mater 24: 115–120.
8. Rapoport N (2007) Physical stimuli-responsive polymeric micelles for anti-cancer drug delivery. Prog Polym Sci 32: 962–990.
9. Sun Q, Cheng D, Yu X, Zhang Z, Dai J, et al. (2011) A pH-sensitive polymeric nanovesicle based on biodegradable poly(ethylene glycol)-b-poly(2-(diisopropylamino)ethyl aspartate) as a MRI-visible drug delivery system. J Mater Chem 21: 15316–15326.
10. Chiang WH, Ho VT, Huang WC, Huang YF, Chern CS, et al. (2012) Dual stimuli-responsive polymeric hollow nanogels designed as carriers for intracellular triggered drug release. Langmuir 28: 15056–15064.
11. Al-Ahmady ZS, Al-Jamal WT, Bossche JV, Bui TT, Drake AF, et al. (2012) Lipid-peptide vesicle nanoscale hybrids for triggered drug release by mild hyperthermia in vitro and in vivo. ACS Nano 6: 9335–9346.
12. Du JZ, Du XJ, Mao CQ, Wang J (2011) Tailor-made dual pH-sensitive polymer-doxorubicin nanoparticles for efficient anticancer drug delivery. J Am Chem Soc 133: 17560–17563.
13. Chiu HC, Lin YW, Huang YF, Chuang CK, Chern CS (2008) Polymer vesicles containing small vesicles within interior aqueous compartments and pH-responsive transmembrane channels. Angew Chem Int Ed 47:1875–1878.
14. Zheng C, Yao X, Qiu L (2011) Novel polymeric vesicles with pH-induced deformation character for advanced drug delivery. Macromol Biosci 11: 338–343.

15. Huang YF, Chiang WH, Tsai PL, Chern CS, Chiu HC (2011) Novel hybrid vesicles co-assembled from a cationic lipid and PAAc-g-mPEG with pH-triggered transmembrane channels for controlled drug release. Chem Commun 47: 10978–10980.
16. Sun P, Zhou D, Gan Z (2011) Novel reduction-sensitive micelles for triggered intracellular drug release. J Control Release 155: 96–103.
17. Li J, Huo M, Wang J, Zhou J, Mohammad JM, et al. (2012) Redox-sensitive micelles self-assembled from amphiphilic hyaluronic acid-deoxycholic acid conjugates for targeted intracellular delivery of paclitaxel. Biomaterials 33: 2310–2320.
18. Zhang L, Xue H, Cao Z, Keefe A, Wang J, et al (2011) Multifunctional and degradable zwitterionic nanogels for targeted delivery, enhanced MR imaging, reduction-sensitive drug release, and renal clearance. Biomaterials 32: 4604–4608.
19. Chiang WH, Hsu YH, Lou TW, Chern CS, Chiu HC (2009) Effects of mPEG grafts on morphology and cross-linking of thermally induced micellar assemblies from PAAc-based graft copolymers in aqueous phase. Macromolecules 42: 3611–3619.
20. Dai J, Lin S, Cheng D, Zou S, Shuai X (2011) Interlayer-crosslinked micelle with partially hydrated core showing reduction and pH dual sensitivity for pinpointed intracellular drug release. Angew Chem Int Ed 50: 9404–9408.
21. Li YL, Zhu L, Liu Z, Cheng R, Meng F, et al. (2009) Reversibly stabilized multifunctional dextran nanoparticles efficiently deliver doxorubicin into the nuclei of cancer cells. Angew Chem Int Ed 48: 9914–9918.
22. Lee HJ, Kim SE, Kwon IK, Park C, Kim C, et al. (2010) Spatially mineralized self-assembled polymeric nanocarriers with enhanced robustness and controlled drug-releasing property. Chem Commun 46: 377–379.
23. Han SY, Han HS, Lee SC, Kang YM, Kim IS, et al. (2011) Mineralized hyaluronic acid nanoparticles as a robust drug carrier. J. Mater. Chem. 21: 7996–8001.
24. Chen Z, Li Z, Lin Y, Yin M, Ren J, et al. (2013) Biomineralization inspired surface engineering of nanocarriers for pH-responsive, targeted drug delivery. Biomaterials 34: 1364–1371.
25. Lee SM, Song Y, Hong BJ, MacRenaris KW, Mastarone DJ, et al. (2010) Modular polymer-caged nanobins as a theranostic platform with enhanced magnetic resonance relaxivity and pH-responsive drug release. Angew Chem Int Ed 49: 9960–9964.
26. Ning S, Huang Q, Sun X, Li C, Zhang Y, et al. (2011) Carboxymethyl dextran-coated liposomes: Toward a robust drug delivery platform. Soft Matter 7: 9394–9401.
27. Lee SM, Chen H, O'Halloran TV, Nguyen ST (2009) "Clickable" polymer-caged nanobins as a modular drug delivery platform. J Am Chem Soc 131: 9311–9320.
28. Hsu YH, Chiang WH, Chen CH, Chern CS, Chiu HC (2005) Thermally responsive interactions between the PEG and PNIPAAm grafts attached to the PAAc backbone and the corresponding structural changes of polymeric micelles in water. Macromolecules 38: 9757–9765.
29. Hsu YH, Chiang WH, Chen MC, Chern CS, Chiu HC (2006) Effects of SDS on the thermo- and pH-sensitive structural changes of the poly(acrylic acid)-based copolymer containing both poly(N-isopropylacrylamide) and monomethoxy poly(ethylene glycol) grafts in water. Langmuir 22: 6764–6770.
30. Smith AE, Xu X, Kirkland-York SE, Savin DA, McCormick CL (2010)"Schizo-"Schizophrenic" self-assembly of block copolymers synthesized via aqueous RAFT polymerization: from micelles to vesicles. Macromolecules 43: 1210–1217.
31. Dou HJ, Jiang M, Peng HS, Chen DY, Hong Y (2003) pH-Dependent self-assembly: micellization and micelle-hollow-sphere transition of cellulose-based copolymers. Angew Chem Int Ed 42: 1516–1519.
32. Wan WM, Sun XL, Pan CY (2009) Morphology transition in RAFT polymerization for formation of vesicular morphologies in one pot. Macromolecules 42: 4950–4952.
33. Huang WC, Chiang WH, Lin SJ, Lan YJ, Chen HL, et al. (2012) Lipid-containing polymer vesicles with pH/Ca^{2+}-ion-manipulated, size-selective permeability. Adv Funct Mater 22: 2267–2275.
34. Manocha B, Margaritis A (2010) Controlled release of doxorubicin from doxorubicin/γ-polyglutamic acid ionic complex J Nanomater 2010: 1–9.
35. Bae HH, Cho MY, Hong JH, Poo H, Sung MH, et al. (2012) Bio-derived poly(gamma-glutamic acid) nanogels as controlled anticancer drug delivery carriers. J Microbiol Biotechnol 22: 1782–1789.
36. Poon Z, Chang D, Zhao X, Hammond PT (2011) Layer-by-layer nanoparticles with a pH-sheddable layer for in vivo targeting of tumor hypoxia. ACS Nano 5: 4284–4292.
37. Cuomo F, Lopez F, Miguel MG, Lindman B (2010) Vesicle-templated layer-by-layer assembly for the production of nanocapsules. Langmuir 26: 10555–10560.
38. Shuai X, Ai H, Nasongkla N, Kim S, Gao J (2004) Micellar carriers based on block copolymers of poly(epsilon-caprolactone) and poly(ethylene glycol) for doxorubicin delivery. J Control Release 98: 415–426.
39. Osaka T, Nakanishi T, Shanmugam S, Takahama S, Zhang H (2009) Effect of surface charge of magnetite nanoparticles on their internalization into breast cancer and umbilical vein endothelial cells. Colloid Surfaces B 71: 325–330.
40. Jung SH, Jung SH, Seong H, Cho SH, Jeong KS, et al. (2009) Polyethylene glycol-complexed cationic liposome for enhanced cellular uptake and anticancer activity. Int J Pharm 382: 254–261.
41. Wang D, Su Y, Jin C, Zhu B, Pang Y, et al. (2011) Supramolecular copolymer micelles based on the complementary multiple hydrogen bonds of nucleobases for drug delivery. Biomacromolecules 12: 1370–1379.
42. Zhang WL, Li YL, Liu LX, Sun QQ, Shuai XT, et al. (2010) Amphiphilic toothbrushlike copolymers based on poly(ethylene glycol) and poly(epsilon-caprolactone) as drug carriers with enhanced properties. Biomacromolecules 11: 1331–1338.
43. Tang R, Ji W, Panus D, Palumbo RN, Wang C (2011) Block copolymer micelles with acid-labile ortho ester side-chains: Synthesis, characterization, and enhanced drug delivery to human glioma cells. J Control Release 151: 18–27.

6

Ergocalciferol and Microcirculatory Function in Chronic Kidney Disease and Concomitant Vitamin D Deficiency: An Exploratory, Double Blind, Randomised Controlled Trial

Gavin Dreyer[1,3], Arthur T. Tucker[4], Steven M. Harwood[3], Rupert M. Pearse[2], Martin J. Raftery[1], Muhammad M. Yaqoob[1,3]*

1 Department of Renal Medicine, Barts Health NHS Trust, London, United Kingdom, **2** Department of Critical Care Medicine, Barts Health NHS Trust, London, United Kingdom, **3** Department of Translational Medicine and Therapeutics, Queen Mary University of London, London, United Kingdom, **4** Ernest Cooke Microvascular Unit, Barts Health NHS Trust, London, United Kingdom

Abstract

Background and Objectives: Vitamin D deficiency and endothelial dysfunction are non-traditional risk factors for cardiovascular events in chronic kidney disease. Previous studies in chronic kidney disease have failed to demonstrate a beneficial effect of vitamin D on arterial stiffness, left ventricular mass and inflammation but none have assessed the effect of vitamin D on microcirculatory endothelial function.

Study Design: We conducted a randomised controlled trial of 38 patients with non diabetic chronic kidney disease stage 3–4 and concomitant vitamin D deficiency (<16 ng/dl) who received oral ergocalciferol (50,000 IU weekly for one month followed by 50,000 IU monthly) or placebo over 6 months. The primary outcome was change in microcirculatory function measured by laser Doppler flowmetry after iontophoresis of acetylcholine. Secondary endpoints were tissue advanced glycation end products, sublingual functional capillary density and flow index as well as macrovascular parameters. Parallel *in vitro* experiments were conducted to determine the effect of ergocalciferol on cultured human endothelial cells.

Results: Twenty patients received ergocalciferol and 18 patients received placebo. After 6 months, there was a significant improvement in the ergocalciferol group in both endothelium dependent microcirculatory vasodilatation after iontophoresis of acetylcholine ($p = 0.03$) and a reduction in tissue advanced glycation end products ($p = 0.03$). There were no changes in sublingual microcirculatory parameters. Pulse pressure ($p = 0.01$) but not aortic pulse wave velocity was reduced. There were no significant changes in bone mineral parameters, blood pressure or left ventricular mass index suggesting that ergocalciferol improved endothelial function independently of these parameters. In parallel experiments, expression of endothelial nitric oxide synthase and activity were increased in human endothelial cells in a dose dependent manner.

Conclusions: Ergocalciferol improved microcirculatory endothelial function in patients with chronic kidney disease and concomitant vitamin D deficiency. This process may be mediated through enhanced expression and activity of endothelial nitric oxide synthase.

Trial Registration: Clinical trials.gov NCT00882401

Editor: Giuseppe Danilo, University of Milan, Italy

Funding: This study was funded by grants from the British Renal Society (www.britishrenal.org) (Grant number BRS 09/010) and the Barts and the London charitable Trust (Barts and the London charitable Trust). The funders had no role in study design, data collection and analysis, decision to publish, or preparation of the manuscript.

Competing Interests: The authors have declared that no competing interests exist.

* Email: m.m.yaqoob@qmul.ac.uk

Introduction

Patients with chronic kidney disease (CKD) are far more likely to die of cardiovascular disease (CVD) than progress to end stage kidney disease (ESKD) [1]. Traditional risk factors including age, hypertension, smoking and diabetes mellitus do not entirely account for the excess of CVD mortality in patients with CKD. Vitamin D deficiency, a non-traditional CVD risk factor in patients with all stages of kidney disease [2,3,4], is highly prevalent in patients with CKD [5,6] and is associated with elevated cardiovascular (CV) morbidity and mortality [7,8,9].

Vitamin D deficiency in patients with CKD has been shown to correlate with impairment in endothelial function [10,11]. In pre-clinical [12] and clinical studies [13], endothelial dysfunction has been identified as a non-traditional risk factor for CVD in CKD with improvements in endothelial function reflecting improved global vascular health and a reduced risk of CVD [14].

Observational studies [15,16,17,18,19,20] have provided support for the protective role of vitamin D therapy in reducing the risk of CVD in patients with CKD and ESKD. However, these studies were heterogeneous in design, therapeutic intervention and patient populations (CKD vs ESKD) and have not elucidated the mechanism by which vitamin D reduces CV risk in this patient group. Several *in vitro*, pre-clinical and clinical studies have demonstrated that endothelial and therefore microcirculatory function can be ameliorated after treatment with both activated and nutritional forms of vitamin D [21,22,23,24,25]. However, none of these studies have included patients with CKD. Two previous studies in patients with non-dialysis and CKD and ESKD evaluating the effect of nutritional vitamin D compounds on endothelial biomarkers and conduit artery function have provided conflicting results [26,27].

The microcirculation, defined as blood vessels <150 μm in diameter [28] located within tissue parenchyma, is intricately linked to endothelial function and predicts the function of the microcirculatory beds in renal and cardiac tissue [29,30,31,32,33]. A review of cardiovascular assessment in patients with CKD [34] has highlighted the need for further assessments of microcirculatory dysfunction in patients with CKD as a method for predicting adverse CV outcomes. To date, there have been no prospective, randomized controlled studies investigating the effect of vitamin D on microcirculatory endothelial function or CV endpoints in patients with CKD [35].

We therefore conducted an exploratory, double blind, randomised, controlled trial to determine if therapy with ergocalciferol compared to placebo improves microcirculatory endothelial function in patients with CKD and concomitant vitamin D deficiency. We also conducted parallel *in vitro* experiments to elucidate the mechanistic pathway of ergocalciferol in cultured human endothelial cells.

Methods

Study design

The protocol for this trial and supporting CONSORT checklist are available as supporting information; see Checklist S1 and Protocol S1. This was a single centre, double blind, exploratory randomised controlled trial comparing oral ergocalciferol to placebo in patients with CKD stage 3–4 (estimated glomerular filtration rate (eGFR) 60–15 ml/min/1.73 m^2) and concomitant vitamin D deficiency (defined as a serum 25 hydroxy vitamin D (25 (OH) D) level of <16 ng/ml). The study was conducted at the Royal London Hospital, UK, between 1/5/2009 and 1/9/2010. All patients provided written informed consent and ethical approval was obtained from the East London Research Ethics Committee. The trial was registered at clinicaltrials.gov (Clinical trials number- NCT00882401, http://clinicaltrials.gov/ct2/show/NCT00882401) and conducted in accordance with the Declaration of Helsinki.

Inclusion/exclusion criteria

The principle inclusion criteria were an eGFR between 15 and 60 ml/min/1.73 m^2 with evidence of 2 consecutive measures of eGFR <60 ml/min/1.73 m^2 by the 4 variable MDRD equation [36] at least 3 months apart, serum 25 (OH) D levels <16 ng/ml, age >18 and <80 years, no evidence of diabetes mellitus (fasting blood sugar <128 mg/dl, not taking any diabetic medication), not receiving nor having had renal replacement therapy in the preceding three months

The principle exclusion criteria were current vitamin D therapy of any type, serum calcium above 10.4 mg/dl (based on the upper limit of the laboratory reference range [37]), pregnant or lactating women, presence of conditions which predispose to hypercalcaemia, renal calculi and presence of a disease other than CKD associated with microcirculatory dysfunction.

Intervention and randomization

Patients were randomised to either ergocalciferol (Sanofi Aventis, New Jersey, USA) or a matching placebo. The dose of ergocalciferol was 50,000 IU weekly for one month followed by 50,000 IU monthly for 5 months resulting in a total dose of 450,000 IU over 6 months. This was in line with existing K/DOQI guidelines for the replacement of vitamin D in patients with CKD at the time the study was designed [37]. The dose of ergocalciferol was standardized for all patients to ensure equal dosing of ergocalciferol over the duration of the study to avoid the potentially confounding effect of varying doses of ergocalciferol based on initial serum concentrations of 25 (OH) D. The control arm received a matching placebo given at the same dose schedule as ergocalciferol. All patients received dietary advice appropriate to their stage of CKD from specialist renal dietitians which included advice on dietary intake of calcium, phosphate, sodium, potassium and protein. Patients were reviewed monthly for 6 months. A 2 week washout period for any vitamin D containing drugs or over the counter supplements was included before randomization, however no subjects required vitamin D washout. The randomization schedule was developed by an independent accountant. Sequentially numbered, sealed envelopes were used to achieve allocation concealment. Envelopes were stored and sequentially dispensed to study patients by the hospital clinical trial pharmacy who were blinded to the intervention and allocation as were the remainder of the study team.

Study endpoints

The primary outcome measure was microcirculatory endothelial function assessed by laser Doppler flowmetry (LDF) over forearm skin after iontophoresis of acetylcholine (ACh). Secondary outcome measures were microvascular parameters including skin autofluorescence (AF) and side stream dark field imaging (SDF) of the sub lingual microcirculation as well as macrovascular parameters including blood pressure, pulse pressure, aortic pulse wave velocity (aPWV), left ventricular mass index (LVMI) and bone mineral parameters (see File S1 for details of all techniques).

Clinical assessments

All patients were reviewed at the Royal London Hospital kidney unit. Patients were instructed to wear loose clothing, avoid caffeine and nicotine for 12 hours prior to assessments and rested for 15 minutes in a temperature and humidity controlled room before microcirculatory assessments.

Iontophoresis and laser Doppler flowmetry

Iontophoresis involves the delivery of charged particles to the local microcirculation, through the skin, using electrically repulsive forces. Laser Doppler flowmetry is a non-invasive technique which uses the Doppler principle to measure flux of erythrocytes in sub dermal capillaries. Increasing red cell flux after iontophoresis reflects microcirculatory vasodilatation as a consequence of improved endothelial function. The combination of these techniques is a validated method for studying endothelial function in the microcirculation in various pathologies including CKD. [38,39,40] A 1% solution of both ACh and sodium nitroprusside (SNP) were iontophoresed on the volar aspect of the non-dominant forearm using a low current protocol to reduce galvanic effect [41] with a maximum achieved dose of 75 μA after 7.5 minutes. To eliminate baseline variability, relative percentage change from baseline flux after the maximum iontophoretic dose is the primary outcome measure (see Figure S1 and Table S1 in File S1) [38].

Skin autofluorescence

Tissue advanced glycation end (AGE) product levels are an independent risk predictor of microcirculatory complications and are predictors of CVD in renal failure [42]. The technique utilises the AGE reader (Diagnoptics, Netherlands) which provides a non-invasive measure of AGE in the skin. AGE products correlate with measures of skin AF provided by the output from the AGE reader device [42].

Side stream dark field imaging of the sublingual microcirculation

This is a non-invasive, real time, imaging tool to assess intra-vital capillary blood flow. An analysis of the moving cells in the recorded video images permits the quantitative measurement of red blood cell flow in the capillaries. SDF images were scored and interpreted according to standard guidelines [43].

Macrocirculatory parameters

Aortic pulse wave velocity (Vicorder device, Skidmore Medical, UK) was measured to determine if changes in microcirculatory function occurred independently of changes in large conduit vessels. LVMI was measured by cardiac magnetic resonance imaging (cMRI) to determine if the hypothesized improved microcirculatory function resulted in reduced peripheral resistance leading to reduced cardiac workload and subsequent reductions in LVMI.

Biochemical analysis

All biochemical tests were performed in our hospital laboratory by a Roche modular unit analyser (F. Hoffmann-La Roche Ltd, Switzerland). Serum vitamin D levels were assessed by UPLC-MS/MS, which is a quantitative ultra-performance liquid chromatography tandem mass spectrometry assay. Parathyroid hormone (PTH) levels were assessed by the Roche E170 intact PTH assay (Roche Diagnostics, Mannheim)

Experimental work

Human aortic endothelial cells (HAEC, Promocell, UK) were cultured and incubated for 24 h using either low (12 ng/dl) or high (120 ng/dl) concentrations of ergocalciferol. Real time polymerase chain reaction (RT-PCR) was used to evaluate the effect of ergocalciferol on the expression of endothelial nitric oxide synthase (eNOS). Nitrite levels in cell supernatant, to evaluate the downstream effect of changes in eNOS expression in cells, were measured by a chemiluminescent technique [44] (see File S1 and figures S1-5 for full description of all techniques).

Statistical analysis

At the time of designing the study, there was insufficient available evidence of the effect of ergocalciferol therapy on microcirculatory parameters to undertake a standard power calculation. Our hypothesis was that ergocalciferol would significantly improve the function of the endothelium in patients with CKD and concomitant vitamin D deficiency. Given the profoundly low levels of 25 (OH) D in this patient group, the expected rise in serum 25 (OH) D levels with ergocalciferol and predicted lack of change of 25 (OH) D levels in the placebo group, we estimated that 30% of patients in the placebo group and 80% of the patients in the ergocalciferol group would have an improvement in peripheral LDF measured by relative change from baseline flux after 6 months of therapy. At 80% power and with a significance level of 0.05, this required 19 patients per arm. An intention to treat analysis was performed.

Clinical trial subjects

The two groups were compared for similarity at baseline and after 6 months of therapy using the Student's t test for normally distributed variables, Mann Whitney tests for non-parametric data and Chi squared tests or Fisher's exact test for proportions. Differences in 25 (OH) D levels and change from baseline flux measured by LDF after iontophoresis were analysed using a two way repeated measures ANOVA test followed by Bonferroni post tests for comparisons at pre determined time points (1, 3 and 6 months). We confirmed our findings using a mixed effects model. Forearm laser Doppler flowmetry is expressed as the percentage increase in flux from baseline after iontophoresis of ACh [38]. Four patients in the ergocalciferol group and 1 in the placebo group completed an initial 3 months on therapy before the end of the predetermined study period and this data was included in the analysis. The analysis of data at 6 months includes data from all remaining patients who completed the full follow up period. SDF imaging of the sublingual microcirculation was expressed as functional capillary density (mm^{-1}) and microvascular flow index as described previously [43]. LVMI, SDF imaging, skin AF and bone mineral parameters were analysed using t tests and Mann Whitney tests based on the distribution of the data. A p value of $<$ 0.05 was considered statistically significant. Analysis was conducted on Stata version 10 (www.stata.com) and GraphPad Prism software version 5 (see File S1 and figures S2–S5 for sub-group analysis).

Cell experiments

RT-PCR data were analyzed with ABI 7900HT Prism sequence detector software (SDS Version 2.3, Applied Biosystems) to determine differential gene expression for eNOS compared to β actin. Differences in nitrite levels were assessed using the Student t-test. Ethanol is included since this was used to dilute the ergocalciferol. Statistical analysis was performed using GraphPad Prism software (version 5).

Results

Patient screening, enrolment and randomization are shown in figure 1. The treatment and placebo groups were similar with respect to demographic, clinical (table 1) and laboratory parameters (table 2). Two patients were lost to follow up in the ergocalciferol arm and 1 in the placebo arm. All patients self reported complete compliance and this was confirmed by manual inspection of study medication bottles at each visit. No patients were taking nitrate containing medications that may have acted as vasodilators through the donation of nitric oxide. After 6 months of treatment with ergocalciferol, 25 hydroxy vitamin D (25 (OH) D) levels increased significantly in the treatment group ($p<0.0001$) (figure 2) but there were no significant changes in other biochemical parameters (table 3).

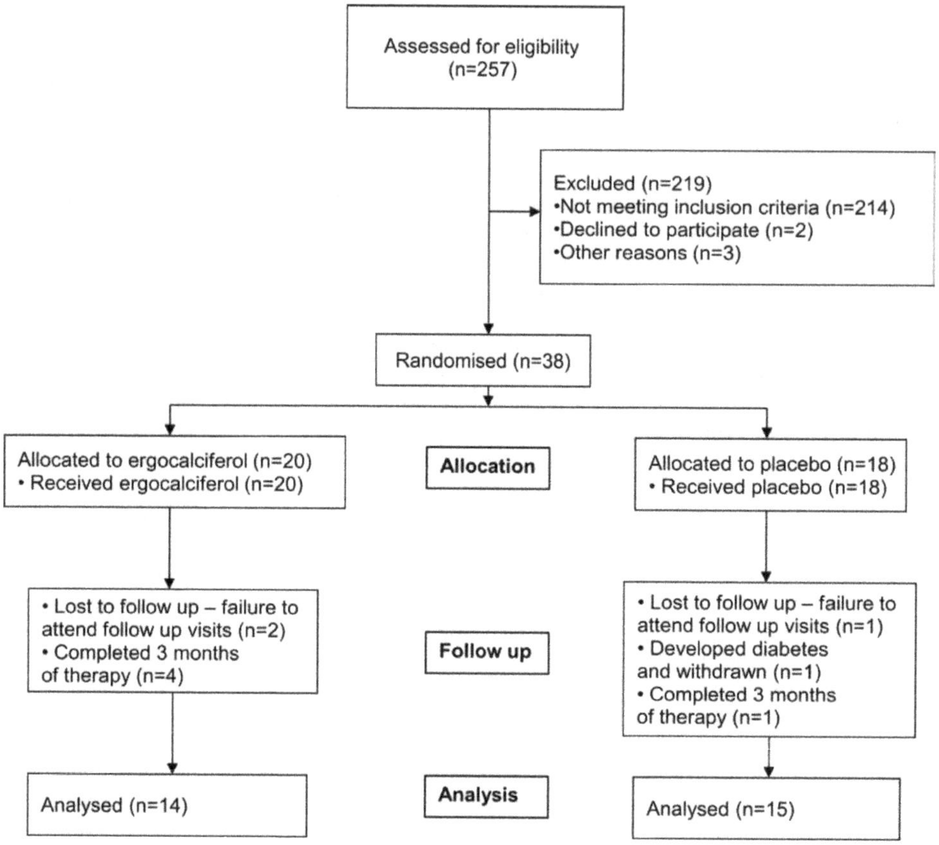

Figure 1. Recruitment schedule for study patients.

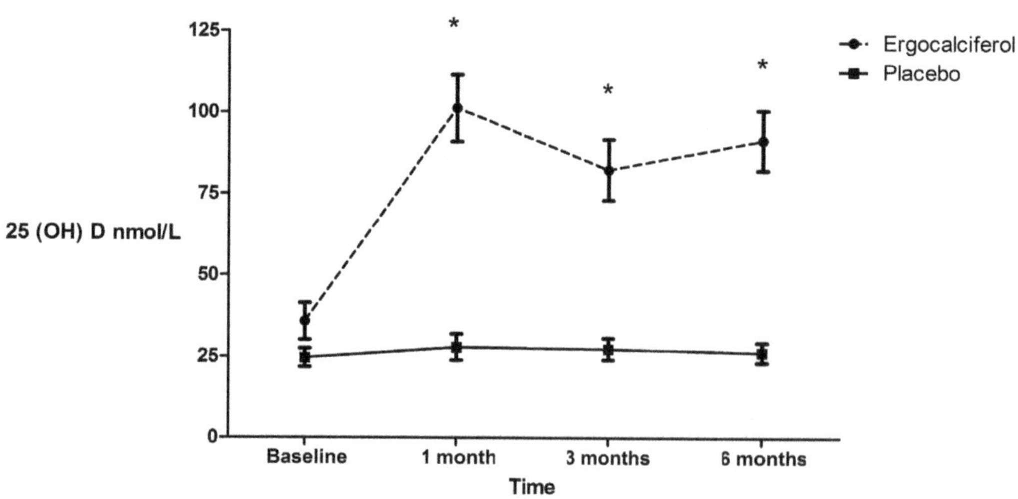

Number at risk

	Baseline	1 month	3 months	6 months
Ergocalciferol	20	19	18	14
Placebo	18	18	16	15

Figure 2. 25 (OH) D levels in patients treated with ergocalciferol and placebo. Bonferroni post tests following two way repeated measures ANOVA at 1,3 and 6 months p<0.0001. (* = statistically significant).

Table 1. Baseline demographic and clinical data for patients.

	Ergocalciferol (n = 20)	Placebo (n = 18)	p value
Age years	45.8 (10.0)	48.8 (12.2)	0.39
Sex (% male)	14 (60.9%)	14 (73.7%)	0.22
Body mass index	30.4 (7.1)	29.2 (3.4)	0.51
Ethnicity			0.57
Caucasian	5 (21.8%)	6 (31.6%)	
Non-Caucasian	15 (78.2%)	12 (68.4%)	
Cause of CKD			0.74
Hypertension	5 (25%)	7 (38.9%)	
Glomerulonephritis	8 (40%)	5 (27.8%)	
ADPKD	2 (10%)	1 (5.6%)	
Other~	5 (25%)	5 (27.7%)	
Smoking status			0.59
Current smoker	1 (5%)	2 (11.1%)	
Never/Ex-smoker	19 (95%)	16 (88.9%)	
Presence of endovascular stent devices	0 (0%)	1 (5.6%)	0.47
ACE-I/ARB	16 (80%)	12 (66.7%)	0.33
β Blocker	7 (35%)	6 (33.3%)	0.57
Statin use	9 (45%)	7 (38.9%)	0.84
Anti platelet therapy	2 (10%)	3 (16.7%)	0.48
Folic acid	1 (5.0%)	1 (5.6%)	1.00
Nitrate containing medications#	0 (0%)	0 (0%)	1.00
Medications containing Vitamin D	0 (0%)	0 (0%)	1.00
BP in past history	15 (65.2%)	11 (57.9%)	0.63
Systolic BP (mmHg)	114 (10)	119 (10)	0.11
Diastolic BP (mmHg)	70 (8)	71 (7)	0.57
MAP (mmHg)	84 (8)	87 (8)	0.29
Pulse pressure (mmHg)	45 (7)	48 (6)	0.08
aPWV (m/s)	8.5 (1.1)	8.5 (1.5)	0.66
LVMI (g/m2)	96.1 (36.3)	87.5 (174)	0.55
Skin AF (AU)	2.8 (0.9)	3.1 (0.9)	0.26
FCD (mm-1)	5.2 (0.5)	5.0 (0.5)	0.78
MFI (AU)	2.5 (0.1)	2.4 (0.1)	0.54

Figures in brackets are standard deviation of the mean or % of total in treatment group. ADPKD – autosomal dominant polycystic kidney disease. BP = blood pressure, ACE-I angiotensin converting enzyme inhibitor, ARB – angiotensin receptor blocker, MAP = mean arterial pressure, aPWV = aortic pulse wave velocity, LVMI – left ventricular mass index, AF – auto fluorescence, FCD – functional capillary density, MFI – microvascular flow index. AU – arbitrary units

#- any form of glyceryl trinitrate, isosorbide mononitrate, isosorbide dinitrate or other esters of nitric acid

~- Additional causes of CKD in ergocalciferol group: tubulo-interstitial nephritis (n = 1), reflux nephropathy (n = 2), unknown (n = 2). Placebo group: reflux nephropathy (n = 2), ischaemic nephropathy presumed due to reno-vascular disease (n = 1), unknown (n = 2).

The effect of ergocalciferol on microcirculatory parameters

Treatment with ergocalciferol compared to placebo was associated with a significant increase in change from baseline flux measured by LDF after iontophoresis of ACh (repeated measures 2 way ANOVA $p = 0.03$) with a significant difference between treatment groups observed at 6 months (Bonferroni post test $p = 0.012$) (figure 3). There were no significant differences in change from baseline flux after the iontophoresis of SNP between treatment groups at 6 months (repeated measures 2 way ANOVA $p = 0.18$) (figure 4). The use of a mixed effects model did not change the significance of these findings (change from baseline after iontophoresis at 6 months follow up: ACh $p = 0.03$, SNP $p = 0.36$).

Skin AF was significantly lower in patients treated with ergocalciferol after 6 months, reflecting reduced levels of tissue oxidative stress ($p = 0.03$). At the end of the follow up period, there were no differences in parameters of functional capillary density (FCD) or microvascular flow index (MFI) assessed by SDF imaging of the sublingual microcirculation (table 4).

The effect of ergocalciferol on macrocirculatory parameters

Pulse pressure was significantly lower in patients treated with ergocalciferol after 6 months ($p = 0.01$) but systolic, diastolic and

Table 2. Baseline laboratory data for CKD patients randomised to either ergocalciferol or placebo.

	Ergocalciferol (n = 20)	Placebo (n = 18)	p value
Creatinine (mg/dl)	2.3 (0.8)	2.0 (1.0)	0.60
eGFR (ml/min/1.73 m^2)	33.0 (13.5)	38.7 (15)	0.39
Stage of CKD			0.33
Stage 3	9 (45%)	13 (72.2%)	
Stage 4	11 (55%)	5 (27.8%)	
Hb (g/dl)	12.8 (1.8)	12.6 (1.4)	0.63
Calcium (mg/dl)	8.8 (0.8)	8.8 (0.8)	0.74
Phosphate (mg/dl)	3.8 (0.6)	3.5 (0.6)	0.16
Calcium phosphate product (mg^2/dl^2)	33.0 (4.2)	31.2 (5.1)	0.25
PTH (pg/L)	102.8 (76.4)	118.9 (103.8)	0.60
CRP (mg/L)	7.6 (17.2)	5.9 (9.8)	0.71
Urine P:CR	190.8 (276.4)	102.7 (147.0)	0.32
Total cholesterol (mg/dl)	201 (53)	185 (39)	0.36
High density lipoprotein cholesterol (mg/dl)	57.5 (24.0)	46.7 (15.9)	0.20

Figures in brackets are standard deviation of the mean. eGFR = estimated glomerular filtration rate, 25 (OH) D = 25 hydroxy vitamin D, Hb = haemaglobin, PTH = parathyroid hormone, CRP = C reactive protein, P:CR = protein:creatinine ratio.

mean arterial pressures were similar between treatment groups. There were no differences between the study groups in aPWV or LVMI after 6 months of therapy (table 4).

Safety data

There were no serious adverse events reported. Three patients in each group experienced episodes of gout that resolved with analgesia. The highest 25 (OH) D level recorded was 68.5 ng/ml. There were no recorded episodes of hypercalcaemia (defined as a serum calcium >10.4 mg/dl).

The effect of ergocalciferol on eNOS expression and nitrite levels in cultured human aortic endothelial cells

RT-PCR analysis for the fold-increase of eNOS compared to β-actin as a control gene demonstrated a dose dependent increase in expression with a 2.4-fold increase in eNOS expression after 24 h of incubation with high concentration ergocalciferol (120 ng/dl) compared to a 1.6 fold increase with low dose ergocalciferol (12 ng/dl) ($p = 0.002$). Only high concentration ergocalciferol resulted in a statistically significant increase in fold expression of eNOS compared to the control experiment ($p < 0.001$) (figure 5). There was no significant difference in nitrite levels between control and low dose ergocalciferol treated cells at 24 h. However, high dose ergocalciferol treatment produced a significant rise in nitrite compared to both low dose ($p = 0.007$) and vehicle control ($p = 0.003$) (figure 6).

Discussion

In this study, ergocalciferol therapy over 6 months in patients with CKD and concomitant vitamin D deficiency was associated with improved endothelium dependent microcirculatory function and a reduction in measures of tissue oxidative stress. The increase

Table 3. Laboratory results in both groups after 6 months of therapy.

	Ergocalciferol (n = 14)	Placebo (n = 15)	p value
Creatinine (mg/dl)	2.4 (0.9)	2.3 (1.1)	0.80
eGFR (ml/min/1.73 m^2)	31.4 (10.6)	35.0 (14.5)	0.44
Hb (g/dl)	12.6 (2.1)	12.4 (1.3)	0.73
Calcium (mg/dl)	9.1 (0.7)	8.9 (0.6)	0.43
Phosphate (mg/dl)	3.7 (0.74)	3.7 (1.2)	0.98
Calcium phosphate product (mg^2/dl^2)	33.6 (8.2)	32.6 (3.5)	0.66
PTH (pg/L)	97.2 (74.5)	135.8 (96.2)	0.26
CRP (mg/L)	7.5 (15.0)	9.7 (19.8)	0.76
Urine P:CR	154.0 (210.3)	117.5 (126.3)	0.62
Total cholesterol (mg/dl)	193 (38)	174 (35)	0.21
High density lipoprotein cholesterol (mg/dl)	54.2 (25.2)	50.8 (15.3)	0.67

Figures in brackets are standard deviation of the mean. eGFR = estimated glomerular filtration rate, 25 (OH) D = 25 hydroxy vitamin D, Hb = haemaglobin, PTH = parathyroid hormone, CRP = C reactive protein, P:CR = protein:creatinine ratio.

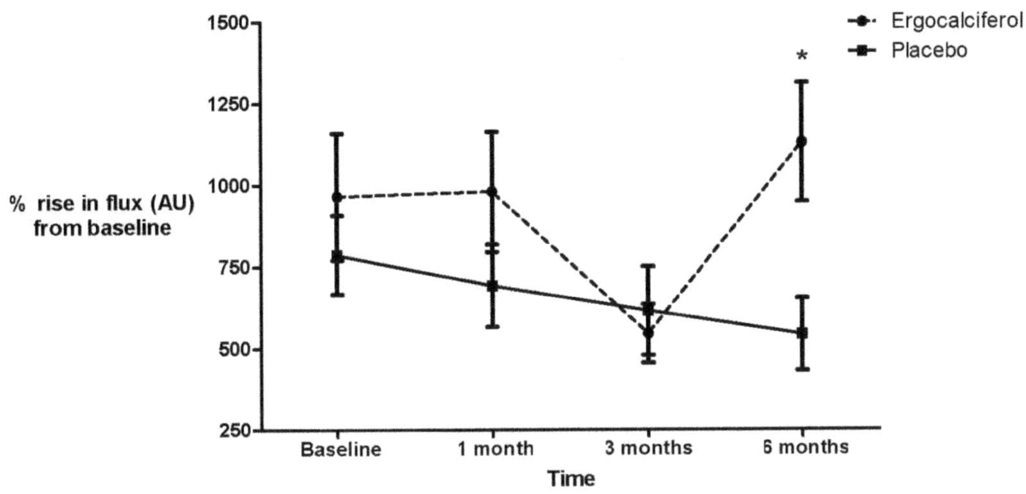

Number at risk

	Baseline	1 month	3 months	6 months
Ergocalciferol	20	19	18	14
Placebo	18	18	16	15

Figure 3. Percentage rise from baseline flux in arbitrary units (AU) after iontophoresis of ACh. Absolute values of percentage change in flux (AU): baseline - ergocalciferol 964.8, placebo 785.9 (p = NS). 1 month - ergocalciferol 979.5, placebo 690.9 (p = NS). 3 months – ergocalciferol 543.7, placebo 613.5 (p = NS). 6 months – ergocalciferol 1130.0, placebo 540.6 (p = 0.012). p values are Bonferroni post test following two way repeated measures ANOVA. (* = statistically significant).

in relative change of flux from baseline after iontophoresis with ACh but not SNP in subjects treated with ergocalciferol indicates improved microcirculatory function occurred through an endothelium dependent mechanism. Reduction in measures of skin AF in the ergocalciferol group correlates with reduced oxidative stress in these patients which will contribute to improved endothelial function and a reduced risk of future CV events [42]. This is in line with previous experimental work that demonstrated the protective effect of calcitriol in human endothelial cells cultured with AGE products [21].

In our study, bone mineral parameters, kidney function, C reactive protein, blood pressure and aPWV were similar at 6

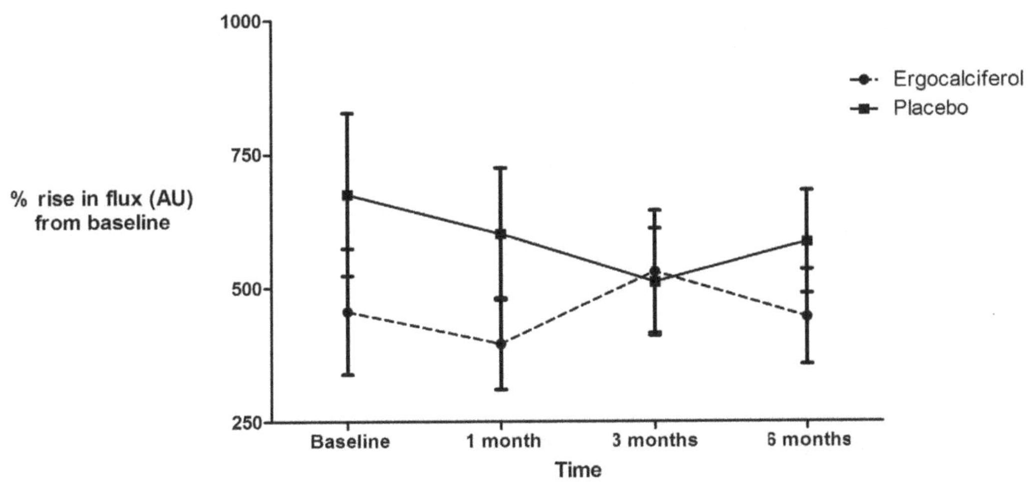

Number at risk

	Baseline	1 month	3 months	6 months
Ergocalciferol	20	19	18	14
Placebo	18	18	16	15

Figure 4. Percentage rise from baseline flux in arbitrary units (AU) after iontophoresis of SNP. Absolute values of percentage change in flux (AU): baseline - ergocalciferol 455.8, placebo 670.1 (p = NS). 1 month - ergocalciferol 395.5, placebo 601.3 (p = NS). 3 months – ergocalciferol 530.2, placebo 511.2 (p = NS). 6 months – ergocalciferol 445.7, placebo 585.9 (p = NS). p values are Bonferroni post test following two way repeated measures ANOVA.

Table 4. Measures of macrovascular parameters in both groups after 6 months of therapy.

	Ergocalciferol (n = 14)	Placebo (n = 15)	p value
Systolic BP (mmHg)	118 (10)	123 (15)	0.26
Diastolic BP (mmHg)	74 (6)	70 (9)	0.15
MAP (mmHg)	89 (7)	88 (10)	0.77
Pulse pressure (mmHg)	44 (8)	53 (12)	0.01
aPWV (m/s)	8.4 (1.3)	8.5 (1.2)	0.78
LVMI (g/m^2)	94.7 (28.4)	110 (54.3)	0.44
Skin AF (AU)	2.8 (0.6)	3.5 (0.9)	0.03
FCD (mm^{-1})	5.3 (0.7)	5.4 (0.8)	0.90
MFI (AU)	2.4 (0.2)	2.4 (0.2)	0.81

Figures in brackets are standard deviation of the mean. BP = blood pressure, MAP = mean arterial pressure, aPWV = aortic pulse wave velocity, LVMI – left ventricular mass index, AF – auto fluorescence, FCD – functional capillary density, MFI – microvascular flow index. AU – arbitrary units.

month follow up suggesting that functional changes to the microcirculation occurred independently of these parameters, adding strength to the argument that ergocalciferol may have a specific mechanism of action within the microcirculation. In contrast to other studies [45,46], proteinuria was unaffected in the ergocalciferol group although the differences in vitamin D compounds, dose schedule, study duration and populations between those studies and ours may explain this difference. aPWV did not decrease in line with the reduction in pulse pressure and this finding may reflect the short duration of the study. Studies with a longer follow up duration are more likely to demonstrate a fall in pulse wave velocity which may occur after a reduction in pulse pressure

After 6 months of therapy with ergocalciferol, there was no increase in the functional capillary density or flow within the microcirculation. This implies that the observed improvements in endothelium dependent microcirculatory function did not involve the recruitment of extra functionally relevant capillaries or changes in blood flow but rather that the endothelium dependent function of the existing microcirculatory network was improved by the direct effect of ergocalciferol.

This hypothesis is supported by the results of parallel *in vitro* experiments in which ergocalciferol, in a dose dependent manner, upregulated eNOS expression measured by RT-PCR. Nitric oxide generation compared to vehicle was numerically but not statistically significantly increased with low dose ergocalciferol but was significantly increased with high dose ergocalciferol. This suggests that higher doses of ergocalciferol are required to increase the functional effect of ergocalciferol on the endothelium and therefore that there may be a threshold 25 (OH) D concentration

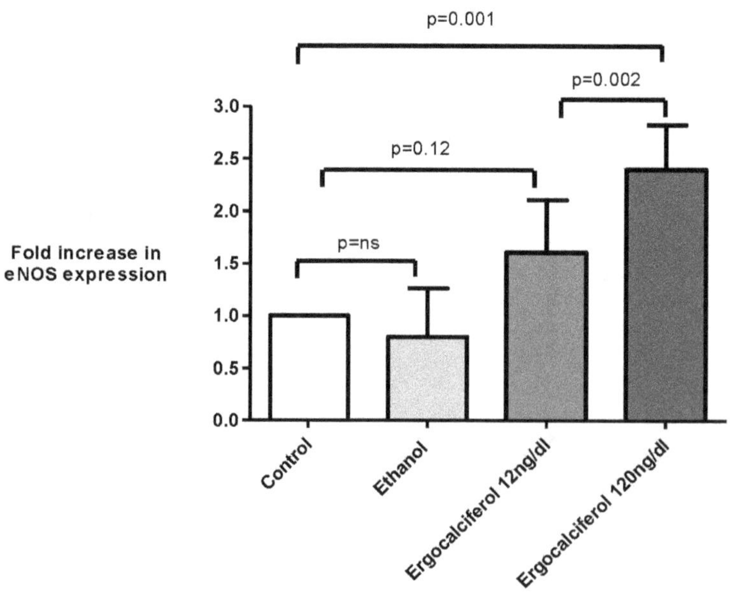

eNOS – endothelial nitric oxide synthase

Figure 5. Fold increase in eNOS expression by RT-PCR in cultured HAEC.

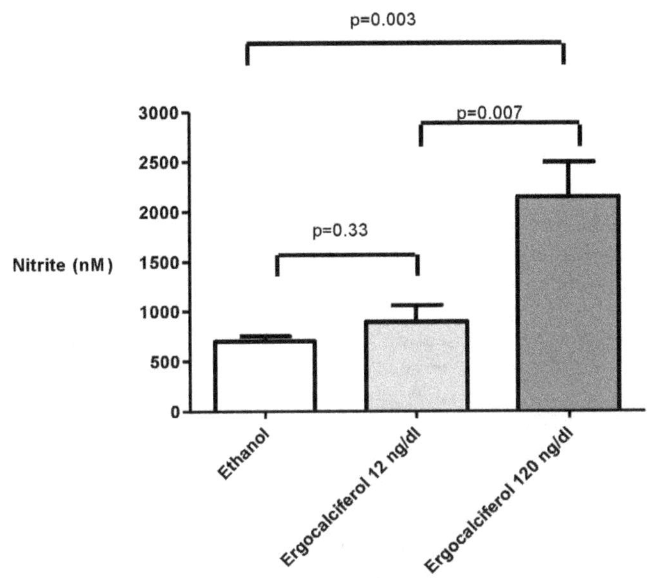

Figure 6. Nitrite levels in supernatants of HAEC. Cultured in low dose (12 ng/dl) and high dose (120 ng/dl) ergocalciferol after 24 h incubation.

above which the maximum effects of ergocalciferol on the microcirculation are achieved.

The present study is the first of its kind to explore the effect of vitamin D on microcirculatory function in patients with CKD and concomitant vitamin D deficiency. The exclusion of patients with diabetes mellitus allowed us to evaluate the effect of ergocalciferol on the microcirculation in CKD without the potentially confounding effect of diabetes on endothelial function.

Prospective studies of the effect of vitamin D therapy in patients with CKD have so far failed to show a beneficial effect of vitamin D on endpoints including LVMI, aPWV, blood pressure and inflammatory biomarkers. [27,47] The effect of nutritional vitamin D compounds on endothelial biomarkers and conduit artery endothelial function in kidney disease has been evaluated in two studies which have produced conflicting results. Marckmann *et al.* [27] compared the effect of 8 weeks of 40,000 IU of weekly cholecalciferol compared to a placebo in patients with both CKD and ESKD treated with haemodialysis. Patients in the control and intervention group were similar at baseline including cause of kidney disease, dialysis status and serum 25 (OH) D, 1,25 $(OH)_2$ D_3 and bone mineral parameters (PTH, Ca, PO_4) levels. There was a significant increase in 25 (OH) D levels in the treatment compared to control group (154.7 nmol/L vs 23.5 nmol/L) and a significant increase in 1,25 $(OH)_2$ D_3 levels although the increase in 1,25 $(OH)_2$ D_3 levels was higher in non-dialysis compared to dialysis requiring CKD (median increase in the CKD group 49 pmol/L ($p<0.01$) compared to 14 pmol/L in the dialysis group ($p>0.05$)). After 8 weeks of treatment, PTH fell significantly in non-dialysis CKD patients but not in dialysis requiring CKD patients. Despite the significant increase in vitamin D levels in the cholecalciferol group, there was no reduction in markers of endothelial dysfunction including D-dimer, von Willebrand factor, fibrinogen and interleukin (IL) 8 or C reactive protein. Additionally, blood pressure, aPWV and aortic augmentation index did not change between the two groups. Specifically, there were no significant differential effects on these parameters when comparing cholecalciferol treated and untreated patients in the dialysis and non-dialysis groups.

Assimon *et al.* [26] have evaluated the effect of ergocalciferol (n = 20 on ergocalciferol for a mean of 39.2 weeks and n = 20 not receiving ergocalciferol) on markers of vascular endothelial adhesion in a case control study of 40 patients undergoing maintenance haemodialysis. There were no significant differences in baseline parameters including dialysis vintage and both groups were receiving an equivalent dose of doxercalciferol. Serum 25 (OH) D levels were higher in the ergocalciferol group (90.8 nmol/L compared to 60.2 nmol/L, $p = 0.03$). In the ergocalciferol group, there was reduction in levels of vascular adhesion molecules sVCAM-1, sICAM-1, P-selectin and in all patients there was a significant negative correlation between serum 25 (OH) D levels and P-selectin and E-selectin. There was no difference in inflammatory biomarkers including IL-6 and TNF-α. However, the functional response of the endothelium was not evaluated and the case control design of this study means that the causal relationship between endothelial adhesion molecules and ergocalciferol cannot be established.

Despite the prompt and sustained rise in 25 (OH) D levels in our patients, significant differences in key microcirculatory end points were only observed after 6 months of therapy with ergocalciferol even though 25 (OH) D levels were similar at 1,3 and 6 months. Previous clinical studies using high dose ergocalciferol or cholecalciferol in healthy and diabetic patients without significant kidney disease demonstrated improved microcirculatory function between 8–12 weeks [24,25,48]. The delay in attainment of significantly improved microvascular function in the current study and lack of improvement over 8 weeks in Marckmann *et al.* study [27] may be a consequence of the uraemic milieu reducing the response of the microcirculation both to the upregulation of eNOS [49] and its downstream effects [50] in increasing availability of vasodilator moieties.

The findings from our study suggest that treatment with high dose ergocalciferol over an extended period of time is required before there is an improvement in microcirculatory endothelial function. This concept will have important implications for determining both the optimum duration of therapy of ergocalciferol and the optimum serum 25 (OH) D level to ensure a maximally beneficial effect on the microcirculation.

The strengths of our study are its double blind randomised placebo control design, replacement of vitamin D in line with international guidelines [37] that was standardised for all patients and commensurate with baseline serum concentrations of 25 (OH) D as well as the use of techniques that specifically assessed both conduit artery and microcirculatory endothelial function. At the time of designing this study, microcirculatory endothelial function had not previously been evaluated in patients with CKD and concomitant VDD in a clinical trial setting. Iontophoresis has been used in the setting of clinical trials to evaluate endothelial function. [51,52,53,54] The experimental conditions and iontophoretic protocol in the present study were standardised and changes in endothelial function were compared with baseline prior to treatment with ergocalciferol. The use of a low current iontophoresis protocol will have reduced the direct galvanic effect from the iontophoretic process on the endothelium seen when a higher current is used. [41] Therefore, any change seen in LDF after iontophoresis must be due to the direct effect of ergocalciferol itself on microvascular endothelial function.

Limitations of this study include the short follow up time and small sample size. The study duration is insufficient to detect significant differences between treatment groups in key outcome measures including CV events. Excluding patients with diabetes mellitus has limited the external validity but improved the internal validity and precision of the present study. Human aortic endothelial cells were not cultured in media consistent with the degree of CKD in the clinical trial subjects due to the complexity of establishing a culture medium that accurately reflects the earlier rather than more advanced stages of CKD. Consequently, the results from the *in vitro* experiments cannot be directly generalised to the uraemic milieu associated with CKD stage 3–4. The current study did not assess the effect of ergocalciferol on endothelial progenitor cells which are important mediators of endothelial repair and function and are reduced in patients at high risk of CVD [55]. Additional studies are required to address the effect of ergocalciferol on endothelial cells cultured in a medium more representative of the earlier stages of CKD as well as the effect of ergocalciferol on EPC number and function in CKD stage 3–4.

Conclusions

High dose ergocalciferol therapy over 6 months improved microcirculatory function and reduced tissue oxidative stress in patients with CKD stage 3–4 and concomitant vitamin D deficiency. *In vitro* studies suggest this effect is mediated through increased expression of eNOS and greater generation of nitric oxide. The primary endpoint of the study reflects global vascular health [14] and it is therefore logical to consider that the observed improvements in microcirculatory function will translate into improved clinical outcomes including a reduction in CV events.

To test this hypothesis, studies in patients with CKD and concomitant vitamin D deficiency with longer follow up and adequately powered to detect CV end points are now required to determine both if improved microcirculatory endothelial function through ergocalciferol therapy subsequently reduces CV endpoints and to determine the optimum serum level of 25 (OH) D to maximize microvascular endothelial function.

Supporting Information

Figure S1 Examples of iontophoresis dose response curves after 6 months of treatment for 2 patients after delivery of ACh demonstrating greater relative increase from baseline in flux in the ergocalciferol compared to placebo treated patient. Flux measured in arbitrary units (AU). Epoch reflects sequential dose increments of the iontophoretic protocol.

Figure S2 Percentage rise in flux from baseline after iontophoresis of ACh in patients with hypertension. Absolute values of percentage change in flux (AU): baseline - ergocalciferol 505.9, placebo 889.2 (p = NS). 1 month - ergocalciferol 853.5, placebo 1051.0 (p = NS). 3 months – ergocalciferol 519.2, placebo 1103.0 (p = NS). 6 months – ergocalciferol 671.6, placebo 1024.0 (p = NS). p values are Bonferroni post test following two way repeated measures ANOVA.

Figure S3 Percentage rise in flux from baseline after iontophoresis of SNP in patients with hypertension. Absolute values of percentage change in flux (AU): baseline - ergocalciferol 339.7, placebo 675.1 (p = NS). 1 month - ergocalciferol 866.9, placebo 724.0 (p = NS). 3 months – ergocalciferol 573.2, placebo 735.0 (p = NS). 6 months – ergocalciferol 682.2, placebo 579.0 (p = NS). p values are Bonferroni post test following two way repeated measures ANOVA.

Figure S4 Percentage rise in flux from baseline after iontophoresis of ACh in patients with glomerulonephritis. Absolute values of percentage change in flux (AU): baseline - ergocalciferol 762.9, placebo 1220.0 (p = NS). 1 month - ergocalciferol 1141.0, placebo 483.8 (p = NS). 3 months – ergocalciferol 647.7, placebo 1023.0 (p = NS). 6 months – ergocalciferol 1086, placebo 661.8 (p = NS). p values are Bonferroni post test following two way repeated measures ANOVA.

Figure S5 Percentage rise in flux from baseline after iontophoresis of SNP in patients with glomerulonephritis. Absolute values of percentage change in flux (AU): baseline - ergocalciferol 794.2, placebo 637.4 (p = NS). 1 month - ergocalciferol 690.6, placebo 708.8 (p = NS). 3 months – ergocalciferol 455.6, placebo 830.8 (p = NS). 6 months – ergocalciferol 387.3, placebo 504.1 (p = NS). p values are Bonferroni post test following two way repeated measures ANOVA.

Protocol S1 Full study protocol.

Checklist S1 Study CONSORT check list.

File S1 Full methodology. Contains Table S1, full iontophoresis protocol.

Acknowledgments

We are grateful to Amanda Smith for helpful advice on scoring SDF videos, Mawdsley Brooks UK for assistance with importing of the ergocalciferol, Alex Farrel and Jeanette Hansen for advice about dispensing the study drug, Dr Mark Westwood for advice about cMRI imaging and Dr Alex Milsom for her assistance with measuring nitrite levels. We are grateful to Dr Mavuto Mukaka for statistical advice.

Author Contributions

Conceived and designed the experiments: GD AT SH RP MJR MMY. Performed the experiments: GD SH. Analyzed the data: GD MJR MMY. Contributed reagents/materials/analysis tools: ATT SH RP MMY. Wrote the paper: GD SH MJR MMY. Conceived the original hypothesis: GD MMY Designed and executed the study: GD MJR MMY Provided scientific advice and equipment for microvascular studies: ATT RP Contributed to and have reviewed the final manuscript: GD ATT SH RP MJR MMY.

References

1. Feehally J, Griffith KE, Lamb EJ, O'Donoghue DJ, Tomson CR (2008) Early detection of chronic kidney disease. BMJ 337: a1618.
2. Li YC, Kong J, Wei M, Chen ZF, Liu SQ, et al. (2002) 1,25-Dihydroxyvitamin D(3) is a negative endocrine regulator of the renin-angiotensin system. J Clin Invest 110: 229–238.
3. Muller K, Haahr PM, Diamant M, Rieneck K, Kharazmi A, et al. (1992) 1,25-Dihydroxyvitamin D3 inhibits cytokine production by human blood monocytes at the post-transcriptional level. Cytokine 4: 506–512.
4. de Boer IH, Ioannou GN, Kestenbaum B, Brunzell JD, Weiss NS (2007) 25-Hydroxyvitamin D levels and albuminuria in the Third National Health and Nutrition Examination Survey (NHANES III). Am J Kidney Dis 50: 69–77.
5. Blair D, Byham-Gray L, Lewis E, McCaffrey S (2008) Prevalence of vitamin D [25(OH)D] deficiency and effects of supplementation with ergocalciferol (vitamin D2) in stage 5 chronic kidney disease patients. J Ren Nutr 18: 375–382.
6. LaClair RE, Hellman RN, Karp SL, Kraus M, Ofner S, et al. (2005) Prevalence of calcidiol deficiency in CKD: a cross-sectional study across latitudes in the United States. Am J Kidney Dis 45: 1026–1033.
7. Pilz S, Iodice S, Zittermann A, Grant WB, Gandini S (2011) Vitamin D status and mortality risk in CKD: a meta-analysis of prospective studies. Am J Kidney Dis 58: 374–382.

8. de Boer IH, Katz R, Chonchol M, Ix JH, Sarnak MJ, et al. (2011) Serum 25-hydroxyvitamin D and change in estimated glomerular filtration rate. Clin J Am Soc Nephrol 6: 2141–2149.
9. de Boer IH, Kestenbaum B, Shoben AB, Michos ED, Sarnak MJ, et al. (2009) 25-hydroxyvitamin D levels inversely associate with risk for developing coronary artery calcification. J Am Soc Nephrol 20: 1805–1812.
10. Chitalia N, Recio-Mayoral A, Kaski JC, Banerjee D (2012) Vitamin D deficiency and endothelial dysfunction in non-dialysis chronic kidney disease patients. Atherosclerosis 220: 265–268.
11. Recio-Mayoral A, Banerjee D, Streather C, Kaski JC (2011) Endothelial dysfunction, inflammation and atherosclerosis in chronic kidney disease—a cross-sectional study of predialysis, dialysis and kidney-transplantation patients. Atherosclerosis 216: 446–451.
12. Tatematsu S, Wakino S, Kanda T, Homma K, Yoshioka K, et al. (2007) Role of nitric oxide-producing and -degrading pathways in coronary endothelial dysfunction in chronic kidney disease. J Am Soc Nephrol 18: 741–749.
13. Pannier B, Guerin AP, Marchais SJ, Metivier F, Safar ME, et al. (2000) Postischemic vasodilation, endothelial activation, and cardiovascular remodeling in end-stage renal disease. Kidney Int 57: 1091–1099.
14. Cohn JN, Quyyumi AA, Hollenberg NK, Jamerson KA (2004) Surrogate markers for cardiovascular disease: functional markers. Circulation 109: IV31–46.
15. Teng M, Wolf M, Ofsthun MN, Lazarus JM, Hernan MA, et al. (2005) Activated injectable vitamin D and hemodialysis survival: a historical cohort study. J Am Soc Nephrol 16: 1115–1125.
16. Andress DL (2006) Vitamin D in chronic kidney disease: a systemic role for selective vitamin D receptor activation. Kidney Int 69: 33–43.
17. Shoben AB, Rudser KD, de Boer IH, Young B, Kestenbaum B (2008) Association of oral calcitriol with improved survival in nondialyzed CKD. J Am Soc Nephrol 19: 1613–1619.
18. Tentori F, Hunt WC, Stidley CA, Rohrscheib MR, Bedrick EJ, et al. (2006) Mortality risk among hemodialysis patients receiving different vitamin D analogs. Kidney Int 70: 1858–1865.
19. Wolf M, Thadhani R (2007) Vitamin D in patients with renal failure: a summary of observational mortality studies and steps moving forward. J Steroid Biochem Mol Biol 103: 487–490.
20. Santoro D, Gitto L, Ferraro A, Satta E, Savica V, et al. (2011) Vitamin D status and mortality risk in patients with chronic kidney disease. Ren Fail 33: 184–191.
21. Talmor Y, Golan E, Benchetrit S, Bernheim J, Klein O, et al. (2008) Calcitriol blunts the deleterious impact of advanced glycation end products on endothelial cells. Am J Physiol Renal Physiol 294: F1059–1064.
22. Borges AC, Feres T, Vianna LM, Paiva TB (1999) Effect of cholecalciferol treatment on the relaxant responses of spontaneously hypertensive rat arteries to acetylcholine. Hypertension 34: 897–901.
23. Wong MS, Delansorne R, Man RY, Vanhoutte PM (2008) Vitamin D derivatives acutely reduce endothelium-dependent contractions in the aorta of the spontaneously hypertensive rat. Am J Physiol Heart Circ Physiol 295: H289–296.
24. Shab-Bidar S, Neyestani TR, Djazayery A, Eshraghian MR, Houshiarrad A, et al. (2011) Regular consumption of vitamin D-fortified yogurt drink (Doogh) improved endothelial biomarkers in subjects with type 2 diabetes: a randomized double-blind clinical trial. BMC Med 9: 125.
25. Sugden J DJ, Witham M, Morris A, Struthers A (2007) Vitamin D improves endothelial function in patients with Type 2 diabetes mellitus and low vitamin D levels. Diabetic Medicine 25: 320–325.
26. Assimon MM, Salenger PV, El-Fawal HA, Mason DL (2012) Nutritional vitamin D supplementation in haemodialysis: A potential vascular benefit? Nephrology (Carlton) 17: 237–242.
27. Marckmann P, Agerskov H, Thineshkumar S, Bladbjerg EM, Sidelmann JJ, et al. (2012) Randomized controlled trial of cholecalciferol supplementation in chronic kidney disease patients with hypovitaminosis D. Nephrol Dial Transplant.
28. Clough G, Cracowski JL (2012) Spotlight issue: Microcirculation-from a clinical perspective. Microcirculation 19: 1–4.
29. Pignocchino P, Conte MR, Scarnato S, Grande A (1994) [Study of cutaneous microcirculation using the laser-Doppler method in syndrome X]. Cardiologia 39: 193–197.
30. Economides PA, Caselli A, Zuo CS, Sparks C, Khaodhiar L, et al. (2004) Kidney oxygenation during water diuresis and endothelial function in patients with type 2 diabetes and subjects at risk to develop diabetes. Metabolism 53: 222–227.
31. Tur E, Yosipovitch G, Bar-On Y (1991) Skin reactive hyperemia in diabetic patients. A study by laser Doppler flowmetry. Diabetes Care 14: 958–962.
32. Jung F, Mrowietz C, Labarrere C, Schuler S, Park JW (2001) Primary cutaneous microangiopathy in heart recipients. Microvasc Res 62: 154–163.
33. Shamim-Uzzaman QA, Pfenninger D, Kehrer C, Chakrabarti A, Kacirotti N, et al. (2002) Altered cutaneous microvascular responses to reactive hyperaemia in coronary artery disease: a comparative study with conduit vessel responses. Clin Sci (Lond) 103: 267–273.
34. McIntyre C JS, Jefferies H (2008) Advances in the cardiovascular assessment of patients with chronic kidney disease. NDT Plus 6: 383–391.
35. de Boer IH, Kestenbaum B (2008) Vitamin D in chronic kidney disease: is the jury in? Kidney Int 74: 985–987.
36. Levey AS, Bosch JP, Lewis JB, Greene T, Rogers N, et al. (1999) A more accurate method to estimate glomerular filtration rate from serum creatinine: a new prediction equation. Modification of Diet in Renal Disease Study Group. Ann Intern Med 130: 461–470.
37. (2003) K/DOQI Clinical Practice Guidelines for Bone Metabolism and Disease in Chronic Kidney Disease. Am J Kidney Dis 42: S1–S201.
38. Cupisti A, Rossi M, Placidi S, Caprioli R, Morelli E, et al. (2000) Responses of the skin microcirculation to acetylcholine and to sodium nitroprusside in chronic uremic patients. Int J Clin Lab Res 30: 157–162.
39. Cupisti A, Rossi M, Placidi S, Fabbri A, Morelli E, et al. (2000) Responses of the skin microcirculation to acetylcholine in patients with essential hypertension and in normotensive patients with chronic renal failure. Nephron 85: 114–119.
40. Morris SJ, Shore AC, Tooke JE (1995) Responses of the skin microcirculation to acetylcholine and sodium nitroprusside in patients with NIDDM. Diabetologia 38: 1337–1344.
41. Droog EJ, Henricson J, Nilsson GE, Sjoberg F (2004) A protocol for iontophoresis of acetylcholine and sodium nitroprusside that minimises nonspecific vasodilatory effects. Microvasc Res 67: 197–202.
42. Gerrits EG, Smit AJ, Bilo HJ (2009) AGEs, autofluorescence and renal function. Nephrol Dial Transplant 24: 710–713.
43. De Backer D, Hollenberg S, Boerma C, Goedhart P, Buchele G, et al. (2007) How to evaluate the microcirculation: report of a round table conference. Crit Care 11: R101.
44. Ignarro LJ, Fukuto JM, Griscavage JM, Rogers NE, Byrns RE (1993) Oxidation of nitric oxide in aqueous solution to nitrite but not nitrate: comparison with enzymatically formed nitric oxide from L-arginine. Proc Natl Acad Sci U S A 90: 8103–8107.
45. de Zeeuw D, Agarwal R, Amdahl M, Audhya P, Coyne D, et al. (2010) Selective vitamin D receptor activation with paricalcitol for reduction of albuminuria in patients with type 2 diabetes (VITAL study): a randomised controlled trial. Lancet 376: 1543–1551.
46. Molina P, Gorriz JL, Molina MD, Peris A, Beltran S, et al. (2013) The effect of cholecalciferol for lowering albuminuria in chronic kidney disease: a prospective controlled study. Nephrol Dial Transplant.
47. Thadhani R, Appelbaum E, Pritchett Y, Chang Y, Wenger J, et al. (2012) Vitamin D therapy and cardiac structure and function in patients with chronic kidney disease: the PRIMO randomized controlled trial. JAMA 307: 674–684.
48. Tarcin O, Yavuz DG, Ozben B, Telli A, Ogunc AV, et al. (2009) Effect of vitamin D deficiency and replacement on endothelial function in asymptomatic subjects. J Clin Endocrinol Metab 94: 4023–4030.
49. Rashid G, Benchetrit S, Fishman D, Bernheim J (2004) Effect of advanced glycation end-products on gene expression and synthesis of TNF-alpha and endothelial nitric oxide synthase by endothelial cells. Kidney Int 66: 1099–1106.
50. Arese M, Strasly M, Ruva C, Costamagna C, Ghigo D, et al. (1995) Regulation of nitric oxide synthesis in uraemia. Nephrol Dial Transplant 10: 1386–1397.
51. Witham MD, Adams F, Kabir G, Kennedy G, Belch JJ, et al. (2013) Effect of short-term vitamin D supplementation on markers of vascular health in South Asian women living in the UK - A randomised controlled trial. Atherosclerosis 230: 293–299.
52. Hobbs DA, Goulding MG, Nguyen A, Malaver T, Walker CF, et al. (2013) Acute ingestion of beetroot bread increases endothelium-independent vasodilation and lowers diastolic blood pressure in healthy men: a randomized controlled trial. J Nutr 143: 1399–1405.
53. Tehrani S, Mobarrez F, Lins PE, Adamson U, Wallen HN, et al. (2013) Impaired endothelium-dependent skin microvascular function during high-dose atorvastatin treatment in patients with type 1 diabetes. Diab Vasc Dis Res 10: 483–488.
54. Kaiser SE, Sanjuliani AF, Estato V, Gomes MB, Tibirica E (2013) Anti-Hypertensive Treatment Improves Microvascular Rarefaction and Reactivity in Low-Risk Hypertensive Individuals. Microcirculation.
55. Pellegatta F, Bragheri M, Grigore L, Raselli S, Maggi FM, et al. (2006) In vitro isolation of circulating endothelial progenitor cells is related to the high density lipoprotein plasma levels. Int J Mol Med 17: 203–208.

7

Microfluidic-Enabled Liposomes Elucidate Size-Dependent Transdermal Transport

Renee R. Hood[1]⁹, Eric L. Kendall[2]⁹, Mariana Junqueira[3], Wyatt N. Vreeland[4], Zenaide Quezado[3], Julia C. Finkel[3], Don L. DeVoe[1,2]*

1 Fischell Department of Bioengineering, University of Maryland, College Park, Maryland, United States of America, **2** Department of Mechanical Engineering, University of Maryland, College Park, Maryland, United States of America, **3** Department of Anesthesiology, Sedation, and Perioperative Medicine, Children's National Medical Center, Washington, DC, United States of America, **4** Biomolecular Measurement Division, National Institute of Standards and Technology, Gaithersburg, Maryland, United States of America

Abstract

Microfluidic synthesis of small and nearly-monodisperse liposomes is used to investigate the size-dependent passive transdermal transport of nanoscale lipid vesicles. While large liposomes with diameters above 105 nm are found to be excluded from deeper skin layers past the stratum corneum, the primary barrier to nanoparticle transport, liposomes with mean diameters between 31–41 nm exhibit significantly enhanced penetration. Furthermore, multicolor fluorescence imaging reveals that the smaller liposomes pass rapidly through the stratum corneum without vesicle rupture. These findings reveal that nanoscale liposomes with well-controlled size and minimal size variance are excellent vehicles for transdermal delivery of functional nanoparticle drugs.

Editor: David T. Eddington, University of Illinois at Chicago, United States of America

Funding: This research was funded by a Sheikh Zayed Institute – Clark School of Engineering seed grant and the National Science Foundation through grant CBET0966407. The funders had no role in study design, data collection and analysis, decision to publish, or preparation of the manuscript.

Competing Interests: The authors have declared that no competing interests exist.

* E-mail: ddev@umd.edu

⁹ These authors contributed equally to this work.

Introduction

Transdermal drug delivery offers significant potential as an alternative to oral delivery and hypodermic injection due to the promise of pain-free local or systemic introduction of drugs with controllable delivery rates over extended time periods [1]. Effective delivery of drug through the skin is hampered by poor diffusive transport across the stratum corneum (SC) layer, a 10 μm to 20 μm thick tissue region comprised of a structured lipid/protein matrix [2,3]. Even when employing chemical penetration enhancers, a broad class of skin disrupting molecules including a variety of surfactants, [1,4], transdermal drug delivery has met only limited success. Techniques such as dermabrasion and thermal ablation can temporarily render the SC porous to enhance drug transport, but these methods require active disruption of the skin and do not allow controlled doses to be delivered over long time periods. Similarly, non-invasive active methods such as ionophoresis and ultrasound require specialized equipment and only enhance drug transport for short periods. Nanoparticles offer an alternative strategy for passive transdermal delivery, offering increased drug loading, sustained release, and the potential for tissue-specific targeting. The structure of the SC includes lamellar lipid regions that present sub-nanometer intercellular spaces which can be widened in the presence of nanoparticle colloids to pores with dimensions on the order of several tens of nanometers [3,5]. Inorganic quantum dots ranging from approximately 4 nm to 12 nm in diameter exhibit efficient passive transport across the SC [6,7]. However, the utility of these nanoparticles for drug delivery is limited by high toxicity and low drug loading capacity [8], In contrast, lipid nanoparticles present a highly attractive route for drug delivery due to their excellent biocompatibility [9]. In particular, nanoscale liposomes with lipid bilayers encapsulating aqueous internal volumes offer high loading of both hydrophilic and amphipathic drugs, low toxicity, and tunable stability. However, there is little evidence that lipid vesicles ranging from 60 nm to several micrometers in diameter can traverse the SC in significant numbers [10–13], nor is there clear evidence of intact liposome passage through the SC. As a result, the application of lipid nanoparticles for transdermal drug delivery has largely focused on flexible liposomes such as transfersomes [14] and ethosomes [15], which incorporate surfactants or alcohols to impart a high degree of flexibility to the vesicle membranes, putatively allowing relatively large vesicles to traverse the small intercellular pores within the SC. However, for systemic delivery through the bloodstream, these nanoparticles are not ideal since large and flexible liposomes are subject to rapid opsonization and phagocytotic clearance. Furthermore, whereas both pharmacokinetics and biodistribution of traditional liposomes have been extensively studied and optimized, the behaviors of flexible liposomes remain largely unknown. More fundamentally, recent evidence indicates that ultraflexible transfersomes are highly compromised by passage through the skin, and may be no better than traditional liposomes for transdermal delivery of intact vesicles [16].

In this work we leverage a microfluidic technique that employs hydrodynamic focusing of a stream of solvated lipid sheathed by a sheath flow of aqueous buffer within a continuous-flow process [17–20]. This approach provides the ability to generate well-defined populations of small liposomes with narrow size distributions, enabling the effective study of the size-dependent transport of lipid vesicles across the SC. Conventional bulk methods of liposome production, including membrane extrusion [21] and sonication [22], are limited in their ability to generate well defined populations of liposomes with diameters in the size range expected to support effective transport of nanoparticles through the SC. As a result, prior studies have not shown extensive penetration of traditional liposomes past the SC [10–13]. In the present study, the capacity of the microfluidic technique to produce small liposomes with low polydispersity was exploited to generate populations of dye-laden vesicles that are almost entirely within the 25 nm to 40 nm diameter range previously reported to result in high transdermal flux of other monodisperse nanoparticles [23,24]. Microfluidic-enabled liposome preparations with mean diameters ranging from 31 nm to 308 nm were prepared (Fig. 1). Within this size range, two classes of liposomes were formed that differed by the incorporation of small amounts of either anionic lipids or PEGylated lipids, enabling the influence of surface chemistry on trans-SC flux to be investigated. For all liposome preparations in this study, the polydispersity index of the microfluidic-synthesized liposomes ranged from 0.035 to 0.135; as a comparison, a previous study investigating vesicles as small as 120 nm reported the use of liposomes with polydispersity indices varying from 0.1 to 0.3 [25]. Overall, the microfluidic-enabled liposomes produced here are both smaller and more narrowly distributed in diameter than bulk-scale produced liposomes used in prior passive transdermal drug delivery studies. The use of smaller liposomes is significant due to the hypothesis that liposomes, like other nanoparticles [3,5,23,24] will exhibit size-dependent dermal transport, with vesicles smaller than approximately 40 nm in diameter traversing the SC more effectively than larger nanoparticles. Similarly, the low polydispersity is significant since the total fluorescence signal from a vesicle population with a wide size distribution will be biased by the presence of significant number of liposomes above the mean diameter, prohibiting accurate evaluation of transport as a function of vesicle size. While a French press technique for liposome preparation has been reported to enable the formation of small unilamellar vesicles with diameters below approximately 30~50 nm [26,27], this method does not allow vesicle size to be readily tuned. The exceptionally low polydispersity of the microfluidic-enabled liposomes over a wide range of diameters allows a unique view into size-dependent dermal transport.

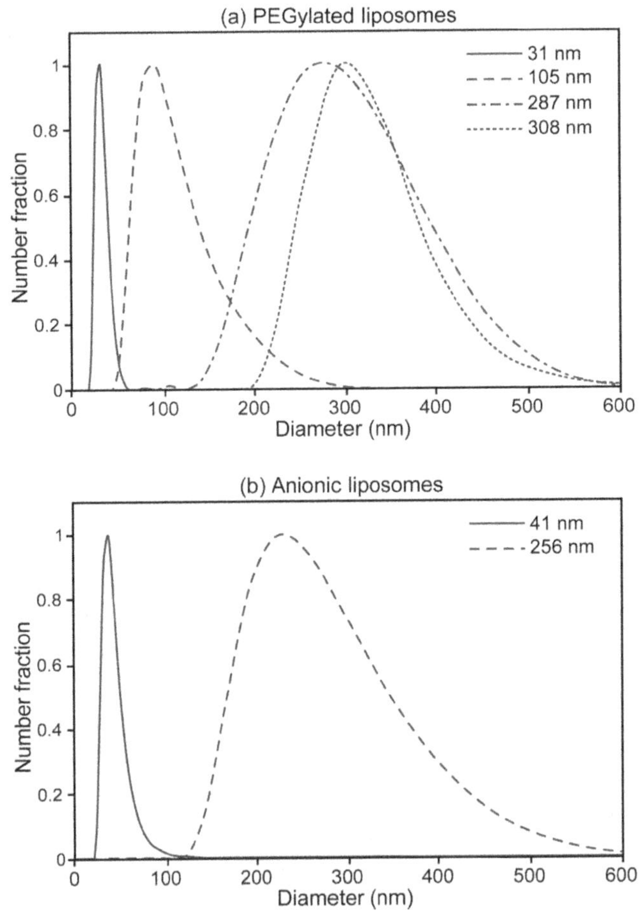

Figure 1. Volume-weighted size distributions of microfluidic-enabled (a) PEGylated and (b) anionic liposomes, revealing narrow size distributions over the full size range from 31 nm to 308 nm.

Results and Discussion

Fluorescence microscopy of microtomed porcine ear tissue after incubation with the various liposome preparations shows a marked difference in the dermal penetration of dyes between tissues exposed to either larger or smaller liposome preparations. Figure 2 shows representative fluorescent images revealing the distribution of DiI dye within the tissue sections. Skin samples exposed to the larger 105 nm to 308 nm liposomes (PEGylated and anionic) consistently exhibit bright bands of fluorescence associated with the SC, with very little fluorescence within deeper skin layers, revealing that these larger liposomes are either physically excluded by the narrow inter-corneocyte spaces, or are ruptured in the process of traversing the SC. In the latter case, the lipids and lipophilic dyes from the ruptured liposomes are likely to adhere to or associate with surrounding cells and extra-cellular material [28]. Conversely, the smaller 31 nm and 41 nm liposomes reveal a more evenly distributed dye profile throughout the skin, appearing to traverse the SC and enter the underlying layers of tissue in multiple instances with less significant accumulation in the SC (Fig. 2). We note that the several bright features that appear in deeper layers within some images are believed to result from imperfections caused by vessels or voids created during cryosectioning. Skin locations with capillaries were excluded due to the known autofluorescence of whole blood between wavelengths of 450–600 nm [29] and the relatively low concentration of fluorescent molecules in the liposome samples. Regions with significant voids created by tearing of the thin tissue sections during microtoming were excluded in order to maintain consistency throughout the samples. In control samples using free SF dye applied to the skin in liposome-free buffer, no penetration beyond the SC was observed. Dye penetration into deeper skin layers shows a strong dependence on liposome size, irrespective of charge state as determined by the presentation of PEG or anionic lipids on the vesicle surfaces. This is consistent with the hypothesis that dermal transport of lipid vesicles is a size-based phenomenon, and the ability of the smallest liposomes to traverse the SC and reach lower layers of skin is a direct result of the reduced liposome diameters. In some samples, bright and highly localized defects were visible in the dermis and epidermis. These features are routinely observed in dermal transport studies, and are the result of enhanced particle transport through hair-follicles, pores, and skin perforations [30,31]. This uneven, defect-based liposome penetration pathway is, by nature, not highly correlated to liposome size [30,31]. The more diffuse, evenly distributed fluorescence signal seen in the epidermis in the small (31 nm and 41 nm) liposome samples is evidence of liposome transport across the SC by a passive inter-corneocyte pathway, a similar phenomenon seen with other nanoparticles below 40 nm in diameter [3,5,23,24]. For tissue samples where hair follicles were present, enhanced transport was observed for all liposomes populations. Results from these samples were omitted from analysis to prevent the confounding influence of follicular transport on analysis of SC penetration.

For quantitative comparison of liposome penetration, ImageJ software was used to obtain plot profiles of fluorescence intensity normal to the tissue surface. Profiles of each tissue section were averaged over 5 representative regions per sample (Fig. 3). These profiles were normalized for maximum fluorescence intensity per profile and aligned to the midpoint of the SC, across all samples. The SC thickness was determined from averaged manual measurements using brightfield images of each tissue, ranging from 15 μm to 40 μm, which is in agreement with previously reported values for porcine skin [32]. The percentage of DiI fluorescence intensity observed beneath the SC compared to the total observed fluorescence signal was calculated from the plot profiles for each sample and compared across different liposome sizes and surface chemistries (Fig. 4). We note that this technique assumes a linear relationship between fluorescence intensity and liposome concentration, an assumption that does not hold for samples where liposomes are highly concentrated in one area causing a local saturation of fluorescence intensity, as observed in some images from the larger (diameter greater than 105 nm) liposomes used in this study. This saturation effect leads to systematic underreporting of liposomes trapped in the SC, and thus a bias toward higher measured penetration efficiencies for these larger liposomes can occur. Detector saturation was avoided as much as possible while maintaining identical imaging conditions across all samples used in this study. We also note that while efforts were made to omit from analysis tissue sections with large voids, blood vessels, or hair follicles, some regions with anomalous fluorescent patches do appear in several images, particularly for the larger 308 nm PEGylated liposomes as seen in Fig. 2.

The small 31 nm PEGylated liposomes pass the SC in large numbers (91%), which is up to 590% greater than the larger 105 nm to 308 nm vesicles studied here. The small 41 nm diameter anionic liposomes show 65% of their total DiI signal under the SC, which is 200% greater than observed with 256 nm diameter liposomes. Both populations of smaller liposomes exhibit significantly enhanced penetration through dermal tissues compared to the larger vesicles, which is consistent with the behavior observed for other nanoparticles smaller than 40 nm in diameter [23,24], and reveals that size-dependent transdermal transport of the microfluidic-enabled liposomes follows the same overall trend observed for other classes of nanoparticles.

Regardless of their transport efficiency, it has been unclear if liposomes can traverse the SC intact. Penetration of fluorescent reporter molecules may occur as a result of liposome rupture or leakage during passage through the SC, with enhanced permeation of free dye possibly resulting from interactions between liposomes and dermal lipid structures. To explore this issue for the case of the microfluidic-enabled liposomes, a combination of hydrophilic dye (SF) and lipophilic dye (DiI) were simultaneously incorporated during liposome formation into the vesicle cores and bilayers, respectively. Due to the lipid structure of the SC, diffusive transport of free hydrophilic and hydrophobic solutes is expected to vary significantly [33,34], such that a lack of spatial correlation between the two dyes would imply that the liposomes had ruptured or leaked, allowing the hydrophilic dye (SF) to permeate through the tissue at a different rate than the lipophilic dye (DiI). Conversely, a high degree of spatial correlation would suggest the presence of intact vesicles. For the case of 31 nm liposomes, two color imaging of the exposed tissue sections reveals strong agreement between the distributions of hydrophilic (green) and lipophilic (red) signals through the SC and into the epidermis for all samples, as revealed through both the images (Fig. 5) and the dye penetration depth profiles taken through the depth of the tissue (Fig. 6). Using Pearson's correlation coefficient (ρ) as a measure of the degree of linear dependence between the spatial distributions of each dye, an average value of $\rho = 0.92$ was determined for the 31 nm PEGylated liposomes, indicating a high degree of correlation between the dye locations. While not conclusive, this evidence strongly suggests that the small liposomes

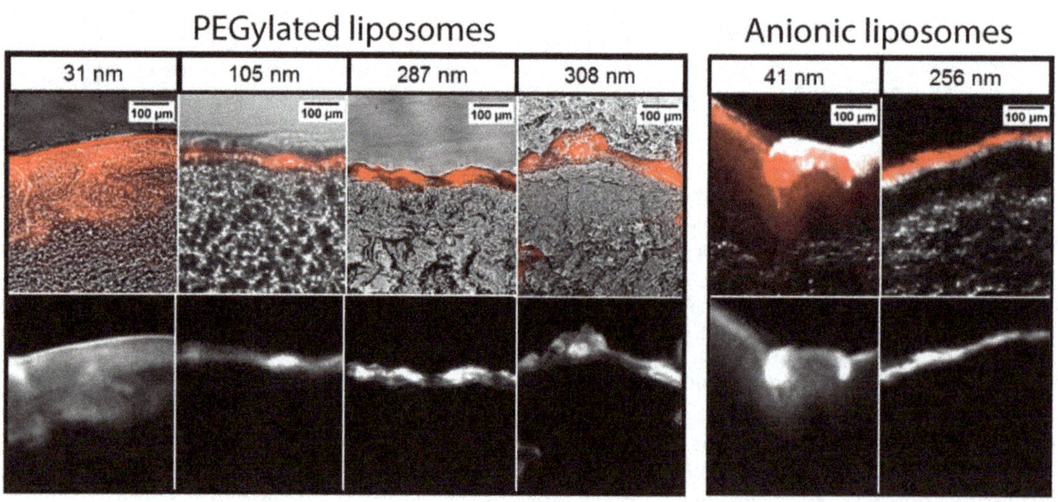

Figure 2. Brightfield/fluorescence image overlays (top) and single-channel fluorescence images (bottom) for microtomed tissue sections following 15 min application of PEGylated or anionic liposome samples of varying diameters containing DiI lipophilic dye. Significant dye penetration past the SC is observed with the smallest liposomes (31 nm diameter PEGylated and 41 nm anionic liposomes), while dye from the larger vesicles does not appear to cross the SC, indicating size-based passive transport independent of surface charge.

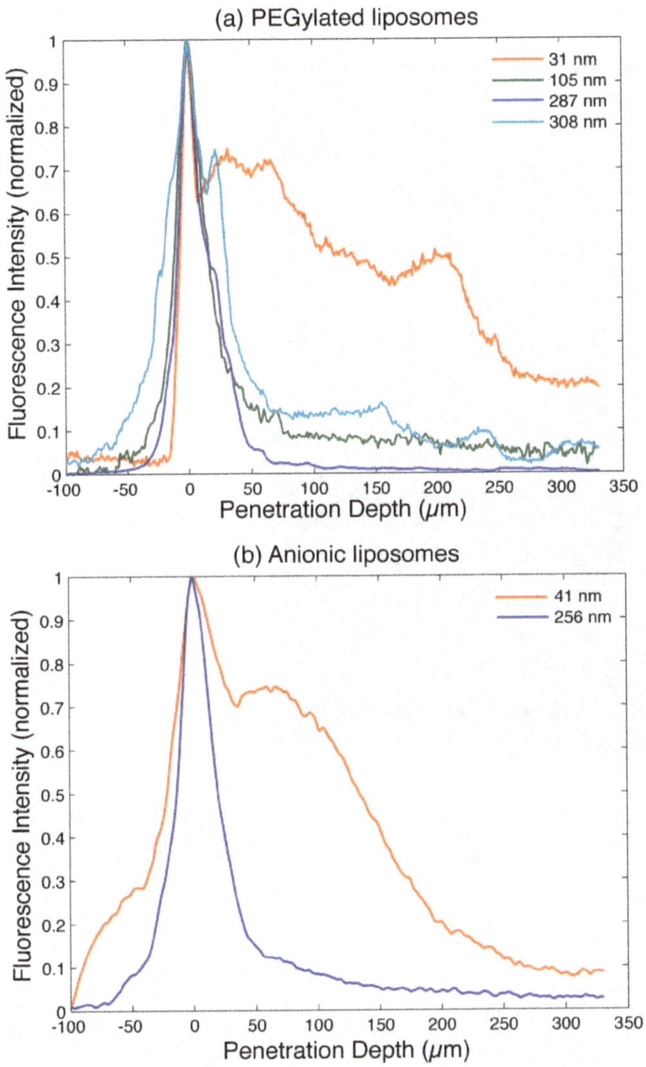

Figure 3. DiI fluorescence intensity plot profiles for (a) PEGylated liposomes and (b) anionic liposomes as a function of porcine skin tissue penetration depth. Measurements were performed 15 minute following liposome application. Each curve is representative of an average of 5 ROIs per image.

successfully penetrate through the SC intact with minimal leakage of their cargo. Experiments performed using larger liposomes resulted in measured values of $\rho = 0.81$ and $\rho = 0.75$ for 308 nm and 105 nm liposomes, respectively. This relatively poor correlation, together with the overall lack of significant dye penetration (Fig. 3), indicates that some degree of vesicle degradation and free dye diffusion occurs for these larger liposomes.

In conclusion, we have leveraged a microfluidic liposome synthesis technique to evaluate size-dependent transdermal delivery of liposomes through *ex vivo* porcine tissues. Compared to larger vesicles, where dye penetration across the SC is presumed to occur primarily through a combination of vesicle rupture and transport along follicular pathways, the smaller 31 nm diameter and 41 nm diameter liposomes traverse and transport their intra-liposomal contents across the full surface of the SC and into deep dermal tissues, with penetration depths of at least several hundred micrometers observed with a short 15 min incubation. Multicolor fluorescence imaging of hydrophilic and hydrophobic dyes

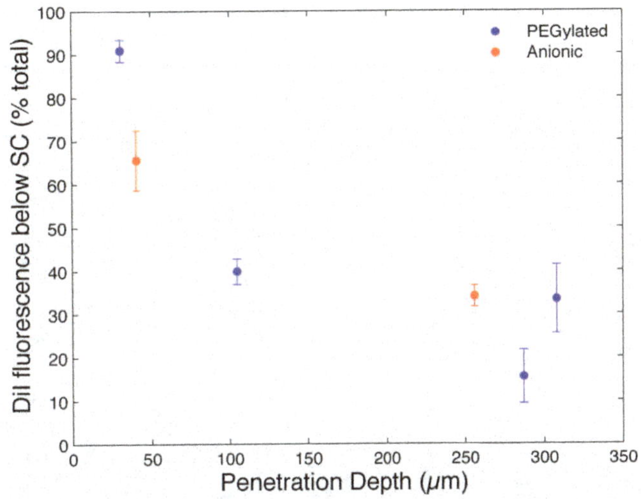

Figure 4. Percentage of total DiI fluorescence signal seen below the SC for the different sizes of PEGylated and anionic liposomes. Each plot reflects the average profile extracted from 5 ROIs per tissue section, with error bars reflecting standard deviation. SC thickness, estimated from averaged manual measurements using brightfield images of each tissue, ranged from 15 μm to 40 μm, in general agreement with previously reported values for porcine skin [32]. The small 31 nm PEGylated liposomes pass the SC in large numbers (91%), which is up to 590% greater than the larger 105 nm to 308 nm diameter liposomes. The small 41 nm anionic liposomes also reveal 65% of their total DiI signal under the SC, which is 200% greater than observed with 256 nm diameter liposomes of the same composition.

incorporated into the liposomes during synthesis further reveals that the smallest 31 nm liposomes are able to traverse dermal layers intact, with implications for clinical applications requiring co-delivery of therapeutic reagents with dissimilar chemical properties, nanoparticle-mediated drug release, or transport of intact nanocarriers to the bloodstream for systemic delivery. The results presented here also represent the first demonstration of passive transdermal diffusion of nanoscale, microfluidic-generated liposomes, opening the door to the use of these nanoparticles for effective delivery of lipophilic, hydrophilic, and amphipathic compounds to underlying dermal layers. The transport of nanoparticles through the SC is a matter of much debate, and the findings of the present study will require additional validation using complementary methods to confirm the size-dependent behavior described here and assess the fate of both liposomes and cargo.

Materials and Methods

Certain commercial equipment, instruments, or materials are identified in this paper to foster understanding. Such identification does not imply recommendation or endorsement by the National Institute of Standards and Technology, nor does it imply that the materials or equipment identified are necessarily the best available for the purpose.

Ethics Statement

This research involved Yorkshire piglets sacrificed as part of a separate parallel study approved by the Institutional Animal Care and Use Committee (IACUC) at the Children's National Medical Center. All procedures were performed in accordance with the National Institutes of Health Guide for the Care and Use of Animals in Research.

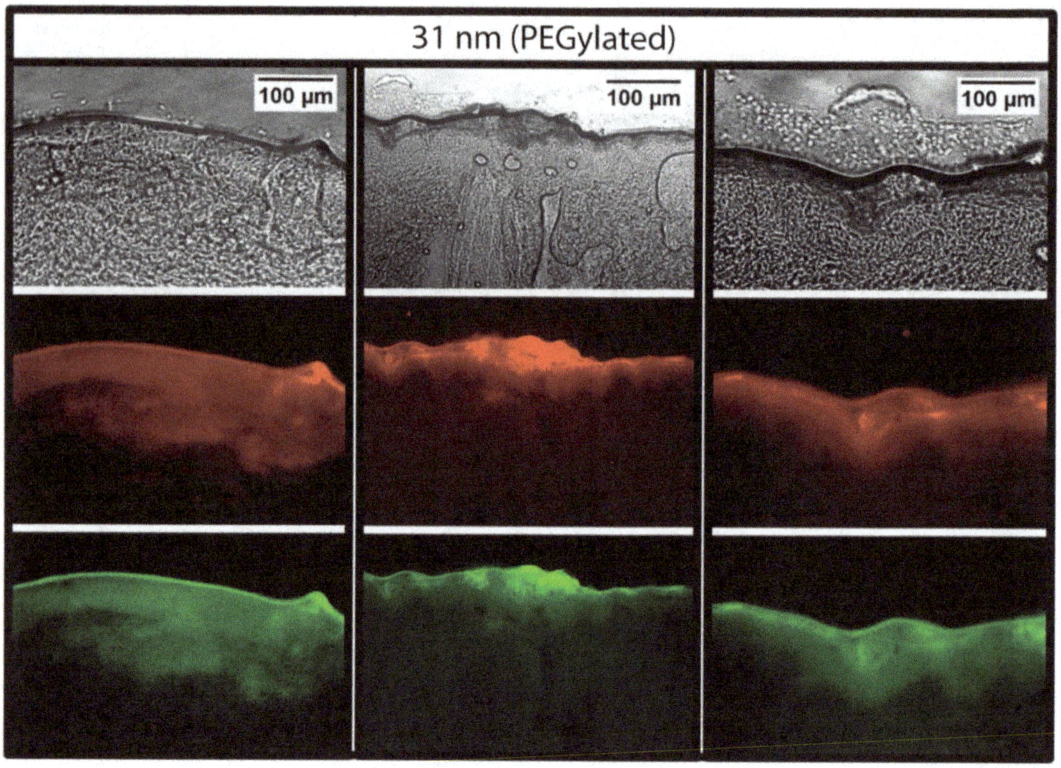

Figure 5. Brightfield images of 3 representative tissue regions following application of 31 nm PEGyated liposomes to porcine skin tissue (top), together with matched single channel fluorescence images for lipophilic DiI (middle) and hydrophilic SF (bottom). Similar fluorescence distributions for both dyes are seen across multiple tissue sections, indicating successful penetration of intact liposomes through the epithelium.

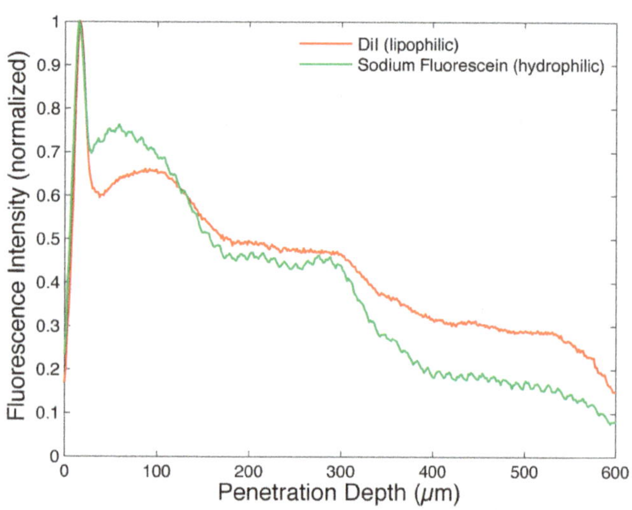

Figure 6. Penetration depth profiles of lipophilic and hydrophilic liposomal dyes within a tissue section following 15 min application of 31 nm PEGyated liposomes simultaneously loaded with both dyes. Each curve is representative of an average of 5 ROIs per image. A Pearson's correlation coefficient of $\rho = 0.92$ reveals a high degree of colocalization between the dyes.

Lipid Mixture and Hydration Buffer Preparation

Two variations of lipid mixtures were prepared to analyze the resulting penetration depth of both PEG-conjugated (PEGylated) and negatively-charged (anionic) into dermal tissue. In addition to enhancing liposome stability, PEG is commonly attached to the exterior of liposomes as a protective shield from the immune system during blood circulation [35], potentially increasing the bioavailability of PEGylated liposomes that are able to reach and enter subcutaneous capillaries after transdermal transport. For PEGylated liposomes, dimyristoylphosphatidylcholine (DMPC), cholesterol, and dipalmitoylphosphatidylethanolamine-PEG 2000 (PEG2000-PE) (Avanti Polar Lipids Inc., Alabaster, AL) were combined in chloroform (Mallinckrodt Baker Inc., Phillipsburg, NJ) at a molar ratio of 70:25:5. For anionic liposomes, DMPC, cholesterol (both from Avanti), and anionic surfactant dihexadecyl phosphate (DCP) (Sigma Aldrich, St. Louis, MO) were mixed in chloroform (Mallinckrodt Baker Inc.) at a molar ratio of 50:40:10. The lipid mixtures were prepared in glass scintillation vials then stored in a vacuum desiccator for at least 24 h for complete solvent removal. The desiccated lipid mixtures were re-dissolved in anhydrous ethanol (Sigma Aldrich) for a total lipid concentration of 40 mM. To assist in fluorescent imaging, a lipophilic membrane dye, 1,1′-dioctadecyl-3,3,3′,3′-tetramethylindocarbocyanine perchlorate (DiI-C_{18}; DiI) (Life Technologies, Carlsbad, CA) was included into the lipid mixtures (1 wt%). A 10 mM phosphate buffered saline (PBS) (Sigma Aldrich) solution at pH 7.4 was used as a hydration buffer, with selected samples containing 1 mM hydrophilic sodium fluorescein salt (SF) (Sigma Aldrich) as a hydrophilic dye. All fluids (solvent and buffer) were passed through

0.22 μm filters (Millipore Corp., New Bedford, MA) before being introduced to the microfluidic device.

Liposome synthesis and characterization

PEGylated and anionic liposomes were prepared using methods described previously [17–20]. Briefly, a flow-focusing microchannel network for liposome synthesis was fabricated following our previous work [36]. All microchannels in the final device were nominally 50 μm wide and 300 μm tall. The prepared lipid-ethanol solution was injected into the microfluidic device between two sheath flows of the aqueous buffer. The flow rate ratio (FRR), defined as the ratio of the volumetric flow rate of the aqueous buffer to the volumetric flow rate of the ethanol, was varied between 5–50 to produce liposomes with modal diameters ranging from 31 nm to 308 nm. Total average linear flow velocity for all FRRs was kept constant (0.125 m/s) for a total volumetric flow rate of 112 μL/min. To enable the formation of smaller vesicles, the temperature of the microfluidic device was controlled by contacting the glass slide of the device with a hot plate at 50°C throughout the entire synthesis process [37]. The resulting liposome populations were characterized for size via dynamic light scattering (Nano ZSP, Malvern Instruments Ltd., UK). Size distribution plots were generated by fitting spline curves to the binned distribution data imported from the dynamic light scattering instrument.

The microfluidic-generated liposomes contained lipophilic DiI in their bilayers and hydrophilic SF in their cores to enable fluorescence imaging of tissue penetration depth. To remove any remaining dye not incorporated into the liposomes during the synthesis process, all liposome samples were purified via size exclusion chromatography on Sephadex G-25 PD-10 columns (GE Healthcare, Piscataway, NJ) equilibrated with PBS immediately before application to the tissue. Gel filtration using the PD-10 columns provides efficient buffer exchange for removal of ethanol used in the liposome formation process, thereby preventing variations in ethanol concentration (2–16%) used for different liposome populations from affecting skin permeation experiments. Final lipid concentrations following gel filtration ranged from 0.56 mM to 4.76 mM, depending on the FRR used for liposome synthesis.

Tissue exposure and cryosectioning

Porcine ear tissue from Yorkshire piglets (4 weeks, 5 kg) was selected due to its morphological and functional resemblance to human skin. Porcine ear skin *in vitro* has shown remarkably similar biophysical properties to human skin *in vivo*, particularly in terms of the diffusivity and permeability coefficient of water across the SC [38]. Studies have also indicated that porcine skin is extremely similar both structurally and chemically to its human counterpart, exhibits chemical properties which are rather consistent across different samples and stable over time at room temperature, therefore porcine skin is a valuable tool for investigating diffusion dynamics of materials with human skin [39]. One ear from each animal was removed following general anesthesia. Liposome solutions were immediately applied in 50 μL aliquots for each size in different locations on the outside of the ear, resulting in spot areas ranging from 0.25–0.5 cm^2, and incubated for 15 min at room temperature. This exposure method was chosen over the use of a perfusion cell since the focus of this study is on short-term SC transport rather than long-term behavior of the nanoparticles within the dermis. For the characterization of size-dependent transport, all liposome solutions covering the full range of size distributions were deposited on ears from a single animal to minimize the influence of tissue morphology variations between animals. Different animals were used for each set of experiments characterizing PEGylated liposome transport, anionic liposome transport, and co-distribution of lipophilic and hydrophilic dyes. Following incubation, the ear tissue was placed in a plastic petri dish and frozen. The frozen tissue was bulk sectioned, embedded using Tissue-Tek Cryo-OCT compound (Fisher Scientific, Pittsburgh, PA), and frozen at −80°C. The frozen tissue blocks were then sectioned into smaller slices, nominally 30 μm thick and revealing dermal tissues at least 300 μm from the surface, using a HM550 cryostat microtome (Richard Allan Scientific, Kalamazoo, MI) and placed onto gelatin-treated glass slides for imaging. Sections were procured from the tissue directly beneath each of the applied liposome volumes, with the plane of each section aligned through the center of its corresponding droplet. Sectioning was performed with the blade oriented perpendicular to the skin surface and the blade path in the direction of the SC to prevent artifacts that could result from mechanical displacement of liposomes, dye, or tissue normal to the SC layer.

Fluorescence microscopy and image processing

The 30 μm thick tissue sections were imaged using a TE-2000 S inverted epifluorescence microscope (Nikon, Melville, NY). Bright-field images and fluorescence images at 528 nm–553 nm (green filter; DiI) and 465 nm–495 nm (blue filter; SF) excitation wavelengths were acquired and overlaid to confirm and evaluate the extent of liposome penetration into the dermal tissue and to assess colocalization of the lipophilic and hydrophilic dyes.

ImageJ software (National Institutes of Health, Bethesda, MD) was used to analyze the images. Fluorescence intensity profiles were extracted using 10 μm wide regions of interest (ROIs), with data from multiple ROIs combined to generate quantitative profiles of liposome penetration depth. The intensity data was averaged across 5 ROIs per sample, then normalized to peak intensity and aligned to reveal the average fluorescence signal seen within each tissue sample below the SC. Dye colocalization was analyzed using the JACoP plugin with ImageJ [40]. In all experiments, image analysis was performed independently for each dye.

Acknowledgments

The authors thank Dr. Nobuyuki Ishibashi of Children's National Medical Center for supplying piglet ear tissue, support of the Maryland NanoCenter FabLab, Dr. Peter Swaan at the University of Maryland School of Pharmacy for Malvern Zetasizer access, and Dr. Adam Hsieh of the University of Maryland College Park for cryostat microtome access.

Author Contributions

Conceived and designed the experiments: RH EK MJ WV ZQ JF DD. Performed the experiments: RH EK. Analyzed the data: RH EK DD. Contributed reagents/materials/analysis tools: MJ WV ZQ JF. Wrote the paper: RH EK DD. Reviewed manuscript: RH EK MJ WN ZQ JF DD.

References

1. Prausnitz MR, Langer R (2008) Transdermal drug delivery. Nat Biotechnol 26: 1261–1268. Available: http://www.pubmedcentral.nih.gov/articlerender.fcgi?artid=2700785&tool=pmcentrez&rendertype=abstract. Accessed 27 February 2013.
2. Schreier H, Bouwstra J (1994) Liposomes and niosomes as topical drug carriers: dermal and transdermal drug delivery. J Control Release 30: 1–15. Available: http://linkinghub.elsevier.com/retrieve/pii/0168365994900396. Accessed 4 July 2013.

3. Cevc G (2004) Lipid vesicles and other colloids as drug carriers on the skin. Adv Drug Deliv Rev 56: 675–711. Available: http://www.ncbi.nlm.nih.gov/pubmed/15019752. Accessed 6 March 2013.
4. Karande P, Jain A, Ergun K, Kispersky V, Mitragotri S (2005) Design principles of chemical penetration enhancers for transdermal drug delivery. PNAS 102: 4688–4693.
5. Bouwstra JA, Honeywell-Nguyen PL, Gooris GS, Ponec M (2003) Structure of the skin barrier and its modulation by vesicular formulations. Prog Lipid Res 42: 1–36.
6. Ryman-Rasmussen JP, Riviere JE, Monteiro-Riviere NA (2006) Penetration of intact skin by quantum dots with diverse physicochemical properties. Toxicol Sci 91: 159–165.
7. Chu M, Wu Q, Wang J, Hou S, Miao Y, et al. (2007) In vitro and in vivo transdermal delivery capacity of quantum dots through mouse skin. Nanotechnology 18: 455103.
8. Schleich N, Préat V (2012) Nanostructured Biomaterials for Overcoming Biological Barriers. Nanostructured Biomaterials for Overcoming Biological Barriers. doi:10.1039/9781849735292-00316.
9. Torchilin VP (2005) Recent advances with liposomes as pharmaceutical carriers. Nat Rev Drug Discov 4: 145–160. doi:10.1038/nrd1632.
10. Du Plessis J, Ramachandran C, Weiner N, Muller DG (1994) The influence of particle size of liposomes on the deposition of drug into skin. Int J Pharm 103: 277–282. doi:10.1016/0378-5173(94)90178-3.
11. Prow TW, Grice JE, Lin LL, Faye R, Butler M, et al. (2011) Nanoparticles and microparticles for skin drug delivery. Adv Drug Deliv Rev 63: 470–491. Available: http://www.ncbi.nlm.nih.gov/pubmed/21315122. Accessed 23 January 2014.
12. Sudhakar CK, Upadhyay N, Jain S, Charyulu RN (2012) Ethosomes as Non-Invasive Loom for Transdermal Drug Delivery Systems. In: Sebastian M, Ninan N, Haghi AK, editors. Nanomedicine and Drug Delivery.Apple Academic Press. pp. 1–15.
13. Sentjurc M, Vrhovnik K, Kristl J (1999) Liposomes as a topical delivery system: the role of size on transport studied by the EPR imaging method. J Control Release 59: 87–97.
14. Cevc G, Gebauer D, Stieber J, Schätzlein A, Blume G (1998) Ultraflexible vesicles, Transfersomes, have an extremely low pore penetration resistance and transport therapeutic amounts of insulin across the intact mammalian skin. Biochim Biophys Acta 1368: 201–215. Available: http://www.ncbi.nlm.nih.gov/pubmed/9459598. Accessed 4 July 2013.
15. Touitou E, Dayan N, Bergelson L, Godin B, Eliaz M (2000) Ethosomes - novel vesicular carriers for enhanced delivery: characterization and skin penetration properties. J Control Release 65: 403–418. Available: http://www.ncbi.nlm.nih.gov/pubmed/10699298. Accessed 28 August 2013.
16. Brewer J, Bloksgaard M, Kubiak J, Sørensen JA, Bagatolli L a (2013) Spatially resolved two-color diffusion measurements in human skin applied to transdermal liposome penetration. J Invest Dermatol 133: 1260–1268. Available: http://www.ncbi.nlm.nih.gov/pubmed/23223136. Accessed 25 April 2013.
17. Jahn A, Vreeland WNNWN, Gaitan M, Locascio LEELE (2004) Controlled vesicle self-assembly in microfluidic channels with hydrodynamic focusing. J Am Chem Soc 126: 2674–2675. Available: http://pubs.acs.org.proxy-um.researchport.umd.edu/doi/pdf/10.1021/ja0318030.
18. Jahn A, Vreeland WN, DeVoe DL, Locascio LE, Gaitan M (2007) Microfluidic Directed Formation of Liposomes of Controlled Size. Langmuir 23: 6289–6293. Available: http://www.ncbi.nlm.nih.gov/pubmed/17451256. Accessed 3 February 2014.
19. Jahn A, Stavis SM, Hong JS, Vreeland WN, DeVoe DL, et al. (2010) Microfluidic Mixing and the Formation of Nanoscale Lipid Vesicles. ACS Nano 4: 2077–2087. doi:10.1021/nn901676x.
20. Hood RR, Shao C, Omiatek DM, Vreeland WN, DeVoe DL (2013) Microfluidic Synthesis of PEG- and Folate-Conjugated Liposomes for One-Step Formation of Targeted Stealth Nanocarriers. Pharm Res 30: 1597–1607. Available: http://www.ncbi.nlm.nih.gov/pubmed/23386106. Accessed 7 March 2013.
21. Batzri S, Korn ED (1973) Single bilayer liposomes prepared without sonication. Biochim Biophys Acta 298: 1015–1019. Available: http://www.ncbi.nlm.nih.gov/pubmed/4738145. Accessed 4 September 2013.
22. Maulucci G, De Spirito M, Arcovito G, Boffi F, Castellano AC, et al. (2005) Particle size distribution in DMPC vesicles solutions undergoing different sonication times. Biophys J 88: 3545–3550. Available: http://www.pubmedcentral.nih.gov/articlerender.fcgi?artid = 1305501&tool = pmcentrez&rendertype = abstract. Accessed 4 September 2013.
23. Vogt A, Combadiere B, Hadam S, Stieler KM, Lademann J, et al. (2006) 40 nm, but not 750 or 1,500 nm, nanoparticles enter epidermal CD1a+ cells after transcutaneous application on human skin. J Invest Dermatol 126: 1316–1322. Available: http://www.ncbi.nlm.nih.gov/pubmed/16614727. Accessed 6 March 2013.
24. Küchler S, Radowski MR, Blaschke T, Dathe M, Plendl J, et al. (2009) Nanoparticles for skin penetration enhancement—a comparison of a dendritic core-multishell-nanotransporter and solid lipid nanoparticles. Eur J Pharm Biopharm Off J Arbeitsgemeinschaft fur Pharm Verfahrenstechnik eV 71: 243–250.
25. Verma DD, Verma S, Blume G, Fahr A (2003) Particle size of liposomes influences dermal delivery of substances into skin. Int J Pharm 258: 141–151. Available: http://linkinghub.elsevier.com/retrieve/pii/S0378517303001832. Accessed 7 March 2013.
26. Barenholzt Y, Amselem S, Lichtenberg D (1979) A new method for preparation of phospholipid vesicles (liposomes) - French press. FEBS Lett 99: 210–214.
27. Hamilton RL, Goerke J, Guo LS, Williams MC, Havel RJ (1980) Unilamellar liposomes made with the French pressure cell: a simple preparative and semiquantitative technique. J Lipid Res 21: 981–992.
28. Elsayed MM a, Abdallah OY, Naggar VF, Khalafallah NM (2007) Lipid vesicles for skin delivery of drugs: reviewing three decades of research. Int J Pharm 332: 1–16. Available: http://www.ncbi.nlm.nih.gov/pubmed/17222523. Accessed 6 August 2013.
29. Gao S, Lan X, Liu Y, Shen Z, Lu J, et al. (2004) Characteristics of blood fluorescence spectra using low-level, 457.9-nm excitation from Ar+ laser. Chinese Opt Lett 2: 160–161.
30. Rolland A, Wagner N, Chatelus A, Shroot B, Schaefer H (1993) Site-specific drug delivery to pilosebaceous structures using polymeric microspheres. Pharm Res 10: 1738–1744. Available: http://www.ncbi.nlm.nih.gov/pubmed/8302759. Accessed 1 August 2013.
31. Mordon S, Sumian C, Devoisselle JM (2003) Site-specific methylene blue delivery to pilosebaceous structures using highly porous nylon microspheres: an experimental evaluation. Lasers Surg Med 33: 119–125. Available: http://www.ncbi.nlm.nih.gov/pubmed/12913884. Accessed 1 August 2013.
32. Jacobi U, Kaiser M, Toll R, Mangelsdorf S, Audring H, et al. (2007) Porcine ear skin: an in vitro model for human skin. Skin Res Technol 13: 19–24. Available: http://www.ncbi.nlm.nih.gov/pubmed/17250528. Accessed 7 March 2013.
33. Akomeah FK, Martin GP, Brown MB (2007) Variability in human skin permeability in vitro: comparing penetrants with different physicochemical properties. J Pharm Sci 96: 824–834.
34. Mitragotri S (2003) Modeling skin permeability to hydrophilic and hydrophobic solutes based on four permeation pathways. J Control Release 86: 69–92. Available: http://www.ncbi.nlm.nih.gov/pubmed/12490374.
35. Immordino ML, Dosio F, Cattel L (2006) Stealth liposomes: review of the basic science, rationale, and clinical applications, existing and potential. Int J Nanomedicine 1: 297–315. Available: http://www.pubmedcentral.nih.gov/articlerender.fcgi?artid = 2426795&tool = pmcentrez&rendertype = abstract. Accessed 3 July 2013.
36. Hood RR, Andar AU, Vreeland WN, DeVoe DL (2013) Microfluidic synthesis of PEGylated and folate receptor-targeted liposomes. Pharm Res in press. doi:10.1007/s11095-013-0998-3.
37. Zook JM, Vreeland WN (2010) Effects of temperature, acyl chain length, and flow-rate ratio on liposome formation and size in a microfluidic hydrodynamic focusing device. Soft Matter 6: 1352. doi:10.1039/b923299k.
38. Sekkat N, Kalia YN, Guy RH (2002) Biophysical study of porcine ear skin in vitro and its comparison to human skin in vivo. J Pharm Sci 91: 2376–2381. Available: http://www.ncbi.nlm.nih.gov/pubmed/12379922. Accessed 30 January 2014.
39. Kong R, Bhargava R (2011) Characterization of porcine skin as a model for human skin studies using infrared spectroscopic imaging. Analyst 136: 2359–2366. Available: http://www.ncbi.nlm.nih.gov/pubmed/21509377. Accessed 7 March 2013.
40. Bolte S, Cordelières FP (2006) A guided tour into subcellular colocalization analysis in light microscopy. J Microsc 224: 213–232. doi:10.1111/j.1365-2818.2006.01706.x.

8

Intracellular Gold Nanoparticles Increase Neuronal Excitability and Aggravate Seizure Activity in the Mouse Brain

Seungmoon Jung[1]◔, Minji Bang[1]◔, Byung Sun Kim[1], Sungmun Lee[2], Nicholas A. Kotov[3], Bongsoo Kim[4], Daejong Jeon[1]*

1 Department of Bio and Brain Engineering, Korea Advanced Institute of Science and Technology (KAIST), Daejeon, Republic of Korea, **2** Department of Biomedical Engineering, Khalifa University of Science, Technology, and Research, Abu Dhabi, United Arab Emirates, **3** Department of Chemical Engineering, University of Michigan, Ann Arbor, Michigan, United States of America, **4** Department of Chemistry, Korea Advanced Institute of Science and Technology (KAIST), Daejeon, Republic of Korea

Abstract

Due to their inert property, gold nanoparticles (AuNPs) have drawn considerable attention; their biological application has recently expanded to include nanomedicine and neuroscience. However, the effect of AuNPs on the bioelectrical properties of a single neuron remains unknown. Here we present the effect of AuNPs on a single neuron under physiological and pathological conditions *in vitro*. AuNPs were intracellularly applied to hippocampal CA1 neurons from the mouse brain. The electrophysiological property of CA1 neurons treated with 5- or 40-nm AuNPs was assessed using the whole-cell patch-clamp technique. Intracellular application of AuNPs increased both the number of action potentials (APs) and input resistance. The threshold and duration of APs and the after hyperpolarization (AHP) were decreased by the intracellular AuNPs. In addition, intracellular AuNPs elicited paroxysmal depolarizing shift-like firing patterns during sustained repetitive firings (SRF) induced by prolonged depolarization (10 sec). Furthermore, low Mg^{2+}-induced epileptiform activity was aggravated by the intracellular AuNPs. In this study, we demonstrated that intracellular AuNPs alter the intrinsic properties of neurons toward increasing their excitability, and may have deleterious effects on neurons under pathological conditions, such as seizure. These results provide some considerable direction on application of AuNPs into central nervous system (CNS).

Editor: Gennady Cymbalyuk, Georgia State University, United States of America

Funding: This work was supported by the Korea Health 21 R&D grant (A120051) funded by Ministry of Health and Welfare, and also supported by the KUSTAR-KAIST Institute, Korea, under the R&D program supervised by the KAIST. The funders had no role in study design, data collection and analysis, decision to publish, or preparation of the manuscript.

Competing Interests: The authors have declared that no competing interests exist.

* E-mail: clark@kaist.ac.kr

◔ These authors contributed equally to this work.

Introduction

In the past decade, nanoparticles (NPs) have been used in biological and biomedical applications such as drug delivery, photothermal therapy, biosensing, and bioimaging [1,2]. NPs are typically transferred into the cells by endocytosis [3]. NPs can be used for delivery of genes or drugs into the cytosol and subcellular organelles, including the nucleus [4]. In particular, intracellular dynamics could be monitored by intracellular delivery of nano-sized contrast agents, and targeting nanomedicine into subcellular organelles could vastly improve the efficacy of therapeutic regimens such as proapoptotic drugs, lysosomal enzymes, gene therapy, and photodynamic therapy [4,5]. However, many toxic effects of NPs on various types of cells have been widely known [6,7].

Gold NPs (AuNPs) are of particular interest due to their excellent stability and various biocompatibility properties, including nontoxicity, non-immunogenicity, and high tissue permeability without hampering cell functionality [8,9]. The distinct properties of AuNPs suggest their potential for the delivery of therapeutic substances—such as drugs or small nucleotides—into the brain for treatment of various neurological diseases or disorders [10]. Although novel AuNPs have been developed as carriers for delivery of therapeutic substances to neuronal cells across the blood-brain barrier (BBB) [11,12], the effect of AuNPs on the electrophysiological activity of neurons has not been investigated. Recently, several NPs, such as silver (Ag), copper oxide (CuO), zinc oxide (ZnO), and tungsten carbide (WC), were reported to alter some properties of ion channels and neuronal excitability [13–19]. Although it remained unclear that these NPs affected inside or outside of neuronal cells, these works suggested some deleterious or toxic effects of NPs on bioelectrical properties of neurons in the brain.

The neuron is a cellular unit of the nervous system. Neuronal activity is represented by changes in membrane potential, such as action potentials (APs), and the related synaptic transmission by means of neurotransmitters, which is associated with receiving, integrating, and transmitting information in the brain [20]. The intrinsic properties of ion channels in neurons determine or regulate neuronal activity [21], and alterations in neuronal activity could impact both physiological and pathophysiological conditions. For instance, abnormal neuronal activity or imbalanced excitation/inhibition is associated with several neurological diseases, such as epilepsy [22,23]. Therefore, for biological and biomedical applications of AuNPs as intracellular carriers of specific molecules (e.g., a drug, antibody, or oligonucleotide) to the brain, a thorough understanding of the interplay between intracellular AuNPs and neuronal intrinsic properties is necessary [24,25].

Patch-clamp recording is an approach to measure bioelectrical properties of the cells, and is especially useful in the study of excitable cells such as neurons [26–28]. One of advantages in whole-cell patch-clamp recordings is to deliver substances directly inside of a living cell through a glass micropipette. Thus, it is possible to investigate the intracellular effect of substances on the bioelectrical properties of a single neuron by whole-cell patch-clamp recordings. In this study, we measured the electrophysiological properties of neurons using the whole-cell patch-clamp technique after delivering AuNPs intracellularly into hippocampal CA1 neurons from the mouse brain. We also investigated the effect of intracellular AuNPs on two *in vitro* seizure models (prolonged sustained repetitive firings and low Mg^{2+}-induced epileptiform burst discharges). Herein is the first report of the effects of AuNPs on the bioelectrical properties of a single neuron under physiological and pathological conditions.

Materials and Methods

Ethics Statement

Animal care and handling were conducted according to the guidelines approved by the Institutional Animal Care and Use Committee (Approval Number: KA2013-33) of the Korea Advanced Institute of Science and Technology (KAIST). All efforts were made to minimize suffering.

Animals

Young male *C57BL/6* mice (4–5 weeks old) were used in the present study. Four mice were housed as a group under a 12-hr light/dark cycle with free access to food and water.

Nanoparticles and application to brain slice

AuNPs (OD 1, stabilized suspension in citrate buffer, negatively charged) of 5- and 40-nm diameter were purchased from Sigma (St. Louis, MO, USA). Fluorophore-labeled (maximum absorbance: 600 nm) spherical AuNPs (40 nm, methyl conjugated) were purchased from Nanopartz Inc. (Loveland, CO, USA). AuNPs were stored at 4°C before use. For intracellular application of AuNPs, the AuNPs were diluted with an intrapipette solution (approximately 1.1×10^{11} NPs/mL for 5-nm AuNPs, and 1.44×10^{8} NPs/mL for 40-nm AuNPs). Electrophysiological recordings with citrate-suspended, non-fluorescent AuNPs were performed 10 min after cell rupture.

Brain slice preparation and patch-clamp recordings

Preparation of hippocampal slices and the whole-cell patch-clamp recording method have been described previously [29,30]. Fully anesthetized mice were decapitated and the horizontal hippocampal slices (310 μm) were prepared in oxygenated (95% O_2, 5% CO_2), cold, ACSF (124 mM NaCl, 3.0 mM KCl, 1.23 mM NaH_2PO_4, 2.2 mM $CaCl_2$, 1.2 mM $MgCl_2$, 26 mM $NaHCO_3$, and 10 mM glucose, pH 7.4). After 1 hr recovery, brain slices were incubated in ACSF and whole-cell recordings were obtained from hippocampal CA1 neurons at 31 °C using glass pipette electrodes (3–6 MΩ). To measure APs and miniature excitatory postsynaptic currents (mEPSCs), glass pipettes were filled with an internal solution (135 mM K-gluconate, 5 mM KCl, 2 mM $MgCl_2$, 5 mM EGTA, 10 mM HEPES, 0.5 mM $CaCl_2$, 5 mM Mg-ATP, and 0.3 mM Na-GTP) which was buffered to pH 7.4 with KOH. APs were triggered by a step-current injection (30 pA steps) from −150 pA to +150 pA in current-clamp mode for 1 sec. The numbers, threshold, and latency of APs evoked by the injected currents in AuNPs-treated and untreated neurons were analyzed. The duration of the first AP was measured at half amplitude above the threshold. The after hyperpolarization (AHP) amplitude was isolated from the first AP. Spontaneous firings in CA1 neurons were measured at −50 mV. After the neurons had been voltage-clamped at −60 mV, the mEPSC experiment was performed in the presence of 1 μM tetrodotoxin (TTX), 10 μM bicuculline ($GABA_A$ receptor antagonist), and 5 μM CGP 55845 ($GABA_B$ receptor antagonist). For the prolonged sustained repetitive firing (SRF) experiment, 80–90-pA currents were injected into the cell under current-clamp configuration for 10 sec [31]. The SRF experiment was conducted more than two times in each of cell. To precipitate epileptiform burst discharges, brain slices were incubated in low-Mg^{2+}/high-K^+ ACSF containing the following (in mM): 124 mM NaCl, 5.0 mM KCl, 1.23 mM NaH_2PO_4, 2.2 mM $CaCl_2$, 26 mM $NaHCO_3$, and 10 mM glucose [32]. After 1 hr incubation, epileptiform activity was measured with the same low-Mg^{2+}/high-K^+ ACSF. The low-Mg^{2+}/high-K^+ ACSF elicited bursts of spikes, and the number of bursts showing more than three spikes was analyzed for 3 min. In all the patch-clamp recordings, large cells in hippocampal CA1 region were visually chosen, and pyramidal neurons and interneurons were identified on the basis of their distinctive intrinsic membrane properties including firing patterns as described previously [33–36]. Cells showing intrinsic membrane properties of interneurons were removed from analysis. Patch-clamp recordings were performed using a MultiClamp 700 B amplifier and a Digidata1440 (Axon instruments), and the acquired data were analyzed using the pCLAMP version 10.2 (Axon Instruments) and Mini-Analysis Program (Synaptosoft).

Statistical analysis

All data are presented as means ± standard error of the mean (SEM). Statistical analyses were conducted using the SPSS software (SPSS, Chicago, IL, USA) and R (Software Foundation, Boston, MA, USA). Data were analyzed by analysis of variance (ANOVA) followed by *post hoc* comparisons. Student's *t*-test was used to identify main effects. A p-value <0.05 was considered to indicate statistical significance.

Results

Altered passive electrical properties by an intracellular application of AuNPs

To investigate the effect of AuNPs on the electrophysiological properties of a single neuron, AuNPs were added to the hippocampal CA1 neurons from a mouse brain slice using a glass micropipette after being mixed with an intrapipette solution. We first verified the intracellular distribution of AuNPs by using fluorophore-conjugated 40-nm AuNPs, which showed fluorescent signals inside of neurons (Figure 1A). The spherical cell shape was clearly displayed by the fluorescent signals, which indicates that the AuNPs were evenly and broadly distributed throughout the cell body and membrane (Figure 1A, right). Then, non-fluorescent AuNPs of 5- and 40-nm diameter were used for the intracellular application throughout the experiments. Passive membrane properties, such as input resistance, threshold potential for AP

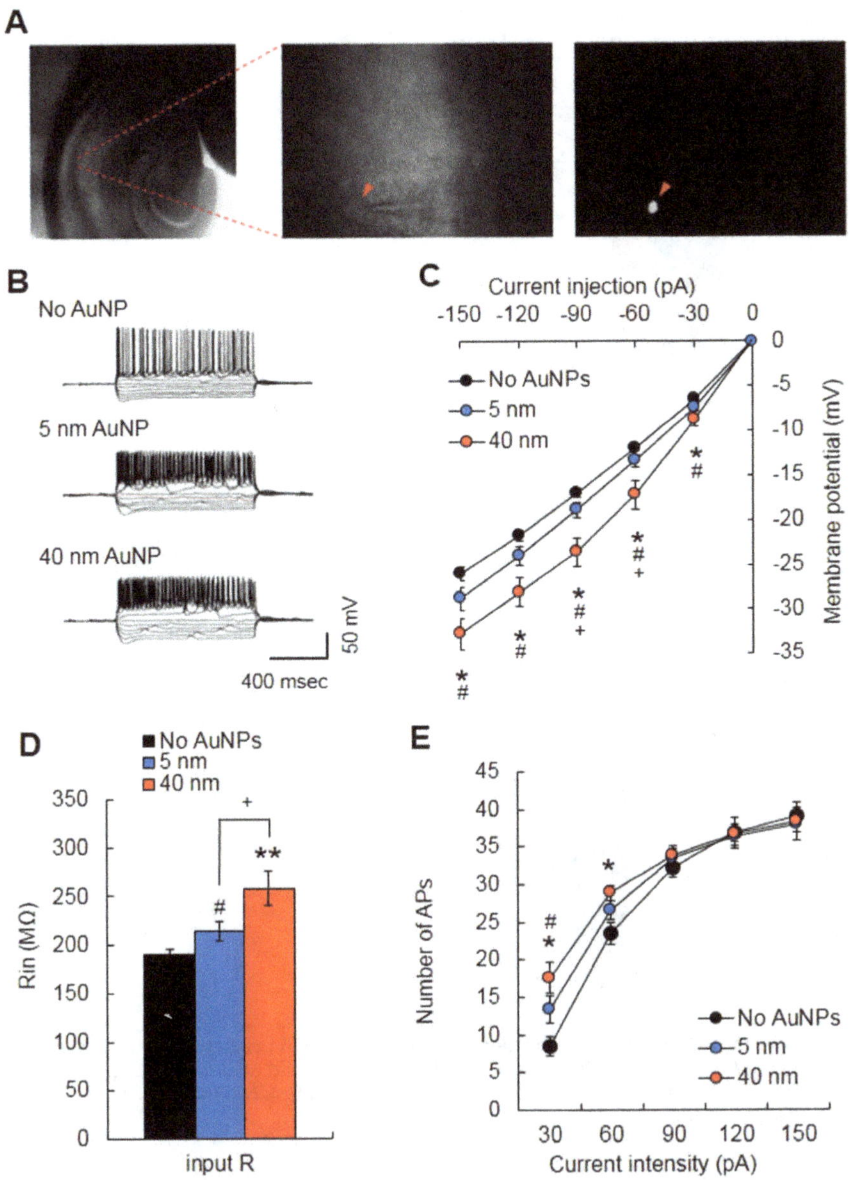

Figure 1. Effects of intracellular treatment with 5- or 40-nm AuNPs on the passive electrical properties of hippocampal CA1 neurons from a mouse hippocampal slice. (A) DIC images of a brain slice (left, 50×) and hippocampal CA1 layer (middle, 630×), and a fluorescence image of CA1 neurons (right, 630×) loaded with fluorophore-conjugated AuNPs through a patch pipette (middle) after breaking the gigaohm seal. The fluorescence signal indicates the infusion of AuNPs into the cell. (B) Representative traces of membrane potential changes and APs elicited by step-current injections for 1 sec from AuNP-treated and untreated (no AuNPs) hippocampal CA1 neurons. (C) AuNPs of both sizes considerably increased the changes in membrane potential. (D) Input resistance was significantly increased by AuNPs of both sizes. (E) The 5- or 40-nm AuNPs increased the number of APs substantially at low current intensity (at 30- or 60-pA depolarizing current injection). $^{*}p<0.05$, $^{**}p<0.01$, Student's *t*-test, No AuNPs *vs.* 40-nm AuNPs; $^{\#}p<0.05$, Student's *t*-test, No AuNPs *vs.* 5-nm AuNPs; $^{+}p<0.05$, Student's *t*-test, 5-nm AuNPs *vs.* 40-nm AuNPs.

generation, and firing frequencies against the amplitude of injected currents, were measured using a current-clamp configuration. APs were generated by current injections with 30 pA steps (Figure 1B). Current-voltage relationships were obtained from values measured at the middle (500 msec) of hyperpolarizing pulses (Figure 1C). The plotted relationship curve shifted downward in both 5- ($n = 18$) and 40-nm ($n = 12$) AuNP-treated neurons compared to non-treated CA1 neurons ($n = 29$) ($F(2,56) = 45.91$, $p<0.001$, two-way ANOVA), and changed more with the 40-nm AuNPs than with 5-nm AuNPs ($F(1,28) = 22.32$, $p<0.001$, two-way ANOVA) (Figure 1C). There was also a significant difference in the input resistance between AuNP-treated and non-treated neurons ($F(2,56) = 11.25$, $p<0.05$, one-way ANOVA). The input resistance was increased in both 5- (214.22±9.94 MΩ, $p<0.05$, Student's *t*-test) and 40-nm (258.1±17.45 MΩ, $p<0.001$, Student's *t*-test) AuNP-treated neurons compared to non-treated CA1 neurons (190.87±5.59 MΩ) (Figure 1D), and changed more with the 40-nm AuNPs than with 5-nm AuNPs ($p<0.05$, Student's *t*-test). As a measure of neuronal excitability, we plotted firing frequencies against the intensity of injected currents. Increased number of

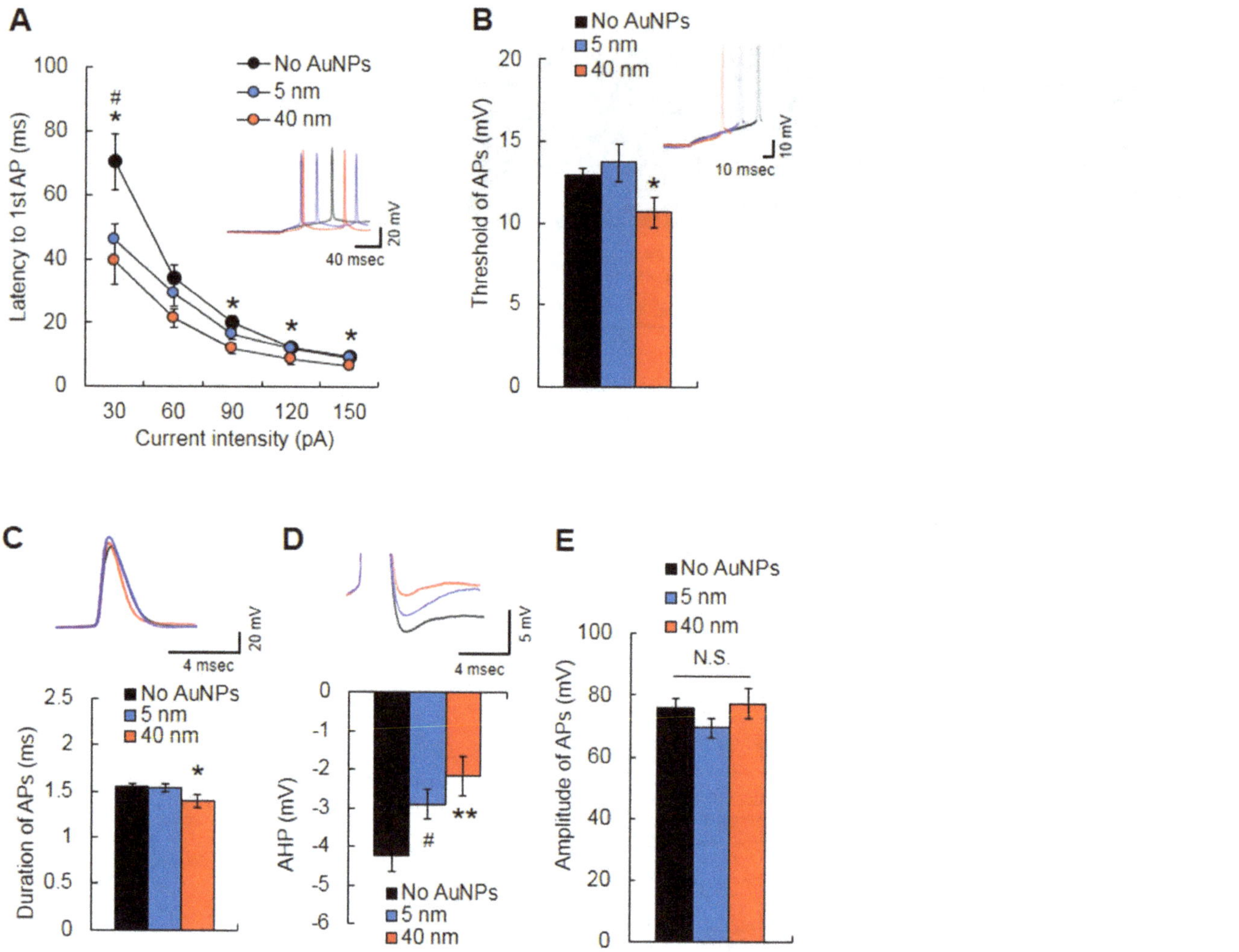

Figure 2. Effects of intracellular treatment with 5- or 40-nm AuNPs on AP properties in hippocampal CA1 neurons. (A) AuNPs of both sizes significantly decreased the latency to the first AP. The 40-nm AuNPs significantly reduced the AP threshold (B) and AP duration (C). (D) AuNPs of both sizes significantly increased AHP. (E) AuNPs did not affect the AP amplitude. *$p<0.05$, **$p<0.01$, Student's *t*-test, No AuNPs *vs.* 40-nm AuNPs; #$p<0.05$, Student's *t*-test, No AuNPs *vs.* 5-nm AuNPs; N.S., no significance.

spikes was observed at low intensities of current injection. Both 5- (13.33±1.76) and 40-nm AuNP-treated neurons (17.58±2.04) showed significantly more spikes at +30 pA injections than the non-treated neurons (8.51±1.22) ($p<0.05$, Student's *t*-test) (Figure 1E). The 40-nm (28.83±0.99), but not 5-nm, AuNP-treated neurons also showed significantly more spikes at +60 pA injections than the non-treated neurons (23.51±1.43) ($p<0.05$, Student's *t*-test). Collectively, these results suggest that intracellular AuNPs alter the basic bioelectrical properties of hippocampal CA1 neurons.

The properties of AP are altered by an intracellular application of AuNPs

Regarding neuronal excitability, we further analyzed the properties of APs in CA1 neurons treated with AuNPs intracellularly. The latency to the first spikes at injection of a current of each intensity was noticeably decreased after the intracellular application of 40-nm AuNP-treated neurons ($F(1,41) = 15.70$, $p<0.001$, two-way ANOVA) (Figure 2A). The 5-nm AuNP-treated neurons showed significant change at only 30 pA injection ($p<0.05$, Student's *t*-test). In addition, 40-nm AuNPs decreased the threshold amplitude of the first AP generation (non-treatment, $n=23$, 12.89±0.43 mV; 40 nm, $n=12$, 10.69±0.91 mV, $p<0.05$, Student's *t*-test) (Figure 2B) and shortened the duration of the first AP (Figure 2C) compared with non-treatment (non-treatment, 1.54±0.03 ms; 40 nm, 1.39±0.07 ms, $p<0.05$, Student's *t*-test). However, 5-nm AuNPs did not affect the threshold amplitude (13.7±1.18 mV) and duration (1.53±0.04 ms) of the first AP generation. The AHP was significantly reduced with both AuNP sizes (5 nm, −2.9±0.39 mV; 40 nm, −2.16±0.51 mV) compared with non-treatment (−4.24±0.39 mV) ($F(2,50)=6.10$, $p<0.005$) (Figure 2D), and there was no significant difference in the AHP amplitude between the 5-nm and 40-nm AuNP-treated neurons. No difference in the amplitude of APs was observed between the AuNP-treated and non-treated neurons (Figure 2E). These results demonstrate that intracellular AuNPs may lead CA1 neurons to become more excitable. Considering the alteration in basic bioelectrical properties, not only the ion channels active in the subthreshold range but also the channels activated during APs are subjected to alterations in CA1 neurons treated intracellularly with AuNP.

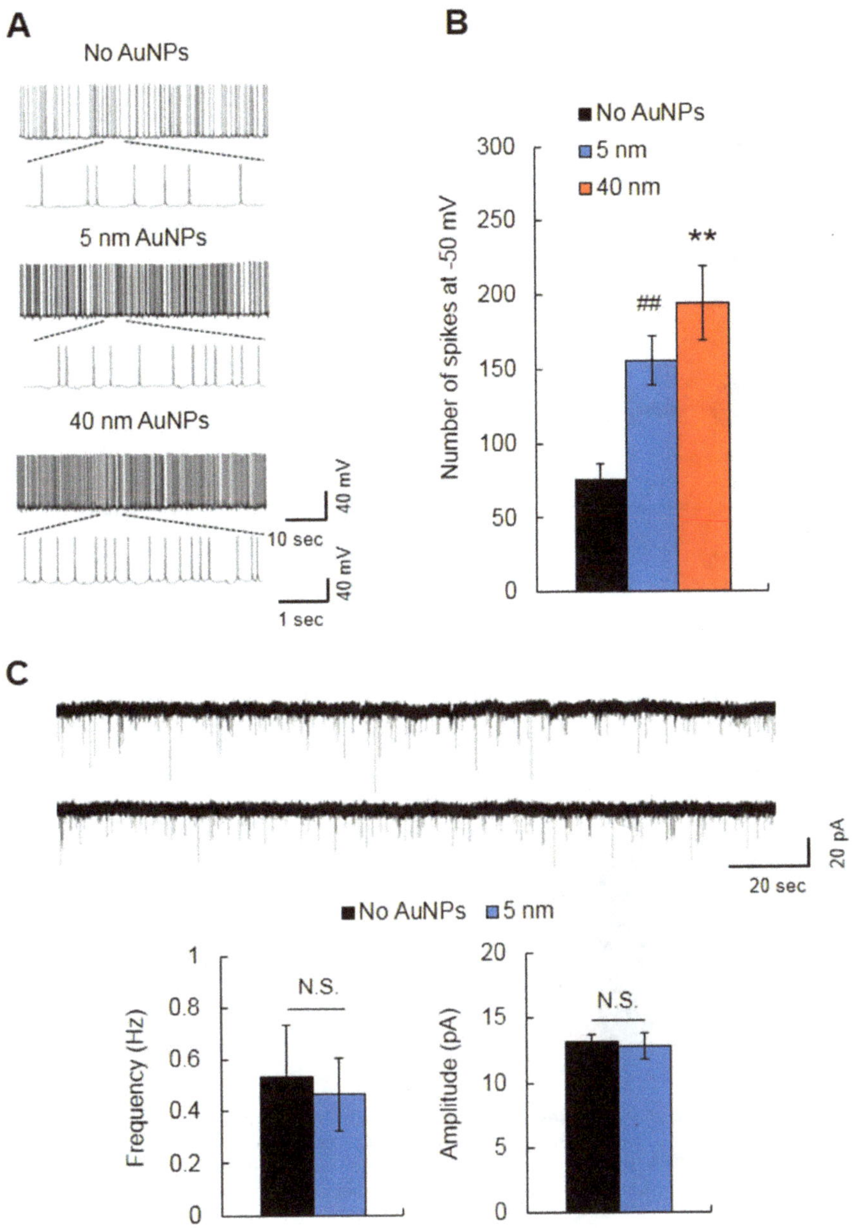

Figure 3. Effects of intracellular treatment with 5- or 40-nm AuNPs on spontaneous firing and excitatory synaptic transmission. (A) The representative traces of spontaneous firing from AuNP-treated and non-treated (No AuNPs) hippocampal CA1 neurons. (B) AuNPs of both sizes significantly increased the rate of spontaneous firing. (C) Neurons treated with 5-nm AuNP showed similar mEPSC frequency and amplitude to non-treated neurons. $^{**}p<0.01$, Student's *t*-test, No AuNPs *vs.* 40-nm AuNPs; $^{\#\#}p<0.01$, Student's *t*-test, No AuNPs *vs.* 5-nm AuNPs; N.S., no significance.

Effects on spontaneous firings and mEPSC of intracellular application of AuNPs

Next, we examined whether spontaneous firings in CA1 neurons are affected by intracellular treatment with AuNPs. Spontaneous APs were measured at −50 mV in current-clamp mode (Figure 3A). The 5- ($n = 7$, 155.86±16.52) and 40-nm ($n = 11$, 194.55±25.29) AuNP-treated neurons displayed more than twice the number of spikes than non-treated neurons ($n = 13$, 75.46±10.73) ($F(2,28) = 12.36$, $p<0.001$, one-way ANOVA) (Figure 3B). To determine whether the AuNPs affected excitatory synaptic transmission—which can alter spontaneous firing—we measured mEPSC in 5-nm AuNP-treated neurons. There was little difference in the frequency (Figure 3C, Left) and amplitude (Figure 3C, Right) of mEPSC between AuNP-treated ($n = 6$) and non-treated neurons ($n = 7$). Thus, the increased firing rate may be due to the altered intrinsic properties of CA1 neurons themselves rather than increased excitatory synaptic transmission. These results indicate that intracellular treatment with AuNPs enhanced the excitability of CA1 neurons.

Effects of AuNPs on prolonged depolarization and low Mg^{2+}-induced epileptiform discharges

Increased excitability can lead to neurological diseases, such as epilepsy. Thus, we investigated the effects of intracellular treatment with AuNPs on two *in vitro* seizure models (prolonged SRF and low Mg^{2+}-induced epileptiform burst discharges) [31,32].

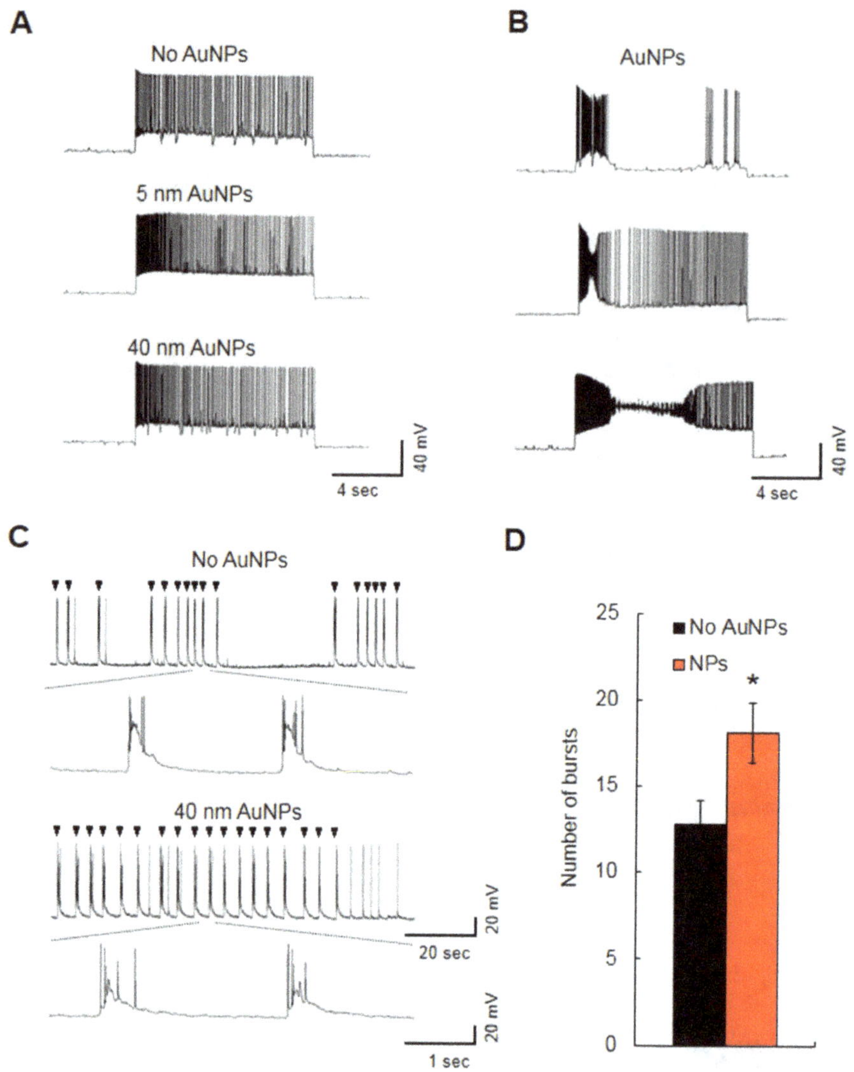

Figure 4. Effects of intracellular treatment with 5- or 40-nm AuNPs on seizure models. (A, B) Prolonged SRF experiment. (A) The representative traces of repetitive firings elicited by long (10 sec) depolarizing current pulses. (B) PDS-like spikes, an epiletiform activity, were observed from a portion of AuNP-treated hippocampal CA1 neurons. (C) The representative traces of low Mg^{2+}-induced bursts of spikes. Arrow head indicates a burst of spikes. (D) Intracellular 40-nm AuNPs increased the number of bursts. Average number of bursts per min were presented. *$p<0.05$, Student's t-test; N.S., no significance.

In prolonged SRF experiment, about 70% of AuNP-treated CA1 neurons showed a similar firing pattern to non-treated neurons (5-nm AuNP-treated, $n=8/11$; 40-nm AuNP-treated, $n=10/14$; untreated CA1 neurons $n=18$) (Figure 4A). However, approximately 30% neurons (7 of 25 neurons) repetitively displayed abnormal eccentric firing behaviors during the long depolarization (Figure 4B). Interestingly, the abnormal firings induced by intracellular AuNPs look very similar to a paroxysmal depolarizing shift (PDS), a cellular manifestation of epileptic seizure caused by excessive ionic currents, an imbalance in the ionic distributions, or dysfunctions of ion channels such as Na^+ or Ca^{2+} channels [37]. The abnormal firing patterns were never observed in non-treated CA1 neurons. With regard to low-Mg^{2+}-induced epileptiform activity, AuNP-treated (40 nm, $n=12$, 18.08 ± 1.74) neurons showed significantly increased number of bursts compared to untreated CA1 neurons ($n=8$, 12.82 ± 1.31) ($p<0.05$, Student's t-test) (Figure 4C and 4D). Taken together, these results indicate that the increased excitability of AuNP-treated neurons is likely to result in the hyperexcitability implicated in pathological conditions such as seizure.

Discussion

The unique physical properties of NPs, including their small size and ability to cross the BBB, are potential advantages for delivering drugs, genes and other small molecules into the brain [38,39]. AuNPs are widely used in biotechnology because of their excellent biocompatibility. However, their physiological influence on neuronal cells has to date not been investigated extensively. In this study, we examined the effects of intracellular application of AuNPs on the activity of a single neuron using patch-clamp recording. Intracellular treatment with AuNPs increased the input resistance and number of spikes, decreased the latency and threshold of AP generation, reduced the AHP, and enhanced spontaneous firing rate in hippocampal CA1 neurons. Furthermore, the AuNPs elicited PDS-like epileptiform activity in a portion of neurons during a long depolarization and increased the number of bursts in low Mg^{2+}-induced *in vitro* seizure model. These results demonstrate that intracellular AuNPs increase the excitability of neurons and aggravate the irritability of neurons in pathological conditions, such as seizure. In this regard, our data suggest that the delivery of AuNPs as vehicles to carry therapeutic agents into CNS should be carefully considered despite their well-known advantage and biocompatibility.

Many studies have reported that NPs including AuNPs have toxicity involving cell damage or death [20,40–42]. The kinetics of bioactive molecules such as a drug or protein, are likely to differ considerably intra- and extracellularly [43,44]. Furthermore, an increasing number of studies on drug delivery to the brain has focused on intracellular labeling of proteins to enhance the effectiveness of the cargo molecules in nanomedicine [4,5]. Recently, application of several NPs, such as Ag, CuO, ZnO, and WC, has been reported to alter the properties of ion channels and excitability in neurons of the brain [13–19]. Ag-NPs have been shown to enhance glutamatergic synaptic transmission and the neuronal firing rate in rat hippocampal slices [15,18]. CuO- and ZnO-NPs were suggested to affect sodium or potassium currents and enhance the excitability of acutely isolated rat hippocampal CA3 neurons [13,14]. In a study of WC-NPs, the NPs reduced the number of APs [19]. However, these studies did not provide the direct evidence on the pathophysiological effects of the NPs on the neuronal cells. The present study showed that intracellular AuNPs led to abnormal firing patterns and aggravated epileptic activity under pathological conditions. Thus, our study suggest a possibility that intracellular AuNPs can cause or worsen neuronal dysfunction or damage in the brain.

In neurons, ions diffuse along the electrochemical gradient, and the passive diffusion of ions through open channels create currents. These currents can then alter neuronal membrane potentials. Ion channels in the plasma membrane are the primary determinant of the bioelectrical properties of neurons in the brain. Various modes of the effects of AuNPs on ionic flow could be hypothesized. Although we could not identify the ion channel affected by AuNPs in this study, AuNPs might interact with Na^+ and K^+ channels. Voltage-gated Na^+ and K^+ channels play a critical role in the generation or shaping of APs [45], and Ca^{2+}-activated K^+ channels together with voltage-gated K^+ channels regulate AHP or spike frequency in neurons [46,47]. In our study, the amplitude of AP was not altered by the AuNPs; therefore, the AuNPs were unlikely to significantly affect the voltage-gated Na^+ channels. However, modulation of the kinetics of voltage-gated Na^+ channels by the AuNPs cannot be ruled out [46]. K^+ channels including Ca^{2+}-activated K^+ channels appear to have the capacity to interact with AuNPs. For instance, pharmacological blocks or genetic mutations of $K_v12.2$, a slowly activating voltage-gated K^+ channel, led to increased input resistance and number of APs in compliance with small electric stimuli [48]. Pharmacological block of Ca^{2+}-activated K^+ channels also cause increased excitability by reducing AHP and increasing the spike frequency in neurons [49]. The intracellular interaction of AuNPs with specific modules of ion channels may be regarded as another aspect of the effects of AuNPs. Voltage-gated ion channels are generally composed of two main parts, the pore-forming transmembrane domains (including voltage-sensing modules), and cytoplasmic loops [50]. Recent studies showed that the pores of ion channels such as hERG and nicotinic acetylcholine receptor (nAChRs) can be directly clogged with ultra-small AuNPs (~1.4-nm diameter) and impede the movement of ions through the channel pore [51,52]. However, the estimated pore sizes of Na^+ and K^+ channels are either below or approximately 10 Å in diameter [53,54]; therefore, the AuNPs used in our study were too large to physically internalize within the channels' pore. Further studies should identify the ion channels affected by the AuNPs by measuring the ionic currents within channels and examine the mechanisms underlying the interaction of the AuNPs with the ion channels.

In conclusion, we demonstrated that intracellular AuNPs caused hippocampal CA1 neurons to be more excitable in terms of generating more APs, which might result from the reduced threshold and duration of AP, increased input resistance, and reduced AHP amplitude. We also examined the effects of AuNPs on *in vitro* pathological conditions. Occasionally, intracellular AuNPs elicited eccentric firing patterns during a long-depolarization, and aggravated epileptiform activity in a seizure model *in vitro*. Thus, the intracellular AuNPs might lead to disturbances in neuronal functions and hyperexcitability in pathological conditions such as seizure. Our results provide valuable information for the use of AuNPs in nanomedicine as an intracellular drug-delivery system.

Author Contributions

Conceived and designed the experiments: SL NAK BK DJ. Performed the experiments: SJ MB. Analyzed the data: BSK DJ. Wrote the paper: SJ BSK SL NAK BK DJ.

References

1. Cho K, Wang X, Nie S, Chen ZG, Shin DM (2008) Therapeutic nanoparticles for drug delivery in cancer. Clin Cancer Res 14: 1310–1316.
2. Selvan ST, Tan TT, Yi DK, Jana NR (2010) Functional and multifunctional nanoparticles for bioimaging and biosensing. Langmuir 26: 11631–11641.
3. Zhang Y, Kohler N, Zhang MQ (2002) Surface modification of superparamagnetic magnetite nanoparticles and their intracellular uptake. Biomaterials 23: 1553–1561.
4. Torchilin VP (2006) Recent approaches to intracellular delivery of drugs and DNA and organelle targeting. Annu Rev Biomed Eng 8: 343–375.
5. Chou LY, Ming K, Chan WC (2011) Strategies for the intracellular delivery of nanoparticles. Chem Soc Rev 40: 233–245.
6. Crosera M, Bovenzi M, Maina G, Adami G, Zanette C, et al. (2009) Nanoparticle dermal absorption and toxicity: a review of the literature. Int Arch Occup Environ Health 82: 1043–1055.
7. Marquis BJ, Love SA, Braun KL, Haynes CL (2009) Analytical methods to assess nanoparticle toxicity. Analyst 134: 425–439.
8. Shukla R, Bansal V, Chaudhary M, Basu A, Bhonde RR, et al. (2005) Biocompatibility of gold nanoparticles and their endocytotic fate inside the cellular compartment: A microscopic overview. Langmuir 21: 10644–10654.
9. Boisselier E, Astruc D (2009) Gold nanoparticles in nanomedicine: preparations, imaging, diagnostics, therapies and toxicity. Chem Soc Rev 38: 1759–1782.
10. Begley DJ (2004) Delivery of therapeutic agents to the central nervous system: the problems and the possibilities. Pharmacol Ther 104: 29–45.
11. Prades R, Guerrero S, Araya E, Molina C, Salas E, et al. (2012) Delivery of gold nanoparticles to the brain by conjugation with a peptide that recognizes the transferrin receptor. Biomaterials 33: 7194–7205.
12. Etame AB, Diaz RJ, O'Reilly MA, Smith CA, Mainprize TG, et al. (2012) Enhanced delivery of gold nanoparticles with therapeutic potential into the brain using MRI-guided focused ultrasound. Nanomedicine 8: 1133–1142.
13. Zhao J, Xu L, Zhang T, Ren G, Yang Z (2009) Influences of nanoparticle zinc oxide on acutely isolated rat hippocampal CA3 pyramidal neurons. Neurotoxicology 30: 220–230.
14. Xu LJ, Zhao JX, Zhang T, Ren GG, Yang Z (2009) In vitro study on influence of nano particles of CuO on CA1 pyramidal neurons of rat hippocampus potassium currents. Environ Toxicol 24: 211–217.
15. Liu Z, Zhang T, Ren G, Yang Z (2012) Nano-Ag inhibiting action potential independent glutamatergic synaptic transmission but increasing excitability in rat CA1 pyramidal neurons. Nanotoxicology 6: 414–423.
16. Shan D, Xie Y, Ren G, Yang Z (2012) Inhibitory effect of tungsten carbide nanoparticles on voltage-gated potassium currents of hippocampal CA1 neurons. Toxicol Lett 209: 129–135.
17. Xie Y, Wang Y, Zhang T, Ren G, Yang Z (2012) Effects of nanoparticle zinc oxide on spatial cognition and synaptic plasticity in mice with depressive-like behaviors. J Biomed Sci 19: 14.

18. Liu Z, Ren G, Zhang T, Yang Z (2009) Action potential changes associated with the inhibitory effects on voltage-gated sodium current of hippocampal CA1 neurons by silver nanoparticles. Toxicology 264: 179–184.
19. Shan D, Xie Y, Ren G, Yang Z (2013) Attenuated effect of tungsten carbide nanoparticles on voltage-gated sodium current of hippocampal CA1 pyramidal neurons. Toxicol In Vitro 27: 299–304.
20. Yang Z, Liu ZW, Allaker RP, Reip P, Oxford J, et al. (2010) A review of nanoparticle functionality and toxicity on the central nervous system. J R Soc Interface 7 Suppl 4: S411–422.
21. Schulz DJ, Baines RA, Hempel CM, Li L, Liss B, et al. (2006) Cellular excitability and the regulation of functional neuronal identity: from gene expression to neuromodulation. J Neurosci 26: 10362–10367.
22. Dube C, Richichi C, Bender RA, Chung G, Litt B, et al. (2006) Temporal lobe epilepsy after experimental prolonged febrile seizures: prospective analysis. Brain 129: 911–922.
23. Sachdev PS (2007) Alternating and postictal psychoses: review and a unifying hypothesis. Schizophr Bull 33: 1029–1037.
24. Paulo CS, Pires das Neves R, Ferreira LS (2011) Nanoparticles for intracellular-targeted drug delivery. Nanotechnology 22: 494002.
25. Wang TT, Bai J, Jiang X, Nienhaus GU (2012) Cellular Uptake of Nanoparticles by Membrane Penetration: A Study Combining Confocal Microscopy with FTIR Spectroelectrochemistry. Acs Nano 6: 1251–1259.
26. Neher E, Sakmann B (1976) Single-channel currents recorded from membrane of denervated frog muscle fibres. Nature 260: 799–802.
27. Hamill OP, Marty A, Neher E, Sakmann B, Sigworth FJ (1981) Improved patch-clamp techniques for high-resolution current recording from cells and cell-free membrane patches. Pflugers Arch 391: 85–100.
28. Hille B (2001) Ion channels of excitable membranes.Sinauer Associates, Inc. 3rd Edition edition.
29. Jeon D, Song I, Guido W, Kim K, Kim E, et al. (2008) Ablation of Ca2+ channel beta3 subunit leads to enhanced N-methyl-D-aspartate receptor-dependent long term potentiation and improved long term memory. J Biol Chem 283: 12093–12101.
30. Jung S, Yang H, Kim BS, Chu K, Lee SK, et al. (2012) The immunosuppressant cyclosporin A inhibits recurrent seizures in an experimental model of temporal lobe epilepsy. Neurosci Lett 529: 133–138.
31. Errington AC, Stohr T, Heers C, Lees G (2008) The investigational anticonvulsant lacosamide selectively enhances slow inactivation of voltage-gated sodium channels. Mol Pharmacol 73: 157–169.
32. Kajsa M, Igelström CHS, Heyward PM (2011) Low-magnesium medium induces epileptiform activity in mouse olfactory bulb slices. J Neurophysiol 106: 2593–2605.
33. Bean BP (2007) The action potential in mammalian central neurons. Nat Rev Neurosci 8: 451–465.
34. Morin F, Beaulieu C, Lacaille JC (1996) Membrane properties and synaptic currents evoked in CA1 interneuron subtypes in rat hippocampal slices. J Neurophysiol 76: 1–16.
35. Martina M, Schultz JH, Ehmke H, Monyer H, Jonas P (1998) Functional and molecular differences between voltage-gated K+ channels of fast-spiking interneurons and pyramidal neurons of rat hippocampus. Journal of Neuroscience 18: 8111–8125.
36. Taverna S, Tkatch T, Metz AE, Martina M (2005) Differential expression of TASK channels between horizontal interneurons and pyramidal cells of rat hippocampus. J Neurosci 25: 9162–9170.
37. Johnston D, Brown TH (1984) The Synaptic Nature of the Paroxysmal Depolarizing Shift in Hippocampal-Neurons. Annals of Neurology 16: S65–S71.
38. Garcia-Garcia E, Andrieux K, Gil S, Couvreur P (2005) Colloidal carriers and blood-brain barrier (BBB) translocation: a way to deliver drugs to the brain? Int J Pharm 298: 274–292.
39. Koziara JM, Lockman PR, Allen DD, Mumper RJ (2003) In situ blood-brain barrier transport of nanoparticles. Pharmaceutical Research 20: 1772–1778.
40. Khlebtsov N, Dykman L (2011) Biodistribution and toxicity of engineered gold nanoparticles: a review of in vitro and in vivo studies. Chem Soc Rev 40: 1647–1671.
41. Pan Y, Neuss S, Leifert A, Fischler M, Wen F, et al. (2007) Size-dependent cytotoxicity of gold nanoparticles. Small 3: 1941–1949.
42. Chen YS, Hung YC, Lin LW, Liau I, Hong MY, et al. (2010) Size-dependent impairment of cognition in mice caused by the injection of gold nanoparticles. Nanotechnology 21: 485102.
43. Hartkoorn RC, Chandler B, Owen A, Ward SA, Bertel Squire S, et al. (2007) Differential drug susceptibility of intracellular and extracellular tuberculosis, and the impact of P-glycoprotein. Tuberculosis (Edinb) 87: 248–255.
44. Schmitt E, Gehrmann M, Brunet M, Multhoff G, Garrido C (2007) Intracellular and extracellular functions of heat shock proteins: repercussions in cancer therapy. J Leukoc Biol 81: 15–27.
45. Hodgkin AL, Huxley AF (1952) a quantitative description of membrane current and its application to conduction and excitation in nerve. J Physiol 117: 500–544.
46. Kress GJ, Mennerick S (2009) Action potential initiation and propagation: upstream influences on neurotransmission. Neuroscience 158: 211–222.
47. Stocker M (2004) Ca(2+)-activated K+ channels: molecular determinants and function of the SK family. Nat Rev Neurosci 5: 758–770.
48. Zhang X, Bertaso F, Yoo JW, Baumgartel K, Clancy SM, et al. (2010) Deletion of the potassium channel Kv12.2 causes hippocampal hyperexcitability and epilepsy. Nat Neurosci 13: 1056–1058.
49. Berkefeld H, Fakler B, Schulte U (2010) Ca2+-Activated K+ Channels: From Protein Complexes to Function. Physiological Reviews 90: 1437–1459.
50. Lehmann-Horn F, Jurkat-Rott K (1999) Voltage-gated ion channels and hereditary disease. Physiological Reviews 79: 1317–1372.
51. Chin C, Kim IK, Lim DY, Kim KS, Lee HA, et al. (2010) Gold nanoparticle-choline complexes can block nicotinic acetylcholine receptors. International Journal of Nanomedicine 5: 315–321.
52. Leifert A, Pan Y, Kinkeldey A, Schiefer F, Setzler J, et al. (2013) Differential hERG ion channel activity of ultrasmall gold nanoparticles. Proc Natl Acad Sci U S A 110: 8004–8009.
53. Doyle DA (1998) The Structure of the Potassium Channel: Molecular Basis of K+ Conduction and Selectivity. Science 280: 69–77.
54. Payandeh J, Scheuer T, Zheng N, Catterall WA (2011) The crystal structure of a voltage-gated sodium channel. Nature 475: 353–358.

9

Effect of Needle Insertion Speed on Tissue Injury, Stress, and Backflow Distribution for Convection-Enhanced Delivery in the Rat Brain

Fernando Casanova[1,3], Paul R. Carney[2], Malisa Sarntinoranont[1]*

1 Department of Mechanical & Aerospace Engineering, University of Florida, Gainesville, Florida, United States of America, **2** Department of Pediatrics, Neurology, Neuroscience, and J. Crayton Pruitt Family Department of Biomedical Engineering, Wilder Center of Excellence for Epilepsy Research, Gainesville, Florida, United States of America, **3** Escuela de Ingeniería Mecánica, Universidad del Valle, Cali, Colombia

Abstract

Flow back along a needle track (backflow) can be a problem during direct infusion, e.g. convection-enhanced delivery (CED), of drugs into soft tissues such as brain. In this study, the effect of needle insertion speed on local tissue injury and backflow was evaluated *in vivo* in the rat brain. Needles were introduced at three insertion speeds (0.2, 2, and 10 mm/s) followed by CED of Evans blue albumin (EBA) tracer. Holes left in tissue slices were used to reconstruct penetration damage. These measurements were also input into a hyperelastic model to estimate radial stress at the needle-tissue interface (pre-stress) before infusion. Fast insertion speeds were found to produce more tissue bleeding and disruption; average hole area at 10 mm/s was 1.87-fold the area at 0.2 mm/s. Hole measurements also differed at two fixation time points after needle retraction, 10 and 25 min, indicating that pre-stresses are influenced by time-dependent tissue swelling. Calculated pre-stresses were compressive (0 to 485 Pa) and varied along the length of the needle with smaller average values within white matter (116 Pa) than gray matter (301 Pa) regions. Average pre-stress at 0.2 mm/s (351.7 Pa) was calculated to be 1.46-fold the value at 10 mm/s. For CED backflow experiments (0.5, 1, and 2 μL/min), measured EBA backflow increased as much as 2.46-fold between 10 and 0.2 mm/s insertion speeds. Thus, insertion rate-dependent damage and changes in pre-stress were found to directly contribute to the extent of backflow, with slower insertion resulting in less damage and improved targeting.

Editor: Timothy W. Secomb, University of Arizona, United States of America

Funding: This work was supported by award number R01NS063360 from the National Institute of Neurological Disorders and Stroke; the Universidad del Valle, Cali, Colombia; and by the Fulbright-COLCIENCIAS-DNP grant. The funders had no role in study design, data collection and analysis, decison to publish, or preparation of the manuscript.

Competing Interests: The authors have declared that no competing interests exist.

* E-mail: msarnt@ufl.edu

Introduction

Successful treatment of neurological disorders requires effective techniques to deliver drugs to the central nervous system (CNS). Systemic delivery can be problematic because of the blood brain barrier (BBB) which prevents passive passage of the majority of large molecules from the bloodstream into the extracellular space [1,2]. Convection-enhanced delivery (CED) is a technique to deliver therapeutic macromolecules directly to the CNS and bypass the BBB [3]. In CED, a cannula (needle) is inserted directly into the parenchyma, and drug infusate is delivered at controlled flow rates into the extracellular space. With convection (advection) as the dominant transport mechanism, this technique can improve local delivery by providing larger distribution volumes than diffusion-dependent methods [3].

CED requires the surgical insertion of a needle into brain tissue, and this raises specific concerns about minimizing penetration injury and ensuring proper targeting. Even with stereotactic positioning, backflow (leakback) along the needle track continues to be a major source of non-specific targeting, especially at high flow rates [4]. With backflow, infusate flows back along the outer needle wall instead of penetrating into tissue at the needle tip. This backflow phenomenon is normally undesirable since large tissue distributions are not achieved, and drugs can reach regions of the brain where they are unintended, not effective, or toxic, resulting in unwarranted side effects [5,6]. Indeed, improper targeting has been implicated as one of the most significant barriers to successful implementation of CED in previous clinical brain tumor trials [6,7]. In these trials, high rates of ineffective delivery resulted in the majority of infusate leaking into CSF spaces [5,8]. These studies employed simple open-ended cannulas that are prone to backflow [8,9]. To reduce backflow, research has focused on developing new cannula designs [10–12], imaging to identify backflow in real-time [13–18], and on modeling to predict the extent of backflow [19–21].

Backflow can be produced by local tissue injury, fluid-tissue interactions, or by a combination of these effects. With needle insertion, tissue disruption and injury may create a fluid-filled gap between the needle and surrounding tissue through which infusate can easily flow with little fluid resistance. Edema may also develop in response to cellular injury or vascular damage, and this abnormal accumulation of fluid can result in swelling and volumetric tissue changes [22]. Expansion of extracellular space may introduce a high hydraulic conductivity (permeability) layer of traumatized tissue around the cannula through which infusate can easily flow [23]. Alternatively, cellular swelling may reduce extracellular space and help to close gaps at the needle-tissue interface. Even when no fluid-filled gap is present at the needle interface, fluid pressure at the needle tip is increased with an increasing infusion flow rate, and this elevated pressure can push soft tissue away from the cannula surface to create a fluid-filled gap (intrinsic backflow) [20,21]. Related to this mechanism, tissue coring, defined as tissue going inside the cannula during the insertion process, has being implicated as another cause of increased backflow [3,14,24]. Peaks in needle fluid pressure which may be required to clear the obstruction also result in a peak in fluid pressure at the needle tip potentially creating a bolus infusion and backflow.

Tissue stresses which are introduced or are pre-existing may also influence the mechanics of backflow. We define pre-stress as the stress that exists around the needle after insertion and before the start of CED infusion. We assume this stress is radially-directed along the needle-tissue interface, and it is created by tissue disruption, displacement, and subsequent compaction around the needle with insertion. The introduction of this stress may reduce backflow since fluid pressure would have to overcome it to separate the tissue from the needle surface [21]. In our previous studies, we have evaluated the effect of pre-stress on CED backflow in hydrogel tissue phantoms [25]. The presence of pre-stress resulted in reduced backflow. However, experimental measures or mechanical analysis of this stress is currently missing for CNS tissues. In CNS tissue, local tissue swelling around the needle can affect backflow if it produces changes in stress distribution before or during infusions. Therefore, local tissue swelling in response to needle injury can result in time-dependent pre-stress and backflow outcomes. In addition, it should be noted that residual stresses already exist in brain tissues even before needle insertion [26,27]. Such residual stresses may also influence backflow by altering the mechanics of tissue disruption, changing fluid-gap dimensions, or changing the magnitude of pre-stress.

Studies of local CNS tissue penetration injury have been previously conducted for insertion of electrodes and needles and for ballistic tests. Blood vessel rupture and hemorrhage have been previously reported as evidence of tissue damage during electrode insertion in cortical tissues [28,29]. Previous CED studies by White et al. [23] observed regions of increased tissue injury with hemorrhage reported mainly within white matter regions, and pressure-induced tissue fracture near the needle tip. Regions of injury were also found to be coincident with backflow. While there are no needle insertion studies measuring acute tissue swelling, early tissue swelling has been detected due to other kinds of brain trauma [30–32].

Few studies have focused on evaluating insertion speed on CNS tissue damage. Previous electrode studies have been conducted in which fast insertions of sharp electrodes and electrode arrays into cortical tissue were shown to cause less vascular rupture and bleeding [28,29]. In our previous study, we have evaluated the influence of needle insertion speed on backflow in a hydrogel tissue phantom [25]. Backflow was considerably reduced if the needle was inserted fast (1.8 mm/s). A pre-stress was estimated, and the existence of this compressive interfacial stress was postulated to contribute to reduced backflow. At a lower speed (0.2 mm/s), hydrogel accumulation at the needle tip produced a damage gap that resulted in backflow. Thus, rate-dependent damage had a great influence on the extent of backflow.

In the CNS, we assume that surgical placement of the infusion cannula creates tissue damage and a volumetric loss of tissue. For example, as cell membranes are irreparably torn by needle penetration, the fluid content of each cell will disperse or be squeezed out into the interstitial space through which it can flow easily to other tissue regions. Also, large strains introduced by needle insertion may result in deformation that results in a permanent track observed along the needle pathway. In this study, the effect of the needle insertion speed on such tissue damage and CED backflow was evaluated *in vivo* in rat brain tissue. The caudate putamen, a gray matter region, was targeted with the needle track passing through both the cortex and external capsule, a white matter structure, before reaching target tissue. Local tissue damage due to needle coring, needle disruption/displacement, and time-dependent swelling was evaluated. The extent of tissue coring was evaluated by monitoring CED infusion pressures. Local tissue damage and time-dependent swelling in the vicinity of the needle were evaluated by histological hole measurements at two time points after needle retraction. Hole measurements were used to reconstruct the tissue penetration damage along the length of the needle track. Hole diameters were also used as an input into a mechanics model to estimate *in vivo* pre-stresses assuming brain tissue to behave as a neo-Hookean material. Finally, these damage assessments were used to understand the influence of rate-dependent injury and pre-stress on backflow. CED experiments infused visible Evans blue albumin (EBA) tracer at varying flow rates and insertion speeds. Backflow was quantified in two ways: percentage of tracer infusate outside the targeted caudate putamen and distance back along the needle track. This study provides a visual way to evaluate mechanical damage along the needle track. Also, to the best of our knowledge it is the first to quantify pre-stress in CNS tissues and study its relation with insertion rate and backflow. The results of this study may be used to better understand and improve the insertion processes of needles, electrodes, probes or other devices in the brain to reduce tissue injury and improve functional outcome.

Methodology

Three series of *in vivo* rat brain experiments were conducted: (1) needle insertion experiments to measure local tissue damage along the needle track (infusion pressure measurements and hole measurements), $n = 12$ rats, (2) additional histological assessment, $n = 3$ rats, and (3) CED backflow experiments, $n = 23$ rats.

Animal preparation and surgical procedures

All experiments were performed on male Sprague-Dawley rats (300–350 g) using protocols and procedures approved by the University of Florida Institutional Animal Care and Use Committee. Anesthesia was initiated with xylazine (10 mg/kg, SQ) and isoflurane (4%) in oxygen delivered at 1.0 L/min. The head was shaven and disinfected with iodine/alcohol. Then animals were placed in a stereotaxic frame (model 900, David Kopf Instruments, Tujunga, CA), and inhalation anesthesia (1.5% in 0.5 L/min of oxygen) was delivered via a nose mask. Body temperature was maintained (~37°C) with a heating pad during the entire procedure. The skull was exposed by a mid-sagittal incision that began between the eyes and extended caudally to the level of the ears to expose the bregma and lambda. Two holes of 2 mm diameter were drilled by hand into the skull above the caudate putamen (CPu). Dura mater was carefully taken off and any residual blood was cleaned with phosphate-buffered saline (1× PBS). The exposed surface of the brain was kept wet with PBS during the course of the experiment.

The CPu was chosen as the target because it is a relatively homogeneous region composed mainly of gray matter and has been previously used for CED backflow studies [4,33–35]. To reach the CPu, the needle must pass through the cortex, which is mainly gray matter and the external capsule (ec) which is a white matter region (Figure 1). The needle was stereotactically inserted at a 5 mm depth within the CPu. Bilateral infusions were conducted on the right and the left sides (AP = 0.5, ML = ±3, DV = −5). After needle insertion, two minutes were allowed for tissue relaxation before infusions. The needle was retracted three minutes after the end of all infusions. The needle was retracted at 0.2 mm/s, and cleaned with 3% hydrogen peroxide followed by 1 ×PBS.

In needle insertion experiments and histology experiments, brain tissues were fixed to avoid further swelling after rat death and to avoid additional distortion and damage during removal and slicing. After needle retraction, rats were immediately euthanized by perfusion fixation using 10% formalin. Brains were removed and put in 10% formalin overnight and then moved to 30% sucrose for 2 days before tissue slicing. To be consistent with previous backflow studies [4], brains used for CED backflow experiments were not fixed, and rats were euthanized by decapitation immediately after needle retraction.

Needle insertion and CED system

For all experiments, a 32 gauge (0.235 mm diameter) blunt tip stainless steel needle (Hamilton, Reno, NV) was used. Blunt tip needles were used because needles of this kind have been used in clinical trials [6], are readily commercially available, and have been used by our lab in previous CED studies [13,14,25]. Moreover, even though new cannulas to minimize backflow have being designed [10–12], the tip geometry of many of these new designs is often a basic blunt tip.

Figure 2 shows a schematic of the experimental set-up used for needle insertion and CED. Needle insertion (*z*-direction) was controlled using a linear stage system (model LP28T, Applied Motion Products, Watsonville, CA) mounted on a machine frame. The needle was coupled to the linear stage using an electrode holder (model 900, David Kopf Instruments, Tujunga, CA) which also provided alignment. The stereotaxic frame and rat were placed on a *x-y* table which was used to position the rat under the needle such that the drilled holes in the rat skull at target AP and ML coordinates was under the needle tip. The infusion system consisted of a syringe pump driving a 100 µL gas-tight syringe (Hamilton, Reno, NV) connected to 40 cm of minimally compliant polyetheretherketone (PEEK) tubing (1 mm inner diameter and 1.58 mm outer diameter). This infusion line was coupled to the needle via a reducing union (Valco Instruments, Houston, TX).

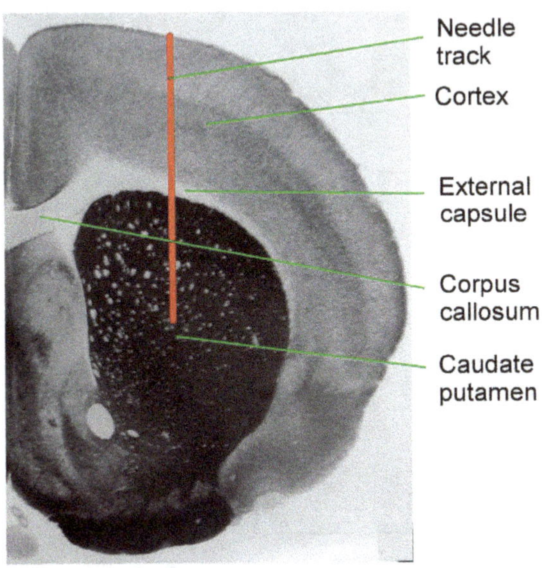

Figure 1. Coronal section of the rat brain schematically showing the needle track (in red) passing through the cortex and the external capsule and targeting the caudate putamen (CPu). Slice picture adapted from [41].

Macromolecular tracer

Evans blue labeled albumin (EBA) was used as the visible macromolecular tracer. EBA was prepared with 20 mg/ml of bovine serum albumin (Sigma-Aldrich, St. Louis, MO) and 1.25 mg/ml of Evans blue (Sigma-Aldrich, St. Louis, MO) in 1× PBS. The concentration of Evans blue was low enough that Evans blue was completely bound to the albumin [37].

Needle insertion experiment

Experiments were conducted at three insertion speeds: 0.2, 2, and 10 mm/s. Four rats were tested at each insertion speed (12 total rats). The first two speed levels were chosen because they are in the range of a previous electrode insertion study [28] and similar to the speed levels of our previous hydrogel CED study [25]. The highest insertion speed was chosen based on a previous microelectrode study [29]. 4 µL of tracer was infused at 2 µL/min to reproduce conditions of backflow and to provide easier identification for hole measurements in fixed tissue sections.

To evaluate changes in our damage parameter, hole diameter, due to acute injury swelling, tissues were fixed at two different time points after needle retraction, 10 and 25 min. Bilateral insertion experiments were conducted on each rat. The second retraction was 15 min after the first one. Then, the rat was immediately euthanized by perfusion fixation using 10% formalin which took ~10 min.

Infusion pressure measurement. In-line infusion pressure provided a separate measure of needle-tissue interaction. In previous studies, spikes in infusion pressures have indicated the occurrence of tissue coring within the needle tip [3,14,24]. In-line pressure measurements were performed for all needle insertion experiments to monitor pressure changes during insertion and CED at 2 µL/min.

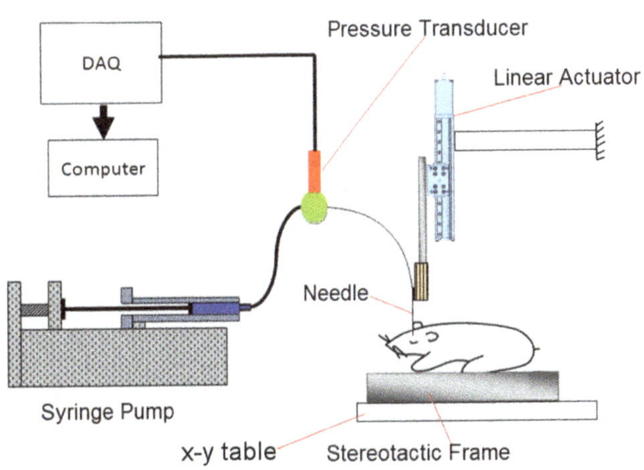

Figure 2. Schematic of the experimental set up used for needle insertion and CED.

Pressures were measured using a custom-designed fiber optic pressure transducer (model FOP-MIV-NS663, FISO Technologies, Quebec, CA) that was connected in-line to the infusion system between the syringe and the needle. Pressure was monitored at 1 Hz during the insertion, infusion, and retraction process. Prior to each brain infusion, a reference pressure was recorded outside the brain with the infusion pump running at the test infusion rate and with the needle at the same stereotaxic level as within the rat brain during CED. This value was a measure of the pressure drop within the infusion line and was subtracted from the *in vivo* pressure measured during infusion in brain to determine pressure at the needle tip.

Hole measurements along the needle track. Fixed brains were sectioned into 100 μm slices in the horizontal plane on a cryostat (~−20°C). Approximately 45 slices were obtained along each needle track. Slices were put in 1× PBS at room temperature for 30 min and then mounted on microscope slides for imaging. Needle holes on each slice were imaged on a microscope (model IX-71, Olympus America Inc., Center Valley, PA) and a digital camera (model SPOT RT3, Diagnostic Instruments, Inc., Sterling Heights, MI) using bright light. Color RGB images of the hole were used to measure the area and the perimeter using a MATLAB script. Images were converted to gray scale and the hole was detected by considering only pixels with intensity higher than a threshold value determined from surrounding tissue in each slice using Otsu's method [36].

Since the holes were not necessarily circular, the measured areas were used to calculate the equivalent diameter, which was defined as the diameter of a circle with the same hole area. The aspect ratio, defined as the ratio between the equivalent perimeter (calculated using the equivalent diameter) and the measured perimeter, was also used to evaluate the shape of the hole. The aspect ratio is 1 for a circular hole, and the aspect ratio goes to zero as the shape becomes more irregular. In some slices, especially those close to the brain surface, the hole was difficult to measure because of excessive bleeding produced during dura mater removal or because the hole was closed. These holes were not included in the data analysis.

Additional histological assessment

In an additional test group ($n = 3$ rats), needles were inserted at the three insertion speeds and 4 μl of albumin in solution with 1×PBS (20 mg/ml) was infused at 2 μL/min. Evans blue was not infused to allow H&E staining. Fixed brain tissue was sliced into 50 μm thick slices in horizontal planes and standard procedures for H&E staining were followed [23].

Pre-stress estimation

Hole diameters were input into a tissue mechanics model to estimate pre-stresses along the length of the needle track. The model assumed that during insertion, tissue was radially displaced and conformed around the inserted needle. This is based our assumption that frictional drag of tissue in the z-direction is small along the main length of the needle and that shear stresses become negligible as the tissue equilibrates around the needle before the start of CED. Also, a plane strain condition was assumed because of the relatively large length of the needle with respect to the diameter. In this way, changes in hole diameters can be related to corresponding radially directed tissue stresses at the needle surface. Axial symmetry and a semi-infinite medium were considered because of the relatively small diameter of the needle compared with the surrounding tissue. Tissue stress was determined at equilibrium after needle insertion; therefore viscoelastic effects were not considered. Pre-stress was calculated at the most immediate tissue fixation time point (10 min) when swelling was minimized. Since swelling and pre-existing residual stresses can change the hole size, the approach to estimating pre-stress considers the net effect of pre-existent stresses and stress generated during needle insertion.

Pre-stress was calculated as the compression load on the surface of the hole necessary to re-expand the equivalent hole diameter (ρ) to the diameter of the inserted needle (a) (**Figure 3**) assuming the solid phase of tissue behaves as a neo-Hookean material [25,37]. By assuming incompressibility of the tissue [38], the Cauchy stress tensor was calculated using [39]

$$\sigma_{ij} = -s\delta_{ij} + F_{ik}\frac{\partial W}{\partial F_{jk}} \tag{1}$$

where s is a material constant, F_{ik} is the gradient deformation tensor, and δ_{ij} is the Kronecker delta tensor. The simplified energy function was

$$W = \frac{1}{2}\mu(F_{ki}F_{ki} - 3) \tag{2}$$

where μ is the shear modulus.

By considering plane strain conditions, stretch ratios were defined as

$$\lambda_r = \frac{1}{\lambda_\theta} = \frac{\rho}{a} \tag{3}$$

The constant s was calculated far away from the needle where stress and displacements go to zero, and the stretch ratio was equal to unity. From Equation 1, s was equal to μ

After calculating the derivative of W, the stress tensor (Equation 1) becomes

$$\sigma_{ij} = -\mu\delta_{ij} + \mu F_{ik}F_{jk} \tag{4}$$

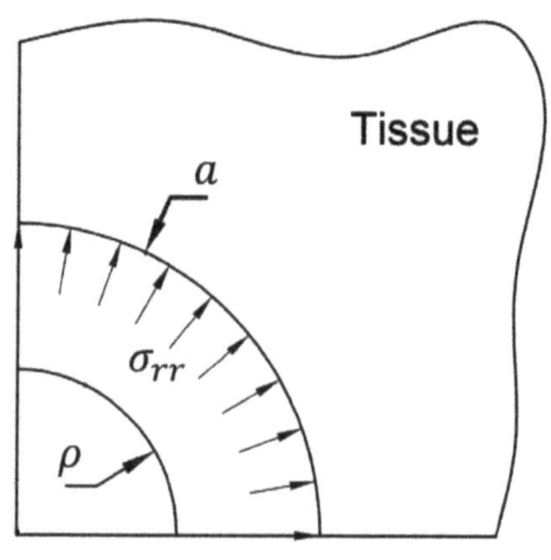

Figure 3. Schematic showing the relation between holes left in tissue after needle retraction and pre-stresses at needle-tissue interface when the needle is in tissue. The hole of diameter ρ can be expanded to the diameter of the needle (a) which introduces compressive pre-stress (σ_{rr}).

The pre-stress is the normal stress in the radial direction

$$\sigma_{rr}=\mu(\lambda_r^2-1) \tag{5}$$

Pre-stress was calculated using equilibrium shear moduli values of 485 Pa for the cortex and 238 Pa for the corpus callosum using values reported by Elkin et al. [40]. In this case, the external capsule was assumed to have similar modulus to the corpus callosum which is a predominately white matter region. This white matter shear modulus was assigned at two points, 2.8 and 2.9 mm depths, corresponding to the ~0.2 mm thick layer of external capsule according to a rat brain atlas [41]. All other points were calculated with the modulus of cortex gray matter.

Backflow experiments

A separate set of experiments was conducted to measure backflow at each insertion speed (0.2, 2, and 10 mm/s). 4 μL of EBA was injected at three flow rates (0.5, 1, and 2 μL/min). Five experiments were performed for each experimental condition for a total of 45 experiments (23 rats with bilateral injections). Following CED experiments, rats were immediately euthanized and freshly excised brains were sectioned into 100 μm slices on the cryostat in the coronal plane. Slices within infused brain regions were mounted on microscope slides and placed on a white surface. White light was projected on each slice, then slices were imaged using a CMOS camera and saved as a RGB file for analysis.

Backflow was quantified by using two different measures: (1) the percentage of tracer infusate outside of the targeted CPu region and (2) the distance from the needle tip to the point of maximum tracer penetration back along the needle track.

Backflow as percentage of tracer infusate outside the target. Previous CED studies have calculated the infused volume using a threshold intensity value and assuming constant concentration in regions with intensity above this threshold. This approach can introduce some error since the concentration of infusate is not necessarily constant throughout infused brain tissues. To avoid this, slice images were converted into concentration maps of Evans blue, which was the visible component of the tracer. The distributed tracer regions were used to calculate the mass of tracer outside the target CPu.

To obtain a gray scale image of each slice and calculate a pixel intensity, the red value (*R*) at every pixel was normalized by the total pixel intensity [10], $I=R/(R+G+B)$ where G is the green component and B is the blue component of the white light. Images were analyzed using a Matlab subroutine, and pixel intensity was converted to dye concentration using a modified Beer's law [42]

$$\ln\left(\frac{I_0}{I}\right)=\alpha LcM+N \tag{6}$$

where L is the path length of light inside the specimen, c is the Evans blue concentration, α is the absorption or extinction coefficient, and I_o is the incident light energy. Beer's law was modified to account for non-transparent tissue such that M is an introduced factor that accounts for the increase in path length of photons that are detected but take a non-straight path, and N is a factor which accounts for the scattering of light. The modified law can then be written as [42]

$$\ln\left(\frac{I_1}{I}\right)=\alpha_1 hc \tag{7}$$

where $I_1=e^{-NI_0}$, $\alpha_1=2M\alpha$, and h is the thickness of the slice, $h=L/2$ because the light was assumed to cross the specimen then reflect back to the camera. The constant I_1 is thus the intensity of the background and was obtained by applying Equation (7) to a reference tissue region without any tracer.

Next, the mass of Evans blue in a given tissue region was determined in terms of image intensity using mass conservation

$$M_E=\int_V c\,dV=\int_V \frac{1}{\alpha_1 h}\ln\left(\frac{I_1}{I}\right)dV=\frac{1}{\alpha_1}\sum_1^{ns}\int_A \ln\left(\frac{I_1}{I}\right)dA \tag{8}$$

where V, dV, A, dA, and ns are volume, differential of volume, area, differential of area, and number of slices, respectively. This relation assumes no capillary clearance or metabolism of EBA over the course of the experiment. To obtain the constant α_1, the total mass of Evans blue introduced into the brain by CED (M_T 1.25 mg/mm^3×4 μL = 5 mg) was compared with intensity data from all slices within the infused region. Once the constants α_1 and I_1 were obtained, Equations 7 and 8 were used to estimate EB concentration and mass accumulated in tissues. An example of a tissue slice image and corresponding Evans blue concentration map within the infused region are shown in **Figure 4**. CPu and white matter regions where easily delineated on each slice as shown in **Figure 4A**. It can be seen that concentration gradients existed inside the CPu and concentrations were not constant (**Figure 4B**).

The backflow percentage (*BF*) was calculated as

$$BF=100\frac{M_T-M_{in}}{M_T} \tag{9}$$

where M_{in} is the mass of Evans blue inside the target CPu. The region with EBA inside the CPu was isolated on each slice using ImageJ software (National Institutes of Health). The mass of Evans blue outside the CPu was not calculated directly from the images because blood was frequently observed outside the CPu, especially in white matter regions.

Backflow distances. Backflow distances from the needle tip to the point of maximum tracer penetration back along the needle track were also determined. For each infusion site, a slice containing the needle track or as close as possible to it was used. Because the position of the needle tip was difficult to identify in the brain slices, backflow distances were calculated as the difference between the total insertion depth (5 mm) and the distance (*d*) from the point of maximum dye penetration along the needle track to the surface of the brain, see **Figure 5**.

Statistical analysis

Analysis of variance (ANOVA) was used in the analysis of experimental data to test whether or not the means of several groups are all equal. One-way ANOVA was used to examine the influence of one factor on the experimental data and two-way ANOVA was used to evaluate the effect of two or more factors. The results of ANOVA can be considered reliable as long as the data are normally distributed. If normal distribution could not be guaranteed, Kruskal-Wallis test was used.

Average infusion peak pressure and steady state pressure was compared for the three insertion speeds by using one-way ANOVA. The total average hole areas, diameters, and pre-stresses, were compared for the three insertion speeds and the two time points by using the Kruskal-Wallis test because data was not normally distributed. Also, the Kruskal-Wallis test was used to compare averages areas, diameters, and pre-stresses among

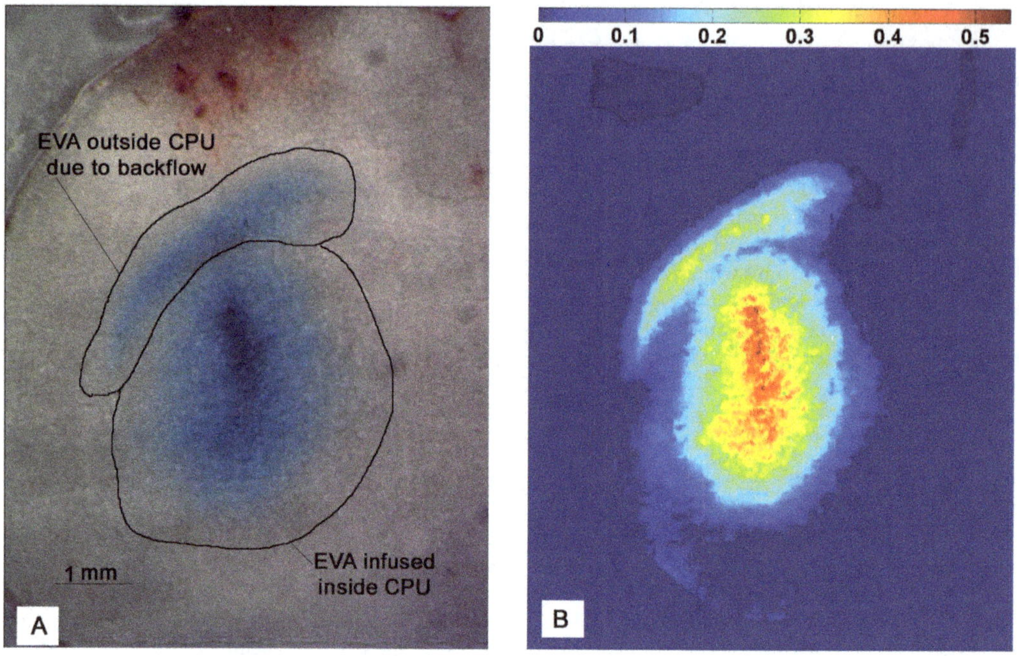

Figure 4. Brain tissue slice showing (A) EBA distribution and (B) corresponding tissue concentration map. The concentration map of Evans blue is in units of mg/mm^3. The needle was inserted at a speed of 0.2 mm/s and CED was at a flow rate of 1 μL/min.

regions in the brain along the needle track (cortex, external capsule, and CPu). Average hole area for each point along the insertion track was compared for the three insertion speeds and for the two time points by using two-way ANOVA. At some depths along the needle track, the hole was difficult to see in images and was not measurable. Therefore statistical analysis was performed only for those depths where the complete data set which consisted of four repetitions was obtained. Average backflow percentage and backflow distances were compared for the three insertion speeds and the three flow rates by using two-way ANOVA. Data are presented as mean ± 1 standard deviation. All p-values of <0.05 were considered significant.

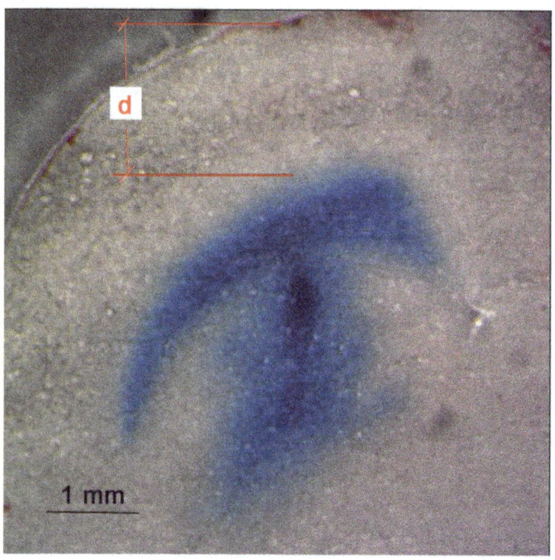

Figure 5. EBA backflow distribution along the needle track. For backflow calculations, distance along the needle track from the brain surface to the top most backflow region (*d*) was measured. Image is of an excised 100 μm brain slice.

Results

Damage assessment

Infusion pressure. Small variations in infusion pressure were observed during needle insertion. Once infusion started, pressure increased to a peak value between 14 and 25 kPa and then decreased to an approximately steady-state value between 2.7 and 7.4 kPa (**Figure 6A**). The peak pressure may be indicative of tissue coring or some other initial tissue resistance which the infusate encounters. After infusion was stopped, infusion pressure decreased to a value just above zero and then went to zero after the needle was fully retracted. For infusions performed with needle insertion speeds of 2 and 10 mm/s, a second small peak (P_B in **Figure 6A**) between 0.2 and 2.46 kPa greater than the local minimum value (P_A) was also observed.

Figure 6B shows the average values of peak pressure, steady state pressure, and the second peak of pressure (P_B) for the different insertion rates. The difference between average peak and steady state values was not significant with respect to insertion speed (p-value = 0.62 for peak pressure; p-value = 0.29 for steady state pressure). That peak pressure did not depend on insertion speed indicated that tissue coring or tissue resistance due to tissue separation was not insertion rate dependent. The difference in the second peak between insertion speed 2 and 10 mm/s was not significant (p-value = 0.6). Magnitude of the second peak of pressure was given by the difference $P_B P_A$. The average of that difference was 0.54 and 0.84 kPa for 2 and 10 mm/s insertion speeds, respectively. The averages of these magnitudes were also not significantly different (p-value = 0.39).

Hole measurements. In the majority of tissue slices, the hole left by the needle appeared as empty space (**Figure 7A**), but in other slices (~5% of slices), especially those close to the surface on

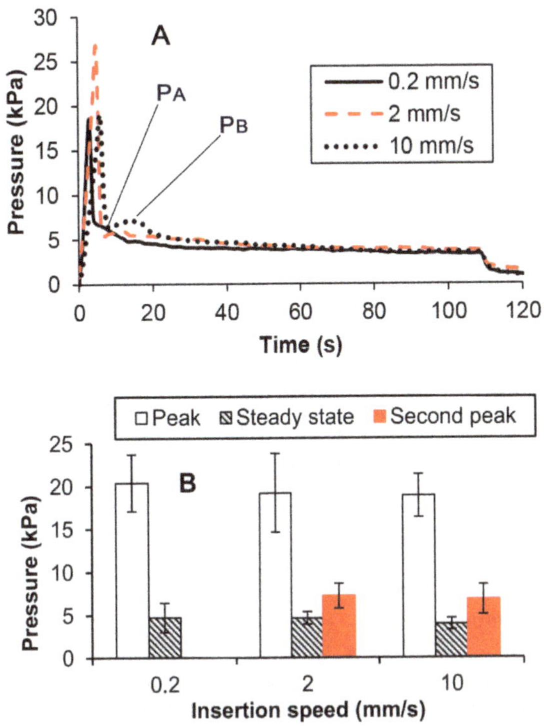

Figure 6. Insertion speed dependence of infusion pressure for CED at 2 μL/min; A) typical pressure profiles during infusion; B) average peak, steady state pressure, and second peak (P_B) for varying needle insertion speeds. (Bars indicate ±1 standard deviation; $n = 8$).

the cortex, the hole appeared as a narrow crack surrounded by EBA (**Figure 7B**). In other cases (~20% of slices), only a region with accumulation of red blood cells was observed (**Figure 7C**) where it was difficult to distinguish the actual track of the needle. These corresponded mainly to locations close to the surface of the brain at insertion depths shallower than 1.4 mm. Data from slices like those shown in Figure 7B and 7C were not considered in any data analysis. Therefore, ~36 hole measurements per needle track were considered.

Measured hole areas were averaged at each spatial location along the needle track for each insertion speed and fixation time point, **Figure 8**. Hole area varied spatially with insertion depth. Track holes increased in size with penetration in the cortex. Between 2 and 3.5 mm depth, hole size reached a maximum, and decreased again for higher depths. The region of maximum hole area corresponded to the white matter region (external capsule). For two experiments performed at 10 mm/s insertion speed, the area of the hole within white matter regions was practically the same as the cross area of the needle (0.0434 mm^2). For the rest of the measured slices, the area of the hole was always considerably smaller than the area of the needle. **Figure 8D** shows the aspect ratios of the holes along the needle track for the 0.2 mm/s insertion speed. Holes were more circular (higher average value and lower standard deviation) between depths of 2 and 3 mm. Holes were found to be less circular at the CPu target site and near the surface of the brain. The aspect ratio profiles for other insertion speeds were found to be similar and are not shown.

Areas of all the holes along the needle track for each insertion speed and time point were averaged and compared by using the Kruskal-Wallis test (**Figure 9A**). As shown in **Figure 9B**, the average area increased for increasing insertion speed, see **Table 1**. Also, average hole area was larger for the earlier fixation, 10 min time point. The total average area for the 10 min fixation time point (0.01624±0.010 mm^2) and for the 25 min time point (0.0139±0.009 mm^2) was also significantly different. Changes in hole area were more sensitive to changes in insertion speed than to fixation time point; the average area for 10 mm/s was 1.87-fold and 1.32-fold the average area for 0.2 mm/s and for 2 mm/s respectively, while the average area for 10 min before fixation was up to 1.17-fold the average area for 25 min after fixation.

Analysis of variance was performed to compare the area of the holes at each point along the needle track, see **Figure 9C**. With respect to insertion speed, difference was significant for the majority of points between 2 and 4 mm depths. Here, increased insertion speed produced increasing hole areas except within a narrow region at ~3 mm depth which likely corresponds to the white matter region. With respect to the fixation time point, hole differences were significant for 12.5% of depth locations.

Figure 9D shows average hole areas for the three main brain regions along the needle track. Average values for the cortex (0.0133±0.011 mm^2), external capsule (0.0218±0.009 mm^2) and CPu (0.016±0.008 mm^2) were significantly different from each other. The maximum difference in average area was between the external capsule and cortex where average area of the external capsule was 1.64-fold the average area in the cortex. This ratio is

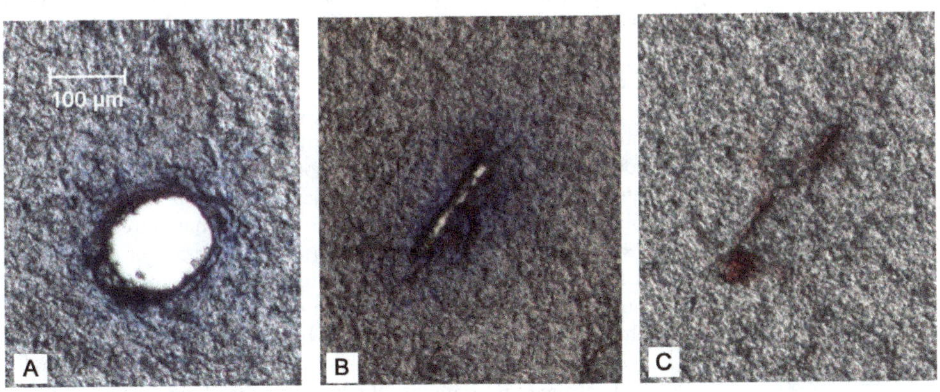

Figure 7. Different types of tissue damage left after needle retraction. A) approximately circular hole surrounded by infused EBA; B) hole as a slender opening/crack; and C) red blood cell accumulation where it was difficult to measure the hole opening. All images are for fixed, 100 μm thick brain tissue slices.

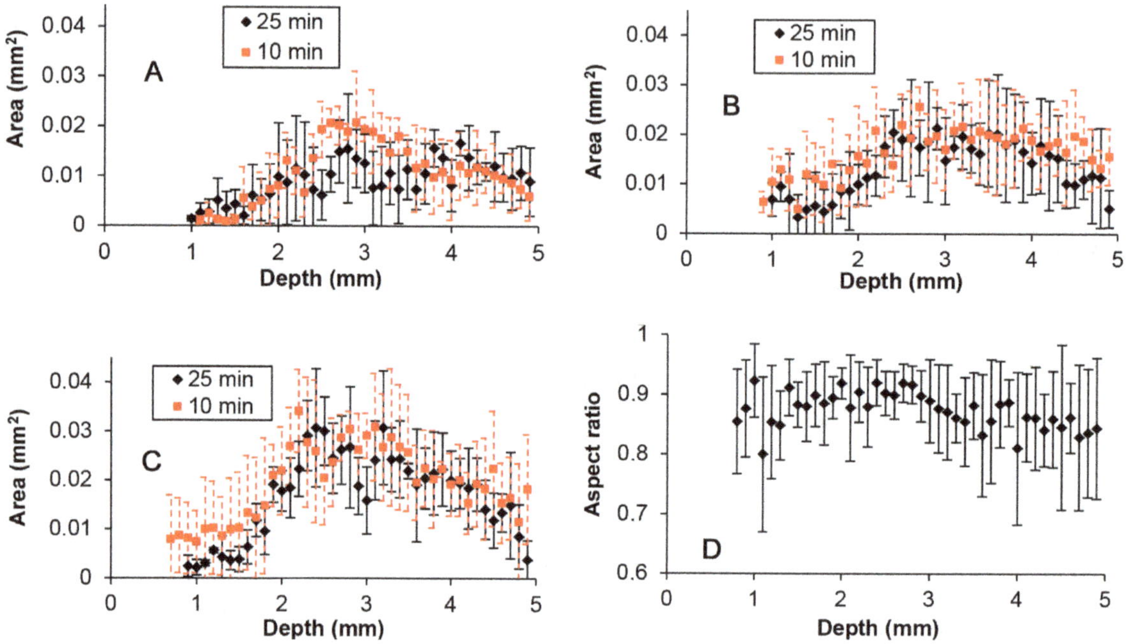

Figure 8. Tissue penetration damage along the length of the needle track. Areas of holes left after needle retraction are plotted as a function of insertion depth for varying fixation time points (10 and 25 minutes) and insertion speeds: A) 0.2 mm/s; B) 2.0 mm/s; and C) 10 mm/s. D) Aspect ratio of holes for an insertion speed of 0.2 mm/s and fixation after 10 min. Each data point corresponds to the average of 4 hole measurements. Bars represent ±1 standard deviation.

smaller than for the ratio between 10 mm/s and 0.2 mm/s insertion speeds. Therefore, tissue damage was more sensitive to insertion speed than brain region over the range of parameters tested.

Average hole diameters and perimeters presented similar trends as the hole areas. These results are summarized in **Table 1**.

Additional histology. Several rupture mechanisms were observed in brain tissue slices. Tissue fracture was defined as a crack or narrow opening with bleeding in interior regions of the tissue slice. The presence of blood indicated that fracturing occurred *in vivo* during needle insertion or retraction and not during tissue processing, e.g. slicing and mounting. **Figure 10A** shows tissue fracture and tissue stained with blood close to the needle hole. Generally, this injury was observed mainly in white matter regions of the external capsule and in the CPu. More intensive bleeding and tissue fracturing was also often observed at higher speeds, 2 and 10 mm/s (**Figure 11B**). Tissue fractures between 20 and 150 μm in length were found. This type of damage was observed in approximately 35% of the needle insertion experiments conducted at 2 or 10 mm/s. At the slower insertion speed, bleeding was only observed close to the hole, and tissue fracturing was not observed.

Individual cell separation from the bulk of tissue was also frequently observed at the surface of holes (**Figure 10A**). Narrow strips of tissue were also separated from the tissue surface (arrow in **Figure 10B**). Layers of cells or fibers were occasionally observed to be curved at the hole boundary, especially at slower insertion speeds of 0.2 mm/s (**Figure 11A**). This provided some evidence of radial tissue compaction.

Pre-stress

Pre-stress was calculated from equivalent hole diameters at the earliest fixation time point for each of the three insertion speeds, see **Figure 12**. Obtained pre-stress values were between 0 and 485 Pa. Pre-stress in white matter was approximately zero at five locations corresponding to locations where the area of the measured holes were practically the same as the needle. Average pre-stress values along the entire needle track are presented in **Table 1**. The average pre-stress for 0.2 mm/s was found to be significantly higher than pre-stress averages at the other two insertion speeds. There was no significant difference between pre-stress averages at 2 and 10 mm/s insertions (p-value = 0.16).

Pre-stress was not constant along the needle track. Maximum values were found in the cortex close to the surface, minimum values were found in the external capsule white matter region, and pre-stress increased with greater depths beyond the external capsule. Average pre-stress values for cortex, external capsule, and CPu regions are shown in **Figure 12D**. The average pre-stress value for the external capsule was significantly different from the other two tissue regions. There was no significant difference between average pre-stress in the cortex and CPu (p-value = 0.5).

CED backflow distributions

CED distributions in brain for varying needle insertion speeds are shown in **Figure 13**. Tracer distributions in tissue were found to be relatively uniform over regions of convective transport with evidence of diffusion at the peripheral front. Backflow was observed as leakage of infusate into white matter regions of the external capsule and corpus callosum (cc) outside of the targeted CPu. Infusate was not observed to flow back into the cortex. In general, backflow increased with increasing insertion speed. In these experiments, evidence of bleeding was frequently found within the external capsule, especially for insertions at 10 mm/s.

Leakage of infusate into the lateral stripe of the striatum (Lss), as shown at the bottom of **Figure 13A, and 13C**, was also frequently found (~65% of cases) independent of flow rate or insertion speed. Leakage to the lateral ventricles was observed in two cases performed at an insertion speed of 10 mm/s. No

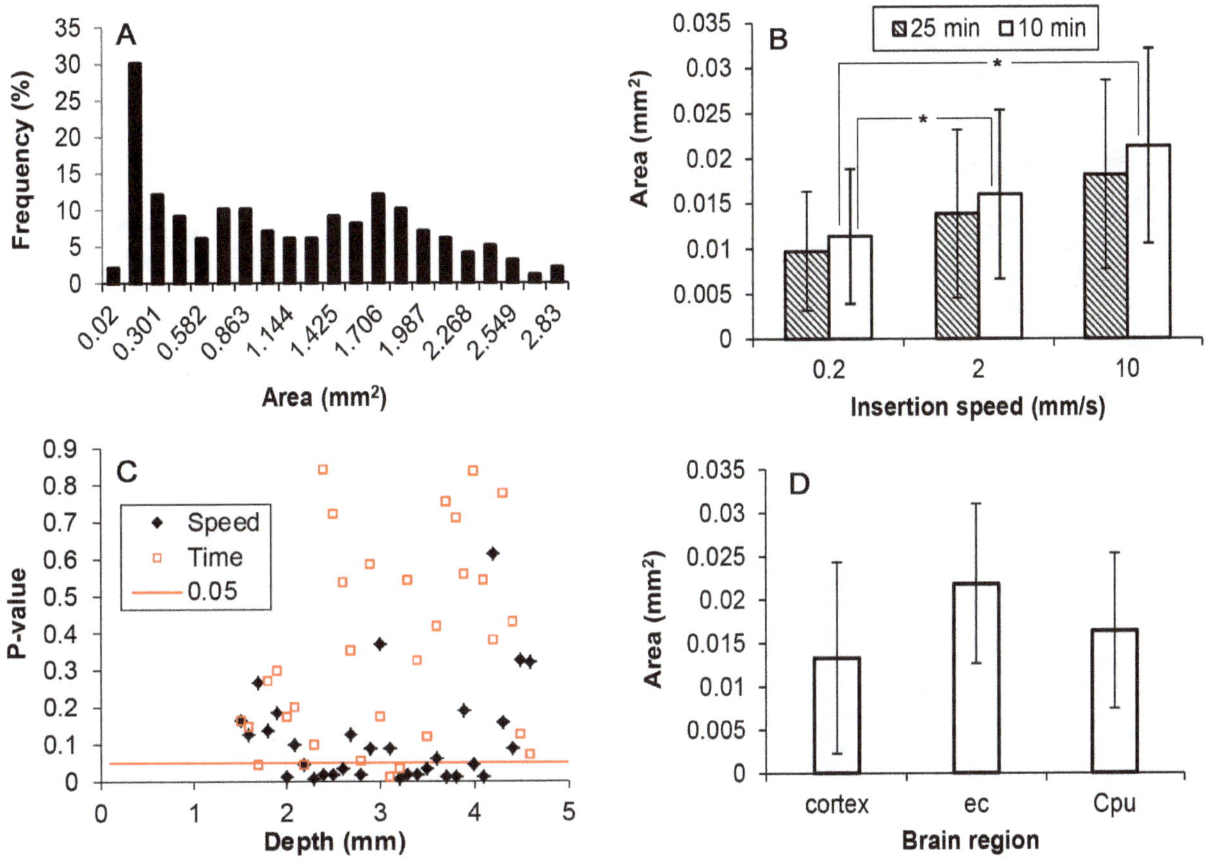

Figure 9. Variation of hole measurements. A) histogram showing non-Gaussian distribution of the hole areas for 10 mm/s needle insertion speed and fixation after 10 min (combined data from 4 needle tracks, 161 total hole measurements); B) average hole areas for the three insertion speeds and the two fixation time points evaluated for depths greater than 1.4 mm. Each bar corresponds to the average of $n = 144$ hole measurements. Significant difference with 10 mm/s is noted by *; C) analysis of variance to evaluate the influence of insertion speeds (0.2, 2, and 10 mm/s) and the influence of fixation time point (10 and 25 min). p-value is plotted for varying insertion depths; D) average area of holes for main tissue regions along the needle track. Each average value was significantly different from each other. Each bar corresponds to the average of $n = 336$, $n = 48$, and $n = 504$ measurements for cortex, external capsule (ec) and caudate putamen (CPu) regions, respectively. For cortex, points between 1.4 and 2.7 mm depth were considered. For external capsule, points at depth 2.8 mm and 2.9 mm were considered. For caudate putamen, points at depth higher than 2.9 mm were considered. Bars represent ±1 standard deviation.

evidence of tracer transport directly between Lss and external capsule regions was observed in any of the slices. For that reason, tracer distributions in the Lss were not considered in backflow calculations.

Average backflow percentages for varying insertion speed and infusion rate are shown in **Figure 14A**. Significant influence of the flow rate and the insertion speed was found. Average backflow percentages for the three insertion speeds were 16.7, 30.8, and 36.6% for flow rates of 0.5, 1, and 2 μL/min, respectively.

Table 1. Needle insertion and CED results for the evaluated needle insertion speeds.

Insertion speed	**0.2 mm/s**	**2 mm/s**	**10 mm/s**
Hole area* (mm^2)	0.0105±0.007	0.0149±0.009	0.0197±0.010
Diameter* (mm)	0.107±0.042	0.137±0.047	0.152±0.046
Perimeter* (mm)	0.383±0.145	0.483±0.153	0.536±0.150
Average pre-stress (Pa)	351.7±92.4	266.7±109.3	240.0±125.1
Backflow percentage (%)**	17.07±11.7	27.7±11.6	39.4±10.4
Backflow distances (mm)**	2.82±0.17	2.86±0.12	2.80±0.14

Average values ±1 standard deviation are presented.
*average for 10 and 25 min fixation time points.
**average for 0.5, 1.0 and 2.0 μL/min flow rates.

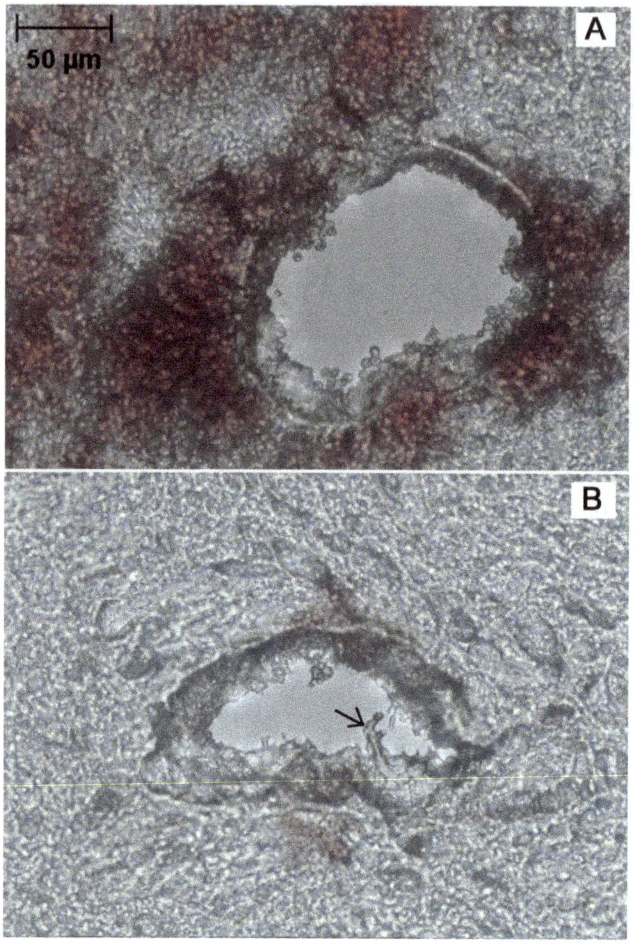

Figure 10. Needle tissue damage at the hole surface. A) cell separation and bleeding in the external capsule for insertion at 10 mm/s, and B) torn fibrous tissue (arrow) in the CPu for insertion at 0.2 mm/s. Both images are for 50 um thick fixed brain tissue slices with no staining.

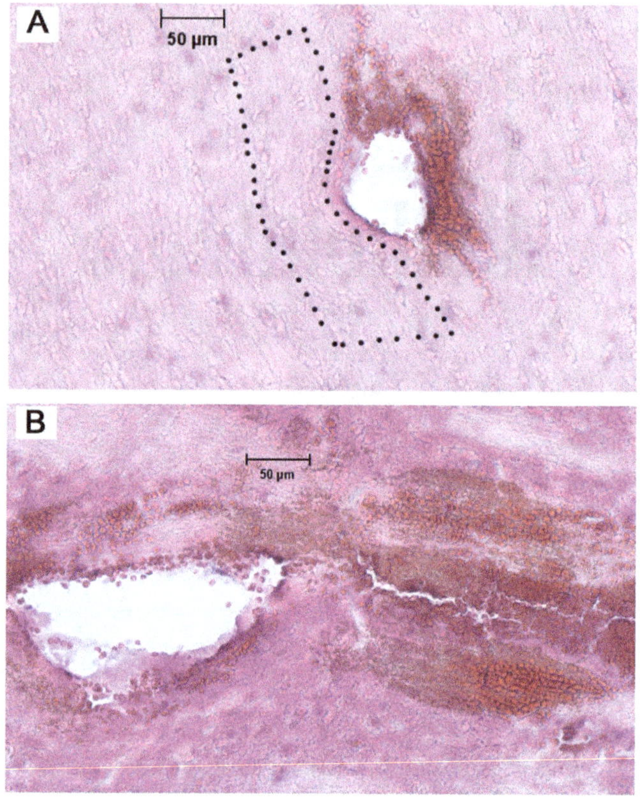

Figure 11. Needle tissue damage observed with H&E staining. A) external capsule region showing deformation and compaction of surrounding tissue. In the enclosed area (dotted lines), layers of cells conform around the hole (needle insertion at 0.2 mm/s); B) CPu region showing extensive bleeding and tissue fracture at some distance away from of the hole (insertion at 10 mm/s).

Average backflow at 0.5 µL/min was significantly different from the average backflow at the other two infusion rates.

Average backflow percentage was also found to increase for increasing insertion speed, see **Table 1**. The average percentage for the three flow rates were all significantly different at the three insertion speeds. Comparing backflow percentages obtained at 10 mm/s with respect to 0.2 mm/s insertion speeds, backflow increased by 2.46, 2.27, and 2.26-fold at 0.5, 1, and 2 µL/min flow rates, respectively. Since backflow was diverted away from the needle track into white matter regions, backflow distances along the needle track were relatively constant over the insertion speeds and flow rates tested (**Figure 14B**). No significant differences between flow rates or insertion speeds for backflow distance was found (p-value = 0.52 for insertion speeds, and p-value = 0.65 for flow rates).

Discussion

In this study, brain tissue damage and backflow during CED was evaluated for varying needle insertion speeds. Histological assessment and hole measurements were used to characterize local tissue damage along needle insertion tracks. This unique approach to characterizing tissue disruption was also used to estimate tissue stresses introduced by needle insertion (pre-stress). To the best of our knowledge, this is the first study to estimate pre-stress around an implant in brain tissue, and this information can be used to improve needle implantation surgical procedures or to improve prediction of backflow.

Tissue damage, evaluated as the size of the hole left by the needle after retraction, bleeding, and tissue fracturing, was found to increase for increasing insertion speeds and was higher within white matter regions. A statistically significant difference in hole areas with respect to insertion speed was found. While there are no previous needle insertion speed studies with which to directly compare, previous electrode insertion studies have noted greater brain surface dimpling and insertion forces with increasing insertion speed [43–45]. These higher deformation and force measures may indicate greater brain tissue damage which is in agreement with the present study. There are also studies which have found that fast insertion of sharp tip electrodes produced less blood vessel rupture and bleeding [28,29]. These differences in rate dependent damage may be due to differences in tip geometry (diameter and tip) or tissue region, since these electrode studies focus mainly on the cortex [28,29]. In the present study, hole measurements were small in the cortex, and no substantial bleeding was observed in the cortex except when it was produced during dura mater removal. Any hemorrhage was observed primarily in white matter regions of the external capsule and the CPu.

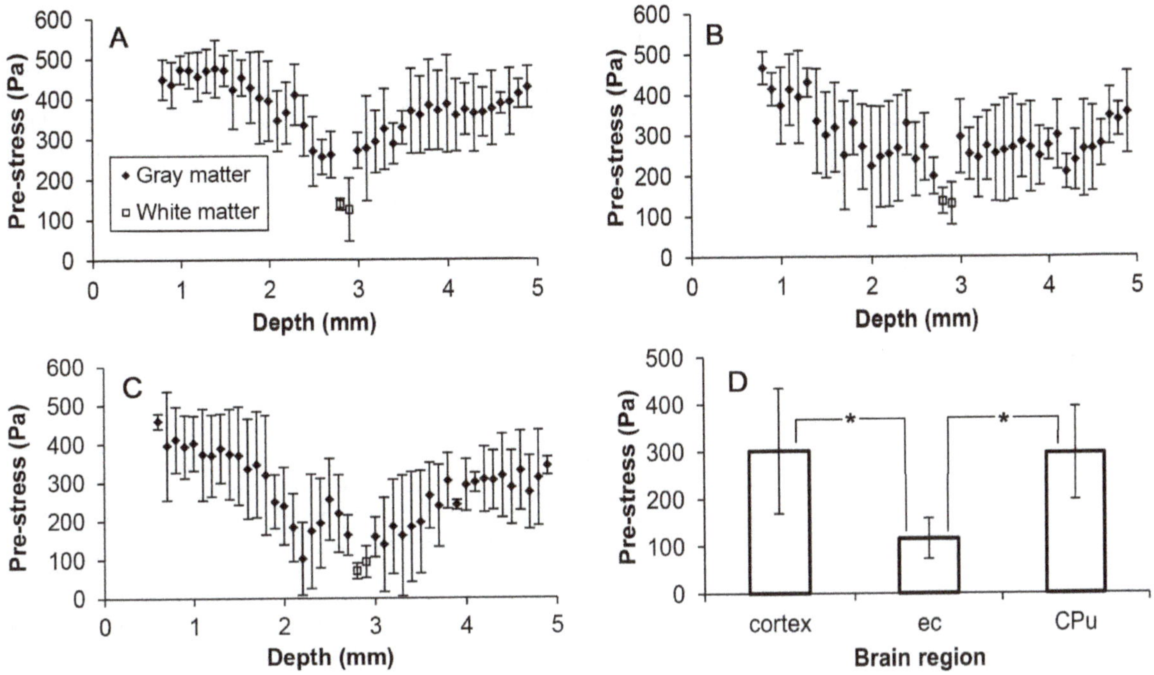

Figure 12. Pre-stress along the needle track for the needle inserted at: A) 0.2 mm/s, B) 2 mm/s, and C) 10 mm/s. (Bars represent the calculated standard deviation, $n = 4$.) D) Average pre-stress values for cortex, external capsule, and CPu regions. Significant difference is noted by *, p-value<0.05. Each bar corresponds to the average of $n = 144$ pre-stress values.

Hole measurements

The hole left in tissue by the needle provided a visual way to reconstruct tissue damage along the needle track. Holes area were relatively small in the cortex, maximum within the white matter region and decreased again in the CPu. The decrease in hole area in the CPu indicated that damage did not accumulate with depth, and that there was negligible tissue accumulation around the needle tip. Hole measurements were more circular in shape within inner cortex and white matter regions and more irregular close to the brain surface and within the CPu. The irregular shape of the hole may have resulted in non-uniform pre-stresses which may have increased the likelihood of backflow in less compacted regions at the needle periphery, i.e., regions of low pre-stress. The variation of the hole area along the needle track is likely because of differences in tissue composition, mechanical properties (modulus, friction, and rupture strength), as well as pre-existing residual

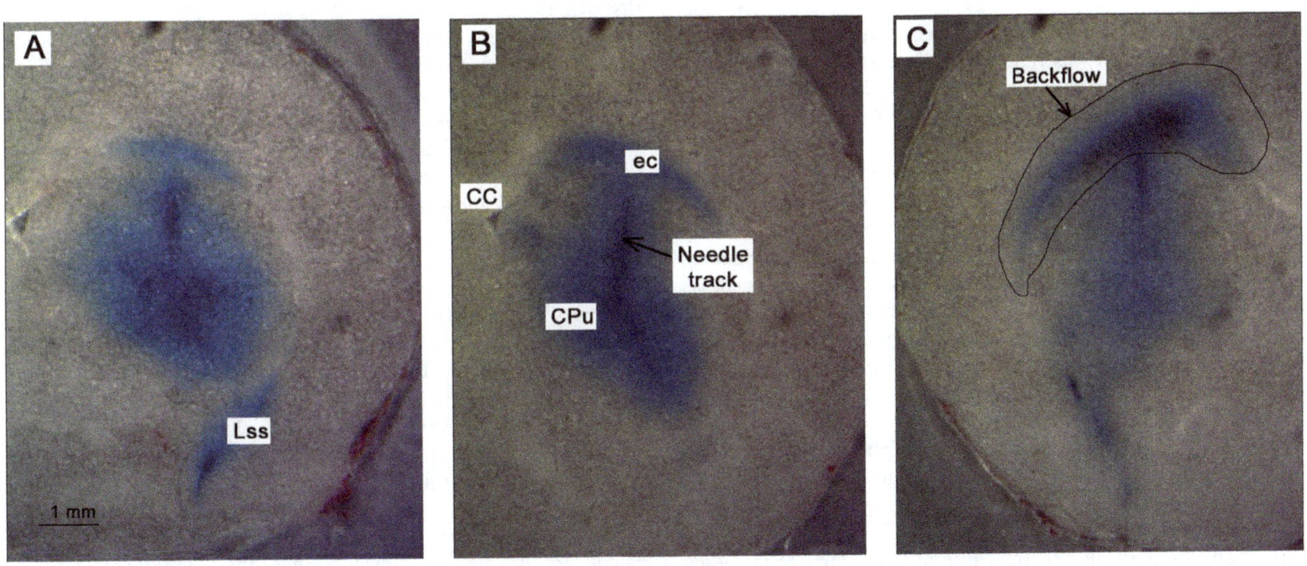

Figure 13. CED backflow in the rat brain. Images show distributions along the needle track after infusion of 4 μL of EBA at 0.5 μL/min. Infusion needles were inserted at varying speeds: A) 0.2 mm/s, B) 2 mm/s, and C) 10 mm/s. Rat brain slices are 100 μm thick slices and unfixed (ec: external capsule, CPu: caudate putamen, Lss: lateral stripe of the striatum, cc: corpus callosum).

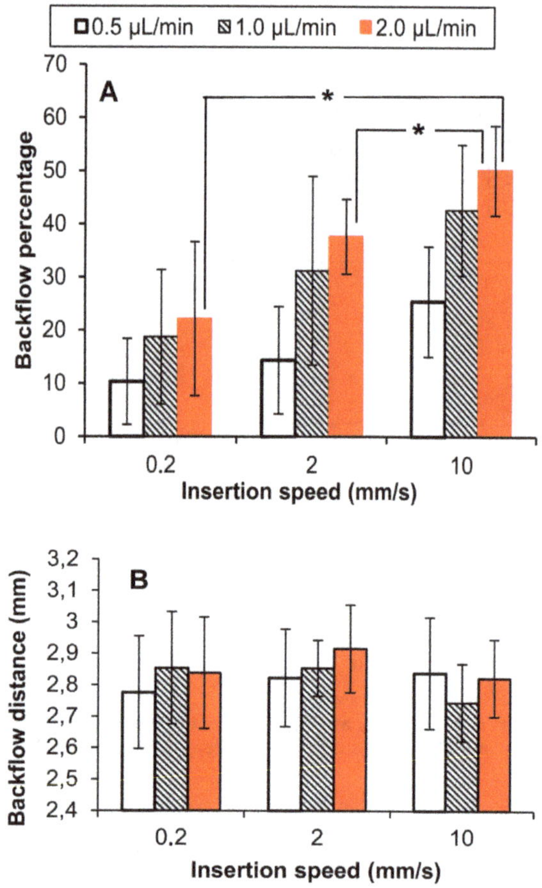

Figure 14. CED backflow following infusion of 4 μL of EBA. A) percentage of the EBA infusate outside the target CPu. Significant difference is noted by *, p-value<0.05 only for 10 mm/s insertion speed. For other flow rates, only the difference between 0.2 mm/s and 10 mm/s was significant. B) Backflow distances. Bars indicate ±1 standard deviation; $n = 5$ for each test group.

stresses in the brain. In a previous study by Xu et al. [26], white matter corpus collosum was reported to be under tensile residual stress that was up to 1.2 kPa. The larger diameter holes observed in the white matter regions of this study may be due to in part to this tensile residual stress.

Local tissue damage was also assessed. More intensive bleeding around the needle was found in white matter regions which is in agreement with hemorrhage patterns seen by White et al. in their CED studies into the rat CPu [23]. This indicates that vasogenic edema is likely. Also, widespread damage to both ECM and cells is possible. A corresponding observation was tissue fracturing observed primarily within white matter regions and the CPu. This is in partial agreement with the study by White et al. [23] where they also reported tissue fracturing but only close to the needle tip (CPu) but not within white matter regions. Greater injury in white matter may be produced by higher rupture stresses as suggested by previous probe insertion force measurements where significant increases in insertion force where found along white matter tracks [43,44]. Larger deformations associated with greater tissue strength may be the cause of more damage in these regions.

With respect to the two fixation time points evaluated, significant difference in the hole size was found. Swelling, inflammation or other injury processes may be increasing tissue volume after initial injury resulting in the measured decreases in hole areas. These results are in agreement with previous studies where brain tissue swelling and increases in intracranial pressure were detected at early time points after injury [30–32]. Therefore, hole measurements include the combined effects of tissue swelling, tissue tearing due to needle insertion, and residual stresses. Reported pre-stress values therefore account for swelling at these specific fixation time points and can be applied to tissue-needle interactions at these time points. Volumetric increases in tissue with swelling will increase pre-stresses with time. If these changes are large enough, they may reduce backflow. However, previous CED studies have not found additional wait time before infusion to be an important influence in preventing backflow [4]. It should be noted that hole damage was found to be less sensitive to changes in fixation time point than to changes in insertion speed.

Tissue coring

If tissue coring occurs during needle insertion, pressure inside the needle increases at the beginning of the infusion in order to expel cored tissue and clear the needle. Infusion pressures were used to determine if higher insertion speeds produce greater coring as another cause of greater backflow; however, pressure measurements showed no significant difference in the peak expulsion pressures. This indicated that tissue coring was not the main cause of insertion rate dependent changes in backflow. The peak and steady state infusion pressures were greater than or similar to those reported in previous studies [3,14,24]. Increased pressures may be due to the use of smaller cannulas which require greater pressure build up than larger cannulas to expel the same volume of tissue. Interestingly, incidence of backflow increased with the appearance of a second small peak in pressure observed at 2 and 10 mm/s insertion speeds. This small peak may be due to dynamic fluid-tissue interactions along the wall or with any cored tissue. Occurrence of a second peak may be a better indicator of backflow than having a high peak pressure value. Decreases in pressure over time may be due to viscoelastic properties of tissue. Slow separation of tissue from the needle (increasing surface area) may also explain decreasing infusion pressure.

Pre-stress

Volumetric tissue changes due to cellular and tissue disruption, tissue swelling and residual stresses ultimately influences internal tissue stresses surrounding the implanted needle. Improved understanding of theses stresses is needed for improved understanding of tissue-infusate interactions that affect backflow. This study provided measure of changes in pre-stress with changes in insertion speed and brain region. Calculated pre-stress was found to be significantly smaller for high insertion speeds because of the greater tissue damage produced at these speeds. Also, pre-stress was determined to be non-uniform along the needle track. It was smallest within the white matter region of the external capsule and it was predicted to be always present and compressive within the cortex and targeted CPu. Thus, the idealized model predicted no gaps between the needle and the tissue within the cortex and CPu. Predicted pre-stress values were low (<500 Pa) in part due to the low shear modulus values of brain tissue and the large extent of tissue disruption introduced by the needle. These low pre-stress values explain the sensitivity of CED to backflow since there is less of a 'seal' at the tissue-needle interface. Consistent with this, calculated pre-stresses were smaller than measured infusion pressures. Applied to CED outcomes, regional variation in pre-stress also supports the observed backflow patterns where infusate moved back up the needle track in the CPu and diverted mainly into adjacent white matter where less of a 'seal' exists. Therefore, pre-stress in the CPu region is the most relevant value when predicting backflow because this is the region where infusion and backflow is initiated.

Reported pre-stress was dependent on the mechanics model chosen and the mechanical properties of brain tissue used. These factors affect the magnitude of the reported pre-stress value. There exist some techniques to directly estimate stress at the tissue-needle interface using probes or microballoons as reported in previous studies [46,47]. However those devices are too large to be used in the rat brain. Moreover, with these techniques only one average value for stress is usually obtained, and information about regional variation along the needle track is missing. Therefore, the combined experiment and modeling approach used in this study establishes a useful way of estimating pre-stresses variation surrounding needles and other brain implants.

Sources of error

Friction and adhesion which were not considered in this study are potentially important parameters for understanding mechanics between the needle and tissue during needle insertion. Further studies measuring insertion forces are needed to estimate these effects.

While fixation was introduced to stop tissue swelling, fixation may also produce volumetric tissue contraction [48] which may be a source of hole measurement and pre-stress error. Hole contraction due to the combined effect of fixation and swelling will result in pre-stress overestimation. We estimated the net effect of these sources of error by incorporating volumetric tissue changes of 8% measured in previous fixation studies [48] and our own swelling analysis assuming uniform contraction in the radial direction. The effect of tissue swelling on hole measures was estimated by linear extrapolation of average hole area at 10 and 25 min time points to a zero time point. This adjusted hole area was resulted in a net decrease in pre-stress of approximately 5% which is small. Moreover, because our tissue analysis is a post-mortem technique, hole measures may be sensitive to tissue preparation, e.g. slicing and mounting. However, it is expected that these errors were uniformly spread along the needle track.

CED Backflow

In all CED experiments, backflow was observed. It was smallest for low flow rate and low insertion speed and significantly increased with higher flow rate and insertion speeds. To induce backflow, tracer infusate likely had to overcome pre-stresses in the CPu to separate tissue and form gap at the needle interface. Once backflow reached the white matter of the external capsule or corpus callosum, it was found to accumulate into these regions. The combination of low pre-stresses and the higher hydraulic conductivity of the white matter with respect to gray matter [49] likely contributed to this diversion of infusate into white matter. There did not seem to be sufficient pressure to open up the tissue gap in the cortex region since no tracers were observed to reach the cortex or the surface of the brain during infusion.

With increasing insertion speed, there was less delivery of EBA to the targeted CPu and greater accumulation in the external capsule and corpus callosum. This reflected greater backflow measured as percentage of the total tracer infused. While backflow distances were not significantly different this was to be expected since tracer was diverted from the needle track to the white matter region. As observed in this study, backflow distances were found to be dependent on the needle pathway and the anatomy of white matter intersection. For this needle pathway, backflow percentage was a better measure of the extent of backflow.

With respect to flow rate, backflow increase with increasing flow rate which was in agreement with numerous previous studies [4,20,21]. With respect to insertion speed, the results of the present study are opposite to that of our previous hydrogel study where material damage and backflow increased for a slow needle insertion speed [25]. Since similar experimental parameters (test system, insertion rates, needle tip) were used, the different outcome is likely due to differences in the mechanical behavior of the materials. At the slow insertion speed in hydrogel, an accumulation of material was observed to form at the needle tip which created a larger zone of damage. In contrast, in brain tissue, no tissue accumulation was noted at the tip based on the tissue damage patterns. In both materials there was still correspondence between pre-stress and backflow. The main difference between both materials was the different failure behavior that resulted in different pre-stress states. Brain tissue has been found to fail after high plastic deformation with a fibrous like fracture [50]. On the other hand, hydrogel fracture occurs with low plastic deformation [51].

Clinical Implications

Backflow has been a persistent problem for CED especially at high flow rates required for clinical applications due to a lack of infusate control. In clinical and primate studies, larger cannulas and designs with step changes in diameter have been used [8,9,52,53]. These needles share the same blunt tip used in our studies which show tissue damage along the needle track to be an important factor affecting backflow. We expect similar dependence of local tissue damage on insertion rate and tissue region. Slow insertion rates that minimize damage should improve targeting. Pre-stresses likely increase with cannula diameter, and increases in tissue compression may partially explain success of step designs in reducing backflow. This effect may also reduce backflow using polymer coated cannulas that swell *in situ* [11]. There are many sources for discrepencies between CED studies (cannula design, cannula alignment, fluidic components, and infusion rates, as well as animal model and infusion site). Tissue rupture and failure initiated at the needle tip is highly dependent on tip geometry, and previous studies have shown sharp or rounded needle tips [20] may reduce the extent of damage and backflow along the needle track. Tissue coring also contributes to pressure build up at the needle tip. Designs that reduce these effects, e.g. side port needles or hollow fiber catheters [10,54], will also reduce backflow. Further studies looking at the effects of needle tip geometry on tissue damage and stress in the vicinity of the needle tip are needed to better understand infusate-tissue interactions that contribute to backflow.

Conclusions

In this study, the effect of needle insertion speed on local tissue injury and backflow was evaluated *in vivo* along a track into the caudate putamen. Fast insertion speeds were found to produce more injury including tissue bleeding and disruption, lower pre-stresses, and greater backflow. New pre-stresses values provide important mechanics information at the tissue-needle interface needed to study fluid-solid interactions and may be used in the future as a predictor of backflow. In addition, patterns of tissue disruption and pre-stress were reported to vary along the length of needle track with difference found between white and gray matter regions. Thus, insertion speed dependent damage and changes in pre-stress were found to directly contribute to the extent and patterns of backflow measured. Overall, slower insertion rates resulting in less damage and improved targeting. Future studies should focus on cellular level injury along needle tracks as well as the influence of different CED parameters, e.g. needle tip geometry and needle pathways, on damage and backflow.

Acknowledgments

We thank Dr. Svetlana Kantorovich, Tatiana Nobrega, K.N. Magdoom and Francisco Delgado for providing valuable discussions.

Author Contributions

Conceived and designed the experiments: FC PC MS. Performed the experiments: FC. Analyzed the data: FC PC MS. Contributed reagents/ materials/analysis tools: PC MS. Wrote the paper: FC MS.

References

1. Abbott NJ, Romero IA (1996) Transporting therapeutics across the blood-brain barrier. Molecular Medicine Today 2(3): 106–113.
2. Nicholson C (2001) Diffusion and related transport mechanisms in brain tissue. Reports on Progress in Physics 64(7): 815–884.
3. Bobo RH, Laske DW, Akbasak A, Morrison PF, Dedrick RL, et al. (1994) Convection-enhanced delivery of macromolecules in the brain. Proceedings of the National Academy of Sciences of the United States of America 91(6): 2076–2080.
4. Chen MY, Lonser RR, Morrison PF, Governale LS, Oldfield EH (1999) Variables affecting convection-enhanced delivery to the striatum: a systematic examination of rate of infusion, cannula size, infusate concentration, and tissue-cannula sealing time. Journal of Neurosurgery 90(2): 315–320.
5. Kunwar S, Prados MD, Chang SM, Berger MS, Lang FF, et al. (2007) Direct intracerebral delivery of cintredekin besudotox (IL13-PE38QQR) in recurrent malignant glioma: A report by the Cintredekin Besudotox Intraparenchymal Study Group. Journal of Clinical Oncology 25(7): 837–844.
6. Sampson JH, Pedain AG, Wembacher SE, Wstphal M, Kunmar S, et al. (2010) Poor drug distribution as a possible explanation for the results of the PRECISE trial Clinical article. Journal of Neurosurgery 113(2): 301–309.
7. Juratli TA, Schackert G, Krex D (2013) Current status of local therapy in malignant gliomas - A clinical review of three selected approaches. Pharmacology & Therapeutics 139(3): 341–358.
8. Sampson JH, Akabani G, Archer GE, Berger MS, Coleman RE, et al. (2008) Intracerebral infusion of an EGFR-targeted toxin in recurrent malignant brain tumors. Neuro-Oncology 10(3): 320–329.
9. Vogelbaum MA, Sampson JM, Kunwar S, Chang SM, Shaffrey M, et al. (2007) Convection-enhanced delivery of cintredekin besudotox (interleukin-13-PE38QQR) followed by radiation therapy with and without temozolomide in newly diagnosed malignant gliomas: phase 1 study of final safety results. Neurosurgery 61(5): 1031–1037.
10. Neeves KB, Lo CT, Foley CP, Saltzman WM, Olbricht WL (2006) Fabrication and characterization of microfluidic probes for convection enhanced drug delivery. Journal of Controlled Release 111(3): 252–262.
11. Vazquez LC, Hagel E, Willenberg BG, Dai W, Casanova F, et al. (2012) Polymer-coated cannulas for the reduction of backflow during intraparenchymal infusions. Journal of Materials Science-Materials in Medicine 23(8): 2037–2046.
12. Yin D, Forsayeth J, Bankiewicz KS (2010) Optimized cannula design and placement for convection-enhanced delivery in rat striatum. Journal of Neuroscience Methods 187(1): 46–51.
13. Astary GW, Kantorovich S, Carney PR, Mareci TH, Sarntinoranont M (2010) Regional convection-enhanced delivery of gadolinium-labeled albumin in the rat hippocampus in vivo. Journal of Neuroscience Methods 187(1): 129–137.
14. Kim JH, Astary GW, Nobrega TL, Kantorovich S, Carney PR, et al. (2012) Dynamic contrast-enhanced MRI of Gd-albumin delivery to the rat hippocampus in vivo by convection-enhanced delivery. Journal of Neuroscience Methods 209(1): 62–73.
15. Lonser RR, Walbridge S, Garmestani K, Butman JA, Walters HA, et al. (2002) Successful and safe perfusion of the primate brainstem: in vivo magnetic resonance imaging of macromolecular distribution during infusion. Journal of Neurosurgery 97(4): 905–913.
16. Szerlip NJ, Walbridge S, Yang L, Morrison PF, Degen JW, et al. (2007) Real-time imaging of convection-enhanced delivery of viruses and virus-sized particles. Journal of Neurosurgery 107(3): 560–567.
17. Varenika V, Dickinson P, Bringas J, LeCouteur R, Higgins R, et al. (2008) Detection of infusate leakage in the brain using real-time imaging of convection-enhanced delivery. Journal of Neurosurgery 109(5): 874–880.
18. Yin D, Valles FE, Fiandaca MS, Bringas J, Gimenez F, et al. (2011) Optimal region of the putamen for image-guided convection-enhanced delivery of therapeutics in human and non-human primates. Neuroimage 54: S196–S203.
19. Garcia JJ, Molano AB, Smith JH (2013) Description and Validation of a Finite Element Model of Backflow During Infusion Into a Brain Tissue Phantom. Journal of Computational and Nonlinear Dynamics DOI:10.1115/1.4007311).
20. Morrison PF, Chen MY, Chadwick RS, Lonser RR, Oldfield EH (1999) Focal delivery during direct infusion to brain: role of flow rate, catheter diameter, and tissue mechanics. American Journal of Physiology-Regulatory Integrative and Comparative Physiology 277(4): R1218–R1229.
21. Raghavan R, Mikaelian S, Brady M, Chen ZJ (2010) Fluid infusions from catheters into elastic tissue: I. Azimuthally symmetric backflow in homogeneous media. Physics in Medicine and Biology 55(1): 281–304.
22. Barzo P, Marmarou A, Fatouros P, Hayasaki K, Corwin F (1997) Contribution of vasogenic and cellular edema to traumatic brain swelling measured by diffusion-weighted imaging. Journal of Neurosurgery 87(6): 900–907.
23. White E, Bienemann A, Malone J, Megraw L, Bunnun C, et al. (2011) An evaluation of the relationships between catheter design and tissue mechanics in achieving high-flow convection-enhanced delivery. Journal of Neuroscience Methods 199(1): 87–97.
24. Prabhu SS, Broaddus WC, Gillies GT, Loudon WG, Chen ZJ, et al. (1998) Distribution of macromolecular dyes in brain using positive pressure infusion: A model for direct controlled delivery of therapeutic agents. Surgical Neurology 50(4): 367–375.
25. Casanova F, Carney PR, Sarntinoranont M (2012) Influence of needle insertion speed on backflow for convection-enhanced delivery. Journal of biomechanical engineering 134(4): 041006–041006.
26. Xu G, Bayly PV, Taber LA (2009) Residual stress in the adult mouse brain. Biomechanics and Modeling in Mechanobiology 8(4): 253–262.
27. Xu G, Kemp PS, Hwu JA, Beagley AM, Bayly PV, et al. (2010) Opening angles and material properties of the early embryonic chick brain. Journal of biomechanical engineering 132(1): 011005–011005.
28. Bjornsson CS, Oh SJ, Al-Loafahi YA, Lim YJ, Smith KL, et al. (2006) Effects of insertion conditions on tissue strain and vascular damage during neuroprosthetic device insertion. Journal of Neural Engineering 3(3): 196–207.
29. Rousche PJ, Normann RA (1992) A method for pneumatically inserting an array of penetrating electrodes in cortical tissue. Annals of Biomedical Engineering 20(4): 413–422.
30. Dubowitz DJ, Dyer EAW, Theilmann RJ, Buxton RB, Hopkins SR (2009) Early brain swelling in acute hypoxia. Journal of Applied Physiology 107(1): 244–252.
31. Qiao M, Latta P, Meng SZ, Tomanek B, Tuor UI (2004) Development of acute edema following cerebral hypoxia-ischemia in neonatal compared with juvenile rats using magnetic resonance imaging. Pediatric Research 55(1): 101–106.
32. Byard RW, Gabrielian L, Helps SC, Thornton E, Vink R (2012) Further Investigations into the Speed of Cerebral Swelling Following Blunt Cranial Trauma. Journal of Forensic Sciences 57(4): 973–975.
33. Haar PJ, Broaddus WC, Chen ZJ, Fatouros PP, Gillies GT, et al. (2010) Quantification of convection-enhanced delivery to the ischemic brain. Physiological Measurement 31(9): 1075–1089.
34. Lieberman DM, Laske DW, Morrison PF, Bankiewicz KS, Oldfield EH (1995) Convection-enhanced distribution of large macromolecules in gray-matter during interstitial drug infusion. Journal of Neurosurgery 82(6): 1021–1029.
35. Neeves KB, Sawyer AJ, Foley CP, Saltzman WM, Olbricht WL (2007) Dilation and degradation of the brain extracellular matrix enhances penetration of infused polymer nanoparticles. Brain Research 1180: 121–132.
36. Sezgin M, Sankur B (2004) Survey over image thresholding techniques and quantitative performance evaluation. Journal of Electronic Imaging 13(1): 146–168.
37. Lee SJ, Sun J, Flint JJ, Guo S, Xie HK, et al. (2011) Optically based-indentation technique for acute rat brain tissue slices and thin biomaterials. Journal of Biomedical Materials Research Part B-Applied Biomaterials 97B(1): 84–95.
38. Libertiaux V, Pascon F, Cescotto S (2011) Experimental verification of brain tissue incompressibility using digital image correlation. Journal of the Mechanical Behavior of Biomedical Materials 4(7): 1177–1185.
39. Mase GT, Mase GE (1999) Continuum Mechanics for Engineers. 2nd ed. New York: CRC Press.
40. Elkin BS, Ilankovan AI, Morrison B (2011) A Detailed Viscoelastic Characterization of the P17 and Adult Rat Brain. Journal of Neurotrauma 28(11): 2235–2244.
41. Paxinos G, Watson C (1989) The Rat Brain in Sterotaxic Coordinates. San Diego, CA: Academic Press.
42. Maikala RV (2010) Modified Beer's Law - historical perspectives and relevance in near-infrared monitoring of optical properties of human tissue. International Journal of Industrial Ergonomics 40(2): 125–134.
43. Andrei A, Welkenhuysen M, Nuttin B, Eberle W (2012) A response surface model predicting the in vivo insertion behavior of micromachined neural implants. J Neural Eng 9(1): 016005.
44. Welkenhuysen M, Andrei A, Ameye L, Eberle W, Nuttin B (2011) Effect of Insertion Speed on Tissue Response and Insertion Mechanics of a Chronically Implanted Silicon-Based Neural Probe. Ieee Transactions on Biomedical Engineering 58(11): 3250–3259.
45. Welsh JP, Schwarz C (1998) Multielectrode recording from the cerebellum. Methods for Neural Ensemble Recordings. CRC Press: Boca Raton.

46. Metz H, McElhane J, Ommaya AK (1970) A comparision of elasticity of live, dead, and fixed brain tissue. Journal of Biomechanics 3(4): 453–458.
47. Yamane K, Shima T, Okada Y, Takeda T, Uozumi T (1994) Acute brain-swelling in cerebral embolization model of rats 1: Epidural pressure monitoring. Surgical Neurology 41(6): 477–481.
48. Quester R, Schroder R (1997) The shrinkage of the human brain stem during formalin fixation and embedding in paraffin. Journal of Neuroscience Methods 75(1): 81–89.
49. Sarntinoranont M, Banerjee RK, Lonser RR, Morrison PF (2003) A computational model of direct interstitial infusion of macromolecules into the spinal cord. Annals of Biomedical Engineering 31(4): 448–461.
50. Franceschini G, Bigoni D, Regitnig P, Holzapfel GA (2006) Brain tissue deforms similarly to filled elastomers and follows consolidation theory. Journal of the Mechanics and Physics of Solids 54(12): 2592–2620.
51. Tsoga A, Kasapis S, Richardson RK (1999) The rubber-to-glass transition in high sugar agarose systems. Biopolymers 49(4): 267–275.
52. Krauze MT, Saito R, Noble C, Tamas M, Bringas J, et al. (2005) Reflux-free cannula for convection-enhanced high-speed delivery of therapeutic agents - Technical note. J Neurosurg 103(5): 923–929.
53. Rosenbluth KH, Luz M, Mohr E, Mittermeyer S, Bringas J, et al. (2011) Design of an in-dwelling cannula for convection-enhanced delivery. Journal of Neuroscience Methods 196(1): 118–123.
54. Oh S, Odland R, Wilson SR, Kroeger KM, Liu C, et al. (2007) Improved distribution of small molecules and viral vectors in the murine brain using a hollow fiber catheter. Journal of Neurosurgery 107(3): 568–577.

10

MRI-Based Computational Model of Heterogeneous Tracer Transport following Local Infusion into a Mouse Hind Limb Tumor

Kulam Najmudeen Magdoom[1], Gregory L. Pishko[1], Lori Rice[2], Chris Pampo[2], Dietmar W. Siemann[2], Malisa Sarntinoranont[1]*

1 Department of Mechanical and Aerospace Engineering, University of Florida, Gainesville, Florida, United States of America, 2 Department of Radiation Oncology, University of Florida, Gainesville, Florida, United States of America

Abstract

Systemic drug delivery to solid tumors involving macromolecular therapeutic agents is challenging for many reasons. Amongst them is their chaotic microvasculature which often leads to inadequate and uneven uptake of the drug. Localized drug delivery can circumvent such obstacles and convection-enhanced delivery (CED) - controlled infusion of the drug directly into the tissue - has emerged as a promising delivery method for distributing macromolecules over larger tissue volumes. In this study, a three-dimensional MR image-based computational porous media transport model accounting for realistic anatomical geometry and tumor leakiness was developed for predicting the interstitial flow field and distribution of albumin tracer following CED into the hind-limb tumor (KHT sarcoma) in a mouse. Sensitivity of the model to changes in infusion flow rate, catheter placement and tissue hydraulic conductivity were investigated. The model predictions suggest that 1) tracer distribution is asymmetric due to heterogeneous porosity; 2) tracer distribution volume varies linearly with infusion volume within the whole leg, and exponentially within the tumor reaching a maximum steady-state value; 3) infusion at the center of the tumor with high flow rates leads to maximum tracer coverage in the tumor with minimal leakage outside; and 4) increasing the tissue hydraulic conductivity lowers the tumor interstitial fluid pressure and decreases the tracer distribution volume within the whole leg and tumor. The model thus predicts that the interstitial fluid flow and drug transport is sensitive to porosity and changes in extracellular space. This image-based model thus serves as a potential tool for exploring the effects of transport heterogeneity in tumors.

Editor: Timothy W. Secomb, University of Arizona, United States of America

Funding: This research was partly funded by grants from the National Institutes of Health (Grant Nos. R21NS05270 and R01NS063360; http://www.nih.gov/) and National Cancer Institute (Public Health Service Grant CA084408; http://www.cancer.gov/). The funders had no role in study design, data collection and analysis, decision to publish, or preparation of the manuscript.

Competing Interests: The authors have declared that no competing interests exist.

* E-mail: msarnt@ufl.edu

Introduction

Cancer treatments based on systemic delivery of therapeutic agents are often hindered due to poor and uneven uptake of drugs within tumors. The unique characteristics of the tumor microenvironment which includes irregular microvasculature and high interstitial fluid pressure (IFP) are known to affect the efficacy of anti-cancer treatments such as chemotherapy. The tumor microvasculature characterized by fenestrated, disorganized vessels, necrotic regions and avascular areas [1–3] leads to heterogeneous extravasation of therapeutic agents [4], while the high IFP may cause inefficient uptake due to decreased transcapillary transport [5].

In recent years, localized drug delivery has emerged as a plausible alternative to systemic delivery for transporting macromolecular therapeutic agents to the tumors [6–11]. By directly injecting into the tumor, this circumvents previously mentioned vascular and interstitial barriers and also reduces side-effects associated with systemic exposure. Amongst the available techniques, convection-enhanced delivery (CED) appears promising because at a given time it can achieve larger distribution volumes than by diffusion alone [12,13]. In CED, an infusion pump delivers the drug at constant flow rate or pressure thereby creating extracellular fluid flow in tissue, to deliver and distribute macromolecules over larger volumes.

Since its advent, CED has been used for delivery of a wide range of substances including nanoparticles [14], liposomes [6,15], cytotoxins [16] and viruses [17,18]. Experimental studies on CED of liposomes into brain tumors (glioma) in rats are encouraging; it was found that the technique effectively distributed liposomes in the tumor and the surrounding normal tissue [6]. On the other hand, a broad heterogeneous distribution was reported to have resulted from CED of cytotoxins into human gliomas [16]. Such an asymmetric distribution was also reported by Boucher and his colleagues in their study with mice involving intratumoral infusion of Evans blue-albumin into sarcoma HSTS 26T [19]. It should however be noted that spherically symmetric distributions for colon adenocarcinoma LS174T were also reported in their study.

Computational modeling of CED has gained attention recently, with pre-clinical and clinical research suggesting the importance of optimization of CED [20,21]. Software taking into account individual characteristics of a patient's anatomy and pathophysiology for the initial plan of CED is likely to be helpful in deciding catheter placement for optimum distribution volume [20]. However, many current tumor models assume theoretical tumor microvasculature (network based) and simplified tumor geometries [22–27]. Eventhough, such models might have the potential to incorporate individual capillary vessels, most of current ones are theoretical and often lack complete transport physics, since accurately reconstructing the entire capillary network and numerically solving for flow physics is computationally intensive. For example, Smith and Humphrey developed a theoretical model for infusions in a spherical tumor with a necrotic core and showed that the flow field was very sensitive to the ratio of vascular conductivity and hydraulic conductivity, and infusion close to the tumor was retarded by the outward flow [22]. Our group has been developing image-based computational porous media models incorporating realistic geometries and spatially-varying transport properties obtained through MRI, for predicting tracer distributions in different tissues [28–32]. For tumors in particular, our group developed a framework which accounts for the realistic tumor leakiness by using dynamic contrast enhanced (DCE)-MRI data to estimate the spatial variation of transport properties (rate transfer constant between plasma and extracellular space, K^{trans} and porosity, ϕ) which were included in a porous media model to solve for interstitial fluid flow and tracer transport using computational fluid dynamics techniques [30–32].

In this study, a DCE-MRI-based computational model was developed for predicting albumin tracer distribution following CED in the lower limb of a mouse (C3H) inoculated with murine sarcoma cells (KHT), as opposed to systemic delivery which was modeled in our previous studies. Direct injections into the interstitial space have the potential to greatly alter the interstitial fluid pressure and velocity fields, and it is the goal of this study to investigate the role of tissue heterogeneity on CED into tumors. Such a model could potentially help assess the efficacy of CED in tumors and provide better understanding of the biophysical IFP and interstitial fluid velocity (IFV) changes due to CED, which are otherwise difficult to measure experimentally. Also DCE-MRI is likely to improve drug efflux estimates of current software models [33], our model being the first one to use DCE-MRI derived parameters (K^{trans} and porosity) to predict CED distributions. Simulations were carried out based on a voxelized modeling approach developed by our group [28,29,32]. In this approach, heterogeneous tissue properties (i.e. K^{trans} and porosity) and anatomical boundaries are assigned from MRI data. These properties are then incorporated into a porous media transport model to predict CED of tracers. This methodology has been previously used by our group to model CED in spinal cord and brain tissues [28,29] and systemic delivery in tumors [31,32]. It should however be noted that the physics, governing equations and resulting physiological flows of the current problem are different. For example, the tumor microenvironment differs significantly from that of the brain due to its aforementioned chaotic vasculature and high IFP. Also porosity dependent formulations for hydraulic conductivity and tracer diffusivity were incorporated in this model, which were not present in our previous studies.

Parameter analysis was performed to study the effects of infusion flow rate, catheter placement and spatially-varying tissue hydraulic conductivity on interstitial fluid flow and albumin tracer transport. This was done to understand the sensitivity of CED distribution to these variables. The flow rate was varied since the capillary fluid exchange is pressure dependent. Catheter placement is also known to be important in CED [13]; studies involving infusions at different locations in the brain have revealed the presence of a optimal site for achieving maximum distribution volumes within a targeted region [29,34]. The tissue hydraulic conductivity, a measure of fluid conductance through the tissue, was also varied because of its direct influence on tumor IFP and convective flow fields in intratumoral infusions. Higher values of hydraulic conductivity are thought to reduce tumor IFP thereby increasing the filtration of fluids and extravasation of macromolecules [19].

Materials and Methods

Mathematical Model

The model requires two components; first, spatially-varying transport properties of the KHT murine sarcoma were estimated using DCE-MRI data following bolus tail vein injection of MR visible tracer gadolinium-diethylene-triamine penta-acetic acid (Gd-DTPA, MW ≈590 Da) in the mice. The MR experimental data presented in [31] was used in this study. DCE-MRI-derived data was used to determine Gd-DTPA concentration in tissue, rate transfer constant (K^{trans}) and porosity (ϕ) maps as in [31]. Briefly, tracer concentration was calculated based on MR signal enhancement due to the tracer, and the resulting concentration was fitted to the following 2-compartment model (plasma and tissue compartments) to obtain K^{trans} and porosity,

$$\frac{dC_t^{\text{MR}}}{dt} = K^{\text{trans}} C_p - \frac{K^{\text{trans}}}{\phi} C_t^{\text{MR}} \tag{1}$$

where C_t^{MR} is the MR derived tracer concentration in the tissue, C_p is the tracer concentration in the blood plasma approximated using an arterial input function (AIF) and t is time. Animal experiments were performed within the principles of the Guide for the Care and Use of Laboratory Animals and approved by the University of Florida Institutional Animal Care and Use Committee (IACUC).

The second part of the study involves incorporating the above calculated variable transport properties into a computational porous media model for predicting extracellular flow and transport following CED, i.e. direct infusion into the tumor. The CED technique along with a K^{trans} and ϕ map are shown in Figure 1, and the modeling methods are summarized in the flow chart shown in Figure 2.

The tissue continuum was modeled as a porous media and the governing equations were solved at each voxel after assigning their respective K^{trans} and ϕ values. For CED, the continuity equation is given by,

$$\nabla.(\phi v^f) = \frac{Q}{\forall_{inf}} \quad \text{At the infusion site} \tag{2a}$$

$$= \frac{K^{\text{trans}}}{\overline{K^{\text{trans}}}} \frac{J_V}{V} - L_{p,ly} \frac{S_L}{V}(p - p_L) \tag{2b}$$

At all other sites in tumor and host tissue

where v^f is the fluid phase velocity (convection velocity in the porous medium), Q is the CED infusion flow rate of albumin infusate, $\forall_{inf}$ is the volume of the direct infusion voxel, $\overline{K^{\text{trans}}}$ is the average value of K^{trans} in host and tumor tissue voxels, $L_{p,ly}$ is lymphatic vessel permeability, S_L/V is the lymphatic vessel surface area per unit volume, p is the IFP and p_L is pressure in the

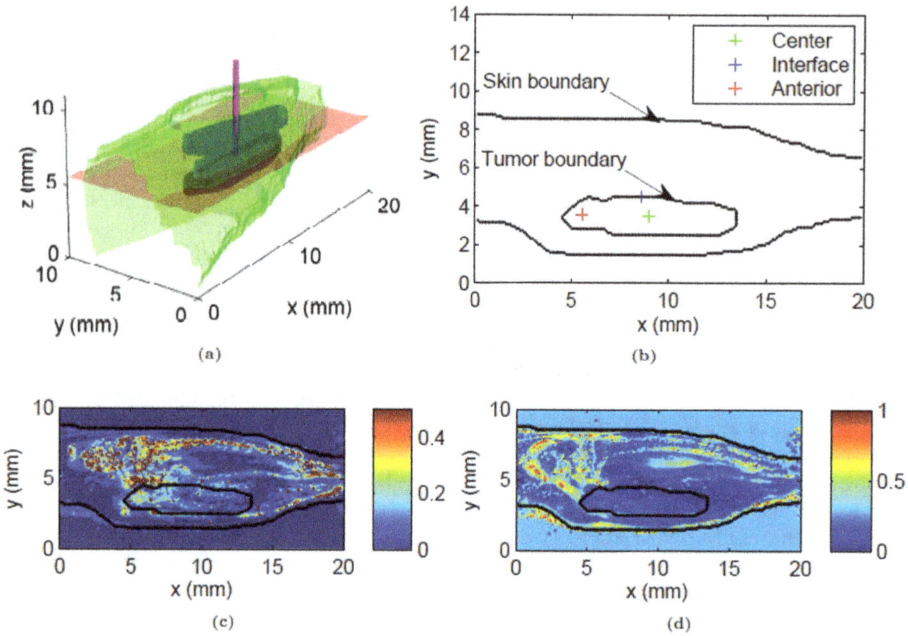

Figure 1. A schematic of the problem along with a sample of the analyzed experimental data. (a) Depiction of baseline CED tumor simulation of tracer spread in hind limb, (b) infusion sites at the mid-plane used in the sensitivity analysis, (c) spatial maps of K^{trans} (min^{-1}) and (d) porosity at the mid-plane calculated from DCE-MRI data. In (a) the skin boundary is shown in green, tumor boundary in blue, tumor midplane in red and infusion cannula in magenta. The infusion cannula is shown for illustration purpose only.

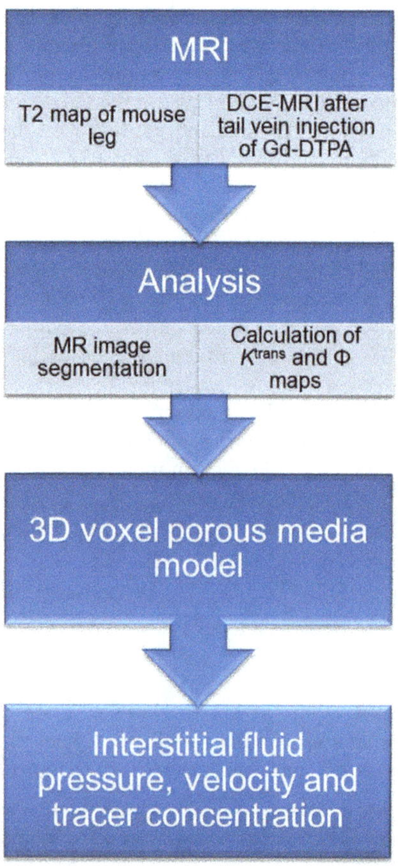

Figure 2. Flow diagram depicting various steps involved in the model.

lymphatic vessels which was set to zero. It should be noted that functional lymphatics were assumed only for normal host tissue as tumors lack functional lymphatics ($L_{p,ly}=0$) [5]. J_V/V is the filtration rate of plasma per unit volume of tissue into the interstitial space which is given by Starling's law as follows [35],

$$\frac{J_V}{V} = L_p \frac{S}{V}(p_v - p - \sigma_T(\pi_v - \pi_i)) \qquad (3)$$

where L_p is the permeability of the microvascular wall, S/V is the blood vessel surface area per unit volume, p_v is the vascular fluid pressure, σ_T is the osmotic reflection coefficient for plasma proteins, π_v, π_i are the osmotic pressures of the plasma and interstitial fluid, respectively.

In the computational fluid dynamics model, properties are assigned on a voxel-by-voxel basis. For voxels that are not infused with albumin infusate, the first term on the right side of the continuity equation (Equation 3) represents the transvascular fluid flux across the microvascular wall per unit volume of the tissue. Assuming similar leakiness patterns for tracer and plasma, this term was scaled by the normalized K^{trans} ($\overline{K^{\text{trans}}}$) to account for leakiness heterogeneity in the model. The second term accounts for the lymphatic drainage from interstitial space per unit volume of tissue. It should be noted that the IFV in the model is given by ϕv^f.

For a porous medium, the momentum equation is given by Darcy's law,

$$\phi v^f = -\text{K}(\mathbf{x})\nabla p \qquad (4)$$

where $\mathbf{x}$ is the position vector, and K is the hydraulic conductivity which is likely to be heterogeneous in tumors and can vary with local changes in porosity of tissues. The following relation, known to predict porosity-dependent variations in hydraulic conductivity for agarose gels and articular cartilage [36], was used

$$\mathrm{K}(\mathbf{x}) = a\left(\frac{\phi(\mathbf{x})}{1-\phi(\mathbf{x})}\right)^m \tag{5a}$$

$$a = \bar{K}\left(\frac{1-\bar{\phi}}{\bar{\phi}}\right)^m \tag{5b}$$

where $\bar{K}, \bar{\phi}$ are the average tissue hydraulic conductivity and porosity for tumor or host tissues respectively, and m is an empirical exponent which characterizes the sensitivity of hydraulic conductivity to porosity. The scaling factor, a in the relation was calculated based on matching the average tissue hydraulic conductivity with average porosity as shown in Equation 5b.

Albumin tracer transport during CED was modeled using the following convection and diffusion equation with no tissue sources or sinks ($\phi(\mathbf{x})$ replaced by ϕ for simplicity), with albumin assumed not to be passively cleared through capillaries within the simulated time points (up to 1 hr).

$$\frac{\partial(\phi C_t)}{\partial t} + \nabla\cdot(\phi v^f C_t) - \nabla^T\cdot(\phi \mathrm{D}_{\mathrm{eff}}(\mathbf{x})\cdot\nabla C_t) = 0 \tag{6}$$

where C_t is the concentration of tracer in the tissue. The expression for the effective diffusivity tensor ($\mathrm{D}_{\mathrm{eff}}$) was based on the following empirical relation for diffusion in porous media [37],

$$\mathrm{D}_{\mathrm{eff}}(\mathbf{x}) = D_{\mathrm{free}}\phi^n(\mathbf{x})\mathrm{I} \tag{7}$$

where D_{free} is the self-diffusion coefficient of albumin in water, n is an empirical exponent set to 1 and I is the Kronecker tensor. The concentration was normalized using the following relation,

$$\hat{C} = \frac{C_t}{C_{(t,i)}\phi_i} \tag{8}$$

where $C_{(t,i)}$ and ϕ_i are the infusate concentration and porosity at the infused voxel, respectively. The values of parameters used in the computational model are listed in Table 1.

MR images also consisted of voxels present outside the mouse which belong neither to tumor or host tissue, i.e. exterior voxels corresponding to surrounding air. In these voxels, the source term for the continuity equation and the diffusivity were set to zero.

Computational Method

The computational method is identical to the one presented in [32]. Briefly, the continuity, momentum and albumin tracer transport equations were solved using the computational fluid dynamics software package, FLUENT (version 12.0.16, ANSYS, Inc., Canonsburg, PA). For the 3D computational tissue model, a rectangular volume ($20\times10\times9$ mm^3) enclosing the tumor was created and meshed with quadrilateral elements (voxels) of size equal to the MRI resolution ($0.104\times0.104\times1$ mm^3) using the meshing software (GAMBIT, Fluent, Lebanon, NH) with one-to-one mapping between the computational fluid dynamics mesh and MR data. Infusion was carried out at the center of the tumor with a tissue hydraulic conductivity parameter, $m=2$ at a flow rate of 0.3 µL/min (baseline case). The value of $m=2$ is the baseline value that was used for both tumor and normal tissue. This value was chosen to closely resemble the Carman-Kozeny equation [38] which has been earlier used to describe the hydraulic permeability in tumors [39]. Although the same value of m was used for both the tumor and normal tissue, it should be noted that the constant a in the relation is different and chosen based on the values reported in literature [31].

Parameter Analysis

The effects of changing the baseline simulation variables (flow rate, catheter placement and value of m) on interstitial flow field and tracer transport were studied separately. The simulation was carried out with two additional flow rates (1 and 3 µL/min) and infusion sites : 1) tumor-host tissue interface and 2) anterior end of the tumor (Figure 1b). The reason for choosing a site at the tumor-host tissue interface was because of the presence of higher convective currents in that region due to the steep decreases in IFP which could result in higher convective velocity. The choice of an infusion site at the anterior end and center of the tumor was to study the distribution at various positions inside the tumor. The effect of changing the tissue hydraulic conductivity was achieved by varying its sensitivity to heterogeneous porosity using the empirical exponent (m). Two additional values of $m=5$ and 10

Table 1. Tissue and vascular parameters used in simulations.

Variable	Description	Value	References
L_p (m/Pa.s)	Vessel permeability	2×10^{-11t}; 3×10^{-12n};	[31]
S/V (m^{-1})	Microvascular surface area per unit volume	20000^t; 7000^n	[49]
$L_{p,ly}S_L/V$ (Pa^{-1}s^{-1})	Lymphatic filtration coefficient	1×10^{-7}	[31]
K_0 (m^2/Pa.s)	Baseline hydraulic conductivity	1.9×10^{-12t}; 3.8×10^{-13n}	[31]
		7.7×10^{-15e}	
p_v (Pa)	Microvascular pressure	2300	[31]
π_i (Pa)	Osmotic pressure in interstitial space	3230^t;1330^n	[31]
π_v (Pa)	Osmotic pressure in microvasculature	2670	[31]
σ_T (Pa)	Average osmotic reflection coefficient for plasma	0.82^t; 0.91^n	[31]
D_{free} (m^2/s)	Self diffusion coefficient of albumin	5.8×10^{-11}	[50]

^{t}- tumor,
^{n}- normal tissue,
^{e}- exterior.

were used to simulate the effect of increased tissue hydaulic conductivity. Vessel permeability and diffusivity (varying n) were not included in the sensitivity analysis based on the results of our previous study on transport in tumors [31], where variations in these parameters did not greatly influence tracer transport.

Infusion simulations were carried out up to $t = 1$ hr and the interstitial distribution of albumin tracer was quantified at intermittent time points, $t = 15$ and 60 mins. Initial conditions for tracer transport assumed no tracer in the tissue, $\hat{C}=0$, except at the infusion site which is one voxel ($0.104 \times 0.104 \times 1\ mm^3$). At this site it was set to a normalized value of 1 at all the times during the transport simulation through an user-defined function. The distribution volume was calculated as the volume occupied by voxels having an albumin concentration greater than 15% of the maximum concentration ($\hat{C}>0.15$). A zero fluid pressure condition, $p=0$, was applied along the cut ends of the tissue volume, and the remaining outer boundaries of the geometry were assigned as a wall boundary, flux = 0. The impermeability condition along the skin boundary was achieved by assigning hydraulic conductivity two orders of magnitude lower than the normal tissue, in the exterior voxels. The assignment of low hydraulic conductivity creates a material that is less penetrable and resistant to fluid motion. For the chosen value of hydraulic conductivity at the exterior voxels, the maximum mean velocity at the skin boundary for all the simulations was calculated to be close to zero (0.02 μm/s).

Results

Baseline case

The predicted IFP inside the tumor was elevated independent of CED as shown in [32]. With CED at 0.3 μL/min, the pressure at the infusion site was increased by approximately 0.33 kPa (≈21% increase) in addition to the overall elevation inside the tumor as shown in the contour plot (Figure 3a). CED created additional pressure gradients (≈0.65 kPa/mm along the infusion plane) around the infusion site which were absent with systemic delivery. There was also significant pressure gradients at the anterior edge of the tumor-host tissue interface (≈0.67 kPa/mm) which was also observed without CED [32]. It should be noted that the pressure gradient outside the skin does not contribute to the extracellular fluid flow due to the very low hydraulic conductivity assigned in those voxels.

The convective velocity is shown in Figure 3b. The predicted velocity field was heterogeneous with maximum velocity near the infusion site (35 μm/s). There were also significant outwardly-directed flows at the tumor-host tissue interface especially near the anterior end of the tumor (≈0.45–3.2 μm/s) which was also observed with systemic delivery [32]. Thus CED has resulted in alterations of endogenous flows closer to the infusion site to a far larger magnitude.

Contours of normalized albumin concentration at various time points following CED infusion are shown in Figures 4a & 4b. Albumin distribution around the infusion site was asymmetric for all the times simulated with high concentration inside the tumor. This is in contrast to systemic delivery [31,32] where the tracer distribution was heterogeneous with high concentration regions outside the tumor. The effect of the skin boundary near the tumor on the distribution pattern was evident at later time points, with gradually increasing tracer accumulation along the skin boundary. Iso-surfaces of the distribution volume at intermittent time points, shown in Figures 4c & 4d, depict the evolution of the concentration profile with time. They show the non-uniform nature of the distribution and the tangential flux of albumin tracer along the skin boundary near the tumor. For the chosen threshold value, albumin was distributed to approximately 48% of the tumor volume after one hour of infusion at 0.3 μL/min. The variation of distribution volume (V_d) with infusion volume (V_i) within the whole leg and tumor, in particular is shown in Figure 5. As expected, plots show a linear relationship between distribution volume and infusion volume for the whole leg; however, a more exponential variation was observed within the tumor and the resultant distribution volume reached a maximum steady-state value in this targeted tumor region (≈48%).

Parameter Analysis

With higher infusion flow rates of 1 and 3 μL/min, IFP close to the infusion site increased by approximately 58% and 226% from the baseline value, respectively (Figures 6a & 6b). With increasing flow rates, convective velocity became orders of magnitude higher inside the tumor than outside (Figures 6c & 6d). The peak fluid velocity values predicted close to the infusion site increased by approximately 228% and 900% from the baseline for infusion flow rates of 1 and 3 μL/min, respectively. These changes were reflected in the predicted tracer distribution in the tissue shown as isosurfaces in Figures 6e & 6f. Increasing the flow rate tended to confine the tracer more within the tumor and reduced spread into adjacent normal tissue. It also reduced the tangential flux of the tracer along the skin boundary close to the tumor. As expected, the distribution volume within the whole leg increased linearly with the infusion volume. However for a given infusion volume, the distribution volume within the whole leg decreased with increasing flow rates (Figure 7a). Within the tumor, higher flow rates resulted in more coverage (Figure 7b) with 85% of the tumor being covered by the tracer infused at a rate of 1 μL/min, and 87% with 3 μL/min for the same amount of infusion volume.

The effect of catheter placement on albumin distribution is shown in Figures 8a & 8b. Asymmetric distributions were observed

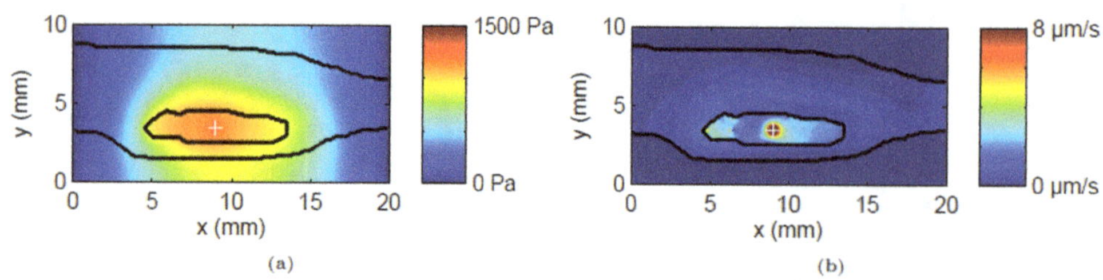

Figure 3. Predicted flow field with local infusion (0.3 μL/min) at the center of the tumor. The interstitial fluid pressure (IFP) and convective fluid velocity within the plane of infusion is shown by its contours (a & b respecively). Tumor and skin boundaries are overlaid on the contours; the infusion site is shown by a plus sign.

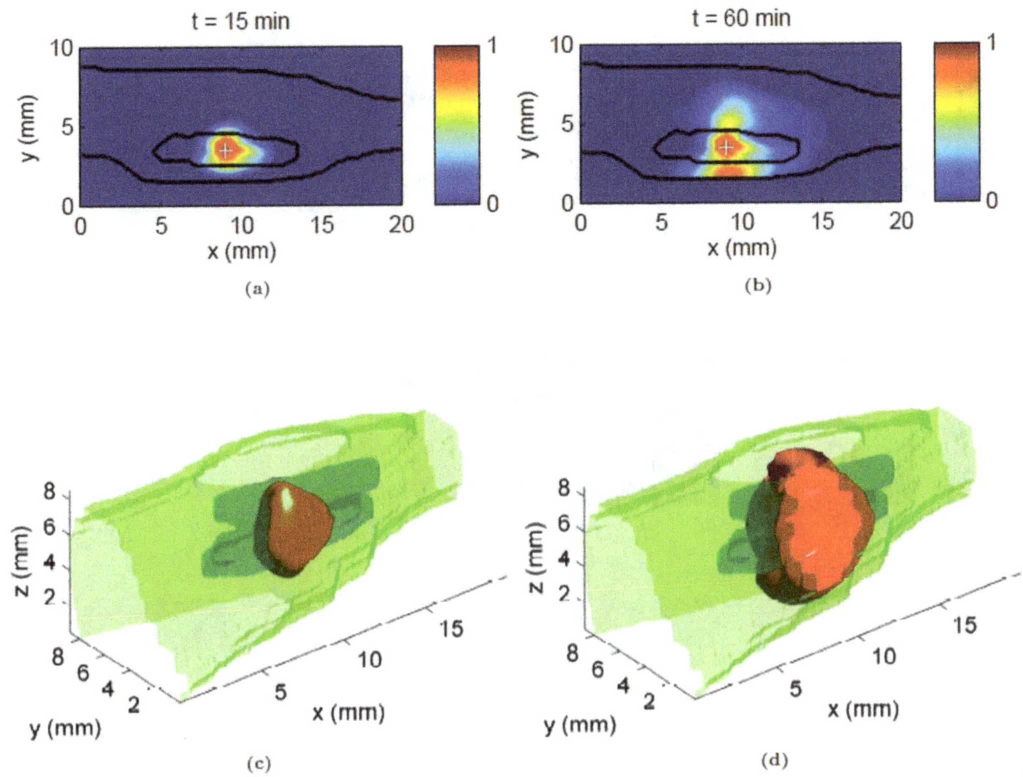

Figure 4. Concentration profile following CED of albumin infusate (0.3 μL/min) at the center of the tumor. (a & b) Normalized albumin tracer concentration contours within the infusion plane at $t = 15$ and 60 min respectively. Tumor and skin boundaries are overlaid on the contours; the infusion site is designated by a plus sign. (c & d) Predicted 3D distributed volume at $t = 15$ and 60 min respectively, shown by an iso-surface of the distribution volume (threshold, $\hat{C} = 0.15$). Visible boundaries are for tumor (blue), skin (green) and distribution volume (red).

for infusions at different locations: tumor-host tissue interface and anterior end of the tumor. Infusion at the interface and anterior end of the leg tended to distribute albumin dorsally and anteriorly within the leg, respectively. For the whole leg, tracer spread again exhibited a linear relation between V_d and V_i, with highest distribution volume for infusion at the tumor center (Figure 8c). Within the tumor, the V_d variation with V_i was also approximately exponential with infusion at the tumor center covering the maximum volume (≈48%) while infusion at the anterior end covered less of the tumor, approximately 11% (Figure 8d).

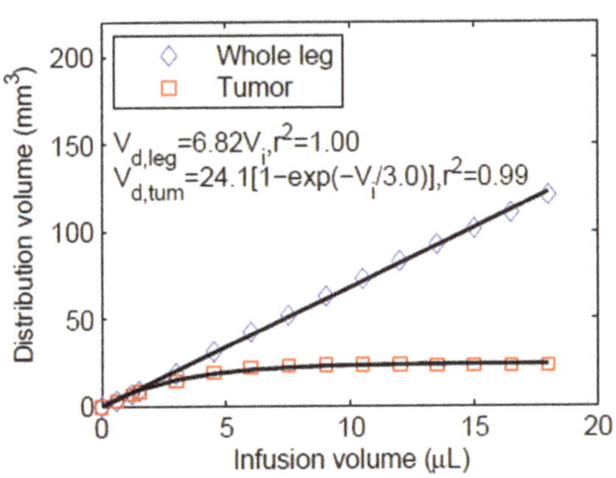

Figure 5. Tracer distribution volumes in tissue for varying infusion volume within the whole leg (tumor and surrounding tissue) and tumor only, following CED at 0.3 μL/min. Distribution volume dependence on infusion volume was fit to linear (whole leg) and exponential (tumor only) models.

For varying hydraulic conductivity sensitivity ($m = 5$ and 10), the model predicted elevated IFP patterns inside the tumor similar to the baseline results albeit with different peak pressure values (Figures 9a & 9b). The simulation results indicated a 50 and 89% reduction in the peak IFP from the baseline value for $m = 5$ and 10, respectively. The convection velocity became more heterogeneous with increasing m (Figures 9c & 9d). The increase in m advected fluid away from the tumor particularly through the anterior end.

Changes in the tracer distribution over time at different values of m are shown in Figures 9e & 9f. Convective effects influenced the distribution pattern with tracer being transported away from the tumor, particularly towards the anterior cut end of the hind limb. This was more apparent for higher values of m. The distribution volume varied linearly with the infusion volume for the whole leg, and exponentially within the tumor for both the values of m (Figure 10). With larger values of m, there was also a reduction in the final distribution volume from baseline values (approximately by 2.5 and 2.15% with $m = 5$, and 9 and 37% with $m = 10$ for the whole leg and tumor, respectively) due to exit of tracer at cut ends. Within the tumor, the distribution volume tended to reach a steady-state value more rapidly with increasing values of m (Figure 10b). One hour of infusion at 0.3 μL/min and $m = 5$ resulted in coverage of approximately 47% of the tumor volume. Whereas for $m = 10$, approximately 30% of the tumor volume was covered.

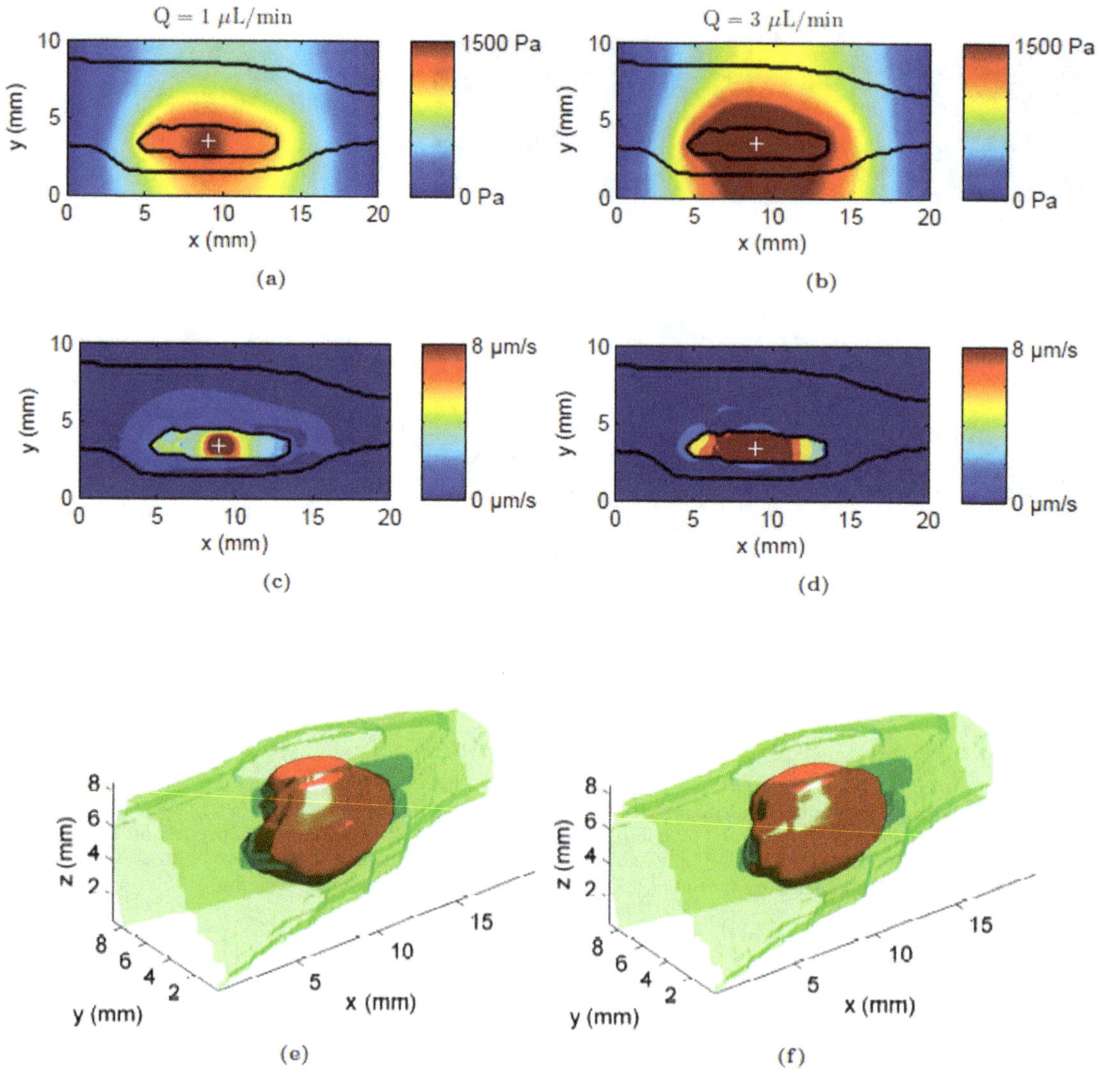

Figure 6. Flow field and tracer distribution following CED of albumin tracer at the center of the tumor for two different flow rates: 1 μL/min and 3 μL/min. (a & b) Interstitial fluid pressure (IFP) contours for $Q=1\&3$ μL/min respectively, and (c & d) convective fluid velocity contours at the infusion plane for $Q=1\&3$ μL/min respectively. Tumor and skin boundaries are overlaid on the contours; the infusion site is designated by a plus sign. (e & f) Predicted 3D tracer distribution volume at the end of infusion (1 hr) shown by an iso-surface of the distribution volume threshold ($\hat{C}=0.15$) for $Q=1\&3$ μL/min respectively. Visible boundaries are for tumor (blue), skin (green) and distribution volume (red).

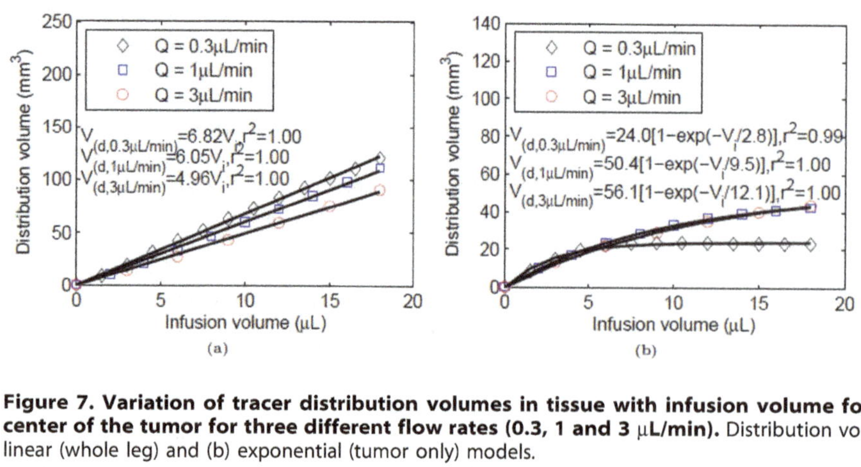

Figure 7. Variation of tracer distribution volumes in tissue with infusion volume for the whole leg and tumor following CED at center of the tumor for three different flow rates (0.3, 1 and 3 μL/min). Distribution volume dependence on infusion volume was fit to (a) linear (whole leg) and (b) exponential (tumor only) models.

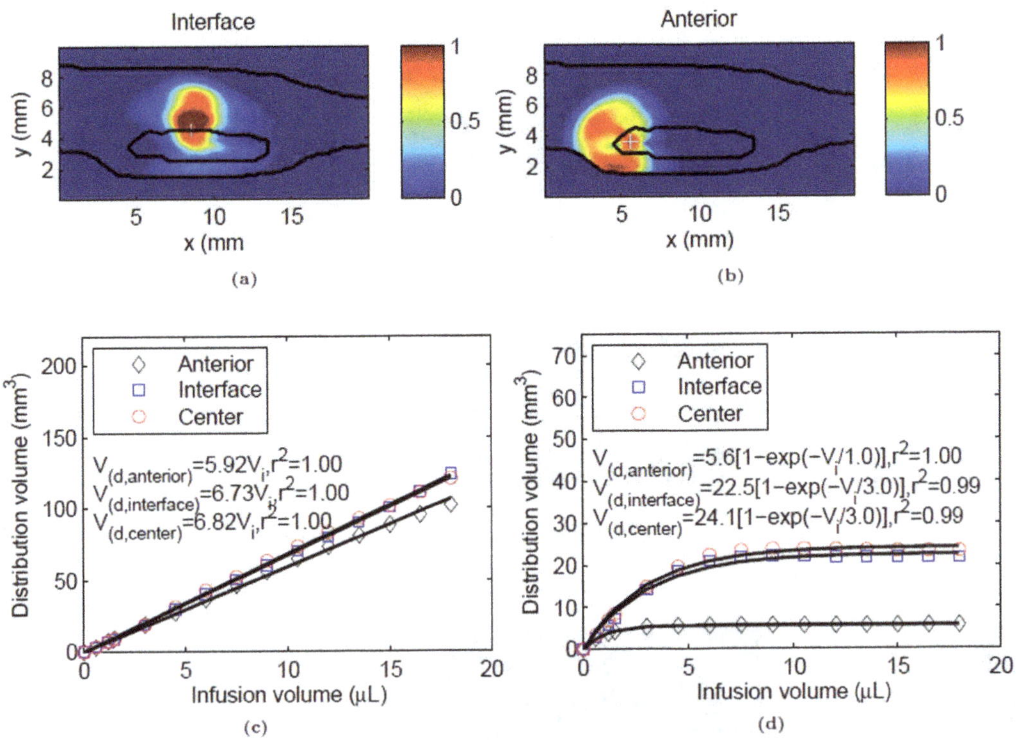

Figure 8. Tracer distribution following CED of albumin (0.3 μL/min) at the tumor-host tissue interface and anterior end of tumor. (a & b) Normalized tracer concentration contours in the infusion plane at the end of infusion (1 hr) in the tumor-host tissue interface and anterior end of tumor respectively. Tumor and skin boundaries are overlaid on the contours, and the infusion site is shown by a plus sign. Variation of tracer distribution volumes in tissue with infusion volume for the (c) whole leg and (d) tumor. Distribution volume dependence on infusion volume was fit to linear (whole leg) and exponential (tumor only) models.

Discussion

A MR image-based computational model (voxelized model) for predicting distribution of a macro-molecular protein tracer following CED in a mouse tumor was developed. The key advancement and contribution is that our model incorporates vasculature as a realistic and heterogeneous entity, which is novel to CED models. By non-invasively probing the vasculature of the tumor and surrounding area, and incorporating heterogeneous transport into our model we have made some interesting discoveries. 1) Penetration of tracer/drug into surrounding tissue was found to be highly dependent on flow rate, tissue boundaries, vascular leakiness and tissue lymphatic clearance which slowed interstitial flows. The predicted tracer distribution was asymmetric, and increasingly confined within the tumor with increasing infusion flow rate. Such distributions can not be captured with spherical tumor models; 2) Our results also make clear and stress the interconnectivity between hydraulic conductivity, vascular leakiness, and tumor interstitial fluid pressure, the delicate balancing act of treatments that target these mechanisms, and the consequences of doing so in relation to CED. The model predicts lower tumor interstitial fluid pressure and tracer distribution volume for increasing the tissue hydraulic conductivity. Thus, if CED is to be used in conjunction with a therapy aimed at lowering IFP, then it may be best to do so after the CED procedure to ensure a large distribution volume of CED-administered drug. Since these results may vary with varying patient-specific pressure patterns; the model results suggest the importance of conducting CED with a priori knowledge of the interstitial pressure patterns. They can be potentially derived from MRI-based computational modeling methods such as those created by our group [31].

Without CED, the predicted IFP reflected previous experimental findings which have shown elevated relatively uniform pressures inside the tumor [40–44]. With CED, the infusion induced an additional local pressure gradient thereby conveying the advantage convection gives in distributing molecules to larger tissue volumes with infusion. Except for near the infusion site, the pressure was relatively uniform inside the tumor and dropped steeply at the periphery which is in agreement with previous experimental findings [5]. Outside the tumor, the tissue boundary condition played a critical role in determining IFP. The close proximity of the tumor to the impermeable skin boundary increased the IFP near its surface approximately by a factor of two (for the baseline case), than at the skin boundary farther from the tumor.

The model predicted heterogeneous convective velocity due to spatially varying pressure gradients induced by CED, porosity and K^{trans} induced by CED. The resulting flow directions reflected the IFP gradient field. High velocities at the infusion site and the anterior end were due to the pressure gradients created due to infusion, and higher leakiness in the region exhibited as increased K^{trans} (Figure 1c). Overall, CED altered the extracellular fluid flows inside the tumor especially in the vicinity of the infusion site.

The model was also able to predict asymmetric distribution of tracer conforming with the previous experimental findings [16,19,45]. The distribution pattern was closely interlinked with the predicted flow field with high concentration at the infusion site, and gradual spread into the adjacent normal tissue. Such a focal CED distribution of the tracer is in contrast with the one obtained

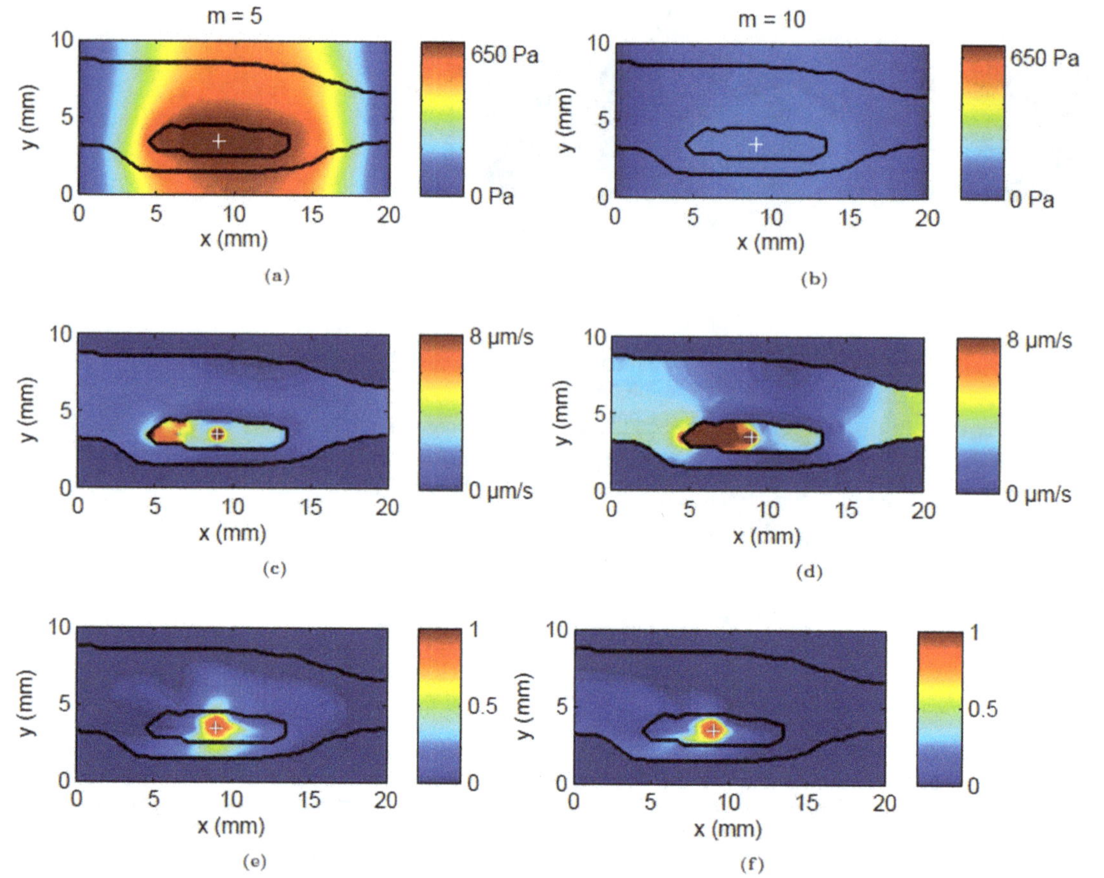

Figure 9. Flow field and tracer distribution following CED of albumin (0.3 μL/min) at the center of the tumor for varying values of the hydraulic conductivity parameter, *m*. (a & b) Interstitial fluid pressure (IFP) contours for $m=5$ & 10 respectively; (c & d) Convective fluid velocity contours for $m=5$ & 10 respectively; (e & f) Normalized tracer concentration contours at the end of infusion (1 hr) for $m=5$ & 10 respectively. All contours are for the plane of infusion with the infusion site designated by a plus sign.

systemically [31], thus making CED delivery a possible alternative to systemic routes. The tracer spread along the skin boundary is due to the close proximity of tumor with the skin. The distribution volume plots (Figure 5) show that the tumor was not entirely covered by the tracer even with longer infusion times. Such a low tumor coverage by the tracer was due to the relatively uniform IFP within the tumor except in the region close to the infusion site (Figure 3a) which restricted the resulting convective velocity (Figure 3b) and tracer filtration within the tumor and directed transport outwards.

Increases in infusion flow rate had profound effects on the tracer distribution as convective velocity outside the tumor was greatly reduced compared to flows enhanced inside the tumor. This was because increasing the flow rate mainly affected the fluid flows

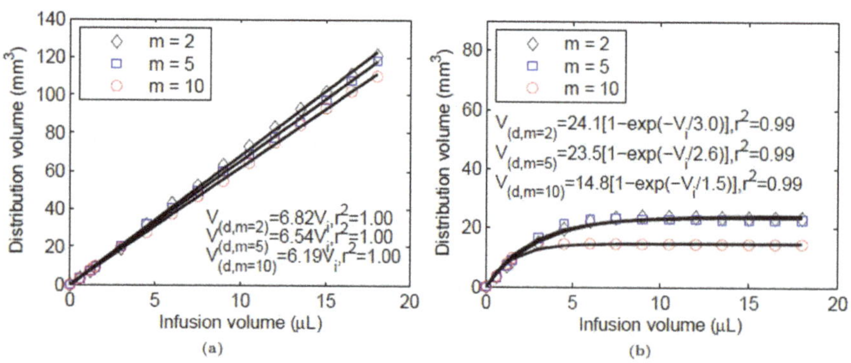

Figure 10. Variation of tracer distribution volumes in tissue with infusion volume for the whole leg and tumor following CED (0.3 μL/min) at the center of the tumor for varying values of the hydraulic conductivity parameter, *m*. Distribution volume dependence on infusion volume was fit to (a) linear (whole leg) and (b) exponential (tumor only) models.

locally close to the infusion site. Although the convective velocity is uniform inside the tumor, it dropped steeply at the tumor periphery (Figure 6d) due to greater lymphatic uptake of interstitial fluid in the normal tissue. Thus the tracer could be expected to be convectively transported well inside the tumor but mainly diffusely at the boundary. This combined with the lack of lymphatics inside the tumor caused more tracer to distribute within the tumor than outside, and this effect became more pronounced at higher flow rates. For the same amount of infusion volume, the tumor was almost fully covered by the tracer at a flow rate of 3 μL/min. The challenge regarding using high infusion rates experimentally is backflow, which our model did not account for. Specially designed cannulas may allow for such infusions at higher flow rates (up to 50 μL/min) without backflow [46,47].

The sensitivity analysis was also used to study tracer distribution at different catheter positions, in an attempt to find a suitable placement which could maximize distribution volume in the target site. For the set of baseline parameters, we found that infusion at the center of the tumor produced the maximum distribution volume within the tumor. Infusion at the tumor-host tissue interface tended to distribute the drug outside the tumor due to enhanced convective effects at the tumor boundary. It should be noted that, the outward flow of albumin from the tumor for infusions at the anterior end of the tumor is also partially due to an unphysical artifact, which is the proximity of the infusion site to the cut ends of the tumor (due to limited field of view) where a zero pressure boundary condition was specified. A similar pattern can be expected for infusions at the posterior end of the tumor. In the future, this approach can be automated to solve infusion in every voxel to determine the optimal infusion site thereby helping with surgical planning on a case-by-case basis.

The possibility of reducing the tumor IFP by increasing the sensitivity of tissue hydraulic conductivity to tissue porosity was also investigated. This analysis was done to partially account for soft tissue swelling and resulted in increased heterogeneous transport. Also several studies have explored the idea of reducing the tumor IFP as a way to overcome the drug delivery barriers [5]. For example, compounds such as VEGF inhibitors, hyaluronidase, mannitol among others have been used to disrupt the heterogeneous tumor microvasculature in an attempt to lower tumor IFP and improve drug delivery [5,48]. By doing so, the underlying tissue hydraulic conductivity may also change [19] and it might be important to study how this affects the drug distribution. Mathematically, this was implemented by varying the empirical parameter m in the expression for tissue hydraulic conductivity (Equation 5a). The parameter m could be thought of as a variable to either amplify or reduce the fluid flows in the heterogeneous pathways in the whole leg determined by the 2-compartmental model. Increasing m caused more interstitial fluid to leak away from the tumor periphery and reduced the tumor IFP as shown in Figure 9. Increasing the hydraulic conductivity has been previously shown to reduce IFP and thus increase extravasation of macromolecules [19]. The results of this sensitivity analysis indicated reduction in peak tumor IFP compared to baseline simulation, however the resulting CED tracer distribution volumes were also reduced. This was because of increase in convective velocity heterogeneity resulting from very high reduction in the tumor IFP, which directed the interstitial fluid and albumin tracer away from the tumor into adjacent normal tissue. The amplified hydraulic conductivity in the whole tissue volume opened up various low resistant fluid pathways through which the tracer got transported away from the tumor. High interstitial velocity at the anterior cut end compared to the posterior side is due to the high K^{trans} described in the earlier paragraph. These results demonstrate the importance of transport heterogeneity and measuring extracellular transport, especially changes in extracellular space for a given tumor, in order to achieve improved understanding of spatial drug distribution within the tumor.

In this study, an image-based tumor model was developed which incorporates realisitic tumor vascular leakiness with anatomical geometries, and used to predict heterogeneous/asymmetric drug distribution following direct infusions. Although the results discussed in this study are restricted to the mouse hind limb tumor under study, it should be noted that the applicability of such a voxelized model to a wide range of tumors is possible. With further experimental validation and measure of tissue properties, this model could be potentially applied towards patient-specific treatments and to more accurately investigate effects of flow patterns on heterogeneous tumor drug delivery. The model however has some limitations at present: 1) model parameter values such as average hydraulic conductivity, diffusivity, scaling factor for the leakiness term ($\frac{J_V}{V}$) obtained from literature varies across tumors and needs to be determined experimentally for a given tumor; 2) modeling heterogeneous tumor microvasculature based on fluid exchange between blood plasma and tissue compartments is only approximate since one assumption is that each MR voxel consists of tissue and blood vessels. Hence at a sufficiently high MR resolution, model predictions could be erroneous in bigger blood vessels, highly vascularized and necrotic regions; and 3) tracer backflow along the infusion needle has not been accounted for. However, even with these limitations, the model is still able to capture major characteristics of heterogeneity and provide important insights into CED tracer transport in tumors.

Acknowledgments

We thank Dr. Thomas Mareci for providing MRI expertise and Dr. Garrett W. Astary for conducting the DCE-MRI experiments.

Author Contributions

Conceived and designed the experiments: MS KNM. Performed the experiments: GLP LR CP. Analyzed the data: KNM. Contributed reagents/materials/analysis tools: MS LR CP DWS. Wrote the paper: KNM. Manuscript feedback/revision: MS GLP DWS LR.

References

1. Jain RK (1988) Determinants of tumor blood flow: a review. Cancer Research 48: 2641–2658.
2. Fu Y, Nagy JA, Dvorak AM, Dvorak HF (2008) Tumor Blood Vessels. Antiangiogenic Agents in Cancer Therapy: 205–224.
3. Huang G, Chen L (2008) Review: Tumor Vasculature and Microenvironment Normalization: A Possible Mechanism of Antiangiogenesis Therapy. Cancer biotherapy & radiopharmaceuticals 23: 661–668.
4. Fukumura D, Duda DG, Munn LL, Jain RK (2010) Tumor microvasculature and microenvironment: novel insights through intravital imaging in pre-clinical models. Microcirculation 17: 206–25.
5. Heldin CH, Rubin K, Pietras K, Ostman A (2004) High interstitial fluid pressure - an obstacle in cancer therapy. Nature Reviews Cancer 4: 806–813.
6. Saito R, Bringas JR, McKnight TR, Wendland MF, Mamot C, et al. (2004) Distribution of lipo-somes into brain and rat brain tumor models by Convection-Enhanced delivery monitored with magnetic resonance imaging. Cancer Research 64: 2572–2579.
7. Wang Y, Wang H, Li C, Yuan F (2006) Effects of rate, volume, and dose of intratumoral infusion on virus dissemination in local gene delivery. Molecular Cancer Therapeutics 5: 362–366.
8. Walter KA, Tamargo RJ, Olivi A, Burger PC, Brem H (1995) Intratumoral chemotherapy. Neu-rosurgery 37: 1129–1145.

9. Engebraaten O, Hjortland GO, Juell S, Hirschberg H, Fodstad O (2002) Intratumoral immunotoxin treatment of human malignant brain tumors in immunodeficient animals. International Journal of Cancer 97: 846–852.
10. Guerin C, Olivi A, Weingart JD, Lawson HC, Brem H (2004) Recent advances in brain tumor therapy: Local intracerebral drug delivery by polymers. Investigational New Drugs 22: 27–37.
11. Wang Y, Hu JK, Krol A, Li Y, Li C, et al. (2003) Systemic dissemination of viral vectors during intratumoral injection. Molecular Cancer Therapeutics 2: 1233–1242.
12. Bobo RH, Laske DW, Akbasak A, Morrison PF, Dedrick RL, et al. (1994) Convection-enhanced delivery of macromolecules in the brain. Proceedings of the National Academy of Sciences 91: 2076–2080.
13. Allard E, Passirani C, Benoit JP (2009) Convection-enhanced delivery of nanocarriers for the treatment of brain tumors. Biomaterials 30: 2302–2318.
14. Perlstein B, Ram Z, Daniels D, Ocherashvilli A, Roth Y, et al. (2008) Convection-enhanced delivery of maghemite nanoparticles: increased efficacy and MRI monitoring. Neuro-oncology 10: 153–161.
15. MacKay JA, Deen DF, Jr FCS (2005) Distribution in brain of liposomes after convection enhanced delivery; modulation by particle charge, particle diameter, and presence of steric coating. Brain Research 1035: 139–153.
16. Sampson JH, Brady ML, Petry NA, Croteau D, Friedman AH, et al. (2007) Intracerebral infusate distribution by convection-enhanced delivery in humans with malignant gliomas: descriptive effects of target anatomy and catheter positioning. Neurosurgery 60: 89–99.
17. Hadaczek P, Yamashita Y, Mirek H, Tamas L, Bohn MC, et al. (2006) The "perivascular pump" driven by arterial pulsation is a powerful mechanism for the distribution of therapeutic molecules within the brain. Molecular Therapy 14: 69–78.
18. Szerlip NJ, Walbridge S, Yang L, Morrison PF, Degen JW, et al. (2007) Real-time imaging of convection-enhanced delivery of viruses and virus-sized particles. Journal of Neurosurgery: Pedi-atrics 107: 560–567.
19. Boucher Y, Brekken C, Netti PA, Baxter LT, Jain RK (1998) Intratumoral infusion of fluid: estimation of hydraulic conductivity and implications for the delivery of therapeutic agents. British Journal of Cancer 78: 1442–1448.
20. Debinski W, Tatter SB (2009) Convection-enhanced delivery for the treatment of brain tumors. Expert review of neurotherapeutics 9: 1519–1527.
21. Dickinson PJ, LeCouteur RA, Higgins RJ, Bringas JR, Larson RF, et al. (2010) Canine spontaneous glioma: a translational model system for convection-enhanced delivery. Neuro-oncology 12: 928–940.
22. Smith JH, Humphrey JAC (2007) Interstitial transport and transvascular fluid exchange during infusion into brain and tumor tissue. Microvasc Res 73: 58–73.
23. Baish JW, Gazit Y, Berk DA, Nozue M, Baxter LT, et al. (1996) Role of tumor vascular architec-ture in nutrient and drug delivery: an invasion percolation-based network model. Microvascular Research 51: 327–346.
24. Secomb TW, Dewhirst MW, Pries AR (2012) Structural adaptation of normal and tumour vascular networks. Basic & clinical pharmacology & toxicology 110: 63–69.
25. Soltani M, Chen P (2011) Numerical modeling of fluid flow in solid tumors. PloS one 6: e20344.
26. Soltani M, Chen P (2013) Numerical modeling of interstitial fluid flow coupled with blood flow through a remodeled solid tumor microvascular network. PloS one 8: e67025.
27. Welter M, Rieger H (2013) Interstitial fluid flow and drug delivery in vascularized tumors: A computational model. PloS one 8: e70395.
28. Kim JH, Astary GW, Chen X, Mareci TH, Sarntinoranont M (2009) Voxelized model of interstitial transport in the rat spinal cord following direct infusion into white matter. Journal of biomechanical engineering 131: 071007.
29. Kim JH, Mareci TH, Sarntinoranont M (2010) A voxelized model of direct infusion into the corpus callosum and hippocampus of the rat brain: model development and parameter analysis. Medical and Biological Engineering and Computing 48: 203–214.
30. Zhao J, Salmon H, Sarntinoranont M (2007) Effect of heterogeneous vasculature on interstitial transport within a solid tumor. Microvascular Research 73: 224–236.
31. Pishko GL, Astary GW, Mareci TH, Sarntinoranont M (2011) Sensitivity analysis of an image-based solid tumor computational model with heterogeneous vasculature and porosity. Annals of Biomedical Engineering 39: 2360–2373.
32. Magdoom KN, Pishko GL, Kim JH, Sarntinoranont M (2012) Evaluation of a voxelized model based on DCE-MRI for tracer transport in tumor. Journal of Biomechanical engineering 134: 091004.
33. Sampson JH, Raghavan R, Brady ML, Croteau D, Friedman AH, et al. (2007) Clinical utility of a patient-specific algorithm for simulating intracerebral drug infusions. Neuro-oncology 9: 343–353.
34. Linninger AA, Somayaji MR, Mekarski M, Zhang L (2008) Prediction of convection-enhanced drug delivery to the human brain. Journal of Theoretical Biology 250: 125–138.
35. Truskey GA, Yuan F, Katz DF (2004) Transport phenomena in biological systems, Upper Saddle River, NJ: Pearson Prentice Hall. p. 473.
36. Mow V, Huiskes R (2004) Basic orthopaedic biomechanics and mechano-biology. Lippincott Williams & Wilkins.
37. Grathwohl P (1998) Diffusion in natural porous media: Contaminant transport, sorp-tion/desorption and dissolution kinetics, Norwell, MA: Kluwer Academic Publishers. p. 31.
38. Nield DA, Bejan A (2006) Convection in porous media. springer.
39. Zhang XY, Luck J, Dewhirst MW, Yuan F (2000) Interstitial hydraulic conductivity in a fibrosar-coma. American Journal of Physiology-Heart and Circulatory Physiology 279: H2726–H2734.
40. Young JS, Llumsden CE, Stalker AL (1950) The significance of the tissue pressure of normal testicular and of neoplastic (brown-pearce carcinoma) tissue in the rabbit. The Journal of Pathology and Bacteriology 62: 313–333.
41. Boucher Y, Baxter L, Jain R (1990) Interstitial pressure gradients in tissue-isolated and subcuta-neous tumors: implications for therapy. Cancer Research 50: 4478–4484.
42. Boucher Y, Kirkwood JM, Opacic D, Desantis M, Jain RK (1991) Interstitial hypertension in superficial metastatic melanomas in humans. Cancer Research 51: 6691–6694.
43. Gutmann R, Leunig M, Feyh J, Goetz AE, Messmer K, et al. (1992) Interstitial hypertension in head and neck tumors in patients: correlation with tumor size. Cancer Research 52: 1993–1995.
44. Nathanson SD, Nelson L (1994) Interstitial fluid pressure in breast cancer, benign breast conditions, and breast parenchyma. Annals of Surgical Oncology 1: 333–338.
45. McGuire S, Yuan F (2001) Quantitative analysis of intratumoral infusion of color molecules. Amer-ican Journal of Physiology-Heart and Circulatory Physiology 281: H715–H721.
46. Krauze M, Saito R, Noble C, Tamas M, Bringas J, et al. (2005) Reflux-free cannula for convection-enhanced high-speed delivery of therapeutic agents. Journal of neurosurgery 103: 923–929.
47. Vazquez L, Hagel E, Willenberg B, Dai W, Casanova F, et al. (2012) Polymer-coated cannulas for the reduction of backflow during intraparenchymal infusions. Journal of Materials Science: Materials in Medicine: 1–10.
48. Jain RK, di Tomaso E, Duda DG, Loeffler JS, Sorensen AG, et al. (2007) Angiogenesis in brain tumours. Nature Reviews Neuroscience 8: 610–622.
49. Baxter LT, Jain RK (1989) Transport of fluid and macromolecules in tumors. I. role of interstitial pressure and convection. Microvascular Research 37: 77–104.
50. Arunyawongsakorn U, Johnson CS, Gabriel DA (1985) Tracer diffusion coefficients of proteins by means of holographic relaxation spectroscopy: Application to bovine serum albumin. Analytical Biochemistry 146: 265–270.

11

Novel Epigenetic Target Therapy for Prostate Cancer

Ilaria Naldi[1,¶], Monia Taranta[1,¶], Lisa Gherardini[1], Gualtiero Pelosi[2], Federica Viglione[2], Settimio Grimaldi[3], Luca Pani[4], Caterina Cinti[1]*

1 Institute of Clinical Physiology, Consiglio Nazionale delle Ricerche (CNR), Experimental Oncology Unit, Siena, Italy, **2** Institute of Clinical Physiology, Consiglio Nazionale delle Ricerche (CNR), Pisa, Italy, **3** Institute of Translational Pharmacology, Consiglio Nazionale delle Ricerche (CNR), Rome, Italy, **4** Institute of Translational Pharmacology, Consiglio Nazionale delle Ricerche (CNR), Cagliari, Italy

Abstract

Epigenetic events are critical contributors to the pathogenesis of cancer, and targeting epigenetic mechanisms represents a novel strategy in anticancer therapy. Classic demethylating agents, such as 5-Aza-2′-deoxycytidine (Decitabine), hold the potential for reprograming somatic cancer cells demonstrating high therapeutic efficacy in haematological malignancies. On the other hand, epigenetic treatment of solid tumours often gives rise to undesired cytotoxic side effects. Appropriate delivery systems able to enrich Decitabine at the site of action and improve its bioavailability would reduce the incidence of toxicity on healthy tissues. In this work we provide preclinical evidences of a safe, versatile and efficient targeted epigenetic therapy to treat hormone sensitive (LNCap) and hormone refractory (DU145) prostate cancers. A novel Decitabine formulation, based on the use of engineered erythrocyte (Erythro-Magneto-Hemagglutinin Virosomes, EMHVs) drug delivery system (DDS) carrying this drug, has been refined. Inside the EMHVs, the drug was shielded from the environment and phosphorylated in its active form. The novel magnetic EMHV DDS, endowed with fusogenic protein, improved the stability of the carried drug and exhibited a high efficiency in confining its delivery at the site of action *in vivo* by applying an external static magnetic field. Here we show that Decitabine loaded into EMHVs induces a significant tumour mass reduction in prostate cancer xenograft models at a concentration, which is seven hundred times lower than the therapeutic dose, suggesting an improved pharmacokinetics/pharmacodynamics of drug. These results are relevant for and discussed in light of developing personalised autologous therapies and innovative clinical approach for the treatment of solid tumours.

Editor: Lucia R. Languino, Thomas Jefferson University, United States of America

Funding: This work was supported by Consiglio Nazionale delle Ricerche (CNR) funding and by European Community funding for POR CReO FESR 2007-2013, BANDO UNICO R&S-ANNO 2012 of Regione Toscana-Project acronym Title: ACTILA. The funders had no role in study design, data collection and analysis, decision to publish, or preparation of the manuscript.

* E-mail: ccinti@ifc.cnr.it

¶ These authors contributed equally to this work.

Introduction

Prostate cancer (PC) is a commonly diagnosed malignancy in developed countries and its incidence dramatically increases with age [1,2]. Despite the proven success of hormonal therapy, surgical castration [3,4] and radiation therapy [5–7], however after being managed a subset of patients manifest disease progression and became resistance to further hormonal manipulation [8–10]. Up to 20% of PC patients treated with radical prostatectomy have the probability to progress to invasive cancer with relapsed metastatic conditions within 5 to 10 years [11]. The median survival of patients with metastatic PC is 12–16 months from the time of diagnosis to death [12]. No curative treatments are available at this stage of the disease. In spite of intensive research efforts, the molecular mechanisms by which prostate cancer cells become resistant to hormone therapy remain poorly characterized.

Epigenetic alterations, involving hypermethylation of genes in critical pathways, such as DNA repair, metabolism, and invasion/metastasis, have been found in prostatic cancer providing new information of the pathogenesis of this tumour [13,14]. Post-translational changes weakening chromatin structure alter gene expression and lead cells to metastatic spreading. However, as epigenetic modifications do not require changing in DNA sequence they are potentially reversible. DNA methyltransferases (DNMTs) involved in the epigenetic silencing of gene expression become therefore a suitable target for epigenetic treatments [15–17].

Decitabine (5-Aza-2'-dC) is a classic demethylating agent approved by FDA for the treatment of patients with myelodysplastic syndromes and Acute Lymphoblastic Leukemia (ALM) [18]. However, the beneficial of Decitabine treatment remains uncertain for patients with solid tumours as the lack of chemical stability in aqueous solution and high incidence of neutropenia have been associated with its use.

Recently the anti-proliferative effect of Decitabine has been tested in different tumour histotypes such as testicular [19], lung [20], breast [21], colorectal cancer cells [22], CNS tumours [23] and prostate cancer [24–26]. These encouraging results indicated that Decitabine could be effective in inhibiting cancer progression and inducing cell differentiation. Notwithstanding these *in vitro* reports, it was emphasised the need for improving drug stability in solution and delivery efficacy, to minimise toxic side effects and prolong epigenetic outcomes *in vivo*.

The remarkable therapeutic potential of Decitabine is in fact hampered by its systemic instability [27]. Its low therapeutic index and the difficulty to calibrate steady state blood concentration have affected several clinical studies.

In recent years drug delivery systems (DDSs) have been developed to improve the specific and localized delivery of therapeutic agents to target tumour tissue while avoiding severe toxic side effects on healthy organs [28,29]. Cell-based drug delivery systems such as erythrocytes are particularly attractive tools for delivering several classes of therapeutics. Erythrocytes are safe and biocompatible carriers that can accommodate molecules of different size, nature and stability and they are particularly useful for those agents that show limited tissue penetration or are rapidly inactivated upon i.v. *in vivo* administration [30–32]. Moreover, erythrocytes also act as circulating bioreactors converting a pro-drugs into its active forms.

A novel erythrocyte-based drug delivery system, endowed with both super-paramagnetic nanoparticles (NPs) inside the erythrocytes and a fusogenic glycoprotein, the filamentous hemagglutinin (FHA), inserted into the cytoplasmic membranes of erythrocytes (Erythro-Magneto-Hemagglutinin Virosomes, EMHVs), was recently patented (WO2010/070620(A1)).

It has been shown that these EMHV improved kinetics of therapeutic compounds into target cells *in vitro*. Efficient drug intracellular release is achieved into host cells due to presence of fusogenic glycoprotein on EMHV membranes [33,34].

The magnetic nature of this drug delivery system allows EMHV to be directed toward the desired tissues/organs *in vivo* upon the application of an external magnetic field.

Here we tested a target "epigenetic therapy" based on use of low dose 5-Aza-2'-dC loaded into EMHVs in two prostate cancer models. Human prostate adenocarcinoma LNCap cells, responsive to hormone therapy, and DU145, hormone refractory cells, have been used [35] *in vitro* and *in vivo* in xenograft tumour models. We show that the pharmacological anticancer activity of 5-Aza-2′-dC is highly increased by our EMHVs delivery system both *in vitro* and *in vivo* suggesting its possible application in future clinical trials.

Materials and Methods

Reagents

Superparamagnetic nanoparticles (NPs) were purchased from nano-screenMAG, Chemicell, Berlin, Germany. Filamentous Hemagglutinin from *Bordetella pertussis* (FHA), 5-aza-2′-deoxicytidine (5-Aza-2'-dC), HPLC grade acetonitrile, N′,N′-dimethylhexylamine (DMHA), cytidine-5′-triphosphate disodium salt (CTP) and 2'-deoxyuridine (dU) were purchased from Sigma-Aldrich, Milan, Italy. Methanol and ammonium acetate were purchased from Carlo Erba, Milan, Italy.

Preparation of 5-Aza-2′-dC-loaded EMHVs (A-EMHVs)

Human erythrocytes were prepared by gradient centrifugation at 400 g for 30 minutes and then washed twice in 1X PBS (1.37 M NaCl, 57 mM KCl, 54 mM Na_2HPO_4, 45 mM KH_2PO_4 pH 7.4). 2×10^9 erythrocytes were lysed in 250 µl lysis buffer 1 (10 mM TRIS, 0.1 mM EDTA, 1 mM $MgCl_2$ pH 7.2) for 60 minutes at 0°C. The isotonicity was then restored by adding 130 µl of resealing buffer (65 µl of 10X PBS pH 7.4 and 65 µl of 15 mM $MgCl_2$ pH 7.4), supplemented with 2 µg of FHA, 0.1 mg of 100 nm super-paramagnetic NPs and 75 µg of 5-Aza-2'-dC.

The suspension was incubated for 45 minutes at 37°C under mild agitation to promote resealing and obtain engineered erythrocytes loaded with 5-Aza-2′-dC (A-EMHVs). A-EMHVs were then collected by centrifugation at 8,000 g for 15 minutes at 4°C. Successively the erythrocyte suspension was washed twice with 1X PBS by centrifugation at 8,000 g for 15 minutes at 4°C, re-suspended in 1X PBS and conserved at 4°C until used.

Cell culture

LNCap and DU145 prostate cancer cell lines were obtained from American Type Culture Collection (ATCC, Rockville, MD) and maintained in culture medium RPMI 1640 supplemented with 10% Fetal Bovine Serum, 2 mM L-glutamine, in presence of 100 U/ml penicillin-streptomycin, at split ratio of 1:3 twice a week. These prostate cancer cells were used for both *in vitro* and *in vivo* experiments.

Confocal Laser Scanning Microscopy (CLSM) analysis

DU145 cells at a density of 1.5×10^5 were seeded in 6-well microtiter plates. On the bottom of the culture plates glass coverslips were placed on which the cells were let to grow until 60–80% confluence. After 24 hours, the culture medium was replaced with media containing 1.5×10^8 A-EMHVs. In a sample, fresh medium was replaced with no adding of EMHVs to visualize naïve cell structure (control). After 6, 24 and 48 hours of incubation, coverslips were retrieved and cells were washed in 1X PBS buffer and fixed with 4% paraformaldehyde. Cell nuclei were counter stained with DAPI, washed with 1X PBS and the whole coverslip is mounted on a slide using anti-fade medium. Fluorescence and bright-field images were captured by CSLM, Leica TCS SP5 inverted microscope system, equipped with sources emitting from the UV to the visible. DAPI fluorescence was detected using excitation at 405 nm and recording emission at 454 nm while the red fluorescence of super-paramagnetic NPs was excited at 543 nm and its emission was detected at 613 nm.

Liquid chromatography–mass spectrometry (HPLC-MS) analysis of 5-Aza-2′-dC loaded into EMHVs

To quantify the total amount of 5-Aza-2'-dC inside the modified erythrocytes, 2×10^9 freshly prepared A-EMHVs were lysed in 200 µl of lysis buffer 2 (155 mM NH_4Cl, 10 mM $KHCO_3$, 0.1 mM EDTA, pH 7.2) for 10 minutes at room temperature and then centrifuged at 12,000 g for 15 minutes at 4°C. The supernatant was transferred into a Microcon centrifugal filter device with MWCO 30,000 Da (Amicon YM-10, Millipore, Vimodrone MI, Italy) and then centrifuged at 14,000 g for 2 hours at 4°C. Filtered samples were kept at −80°C until analysis. The HPLC system used was a Dionex 3,000 Ultimate series LC (Sunnyvale, CA, USA) connected to a linear ion trap LTQ-Orbitrap mass spectrometer (Thermo Fisher Scientific, USA), equipped with an electrospray ion source. Data were acquired and processed with Excalibur 2.1 software. Compounds were separated on a Mediterranea Sea18 reverse-phase column (150 mm, 2.1 mm I.D. and 5 µm particle size) from Teknokroma (Analytical Technology S.r.l., Brugherio Milan, Italy). The column was set at a flow rate of 0.25 ml/minute, at a temperature of 36°C, and sample volumes of 10 µl were injected. The mobile phase consisted of 5 mM ammonium acetate (solvent A) and acetonitrile (solvent B). The first 13 minutes were an isocratic run with solvent A; between 13 and 20 minutes the percentage of mobile phase B was increased to 35%, maintained for 2 minutes and then the initial the mobile phase was re-established within 2 minutes. The mass spectrometer was operated in positive electrospray mode and the collision energy was 35 eV. The transitions monitored were m/z 229--->113 for 5-Aza-2'-dC; m/z 219--->103 for guanylurea derivatives; m/z 247--->131 for formulated derivatives of 5-Aza-2'-dC. To search for possible phosphorylated forms of 5-Aza-2'-dC, 2×10^9 freshly prepared A-EMHVs were left at 37°C for 24 hours. Successively, samples were lysed and filtered as above described and 400 ng of CTP were added to the samples as internal standards. The mobile phase consisted of 20 mM DMHA pH 7.0 (solvent A) and methanol-water 80:20 (solvent B). The first 12 minutes were an isocratic run with 10% solvent B; between 12 and 15 minutes the percentage of mobile phase B was increased to 80%, maintained for 1 minute and then the initial the mobile phase was re-established within 2 minutes. The mass spectrometer was operated in negative electrospray mode and the collision energy was 15 eV. The transitions monitored were m/z 482---> 384 for CTP; m/z 467--->369 for 5-Aza-2'-dC triphosphate; m/z 387--->289 for 5-Aza-2'-dC diphosphate; m/z 307--->208 for 5-Aza-2'-dC monophosphate corresponding to the elimination of a neutral molecule of H_3PO_4. For the calibration curve, six different CTP standard solutions were used. The peak area ratio of sample/CTP was used for quantization.

Cytofluorimetric (FACS) analysis

LNCap and DU145 cells at a density of 1.5×10^5 were seeded in 6-well microtiter plates for cell cycle assays. After 24 hours, the culture medium was replaced with media containing: no drug (CTRL); free 5-Aza-2'-dC at doses 6.8 µg or 120 ng; 1.5×10^8 A-EMHVs (containing approximately 120 ng 5-Aza-2'-dC).

After 24, 48 and 96 hours of incubation, control and treated cells were harvested and analysed by FACS. Nuclei were stained with 10 µg/ml propidium iodide (PI) in hypotonic solution (1X PBS containing 0.1% sodium citrate and 0.1% Triton X-100) for 30 minutes at 4°C in the dark for assessment of cell cycle phases.

Apoptotic cells were detected by Annexin V test (BioVision). The treated and untreated cells were suspended in 1X binding buffer and incubated at room temperature for 15 minutes with Annexin V-FITC and Propidium Iodide (PI) was added for nuclei staining following manufacturer's instructions.

Flow-cytometry was carried using Becton–Dickinson FACScan CentroII and data were analysed by FlowJo software.

Animals

For the experiments carried out at the animal facility of Marshall University, congenital athymic BALB/c Nude mice, homozygous for the *nu/nu* allele, were bred in house. The colony of 8- to 12-week-old male mice was developed from breeding stock obtained from Charles Rivers Laboratories (Wilmington, MA). These animals were used for LNCap xenograft experiments.

Animals used in experiment carried out at "Toscana Life Sciences" animal facility were athymic Nude-Foxn1*nu* male mice, 6 weeks of age, purchased from Harlan Laboratories (Udine, Italy). These animals were used for DU145 xenografts.

In both cases, animals were housed in micro-isolators in autoclaved cages with polyester fiber filter covers, under germ-free conditions. All food, water, and bedding were sterilized and the animals were maintained in an ambient temperature of 23±2°C in rooms having a 12 hours light/dark cycle.

X-ray imaging

Athymic BALB/c Nude mice were injected with 1.5×10^8 EMHVs suspended in 150 µl of 1X PBS.

Following EMHVs tail vein injection, one group of animal were exposed to external magnetic field by placing two earth magnets on the lower lateral abdominal region for 30 minutes (EMHVs-MF), while mice were kept under 2% isofluorane anesthesia. Neodinium magnets (round shaped 5.0 mm) with approximately coercive force of 1,000 KOersted, were used. A control group of mice was tail vein injected with EMHVs as previously described but no external magnetic field was applied (EMHVs-NMF). One hour after the treatment, mice were sacrificed by CO_2 asphyxiation and the accumulation of ferrous beads was assessed by X-ray imaging. The imaging analysis was performed using a Philips DigitalDiagnost direct digital radiography system with flat detector technology (Philips, Hamburg, Germany) with a dose of 60 kVp at 5 mAs.

Tumour xenograft procedures

Both athymic BALB/c Nude and Nude-Foxn1*nu* mice were anesthetized by 2.5% isoflurane during manipulation.

The setting of the models: LNCap or DU145 cells were concentrated to 7×10^6 or 4.5×10^6 respectively in 1X PBS and injected subcutaneously 1:1 with MatrigelTM basement membrane matrix (BD Biosciences, Franklin Lakes, NJ) into the left flank of each mouse (total volume 200 µl). Once xenografts started growing, their sizes (mm^3) were measured twice a week with digital caliper and the volume was calculated by using the standard formula: length x width^2/2. Tumour xenografts were allowed to grow approximately up to 100 mm^3 and this volume was selected as the initial stage for beginning the treatment. Mice were randomized (n = 6), anesthetized and prepared for tail vein injection with the selected treatment. Before each injection, tumours were measured and compared to the corresponding initial volumes, in order to normalize the data (X = 100 x volume$_1$/volume$_0$). Randomisation: Mice were assigned to seven different groups in both experimental settings (LNCap or DU145 xenografts) and they were treated as follow: 1X PBS (CTRL); 85 µg 5-Aza-2'-dC (2.5 mg/kg) (A1); 120 ng 5-Aza-2'-dC (A2); 1.5×10^8 unloaded EMHVs in absence of static magnetic field (EMHVs-NMF); 1.5×10^8 unloaded EMHVs and static magnetic field applied on tumour (EMHVs-MF); 1.5×10^8 EMHVs containing 120 ng 5-Aza-2'-dC (A-EMHVs-NMF); 1.5×10^8 EMHVs containing 120 ng 5-Aza-2'-dC and static magnetic field applied on tumour (A-EMHVs-MF).

Injection protocol: Mice were biweekly administered intravenously with 150 µl treatment per inoculation, over 3 weeks. After each injection in those groups selected to be treated also with static magnetic field (EMHVs-MF and A-EMHVs-MF), two earth magnets (1,000 KOersted) were applied to the xenograft mass for 30 minutes to ensure intra-tumour accumulation. Mice were then allowed recovering and monitored for signs of distress. At the end of the treatment course or when the tumour volume reached approximately 400 mm^3, mice were sacrificed by CO_2 asphyxiation and the prostate tumour mass, liver, kidneys were harvested and stored at -80°C until additional analysis.

Morphological and immunohistochemical analysis of tumour xenografts

Frozen samples stored at -80°C were equilibrate at −20°C overnight before sectioning by cryostat (Microm HM 500 W) following embedding in OCT.

Consecutive serial cryosections of 5–6 µm thickness were obtained from the middle (largest) portion of each samples, placed on positively charged slides, dried in air for a few minutes and then fixed with cold acetone. Two-four sections were stained with Mayer's hematoxylin for histopathologic examination.

After washing in 1X PBS and incubation in H_2O_2 at room temperature to block endogenous peroxidase, the section were incubated with diluted normal blocking serum prepared from the

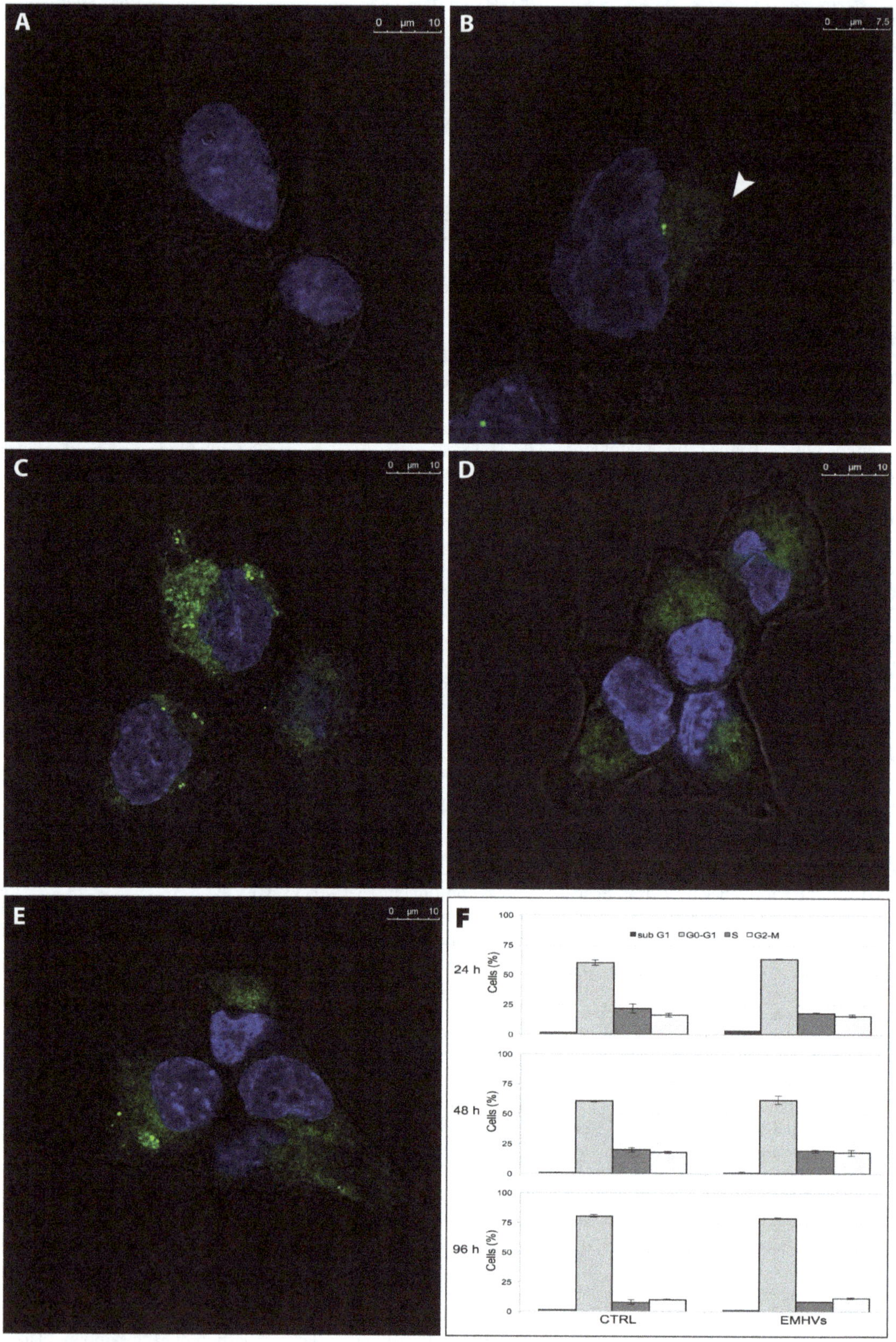

Figure 1. Qualitative and quantitative analysis of the distribution and effect of EMHVs treatment in DU145 prostate cancer cells. Representative CLSM images of EMHVs internalization and released nanoparticle distribution (green fluorescence signal, **B–E**) into the host cell cytoplasm at several time points are depicted. Naïve cells (**A**) are reported as control. In (**B**), after 6 hours of treatment, an intact EMHV is present in the cytoplasm (arrow). At 24 hours (**C**) the particles appeared to have been released from the EMHVs. In the pictures taken at 48 (**D**) and 96 (**E**) hours, nanoparticles appear to have homogeneously distributed throughout the cytoplasm. Lack of toxic effect of erythrocyte drug delivery system treatment was evaluated by FACS analysis (**F**) where cell profile of the treated cells (EMHVs) at selected time points show no significant changes in sub-phase distributions with respect to control (CTRL).

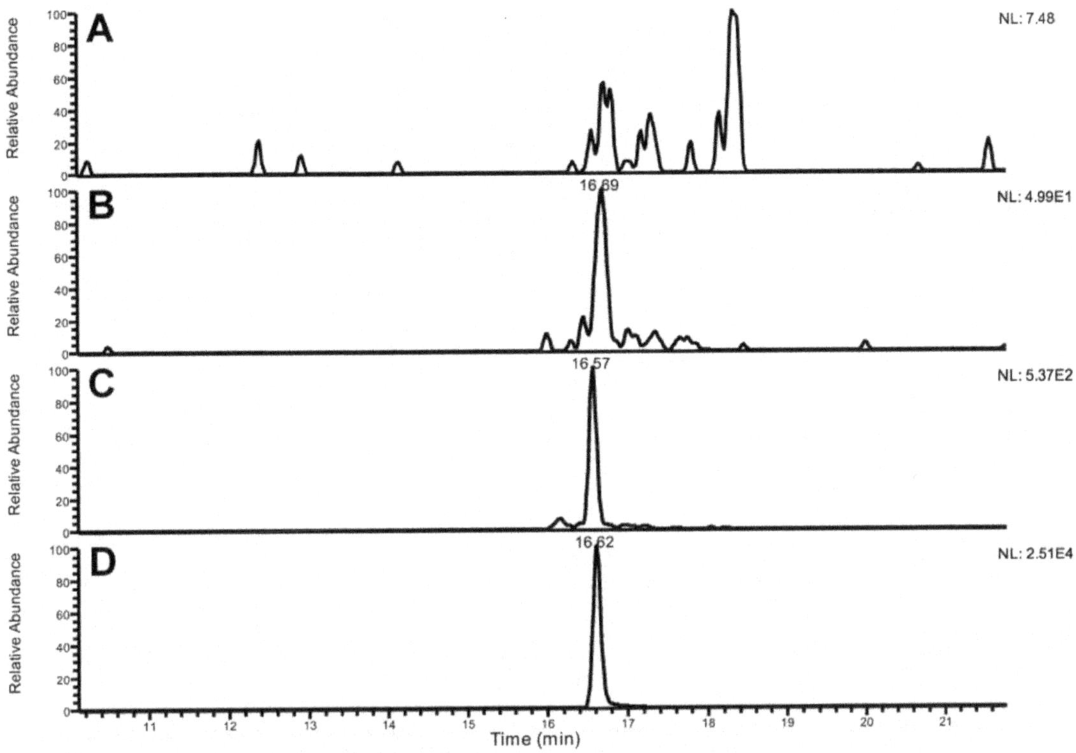

Figure 2. HPLC-MS chromatogram of the phosphorylated forms of 5-Aza-2′-dC. (**A**) chromatograms for 5-Aza-2′-dC mono-phosphate; (**B**) di-phosphate (RT: 16.6); (**C**) tri-phosphate (RT: 16.5) and (**D**) internal standard CTP (RT: 16.5).

species in which the secondary antibody is made. Slides were incubated in humid chamber overnight at 4°C with primary human reactive antibodies for Ki67 (clone SP6, rabbit monoclonal antibody, Thermoscientific) at a dilution 1:200 and DNMT3b (clone 52A1018, mouse monoclonal antibody, IMGENEX) at the dilution 1:150. Following 30 min secondary biotinylated antibody and 30 min Vectastain Elite ABC reagent the slides were then incubation with peroxidase substrate solution (DAB). Slides were counterstained with Mayer's hematoxylin for 1 min, and mounted in aqueous Mount Quick (Bioptica). Microscopic examination was carried out from 2x to 40x magnification under an Olympus BX43 light microscope interfaced to a videocamera for digital acquisition and imaging analysis (DP20 Olympus). The values of DNMT3b and Ki67 positive nuclei were expressed as percentage of positive or negative cells over the counting at least 500 total cells at 20x original magnification.

Statistical analysis

The cell cycle phases are expressed as mean ± SD of at least n = 3. Three-Ways ANOVA were applied to compare the effect of different treatments (CTRL, 6.8 μg 5-Aza-2'-dC; 120 ng 5-Aza-2'-dC; 1.5×10^8 A-EMHVs) on cell cycle phases (sub G1, G0-G1, S, G2-M) and One-Way ANOVA was used to compare the effect of A-EMHVs treatment at selected time points (24, 48 and 96 hours).

The apoptotic cells were expressed as mean ± SEM of at least n = 3. Statistical analysis was performed with One-Way ANOVA independently for early and late apoptosis on log transformed data to improve normalization. Pairwise comparisons were tested using Tukey's honestly significant difference criterion.

The *in vivo* results are expressed as mean ± SEM of n = 6. One-Way ANOVA was applied to compare the tumour mass reduction in the evaluation of the xenograft implant after selected treatment using data collected at the last injection. To describe tumour mass reduction rate (50%) in mice after selected treatments, Kaplan-Meier analysis was applied followed by log-rank test.

Ethics statements

Human red blood cells were obtained from transfusion bags collected from anonymous healthy voluntary donors, which have given their written informed consent carried out in accordance with Italian Government law. It was not necessary the approval from an institutional review board (ethics committee) since neither direct human participation nor involvement of human studies have been foreseen in this work. Samples have been provided by Azienda Ospedaliera Universitaria Senese.

The preclinical study was carried out in strict accordance with the recommendations in the Guide for the Care and Use of Laboratory Animals of the International guidelines on handling of laboratory animals and applying the 3Rs to experiments (in accordance with NIH and European Commission recommendations).

The protocols for Animal Experiments were approved by the Ethics Committee of the Marshall University (Huntington, WV, USA) (Permit Number: # 458/2010) and by the Ethics Committees of the Toscana Life Sciences and the Istituto Superiore di Sanità (ISS) on behalf of Italian Minister of Health (Permit Number: # CNR-270111 exp1/prot1). Animal well-being was monitored accordingly to Langford et al, 2010. [36] "

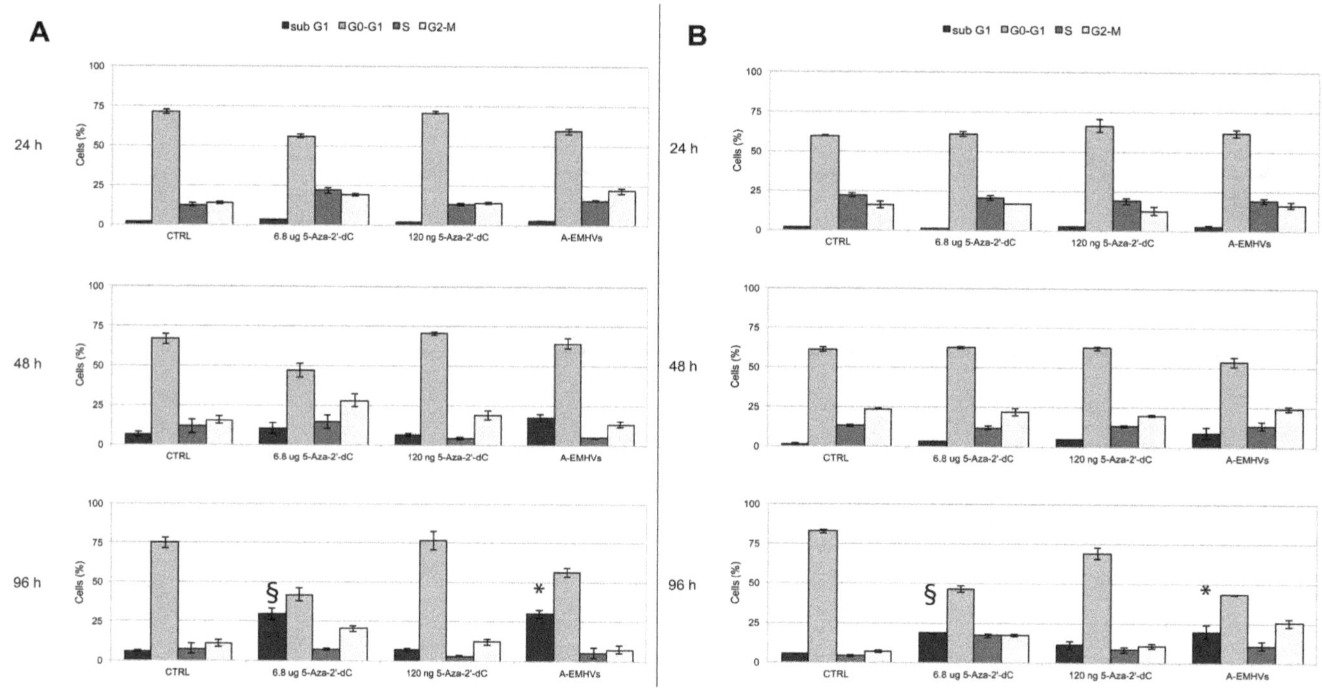

Figure 3. The effect of A-EMHVs on the cell cycle arrest of LNCap, hormone sensitive and DU145 hormone refractory cells. 1.5×10^8 A-EMHVs treatment, containing 120 ng internal 5-Aza-2′-dC, was compared with 6.8 µg free 5-Aza-2′-dC and 120 ng free 5-Aza-2′-dC treatments at 24 (top) 48 (middle) 96 (bottom) hours. Untreated cells were used as control (CTRL). In both LNCap (**A**) and DU145 (**B**) cell lines, A-EMHVs treatment induced a significant enrichment in sub G1 cell distribution (black bars) already detectable at 48 hours after treatment (**A** and **B** middle panel, respectively) that last up to 96 hours (*ANOVA $p<0.05$). Similar shift toward sub G1 distribution was also obtained using 6.8 µg of free 5-Aza-2′-dC (§ANOVA $p<0.05$) but only detected at 96 hours. No shift in cell cycle distribution was detected for free 120 ng 5-Aza-2′-dC, not differing from controls.

Results

Characterization of novel anticancer formulation in erythrocyte-based drug delivery system

To enhance the performance profile of 5-Aza-2′-dC pro-drug, with respect to chemical stability, pharmacokinetics and pharmacodynamics, engineered magnetic erythrocytes carriers (EMHVs) were used as drug delivery system (DDS). The kinetics of EMHV DDS internalization and its toxicity as well as the efficiency and efficacy of this novel anticancer 5-Aza-2′-dC formulation were tested firstly *in vitro* in hormone sensitive (LNCap) and resistant (DU145) prostate cancer cells.

Internalisation of the EMHVs carrier into tumour cell *in vitro*. The kinetic of EMHVs internalization into both LNCap and DU145 prostate cancer cells was confirmed by Confocal Laser Scanning Microscopy analysis (CSLM) by monitoring the distribution of released fluorescent NPs (green) into the cytoplasm of target cells (Fig. 1). An example of DU145 naïve cells is shown in Fig. 1A. Internalization is already taking place at 6 hours after treatment, when EMHVs were found inside the cytoplasm of DU145 cells. At this stage EMHVs still retain their intact membrane and their content of NPs (Fig. 1B). Similarly to what found in our previous work [33], after internalization the EMHV membrane fuses with membrane of host cell releasing the fluorescent content in the whole cytoplasmic space (Fig. 1C–E). At the latest time points (48–96 hours) a wide spread fluorescence of NPs is detectable in the cytoplasm although host cells appear morphologically healthy and no cytotoxic effect is visible (Fig. 1D–E).

Lack of toxicity of the EMHV carriers on cell models. The toxicity of EMHV DDS against host cells was assessed by analysing cell cycle phases of target cells. When treated with unloaded EMHVs for 48 and 96 hours, no shift in LNCap and DU145 cell phase distribution was detectable and cells retained their normal cell cycle for the duration of the treatment (Fig. 1F). This finding suggests that EMHVs drug delivery system did not exert any toxic effect on cancer cells per se.

Chemical stability of 5-Aza-2'-dC into EMHV bioreactor system (A-EMHVs). 5-Aza-2'-dC is a pro-drug and it requires to be activated by phosphorylation to a nucleoside triphosphate before exerting inhibition on DNA methylation [37].

Recently it has been shown that erythrocytes act as bioreactors due to their enzymatic systems [34]. This makes them suitable for encapsulation of pro-drugs that will subsequently be transformed into the active drug [38]. Loading 5-Aza-2'-dC pro-drug into EMHV bioreactor system was achieved according to a standardized protocol (see materials and methods). HPLC-MS was used to quantify the total amount of drug inside the DDS (A-EMHVs) and to detect the presence of its active phosphorylated forms. The chromatogram of samples incubated for 24 hours at 37°C highlighted a mixture of different phosphorylated forms of 5-Aza2′-dC (Fig. 2). Di- and tri-phosphate forms of phosphorylated 5-Aza2′-dC elute at RT 16.6 and RT 16.5 respectively (Fig. 2B and 2C). Figure 2D shows the peak of cytidine thriphosphate (CTP; RT: 16.5), an internal standard that we added to our samples as control. It appears that the tri-phosphate form of 5-Aza2′-dC overbears the other phosphorylated forms proving the high efficiency of EMHVs as bioreactors. We found that 1.5×10^8 A-EMHVs accommodates about 120 ng of total drug and that the

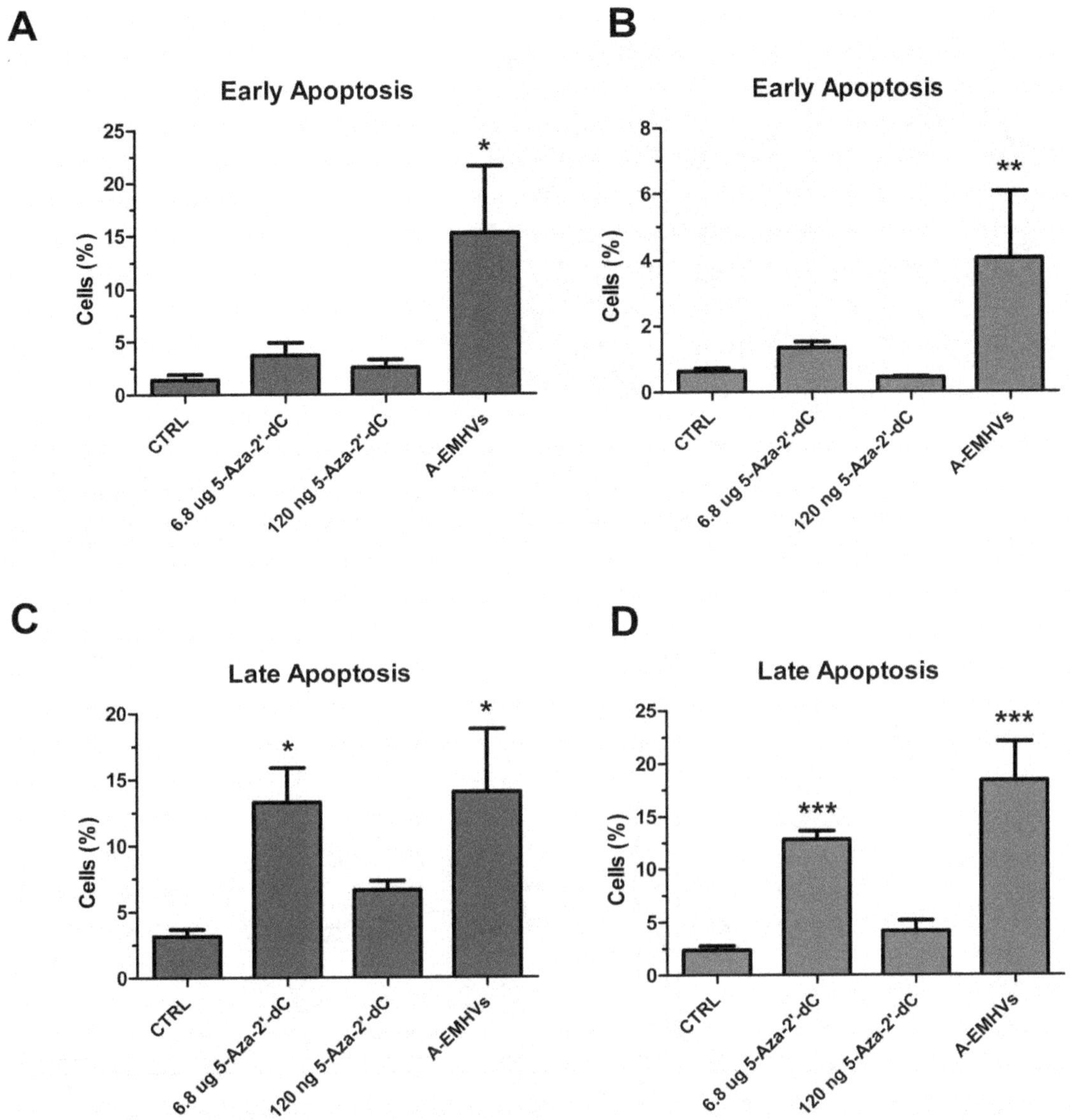

Figure 4. The pro-apoptotic effect of A-EMHVs on LNCap, hormone sensitive and DU145, hormone refractory cells. 1.5×10^8 A-EMHVs treatment, containing 120 ng internal 5-Aza-2′-dC, was compared with 6.8 μg free 5-Aza-2′-dC and 120 ng free 5-Aza-2′-dC treatments at 96 hours. Untreated cells were used as control (CTRL). In both LNCap (**A**) and DU145 (**B**) cell lines, A-EMHVs treatment induced a significant enrichment in early apoptosis (*ANOVA $p<0.05$ and **ANOVA $p<0.01$, respectively). Using 6.8 μg or 120 ng of free 5-Aza-2′-dC, no effect in early apoptosis was detected in any cell lines at 96 hours. Significant increase in late apoptosis response was observed in LNCap (**C**) and DU145 (**D**) after treatment with A-EMHVs as well as with 6.8 μg of free 5-Aza-2′-dC (*ANOVA $p<0.05$ and ***ANOVA $p<0.001$, respectively), whereas no change in late apoptosis was detected after lower free 5-Aza-2′-dC treatment at 96 hours in any of the cell lines.

active phosphorylated forms of 5-Aza-2'-dC represents the 50% of total loaded drug into the A-EMHVs.

The anti proliferative activity of A-EMHVs *in vitro*. The anti-proliferative effect of A-EMHV in inducing cell cycle arrest and apoptosis was tested in both prostate cancer models: hormone sensitive LNCap cells and androgen independent prostatic cancer DU145 cell line where traditional therapeutic approaches are hampered by the lack of responsiveness to hormone therapy and PSA antigen expression on the cell membrane.

The effect of 1.5×10^8 A-EMHVs treatment, containing approximately 120 ng internal 5-Aza2′-dC, has been compared with that of free 5-Aza-2'-dC used at the dose of 2.5 μM (total of 6.8 μg) scaled down from the therapeutic dose used in clinics. We also compared the effect of the same amount of 5-Aza-2′-dC contained inside the A-EMHVs (120 ng) used as free drug solution.

On hormone responsive LNCap cells (Fig. 3A), the A-EMHVs treatment induced a significant enrichment in sub G1 suggesting a possible activation of apoptotic response (Fig. 3A). This shift was already detectable at 48 hours after treatment (Fig. 3A middle panel) and reached statistic significance at 96 hours (ANOVA $p<0.05$). A similar shift toward sub G1 distribution was obtained also using 6.8 μg of free 5-Aza-2'-dC (ANOVA $p<0.05$), however this dose is more than 50 times higher than the 5-Aza-2'-dC loaded into the A-EMHVs. Moreover, the effect of 6.8 μg free 5-Aza-2'-dC treatment seems to have a later onset comparing to A-EMHVs. This is probably due to the fact that 5-Aza-2'-dC, encapsulated into the EMHVs is readily turned into phosphorylated forms

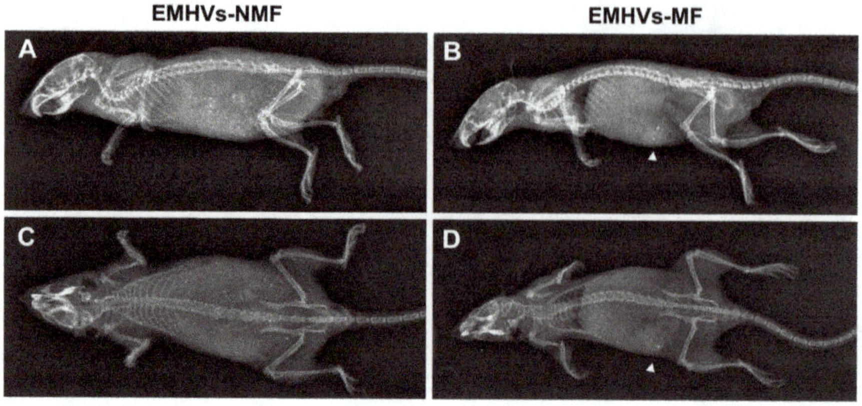

Figure 5. Localized targeted in vivo distribution of EMHVs after systemic tail vein administration in mice. Representative X-ray images of mice injected with EMHVs and treated with null (**A** and **C**) or 1,000 KOersted external static magnetic field (**B** and **D**) applied for 30 min in correspondence of the abdomen, are depicted. After 1 hour from the injection, a rather sparse distribution of nanoparticles (white irregular shadow/dots) was found inside metabolic organs and tissues exposed to null magnetic field (EMHVs-NMF, **A** sagittal and **C** frontal planes, respectively). After exposure to the magnetic field (EMHVs-MF, **B** sagittal and **D** frontal planes, respectively), nanoparticles concentrated in the target tissue (abdomen) resulting in a sharp intense signal (arrow).

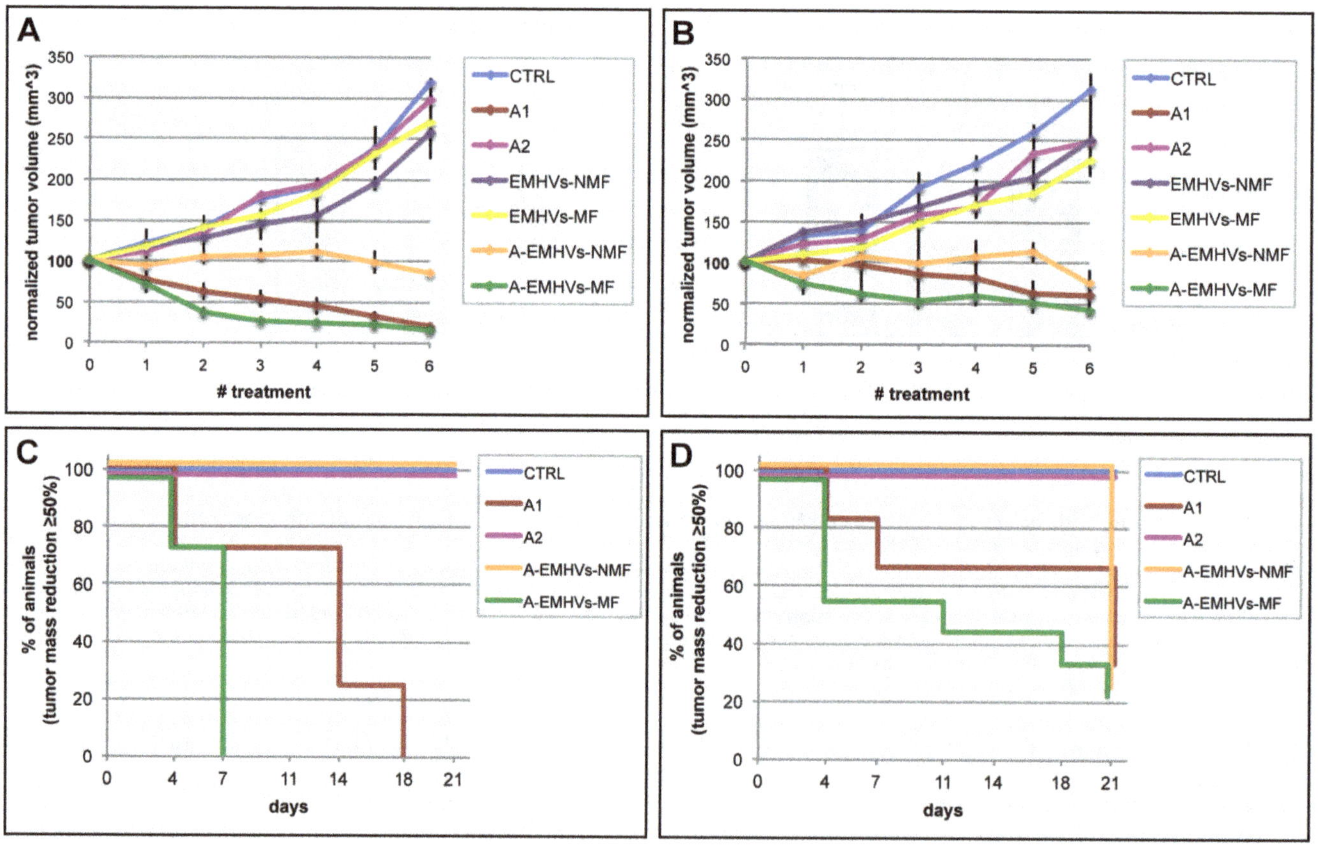

Figure 6. The anticancer effect of A-EMHVs treatment *in vivo*. Mass tumour growth curves for all experimental group are depicted in panel **A** and **B**. The treatments are Control (CTRL, cyan); therapeutic dose (A1, red); low dose equivalent to that inside the erythrocytes (A2, purple); EMHVs and no magnetic field applied (EMHVs-NMF, blue); EMHVs undergoing magnetic field (EMHVs-MF, yellow); loaded EMHVs and no magnetic field applied (A-EMHVs-NMF, orange); loaded EMHVs undergoing magnetic field application (A-EMHVs-MF, green). In (**A**) LNCap xenograft, the most significant mass reduction was measured both in A-EMHVs-MF and A1, while other treatments exerted intermediate effect with respect to controls (One-Way ANOVA $p<0.05$ at time of the sixth injection). In (**B**) DU145 xenograft, mass showed a similar trend with A-EMHVs-MF and A1 treatments being the most effective (One-Way ANOVA $p<0.05$). In **C** and **D**, Kaplan-Meier estimator curve was used to determine the percentage of treated mice showing a reduction of tumour mass volume (≥50%) during treatment. In (**C**) the trend of reduction is depicted for LNCap xenograft model: 100% of animals show ≥50% tumour volume reduction after A-EMHVs-MF (day 7th) and A1 (day18th) treatments. In DU145 xenograft model (**D**), A-EMHVs-MF (green) is the most effective anti-tumour treatment (e.g. CTRL or A2 vs A-EMHVs-MF, log rank=4.52 at day 21st).

improving 5-Aza-2'-dC pharmacokinetics/pharmacodynamics. Notably low doses of free 5-Aza-2'-dC (120 ng) did not exert sub G1 shift effect and the cell cycle distribution profile did not differ from controls up to 96 hours.

A similar trend towards sub G1 phase was described in hormone resistant DU145 cell line (Fig. 3B) after either treatment with A-EMHVs or 6.8 µg free 5-Aza-2'-dC at 96 hours (Fig. 3B lower panel, ANOVA $p<0.05$) while no change in cell cycle was detected after lower free 5-Aza-2'-dC treatment at any time points. Because a hypermethylation of some tumour suppressor genes was found in DU145, this suggests that a reprogramming of these drug resistant cells towards susceptibility of cells to apoptosis was achieved following epigenetic therapy.

To assesse if the treatments can induce the activation of pro-apoptotic response, Annexin V test has been performed. The analysis indicates that A-EMHVs exert a pro-apoptotic effect in both prostate cancer cell lines (Fig. 4). In particular the A-EMHVs treatment induced enrichment in early and late apoptosis at 96 hours after treatment (Fig. 4A and 4C) on LNCap cells, reaching statistic significance in both cases (ANOVA $p<0.05$). A similar result, but only for late apoptosis, was obtained using 6.8 µg of free 5-Aza-2'-dC (ANOVA $p<0.05$), whereas the level of early apoptosis, induced by treatment, does not statistically differ from control. A similar trend for both early and late apoptosis was described in hormone resistant DU145 cells (Fig. 4B and 4D), after treatment with A-EMHVs at 96 hours (ANOVA $p<0.01$ and $p<0.001$, respectively). Using 6.8 µg of free 5-Aza-2'-dC, a significant increase in late apoptosis was obtained, while no effect was detected for early apoptosis. No change in apoptosis was detected after lower free 5-Aza-2'-dC treatment at 96 hours in either of the cell lines.

Characterization of novel anticancer formulation *in vivo*

To set-up an efficient and effective target epigenetic therapy for solid tumours and overcome the obstacles represented by the use of demethylating agents in clinical practice [39,40], we investigated the therapeutic potential of 5-Aza-2′-dC (Decitabine) in a novel anticancer formulation *in vivo*.

***In vivo* selective concentration of EMHV by magnetic field.** To verify that systemic intravenous (i.v) administration of A-EMHVs could benefit the localised treatment of solid tumour, we first assessed if EMHV DDS could be efficiently driven to reach selected body compartments. Naïve animals were i.v. injected with 1.5×10^8 EMHVs. Immediately after injection a group of animals was exposed to an external static magnetic field applied for 30 minutes to their lower lateral abdominal region (EMHVs-MF). Control animal only received the injection and no magnetic field was applied (EMHVs-NMF).

X-ray imaging, acquired 1 hour after the injection, shows specific localization of the EMHVs in a mouse treated with EMHVs in presence of magnetic field (Fig. 5B sagittal plane and Fig. 5D frontal plane representative pictures). This animal displays few well-defined localized bright spots in the abdomen, in correspondence to the site of magnet application (1,000 KOersted). No specific accumulation was evident in the control, treated in absence of the magnetic field (EMHVs-NMF Fig. 5A and 5C, sagittal and frontal planes, respectively), where a rather sparse distribution of nanoparticles was found in the abdomen area, apparently proximal to the liver and kidneys organs.

Effect of A-EMHVs on human hormone responsive LNCap prostate cancer xenograft models. The therapeutic potential of the novel 5-Aza-2'-dC anticancer formulation (A-EMHVs) was investigated *in vivo* on animals bearing flank cancer xenografts. In LNCap xenografts (Fig. 6A), a constant increased tumour mass volume was measured in control animals (CTRL) as well as in the groups treated with unloaded 1.5×10^8 EMHVs either in absence (EMHVs-NMF) or presence (EMHVs-MF) of static magnetic field. In CTRL, volume reached 318.10 ± 5.90 mm^3, while in EMHVs-NMF and EMHVs-MF reached 257.80 ± 31.78 and 268.84 ± 7.72 mm^3 respectively, confirming that unloaded EMHVs delivery system does not induce any cytotoxic effect on target tissues per se (see also Fig. 1F, *in vitro* data). Interestingly, also the lower dose of free 5-Aza-2'-dC, (120 ng, A2), similar to those entrapped into A-EHMVs, did not alter tumour mass growth that increased up 296.19 ± 21.55 mm^3, similar to controls.

On the contrary, a constant reduction of LNCap tumour mass growth was observed in both A1 group treated with 85 µg free 5-Aza-2'-dC (2.5 mg/kg) and the group treated with A-EMHVs in presence of magnetic field (A-EHMVs-MF). More specifically, all A-EMHVs-MF animals showed a reduction in tumour volume as early as the second/third injection (A-EMHVs-MF 35.91 ± 6.29 mm^3 and 27.18 ± 3.97 mm^3) and this trend was maintained up to the latest 6th injection (A-EMHVs-MF 15.96 ± 2.77 mm^3). Similarly, a significant volume reduction was measured in A1 group after fourth/fifth injection (A1 45.24 ± 10.94 mm^3 and 21.35 ± 6.50 mm^3) and this trend was maintained up to the latest 6th injection (A1, 20.63 ± 4.59 mm^3). Therefore, although A-EMHVs-MF contains 700 times lower dose (120 ng) than A1 therapeutic dose (85 µg/i.v.), it results significantly more effective than the therapeutic dose (Two-Ways ANOVA RM $p<0.01$).

In absence of static magnetic field (NMF), A-EMHVs treatment exerts a strong cytostatic action, inhibiting the tumour growth already after the first up to the latest injection (A-EMHVs-NMF 84.87 ± 2.09 mm^3), although its effect is significantly lower in respect to A-EMHVs-MF and A1 treatment (Two-Ways ANOVA RM $p<0.001$).

The effect of A-EMHVs on non-responsive prostate cancer DU145 xenograft model. Similarly to what described *in vitro*, DU145 xenograft model is responsive to anti-cancer treatments (Fig. 6B). As expected DU145 tumour mass grew steadily during the entire duration of the experiment in CTRL, EMHVs-NMF and EMHVs-MF groups (values at sixth injection: CTRL 312.54 ± 28.23 mm^3; EMHVs-NMF 250.86 ± 19.25 mm^3; EMHVs-MF 224.50 ± 10.85 mm^3). Moreover, also the low amount of free 5-Aza-2'-dC was not sufficient to stop tumour growth (value at sixth injection A2 group 248.94 ± 70.25 mm^3). Nonetheless, tumour volume reduction of *circa* 50% was visible after the third injection of A-EMHVs in presence of magnetic field (A-EMHVs-MF 51.65 ± 8.65 mm^3) up to the last measurement at time of the sixth injection (A-EMHVs-MF 40.43 ± 5.29 mm^3). Interestingly, this reduction was not visible in A1 group. In the case of DU145 hormone resistant cells, treatment with therapeutic dose (85 µg/injection) of free 5-Aza-2′-dC (value at sixth injection A1 group 75.82 ± 21.9 mm^3) was significantly less effective than carrier delivered therapy, although the amount of injected free 5-Aza-2-dC was 700 times higher with respect to those contained in A-EMHVs as verified by Two-Ways ANOVA RM (A-EMHV-MF versus and A1, $p<0.05$).

A-EMHVs in absence of magnetic field (value at time of sixth injection A-EMHVs-NMF 127.88 ± 17.59 mm^3) only exerted a slight cytostatic activity on tumour mass and was significantly less effective than A-EMHV-MF (Two-Ways ANOVA RM: A-EMHV-NMF vs A-EMHV-MF $p<0.001$) and A1 treatment (Two-Ways ANOVA RM: A-EMHV-NMF vs A1 $p<0.05$).

Estimation of mass reduction rate *in vivo*. The introduction of the magnetic field therefore re-enforces the anticancer effect of A-EMHVs (A-EMHVs-MF vs A-EMHVs-NMF). This is

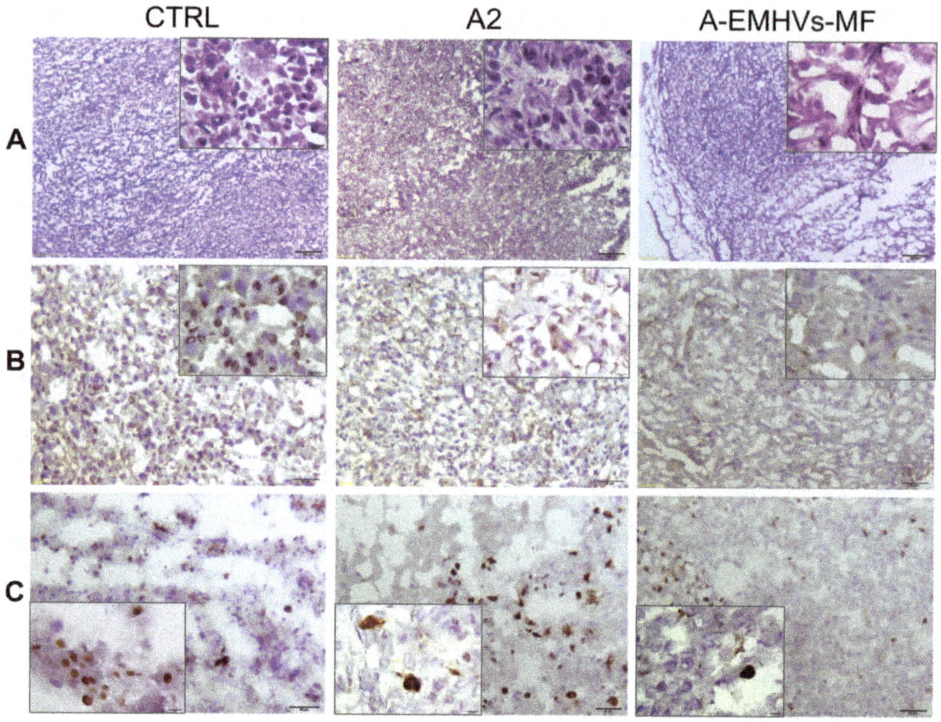

Figure 7. Histological and immunohistochemical features of explanted xenografts. Representative sections of controls (CTRL), 120 ng of free 5-Aza-2′-dC (A2) and A-EMHVs-MF treated animals. Top panels (**A**) show H&E stain at low power (2x original magnification) and high power (40x original magnification, insets) micrographs. In **B**, immunohistological reactivity, positive for nuclear DNMT3b methyltrasferase (DNA methyltransferase 3b) as a marker of tumour cells de novo methylation is shown (positive nuclei: dark brown, negative nuclei: blue. Original magnification 10x and insets at 40x). In the bottom panels (**C**) proliferating tumour cells are visualized using Ki67 marker (positive nuclei: dark brown, negative nuclei: blue. Original magnification 10x and insets at 40x).

depicted in the Kaplan-Meier estimator curve for both prostate cancer xenograft models (Fig. 6C and 6D). We chose ≥50% tumour volume reduction as the significant event to estimate and analyse the percentage of animals that demonstrated this reduction in time course.

In A-EMHVs-NMF as well as A2 and CTRL groups, the treatments are not able to exert a beneficial reduction ≥50% of tumour volume, neither in LNCap nor DU145 xenograft models.

A strong anti-cancer effect of the treatments was detected in both A-EMHV-MF and A1 groups of LNCap xenograft as 100% animals showed reduction of their mass volume more that 50% at the 7th day and 18th day, respectively (log-rank test >3.84 A-EMHV-MF or A1 vs CTRL). Similar although milder anticancer therapeutic effect was measured in DU145 xenografts with 78% of animals showing reduction of tumour volume of ≥50% in A-EMHVs-MF group (log-rank test >3.84 A-EMHVs-MF vs CTRL) and the 50% of A1 animals at day 21st. See also Figures S1 and S2 showing representative images of mice bearing tumours and intact severed specimens.

Therefore, comparing the new anticancer formulation with the free administration of therapeutic dose either in hormone sensitive and resistant forms of prostate cancer, the effect of this novel Decitabine formulation on tumour volume reduction seems to exert a stronger and faster effect with respect to drug free (A1)

Table 1. Evaluation of cell proliferation after treatments.

	CTRL		A2		A-EMHVs-MF	
	absolute value	**%**	**absolute value**	**%**	**absolute value**	**%**
DNMT3 +	93	15,7%	76	14,7%	64	10,4%
DNMT3 −	502	84,3%	575	88,3%	555	89,6%
total cell count	**595**		**651**		**619**	
Ki67 +	124	20,3%	95	16,8%	37	6,5%
Ki67 −	488	79,7%	469	83,2%	535	93,5%
total cell count	**612**		**564**		**572**	

Immuno-histochemical positivity for DNMT3b and Ki67. The results are expressed as cumulative number of and the percentage of reactive cells. Controls samples showed the highest number of reactive cells in comparison to either A2 or A-EMHVs-MF treatments.

therapy although the amount of 5-Aza-2′-dC contained into the formulation in each injected dose is much lower that the free administered drug.

Histological and immunohistochemical evidence of epigenetic A-EMHV-MF treatment. A-EMHVs-MF induced the most significant morphological changes in the tumour mass severed from xenograft implants when compared with CTRL or the equal dose (120 ng) of free 5-Aza-2′-dC treatment (A2). A first qualitative analysis of tumour mass sections indicates that the A-EMHVs-MF treatment induced a visible reduction of the slice volume occupied by tumour cells associated with an extensive replacement of death cells by fibrous tissue around the residual tumour mass. Some fibrocytes and fibroblasts were visible within the capsular tissue surrounding the tumour mass as well as replacing the necrotic tumour cells.

A thorough investigation using standard H&E stain confirmed that A-EMHVs-MF was the most effective treatment in promoting tumour cells death as highlighted by loss of nucleic staining (right inserts) and fibrous repair (Fig. 7 panel A). On the other hand, no microscopically detectable changes in sparse fibrocytes and fibroblasts were found across CTRL and A-EMHVs-MF samples stained with H&E, suggesting that the A-EMHVs-MF treatment did not induced any significant damage or toxic site effect on normal cells.

As to confirm the epigenetic nature of the therapy, a higher immunoreaction positivity for DNMT3b (DNA methyltransferase 3b) was found in tumour cells nuclei of control animals, (15.7% positivity of a cumulative number of 595 cells, Table 1) (Fig. 7 panel B, CTRL), and in animals treated with 120 ng free 5-Aza-2'-dC (14.7%, of 651 cells; Fig. 7 panel B, A2) as compared to animals treated with A-EMHVs in presence of MF (10.4% of 619 cells; Fig. 7 panel B, A-EMHVs-MF). These results suggest that loading 5-Aza-2'-dC into the erythrocytes (120 ng per dose) leads to a more efficient inhibition of DNMT3b and in turn to increased rate of tumour cell death. These data correlate with the observation that nuclear immunoreactivity of the Ki67 cell proliferating marker (Fig. 7 panel C) markedly decreases after A-EMHVs-MF treatment (6.5% positive nuclei of a total nuclear count of 572 cells) as compared to CTRL and A2 (20.3% and 16.8% positive nuclei, respectively), suggesting that A-EMHVs-MF hampers cell replicating activity within tumour mass.

All together the *in vivo* data indicate that the administration of 5-Aza-2′-dC-loaded EMHVs in mice could be considered as a locally effective epigenetic therapy. In fact it induced a significant improvement in the pharmacokinetics of drug given that low dosage of the demethylating agent was sufficient to reduce expression of DNMT and to reprogram cell fate.

Discussion

The potential of novel target epigenetic therapy, based on the use of engineered magnetic erythrocyte (EMHVs) drug delivery system, has been demonstrated in this work both *in vitro* and *in vivo* in hormone sensitive and resistant prostate cancer models opening new therapeutic prospective for its future clinical application against other solid tumours.

Using EMHVs, we were able to maximise the anti-cancer effectiveness of 5-Aza-2'-dC demethylating agent and to improve the bioavailability as well as pharmacokinetic and pharmacodynamics of drug. 5-Aza-2'-dC loaded into the carriers exhibited a significant anti-proliferative effect comparable only to the use of much higher doses of free Decitabine. This effect is likely to be related to the phosphorylation of Decitabine, critical step for anticancer activity occurred inside the EMHVs that acted as bioreactors as demonstrated by HPLC analysis. The shield provided by EMHVs to the phosphorylated active form of drug protects it from host enzyme degradation and promotes the pro-drug to active drug transition. This would improve Decitabine transient therapeutic effect and reduce inter-patient variability to therapy response [41]. This is in good agreement with recent data on Decitabine-loaded nanogels synthesized to deliver low amount of drug to chemo-resistant breast cancer cells *in vitro*. In this work the prolonged anti-proliferative effect of Decitabine was ascribed to the sustained delivery rate achieved with the use of nanogels that sustained DNMT1 depletion [21].

In vivo however, Decitabine epigenetic prolonged effect is strictly dose schedule dependent and drug concentration and bioavailability influence administration regime [27,39]. Here we were able to further improve Decitabine pharmacokinetics *in vivo*, by confining and concentrating the circulating drug-loaded EMHVs at the site of action through the application of external static magnetic field on animal xenograft tumours.

As shown in *in vitro* experiments, the fate of drug-loaded EMHVs, reaching their target, is to fuse with and release their content directly inside the host cells.

Kaplan-Meier estimator analysis demonstrated in fact a highly significant reduction in growth of tumour mass in animals treated with loaded EMHVs and magnetic field application, when compared with free Decitabine treatment. This result derived from two synergistic effects: the initial burst of delivery driven by the magnetic field application and the subsequent cytostatic effect that drug-loaded EMHVs provided as they remained in the blood pool acting as a circulating reservoir of active drug that continued to exert its anticancer activity after magnetic field removal.

The safety of the EMHVs delivery system was ascertained neither *in vitro* nor *in vivo* as undesired toxic effect was detected. In previous work we demonstrated that EMHVs are indistinguishable from host erythrocytes therefore physiological RES processing is awaiting EMHVs that might not be held by the applied magnetic force. Toxicity tests *in vivo* demonstrated the safety of EMHVs carrier in immune competent mice [34]. Thus the use of loaded EMHVs would provide a low dose, safe targeted therapy effect probably reducing possible toxic side-effects, such as granulocytopenia often observed in patients treated with Decitabine.

Moreover, the magnetic nanoparticles within engineered erythrocytes are approved by FDA for use with Magnetic Resonance Imaging (MRI) as a contrast agent to provide an improved image of body organs and tissues in diagnostic routine. It has been shown that these nanoparticles are eliminated predominantly via the kidneys and their use appear in general to be safe and well tolerated [42]. We demonstrated that EMHVs carrying magnetic nanoparticles could be concentrated into selected superficial or internal body districts by means of application of a biocompatible external magnetic field thus reducing the risk factors that could emerge by intravenous administration of free magnetic nanoparticles. This no invasive application uses similar magnetic force field employed in MRI practice, suggesting the possibility of developing loaded EMHVs formulation as a specific locally driven theranostic agent, thus opening new therapeutic prospective for the use of 5-Aza-2′-dC-EMHVs formulation in other solid tumours.

Because aberrant DNA methylation associated with inappropriate gene silencing is a common feature of solid tumours, DNA methylation inhibitors might contribute an alternative therapy especially for those tumours no responsive to conventional chemotherapy. Recent works identified aberrant methylation of some genes in LNCap and DU145 cells and highlight the potential therapeutic value of demethylating agents in prostate cancer that poor respond to conventional therapy [43,44].

Notably, we were able to tackle proliferation in prostate hormone resistant cancer cells suggesting that the epigenetic mechanisms are pivotal in development of resistant phenotype. Future work should involve screening of reprogrammed methylation and reactivated gene expression in this unresponsive model to correlate with anti-proliferative profile, which in turn would result in halting of cancer metastatic fate. Although the exact anticancer mechanism of 5-Aza-2′-dC is controversial, however our results suggest its possible role in the reduction of DNMT expression. The majority of the reports used somatic cells to assess anticancer activity of Decitabine at high dosage. There is evidence that incorporation of 5-Aza-2′-dC in DNA lead to the sequestration of DNMT enzymes and in turn to hypomethylation of specific genes suppressing DNA repair activity [45]. Recently, a specific sensitivity to low 5-Aza-2′-dC dose (10 nM) by human embryonic carcinoma cells (EC) was described in testicular germ cell tumours. More specifically, hypersensitivity was correlated with high expression of DNMT3b proper of embryonic and cancer stem cells. In these cells, the early effect on DNMT3 depletion and gene methylation was evident within 72 hours of treatment [19]. Similarly we found that the anti-proliferative effect due to loaded EMHVs administration (120 ng 5-Aza-2′-dC) in both LNCap and DU145 was significantly higher at 24 and lasted up to 96 hours in culture. A-EMHVs treatment resulted in a fast and strong shift of cell cycle phase distribution towards sub G1, inducing the cell cycle arrest. In fact apoptotic response was stronger after A-EMHVs treatment, comparing free 5-Aza-2′-dC conventional treatment, likely due to the fact that EMHVs directly release and enriched the therapeutic phosphorylated active drug inside the cells.

Moreover, 5-Aza-2'-dC was also found to regulate gene re-expression in a DNA methylation-independent manner through the breaking up complex protein interactions by inhibition and removal of DNMTs from the nucleus. It is likely that this pronounced A-EMHVs-MF effect on prostate hormone responsive and non-responsive tumour cells could be mediated by the intrinsic direct inhibitory activity exerted by 5-Aza-2'-dC on the DNA methyltransferases [37,46,47]. Indeed immunohistochemical findings in specimens from *in vivo* xenografts suggested a specific involvement of DNMT3b inhibition exerted by the low dose 5-Aza-2′-dC-loaded EMHVs (120 ng) in presence of magnetic field causing apoptotic response on target cancer cells. A reduce expression of DNMT3 was in fact found in tumour mass sections after treatment with A-EMHVs-MF, while the same 5-Aza-2′-dC concentration administered free was not able to exert any changes in immunohistochemical staining or cytotoxic effect.

Coincidently the expression of Ki67 pro-proliferative factor is highly down regulated in tumour cells of animal group treated with A-EMHVs-MF, suggesting that reprogramming of the tumour suppressor gene methylation might take place and re-establishing chemotherapy sensitivity would prompt those cancer cells to respond to a subsequent conventional chemotherapy. Interestingly, no morphological damages were visible in fibrocytes and fibroblasts surrounding and infiltrating tumour mass suggesting the A-EMHVs-MF treatment did not exerted any local toxicity to normal cells.

EMHVs are versatile carriers that have been used to target the delivery of different types of molecule and for the treatment of diseases other that cancer. Recently, their use for a gene therapy in a vascular restenosis models has been reported [48]. Similarly, in this work erythrocyte-based delivery of bio-drugs resulted more efficient than the delivery by other conventional vehicles. Up to now the need for *ex-vivo* manipulations with RBCs, a relatively limited shelf life, concerns related to the safety of donors matching and blood-born infections have limited their use as DDS carriers. The development of a personalized medicine for cancer or other diseases based on the use of autologous loaded EMHVs is getting nonetheless more and more feasible, as progress in modulating the RBC membrane to produce transferable stealth donor RBCs have been made. Indeed, the use of autologous blood (re-infusion) would minimize the safety concerns. Loaded EMHVs may be easily produced on the daily bases by self-donation of patients that could lately receive the therapy with minimal discomfort and total safety. This would encourage the "bench to bedside" translation of innovative clinical approaches.

Conclusions

The scientific rationale for this investigation is the urgent need to find new safe strategies for tackling common forms of cancer, such as prostate cancer that often develops into metastatic and untreatable forms. Increasing evidence suggests that epigenetic events are causally implicated in prostate cancer development as epigenetic silencing of androgen receptor expression has been observed in 8% of primary prostate cancers. In the present work we exploited the therapeutic potential of classic demethylating agent Decitabine to induce tumour cell reprogramming by loading it into an erythrocyte-based delivery system to improve pharmacokinetics and pharmacodynamics. This approach represents a novel formulation of anticancer treatment that can be easily localised at site of action by a non-invasive safe magnetic system. Interestingly this novel Decitabine formulation might find new application in unresponsive forms of carcinoma, such as hormone refractory prostate cancer. As several challenges exist to successfully translate the outcomes from animal research to humans in a clinical setting we foresee future investigation to confirm EMHVs effectiveness in orthotopic animal model of cancer before beginning studies in patients.

Supporting Information

Figure S1 Representative images of mice bearing tumours and intact severed specimens of LNCap xenograft groups after the sixth injection. CTRL animal treated with 1X PBS; **A1** animal treated with 85 µg 5-Aza-2'-dC (2.5 mg/kg); **A2** animal treated with 120 ng 5-Aza-2'-dC; **EMHVs-NMF** animal treated with 1.5×10^{8} unloaded EMHVs drug delivery system in absence of static magnetic field; **A-EMHVs-NMF** animal treated with 1.5×10^{8} EMHVs containing 120 ng 5-Aza-2'-dC in absence of static magnetic field; **A-EMHVs-MF** animal treated with 1.5×10^{8} EMHVs containing 120 ng 5-Aza-2'-dC and static magnetic field applied on tumour.

Figure S2 Representative images of mice bearing tumours and intact severed specimens of DU145 xenograft groups after the sixth injection. CTRL animal treated with 1X PBS; **A1** animal treated with 85 µg 5-Aza-2'-dC (2.5 mg/kg); **A2** animal treated with 120 ng 5-Aza-2'-dC; **EMHVs-NMF** animal treated with 1.5×10^{8} unloaded EMHVs drug delivery system in absence of static magnetic field; **A- EMHVs-NMF** animal treated with 1.5×10^{8} EMHVs containing 120 ng 5-Aza-2'-dC in absence of static magnetic field; **A- EMHVs-MF** animal treated with 1.5×10^{8} EMHVs containing 120 ng 5-Aza-2'-dC and static magnetic field applied on tumour.

Acknowledgments

The authors wish to acknowledge Dr. Pier Paolo Claudio for his support in *in vivo* experiments started at Marshall University of Huntington, WV, USA and stimulating discussions. The author also thanks Dr. Claus A. Andersen for English editing.

Author Contributions

Conceived and designed the experiments: IN MT CC SG. Performed the experiments: IN MT GP FV. Analyzed the data: IN MT LG GP LP. Contributed reagents/materials/analysis tools: CC SG GP. Wrote the paper: LG CC.

References

1. Jemal A, Siegel R, Ward E, Hao Y, Xu J, et al. (2008) Cancer statistics, 2008. CA Cancer J Clin 58: 71–96.
2. Scosyrev E, Messing EM, Mohile S, Golijanin D, Wu G (2012) Prostate cancer in the elderly: frequency of advanced disease at presentation and disease-specific mortality. Cancer 118: 3062–3070.
3. Schmitges J, Trinh QD, Walz J, Graefen M (2011) Surgery for high-risk localized prostate cancer. Ther Adv Urol 3: 173–182.
4. Gnanapragasam VJ, Mason MD, Shaw GL, Neal DE (2012) The role of surgery in high-risk localised prostate cancer. BJU Int 109: 648–658.
5. Shipley WU, Thames HD, Sandler HM, Hanks GE, Zietman AL, et al. (1999) Radiation therapy for clinically localized prostate cancer: a multi-institutional pooled analysis. JAMA 281: 1598–1604.
6. Zietman AL, DeSilvio ML, Slater JD, Rossi CJ, Jr., Miller DW, et al. (2005) Comparison of conventional-dose vs high-dose conformal radiation therapy in clinically localized adenocarcinoma of the prostate: a randomized controlled trial. JAMA 294: 1233–1239.
7. Peeters ST, Heemsbergen WD, Koper PC, van Putten WL, Slot A, et al. (2006) Dose-response in radiotherapy for localized prostate cancer: results of the Dutch multicenter randomized phase III trial comparing 68 Gy of radiotherapy with 78 Gy. J Clin Oncol 24: 1990–1996.
8. Saraon P, Jarvi K, Diamandis EP (2011) Molecular alterations during progression of prostate cancer to androgen independence. Clin Chem 57: 1366–1375.
9. Yadav N, Heemers HV (2012) Androgen action in the prostate gland. Minerva Urol Nefrol 64: 35–49.
10. Sartor AO (2011) Progression of metastatic castrate-resistant prostate cancer: impact of therapeutic intervention in the post-docetaxel space. J Hematol Oncol 4: 18.
11. Siegel R, Naishadham D, Jemal A (2013) Cancer statistics, 2013. CA Cancer J Clin 63: 11–30.
12. Heidenreich A, Sommer F, Ohlmann CH, Schrader AJ, Olbert P, et al. (2004) Prospective randomized Phase II trial of pegylated doxorubicin in the management of symptomatic hormone-refractory prostate carcinoma. Cancer 101: 948–956.
13. Patra A, Deb M, Dahiya R, Patra SK (2011) 5-Aza-2'-deoxycytidine stress response and apoptosis in prostate cancer. Clin Epigenetics 2: 339–348.
14. Goering W, Kloth M, Schulz WA (2012) DNA methylation changes in prostate cancer. Methods Mol Biol 863: 47–66.
15. Gnyszka A, Jastrzebski Z, Flis S (2013) DNA methyltransferase inhibitors and their emerging role in epigenetic therapy of cancer. Anticancer Res 33: 2989–2996.
16. Tsai HC, Baylin SB (2011) Cancer epigenetics: linking basic biology to clinical medicine. Cell Res 21: 502–517.
17. Mishra MV, Bisht KS, Sun L, Muldoon-Jacobs K, Awwad R, et al. (2008) DNMT1 as a molecular target in a multimodality-resistant phenotype in tumor cells. Mol Cancer Res 6: 243–249.
18. Kantarjian H, Issa JP, Rosenfeld CS, Bennett JM, Albitar M, et al. (2006) Decitabine improves patient outcomes in myelodysplastic syndromes: results of a phase III randomized study. Cancer 106: 1794–1803.
19. Biswal BK, Beyrouthy MJ, Hever-Jardine MP, Armstrong D, Tomlinson CR, et al. (2012) Acute hypersensitivity of pluripotent testicular cancer-derived embryonal carcinoma to low-dose 5-aza deoxycytidine is associated with global DNA Damage-associated p53 activation, anti-pluripotency and DNA demethylation. PLoS One 7: e53003.
20. Momparler RL (2013) Epigenetic therapy of non-small cell lung cancer using decitabine (5-aza-2'-deoxycytidine). Front Oncol 3: 188.
21. Vijayaraghavalu S, Labhasetwar V (2013) Efficacy of decitabine-loaded nanogels in overcoming cancer drug resistance is mediated via sustained DNA methyltransferase 1 (DNMT1) depletion. Cancer Lett 331: 122–129.
22. Mossman D, Kim KT, Scott RJ (2010) Demethylation by 5-aza-2'-deoxycytidine in colorectal cancer cells targets genomic DNA whilst promoter CpG island methylation persists. BMC Cancer 10: 366.
23. Chu SH, Ma YB, Feng DF, Zhang H, Qiu JH, et al. (2012) Effect of 5-Aza-2'-deoxycytidine on SLC22A18 in glioma U251 cells. Mol Med Rep 5: 138–141.
24. Hagelgans A, Menschikowski M, Fuessel S, Nacke B, Arneth BM, et al. (2013) Deregulated expression of urokinase and its inhibitor type 1 in prostate cancer cells: role of epigenetic mechanisms. Exp Mol Pathol 94: 458–465.
25. Tian J, Lee SO, Liang L, Luo J, Huang CK, et al. (2012) Targeting the unique methylation pattern of androgen receptor (AR) promoter in prostate stem/progenitor cells with 5-aza-2'-deoxycytidine (5-AZA) leads to suppressed prostate tumorigenesis. J Biol Chem 287: 39954–39966.
26. Fialova B, Smesny Trtkova K, Paskova L, Langova K, Kolar Z (2013) Effect of histone deacetylase and DNA methyltransferase inhibitors on the expression of the androgen receptor gene in androgen-independent prostate cancer cell lines. Oncol Rep 29: 2039–2045.
27. Karahoca M, Momparler RL (2013) Pharmacokinetic and pharmacodynamic analysis of 5-aza-2'-deoxycytidine (decitabine) in the design of its dose-schedule for cancer therapy. Clin Epigenetics 5: 3.
28. Li W, Zhang L, Zhang G, Wei H, Zhao M, et al. (2013) The finely regulating well-defined functional polymeric nanocarriers for anti-tumor immunotherapy. Mini Rev Med Chem 13: 643–652.
29. Niemirowicz K, Markiewicz KH, Wilczewska AZ, Car H (2012) Magnetic nanoparticles as new diagnostic tools in medicine. Adv Med Sci 57: 196–207.
30. Hu CM, Fang RH, Zhang L (2012) Erythrocyte-inspired delivery systems. Adv Healthc Mater 1: 537–547.
31. Magnani M, Pierige F, Rossi L (2012) Erythrocytes as a novel delivery vehicle for biologics: from enzymes to nucleic acid-based therapeutics. Ther Deliv 3: 405–414.
32. Hamidi M, Zarrin A, Foroozesh M, Mohammadi-Samani S (2007) Applications of carrier erythrocytes in delivery of biopharmaceuticals. J Control Release 118: 145–160.
33. Cinti C, Taranta M, Naldi I, Grimaldi S (2011) Newly engineered magnetic erythrocytes for sustained and targeted delivery of anti-cancer therapeutic compounds. PLoS One 6: e17132.
34. Taranta MN, I; Grimaldi, S; Salvini, L; Claudio, PP; Rocchio, F; Munoz, AF; Prete, S; Cinti, C;. (2011) Magnetically driven bioreactors as new tools in drug delivery. Bioanalysis and biomedicine 2011, s5.
35. Chiam K, Centenera MM, Butler LM, Tilley WD, Bianco-Miotto T (2011) GSTP1 DNA methylation and expression status is indicative of 5-aza-2'-deoxycytidine efficacy in human prostate cancer cells. PLoS One 6: e25634.
36. Langford DJ, Bailey AL, Chanda ML, Clarke SE, Drummond TE, et al. (2010) Coding of facial expressions of pain in the laboratory mouse. Nat Methods 7: 447–449.
37. Christman JK (2002) 5-Azacytidine and 5-aza-2'-deoxycytidine as inhibitors of DNA methylation: mechanistic studies and their implications for cancer therapy. Oncogene 21: 5483–5495.
38. Gutierrez Millan C, Zarzuelo Castaneda A, Sayalero Marinero ML, Lanao JM (2004) Factors associated with the performance of carrier erythrocytes obtained by hypotonic dialysis. Blood Cells Mol Dis 33: 132–140.
39. Momparler RL (2005) Pharmacology of 5-Aza-2'-deoxycytidine (decitabine). Semin Hematol 42: S9–16.
40. Liu Z, Marcucci G, Byrd JC, Grever M, Xiao J, et al. (2006) Characterization of decomposition products and preclinical and low dose clinical pharmacokinetics of decitabine (5-aza-2'-deoxycytidine) by a new liquid chromatography/tandem mass spectrometry quantification method. Rapid Commun Mass Spectrom 20: 1117–1126.
41. Graham JS, Kaye SB, Brown R (2009) The promises and pitfalls of epigenetic therapies in solid tumours. Eur J Cancer 45: 1129–1136.
42. Kirchin MA, Runge VM (2003) Contrast agents for magnetic resonance imaging: safety update. Top Magn Reson Imaging 14: 426–435.
43. Sabatino MA, Geroni C, Ganzinelli M, Ceruti R, Broggini M (2013) Zebularine partially reverses GST methylation in prostate cancer cells and restores sensitivity to the DNA minor groove binder brostallicin. Epigenetics 8: 656–665.
44. Lenka G, Weng WH, Chuang CK, Ng KF, Pang ST (2013) Aberrant expression of the PRAC gene in prostate cancer. Int J Oncol 43: 1960–1966.
45. Kim HJ, Kim JH, Chie EK, Young PD, Kim IA, et al. (2012) DNMT (DNA methyltransferase) inhibitors radiosensitize human cancer cells by suppressing DNA repair activity. Radiat Oncol 7: 39.
46. Ghoshal K, Datta J, Majumder S, Bai S, Kutay H, et al. (2005) 5-Aza-deoxycytidine induces selective degradation of DNA methyltransferase 1 by a proteasomal pathway that requires the KEN box, bromo-adjacent homology domain, and nuclear localization signal. Mol Cell Biol 25: 4727–4741.
47. Robertson KD, Ait-Si-Ali S, Yokochi T, Wade PA, Jones PL, et al. (2000) DNMT1 forms a complex with Rb, E2F1 and HDAC1 and represses transcription from E2F-responsive promoters. Nat Genet 25: 338–342.
48. Lande C, Cecchettini A, Tedeschi L, Taranta M, Naldi I, et al. (2012) Innovative erythrocyte-based carriers for gene delivery in porcine vascular smooth muscle cells: basis for local therapy to prevent restenosis. Cardiovasc Hematol Disord Drug Targets.

12

Analysis of Vaginal Microbicide Film Hydration Kinetics by Quantitative Imaging Refractometry

Matthew Rinehart[1]*, Sheila Grab[2], Lisa Rohan[2], David Katz[1,3], Adam Wax[1]

1 Department of Biomedical Engineering, Duke University, Durham, North Carolina, United States of America, **2** University of Pittsburgh, School of Pharmacy, Magee Womens Research Institute, Pittsburgh, Pennsylvania, United States of America, **3** Department of Obstetrics and Gynecology, Duke University, Durham, North Carolina, United States of America

Abstract

We have developed a quantitative imaging refractometry technique, based on holographic phase microscopy, as a tool for investigating microscopic structural changes in water-soluble polymeric materials. Here we apply the approach to analyze the structural degradation of vaginal topical microbicide films due to water uptake. We implemented transmission imaging of 1-mm diameter film samples loaded into a flow chamber with a 1.5×2 mm field of view. After water was flooded into the chamber, interference images were captured and analyzed to obtain high resolution maps of the local refractive index and subsequently the volume fraction and mass density of film material at each spatial location. Here, we compare the hydration dynamics of a panel of films with varying thicknesses and polymer compositions, demonstrating that quantitative imaging refractometry can be an effective tool for evaluating and characterizing the performance of candidate microbicide film designs for anti-HIV drug delivery.

Editor: Bing Xu, Brandeis University, United States of America

Funding: This work was funded by grants from the National Science Foundation (MRI-1039562) and the National Institutes of Health (RO1 HD072702 and DAIDS IPCP U19 AI082639). The funders had no role in study design, data collection and analysis, decision to publish, or preparation of the manuscript.

Competing Interests: The authors have declared that no competing interests exist.

* E-mail: matt.rinehart@duke.edu

Introduction

Thin polymeric films have been utilized as dosage forms for oral and topical delivery of drugs. Vaginal films have been commercially available as contraceptive products for many years [1–4]. Now, vaginal films are being developed as topical drug delivery vehicles for the prevention of infection and spread of HIV/AIDS [5–7]. They have many favorable qualities as drug delivery platforms: films allow localized drug delivery at the most common site of transmission (the vagina), are inexpensive to manufacture, may be applied without an applicator, do not leak, and are highly-stable, portable products that are easily stored for long periods of time without risk of drug degradation [8].

Topical drug delivery by films and other vaginally administered microbicide products (e.g. gels) places requirements not only on the drug release rate but also on subsequent spatial distribution of the active pharmaceutical ingredient (API). This derives from the spreading and hydration behavior of the delivery vehicle [9–11]. However, most quantitative methods of evaluation of these products have focused on measuring bulk material physicochemical properties and macroscopic disintegration and dissolution/drug release rates. Film disintegration testing is regularly a part of product development efforts. However, standard USP methods for disintegration testing require testing in large volumes of medium. In order to create a more biorelevant assessment of disintegration, a subjective visual assessment has been used in a lower volume of medium reflective of the small amount of fluids present in the vagina [12,13]. Although film uptake of fluid and consequent swelling, disintegration, and dissolution, are central to drug delivery by the film, there has been little study of the spatial behavior of film swelling, which underlies the drug release and delivery [12,13]. As computational film dissolution models are developed [14] and more advanced films are designed with complex dissolution and delivery characteristics, there is a need for objective and quantitative methodology that can verify that film formulations function as intended, delivering APIs to tissue with both the requisite spatial and temporal concentration distributions.

We have previously demonstrated an optical characterization method based on quantitative phase microscopy (QPM) to measure spatial distributions of polymer volume fractions of dissolving polymer films [15]. This technique produces spatial maps of the integral refractive index (RI) throughout a film sample from a single temporal imaging frame. Interferometric phase microscopy has also been used in several cell studies as an effective method for analyzing dynamic changes in water content and cell dry mass [16–18]. In the work presented here, we further develop our technique into a quantitative assay and incorporate spatio-temporal analysis of mass transport to present the first comparison of the structural changes of different antiretroviral containing films with varied compositions and geometries.

First, we describe an optimized optical configuration for standardized and comparable experiments. Then, using reference measurements of the refractive index of each sample, we show how to compute the volume fraction and mass density of the film material and water, yielding two-dimensional spatial maps of hydration and structural disintegration. We compare these data for a panel of film candidates loaded with tenofovir (TFV), an antiretroviral drug being studied for vaginal administration for topical pre-exposure prophylaxis. This drug is in the midst of multiple clinical trials, the first of which showed its promise in topical vaginal prophylactic against HIV infection [19–21]. Finally, we show that both the polymer composition and film geometry affect not only film hydration rate, but also the spatial distributions of polymer film material.

Methods

2.1 Quantitative Phase Microscopy Setup

The imaging device used for these experiments is a custom interferometer designed for quantitative phase microscopy, as illustrated in fig. 1A [15]. A beam from a helium-neon laser ($\lambda = 632.8$ nm) is spatially-filtered and magnified using lenses L1 and L2 along with aperture A, and is then split into sample and reference arms, S and R, at BS1. The light from the sample arm passes through the sample, which imparts a spatial pattern of phase delays upon this beam. Microscope objective MO1 (2.5× A-plan, Zeiss) is in a 4F imaging configuration with tube lens TL and produces a magnified image of a 2.0 mm×1.5 mm field of view onto the plane of the camera (Flea3.0, Point Grey). The light from the reference arm passes through a matched objective MO2 and recombines with the sample light at beam splitter BS2 before being imaged onto the camera by TL. A lateral shift in the alignment of both the reference beam and MO2 relative to the signal beam path produces a high frequency linear fringe pattern.

2.2 Phase Image Processing

After image acquisition, the off-axis interferograms are digitally processed to recover phase images of the relative optical delays associated with the sample [15,22]. The Fourier transform of this off-axis interference pattern yields distinct autocorrelation and crosscorrelation terms arising from the optical mixing of the reference and sample light fields. One of the cross correlation terms is first isolated by spatial filtering, then re-centered in frequency space, and is finally inverse Fourier transformed to recover the complex wave information [22]. Taking the phase of this complex-valued data produces a two-dimensional map of the relative phase difference between the reference beam and the sample beam. The recovered phase delays are mathematically limited in range to $\pm\pi$, with longer or shorter delays being ambiguously measured modulo-2π. In order to recover a true representation of the relative phase delays across the field of view, spatial [23] and temporal [24] unwrapping algorithms are combined as described previously [15]. Under the assumption that the true phase distribution does not change by more than $\pi/2$ between two adjacent data points in either time or space, these algorithms produce unambiguous phase images.

The recovered quantitative phase measurements are further processed to produce film polymer volume fraction and hydration maps. First, a phase image of the flow chamber filled with water is subtracted from each image to remove system phase artifacts and yield the relative phase delays induced by only the film material, $\Delta\varphi(\vec{r},t)$. Then, using the chamber height as measured with digital calipers ($d_{chamber} = 250\mu m \pm 10\mu m$), the average refractive index, $\bar{n}(\vec{r},t)$, is calculated as:

$$\bar{n}(\vec{r},t) = \frac{\Delta\varphi(\vec{r},t)}{d_{chamber}}\frac{\lambda}{2\pi} \quad (1)$$

It is important to note that $\bar{n}(\vec{r},t)$ is the average RI over the entire axial thickness of the chamber sample, and therefore represents a linear combination of the component refractive indices weighted by their relative heights as given in eqn. 2:

$$n_{h_2o}d_{h_2o} + n_f d_f = \bar{n}(d_{h_2o} + d_f) \quad (2)$$

The height of the sample chamber along with the xy-lateral dimensions of the microscope form a voxel whose RI is a linear combination of the RIs of the water, n_{h_2o}, and film, n_f, components weighted by the heights of the water and film, d_{h_2o} and d_f, respectively. Upon decomposition of the measured RI

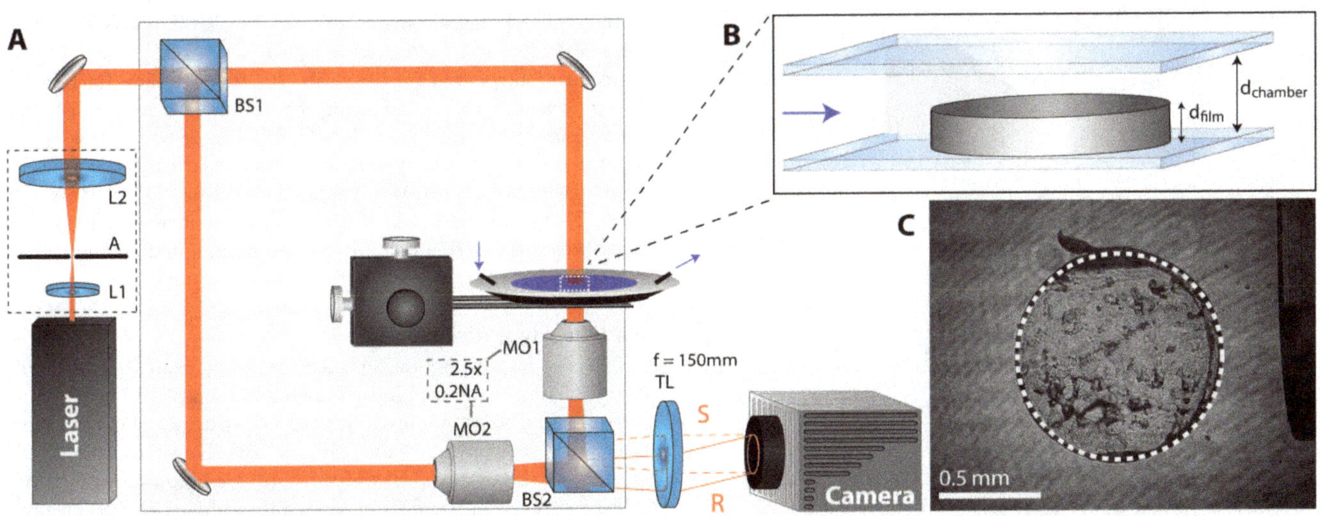

Figure 1. Microscope setup and hydration assay configuration. (A) Experimental schematic of quantitative phase microscope. (B) Film geometry within the chamber at time t = 0. The blue arrow indicates lateral water flow which initiates hydration. (C) Typical interferogram of a 1-mm-diameter film sample with the phase calibration ramp visible in the microscope's field of view (right edge).

Table 1. Refractive indices & measured dissolution parameters of specific film formulations.

	dn/dc (ml/ml)	Density, ϱ^f (g/ml)	α (ml/g)	Refractive Index	τ_H (m:ss)	Λ	Γ
H_2O		1.000		1.3329±.0001			
T1A	0.154±.002	1.183	0.130±.002	1.486±.002	5:16	.076±.002	0.165±.033
T2A	0.144±.001	1.118	0.129±.001	1.477±.001	5:44	.105±.003	0.253±.100
T3A	0.151±.008	1.315	0.115±.006	1.485±.008	8:52	.016±.001	0.061±.031
T1B	0.154±.002	1.180	0.130±.002	1.486±.002	7:48	.116±.003	0.125±.007

α values are given as mean ±95% CI. τ_H is hydration time; Λ and Γ given as mean ± standard deviation.

values into percent-volumes of film polymer and water, quantitative maps are produced. From these, the percent volume of film, *F*, (i.e. volume fraction of polymer) at each spatial point is calculated:

$$F = \%vol.Film = \frac{\bar{n} - n_{h_2o}}{n_f - n_{h_2o}} * 100$$

The quantitative phase microscope and processing methods described above achieve a temporal phase stability of 13.5 mrad, corresponding to a refractive index sensitivity of $\sigma_{\bar{n}} = 5.5 \times 10^-6$ [15]. This measurement sensitivity along with the measurements and uncertainties of $n_{h_2}o$

The quantitative phase microscope and processing methods described above achieve a temporal phase stability of 13.5 mrad, corresponding to a refractive index sensitivity of $\sigma_{\bar{n}} = 5.5 \times 10^-6$ [15]. This measurement sensitivity along with the measurements and uncertainties of $n_{h_2}o$ and each film's n_f (Table 1) are propagated through eqns. 3 and 4 to yield a film fraction measurement precision ranging from $\sigma_F = 0.0035 - 0.0038$ percentage points (pp).

2.3 Microbicidal Film Characterization

Microbicidal films were manufactured in sheets that are approximately 8 inches × 12 inches using a solvent casting method similar to that described by Akil, et al [12]. Films were cast onto substrate and dried before being cut into 1 inch by 2 inch individual film strips using a die press. Individual film strips were analyzed for drug content using high pressure liquid chromatography methods and were found to contain approximately 20 mg of tenofovir. Water content was measured using a Karl Fisher titration apparatus. Film thickness was measured with mechanical calipers with a measurement resolution of ±10 μm. Finally, the RIs of each distinct film composition, as well as that for the deionized water used for the flow experiments, were measured separately using a bulk refractometer (Bellingham & Stanley, RFM 340). Since this is a surface measurement device, equilibrium serial dilutions of the polymer film samples with water were prepared. Fitting the RI measurements of each film's dilution series to a linear model as $n(C) = dn/dC_v * C_v + n_{h_2o}$ where C_v is the volume concentration, yielded a value of dn/dC_v for each film. Each film's density was then calculated according to the compositions listed in Table 2 and used to convert dn/dC_v to RI increments, α, which is a parameter that is widely used in interferometric mass analysis of biomaterials [18,25,26]. We evaluated four distinct films (Table 2): T1A, T2A, and T3A, which are tenofovir-loaded films, 120 μm thick, which differed in polymer composition, and T1B, which has the same composition as T1A but is twice as thick.

2.4 Film Hydration Assay

Samples for the hydration assay were cut from the film strip using a 1 mm-diameter biopsy punch and then placed on a round coverslip in close proximity to a reference structure. This structure is a transparent physical ramp (Sylgard 184, Dow Corning) that is epoxied to the coverslip in order to provide a constant refractive index reference in the field of view during the experimental time course [15]. Gentle pressure was applied to the film with a blunt pair of tweezers in order to partially attach the sample to the coverslip. This ensured that the film remained centered in the field of view when water was added at the beginning of the experiment.

Table 2. Composition and thicknesses of films analyzed in the study.

	Composition prior to evaporation									Post-evaporation properties		
	PVP	MC	HPMC	HEC	Na CMC	TFV	GLYC	NaOH	H_2O	H_2O	Thickness (μm)	RI
T1A	-	-	6	6	2	2	2	0.28	81.72	5.47	120	1.486
T2A	-	-	7	7	-	2	2	0.28	81.72	7.15	120	1.477
T3A	10	2	-	-	2	2	3.6	0.28	80.12	10.51	120	1.485
T1B	-	-	6	6	2	2	2	0.28	81.72	7.31	240	1.486

All values are given as % w/w, except for thicknesses and RIs.
Ingredient abbreviations: hydroxyethyl cellulose (HEC), hydroxypropyl methylcellulose (HPMC), carboxymethylcellulose sodium (NaCMC), Tenofovir (TFV), glycerin (GLYC), sodium hydroxide (NaOH), polyvinylpyrrolidone K90 (PVP), methyl cellulose (MC), water (H_2O).

After placement of a film sample, a coverslip was inserted as the top of a lateral flow chamber (Bioptechs, FCS3 chamber). A 250 μm thick gasket sealed the chamber and thus allowed both top and bottom coverslips to make contact with the calibration ramp structure. The sample was centered in the QPM field of view, and then water was injected with a hand syringe into the chamber from an inlet port until it completely immersed the sample and flowed to the outlet port. As soon as the water reached the outlet port (~2–3 seconds after film immersion), flow was halted. Images were acquired at 2 s intervals over a time course of 20 minutes as the film dissolved. After a defined 20 minute hydration period, a large volume of water was flushed through the chamber to clear all film material from the field of view. An interferogram was then captured with the water-filled chamber as a reference phase measurement. Each interference image was then processed as described in section 2.1 to yield film volume fraction data (approx. 2 s per image, 20 min total processing time per dataset), which became an output measure of hydration for comparison across repeated experiments and varied film compositions. The hydration assay was repeated three times for each film type.

2.5 Comparative Analysis of Films

Film volume fraction images were calculated from the QPM measurements as described in section 2.2. Although films T1A–T3A have unique compositions and densities, their initial geometries are identical and therefore their volume fractions are directly comparable during hydration and dissolution. Representative images of film volume fraction were selected for direct comparison at specific time points. The volume fraction of film material remaining within the initial area was also compared by manually selecting the center location of each sample and averaging the volume fraction remaining within a 1 mm-diameter area (fig. 1C).

Additionally, differences in hydration dynamics were analyzed by quantifying spatial distributions of the polymer dry mass. The mass density, which indicates polymer concentration, was calculated from volume fraction data using the known geometry of the flow chamber and the density of each film (ϱ_f in g/ml, see Table 1):

$$M(x,y,t) = F(x,y,t) * 250 \times 10^-6 \frac{ml}{mm^2} * \varrho_f.$$

Mass density images were interpolated from Cartesian (x, y) to polar (r, θ) coordinates, (Figs. 2A and B), and axiosymmetric radial profiles were calculated by taking the median value over θ as a robust measure of central tendency.

Hydration dynamics of the varied polymer films were further compared using spatial Fourier analysis (SFA) of the mass density distributions. Polar mass density distributions (Fig. 2B) were Fourier transformed in r, and averaged over θ to produce $\langle \hat{M}(\rho,t) \rangle_\theta$, which is a measure of how each radial spatial frequency evolves over time (Figs.2B and C). The dynamics of each film's hydration process were then compared by examining the temporal dynamics of specific spectral components (Fig. 2D).

Results

3.1 Film Characteristics Summary

Table 2 summarizes the initial compositions, the residual water content after evaporation, thickness, and refractive indexes of the film compositions analyzed in this study. Films T1A and T2A are more chemically similar to each other than T3A, containing only a

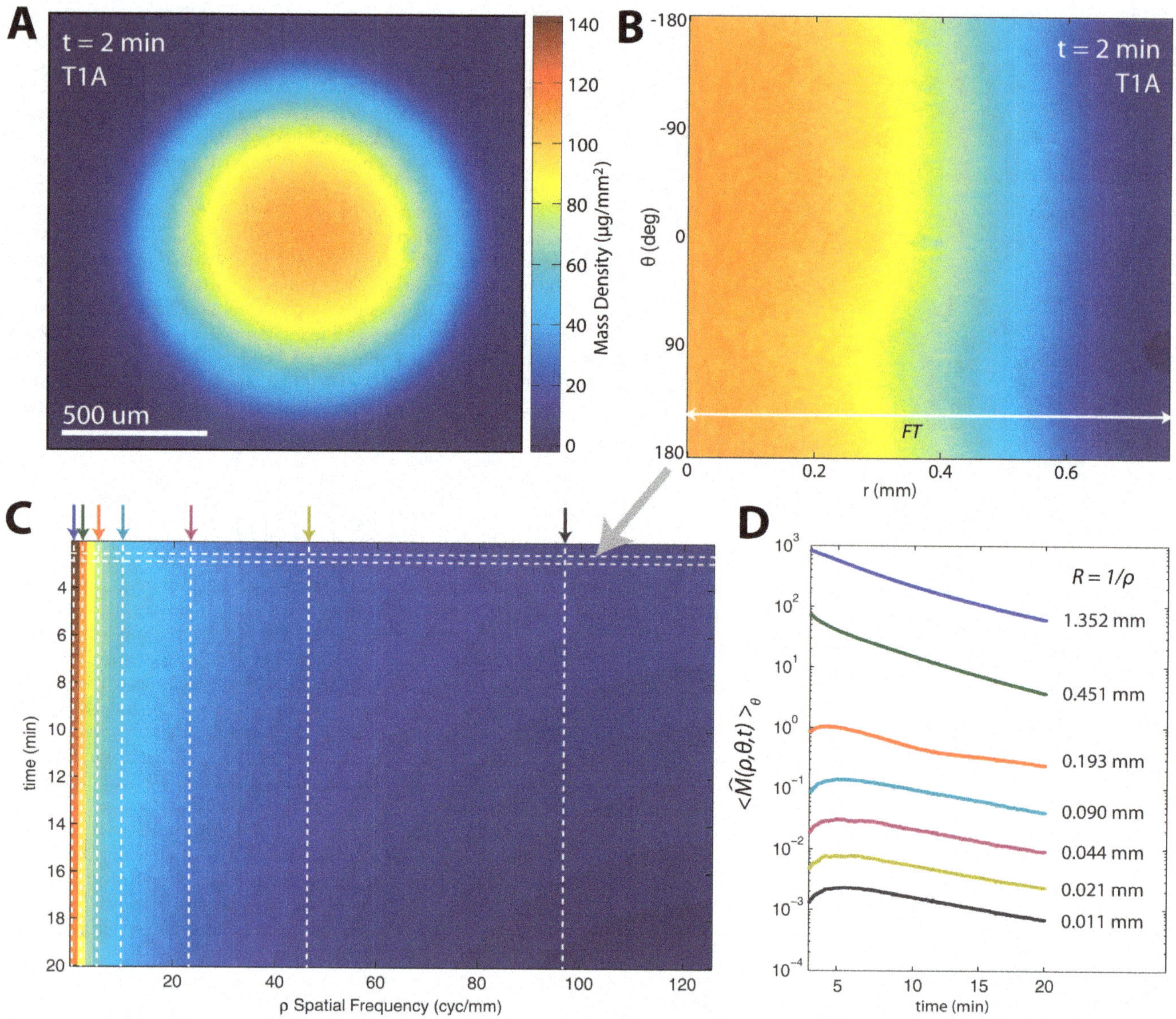

Figure 2. Spatial Fourier analysis of mass density: (A) Mass density image of film T1A at t = 2 min; (B) Polar-coordinate representation of data in (A). Mass density distributions are then Fourier-transformed in the radial direction and averaged azimuthally to produce (C) power spectral density over time. (D) As the film hydrates and dissolves, each spatial frequency component decays with different temporal dynamics.

2% difference in fractional composition. Meanwhile, T3A substitutes two unique polymers and contains almost double the content of glycerin relative to T1A and T2A. Notably, films T1A and T3A contain NaCMC (n = 1.515) and have higher refractive indices than T2A, which does not contain NaCMC.

3.2 Refractive Index Measurements of Water and Film Samples

Table 1 summarizes the RI increments (see section 2.3) and extrapolated RI values of the water and three distinct film polymer compositions used in the hydration experiments. The error bars correspond to the 95% confidence bounds of the fit model. Films T1A, T2A and T1B all exhibit similar RI increments, α, while T3A was found to have a significantly lower refractive index increment.

3.3 Effects of Film Thickness on Hydration Behavior

Figure 3 compares representative film volume fraction images (fig. 3A) and summary (volume average over the entire film, r = 0 mm to r = 0.5 mm) volume fraction time curves (fig. 3B) for two film types with identical polymer compositions but different thicknesses, T1A and T1B. The hydration data contains several notable features. First, T1A is half as thick as T1B and thus contains half the volume of polymer material as T1B initially. Additionally, the volume of T1A polymer within the initial area is about half that of T1B at each time point because both films spread at approximately the same rate. Finally, the thicker film, T1B, exhibited phase wrapping artifacts for the initial 7 minutes of the experimental time course, whereas the phase data from the thinner film T1A were free of wrapping artifacts within 2 minutes of initial hydration. The consequence of this behavior difference is discussed below.

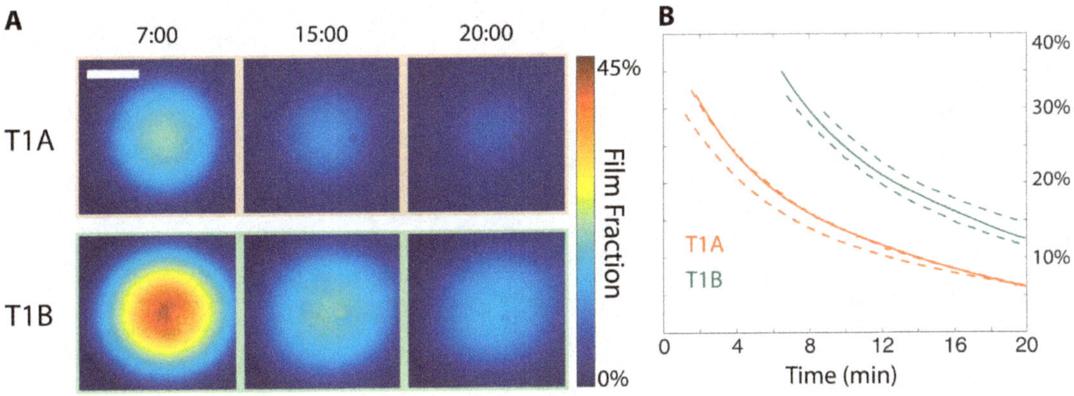

Figure 3. Comparison of two films with different thicknesses, T1A (120 μm) and T1B (240 μm). (A) Calculated film fraction at 7, 15, and 20 minutes. (B) Film fraction remaining within the initial circular film area during hydration. The three repeats of T1A (red) show a distinctly faster hydration rate than the repeated measurements of samples from the T1B film (blue). Solid lines indicate experimental data depicted in (A), while dashed lines are data from repeated experiments with identical conditions. Scale bar: 0.5 mm.

3.4 Film Hydration Comparison: Varying Polymer Composition

The hydration experiments were repeated with the three films of different compositions, to explore the effect of composition on hydration dynamics (fig. 4). Here, T1A and T3A appear to have similar temporal hydration profiles but exhibit early kinetic differences, along with a potential variation in initial thickness of ±10 μm. These result in different film volume fractions after the first two minutes of the experimental time course. While T2A appears to contain the largest volume fraction of film material at its center two minutes after hydration, this central concentration diminishes rapidly and contains the least fraction of film material after 20 minutes.

3.5 Azimuthally-averaged radial profiles

The effects of varied polymer compositions and thickness are further examined in concentration profiles shown in fig. 5. Azimuthal averaging has removed small-scale features and allows examination of the macroscopic radial shapes exhibited by the polymers during dissolution. T1A and T2A exhibit a pronounced central core: after initial hydration, the films retain an inflection point within the field of view that migrates inward during further dissolution. T3A differs significantly in composition (see Table 2), and lacks this inflection feature. Interestingly, the thicker film T1B, which is compositionally identical to T1A, lacks this feature as well. Because T1A's inflection point is near the edge of the field of view, we expect that the same feature is not seen in T1B's mass density profiles both because it occurs beyond the field of view and also because the inward migration of the inflection point is expected to occur later than the final time point of this experiment.

3.6 Spatial Frequency Analysis

Spatial frequency analysis indicates distinct behavior at characteristic length-scales given by $R = 1/\rho$. Relative increases and

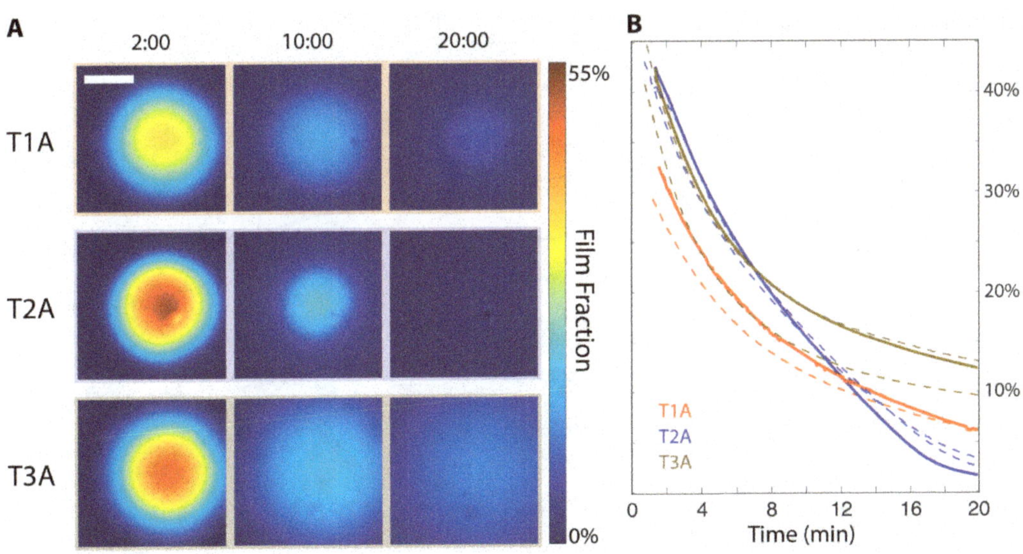

Figure 4. Comparison of three distinct film formulations as summarized in Table 2. (A) Calculated film fraction at 2, 10, and 20 minutes. (B) Film fraction remaining within the initial circular film area during hydration; Solid line corresponds to the hydration time course represented in (A), dashed lines correspond to triplicate repeat experiments and demonstrate assay variability/repeatability.

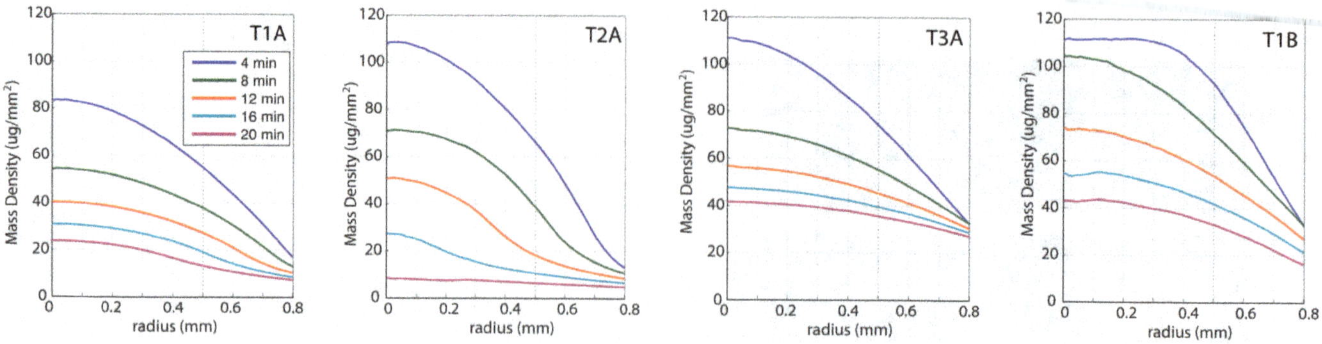

Figure 5. Azimuthally-averaged radial mass density profiles.

decreases in the amplitude of specific length scales occur as dissolution proceeds by mechanisms such as polymer chain disentanglement, fragmentation, swelling, and diffusion [27–29]. Pure diffusion, as governed by Fick's second law, predicts that the power in each spatial frequency component will decay as:

$$\hat{M}(\rho,\theta,t) = \hat{M}(\rho,\theta,0)e^{-4\pi^2 D\rho^2 t}$$

where $\hat{M}(\rho,\theta,0)$ is the initial mass density distribution and D is the diffusion coefficient [30,31]. Figure 6 illustrates that diffusion does not appear to be the dominant mechanism of mass transport for any of the compositions or thicknesses, although each film's hydration behavior differs significantly. For all films, amplitudes for characteristic length scales less than 0.27 mm increase in relative contribution during the first several minutes of hydration, which we attribute to swelling and polymer chain disentanglement. As dissolution continues, all curves approach uniform decay rates. Films T1A and T2A also exhibit damped oscillations in length scales 0.2 mm$<$R$<$0.5 mm due to complex polymer-solvent interactions. The smallest length scales correspond to the resolution limit of the interferometric imaging system.

Each spatial frequency time series calculated by SFA is divided into two regimes: (1) an initial hydration regime and (2) a dissolution regime. These two regimes are divided at τ_H, the time where all spatial frequencies have passed their maximum value. The hydration times for films T1A and T2A, which have similar polymer compositions, are 5:16 and 5:44, respectively (times represented as m:ss). T3A has a much longer τ_H of 8:52. Doubling the film thickness while keeping the polymeric composition identical (T1A = 120 μm, T1B = 240 μm) increases τ_H from 5:16 to 7:48.

Once in the dissolution regime, each characteristic length scale amplitude curve is fit to an exponential decay of the form: $e^{-\lambda(R)t}$ to determine the decay rate, λ. There is a clear difference in decay behavior above and below R = 200 μm (see fig. 7A), where long length scales indicate bulk dissolution dynamics and the small length scales indicate the micron-scale particle behavior of the film. Fig. 7B shows the average decay rates of each film sample's bulk ($\Gamma = \langle\lambda\rangle_{R>200\mu m}$) and micron-scale ($\Lambda = \langle\lambda\rangle_{R<200\mu m}$) features. While T1A–T3A all have the same physical geometry, T3A exhibits both a lower bulk decay rate as well as slower dissolution of micron-sized particles. All three of these films have larger decay rates at long length scales and approximately constant decay rates at length scales smaller than 200 μm; In contrast to the 120 μm-thick films, T1B's Γ and Λ decay rates are similar. The variation in decay rates Γ and Λ indicates that polymer composition and geometry affect not only the bulk rate of dissolution, but also the

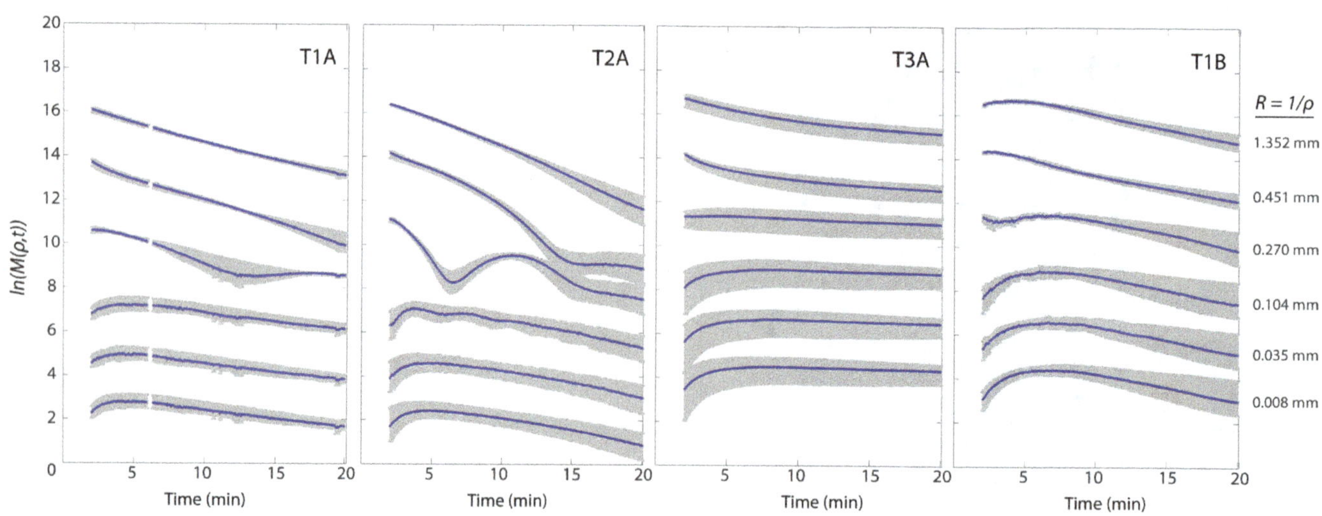

Figure 6. Spatial frequency time dynamics. Selected characteristic length scales demonstrate early hydration and subsequent dissolution. Blue lines and error bars correspond to the mean and standard deviation of three repeats of each film type.

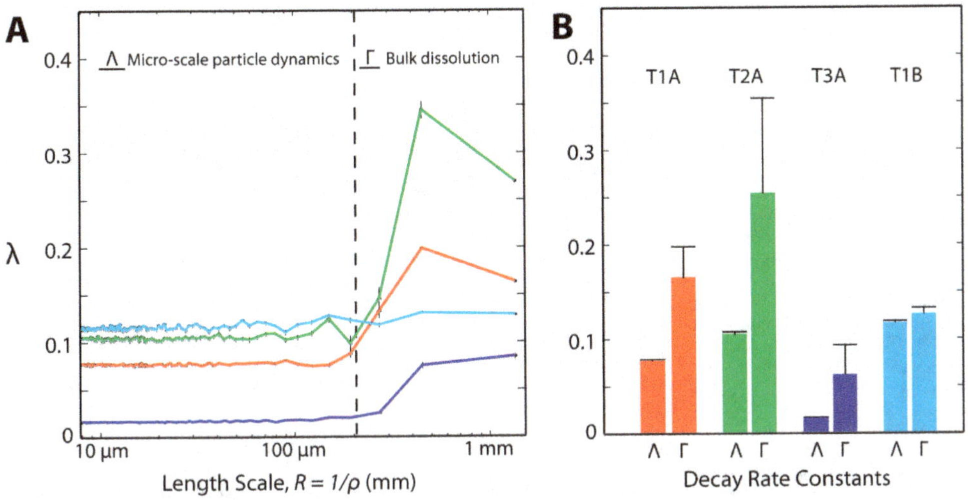

Figure 7. Spatial frequency decay rates. (A) Each characteristic length scale is fit over the time interval of (τ_H,20:00) to an exponential decay, $e^{-\lambda(R)t}$. 95% confidence intervals of the fits are shown as black bars. (B) Average bulk decay rates (Γ) and micron-scale particle decay rates (Λ) of each sample. Black bars show standard deviation (See Table 1 for summary).

rate at which smaller-sized objects are generated and decay. Each parameter is expected to have a distinct influence on the film's ability to spread across and deliver API to a target tissue.

Discussion and Conclusion

In this study, we have demonstrated that quantitative imaging refractometry can be an objective, quantitative tool for investigating differences in the water uptake, hydration, and dissolution behaviors of microbicide films with varying compositions and thicknesses. These processes impact drug release profiles and ultimately underlie drug pharmacokinetics. We have introduced the methodology and illustrated its use for a set of prototype films being evaluated for vaginal delivery of the topical anti-HIV microbicide Tenofovir. To date, no method exists to study the initial stages of film hydration, which are critical to drug release. Thus, the methodology presented here represents a novel technique for studying the spatial distributions of hydration parameters *in vitro*, which can aid in film formulation development and understanding of *in vivo* film behavior.

In the experiments presented here, we compared film prototypes with different thicknesses as well as polymeric compositions. Refractive index measurements of the films enabled calculation of film volume fractions (local, average), mass density profiles, and spatial Fourier analysis that can be used in comparing various film designs. Film T1A (d = 120 μm) dissolved consistently quicker than the 240 μm-thick film of the same formulation, and contained approximately half as much material in the initial film area after 20 minutes of hydration (T1A = 6.2%, T1B = 12.5%). Variations in polymer formulation produced films of identical thickness that dissolved at different rates, as demonstrated by the fitted Λ and Γ values. Notably, results here showed that composition and geometry can be altered to produce not only different hydration rates, but distinct bulk- and micro-scale particle dissolution rates that can vary independently. These results illustrate that our new methodology will provide a reference for future modeling and analysis that seek to understand how polymer-solvent kinetics (including polymer chain disentanglement, material cracking, and formation of a glassy transition layer) govern film vehicle spreading as well as microbicidal drug release and delivery to tissues of interest.

The precision, accuracy, and fidelity of this method are bounded by several factors. Each 2π wrapping artifact contributes an error of 2.5×10^{-3} refractive index units, which corresponds to a film volume fraction error of 1.65–1.76 pp depending on the specific refractive index of the film. In comparison, the spatio-temporal phase fluctuations, as limited by the inherent noise of the interferometer, yield a refractive index sensitivity of $\sigma = 5.5\times10^{-6}$ [15], corresponding to film fraction measurement precision of 0.0035–0.0038 pp and a mass density measurement precision of $\sigma_M = 0.98 - 1.25 \mu g/mm^2$. The accuracy of the measured film fractions is bounded by the error of the refractive index measurements given in Table 1. While the absolute differences across the four film samples contain some uncertainty due to these calibration measurements, the system precision suggests that the differences in hydration kinetics between specific film repeat measurements (figs.3–7) are deterministically attributable to sample geometric and kinetic variability. It is important to note that the measured phase data contain large errors due to wrapping artifacts during the initial minutes following hydration, rendering data at these early times unsuitable for analysis. After a short period of hydration, the phase images become smooth and easily unwrapped, and thus produce high quality data for the remainder of each experiment.

In conclusion, we have presented and applied a novel methodology for the first objective, quantitative imaging comparison of microbicide film polymer hydration kinetics. Our results demonstrate that film geometry and polymer composition each can have a significant effect on not only the time to hydrate, but also on the specific behavior of the spatiotemporal dissolution profiles. These results can be input to mechanistic analyses of film hydration, disintegration, drug dissolution and release [14], helping to improve our understanding of the determinants of those processes. In turn, they can contribute to improved design of films for effective vaginal delivery of anti-HIV microbicides.

Author Contributions

Conceived and designed the experiments: MR LR DK AW. Performed the experiments: MR. Analyzed the data: MR. Contributed reagents/

materials/analysis tools: LR AW. Wrote the paper: MR SG LR DK AW. Built the imaging refractometry system: MR. Manufactured and characterized film samples: SG.

References

1. Frankman O, Raabe N, Ingemansson CA (1975) Clinical evaluation of C-Film, a vaginal contraceptive. J Int Med Res 3: 292–296.
2. Neurath AR, Strick N, Li Y-Y (2003) Water dispersible microbicidal cellulose acetate phthalate film. BMC Infect Dis 3: 27.
3. Dobaria NB, Badhan AC, Mashru RC (2009) A Novel Itraconazole Bioadhesive Film for Vaginal Delivery: Design, Optimization, and Physicodynamic Characterization. AAPS PharmSciTech 10: 951–959. doi:10.1208/s12249-009-9288-0.
4. Younus Pasha M, Bhat SR, Hani U (2012) Formulation design and evaluation of bioadhesive vaginal films of metronidazole for vaginal candidiasis. Lat Am J Pharm 31.
5. Machado RM, Palmeira-De-Oliveira A, Martinez-De-Oliveira J, Palmeira-De-Oliveira R (2013) Vaginal films for drug delivery. J Pharm Sci 102: 2069–2081. doi:10.1002/jps.23577.
6. Stone A, Harrison PF (2010) Microbicides: Ways Forward. Alliance for Microbicide Development, Silver Spring, MD.
7. Rustomjee R, Abdool Karim Q, Abdool Karim SS, Laga M, Stein Z (1999) Phase 1 trial of nonoxynol-9 film among sex workers in South Africa. AIDS Lond Engl 13: 1511–1515.
8. Garg S, Goldman D, Krumme M, Rohan LC, Smoot S, et al. (2010) Advances in development, scale-up and manufacturing of microbicide gels, films, and tablets. Antiviral Res 88: S19–S29.
9. Garg S, Vermani K, Garg A, Anderson RA, Rencher WB, et al. (2005) Development and characterization of bioadhesive vaginal films of sodium polystyrene sulfonate (PSS), a novel contraceptive antimicrobial agent. Pharm Res 22: 584–595. doi:10.1007/s11095-005-2490-1.
10. Geonnotti AR, Katz DF (2006) Dynamics of HIV Neutralization by a Microbicide Formulation Layer: Biophysical Fundamentals and Transport Theory. Biophys J 91: 2121–2130. doi:10.1529/biophysj.106.086322.
11. Katz DF, Gao Y, Kang M (2011) Using modeling to help understand vaginal microbicide functionality and create better products. Drug Deliv Transl Res 1: 256–276. doi:10.1007/s13346-011-0029-z.
12. Akil A, Parniak MA, Dezzutti CS, Moncla BJ, Cost MR, et al. (2011) Development and characterization of a vaginal film containing dapivirine, a non-nucleoside reverse transcriptase inhibitor (NNRTI), for prevention of HIV-1 sexual transmission. Drug Deliv Transl Res 1: 209–222. doi:10.1007/s13346-011-0022-6.
13. Ham AS, Rohan LC, Boczar A, Yang L, W. Buckheit K, et al. (2012) Vaginal Film Drug Delivery of the Pyrimidinedione IQP-0528 for the Prevention of HIV Infection. Pharm Res 29: 1897–1907. doi:10.1007/s11095-012-0715-7.
14. Tasoglu S, Rohan LC, Katz DF, Szeri AJ (2013) Transient swelling, spreading, and drug delivery by a dissolved anti-HIV microbicide-bearing film. Phys Fluids 25: 031901. doi:10.1063/1.4793598.
15. Rinehart MT, Drake TK, Robles FE, Rohan LC, Katz D, et al. (2011) Time-resolved imaging refractometry of microbicidal films using quantitative phase microscopy. J Biomed Opt 16: 120510. doi:10.1117/1.3665439.
16. Rappaz B, Marquet P, Cuche E, Emery Y, Depeursinge C, et al. (2005) Measurement of the integral refractive index and dynamic cell morphometry of living cells with digital holographic microscopy. Opt Express 13: 9361. doi:10.1364/OPEX.13.009361.
17. Shaked NT, Finan JD, Guilak F, Wax A (2010) Quantitative phase microscopy of articular chondrocyte dynamics by wide-field digital interferometry. J Biomed Opt 15: 010505. doi:10.1117/1.3290242.
18. Popescu G, Park Y, Lue N, Best-Popescu C, Deflores L, et al. (2008) Optical imaging of cell mass and growth dynamics. AJP Cell Physiol 295: C538–C544. doi:10.1152/ajpcell.00121.2008.
19. Abdool Karim Q, Abdool Karim SS, Frohlich JA, Grobler AC, Baxter C, et al. (2010) Effectiveness and Safety of Tenofovir Gel, an Antiretroviral Microbicide, for the Prevention of HIV Infection in Women. Science 329: 1168–1174. doi:10.1126/science.1193748.
20. National Institute of Allergy and Infectious Diseases (NIAID); Microbicide Trials Network. Safety and Effectiveness of Tenofovir 1% Gel, Tenofovir Disproxil Fumarate, and Emtricitabine/Tenofovir Disoproxil Fumarate Tablets in Preventing HIV in Women. (2000) In: ClinicalTrials.gov [Internet]. Bethesda (MD): National Library of Medicine (US). Available: http://clinicaltrials.gov/ct2/show/NCT00705679 NLM Identifier: NCT00705679. Accessed 2013 Sept 23.
21. CONRAD; Follow-on African Consortium for Tenofovir Studies (FACTS); United States Agency for International Development (USAID) (2013) Safety and Effectiveness of Tenofovir Gel in the Prevention of Human Immunodeficiency Virus (HIV-1) Infection in Women and the Effects of Tenofovir Gel on the Incidence of Herpes Simplex Virus (HSV-2) Infection. In: ClinicalTrials.gov [Internet]. Bethesda (MD): National Library of Medicine (US). Available: http://clinicaltrials.gov/show/NCT01386294 NLM Identifier: NCT01386294. Accessed 2013 Sept 23.
22. Shaked NT, Zhu Y, Rinehart MT, Wax A (2009) Two-step-only phase-shifting interferometry with optimized detector bandwidth for microscopy of live cells. Opt Express 17: 15585–15591. doi:10.1364/OE.17.015585.
23. Ghiglia D, Pritt M (1998) Two dimensional phase unwrapping: theory, algorithms & software. Wiley Interscience.
24. Huntley JM, Saldner H (1993) Temporal phase-unwrapping algorithm for automated interferogram analysis. Appl Opt 32: 3047. doi:10.1364/AO.32.003047.
25. Davies HG, Wilkins MHF (1952) Interference Microscopy and Mass Determination. Nature 169: 541–541. doi:10.1038/169541a0.
26. Barer R (1952) Interference Microscopy and Mass Determination. Nature 169: 366–367. doi:10.1038/169366b0.
27. Lee PI, Peppas NA (1987) Prediction of polymer dissolution in swellable controlled-release systems. J Controlled Release 6: 207–215. doi:10.1016/0168-3659(87)90077-0.
28. Kolin DL, Ronis D, Wiseman PW (2006) k-Space Image Correlation Spectroscopy: A Method for Accurate Transport Measurements Independent of Fluorophore Photophysics. Biophys J 91: 3061–3075. doi:10.1529/biophysj.106.082768.
29. Miller-Chou BA, Koenig JL (2003) A review of polymer dissolution. Prog Polym Sci 28: 1223–1270. doi:10.1016/S0079-6700(03)00045-5.
30. Tsay TT, Jacobson KA (1991) Spatial Fourier analysis of video photobleaching measurements. Principles and optimization. Biophys J 60: 360–368. doi:10.1016/S0006-3495(91)82061-6.
31. Berk DA, Yuan F, Leunig M, Jain RK (1993) Fluorescence photobleaching with spatial Fourier analysis: measurement of diffusion in light-scattering media. Biophys J 65: 2428–2436. doi:10.1016/S0006-3495(93)81326-2.

13

Autonomous Device for Application in Late-Phase Hemorrhagic Shock Prevention

Vlad Oncescu[1], Seoho Lee[1], Abdurrahman Gumus[2], Kolbeinn Karlsson[2], David Erickson[1]*

1 Sibley School of Mechanical and Aerospace Engineering, Cornell University, Ithaca, New York, United States of America, 2 Electrical and Computer Engineering, Cornell University, Ithaca, New York, United States of America

Abstract

Hemorrhagic shock (HS) is the leading cause of death for people with traumatic injuries. The onset of HS is correlated with marked changes in the plasma vasopressin levels and some studies indicate that administrating vasopressin in the bloodstream can help stabilize the situation. This situation calls naturally for the use of implantable devices for both the monitoring and treatment of HS. In this work, we present a self-powered hemorrhagic-shock autonomous integrated device (hemoAID) that continuously monitors vasopressin levels and releases vasopressin automatically when levels drop below a certain threshold. We demonstrate that the device can operate at physiological concentrations of vasopressin, in sheep serum, thus paving the way towards the development of an autonomous implantable device for HS prevention.

Editor: Leo T.O. Lee, University of Hong Kong, Hong Kong

Funding: The authors wish to acknowledge the support of the Office of Naval Research (ONR) under award number N000141010115 "Autonomous Microfluidic Devices for Battlefield Health Assessment and Treatment". In addition, V.O. wishes to acknowledge the support of the Canadian institution NSERC through a fellowship. Some elements of the integration were also carried out with the support of NSF grant #1014891. The funders had no role in study design, data collection and analysis, decision to publish, or preparation of the manuscript.

Competing Interests: The authors have declared that no competing interests exist.

* E-mail: de54@cornell.edu

These authors contributed equally to this work.

Introduction

Over the past decade, implantable autonomous microsystems have been developed to counter life-threatening medical conditions and to improve patient care by replacing cumbersome treatment procedures [1–3]. As such, a growing number of patients now depend on implantable cardioverter defibrillators [4], gastric stimulators [5], cardiac pacemakers [6] and artificial organs [7–9] for survival. In such cases, the severity and urgency of the medical condition override the high cost and risk of the invasive surgery that is required. On the other hand, some situations call naturally for implantable medical devices to continuously monitor physiological changes in patients or to deliver treatment through pre-determined and repeated drug delivery. For instance, continuous glucose monitoring devices have found their market by increasing the efficacy of diabetes treatment and by helping patients monitor real-time variations in their blood glucose levels due to insulin and food intake, exercise, and other factors. Recently, Farra *et al.* [10] demonstrated an implantable drug delivery microchip that operates for up to 3 weeks and eliminates the need for daily physician-assisted injections for patients with osteoporosis. While these developments have been successful at independently performing sensing [11,12] and drug delivery [13], developing implantable medical devices capable of achieving both of those functions simultaneously would be suitable for a number of applications [14]. One such case is the detection and treatment of traumatic injuries such as hemorrhagic shock (HS).

Studies have correlated the onset of HS with marked changes in the plasma vasopressin levels [15,16]. Morales *et al.* [15] have conducted a set of canine experiments where vasopressin levels showed a marked increase at the onset of hemorrhage (to as much as 319 pg/mL) followed by a fall to well below the normal physiological level (29 pg/mL) as hemorrhage progressed. In addition, evidence suggests that replenishment of vasopressin at this stage can reverse hypotension in patients [17,18]. Krismer *et al.* [19] have reported case studies where dosages of 100–160 IU vasopressin led to hemodynamic stability with sinus rhythm in HS patients within 2 min and patient survival without additional treatment of up to 90 min. Therefore, vasopressin can serve as both a biomarker indicative of a critical injury state and a therapeutic agent for treating it. Developing an implantable autonomous device that can provide initial medical treatment when physician care is not readily available is highly suitable in this case.

In this paper, we present a self-powered hemorrhagic-shock prevention autonomous integrated device (hemoAID) that continuously monitors vasopressin levels in solution and releases vasopressin automatically when vasopressin levels drop below a certain threshold. We demonstrate that the device works at physiological concentrations of vasopressin in sheep serum. This represents the first steps towards the development of an implantable, self-powered microfluidic device for late-phase HS prevention. In the next sections, we introduce the hemoAID and discuss the fabrication and integration of its major components. We then demonstrate the operation of the device during rapid changes in vasopressin concentration and proceed by discussing the characteristics of the sensing, drug delivery and power units. Finally in the "Conclusion and Future Prospective" section, we discuss some of the issues that need to be addressed in order to move toward a fully integrated autonomous implantable hemoAID.

Materials and Methods

System Design and Assembly

The hemoAID device shown in Fig. 1a consists of a nanowire biosensor for detecting changes in vasopressin levels, an on-board electrochemically driven drug delivery system for administration of vasopressin, and a non-enzymatic glucose fuel cell for powering the system. Those three main functional components are integrated inside a 3 cm^3 package. In this prototype version, the electronic control system is external to the system and uses the circuit shown in Fig. 1b. External housing of the circuitry was done to facilitate prototype development and could be integrated into the system in the future.

The non-enzymatic glucose fuel cell is used to continuously charge a small rechargeable battery (Thinergy MEC225) that is then used to power a low power microcontroller (MSP430F2012, Texas Instruments, TX, USA). This set-up allows the device to operate steadily even with significant fluctuations in the power output of the fuel cell unit. During device operation, the sensor is driven by an adjustable 2-terminal current source (LT3092, Linear Technology, Milpitas, CA, USA) at 60 mA. The resistance of the sensor changes with the amount of vasopressin in solution, which results in detectable voltage change over the biosensor. In order to improve sensitivity, the voltage is amplified using a non-inverting amplifier (Maxim Integrated, CA) before being detected using a low power microcontroller's analog to digital converter (ADC). If the voltage is lower than the pre-determined threshold, the microcontroller enables the corresponding output pin to activate the drug delivery system. In order to increase the discharge rate of vasopressin in the drug delivery device, the base voltage (3 V) is converted to 35 V with a micropower step-up DC/DC converter (LT3464, Linear Technology, Milpitas, CA, USA).

Biosensor Fabrication

The biosensor consists of gold electrodes and a carbon nanotube (CNT) based detection region on which aptamer molecules are immobilized [20]. The detection region of the sensor was patterned on a 4-inch silicon wafer using general photolithography and surface-treated with (3-aminopropyl)trimethoxysilane (APTMS) using Molecular Vapor Deposition Tool (MVD 100). The aminosilanes from the surface treatment were covalently linked with COOH-functionalized multiwalled CNT (Cheap Tubes Inc.) to serve as carriers of aptamer receptors. The scanning electron microscope (SEM) images of immobilized CNT have been reported in our previous work [20]. Electrodes to the detection zone were lithographically patterned, followed by 5 nm chromium/60 nm gold deposition using a CHA Mark 50 e-Beam Evaporator. The wafer was diced into 0.8 cm×0.5 cm pieces which represents significant size reduction from the previous design that measures 5 cm×5 cm.

To immobilize the aptamer molecules on the CNT surface, an activation layer was first created by pipetting a mixture of 0.4 M 1-ethyl-3-(3-dimethylaminopropyl) carbodiimide (Geno Technology) and 0.1 M N-hydroxysuccinimide (MP Biomedicals LLC) in 1:1 volume ratio. The droplet was maintained for 3 h at room temperature and cleaned with DI H_2O wash and N_2 dry. Subsequently, 0.1 μM aptamer solution was pipetted on the surface-treated CNT and maintained for 24 h at room temperature. The premature drying of the droplets for surface modifications was prevented by placing the sensors in a humidified chamber.

Drug Delivery Device Fabrication

The drug delivery consists of three subcomponents: a top layer with a patterned gold electrode and suspended capping membrane, a bottom layer with a patterned gold counter-electrode and custom packaging to hold the two layers and define a micro-reservoir for vasopressin storage. Fabrication procedures for the top silicon structure are described in details in a previous publication [13]. Briefly, silicon nitride was deposited on both sides of a silicon wafer using low pressure chemical vapor deposition (LPCVD) followed by gold deposition on the top and patterning for reservoir location on the bottom. The wafer was later immersed in potassium hydroxide (KOH) overnight and reactive ion etching was used to remove the silicon nitride in the

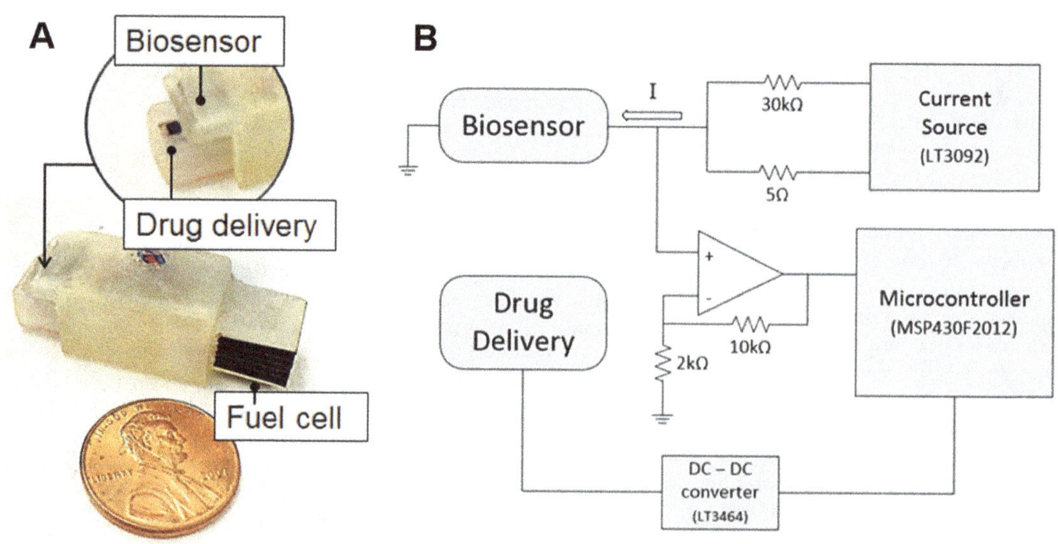

Figure 1. hemoAID device and schematic of electrical connections. A) Integrated device consisting of a biosensor, drug delivery and fuel cell unit B) schematic of the electrical connections between the different components of the hemoAID.

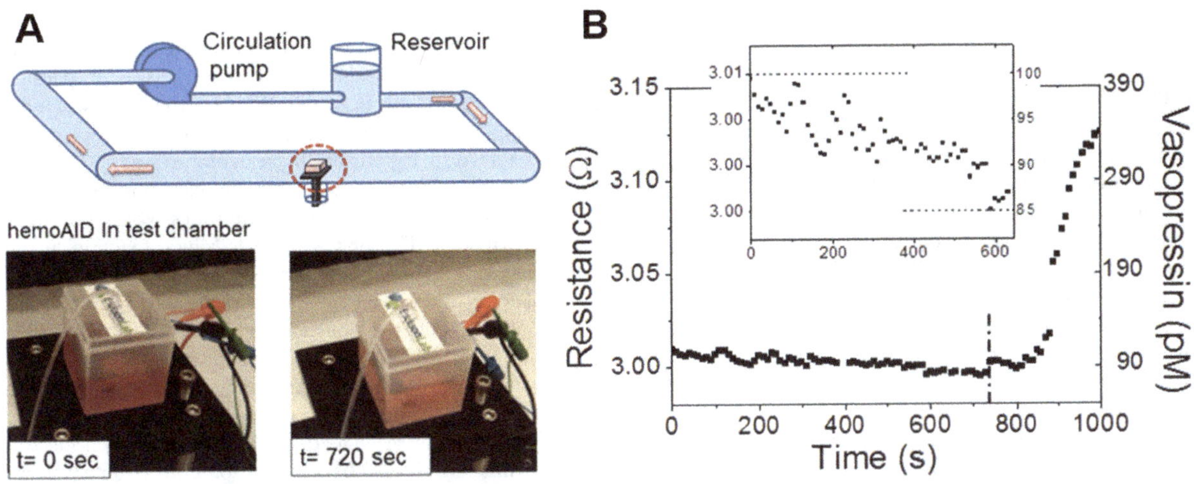

Figure 2. Setup and experiment demonstrating application of hemoAID to late-phase HS prevention. A) Setup for integrated device testing simulating late-phase HS B) resistance change, and associated vasopressin concentration change, detected by the biosensor during integrated experiment simulating late phase HS changes in vasopressin concentration. For the first 720 s the vasopressin concentration is gradually lowered until the drug delivery is autonomously activated to counteract the drop in vasopressin (at 15% drop). The line at 720 s shows the point at which drug delivery is activated. The inset shows the vasopressin drop before the drug delivery is activated (simulating the onset of late-phase HS).

patterned reservoir location, leaving a 100 μm×100 μm gold capping membrane. Modifications in our new architecture regard the other two components of the device and serve to facilitate subcomponent fabrication and assembly. The replacement of a gold deposited Pyrex layer with a single gold electrode eliminates the standard lift-off processing before the gold deposition. Furthermore, the custom packaging is used in place of PDMS in order to facilitate assembly protocol and reduce leakage of vasopressin through the PDMS. The assembled components were sealed with epoxy adhesive.

Power Unit Integration

A non-enzymatic glucose fuel cell unit, connected to a rechargeable battery, is used to power the microcontroller and other electrical components of the hemoAID. Lithium batteries were not used here since their short life-time makes them unsuitable for long term autonomous implantable devices with power requirements superior to that of pacemakers [21]. Non-enzymatic glucose fuel cells are promising power sources in such devices due to good long-term stability and adequate power density. Here, we are using the stacked single layer configuration that we have presented previously [22] to demonstrate integration within the hemoAID. The 1 cm^2 single layer fuel cells are patterned directly on 500 μm thick fused silica substrates. A Raney-type Pt/Ni alloy was used as anode for glucose oxidation and a Pt/Al alloy as cathode for oxygen reduction because of increased selectivity as discussed elsewhere [23,24]. The fuel cell unit is composed of 12 single layer fuel cells that are connected externally in parallel to form a fuel cell stack and integrated inside of custom holder with a volume of approximately 1 cm^3.

Results and Discussion

Integrated Device Operation in Flow Network

In order to demonstrate its operation, the hemoAID device was placed inside a closed chamber within a fluid network designed to simulate the physiological vasopressin states of late-phase HS patients. According to a clinical study by Jochberger *et al.* [25] vasopressin concentration for patients with hemorrhagic shock rises from the normal 6±3 pM range to 52±30 pM as the body tries to reverse hypotension by releasing vasopressin. Following this initial increase, the level of vasopressin starts decreasing, which indicates the onset of late phase hemorrhagic shock. At that point, administering a high dose of vasopressin can temporarily stabilize the situation. Here, we demonstrate the operation of the hemoAID at those physiologically relevant vasopressin concentrations. The test chamber housing the integrated device (Fig. 2a) is initially filled with 100 pM vasopressin solution, which corresponds to the high initial value (52±30 pM) of blood vasopressin for patients prior to late-phase HS onset. The vasopressin concentration is then progressively lowered by introducing 10 pM solution into the chamber using a VWR Mini-Pump at a flow-rate of 0.115 ml/s. The decrease in vasopressin concentration, indicating late-phase HS, causes a decrease in resistance resulting in a voltage output drop across the nanowire sensor at constant current. This resistance drop across the sensor can be correlated to the vasopressin concentration. As shown in Fig. 2b, the sensor's resistance decreased over 14 min in response to the decrease in vasopressin levels. Upon reaching a pre-determined 15% decrease in vasopressin concentration, corresponding to 0.25% resistance decrease ratio, the drug delivery is activated autonomously by the application of 35 V between the top and bottom electrodes which results in the release of 16 μL of highly concentrated (200 μM) vasopressin. The localized vasopressin release was detected successfully by the sensor as can be seen in Fig. 2b. This temporary increase in vasopressin would allow a patient to survive until further medical assistance can be provided.

The data obtained from the sensor is in the form of a voltage at the supplied current of 60 mA. This can be transformed into a resistance change that is related to the vasopressin concentration change in solution via the following experimentally derived equation:

$$\Delta[VP]=57.64\Delta R+102.68 \tag{1}$$

In the above equation Δ[VP] is in pM and ΔR is a % change in resistance. The relationship between changes in resistance and concentration is further discussed in the next section and is based on experiments presented elsewhere [20].

Biosensing Ability of Integrated Device

The nanowire biosensor we have developed and integrated in the hemoAID allows for the detection of pM changes in vasopressin concentration. Immobilized aptamer molecules on the nanowire biosensor act as electrical bioreceptors for the surrounding vasopressin. Reversible vasopressin binding leads to changes in conductivity through the CNT detection zone. The sensor is based on a device developed previously with a limit of detection of 43 pM in standard solution [20]. In this section, we demonstrate the sensing ability of the hemoAID for gradual changes in vasopressin levels by performing several characterization experiments. First, we show the reversibility of our sensor's detection mechanism by monitoring the sensor response to alternating vasopressin concentrations in a single experiment. The biosensor was placed into a custom packaging with microchannels as shown in Fig. 3a and 0.01 M Phosphate Buffer Saline (PBS) solution was introduced through one inlet until the output current was stabilized. The flow of 0.01 M PBS was stopped after 20 s and 10 μM vasopressin was allowed to flow through the other inlet, which was again replaced by a PBS injection after another 45 s. As shown in Fig. 3b, the initial introduction of a high-concentration 10 μM vasopressin solution results in a current decrease, and resistance increase, through the sensor almost instantaneously which is a consequence of depletion of charge carriers on the CNTs due to vasopressin to aptamer binding. The recovery of current upon 0.01 M PBS injection at $t = 50$ s is due to the release of vasopressin molecules from the immobilized aptamer which demonstrates the reversible nature of the binding events. The slower rate of current change during the dilution is due to the low dissociation constant of aptamer-vasopressin complex, confirming the high affinity of aptamer molecules to vasopressin [26]. This experiment demonstrates the biosensor's rapid reversibility even when a high vasopressin concentration causes large changes in resistance, uncommon under normal physiological conditions.

In addition, we show that the sensor can be used to monitor physiologically relevant changes in serum vasopressin concentration. In Fig. 3c, the biosensor is subjected to continuous variations in vasopressin by flowing sheep serum (Valley Biomedical Inc.) with 100 pM, 50 pM, 10 pM and 0 pM of added vasopressin in the respective order for a period of 150 s at each concentration. With each dilution, the current through the sensor increases as expected due to the release of vasopressin from the immobilized aptamers. In Fig. 3d we show the percentage change in current from the initial no vasopressin case due to the addition of 10 pM, 50 pM and 100 pM vasopressin. The bar graph represents the average of 5 experiments that were performed by continuously varying the concentration of vasopressin as shown in Fig. 3c, with the error bar representing the range between the highest and lowest reading. These experiments demonstrate that the sensor can detect physiologically relevant changes in vasopressin in serum.

The high current used to increase the sensitivity of the sensor in the previous section can be decreased by changing the design of the sensor to increase its resistance either by decreasing the thickness of the nanowire sensing area on which APTMS is immobilized or by integrating several such nanowires in series. With these improvements, the sensor can be used for detection of vasopressin in interstitial fluid where changes in vasopressin are gradual and not affected by pressure changes in the bloodstream.

Stabilizing Vasopressin Levels through Drug Delivery

In this section we demonstrate the integrated device's mechanism to stabilize vasopressin levels through the in-parallel operation of the drug delivery system (Fig. 4a) with the biosensor. Time-controlled ejection of vasopressin based on electrochemical principles as shown in Fig. 4b has been demonstrated in previous publications [13,27]. To release vasopressin, electrical potential is applied between the top and bottom electrodes which results in two distinct reactions. The first is the electrolytic reaction in the reservoir that causes gas bubble formation and pressure build-up as a result. The second is the reaction between the chlorine ions in the buffer solution and the gold capping membrane to form a water soluble complex that gradually dissolves until it ruptures with increasing pressure of the reservoir. In the experiment presented in Fig. 4c, the sensor and the capping membrane of the drug delivery system were aligned 50 mm apart using a custom holder and immersed in a 0.01 M PBS solution. After approximately 162 s, the voltage output has stabilized (at $t = 0$ s on the graph), and the drug delivery was initiated by the application of a 35 V potential between the top and bottom electrodes of the drug delivery system. The electrochemical ejection procedure has been imaged to suggests the onset of gold membrane rupture 5 s after the potential application [27] and a sustained spike in voltage is first observed after 25 s. The small magnitude of this signal (0.25 mV) and the slow response of the sensor are due to large distance between the sensor and the drug delivery device. In the integrated hemoAID device, and the experiment in Fig. 2b the sensor is placed 5 mm in front of the sensor and the release of 16 μL vasopressin solution at 200 μM causes a much more rapid and larger voltage increase of 3.7%. This experiment demonstrates the ability of the sensor to monitor sudden changes in vasopressin concentration due to drug delivery by measuring the increase in voltage even when the two components are not in direct proximity.

Powering of Integrated Device

Instead of using the fuel cell unit directly to power the device, a small rechargeable battery shown in Fig. 5a is used as an intermediate in order to decrease power supply fluctuations. In addition this also allows excess energy to be stored and used for the one-time operation of the drug delivery device.

The power consumption for the integrated device with the sensor operated continuously is around 60 mA at 3 V. This is well above what can be supplied by a 1 cm^3 fuel cell unit (20 μA at 0.15 V) however most of the power is required by the biosensor since the change in resistance across the detection area is directly proportional to the current applied. Although decreasing the current supply is in theory possible, this results in lower detection sensitivity. However, the microcontroller only requires 60 to 70 μA at 3 V to operate and we can operate the sensor at discrete time intervals, thus greatly reducing the power consumption of the system and making it possible to operate the system using a 1 cm^3 fuel cell unit. In Fig. 5b we show the chronoamperometric response of the fuel cell unit (composed of 12 stacked single layers) at 0.1 V in 0.01 M PBS solution (pH 7.4) and physiological levels of glucose and oxygen (5 mM glucose, 8% oxygen saturation) over a period of 10 h. In Fig. 5c we show the discharge profile of the Thinergy MEC225 with an operating current of 100 μA. By continuously charging the Thinergy battery the system can operate continuously over a long period of time and avoid the power fluctuations typical of glucose fuel cell units (±4% as can be seen in Fig. 5b).

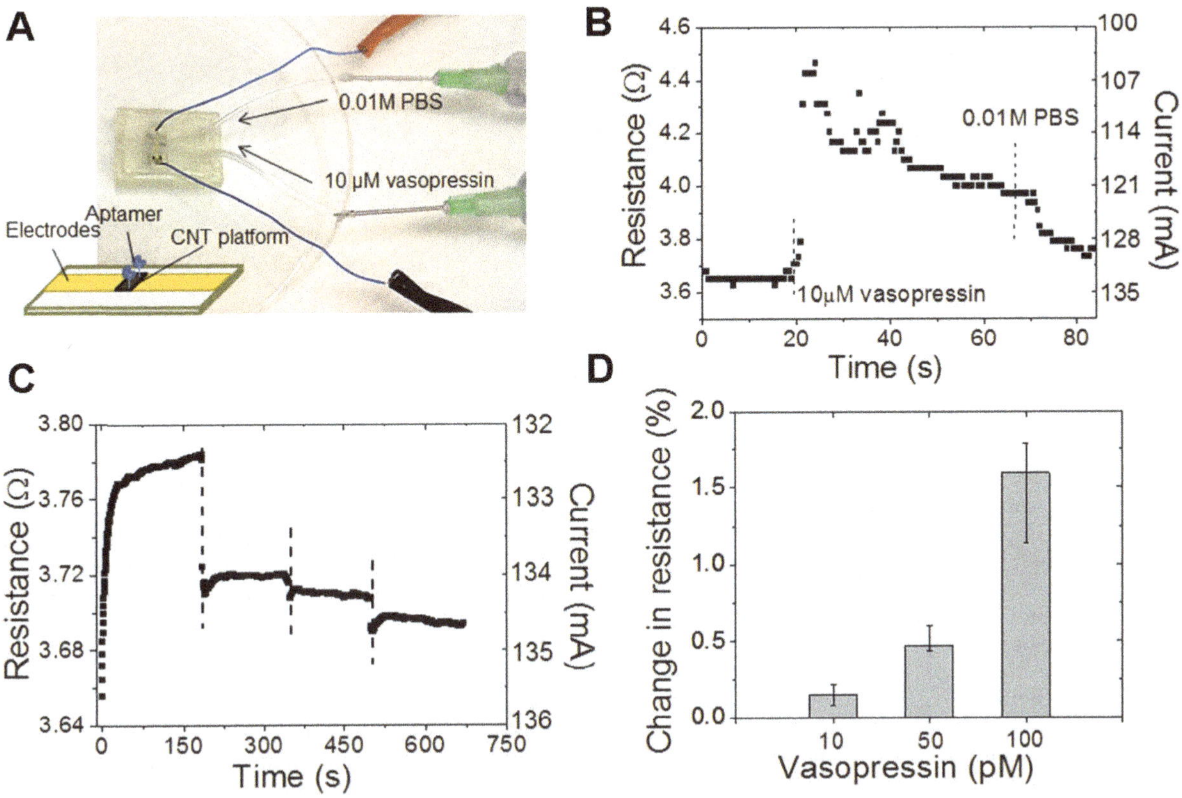

Figure 3. Setup and experiments for sensor characterization. A) Schematic of the nanowire biosensor and picture of the flow through system B) demonstration of sensor reversibility C) resistance, and associated current, change due to continuous decrease in vasopressin concentration in sheep serum. At t = 0 sheep serum with 100 pM vasopressin is introduced, followed by 50 pM, 10 pM and with no additional vasopressin D) Percentage change in resistance from the initial no vasopressin case caused by the flow of sheep serum with different vasopressin concentrations (average of 5 experiments with the error bars representing the highest and lowest reading).

Conclusion and Future Perspectives

In this paper, we have introduced the hemoAID, a device that can be used to detect a gradual drop in vasopressin concentration, corresponding to the onset of late-phase hemorrhagic shock, and deliver a highly concentrated dose of vasopressin to help stabilize the situation. We have demonstrated its operation in a controlled fluidic environment in which a 15% drop in vasopressin concentration was sensed and automatically triggered the activation of the drug delivery system. We discussed the sensor's mechanism and ability to operate in a complex medium such as sheep serum thus opening the door to the development of an implantable device for late phase hemorrhagic shock prevention.

Miniaturization and *in-vivo* testing are the next steps in the development of an implantable hemoAID. The operation of the individual components of this device, or similar technologies, have been demonstrated elsewhere *in-vivo* or in serum. The vasopressin drug delivery system presented here is based on a device, by Chung *et al.*, that allows controlling the rate of drug ejection and has been later shown to operate *in-vivo* in *Manduca sexta* moths [28].

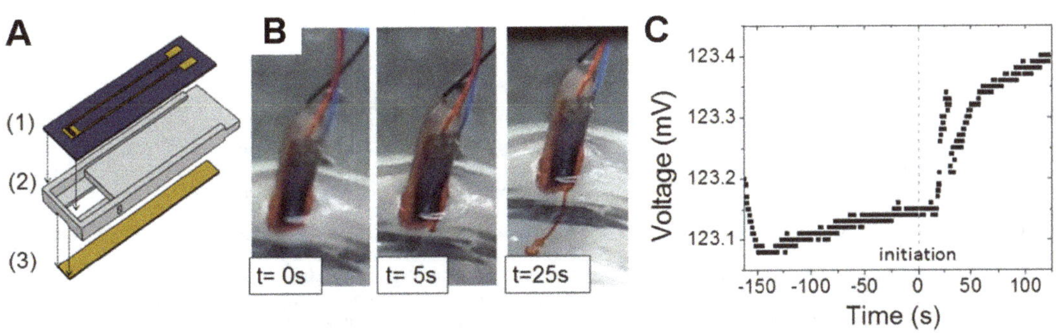

Figure 4. Drug delivery device activation. A) Assembly of the drug delivery unit B) vasopressin ejection over 25 s of applied voltage C) increase in biosensor voltage due to drug delivery. The vertical dotted line indicates when the potential was applied (at t = 0 s) and the a sustained spike in voltage occurs after 25 s.

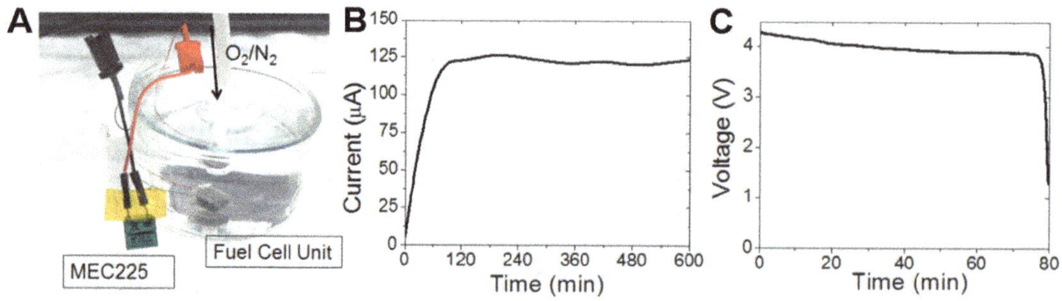

Figure 5. Power unit characterization. A) Power unit consisting of a 1 cm^3 fuel cell unit in 5 mmol glucose solution at 8% O_2 saturation and an external rechargeable battery B) chronoamperometric response of the fuel cell unit at 0.1 V in 0.01 M PBS solution and 5 mmol/L glucose solution over a period of 10 h C) discharge profile for the rechargeable battery at an operating current of 100 μA.

In that work the drug delivery devices are sealed using biocompatible wax and implanted in the moths for over 2 days demonstrating stability of vasopressin during storage and upon electrochemical ejection. Other groups have developed similar micro-electro-mechanical-systems (MEMS) for rapid delivery of vasopressin and have demonstrated biocompatibility and long term vasopressin storage without degradation [29]. Some preliminary *in-vivo* studies in rabbits have been reported by H. L. Ho. Duc where a 20 μL dose of 100 μg/kg vasopressin solution is delivered subcutaneously and an increase in plasma vasopressin levels was observed to reach a stable concentration after about 1 h [30]. These experiments demonstrate that such drug delivery technology is suitable for implantation and that the amount of vasopressin required is not an obstacle. The hemoAID reservoir contains approximately 16 μL of concentrated vasopressin solution (200 μM) or approximately 1.4 IU. When the device is loaded with a saturated solution of Arg8-vasopressin (400 IU/mg with 20 mg/ml solubility [31]) it is able to deliver a maximum of 128 IU. This falls within the range of vasopressin levels required to temporarily maintain a late-HS patient alive as discussed previously. Multiple drug delivery reservoirs can be integrated to deliver vasopressin over a longer period of time without substantially increasing the volume of the device as was done by Chung *et al.* [32].

In our previous work we have demonstrated the *in-vivo* operation of the drug delivery system after a 2 day implantation period in moths [28]. For a longer implantation period, as would be required for late phase sceptic shock prevention, a two reservoir system can be used in order to allow the drug to remain in solid lyophilized form until the device is electrochemically activated [30]. The operation principle of the drug delivery system would remain the same; however one reservoir would contain the lyophilized drug and the other the reconstruction media. The stability of vasopressin following electrochemical ejection from our device was investigated using MALDI-TOF/TOF mass spectroscopy in the appendix of a previous work [13]. Strong vasopressin peaks were observed for the ejected contents after application of a 12 V potential for 5 min indicating that only a small fraction of the vasopressin was oxidized during the ejection process.

In the current form, the device is integrated in a 3 cm^3 packaging with the fuel cell occupying about 1 cm^3 and the circuitry being external to the device. The miniaturization of similar circuitry has been demonstrated by Gumus *et al.* for application in *in-vivo* uric acid sensing on domestic chicken [33]. We envision the final version of the hemoAID, with multiple vasopressin drug delivery reservoirs, on-board circuitry and coated in biocompatible wax, to be suitable for sub-cutaneous implantation.

Acknowledgments

The fabrication steps described in this paper were carried out at the Cornell Nanoscale Facility (CNF) and the Nanobiotechnology Center at Cornell University (NBTC).

Author Contributions

Conceived and designed the experiments: VO SL DE. Performed the experiments: VO SL AG KK. Analyzed the data: VO SL. Contributed reagents/materials/analysis tools: DE. Wrote the paper: VO SL DE.

References

1. Receveur RAM, Lindemans FW, de Rooij NF (2007) Microsystem technologies for implantable applications. Journal of Micromechanics and Microengineering 17: R50–R80.
2. Bazaka K, Jacob M (2012) Implantable Devices: Issues and Challenges. Electronics 2: 1–34.
3. Onuki Y, Bhardwaj U, Papadimitrakopoulos F, Burgess DJ (2008) A review of the biocompatibility of implantable devices: current challenges to overcome foreign body response. J Diabetes Sci Technol 2: 1003–1015.
4. Adler A, Halkin A, Viskin S (2013) Wearable Cardioverter-Defibrillators. Circulation 127: 854–860.
5. Arriagada AJ, Jurkov AS, Neshev E, Muench G, Andrews CN, et al. (2011) Design, implementation and testing of an implantable impedance-based feedback-controlled neural gastric stimulator. Physiological Measurement 32: 1103–1115.
6. Liu SS, Monti J, Kargbo HM, Athar MW, Parakh K (2013) Frontiers of Therapy for Patients With Heart Failure. American Journal of Medicine 126: 6-U45.
7. Ricotti L, Assaf T, Dario P, Menciassi A (2013) Wearable and implantable pancreas substitutes. Journal of Artificial Organs 16: 9–22.
8. Krabatsch T, Schweiger M, Stepanenko A, Drews T, Potapov E, et al. (2011) Improvements in implantable mechanical circulatory support systems. Literature overview and update. Herz 36: 622–629.
9. Cebotari S, Tudorache I, Schilling T, Haverich A (2010) Heart valve and myocardial tissue engineering. Herz 35: 334–340.
10. Farra R, Sheppard NF, McCabe L, Neer RM, Anderson JM, et al. (2012) First-in-Human Testing of a Wirelessly Controlled Drug Delivery Microchip. Science Translational Medicine 4: 122ra121.
11. Fojtik M, Daeyeon K, Chen G, Yu-Shiang L, Fick D, et al. (2013) A Millimeter-Scale Energy-Autonomous Sensor System With Stacked Battery and Solar Cells. Solid-State Circuits, IEEE Journal of 48: 801–813.
12. Li H, Mu X, Wang Z, Liu X, Guo M, et al. (2012) Wearable autonomous microsystem with electrochemical gas sensor array for real-time health and safety monitoring. Conf Proc IEEE Eng Med Biol Soc: 6345978.
13. Chung AJ, Huh YS, Erickson D (2009) A robust, electrochemically driven microwell drug delivery system for controlled vasopressin release. Biomed Microdevices 11: 861–867.
14. Esquivel JP, Colomer-Farrarons J, Castellarnau M, Salleras M, del Campo FJ, et al. (2012) Fuel cell-powered microfluidic platform for lab-on-a-chip applications:

Integration into an autonomous amperometric sensing device. Lab on a Chip 12: 4232–4235.
15. Morales D, Madigan J, Cullinane S, Chen J, Heath M, et al. (1999) Reversal by vasopressin of intractable hypotension in the late phase of hemorrhagic shock. Circulation 100: 226–229.
16. Voelckel WG, Convertino VA, Lurie KG, Karlbauer A, Schochl H, et al. (2010) Vasopressin for hemorrhagic shock management: revisiting the potential value in civilian and combat casualty care. J Trauma 69.
17. Anand T, Skinner R (2012) Arginine vasopressin: the future of pressure-support resuscitation in hemorrhagic shock. J Surg Res 178: 321–329.
18. Wenzel V, Raab H, Dunser MW (2008) Arginine vasopressin: a promising rescue drug in the treatment of uncontrolled haemorrhagic shock. Best Pract Res Clin Anaesthesiol 22: 299–316.
19. Krismer AC, Wenzel V, Voelckel WG, Innerhofer P, Stadlbauer KH, et al. (2005) Employing vasopressin as an adjunct vasopressor in uncontrolled traumatic hemorrhagic shock. Three cases and a brief analysis of the literature. Anaesthesist 54: 220–224.
20. He P, Oncescu V, Lee S, Choi I, Erickson D (2013) Label-free electrochemical monitoring of vasopressin in aptamer-based microfluidic biosensors. Analytica Chimica Acta 759: 74–80.
21. Vincent CA (2000) Lithium batteries: a 50-year perspective, 1959–2009. Solid State Ionics 134: 159–167.
22. Oncescu V, Erickson D (2013) High volumetric power density, non-enzymatic, glucose fuel cells. Scientific reports 3.
23. Kerzenmacher S, Ducrée J, Zengerle R, von Stetten F (2008) Energy harvesting by implantable abiotically catalyzed glucose fuel cells. Journal of Power Sources 182: 1–17.
24. Oncescu V, Erickson D (2011) A microfabricated low cost enzyme-free glucose fuel cell for powering low-power implantable devices. Journal of Power Sources 196: 9169–9175.
25. Jochberger S, Morgenthaler NG, Mayr VD, Luckner G, Wenzel V, et al. (2006) Copeptin and arginine vasopressin concentrations in critically ill patients. J Clin Endocrinol Metab 91: 4381–4386.
26. Maehashi K, Matsumoto K, Takamura Y, Tamiya E (2009) Aptamer-Based Label-Free Immunosensors Using Carbon Nanotube Field-Effect Transistors. Electroanalysis 21: 1285–1290.
27. Cordovez B, Chung AJ, Mak M, Erickson D (2011) A novel polymer microneedle fabrication process for active fluidic delivery. Microfluidics and Nanofluidics 10: 785–791.
28. Chung AJ, Erickson D (2009) Engineering insect flight metabolics using immature stage implanted microfluidics. Lab Chip 9: 669–676.
29. Elman NM, Ho Duc HL, Cima MJ (2009) An implantable MEMS drug delivery device for rapid delivery in ambulatory emergency care. Biomed Microdevices 11: 625–631.
30. Ho Duc HL (2009) Emergency delivery of Vasopressin from an implantable MEMS rapid drug delivery device: Massachusetts Institute of Technology.
31. Dawson RMC, Elliott DC, Elliott WH, Jones KM (1986) Data for biochemical research. Oxford University Press 3: 31–32.
32. Chung A, Cordovez B, Jasuja N, Lee D, Huang X, et al. (2012) Implantable microfluidic and electronic systems for insect flight manipulation. Microfluidics and Nanofluidics 13: 345–352.
33. Gumus A, Lee S, Karlsson K, Gabrielson R, Winkler DW, et al. (2013) Real-time in-vivo uric acid biosensor system for biophysical monitoring of birds. Analyst (Accepted).

14

ICAM-1 Targeted Nanogels Loaded with Dexamethasone Alleviate Pulmonary Inflammation

M. Carme Coll Ferrer[1,3], Vladimir V. Shuvaev[2], Blaine J. Zern[2], Russell J. Composto[3], Vladimir R. Muzykantov[2], David M. Eckmann[1]*

1 Department of Anesthesiology and Critical Care, University of Pennsylvania, Philadelphia, Pennsylvania, United States of America, **2** Department of Pharmacology and Center for Targeted Therapeutics and Translational Nanomedicine, University of Pennsylvania, Philadelphia, Pennsylvania, United States of America, **3** Materials Science and Engineering, University of Pennsylvania, Philadelphia, Pennsylvania, United States of America

Abstract

Lysozyme dextran nanogels (NG) have great potential *in vitro* as a drug delivery platform, combining simple chemistry with rapid uptake and cargo release in target cells with "stealth" properties and low toxicity. In this work, we study for the first time the potential of targeted NG as a drug delivery platform *in vivo* to alleviate acute pulmonary inflammation in animal model of LPS-induced lung injury. NG are targeted to the endothelium via conjugation with an antibody (Ab) directed to Intercellular Adhesion Molecule-1(ICAM-NG), whereas IgG conjugated NG (IgG-NG) are used for control formulations. The amount of Ab conjugated to the NG and distribution in the body after intravenous (IV) injection have been quantitatively analyzed using a tracer isotope-labeled [^{125}I]IgG. As a proof of concept, Ab-NG are loaded with dexamethasone, an anti-inflammatory therapeutic, and the drug uptake and release kinetics are measured by HPLC. *In vivo* studies in mice showed that: i) ICAM-NG accumulates in mouse lungs (~120% ID/g vs ~15% ID/g of IgG-NG); and, ii) DEX encapsulated in ICAM-NG, but not in IgG-NG practically blocks LPS-induced overexpression of pro-inflammatory cell adhesion molecules including ICAM-1 in the pulmonary inflammation.

Editor: Tobias Stoeger, Helmholtz Zentrum München, Germany

Funding: The National Institutes of Health provided support via grant NIH R01 EB006818 (DME). A pilot grant from NSF Nano-Bio Interface Center DMR08-32802 (RJC) facilitated this work, as well as partial support from NSF DMR09-07493 (RJC). Facilities at the Nanoscale Characterization Center supported by NSF/CEMRI (DMR11-20901) are acknowledged. Research reported in this publication was supported in part by the Center for Translational Targeted Therapeutics and Nanomedicine (CT3) of the National Center for Advancing Translational Sciences of the National Institutes of Health under award number UL1TR000003. The funders had no role in study design, data collection and analysis, decision to publish, or preparation of the manuscript.

Competing Interests: The authors have declared that no competing interests exist.

* Email: eckmanndm@uphs.upenn.edu

Introduction

The endothelial monolayer lining the vasculature represents a multifunctional regulatory interface between blood and tissues [1–5]. Endothelial abnormalities are implicated in the pathogenesis of cardiovascular, neurological, pulmonary, metabolic, and other conditions [6–8]. In these conditions, endothelial cells represent an important participant, victim and therapeutic target [9–12]. In particular, the pulmonary endothelium is an important target for treatment of acute inflammation, such as acute lung injury/acute respiratory distress syndrome [1].

Acute lung injury causes disruption of the lung endothelial and epithelial barriers. As a consequence, the lungs mechanics change (i.e., lungs become stiffer) and the number of pores media available for gas exchange are compromised. Most current treatments involve ventilatory strategies, which further traumatize the lung. Other pharmacological treatments attempted in clinical trials have yet not been effective in reducing mortality [13]. In the US, the incidence of acute lung injury is estimated at 200,000 cases with a mortality rate of 40% and is mainly associated with intensive care unit disorders such as sepsis, pneumonia and trauma [14].

Most drugs and drug carriers have no natural affinity to endothelium [15,16]; hence only a minor fraction of the dose acts in this target, despite its accessibility to the bloodstream. As a result, systemic drug delivery and effective pharmacotherapies intended to treat abnormalities of pulmonary endothelium are not sufficient to cope with acute grave disorders like acute lung injury/acute respiratory distress syndrome. In order to achieve this goal, we conjugate drugs and drug carriers with antibodies and other affinity ligands that bind to endothelial cells [17–19]. Pulmonary vasculature represents ~25% of the total endothelial surface and receives essentially the entirety of the right-sided cardiac output; hence these compounds targeted to the endothelium accumulate in the lungs [20–22].

Surface receptors of endothelial cells include intracellular adhesion molecules (ICAM-1), a transmembrane glycoprotein. Its antibody, Anti-ICAM-1, is known to accumulate in the lungs after intravenous (IV) injection and has been used for drug targeting to the endothelium [23,24].

Dexametasone (DEX) is a potent long lasting synthetic glucocorticoid known to inhibit the inflammatory cascade. DEX mainly acts by suppressing expression of proinflammatory cytokines (IL-1, IL-6, IL-8 and TNF-α) and cell adhesion molecules (endothelial leucocyte adhesion molecule-1 and ICAM-1) involved in the migration of leucocytes into the extravascular space [25]. Although DEX is utilized frequently in hospital and out-patients to relieve inflammation in different parts of the body including the lungs, DEX can cause systematic side effects. Consequently, efforts have focused on delivery DEX via drug delivery system such as immunoconjugates [26], polymeric nanocarriers [27] and liposomes [28]. Alternatively, we proposed to deliver DEX locally to the inflammation site via a nanogel system.

Nanogels are nanosized networks that can absorb large amounts of water while preserving their structure via physical or chemical crosslinks [29,30]. In the swollen state, nanogels behave as soft gels known to minimize non-specific interactions with *fluid-like transport properties*. In contrast to traditional nanoparticles (i.e., stiffer gels/ nanocarriers), nanogels can deform to pass physiological filters resulting in greater delivery efficiency than can be reached using stiffer nanoparticles. Additionally, nanogels overcome limitations of other delivery systems such as liposomes. These include limited drug loading capacity of immunoconjugates, greater stability, easiness for sterilization and lower clearance due to non-specific uptake.

In previous work, we developed biocompatible nanogels composed of a rhodamine-labeled dextran shell and a lysozyme core (NG) and examined their viability for drug delivery with a fluorescent molecular probe as a mock drug in two *in vitro* models. Human umbilical vein endothelial cells (HUVEC) were used as a cell culture model to verify NG uptake, drug release and assess cytotoxicity whereas differentiated macrophages (THP-1 cells stimulated with PMA) were used as a model of the mononuclear phagocyte system. These NG showed great potential based on their lack of cytotoxicity and rapid release of the drug in HUVEC before reaching the lysosomes, as compared to their slow uptake by macrophages [31]. In other work, we also highlighted the potential of similar NG for antimicrobial therapy applications when loaded with Ag NPs by *in situ* reaction in the NG solution [32,33].

In this study, we aim to enhance delivery of DEX to the lungs while reducing the toxicity of free DEX to non-target organs. This is accomplished by grafting these biocompatible NG with anti-ICAM (ICAM-NG) directed to the pulmonary endothelium. Naïve mice are used to verify *in vivo* targeting of ICAM-NG. Furthermore, ICAM-NG are loaded with DEX (ICAM-NG-DEX), and their potential to alleviate pulmonary inflammation is studied in a mouse model of inducible inflammatory state. As control formulations, IgG-conjugated NG (IgG-NG) are used.

Materials and Methods

Materials

Rhodamine B isothiocyanate–dextran from *Leuconostoc* ssp. (64–76 kDa molecular weight), lysozyme from chicken egg white, lipopolysaccharides (LPS, from *E. coli* O55:B5) and dexamethasone (DEX) were obtained from Sigma-Aldrich (St. Louis, MI). Anti-ICAM monoclonal antibody (mAb) used was mAb YN1/ 1.7.4, a rat mAb directed against murine Intercellular Adhesion Molecule-1 (ICAM) [34]. Rat IgG was purchased from Equitech Bio, Inc. (Kerrville, TX). Millipore water (18.2 MΩ.cm) was used.

Methods

DLS analysis. The particle size and size distribution of the hydrated NG was determined by dynamic light scattering using a ZS90 Malvern Zetasize Nano series instrument (Malvern, Westborough, MA) equipped with a 22 mW He-Ne laser operating at a wavelength of 633 nm.

Cryo-TEM analysis. Nanogel morphology was imaged by cryo-transmission electronic microscopy on a FEI tecnai-12 operated at 120 keV. The images were recorded on a Gatan ultrascan 1000 CCD camera (2048×2048 pixels, with each pixel dimension at 14 μm).

γ-Counter analysis. Radioactivity was determined using 2470 WIZARD^2 Automatic Gamma Counter (PerkinElmer Inc., Waltham, MA). The amount of dexamethasone released was analyzed using HPLC (Beckman-Coulter, Inc., Brea, CA). Analysis was performed at 246 nm using a Beckman-Coulter 250 mm reversed-phase ultrasphere ODS column with a mobile phase of 40% 2 mM acetate buffer (pH 4.8) and 60% acetonitrile flowing at 1 mL min^{-1} at room temperature.

Synthesis of NG, conjugation of antibodies (Ab) and loading of dexamethasone

The synthesis of NG was performed as previously reported [31,35]. Briefly, Rhodamine B isothiocyanate–dextran and lysozyme were dissolved at 1:1 molar ratio in water, the pH was adjusted to between 7 and 8 using 0.1 N sodium hydroxide and the solution was lyophilized. The lyophilized powder was allowed to react at 60°C under 79% relative humidity in a desiccator containing saturated KBr solution for 18 to 24 h. The reacted powder was dissolved in water (5 mg/mL, based on dextran and lysozyme together), the pH was adjusted to 10.7 using 0.1 N sodium hydroxide, and the solution was further reacted at 80°C for 30 min. The NG were stored at 4°C.

A schematic showing the conjugation of antibodies (Ab) to the NG (Ab-NG) and loading of DEX (Ab-NG-DEX) is illustrated in Figure 1. Prior to Ab conjugation, the NG were activated using sodium periodate ($NaIO_4$) under mild conditions (i.e., room temperature, 3 days) at 1:0.01 molar ratio of dextran:$NaIO_4$ to generate formyl groups [36] and when required, the NG were loaded with DEX. To do so, NG (400 μL) were concentrated to 35 μL by ultracentrifugation (Amicon, Millipore, Billerica, MA), dispersed with 100 μL $NaIO_4$ 0.01 M, 100 μL NaCl 25 wt% and 265 μL deionized water, and allowed to react over 3 days on a shaker at room temperature in the dark. Following reaction, the NG were spun down and dispersed to 500 μL with deionized water twice sequentially. To load them with DEX (NG-DEX), NG (0.22 wt. %) were incubated on a shaker with DEX at a final concentration of 645 μg/mL for 1 day at 37°C. For conjugation, 100 μg of Ab (either IgG (IgG-NG) or anti-ICAM (ICAM-NG), in PBS containing ≤0.09% sodium azide) was added to 300 μL of NG (or NG-DEX) suspension in DI water and placed on a shaker overnight at 4°C. Following Ab conjugation, Ab-NG (or Ab-NG-DEX) mixture was centrifuged at 16,000×g for 15 min to remove unbound Ab (and free DEX). The Ab-NG (or Ab-NG-DEX) pellet was then dispersed via sonication into 1 wt% BSA/PBS.

Anti-ICAM coating efficiency of ICAM-NG

The ICAM-NG were formulated with a trace amount of conjugated [^{125}I]IgG (~2 μCi) in 200 μL 1 wt% BSA/PBS following same procedure described above. The anti-ICAM coating efficiency was determined by measuring [^{125}I]IgG

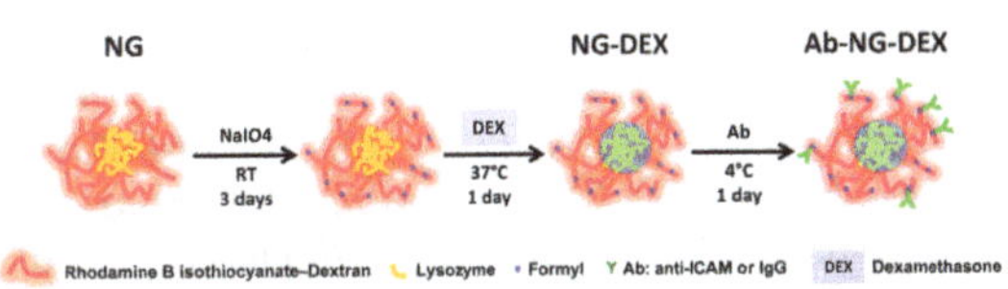

Figure 1. Schematic illustrating the conjugation of Ab to NG and loading of DEX.

conjugated onto NG relative to the IgG mass added. Briefly, ICAM-NG were centrifuged at 16,000×g for 15 min to remove unbound [^{125}I]IgG. The ICAM-NG was then dispersed via sonication into PBS. The coating efficiency was then calculated as [^{125}I]IgG free/[^{125}I]IgG bound [37]. The number of IgG molecules per NG was calculated based on NG surface area, ($A = 4\pi r^2$, assuming NP diameter is 105 nm) and treating mAb as a block (footprint equates to ~120 nm^2). Ultimately, this corresponded to ~250 mAbs/NP.

In vitro release kinetics of DEX from IgG-NG-DEX

Fresh purified IgG-NG-DEX pellet dispersed via sonication into 1 wt% BSA/PBS was placed on a shaker at 37°C for DEX release kinetics study. At each time point studied, the IgG-NG-DEX were centrifuged at 14,000×g for 15 min to remove free DEX, redispersed via sonication into 1 wt% BSA/PBS and returned to the shaker at 37°C. The concentration of free DEX in the natants, as well as the drug encapsulation efficiency, was measured by HPLC. To account for the free DEX that may have released out of IgG-NG-DEX while preparing them for injection into mice (i.e., under static conditions at room temperature), fresh purified IgG-NG-DEX pellet were allowed to sit at room temperature for 30 min before centrifugation to obtain a measure of free DEX drug loss. This amount was proportionately subtracted from the 15 min and 30 min time points. The corrected drug encapsulation efficiency of IgG-NG-DEX was 17%. The experimental data were fitted to an extended Langmuir model (LangmuirEXT1, Simplex) with OriginPro software (Northampton, MA).

In vivo studies

All animal studies were carried out in strict accordance with the recommendations in the Guide for the Care and Use of Laboratory Animals of the National Institutes of Health. The protocol was approved by the Committee on the Ethics of Animal Experiments of the University of Pennsylvania (Permit Number: 803375). All surgery was performed under ketamine/xylazine anesthesia, and all efforts were made to minimize suffering.

Biodistribution studies of Ab-NG in mice

This study was performed on 6 to 8 week-old female C57BL/6 mice (18 to 22 g; $n = 3$ to 5 per group). Mice were anesthetized and injected IV via the jugular vein with ICAM-NG or IgG-NG. Mice were injected with approximately 2.2 mg of Ab-NG formulated with a trace amount of conjugated [^{125}I]IgG (~2 μCi) in 200 μL 1 wt% BSA/PBS. At 30 min post-injection of Ab-NG, blood was collected from the retro-orbital sinus, the animals were euthanized and organs (heart, kidneys, liver, spleen, lungs, and brain) were extracted, weighed and blotted. Tissue radioactivity was measured in a γ-counter, and NG targeting parameters defined by percent of injected dose per gram of tissue (% ID/g). The total activity in blood was calculated assuming a total blood volume representing 7% of the mouse body weight.

Endotoxemia model in mice

This study was performed on 6 to 8 week-old male C57BL/6 mice (20 to 25 g, $n = 5$ to 7 per group). Mice were anesthetized and either 2.2 mg of ICAM-NG-DEX or control (IgG-NG-DEX, ICAM-NG or 1 wt% BSA/PBS) in approximately 200 μL was injected 15 min prior to LPS administration (200 μg/kg) via the tail vein [38]. After 24 h elapsed from initiation of the LPS challenge, the mice were euthanized and the lungs were perfused and harvested. Lungs were homogenated and VCAM-1 and ICAM-1 expression levels were assayed by Western blot.

Western blot analysis

Lung homogenates were subjected to 4–15% gradient gel. Gels were transferred to PVDF membranes (Millipore) and the membranes were blocked with 3% nonfat dry milk in TBS-T (100 mM Tris (pH 7.5), 150 mM NaCl, 0.1% Tween 20) for 1 h. Proteins were detected using goat polyclonal anti-VCAM (R&D Systems, Minneapolis, MN) and anti-ICAM (Santa Cruz Biotechnology, Inc., Santa Cruz, CA), and anti-actin-HRP (Abcam, Cambridge, MA).

Statistical analysis

Data are presented as mean ± SD, unless otherwise noted. Statistical significance between two groups was assessed via t-test, while multiple groups were compared via ANOVA followed by Student's t-test (OriginLab, Northampton, MA). Values of $p < 0.05$ were considered statistically significant.

Results

Synthesis and characterization of Ab conjugated NG

A schematic describing the steps for conjugation of Ab to NG and loading of DEX is given in Figure 1. For Ab conjugation, the dextran present on the outer layer of the NG was oxidized with a reducing agent, $NaIO_4$, to yield reactive formyl groups. These formyl groups were then reacted with Ab molecules via primary amine groups. The latter reaction was carried out at 4°C to minimize Ab degradation and/or inactivity. Independent of Ab conjugation, the NGs diameters displayed Gaussian distributions as measured by DLS (Figure 2a). The particle size (z-average) increased 17% upon Ab conjugation, from 137 nm (pdi = 0.081) to 160 nm (pdi = 0.095). By volume distribution, similar particle sizes were observed (139±47 for NG, 173±61 for Ab-NG) suggesting modal distribution of particles. Considering the hydrodynamic radius of IgG is 5.3 nm [39], the NG size increased as expected with Ab conjugation.

To target the pulmonary vasculature, NGs were coated with Ab directed to endothelial determinant ICAM-1(ICAM-NG) or control IgG (IgG-NG). The amount of Ab conjugated to the NG (Figure 2b) was quantified by gamma radiation using

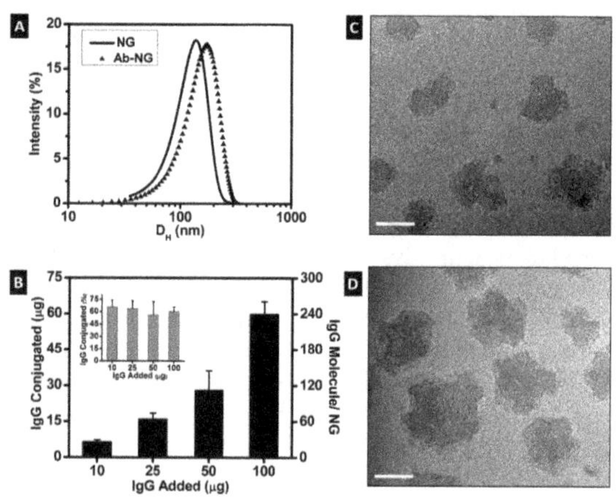

Figure 2. Characterization of Ab-NG. (a) Size distribution of nanogel before (NG) and after Ab coating (Ab-NG), as measured by DLS. The particle size (z-average) is 137 nm (pdi = 0.081) and 160 nm (pdi = 0.095) for NG and Ab-NG, respectively. (b) Summary of anti-ICAM coverage of NGs, [^{125}I]IgG conjugation increases with [^{125}I]IgG added to the NGs. Representative cryo-TEM images of NG before (c) and after (d) anti-ICAM coating (ICAM-NG). Scale bar: 50 nm.

radiolabeled [^{125}I]IgG. The Ab conjugated to the NG was optimized and reaction efficiency of 60% IgG conjugation was observed within the concentrations of IgG studied (10 to 100 μg). At the highest IgG concentration studied, NG were decorated with ~250 Ab molecules per NG.

The morphology of the nanogels in the hydrated state, prior (NG) and subsequent to anti-ICAM conjugation (ICAM-NG), was visualized by cryo-TEM (Figure 2c–d). The nanogels were well-dispersed and irregularly shaped, consistent with lightly crosslinked (i.e., highly hydrated) structures. The average size of the hydrated nanogels observed by TEM was significantly smaller than the hydrodynamic diameter measured by DLS. These divergences are explained based on both techniques limitations. On one side, DLS assumes transparent solutions of diluted spherical colloids. However, the nanogels used in this study, scatter, fluoresce and are irregularly shaped. Moreover, the hydrodynamic diameter measured by DLS, corresponds to the diameter of the nanogels plus the thickness of its solvation layer and therefore, can easily overestimate diameters. By comparison, cryo-TEM is based on electron density contrast particularly near the periphery of the nanogel and therefore poor electron density contrast of the nanogel due to a highly swollen network can underestimate diameters [40].

In vivo targeting of [^{125}I]Ab-NG to pulmonary vasculature

In vivo biodistribution analyses confirmed that the anti-ICAM conjugated to NG (ICAM-NG) was still bioactive (Figure 3). Analyses of different tissues and blood after injection of ICAM-NG targeted to endothelial cells showed preferential location (~12-fold increase in tissue level) of the NG in the pulmonary vasculature compared to non-specific control experiments (IgG-NG). At lower extent, ICAM-NG and IgG-NG were also taken up by organs in the mononuclear phagocyte system, such as the liver and the spleen. Interestingly, the hepatic uptake of ICAM-NG was markedly lower (30%) as compared to IgG-NG, indicating that specific targeting to endothelium, first of all, in the lungs, competes successfully with non-specific uptake in the mononuclear phagocyte system. A more accurate measure of NG targeting efficiency can be obtained by comparing the specific targeting (ICAM-NG) relative to non-specific targeting (IgG-NG) of the nanogels to the target (lungs) versus a clearance organ (liver). By this measurements, the targeting efficiency of ICAM-NG to the lungs was 18-fold that of the liver. Furthermore, blood and other organs studied showed minimum Ab-NG uptake (<10%).

Loading of DEX and in vitro release

The Ab-NG were loaded 5% of their weight with DEX at 37°C. Significantly lower DEX payloads were measured when following attempts to load the drug at 4°C (data not shown). The *in vitro* release of DEX (at 37°C with agitation) is plotted in Figure 4 as accumulative release over time. An initial release burst was observed during the first hour as ~80% of DEX was released. At longer time, DEX released slower, reaching complete release within 3 h. The experimental data followed an extended Langmuir model, represented by:

$$y = \frac{abx^{(1-c)}}{1 + bx^{(1-c)}}$$

where a = 104, b = 3.1 E-4 and c = −1.2 (R^2 = 0.95).

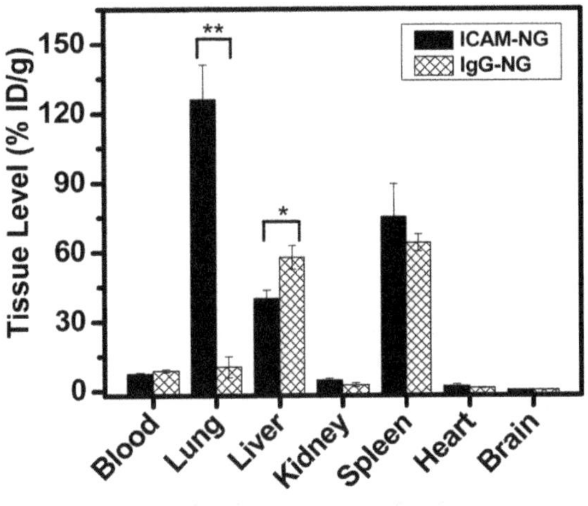

Figure 3. *In vivo* targeting of [^{125}I]Ab-NG. Organ uptake of [^{125}I]ICAM-1 targeted and [^{125}I]IgG-NG were analyzed at 30 min post-IV administration. **$p<0.005$, *$p<0.05$.

In vivo administration of ICAM-NG-DEX in endotoxemia model mice

An endotoxemia model (LPS) was used to induce a systemic inflammatory response in mice. This challenge resulted in approximately 3-fold elevation of expression of an inflammatory marker, ICAM-1, in the inflamed pulmonary vasculature after 24 h (data not shown), in agreement with the literature [37].

The potential of ICAM-NG-DEX to reduce pulmonary vasculature inflammation in mice was measured as % protection based on the protein levels in the lungs of two inflammatory markers, ICAM-1 and VCAM-1, assessed 24 h after therapeutic injection (Figure 5). As controls, naïve mice (100% protection), bare endotoxemia model mice (+LPS, 0% protection) and endotoxemia model mice previously injected with non-specific NG loaded with DEX (+LPS, +IgG-NG-DEX) or specific NG with no drug (+LPS, ICAM-NG) were used. In the animals given the targeted, therapeutic-laden nanogels ICAM-NG-DEX, there was drastic reduction in pulmonary vasculature inflammation to levels found in naïve mice. In particular, injection of ICAM-NG-DEX provided 93% and 84% protection against inflammation expression of ICAM-1 and VCAM-1 in lung tissue, respectively. As expected, neither injection of NG loaded with DEX but lacking targeting, IgG-NG-DEX, nor injection of NG with targeting but lacking DEX, suppressed inflammation in mice.

Discussion

In this study, we have developed for the first time NG targeted to the lungs by direct covalent immobilization of Ab against endothelium determinant, ICAM-1, using simple and direct chemistry (i.e., single step, no Ab modification required, Figure 1).

This novel methodology introduces advantages over ICAM-1 targeted nanocarriers prepared via electrostatic/hydrophobic interactions [37]. In our NGs, the dextran shell of the NG was activated to generate free aldehydes, for subsequent Ab immobilization via free amines. The covalent bond prevents Ab displacement by proteins and leaching off the surface, favors stability of the attached Ab (i.e., prevents denaturation) and allows for better control of the number/location of Ab binding sites [41]. Using this aldehyde-mediated direct chemistry we demonstrated conjugation of Ab onto NG by DLS, gamma radiation and cryo-TEM (Figure 2). In particular, we conjugated the NG with anti-

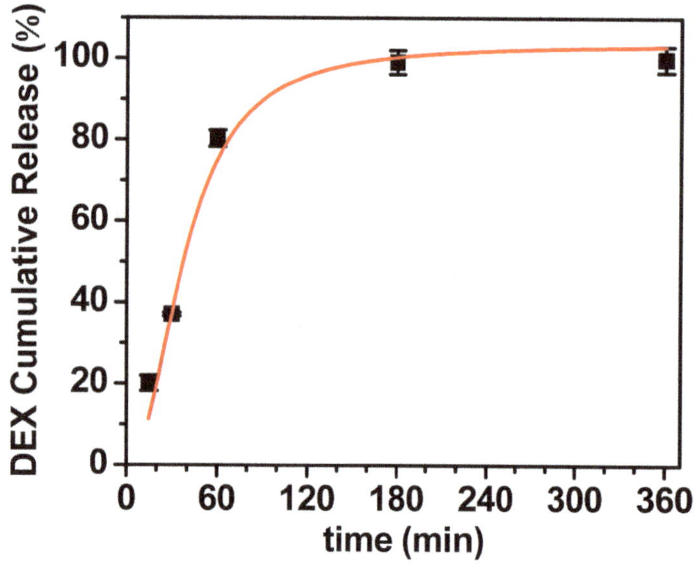

Figure 4. *In vitro* DEX release kinetics of IgG-NG in 1 wt% BSA/PBS. The red line is extended Langmuir model fit.

ICAM to target the pulmonary endothelium or IgG to use as a control (i.e., non-specific targeting). Complete saturation of Ab (~60%) at the highest concentration of IgG studied led to ~240 Ab molecules per NG particle, which is consistent with our geometric estimates of ~250 Ab molecules per NG particle indicated above. This surface coverage has shown 100% endothelium *in vivo* targeting with anti-ICAM molecules in mice when using polystyrene beads (100 nm) as a nanocarrier [42].

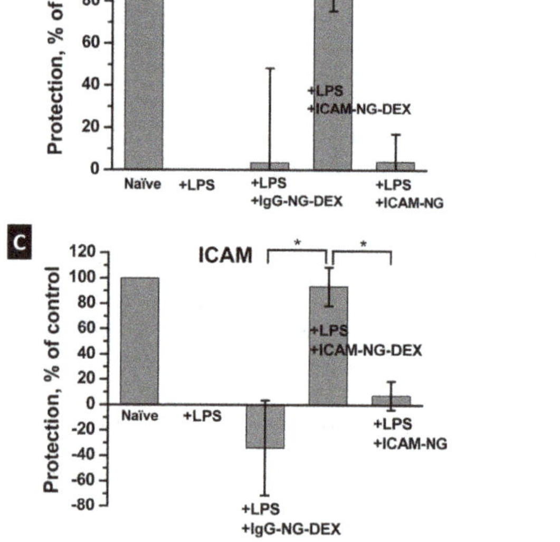

Figure 5. *In vivo* VCAM and ICAM protein expression in lung tissue for naïve and LPS-treated (+LPS) mice following injection for the different treatments studied. (a) Representative Western blot detection, (b) summary of % protection for VCAM expression, (c) summary of % protection for ICAM expression. *$p<0.05$.

Importantly, the Ab in our ICAM-NG maintained their biological activity (Figure 3). This result suggests that possible drawbacks associated with Ab conjugation by direct chemistry are kept to a minimum (i.e., no site-specificity, uncontrolled Ab orientation, and need for a further step reduction of the imine bond to amine). Most importantly, we demonstrated that our ICAM-NG effectively targeted specific anatomical tissue/cells *in vivo* (i.e., pulmonary endothelium, Figure 3) in the resting state while showing low specificity for clearance tissues involved in the mononuclear phagocyte system (i.e., liver, spleen). Note that in the resting state, the levels of ICAM expressed by endothelial cells were about 3-fold lower than in the activated state. This result further highlights ICAM-NG extraordinary specificity. Relative to the liver, the amount of ICAM-NG that reached the lungs was 18-fold higher than IgG-NG.

As a proof of concept, the potential of ICAM-NG to upload and offload drugs via diffusion was tested using DEX. Ab-NG-DEX exhibited a fast onset of DEX action. A DEX upload of 5 wt% of the Ab-NG-DEX particle's own weight was released continuously and rapidly within 1 h (~80% released) whereas the remainder of the drug was entirely released at a slower pace within 3 h (Figure 4), following an extended Langmuir model fit. This fast onset of DEX action is particularly important when used for prophylaxis in surgery to minimize postoperative inflammation, pain, nausea and vomiting [43]. A single preoperative dose of DEX (~8 to 10 mg/kg in adults) has shown benefits in various surgeries [44], such as cardiac [45] and thyroid operations [46]. However, free drug has also been associated with toxicity to non-target organs. Alternatively, drugs can be delivered specifically using targeted nanocarriers, which would, ideally, maintain the therapeutic efficiency of the drug while reducing its toxicity to other organs [47]. We chose endothelium determinant ICAM-1 because is expressed in the rested and pathological activated state [48]. Therefore, our ICAM-NG-DEX can be administered prophylactically to prevent inflammation from occurring.

In vivo studies demonstrated the therapeutic efficiency of ICAM-NG-DEX in mice. These NG targeted to the lungs succeeded to deliver DEX, as indicated by the low levels of pro-inflammatory cytokines measured in the lungs of endotoxemic mice pretreated with ICAM-NG-DEX (Figure 5). The importance of targeting the drug-loaded NG is further confirmed by the lack of action to minimize lung inflammation in endotoxemic mice when IgG-NG-DEX is used instead of ICAM-NG-DEX or when DEX is not loaded in the NG (ICAM-NG).

These results highlight the potential of our NGs to selectively deliver drug intracorporeally by intravascular injection. By changing the Ab, this methodology can be easily extended to prepare NGs aimed at other targets (i.e., cells types, tissue, organs). As a proof of concept, we have demonstrated that the NG can effectively deliver a drug, in this case the anti-inflammatory steroid DEX, to the target cells while minimizing drug offloading into the other organs, and minimizing early drug loss via clearance mechanisms involving the RES. Future studies will focus on optimization of uptake/offloading of different drugs into these NG.

Conclusions

A novel approach to prepare nanogels targeted to the lungs is demonstrated by conjugating them with anti-ICAM antibodies. These NG loaded with dexamethasone and administered prophylactically successfully minimize inflammatory response in acute lung injury in endotoxemia model mice.

Acknowledgments

We thank Dr. D. R. Williams for TEM imaging and Dr. Q. C. Meng for performing HPLC analyses. We are grateful to Evguenia Arguiri for assistance with *in vivo* experiments. The content of this paper is solely the responsibility of the authors and does not necessarily represent the official views of the National Institutes of Health.

Author Contributions

Conceived and designed the experiments: MCCF VVS BZ VRM RJC DME. Performed the experiments: MCCF VVS BZ. Analyzed the data: MCCF VVS BZ. Contributed reagents/materials/analysis tools: VRM RJC DME. Contributed to the writing of the manuscript: MCCF VVS BZ RJC VRM DME.

References

1. Howard MD, Hood ED, Zern B, Shuvaev VV, Grosser T, et al. (2014) Nanocarriers for vascular delivery of anti-inflammatory agents. Annu Rev Pharmacol Toxicol 54: 205–226.
2. Cheng Z, Al Zaki A, Hui JZ, Muzykantov VR, Tsourkas A (2012) Multifunctional nanoparticles: cost versus benefit of adding targeting and imaging capabilities. Science 338: 903–910.
3. Buxton DB (2009) Nanomedicine for the management of lung and blood diseases. Nanomedicine (Lond) 4: 331–339.
4. Pan H, Myerson JW, Hu L, Marsh JN, Hou K, et al. (2013) Programmable nanoparticle functionalization for in vivo targeting. FASEB J 27: 255–264.
5. Simionescu M, Gafencu A, Antohe F (2002) Transcytosis of pla sma macromolecules in endothelial cells: a cell biological survey. Microsc Res Tech 57: 269–288.
6. Cybulsky MI, Gimbrone MA Jr (1991) Endothelial expression of a mononuclear leukocyte adhesion molecule during atherogenesis. Science 251: 788–791.
7. Iiyama K, Hajra L, Iiyama M, Li H, DiChiara M, et al. (1999) Patterns of vascular cell adhesion molecule-1 and intercellular adhesion molecule-1 expression in rabbit and mouse atherosclerotic lesions and at sites predisposed to lesion formation. Circ Res 85: 199–207.
8. Muro S, Muzykantov VR (2005) Targeting of antioxidant and anti-thrombotic drugs to endothelial cell adhesion molecules. Curr Pharm Des 11: 2383–2401.
9. Charoenphol P, Mocherla S, Bouis D, Namdee K, Pinsky DJ, et al. (2011) Targeting therapeutics to the vascular wall in atherosclerosis-Carrier size matters. Atherosclerosis 217: 364–370.
10. Greineder CF, Howard MD, Carnemolla R, Cines DB, Muzykantov VR (2013) Advanced drug delivery systems for antithrombotic agents. Blood 122: 1565–1575.
11. Howard MD, Hood ED, Zern B, Shuvaev VV, Grosser T, et al. (2014) Nanocarriers for Vascular Delivery of Anti-Inflammatory Agents. Annual Review of Pharmacology and Toxicology, Vol 54. pp. 205–226.
12. Maruyama K, Holmberg E, Kennel SJ, Klibanov A, Torchilin VP, et al. (1990) Characterization of Invivo Immunoliposome Targeting to Pulmonary Endothelium. Journal of Pharmaceutical Sciences 79: 978–984.
13. Johnson ER, Matthay MA (2010) Acute Lung Injury: Epidemiology, Pathogenesis, and Treatment. Journal of Aerosol Medicine and Pulmonary Drug Delivery 23: 243–252.
14. Rubenfeld GD, Caldwell E, Peabody E, Weaver J, Martin DP, et al. (2005) Incidence and outcomes of acute lung injury. New England Journal of Medicine 353: 1685–1693.
15. Cliffel DE, Turner BN, Huffman BJ (2009) Nanoparticle-based biologic mimetics. Wiley Interdisciplinary Reviews-Nanomedicine and Nanobiotechnology 1: 47–59.
16. Mochalin VN, Shenderova O, Ho D, Gogotsi Y (2012) The properties and applications of nanodiamonds. Nature Nanotechnology 7: 11–23.
17. Liu J, Weller GE, Zern B, Ayyaswamy PS, Eckmann DM, et al. (2010) Computational model for nanocarrier binding to endothelium validated using in vivo, in vitro, and atomic force microscopy experiments. Proc Natl Acad Sci U S A 107: 16530–16535.
18. Muzykantov VR, Christofidou-Solomidou M, Balyasnikova I, Harshaw DW, Schultz L, et al. (1999) Streptavidin facilitates internalization and pulmonary targeting of an anti-endothelial cell antibody (platelet-endothelial cell adhesion molecule 1): a strategy for vascular immunotargeting of drugs. Proc Natl Acad Sci U S A 96: 2379–2384.
19. Muzykantov VR, Atochina EN, Ischiropoulos H, Danilov SM, Fisher AB (1996) Immunotargeting of antioxidant enzyme to the pulmonary endothelium. Proc Natl Acad Sci U S A 93: 5213–5218.
20. Christofidou-Solomidou M, Scherpereel A, Wiewrodt R, Ng K, Sweitzer T, et al. (2003) PECAM-directed delivery of catalase to endothelium protects against pulmonary vascular oxidative stress. American Journal of Physiology-Lung Cellular and Molecular Physiology 285: L283–L292.
21. Danilov SM, Muzykantov VR, Martynov AV, Atochina EN, Sakharov IY, et al. (1991) Lung Is the Target Organ for a Monoclonal-Antibody to Angiotensin-Converting Enzyme. Laboratory Investigation 64: 118–124.
22. Muro S, Garnacho C, Champion JA, Leferovich J, Gajewski C, et al. (2008) Control of endothelial targeting and intracellular delivery of therapeutic enzymes by modulating the size and shape of ICAM-1-targeted carriers. Molecular Therapy 16: 1450–1458.
23. Carnemolla R, Shuvaev VV, Muzykantov VR (2010) Targeting antioxidant and antithrombotic biotherapeutics to endothelium. Seminars in Thrombosis and Hemostasis 36: 332–342.
24. Chittasupho C, Xie S-X, Baoum A, Yakovleva T, Siahaan TJ, et al. (2009) ICAM-1 targeting of doxorubicin-loaded PLGA nanoparticles to lung epithelial cells. European Journal of Pharmaceutical Sciences 37: 141–150.
25. Rocksen D, Lilliehook B, Larsson R, Johansson T, Bucht A (2000) Differential anti-inflammatory and anti-oxidative effects of dexamethasone and N-acetylcysteine in endotoxin-induced lung inflammation. Clinical and Experimental Immunology 122: 249–256.
26. Everts M, Kok RJ, Asgeirsdottir SA, Melgert BN, Moolenaar TJM, et al. (2002) Selective intracellular delivery of dexamethasone into activated endothelial cells using an E-selectin-directed immunoconjugate. Journal of Immunology 168: 883–889.
27. Zhang N, Chittasupho C, Duangrat C, Siahaan TJ, Berkland C (2008) PLGA nanoparticle-peptide conjugate effectively targets intercellular cell-adhesion molecule-1. Bioconjugate Chemistry 19: 145–152.
28. Asgeirdottir SA, Kamps JAAM, Bakker HI, Zwiers PJ, Heeringa P, et al. (2007) Site-specific inhibition of glomerulonephritis progression by targeted delivery of dexamethasone to glomerular endothelium. Molecular Pharmacology 72: 121–131.
29. Kabanov AV, Vinogradov SV (2009) Nanogels as Pharmaceutical Carriers: Finite Networks of Infinite Capabilities. Angewandte Chemie-International Edition 48: 5418–5429.
30. Vinogradov SV, Bronich TK, Kabanov AV (2002) Nanosized cationic hydrogels for drug delivery: preparation, properties and interactions with cells. Advanced Drug Delivery Reviews 54: 135–147.
31. Ferrer MCC, Sobolewski P, Composto RJ, Eckmann DM (2013) Cellular uptake and intracellular cargo release from dextran based nanogel drug carriers. Journal of Nanotechnology in Engineering and Medicine 4:011002: 1–8.
32. Ferrer MCC, Dastgheyb S, Hickok NJ, Eckmann DM, Composto RJ (2014) Designing Nanogel Carriers for Antibacterial Applications. Acta biomaterialia In Press.
33. Ferrer MCC, Ferrier RC Jr, Eckmann DM, Composto RJ (2013) A facile route to synthesize nanogels doped with silver nanoparticles. Journal of Nanoparticle Research 15: 1–7.
34. Takei F (1985) Inhibition of Mixed Lymphocyte-Response by a Rat Monoclonal-Antibody to a Novel Murine Lymphocyte-Activation Antigen (Mala-2). Journal of Immunology 134: 1403–1407.

35. Li J, Yu SY, Yao P, Jiang M (2008) Lysozyme-dextran core-shell nanogels prepared via a green process. Langmuir 24: 3486–3492.
36. Ferrer MCC, Hickok NJ, Eckmann DM, Composto RJ (2012) Antibacterial biomimetic hybrid films. Soft Matter 8:2423–2431.
37. Zern BJ, Chacko A-M, Liu J, Greineder CF, Blankemeyer ER, et al. (2013) Reduction of Nanoparticle Avidity Enhances the Selectivity of Vascular Targeting and PET Detection of Pulmonary Inflammation. Acs Nano 7: 2461–2469.
38. Shuvaev VV, Han J, Yu KJ, Huang S, Hawkins BJ, et al. (2011) PECAM-targeted delivery of SOD inhibits endothelial inflammatory response. Faseb Journal 25: 348–357.
39. Armstrong JK, Wenby RB, Meiselman HJ, Fisher TC (2004) The hydrodynamic radii of macromolecules and their effect on red blood cell aggregation. Biophysical Journal 87: 4259–4270.
40. Mittal V, Matsko NB (2012) Analytical imaging techniques for soft matter. Berlin Heidelberg: Springer-Verlag.
41. Arruebo M, Valladares M, Gonzalez-Fernandez A (2009) Antibody-Conjugated Nanoparticles for Biomedical Applications. Journal of Nanomaterials 2009: 1–24.
42. Liu J, Weller GER, Zern B, Ayyaswamy PS, Eckmann DM, et al. (2010) Computational model for nanocarrier binding to endothelium validated using in vivo, in vitro, and atomic force microscopy experiments. Proceedings of the National Academy of Sciences of the United States of America 107: 16530–16535.
43. Henzi I, Walder B, Tramer MR (2000) Dexamethasone for the prevention of postoperative nausea and vomiting: A quantitative systematic review. Anesthesia and Analgesia 90: 186–194.
44. Eberhart LHJ, Morin AM, Georgieff M (2000) Dexamethasone for prophylaxis of postoperative nausea and vomiting - A meta-analysis of randomised controlled studies. Anaesthesist 49: 713–720.
45. El Azab SR, Rosseell PMJ, de Lange JJ, Groeneveld ABJ, van Strik R, et al. (2002) Dexamethasone decreases the pro- to anti-inflammatory cytokine ratio during cardiac surgery. British Journal of Anaesthesia 88: 496–501.
46. Chen C-C, Siddiqui FJ, Chen T-L, Chan ES-Y, Tam K-W (2012) Dexamethasone for Prevention of Postoperative Nausea and Vomiting in Patients Undergoing Thyroidectomy: Meta-analysis of Randomized Controlled Trials. World Journal of Surgery 36: 61–68.
47. De Jong WH, Borm PJA (2008) Drug delivery and nanoparticles: Applications and hazards. International Journal of Nanomedicine 3: 133–149.
48. Hua S (2013) Targeting sites of inflammation: intercellular adhesion molecule-1 as a target for novel inflammatory therapies. Front Pharmacol 4: 127.

15

Therapeutic Efficacy of Combining PEGylated Liposomal Doxorubicin and Radiofrequency (RF) Ablation: Comparison between Slow-Drug-Releasing, Non-Thermosensitive and Fast-Drug-Releasing, Thermosensitive Nano-Liposomes

Alexander V. Andriyanov[1], Erez Koren[1], Yechezkel Barenholz[1*¶], S. Nahum Goldberg[2¶]

1 Laboratory of Membrane and Liposome Research, Department of Biochemistry, Institute for Medical Research Israel-Canada, Hebrew University-Hadassah Medical School, Jerusalem, Israel, 2 Radiology Department, Hadassah Hebrew University Medical Center, Ein Kerem, Jerusalem, Israel and Beth Israel Deaconess Medical Center, Boston, Massachusetts, United States of America

Abstract

Aims: To determine how the accumulation of drug in mice bearing an extra-hepatic tumor and its therapeutic efficacy are affected by the type of PEGylated liposomal doxorubicin used, treatment modality, and rate of drug release from the liposomes, when combined with radiofrequency (RF) ablation.

Materials and Methods: Two nano-drugs, both long-circulating PEGylated doxorubicin liposomes, were formulated: (1) PEGylated doxorubicin in thermosensitive liposomes (PLDTS), having a burst-type fast drug release above the liposomes' solid ordered to liquid disordered phase transition (at 42°C), and (2) non-thermosensitive PEGylated doxorubicin liposomes (PLDs), having a slow and continuous drug release. Both were administered intravenously at 8 mg/kg doxorubicin dose to tumor-bearing mice. Animals were divided into 6 groups: no treatment, PLD, RF, RF+PLD, PLDTS, and PLDTS+RF, for intra-tumor doxorubicin deposition at 1, 24, and 72 h post-injection (in total 41, mice), and 31 mice were used for randomized survival studies.

Results: Non-thermosensitive PLD combined with RF had the least tumor growth and the best end-point survival, better than PLDTS+RF ($p<0.005$) or all individual therapies ($p<0.001$). Although at 1 h post-treatment the greatest amount of intra-tumoral doxorubicin was seen following PLDTS+RF ($p<0.05$), by 24 and 72 h the greatest doxorubicin amount was seen for PLD+RF ($p<0.05$); in this group the tumor also has the longest exposure to doxorubicin.

Conclusion: Optimizing therapeutic efficacy of PLD requires a better understanding of the relationship between the effect of RF on tumor microenvironment and liposome drug release profile. If drug release is too fast, the benefit of changing the microenvironment by RF on tumor drug localization and therapeutic efficacy may be much smaller than for PLDs having slow and temperature-independent drug release. Thus the much longer circulation time of doxorubicin from PLD than from PLDTS may be beneficial in many therapeutic instances, especially in extra-hepatic tumors.

Editor: Dimitris Fatouros, Aristotle University of Thessaloniki, Greece

Funding: This work was supported by NCI grant 5U54CA151881-04 to SNG, the Barenholz Fund, the Israel Ministry of Health, and the Israel Science Foundation. The Barenholz Fund is originated from royalties Hebrew University received from YB's commercialized projects, and this money is used to support YB's research activities. The funders had no role in study design, data collection and analysis, decision to publish, or preparation of the manuscript.

Competing Interests: The authors have read the journal's policy and have the following conflicts: Yechezkel Barenholz is one of the inventors on two already expired (March 2010) patents relevant to Doxil: 1. Yechezkel Barenholz and Gilad Haran: "Method of Amphipathic Drug Loading in Liposomes by pH Gradient". U.S. Patent No. 5,192,549, March 9, 1993. on Water". U.S. Patent 5,244,574, September 14, 1993 2. Yechezkel Barenholz and Gilad Haran: "Liposomes: Efficient Loading and Controlled Release of Amphipathic Molecules". U.S. Patent 5,316,771, May 31, 1994. Yechezkel Barenholz is a stock holder of LipoCure Ltd., which prepared the DOX-NP (a Doxil-like PLD) for research applications, which is distributed by Avanti Polar lipids. S. Nahum Goldberg has unrelated sponsored research and consulting with Angiodynamics and Cosman Company, both of whom produce RF devices for tumor ablation.

* E-mail: chezyb@gmail.com

¶ YB and SNG are joint senior authors on this work

Introduction

A main impediment of current anticancer chemotherapy is low tumor selectivity and the resultant generation of undesirable side effects [1]. The use of pharmaceutical nanoparticle carriers such as liposomes has been proposed as an effective approach to overcome these obstacles [2]. Nonspecific liposomal targeting is based on the pathophysiological phenomenon characterized as the enhanced permeability and retention (EPR) effect [3]. This occurs primarily in two main pathological states: inflammation and cancer, in which particles of approximately 100 nm or less preferentially accumulate in the diseased tissues. Benefits for liposome-delivered treatment of inflammation [4,5] and cancer treatment [6,7] have been reported *in vivo*. For nano-drugs to benefit from the EPR effect, the liposomes are required to evade the immune system. This is achieved by including a lipopolymer such as PEG-DSPE in the liposome membrane [8]. However, a selective accumulation at the tumor site by itself is not sufficient to achieve therapeutic efficacy. There is an obligatory need for a sufficient spontaneous drug release from the liposomes *in situ*.

Doxil is the first FDA-approved (and still extensively used clinically) liposomal nano-drug. The active pharmaceutical ingredient (API), doxorubicin, is remotely-loaded into PEGylated liposomes [8]. For Doxil, drug release at the tumor is assumed to be higher than in plasma in order to achieve the observed therapeutic efficacy. In the case of remotely-loaded Doxil, this drug release is also demonstrated by the presence of doxorubicin metabolites in the tumor tissue [8]. This is not the case for the passively-loaded "Stealth" cisplatin liposomes, which although they benefit from the EPR effect, unlike Doxil, do not show sufficient therapeutic efficacy *in vivo* due to insufficient spontaneous drug release at the tumor site [9,10]. Although the mechanism of drug release in tumors from liposomes is not fully known, it is clear that it is dependent on three main factors: the mechanism of drug loading (remote versus passive), liposome membrane composition, and the tumor microenvironment [2,8,11].

Many studies have shown that external energy sources combined with appropriate lipid compositions resulted in improving controlled drug release at the tumor site, followed by improved therapeutic efficacy. Examples of external energy sources include heat, radiofrequency, ultrasound, and light [12–14]. Lipid composition of the liposome membrane is an important parameter which, in combination with energy use, controls the desired drug-release profile [5,15,16]. Liposomal membrane lipid composition influences drug release rate as a response to exposure to specific energy sources. For example, light-induced photochemical activation of content release from liposomes was previously designed to employ destabilization of membrane lipids by isomerization (azobenzene, retinoyl phospholipids, spiropyran, stilbene); cleavage (NVOC-DOPE, *o*-nitrobenzyl, coumarin);s or by polymerization (bis-sorb PC, diacetylene PC) of its components [17]. Furthermore, the use of *lyso*-phospholipids when combined with the lack of cholesterol for the construction of temperature-sensitive liposomes is a well-established strategy to achieve a fast burst release, as was demonstrated with ThermoDox [18].

Doxil membrane lipid composition, being based on the combination of high-Tm (53°C) hydrogenated soy phosphatidylcholine as the "liposome-forming lipid" [19] and a high mole % of cholesterol causes the liposome membrane to be in a liquid ordered (LO) phase, lacking the solid ordered (SO) to liquid disordered (LD) phase transition. This phase transition is typical of most phospholipids when cholesterol is missing from the lipid bilayer [15,20,21]. A lipid bilayer such as that of the non-thermosensitive liposomes, PLD, is expected to demonstrate a very slow, almost negligible zero-order release rate at 37°C *in vitro* in buffer and plasma, 5% after 30 h of incubation, as was shown previously [22], and also a slow release rate *in vivo* was shown by us (unpublished data). These liposomes are referred to as temperature insensitive liposomes. On the other hand, liposomal formulations that lack cholesterol exhibit a SO to LD phase transition at Tm's, which depend on the exact lipid composition. Such liposomes are referred to as temperature-sensitive liposomes (PLDTS), and they burst-release their intra-liposome aqueous phase content upon passing through the phase transition [23]. One such PEGylated liposomal doxorubicin PLDTS formulation, referred to as ThermoDox, was developed by Needham and co-workers [24,25]. This formulation showed promise in pre-clinical studies; However, recently it failed in a Phase III clinical trial for the treatment of liver cancer [26,27]. This PLDTS lipid composition was designed to have its phase transition at 41.5°C, and once these liposomes are exposed to 42°C or higher they demonstrate a fast burst-type release of almost all loaded doxorubicin in less than 5 min. [28–31].

Given the availability of two very different liposomal formulations for the delivery of drugs such as doxorubicin, we can use them to optimize the therapy achieved by combining the liposomal drug delivery with RF. For this we have to answer two very critical questions:

1. What is the optimal drug release rate at the tumor tissue?
2. How stable should drug-loaded liposomes be in plasma?

It is also important to note that the answers to these queries may also depend on the mechanism of action of the anticancer drug [32,33]. It may involve "phase-specific drugs", which are most active against cells in a specific phase of the cell cycle (e.g. vincristine, which is specific to the mitosis phase) or for cell-cycle-specific drugs. The latter are effective while cells are actively in cycle, but do not depend on the cell's being in a particular phase (doxorubicin belongs to this group). The third group is cell-cycle non-specific drugs (e.g. alkylating agents). The lack of answers to these two questions is often a barrier to achieving effective therapy.

PLDTS and Doxil (PLD) are two different approaches to deliver doxorubicin to ablated tissues, and represent two extreme situations. The PLDTS are long-circulating liposomes that demonstrate a solid ordered to liquid disordered phase transition (Tm of 41.5°C) and therefore have a heat-sensitive delivery of high doses of rapidly released drugs [34], whereas the second preparation (Doxil) are long-circulating liposomes, which, due to the high level of cholesterol, lack such a phase transition and, due to their high content of HSPC (Tm of 53°C), show a very slow release profile [5,8,35]. Thus, these two strategies offer two types of release kinetics that may lead to quite different strategies of doxorubicin delivery and of treatment clinical outcome. Both nano-drugs have been reported as exhibiting synergistic effects when combined with radiofrequency (RF) ablation [29,36–38], gaining increasing clinical adoption with minimally invasive image-guided tumor therapy of focal hepatic, lung, renal, and bone tumors [39–41]. Increases in intra-tumoral drug deposition of 4–6 fold have been reported for both approaches [29,36–38]. Since direct comparison of the two approaches has to our knowledge not yet been performed, we decided to compare them side-by-side using the same appropriate animal model. Specifically, in our current study, nude mice with human medulloblastoma [42] were treated with RF and two PEGylated liposomal doxorubicin preparations, as this chemotherapeutic is reported as a potent and active anticancer element for this type of cancer [43,44].

Materials and Methods

Lipids and Doxorubicin

1,2-dipalmitoyl-*sn*-glycero-3-phosphatidylcholine (DPPC), 1-stearoyl-2-hydroxy-*sn*-glycero-3-phosphatidylcholine (MSPC) and N-carbamyl-poly-(ethylene glycol methyl ether)-1,2-distearoyl-*sn*-

Table 1. Liposome characterization.

Nano-drug name	Lipid composition	Mole lipid ratio	Size (Z-average, nm)	PDI	ζ-potential (mV)	Tm (°C)
PLD	HSPC; Cholesterol; PEG-DSPE	57/38/5	84.4	0.05	−2.7±0.2	No phase transition*
PLDTS	DPPC; MSPC; PEG-DSPE	86/10/4	97.5	0.1	−1.7±0.2	42

*No phase transition is explained by the high mole % of cholesterol.

glycero-3-phosphoethanolamine sodium salt (PEG_{2k}-DSPE) were obtained from Lipoid (Ludwigshafen, Germany). Doxorubicin hydrochloride (Dox) was obtained from Pharmachemie B.V. (Harlem, The Netherlands).

Doxil-like DOX-NP, PEGylated nano-liposomes remote-loaded with doxorubicin (PLD) by transmembrane ammonium sulfate gradient, was obtained from Avanti Polar Lipids (for details see: *http://avantilipids.com/index.php?option= com_content&view=article&id=2331&Itemid=607*) catalog #300102. DOX-NP (PLD) and PLDTS were characterized by us as described in Table 1 using the methodologies as described in [45] and reviewed in [8].

Liposomal Preparation

PLDTS (PEGylated thermosensitive nano-liposomes remote-loaded with doxorubicin) were prepared according to previously reported methods [24,25,46]. Briefly, PLDTS were fabricated by lipid film hydration, followed by down-sizing using extrusion. Doxorubicin was remote loaded by transmembrane pH gradient using sodium citrate buffer as intra-liposome low-pH medium. Unloaded drug was removed by the cation exchange resin Dowex 50WX-4 (Sigma-Aldrich, St. Louis, MO, USA) or cation exchange column Stata-X-C Polymeric Strong Cation 200 mg/3 ml (Phenomenex, Torrence, CA, USA) [47]. The final amounts of intraliposomal doxorubicin were determined by using intensity of absorption at 480 nm using Synergy 4 Multi-Mode Microplate Reader (Biotek Instruments, Winooski, VT, USA), as previously described by Amselem et al. [48].

Liposomal Characterization

Liposomes were characterized for their zeta-potential and size distribution by Malvern's Zetasizer Nano ZS instrument (Worcestershire, UK), as described by Garbuzenko et al. [49]. Phospholipid concentration was determined using a modified Bartlett procedure [45,50]. Differential scanning calorimetry (DSC) analysis was performed as previously described by Biltonen and Lichtenberg [51] using a MicroCal VP-Capillary DSC system (GE Healthcare, Uppsala, Sweden).

Cryo-transmission Electron Microscopy (Cryo-TEM)

Cryo-TEM was used to confirm liposome size distribution measured by dynamic light scattering (DLS) and to characterize the detailed structure of the PLDTS before and after heat activation, as well as the physical state of the encapsulated drugs, as previously described [13].

Drug Administration

The total amount of doxorubicin injected into the tail vein of each mouse in all groups, except control and RF only, was 8 mg/kg (up to 200 μL per mouse weighing about 25 g) [38,41].

RF Application

Conventional monopolar RF was applied by using a 500-kHz RFA generator (Model 3E; Radionics, Burlington, MA, USA). To complete the RF circuit, the animal was placed on a standardized metallic grounding pad (Radionics). Contact was assured by shaving the animal's fur and liberally applying electrolytic contact gel. Initially, the 1-cm tip of a 21-gauge electrically insulated electrode (SMK electrode; Radionics) was located at the midpoint of the tumor. For all studies, duration of RF was 3 min, with the generator output titrated to maintain a designated tip temperature (70±2°C). This standardized method of RF application and the parameters chosen have been demonstrated previously to provide specific, constant dimensions of ablation with reproducible coagulation volumes, thereby enabling straightforward comparison of the effects of adjuvant drug administration [52].

Our protocols for administering liposomal doxorubicin in relation to the RF were optimized to maximum effect of either RF tissue changes (Doxil-PLD) [38,53] or the equivalent of clinical recommendations for Phase III clinical trials combining thermally sensitive liposomes and RF [26]. These well-established treatment protocols are described in Schemes 1,2 (See supplementary data). For PLD treatment, drug was injected IV 15 min post-RF treatment to permit, on the one hand, induced changes in the tumor microenvironment that await the PLD, while at the same time allowing the tumor to be cooled and returned to baseline temperature [52,54]. For PLDTS treatment, the opposite order was performed. PLDTS was administrated IV, and 15 minutes later the tumor was exposed to the RF, as a similar protocol was used previously by others including that for ThermoDox [26].

In vivo Animal Model

Approval by the Institutional Animal Care and Use Committee of the Hebrew University (#MD-07-10404-5) was obtained before the initiation of these studies. The human medulloblastoma cell line (Daoy) was purchased from American Type Culture Collection (Manassas, VA, USA). Approximately 4 million Daoy cells were inoculated s.c. in the back of 4–5 week old NUDE-Hsd:Athymic mice (Harlan Laboratories, Jerusalem, Israel) [7]. For the bio-distribution study, and in order enable direct pair-wise comparison of the specific RF effect on the same mouse, two subcutaneous tumors were established by injecting 4 million Daoy cells in both the lower left and right flanks of each mouse. Four to six weeks after cell injection, tumors grew to the desired size (13±2 mm diameter for quantitation studies, and 11±2 mm for the survival study). For all experiments and procedures, anesthesia was induced with intraperitoneal injection of a mixture of ketamine (50 mg/kg, Ketaset; Fort Dodge Animal Health, Fort Dodge, Iowa, USA) and xylazine (5 mg/kg, Sedaxylan; Eurovet Animal Health B.V., Bladel, The Netherlands). Animals were sacrificed with an overdose of double the amounts of these drugs.

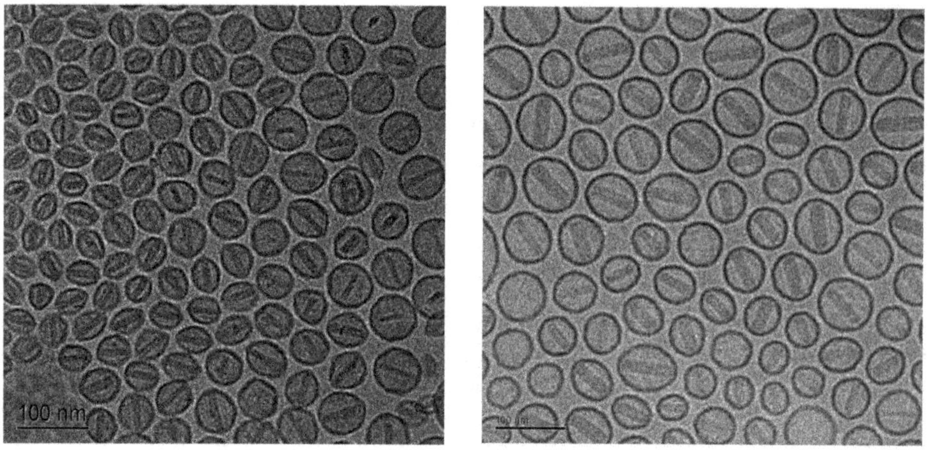

a b

Figure 1. Cryo-TEM micrographs of PLDTS (a) and PLD (b) liposomal formulations at 25°C. Clearly seen are the ellipsoid liposomes containing the loaded doxorubicin, similar to what was previously observed for doxorubicin-loaded liposomes (Doxil/Myocet) [8,23,62].

Pharmacokinetics and Biodistribution

An initial group of 41 mice was randomized to six groups and sacrificed at 1, 24 and 72 h after the liposome intravenous administration (three time-points for each liposomal formulation, PLDTS and PLD). As mentioned above, in order to enable direct pair-wise comparison of the specific RF effect on the same mouse, RF was applied to all mice in one tumor only. An additional group of 8 mice (4 for each drug) was used for a 6-hour study. Recovered doxorubicin was evaluated in the most relevant tissues, including plasma, tumor (with or without RF treatment), and liver of all animals. Organs were harvested at the defined sacrifice times with samples stored at −80°C until analysis. The organs were homogenized in acidic isopropanol as described by Gabizon et al. [55]. Measurements were made by determining the fluorescence emission intensity at emission wavelength filter of 600±20 nm and excitation wavelength of 485 nm using Synergy 4 Multi-Mode Microplate Reader from Biotek Instruments (Winooski, VT, USA). The ability to distinguish between free and liposomal doxorubicin stems from the fact that the free doxorubicin at the concentration present in the plasma shows a lack of fluorescence quenching and demonstrates a linear increase of fluorescence with increasing doxorubicin concentration. On the other hand, the fluorescence of the Doxil liposome (encapsulated doxorubicin) is fully quenched [46]. When free and liposomal doxorubicin are mixed, only the fluorescence of free doxorubicin is expressed. Therefore, to determine plasma free doxorubicin concentrations for both formulations, we diluted 10 μL of plasma in 90 μL of physiological saline. For determination of total (free plus liposomal) doxorubicin, we dissolved the liposomal membrane by diluting 10 μL of plasma in 90 μL of acidic isopropanol [55], thereby releasing all liposome doxorubicin, as this large dilution from the very small trapped volume of the nano-liposomes to 100 μL causes a complete fluorescence dequenching allowing for the accurate determination of total (liposomal plus free) plasma doxorubicin.

The liposome-encapsulated doxorubicin was calculated by subtraction of free doxorubicin from total doxorubicin. For precise definition of tissues' doxorubicin concentration (calculated following tissue weight measurements) presented as % of injected dose (%ID), we created a doxorubicin calibration curve and calculated the fraction of doxorubicin uptake into the various tissues based upon the following formula:

$$\%\text{ of Injected Dose }(\%\text{ID}) = \frac{\text{Measured value of Dox in 1 g tissue ((mg of Dox)/(g of tissue))} \times \text{weight of tissue (g)}}{\text{Total amount of Dox injected into mouse (mg)}} \times 100\%$$

Therapeutic Efficacy

On day zero, 31 mice with tumor size of 12×9±1 mm were randomized to six groups and treated as specified:

1. Mono therapy – injection of PLDTS
2. Mono therapy – injection of PLD
3. RF ablation alone
4. Combined therapy: PLDTS injection 15 minute before RF application [26]
5. Combined therapy: PLD injection 15 minute after RF treatment [52,54,56]
6. Control (non-treated mice)

Two primary endpoints were determined: growth rate and time to reach surrogate endpoint survival (burden of tumor more than 1000 mg). Tumor weights were calculated according to the equation:

$$\text{Tumor Weight (g)} = \frac{\text{Length} \times (\text{Width})^2}{2}$$

Direct caliper measurements were used for determination of tumor size [7,57,58].

Tumor size, survival, and body weight were monitored 2–3 times per week.

Statistical analysis

Additional post-hoc analysis was performed with paired, two-tailed Student's *t*-test, by using Prism 4 software (GraphPad Software, San Diego, CA, USA). A p-value of less than 0.05 was

Table 2. Biodistribution of doxorubicin following PLD and PLDTS administration.

Nano-drug name	Time (h)	% of total Injected doxorubicin/organ					
		Tumor+RF	Tumor (no RF)	Liver	Plasma Free Dox	Plasma Liposomal Dox	Total Dox recovered in evaluated tissues
PLD	1	1.1±0.18	0.3±0.1	8.8±0.8	4.2±1.3	76.3±4.7	90.8±7.1
PLD	24	2.5±0.5	0.3±0.2	9.2±0.8	8.2±1.0	47.9±5.1	68.2±7.6
PLD	72	4.6±1.0	0.8±0.2	7.3±1.5	0.7±0.1	6.1±1.2	19.6±4.1
PLDTS	1	6.4±1.9	1.1±0.3	33.8±1.6	6.3±1.1	42.1±1.9	89.6±6.9
PLDTS	24	1.2±0.3	0.2±0.1	10.7±1.4	0.2±0.06	0.5±0.1	12.8±2.0
PLDTS	72	0.6±0.1	0.03±0.02	5.0±0.6	0.02±0.01	0.2±0.1	5.8±1.0

considered significant. The statistical significance between different treatment groups was determined using the 1-way ANOVA test for tumor volume and the log-rank (Mantel-Cox) test for comparison of Kaplan-Meir curves [59]. For determination of group diversity we used standard error values [60].

Results

Characterization of Liposome-loaded Drugs

Table 1 shows the PLD and PLDTS formulation parameters. The mean diameter of PLDTS was 97.5 nm with a polydispersity index (PDI) of 0.1. PLD showed mean a size of 84.4 nm with a PDI of 0.05. These results are similar to previously published data [8,49].

Remote-loading efficiency of doxorubicin using ammonium sulfate gradient was ~95% for PLD and ~80.5% for PLDTS, in agreement with prior reports [28,61]. Additionally, results of cryo-TEM show PLD and PLDTS remotely-loaded with doxorubicin (Fig. 1) with a similar liposomal doxorubicin "coffee bean shape" as previously demonstrated for Doxil [8], and for pH-gradient doxorubicin-loaded liposomes such as Myocet [62].

Doxorubicin Pharmacokinetics and Biodistribution

The objective of the current study was to determine the thermogenic therapeutic effect of a PLD+RF combination therapy and to elucidate its mechanism of action (MoA). We compared two well-established tumor cancer treatment modalities: one, based on PLD, which has been previously shown to have a temperature-independent, slow zero-order release kinetics of doxorubicin [8] and the second, based on PLDTS, a temperature-sensitive and -dependent liposomal drug carrier, which shows fast burst-type release with almost complete release at temperatures slightly above the liposome membrane Tm of 41.5°C from solid ordered to liquid disordered, as described elsewhere [18] and confirmed by us using DSC for this study (data not shown). Our doxorubicin-release *in vitro* kinetics studies for both PLD and PLDTS liposomes were equivalent to those reported by others [34], confirming the relative equivalence of our preparations to theirs. Specifically, exposure of PLD in buffered saline to 4°C, 25°C, 37°C, and 42°C showed minimal release (i.e. less than 5% of the drug encapsulated) even after 48 h of incubation in a relatively temperature-independent manner. However, exposure of PLDTS formulation was highly temperature dependent and showed a burst release (81% over a 3 min exposure) at 42°C, above the liposome solid to liquid ordered phase transition temperature, as reported previously by others [25,34] and complete drug release at 30 min exposure. The three lower temperatures tested (4°C, 25°C, and 37°C) showed only 0.3–0.5% drug release from PLDTS after three minutes, while after 30 min exposure the PLDTS showed a temperature-dependent release of 1.2%, 4.1%, and 9.7% of encapsulated doxorubicin at 4°C, 25°C and 37°C, respectively. This is related to the absence of cholesterol in the PLDTS and having DPPC as its liposome-forming lipid. One hour post-treatment initiation (See Table 2), both PLD and PLDTS modalities show a similar total doxorubicin fraction in evaluated tissues (with total recovery of ~90%ID), which differ in their distributions between plasma and liver doxorubicin ratios ([free Dox+liposomal Dox]/[liver Dox]) (9.15 and 1.44 for PLD and PLDTS, respectively). In addition, percent of free Dox relative to total Dox plasma levels, as measured one hour post-treatment initiation, showed 13% and 5.0% of ID for PLDTS and PLD, respectively ([plasma free Dox]/[total plasma Dox]x100%). While one hour post-treatment initiation, plasma PLD doxorubicin was 76%ID, while for PLDTS doxorubicin it was only 42%ID,

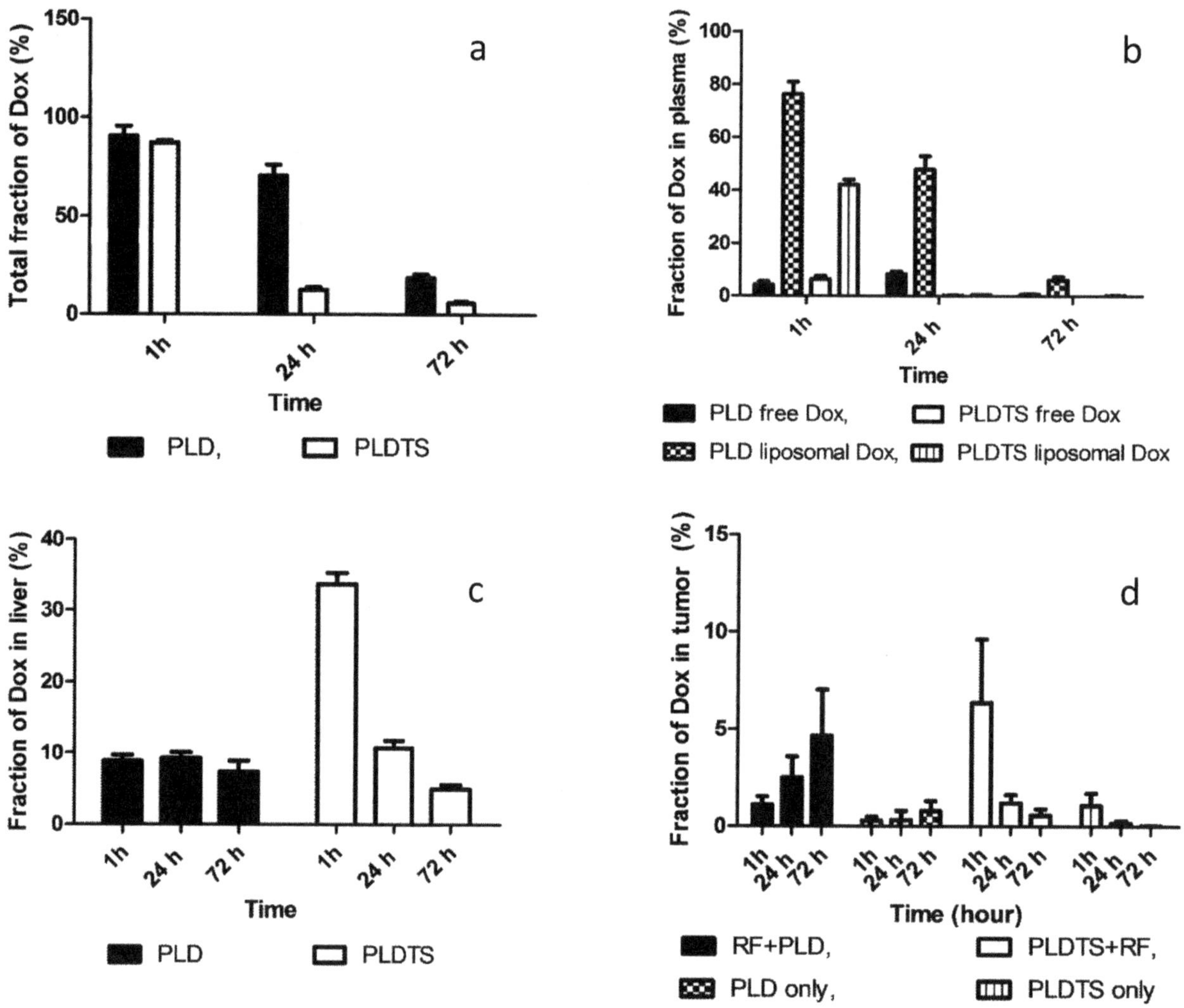

Figure 2. Doxorubicin biodistribution following PLD. (a) Total doxorubicin recovered in evaluated most relevant tissues; (b) Doxorubicin fraction in plasma, free and liposomal forms; (c) Doxorubicin fraction in liver; and (d) Fraction of intra-tumoral doxorubicin, with or without RF treatment. n = 4–7 per group. Statistically significant difference ($p \leq 0.05$).

suggesting much faster clearance of PLDTS doxorubicin from the circulation already at 1 h post-treatment initiation.

Total doxorubicin levels in the most relevant tissues, plasma, liver, and tumors, were calculated for all time points of the experiment as the sum of all organs tested (Fig. 2a). It is clear that there was a reduction of doxorubicin levels over time in both PLD and PLDTS formulations. Nevertheless, the rate of decrease in total doxorubicin levels in the PLTDS-treated mice already at 24 h post-treatment (and very likely even earlier) is much larger, and this may shed light on the differences between the two formulations in therapeutic efficacy (to be discussed later). Our results show that from a similar starting point of ~90% of ID, at 24 h post-treatment, the total doxorubicin recovered levels in evaluated tissues for PLDTS was reduced to 12.4% of ID, compared with 58% of ID for PLD ($p \leq 0.01$). Seventy-two hours post-treatment, the same trend is kept, although absolute values were lower for PLDTS (5.8% of ID for PLDTS and 19% of ID for PLD; $p \leq 0.01$).

Plasma levels analysis was conducted for both liposomal doxorubicin and free drug in plasma. At 1 h post-treatment, the fraction of free drug in plasma for both formulations lacked statistical significance (Fig. 2b). However a large (~1.8 times higher) level of liposomal doxorubicin was observed for PLD. At 24 h, the difference between PLD and PLDTS was much more dramatic: for PLDTS the level of total doxorubicin was reduced drastically to less than 1% of ID, compared with more than 50% of ID for PLD-treated mice. Three days post-treatment, both nano-drugs show lack of free doxorubicin. The level of plasma liposomal doxorubicin 72 h post-treatment was still significant for PLD (6.1% of ID) but was at the limit of detection for the PLDTS-treated mice (0.2% of ID).

For the liver, an almost constant fraction of doxorubicin (7–9% of ID) was seen in mice treated with PLD (Fig. 2c) at all three tested time points (1, 24 and 72 h). However, with PLDTS, a rapid elevation at 1 h post-injection to ~34% of ID, followed by a fast decline to 10.7% of ID at 24 h and 5% of ID at 72 h was observed, suggesting that a large fraction of doxorubicin was released from the PLDTS and reached the liver as a free drug.

The results of intra-tumoral drug concentrations (Fig. 2d) show different kinetics and maximal levels of doxorubicin for both treatment modalities, either for the nano-drugs alone or in combination with RF ablation. For combined PLDTS and RF ablation, maximum intra-tumoral drug was seen 1 h post-treatment initiation, while for PLD-RF treatment the highest

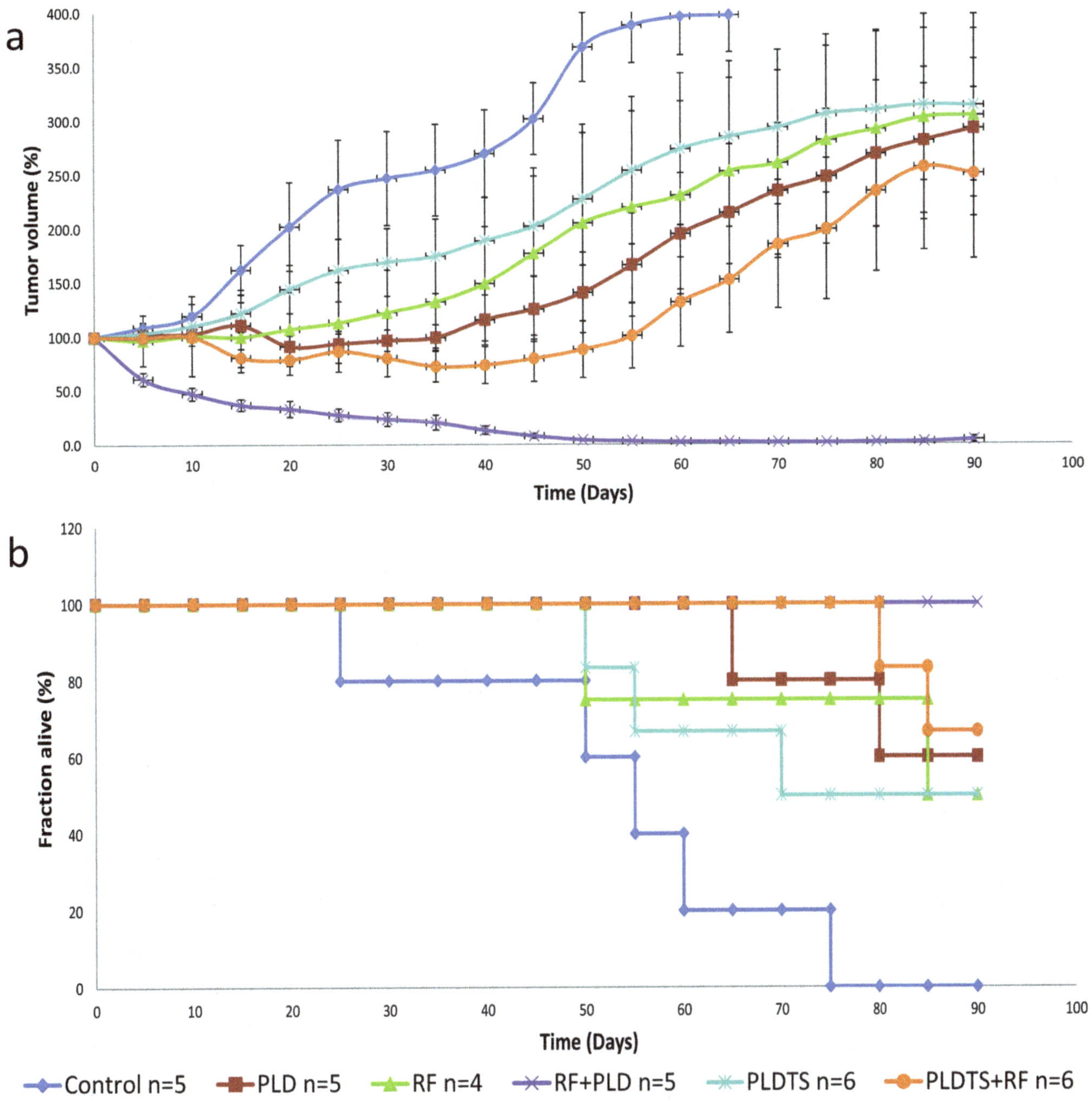

Figure 3. Mice tumor model therapeutic efficacy studies using PLD and PLDTS with and without RF ablation. (a) Effect of the various treatments on tumor volume during 90 days duration, and (b) survival of mice by using surrogate end point.

accumulation was observed at the last time point checked, 72 h post-treatment initiation. It is possible that drug levels would be even higher at longer times post-administration [37,38]. One hour post-injection, the PLDTS shows 6-fold higher intra-tumoral doxorubicin levels when compared to PLD (6.4% and 1.1% of ID, respectively). At 24 h post-injection, the doxorubicin tumor levels were reduced dramatically for PLDTS treatment (1.2% ID), while it doubled for PLD (2.5%ID). Of special interest are the findings that tumor accumulation for the PLD treatment kept increasing with time, reaching at 72 h the level of 4.6% of ID compared with very low levels of only 0.6%ID for PLDTS. Thus, reversed trends of increasing intra-tumoral drug for PLD and decreasing drug for PLDTS were found. The nano-drug with RF combination treatment was shown to be more efficacious than PLD or PLDTS treatments alone for both nano-drugs. However, since prolonged exposure of cancer cells to doxorubicin is clinically preferable and is a more efficient treatment approach, the PLD and RF ablation combination clearly implies a superior protocol (in respect to tumoral doxorubicin fraction) compared to the other treatment protocols evaluated in this study at 72 h post-treatment initiation and resulted in the highest doxorubicin fraction of %ID.

End-point Survival Studies

Comparison of the two therapeutic approaches was assessed via a survival study during 90 days follow-up. The analysis is based on using the "humane end point" of 4-fold tumor growth (as required by the animal ethics committee). Change in tumor volume was seen in mice of all groups (Fig. 3a). All single therapy groups (RF, PLD, and PLDTS) did not show statistically significant differences among them, and all displayed increased survival compared to the control group ($p<0.0001$) but lower survival compared to both combination therapy groups (PLDTS with RF [$p<0.005$] and PLD with RF [$p<0.0001$]).

Most importantly, the combination of RF with PLD was much superior to RF+PLDTS, with high statistical significance. Only the RF+PLD treatment showed significant long-term reduction of tumor volume and macroscopic disappearance of tumor. This is also the only group that showed 100% survival (by the humane end point) for at least 90 days compared to all other treatment protocols.

Kaplan-Meier survival curve results (Fig. 3b) demonstrate that all mice from the group treated with combined therapy of RF and PLD survived to the last day of experiment. By contrast, the last mouse from the control group was sacrificed at day 70. 50% of mice from the two single-therapy groups: RF and PLDTS were alive on the last day of experiment. 67% and 60% of mice treated with PLDTS plus RF and with PLD alone, respectively, survived to the end of the experiment. Thus, we observed a statistically significant differences between mice treated with the combination therapies (RF with PLD and RF with PLDTS) ($p<0.05$).

Almost all comparisons except RF vs. PLD, RF vs. PLDTS, and PLDTS+RF vs. PLD had statistically significant differences between them ($p<0.05$).

Discussion

Tumor microenvironment can be altered following RF ablation, and therefore timing between the combined treatments is crucial for success. Goldberg et al. [63] treated several different liver malignancies, including 4 patients with hepatocellular carcinoma, and were able to attain 25–30% increases in coagulation volume by administering liposomal doxorubicin 24 h before RF application. Follow-up imaging studies demonstrated that this particular form of adjuvant therapy resulted in more complete tumor destruction because coagulation progressed over time to include residual tumor foci and patent intra-tumoral blood vessels. Thus, measured pathological changes and coagulation diameter over time can serve as an effective estimation tool to elucidate the described combined treatment. Accordingly, it was previously shown [52] in a rat breast cancer tumor model treated with combined RF and liposomal doxorubicin-loaded liposomes that for tumors treated with both liposomal doxorubicin and RF ablation therapy, the increase in observed coagulation diameter was progressive to 48 h post-RF ablation, with equivalent coagulation diameters observed when the liposomal doxorubicin was administered 3 days before to 24 h after RF application. It was also previously shown [38] that radiofrequency thermal ablation sharply increases intra-tumoral liposomal doxorubicin accumulation as well as tumor coagulation, with intra-tumoral doxorubicin accumulation increased to a maximum at 72 h with greater uptake in the RF-ablated tumors compared with controls or with liposomal doxorubicin alone at all time points in the R3230 mammary adenocarcinoma rat model. Additionally, RF enabled even greater uptake in tumor compared with liver. Further proof of liposomal doxorubicin altering the RF ablation-induced microenvironment has recently been published by our group [16], noting that RF ablation induces morphologic changes to vessels within the ablation zone lasting 12–24 hours after treatment, but that the addition of liposomal doxorubicin causes early vessel contraction and a reduction in peri-ablational microvascular patency, and continuing: "Such changes would likely need to be considered when determining optimal drug administration and imaging paradigms".

Two different mechanisms can be suggested to explain Doxil's doxorubicin internalization into tumor cells in vivo:

1. Uptake of intact Doxil liposomes by cells, followed by intracellular drug release;
2. Doxorubicin release in the tumor interstitial fluid, from where it is taken up by cells as a free drug.

The contribution of the intact Doxil uptake by tumor cells must be minimal, as intact cisplatin Stealth nano-liposomes, which have a similar lipid composition and size distribution as Doxil, did not show uptake of cisplatin by tumor cells and therefore showed lack of therapeutic efficacy (see [9]). Therefore, we are left with the second option of tumor cells' uptake of drug that was released in the tumor interstitium. Factors leading to doxorubicin release from Doxil may include collapse or partial collapse of the ammonium sulfate gradient and/or the destabilization of Doxil liposomes by phospholipases that hydrolyze the liposome phospholipids (see review by Mouritsen and Jørgenson [64], thereby enabling faster doxorubicin release. However, there are two major objections to the latter phospholipase related drug release explanation. The first one is the fact that there is no drug release in vivo from Stealth cisplatin, which is identical in size and lipid composition to Doxil; the second is that the presence of cholesterol in the liposome membrane inhibits drastically phospholipase activity [64]. Therefore, we are left with the default, which suggests that the collapse of the ammonium sulfate gradient plays a more major role in doxorubicin release of Doxil in vivo. However, the latter assumption is as yet unproven and its proof requires further in-depth investigation. In the present communication, we compared two clinically-relevant methods of combining long-circulating PEGylated nano-liposomes encapsulating doxorubicin and RF ablation for the treatment of human medulloblastoma cancer using an extrahepatic tumor xenograft mouse model. To achieve this goal, we formulated PLD and PLDTS liposomes and we showed that they have similar properties to those previously reported [18] (see Table 1). Both nano-drugs used are PEGylated nano-liposomes, are of a similar size distribution and both include a similar mole fraction of 2000-Da PEG-DSPE, and therefore the liposomes in both cases are long-circulating sterically-stabilized. Structure analysis based on cryo-TEM shows that both formulations, when loaded with doxorubicin, show a similar ellipsoid "coffee-bean" structure, as previously described for PLD [8,62]. The large and quantitive burst in drug release at or above Tm is a well-established phenomenon [15] and was confirmed in this study as well (data not shown). Such rapid release of drug from the liposomes is dramatically increased when *lyso*-palmitoyl phosphatidylcholine (LPC) is a liposome-membrane component [28–31,65]. A complete and fast drug release from PLDTS above the solid ordered to liquid disordered phase transition temperature is contributed by the presence of LPC. These results are in agreement with previously reported heat-induced doxorubicin release of ~90% from PLDTS in the first 5 min of exposure to 42°C [25], as was also confirmed by us.

PEGylated liposomes or other nano-drugs can passively accumulate in targets via the EPR effect [3]. Furthermore, when designing a "smart" drug delivery platform, specific characteristics of tumor microenvironment can further enhance the delivery or release of a variety of agents to a desired target, with extracellular release or intracellular distribution to specific organelles [66]. Tumor microenvironment-sensitive carriers were previously designed and demonstrated *in vitro* and *in vivo* changrs by manipulation of the carrier's swelling behavior, network structure, permeability, or stability in response to tumor-environmental changes (e.g. pH, ionic strength), as well as following local exposure to elevated temperature by ultrasound or RF ablation [12,13,67,68]. In relation to the drug carrier used, an absence of these factors can potentially lead to an unsatisfactory drug release profile and low drug levels at the desired site. The outcome might be a dysfunction of therapy, as noted for liposomal cisplatin, where poor anticancer therapy has been attributed to a lack of sufficient intra-tumoral drug release in spite of superior intra-tumoral accumulation of the nano-drugs [8,10]. Earlier, we studied the use of RF ablation combined with intravenously administered PLD, and compared this with the use of RF ablation or doxorubicin alone [57]. These studies demonstrated that the RF+PLD combination facilitated and increased tissue coagulation and tumor interstitial drug accumulation in animal models [38]. However, the optimal drug release rate at the tumor site and its potential concomitant effect of altering the tumor microenvironment remained an open question whose answer may be highly beneficial for further improving the therapeutic efficacy of liposome-based nano-drugs.

Therefore, here we purposefully compared the two extremely different situations: (a) temperature-driven, fast burst-type release and (b) passive, temperature-insensitive, slow drug release. For both cases we compared the performance of the two systems with and without changing the tumor microenvironment using RF. Our PLD was constructed to be identical to Doxil, a non-thermosensitive liposome where membrane is in the liquid-ordered (LO) phase. Doxil was approved by the FDA in 1995 and has been in clinical use since [69]. Our second formulation, PLDTS, was constructed to be similar to ThermoDox, a formulation that recently has been studied in Phase III clinical trials [26]. It has a fast drug release above its 41.5°C Tm. Our injection protocol is designed in such a way that a significant local (at site of RF) drug release from the liposomes occurs upon exposure to RF heating. It also worth noting that for PLDTS, 1 h post-injection, after the exposure to RF, almost 90% of doxorubicin ID was still retained in the animal body, mainly in the plasma (48.4%ID total plasma concentration, 42.1%ID encapsulated and 6.3%ID free) and in the liver (~34%ID) (Table 2). However, these values decay very fast with time (Table 2). This significantly poorer performance of PLDTS is related to the fast release of doxorubicin from the PLDTS even without exposure to RF, as is obvious from the very low drug retention in the total evaluated doxorubicin levels in plasma, liver, and tumors of PLDTS-treated mice (Table 2). Specifically, doxorubicin retention after administration of PLDTS is too low to enable drug-loaded liposome accumulation at the tumor site.

For PLD (which is not thermosensitive) we used a different established protocol. Here, the tumor was first exposed to RF to induce changes in tumor microenvironment, and 15 min post-irradiation (after the tumor cooled to baseline) PLD was injected. As described above, PK, BD, and efficacy of the two formulations differed to a large extent. Data analysis of biodistribution experiments shows that 1 h after injection, most of the drug measured in the plasma was retained in the liposome. This strongly suggests that at 15 min post-PLDTS injection, immediately before the time of tumor exposure to RF, the level of plasma PLDTS doxorubicin was significantly higher than 48.4% of ID (total plasma concentration) at 1 h and mostly as liposomal drug. This observation, however, raises an important question: why with RF ablation 6 h post-PLDTS injection do we not achieve similar levels of doxorubicin in the tumor or plasma as we observed for the PLD? We hypothesize that for this treatment protocol and this liposomal composition, liposomes might be "empty", namely lacking a significant level of doxorubicin, which probably occurred due to the much faster release than from the PLD, which show very slow drug release in plasma.

For PLDTS, the short interval between the injection and the exposure to RF was a must, as we wanted to have enough drug-loaded liposomes remaining in the blood circulation. We demonstrated that when RF exposure is performed much later post-injection, there are insufficient drug-loaded liposomes in the circulation. It is suggested that this is due to fast doxorubicin release from the PLDTS, which at 37°C show ~10% (zero order) release in the 30-min incubation. This explains the lack of doxorubicin in plasma 6 h after PLDTS administration (data not shown), leaving behind circulating "empty" PLDTS. Therefore, the desired efficacy is not achieved.

The difference in release rate is related to the PLDTS lacking cholesterol and also having DPPC (Tm at 41.5°C) as the liposome-forming lipid, while the PLD is based on the high-Tm (53°C) HSPC as the liposome-forming lipid and on a high mole % cholesterol, which abolishes the phase transition. Therefore, as expected, the PLD is much more release-resistant than the PLDTS and as the process of tumor nano-drug accumulation is a slow process, PLD has a large advantage over the fast-releasing PLDTS. It is important to note that although the role of cholesterol in this effect is dominant, the contribution of the PC used cannot be ignored. Long ago we showed that PLD based on DPPC as a liposome-forming lipid has poorer drug retention, when compared with PLD based on HSPC as the liposome-forming lipid. That is one of the main reasons why HSPC was the liposome-forming lipid of choice for Doxil [46].

As expected, determination of doxorubicin concentration in liver, plasma, and tumor demonstrates that PLDTS and PLDs result in two very different pharmacokinetics profiles. The relatively fast decrease of total doxorubicin fraction of PLDTS compared to PLD may be explained by zero-order kinetics in the case of PLD, compared to first or even second-order kinetics in the case of PLDTS. Thus, whereas the liver drug fraction after injection of PLD was constant from 1 to 72 h (about 10%), those after PLDTS injection displayed an exponential decay with drug concentrations significantly higher (33% of ID) at 1 h ($p<0.0001$) and only 5% by 72 h. This may be predicted by the significant decrease in plasma total doxorubicin levels 1 h post-PLDTS injection, from 48.4% total plasma concentration (while total body doxorubicin is ~90%ID) to 0.7% total plasma concentration at 24 h (with total body doxorubicin of 12.8%ID). This profile of rapid clearance was also observed by Poon and Borys in clinical studies [29] and by Gasselhuber et al. in another small animal model [70]. Likewise, the presence of PLD liposomes in the blood stream for at least three days is similar to that noted previously [8,70].

Key findings of our work include that there are substantial differences in drug profile dynamics observed in the most clinically relevant tissue assessed, the intra-tumoral doxorubicin fraction. These differences were magnified especially in combination with RF, as the application of heat fulfilled a different adjunctive role for each nano-drug. In the case of PLDTS, RF heating essentially acts as a trigger for drug release, and thus RF was applied in the presence of nano-drug in the body. Thus, although for both preparations, combined therapy leads to a significantly high doxorubicin fraction, for PLDTS the maximum of drug fraction in tumor was observed after the first hour. By contrast, in the case of PLD, RF was performed immediately prior to drug injection to specifically lead to the intensification of EPR effect due to change in tumor microenvironment. The concentration of the long-circulating drug, even after the RF-ablation heat effect was no longer present, was higher for PLD, but even for the PLDTS it was still significant and may result in better therapeutic efficacy if drug retention in plasma liposomes could be improved. Thus, the use of PLD benefits from RF's inflammatory reaction without bursting the nano-carrier [41]. Accordingly, the intra-tumoral fraction of doxorubicin in the first hour was minimal and reached its maximum after three days or even longer.

The biodistribution study largely forecast the results of our therapeutic efficacy study. Based upon prior reports [37], it is not surprising that improved anticancer effects were obtained with combined therapy. Specifically, for the first 40 days, RF combined with either liposomal preparation resulted in negative tumor growth, whereas, by comparison, all single therapy groups, as well as control demonstrated positive tumor growth. Yet, over the next 50 days, differences between the two preparations in combination with RF began to become apparent, as PLDTS+RF likewise began to demonstrate tumor growth while RF+PLD did not show tumor growth. Indeed, no RF+PLD mouse demonstrated recurrence of tumor and as a result demonstrated 100% survival. However, for the other groups, end-point mortality was proportional to the rate of tumor growth, being markedly reduced in the combined therapy of the RF and PLDTS group and maximal in the control group.

We initially performed experiments to determine whether greatest synergy between RF and doxorubicin occurred with high doses of drug released immediately during the ablation process (facilitated by a thermally sensitive liposomal carrier) vs. a process of exposing the partially RF-treated tumor to a relatively long exposure of drug (using a long-circulating liposomal carrier). In a manner akin to Aesop's famous fable of the tortoise and the hare, our results confirmed greater intra-tumoral drug concentrations at 72 h and greater survival of the Daoy cell-line-bearing mice for the PLD preparation. Furthermore, we noted that for extra-hepatic tumors in mice, the much faster release of doxorubicin from PLDTS, ironically, did not have the intended effect of greater long-term intra-tumoral drug concentrations, as the overwhelming majority of freed doxorubicin was found in the liver within the first hour of drug delivery and ablation. Indeed, overall, more drug stayed in the extra-hepatic tumor over a longer period of time when using PLD, and this is likely to have influenced the difference in survival noted. Thus, our results again underscore that it is not enough to deliver a drug to the target site, but that our goal must be modified to have long and sufficient exposure to released drug in order to have the desired local therapeutic target effects. Clearly, for some tumors and/or chemotherapeutics (such as for doxorubicin [71]), contact time is paramount as it may give more opportunities for a drug to interact favorably with its intended target. For drugs that are most efficacious in dividing or growing cells, a longer window of opportunity enables a larger portion of cells to be affected. By the same token, one can ask of the thermally-sensitive liposome approach: if we burst the liposomes, release the contents, and the active agent doesn't stay *in situ* long enough to have optimal effect, of what benefit was using the liposome to increase the intra-tumoral concentration in the first place?

Our study also highlights ways to improve RF ablation therapy. One important item to note in our study is the fact that we used clinically relevant drugs and therefore translations to early clinical trials as a next step are certainly feasible [41]. The double stress caused by both RF and the drug selected showed anti-tumoral synergism, making this work more clinically relevant.

We understand the limitations of our present work. Most importantly, we acknowledge that we used only one animal model. Thus, it is quite possible that a strategy involving thermally sensitive liposomes may perform better in other models. There is an abundant literature advocating high first-pass concentration chemo for hepatocellular carcinoma that may support a PLDTS approach for hepatic cancer [72,73].

Nevertheless, our study sets the stage for a call for study on a cancer-by-cancer basis in clinical trials. Further work on other nano-drugs and understanding their effect over time also needs to be performed, as well as the effects of other doses of RF energy and other thermal energy sources clinically used, such as microwave, ultrasound, and laser [12].

Conclusions

Substantial variability in outcome can be seen when using different strategies for administering liposomal drugs in relation to RF ablation. Specifically, we report that a strategy based on using RF ablation with long-circulating liposomes resulted in longer intra-tumoral drug retention and end-point survival than a strategy based on a thermally-dependent burst of nanoparticles leading to overload of anticancer agent in the Daoy mouse tumor model. Thus, at least for some tumors, the timing and length of exposure to doxorubicin may be more important than shorter courses of high concentration chemotherapeutics. Our study stresses that the stability of the nano-drug, especially with respect to drug release in plasma at body temperature is critical for the nano-drug performance. Therefore, the evaluation of PLDTS formulations, with better liposomal drug retention *in vivo* than the PLDTS used here, is needed to better understand the potential of PLDTS as nano-drugs. The large impact of RF on the therapeutic efficacy of nano-drugs described here and before [26,37–41,52,54,74] encourages further research aimed at exploring optimal methods of combining ablation therapy and nano-drugs.

Supporting Information

Data S1 Experimental design, PK.

Data S2 Experimental design, Survival.

Acknowledgments

The authors thank Dr. Einat Nativ-Roth (Electron Microscopy Unit, Ben-Gurion University) for transmission electron microscopy and Mr. Yizhak Nissenbaum (Radiology Department, Hadassah Medical Center) for advice on using the RF instrument. We also thank Mr. Sigmund Geller for his help in editing the manuscript.

Author Contributions

Conceived and designed the experiments: AVA EK YB SNG. Performed the experiments: AVA EK. Analyzed the data: AVA EK YB SNG. Contributed reagents/materials/analysis tools: AVA EK. Wrote the paper: AVA EK YB SNG.

References

1. Gregoriadis G (1981) Targeting of drugs: implications in medicine. Lancet 2: 241–246.
2. Torchilin VP (2010) Passive and active drug targeting: drug delivery to tumors as an example. Handb Exp Pharmacol: 3–53.

3. Maeda H, Wu J, Sawa T, Matsumura Y, Hori K (2000) Tumor vascular permeability and the EPR effect in macromolecular therapeutics: a review. J Control Release 65: 271–284.
4. Schroeder A, Sigal A, Turjeman K, Barenholz Y (2008) Using PEGylated nano-liposomes to target tissue invaded by a foreign body. J Drug Target 16: 591–595.
5. Avnir Y, Turjeman K, Tulchinsky D, Sigal A, Kizelsztein P, et al. (2011) Fabrication principles and their contribution to the superior in vivo therapeutic efficacy of nano-liposomes remote loaded with glucocorticoids. PLoS One 6: 1–14.
6. Zucker D, Andriyanov AV, Steiner A, Raviv U, Barenholz Y (2012) Characterization of PEGylated nanoliposomes co-remotely loaded with topotecan and vincristine: relating structure and pharmacokinetics to therapeutic efficacy. Journal of controlled release 160: 281–289.
7. Zucker D, Barenholz Y (2010) Optimization of vincristine-topotecan combination–paving the way for improved chemotherapy regimens by nanoliposomes. J Control Release 146: 326–333.
8. Barenholz Y (2012) Doxil(R)–the first FDA-approved nano-drug: lessons learned. J Control Release 160: 117–134.
9. Bandak S, Goren D, Horowitz A, Tzemach D, Gabizon A (1999) Pharmacological studies of cisplatin encapsulated in long-circulating liposomes in mouse tumor models. Anticancer Drugs 10: 911–920.
10. Lasic DD, Vallner JJ, Working PK (1999) Sterically stabilized liposomes in cancer therapy and gene delivery. Curr Opin Mol Ther 1: 177–185.
11. Barenholz Y (2013) and co-authors; In preparation.
12. Torchilin VP (2005) Recent advances with liposomes as pharmaceutical carriers. Nat Rev Drug Discov 4: 145–160.
13. Schroeder A, Avnir Y, Weisman S, Najajreh Y, Gabizon A, et al. (2007) Controlling liposomal drug release with low frequency ultrasound: mechanism and feasibility. Langmuir 23: 4019–4025.
14. Volodkin DV, Skirtach AG, Möhwald H (2009) Near-IR Remote Release from Assemblies of Liposomes and Nanoparticles. Angewandte Chemie International Edition 48: 1807–1809.
15. Barenholz Y, Cevc G (2000) Physical Chemistry of Biological Interfaces. In: Baszkin A, Norde W, editors. New York: Marcel Dekker. 171–241.
16. Moussa M, Goldberg SN, Tasawwar B, Sawant RR, Levchenko T, et al. (2013) Adjuvant Liposomal Doxorubicin Markedly Affects Radiofrequency Ablation–induced Effects on Periablational Microvasculature. Journal of Vascular and Interventional Radiology 24: 1021–1033.
17. Leung SJ, Romanowski M (2012) Light-activated content release from liposomes. Theranostics 2: 1020–1036.
18. Needham D, Park JY, Wright AM, Tong J (2013) Materials characterization of the low temperature sensitive liposome (LTSL): effects of the lipid composition (lysolipid and DSPE-PEG2000) on the thermal transition and release of doxorubicin. Faraday Discuss 161: 515–534; discussion 563–589.
19. Garbuzenko O, Barenholz Y, Priev A (2005) Effect of grafted PEG on liposome size and on compressibility and packing of lipid bilayer. Chem Phys Lipids 135: 117–129.
20. Mouritsen OG, Jorgensen K (1994) Dynamical order and disorder in lipid bilayers. Chem Phys Lipids 73: 3–25.
21. Barenholz Y (2004) Sphingomyelin and cholesterol: from membrane biophysics and rafts to potential medical applications. Subcellular Biochemistry 37: 167–216.
22. Gabizon A, Martin F (1997) Polyethylene glycol-coated (pegylated) liposomal doxorubicin. Rationale for use in solid tumours. Drugs 54 Suppl 4: 15–21.
23. Lasic DD, Frederik PM, Stuart MC, Barenholz Y, McIntosh TJ (1992) Gelation of liposome interior. A novel method for drug encapsulation. FEBS Lett 312: 255–258.
24. Needham D, Dewhirst MW (2001) The development and testing of a new temperature-sensitive drug delivery system for the treatment of solid tumors. Adv Drug Deliv Rev 53: 285–305.
25. Needham D, Anyarambhatla G, Kong G, Dewhirst MW (2000) A new temperature-sensitive liposome for use with mild hyperthermia: characterization and testing in a human tumor xenograft model. Cancer Res 60: 1197–1201.
26. Celsion (2012) Phase 3 Study of ThermoDox With Radiofrequency Ablation (RFA) in Treatment of Hepatocellular Carcinoma (HCC). Available: http://clinical-trials.findthedata.org/l/93100/Phase-3-Study-of-ThermoDox-With-Radiofrequency-Ablation-RFA-in-Treatment-of-Hepatocellular-Carcinoma-HCC.
27. Poon RT, Borys N (2011) Lyso-thermosensitive liposomal doxorubicin: an adjuvant to increase the cure rate of radiofrequency ablation in liver cancer. Future Oncol 7: 937–945.
28. Mills JK, Needham D (2005) Lysolipid incorporation in dipalmitoylphosphatidylcholine bilayer membranes enhances the ion permeability and drug release rates at the membrane phase transition. Biochim Biophys Acta 1716: 77–96.
29. Poon RT, Borys N (2009) Lyso-thermosensitive liposomal doxorubicin: a novel approach to enhance efficacy of thermal ablation of liver cancer. Expert Opin Pharmacother 10: 333–343.
30. Banno B, Ickenstein LM, Chiu GN, Bally MB, Thewalt J, et al. (2010) The functional roles of poly(ethylene glycol)-lipid and lysolipid in the drug retention and release from lysolipid-containing thermosensitive liposomes in vitro and in vivo. J Pharm Sci 99: 2295–2308.
31. Al-Jamal WT, Al-Ahmady ZS, Kostarelos K (2012) Pharmacokinetics & tissue distribution of temperature-sensitive liposomal doxorubicin in tumor-bearing mice triggered with mild hyperthermia. Biomaterials 33: 4608–4617.
32. Skeel RT (2011) Biologic and Pharmacologic Basis of Cancer Chemotherapy, in: Handbook of cancer chemotherapy; Skeel RT, Khleif SN, editors. Boston, MA: Wolters Kluwer Health.
33. Abouzeid AH, Torchilin VP (2013) The role of cell cycle in the efficiency and activity of cancer nanomedicines. Expert Opin Drug Deliv 10: 775–786.
34. Landon CD, Park JY, Needham D, Dewhirst MW (2011) Nanoscale Drug Delivery and Hyperthermia: The Materials Design and Preclinical and Clinical Testing of Low Temperature-Sensitive Liposomes Used in Combination with Mild Hyperthermia in the Treatment of Local Cancer. The Open Nanomedicine Journal 3: 38–64.
35. Tagami T, Ernsting MJ, Li SD (2011) Optimization of a novel and improved thermosensitive liposome formulated with DPPC and a Brij surfactant using a robust in vitro system. J Control Release 154: 290–297.
36. Gasselhuber A, Dreher MR, Negussie A, Wood BJ, Rattay F, et al. (2010) Mathematical spatio-temporal model of drug delivery from low temperature sensitive liposomes during radiofrequency tumour ablation. Int J Hyperthermia 26: 499–513.
37. Monsky WL, Kruskal JB, Lukyanov AN, Girnun GD, Ahmed M, et al. (2002) Radio-frequency ablation increases intratumoral liposomal doxorubicin accumulation in a rat breast tumor model. Radiology 224: 823–829.
38. Ahmed M, Monsky WE, Girnun G, Lukyanov A, D'Ippolito G, et al. (2003) Radiofrequency thermal ablation sharply increases intratumoral liposomal doxorubicin accumulation and tumor coagulation. Cancer Res 63: 6327–6333.
39. Gazelle GS, Goldberg SN, Solbiati L, Livraghi T (2000) Tumor ablation with radio-frequency energy. Radiology 217: 633–646.
40. Dupuy DE, Goldberg SN (2001) Image-guided radiofrequency tumor ablation: challenges and opportunities–part II. J Vasc Interv Radiol 12: 1135–1148.
41. Solazzo SA, Ahmed M, Schor-Bardach R, Yang W, Girnun GD, et al. (2010) Liposomal doxorubicin increases radiofrequency ablation-induced tumor destruction by increasing cellular oxidative and nitrative stress and accelerating apoptotic pathways. Radiology 255: 62–74.
42. Jacobsen PF, Jenkyn DJ, Papadimitriou JM (1985) Establishment of a human medulloblastoma cell line and its heterotransplantation into nude mice. J Neuropathol Exp Neurol 44: 472–485.
43. Mahoney DH Jr, Steuber CP, Sandbach JF, Fernbach DJ (1986) Extraneural metastases from medulloblastoma: long-term survival after sequentially scheduled chemotherapy and radiotherapy. Med Pediatr Oncol 14: 329–331.
44. Hacker S, Karl S, Mader I, Cristofanon S, Schweitzer T, et al. (2011) Histone deacetylase inhibitors prime medulloblastoma cells for chemotherapy-induced apoptosis by enhancing p53-dependent Bax activation. Oncogene 30: 2275–2281.
45. Barenholz Y, Amsalem S (1993) Liposome Technology (Gregoriadis, G., Ed). CRC Press, Boca Raton, FL. 527–616.
46. Haran G, Cohen R, Bar LK, Barenholz Y (1993) Transmembrane ammonium sulfate gradients in liposomes produce efficient and stable entrapment of amphipathic weak bases. Biochim Biophys Acta 1151: 201–215.
47. Storm G, van Bloois L, Brouwer M, Crommelin DJ (1985) The interaction of cytostatic drugs with adsorbents in aqueous media. The potential implications for liposome preparation. Biochim Biophys Acta 818: 343–351.
48. Amselem S, Gabizon A, Barenholz Y (1990) Optimization and upscaling of doxorubicin-containing liposomes for clinical use. J Pharm Sci 79: 1045–1052.
49. Garbuzenko O, Zalipsky S, Qazen M, Barenholz Y (2005) Electrostatics of PEGylated micelles and liposomes containing charged and neutral lipopolymers. Langmuir 21: 2560–2568.
50. Bartlett GR (1959) Phosphorus assay in column chromatography. J Biol Chem 234: 466–468.
51. Biltonen RL, Lichtenberg D (1993) The Use of Differential Scanning Calorimetry as a Tool to Characterize Liposome Preparations. Chem Phys Lipids 64: 129–142.
52. Goldberg SN, Kruskal JB, Oliver BS, Clouse ME, Gazelle GS (2000) Percutaneous tumor ablation: increased coagulation by combining radio-frequency ablation and ethanol Instillation in a rat breast tumor Model. Radiology 217: 827–831.
53. Moussa M, Goldberg S, Tasawwar B, Sawant R, Levchenko T, et al. (2013) Adjuvant Liposomal Doxorubicin Markedly Affects Radiofrequency Ablation-induced Effects on Periablational Microvasculature. Journal of vascular and interventional radiology: JVIR: 1021–1033.
54. Yang W, Ahmed M, Tasawwar B, Levchenko T, Sawant RR, et al. (2011) Radiofrequency ablation combined with liposomal quercetin to increase tumour destruction by modulation of heat shock protein production in a small animal model. International Journal of Hyperthermia 27: 527–538.
55. Gabizon A, Catane R, Uziely B, Kaufman B, Safra T, et al. (1994) Prolonged circulation time and enhanced accumulation in malignant exudates of doxorubicin encapsulated in polyethylene-glycol coated liposomes. Cancer Res 54: 987–992.
56. Goldberg SN, Kruskal JB, Oliver BS, Clouse ME, Gazelle GS (2000) Percutaneous tumor ablation: increased coagulation by combining radio-frequency ablation and ethanol instillation in a rat breast tumor model. Radiology 217: 827–831.
57. Euhus DM, Hudd C, LaRegina MC, Johnson FE (1986) Tumor measurement in the nude mouse. Journal of Surgical Oncology 31: 229–234.

58. Tomayko MM, Reynolds CP (1989) Determination of subcutaneous tumor size in athymic (nude) mice. Cancer Chemotherapy and Pharmacology 24: 148–154.
59. Mantel N (1966) Evaluation of survival data and two new rank order statistics arising in its consideration. Cancer Chemother Rep 50: 163–170.
60. Cumming G, Fidler F, Vaux DL (2007) Error bars in experimental biology. J Cell Biol 177: 7–11.
61. Mayer LD, Tai LC, Bally MB, Mitilenes GN, Ginsberg RS, et al. (1990) Characterization of liposomal systems containing doxorubicin entrapped in response to pH gradients. Biochim Biophys Acta 1025: 143–151.
62. Swenson CE, Perkins WR, Roberts P, Janoff AS (2001) Liposome technology and the development of Myocet (TM) (liposomal doxorubicin citrate). Breast 10: 1–7.
63. Goldberg SN, Kamel IR, Kruskal JB, Reynolds K, Monsky WL, et al. (2002) Radiofrequency ablation of hepatic tumors: increased tumor destruction with adjuvant liposomal doxorubicin therapy. American Journal of Roentgenology 179: 93–101.
64. Mouritsen OG, Jørgensen K (1998) A new look at lipid-membrane structure in relation to drug research. Pharmaceutical research 15: 1507–1519.
65. Zhang X, Luckham PF, Hughes AD, Thom S, Xu XY (2013) Towards an understanding of the release behavior of temperature-sensitive liposomes: a possible explanation of the "pseudoequilibrium" release behavior at the phase transition temperature. J Liposome Res: 167–173.
66. Torchilin V (2012) Next Step in Drug Delivery: Getting to Individual Organelles. Drug Deliv Transl Res 2: 415–417.
67. Kale AA, Torchilin VP (2010) Environment-responsive multifunctional liposomes. Methods Mol Biol 605: 213–242.
68. Koren E, Apte A, Jani A, Torchilin VP (2012) Multifunctional PEGylated 2C5-immunoliposomes containing pH-sensitive bonds and TAT peptide for enhanced tumor cell internalization and cytotoxicity. J Control Release 160: 264–273.
69. Ferrandina G, Corrado G, Licameli A, Lorusso D, Fuoco G, et al. (2010) Pegylated liposomal doxorubicin in the management of ovarian cancer. Ther Clin Risk Manag 6: 463–483.
70. Gasselhuber A, Dreher MR, Rattay F, Wood BJ, Haemmerich D (2012) Comparison of conventional chemotherapy, stealth liposomes and temperature-sensitive liposomes in a mathematical model. PLoS One 7: 1–11.
71. Papahadjopoulos D, Allen TM, Gabizon A, Mayhew E, Matthay K, et al. (1991) Sterically Stabilized Liposomes - Improvements in Pharmacokinetics and Antitumor Therapeutic Efficacy. Proceedings of the National Academy of Sciences of the United States of America 88: 11460–11464.
72. Ku Y, Saitoh M, Iwasaki T, Tominaga M, Maekawa Y, et al. (1993) Intraarterial infusion of high-dose adriamycin for unresectable hepatocellular carcinoma using direct hemoperfusion under hepatic venous isolation. Eur J Surg Oncol 19: 387–392.
73. Lewandowski RJ, Geschwind JF, Liapi E, Salem R (2011) Transcatheter intraarterial therapies: rationale and overview. Radiology 259: 641–657.
74. Ahmed M, Liu Z, Lukyanov AN, Signoretti S, Horkan C, et al. (2005) Combination radiofrequency ablation with intratumoral liposomal doxorubicin: effect on drug accumulation and coagulation in multiple tissues and tumor types in animals. Radiology 235: 469–477.

16

Engineering a Segmented Dual-Reservoir Polyurethane Intravaginal Ring for Simultaneous Prevention of HIV Transmission and Unwanted Pregnancy

Justin T. Clark[1], Meredith R. Clark[2], Namdev B. Shelke[1], Todd J. Johnson[1], Eric M. Smith[1], Andrew K. Andreasen[1], Joel S. Nebeker[1], Judit Fabian[1], David R. Friend[2], Patrick F. Kiser[1,3]*

1 Department of Bioengineering, University of Utah, Salt Lake City, Utah, United States of America, 2 CONRAD, Department of Obstetrics and Gynecology, Eastern Virginia Medical School, Arlington, Virginia, United States of America, 3 Department of Biomedical Engineering, Northwestern University, Evanston IL, United States of America

Abstract

The HIV/AIDS pandemic and its impact on women prompt the investigation of prevention strategies to interrupt sexual transmission of HIV. Long-acting drug delivery systems that simultaneously protect womenfrom sexual transmission of HIV and unwanted pregnancy could be important tools in combating the pandemic. We describe the design, *in silico*, *in vitro* and *in vivo* evaluation of a dual-reservoir intravaginal ring that delivers the HIV-1 reverse transcriptase inhibitor tenofovir and the contraceptive levonorgestrel for 90 days. Two polyether urethanes with two different hard segment volume fractions were used to make coaxial extruded reservoir segments with a 100 μm thick rate controlling membrane and a diameter of 5.5 mm that contain 1.3 wt% levonorgestrel. A new mechanistic diffusion model accurately described the levonorgestrel burst release in early time points and pseudo-steady state behavior at later time points. As previously described, tenofovir was formulated as a glycerol paste and filled into a hydrophilic polyurethane, hollow tube reservoir that was melt-sealed by induction welding. These tenofovir-eluting segments and 2 cm long coaxially extruded levonorgestrel eluting segments were joined by induction welding to form rings that released an average of 7.5 mg tenofovir and 21 μg levonorgestrel per day *in vitro* for 90 days. Levonorgestrel segments placed intravaginally in rabbits resulted in sustained, dose-dependent levels of levonorgestrel in plasma and cervical tissue for 90 days. Polyurethane caps placed between segments successfully prevented diffusion of levonorgestrel into the tenofovir-releasing segment during storage.Hydrated rings endured between 152 N and 354 N tensile load before failure during uniaxial extension testing. In summary, this system represents a significant advance in vaginal drug delivery technology, and is the first in a new class of long-acting multipurpose prevention drug delivery systems.

Editor: Gilda Tachedjian, Burnet Institute, Australia

Funding: Funding was provided under cooperative agreement (GPO-A-00-08-00005-00 and AID-OAA-A-10-0006) between the United States Agency for International Development (USAID) and the Eastern Virginia Medical School. This work was supported by a cooperative agreement from The United States Agency for International Development (USAID). USAID had no role in study design, data collection and analysis, decision to publish, or preparation of the manuscript.

Competing Interests: The authors have declared that no competing interests exist.

* E-mail: patrick.kiser@northwestern.edu

Introduction

The global HIV/AIDS pandemic continues to drive advances in biomedical technologies designed to quell the spread of the virus [1]. The recent USFDA approval of oral Truvada® for HIV pre-exposure prophylaxis (PrEP) in discordant couples is a major biomedical advance [2]. But clinicians have encountered difficulty in consistently demonstrating PrEP efficacy in prevention trials. In the CAPRISA 004 trial, topical vaginal application of the tenofovir (TFV) 1% gel used episodically before and after intercourse resulted in a 39% reduction in HIV infection in women [3]. But the same TFV gel did not reduce transmission rates when used once daily [4]. The variability in trial outcomes has caused consternation and several thoughtful reviews [5,6,7,8,9]. Yet the progress is evident when simultaneously considering the success of oral Truvada, the modest effect in CAPRISA 004, and alongside the accumulating evidence of the protective effect of TFV from non-human primate studies [10,11,12]. It is now conceptually clear that using oral and topical antiretroviral (ARV) drugs to interrupt the early events of sexual HIV transmission and dissemination is biologically and biomedically possible. The poor clinical outcomes result from confounding factors that span across behavioral, biological and pharmacological causes. Since the discovery of low rates of adherence in the Carraguard trial [13] and subsequently in the VOICE trial [4] it has been clear that infrequent use of gels by women likely has been a significant factor contributing to the low rates of effectiveness observed in most gel PrEP trials to date. For many reasons, trial participants are not sufficiently motivated to use the prevention products as instructed. Therefore, if PrEP is to be a technological success, new PrEP modalities are desperately needed that are easier to use and more desirable to women, and are supported by high user demand.

There are two main approaches being explored to increase user demand for PrEP, to either increase device duration or to make devices that are multifunctional and satisfy more than one user need. It is observed across many types of pharmaceutical products that user adherence and dose duration are positively correlated [14,15]. To this end much effort has been directed toward long-acting injectable ARV [16] and ARV eluting intravaginal rings (IVR) [17,18] for PrEP. Adding multiple functions, indications or purposes is also receiving attention as a method for improving user demand. Hormonal contraception is a well established technology in many low income countries impacted by the HIV pandemic. This has motivated the development of biomedical devices, and in particular long-acting IVR [19,20,21] that elute both contraceptive hormones and ARV. The development of multipurpose prevention technologies (MPT) could be ground breaking as there are no approved products that use two drugs to simultaneously address multiple indications. Yet the literature and the drug store shelf are replete with examples of fixed dose drug combinations designed to treat a single indication that were developed to improve ease of use, patient compliance and outcomes [22,23].

As one might expect, there are a host of contraceptive agents and ARV under evaluation for use in MPT. The progestin levonorgestrel (LNG) is a leading contraceptive agent with a long history of clinical use in topical and oral administration. The Mirena® intrauterine system releases up to 20 µg LNG per day for 5 years. The WHO also developed a silicone reservoir IVR that released approximately 20 µg LNG per day for 90 days [24]. In a large multi-center clinical trial, the LNG IVR was over 95% effective in preventing unintended pregnancy. Tenofovir (TFV) is the leading ARV for many reasons including its approval for PrEP, its long clinical safety record (tenofovir prodrug formulations are currently used by 3.5 million people), extended duration of cellular levels following dosing and stability. But simultaneous dosing of TFV and LNG at relevant levels from simple, monolithic IVR is a challenge due to differences in their properties and target release rates, mandating the investigation of customized IVR designs.

We recently demonstrated the three-month zero-order delivery of TFV from a hydrophilic polyether urethane (HPEU) reservoir IVR [25]. In this report we describe the engineering and design of a segmented dual-reservoir IVR for the controlled delivery of TFV and LNG for 90 days. This manuscript illustrates the challenges of designing and integrating a solid, non-swellable LNG-releasing polyether urethane (PEU) reservoir into the existing swellable HPEU reservoir technology. We used a combination of *in silico*, *in vitro* and *in vivo* methodologies to study, engineer and evaluate the combination IVR. We present new insights regarding the use of the chemically diverse class of elastomeric PEU in reservoir-type dosage forms to deliver chemically diverse molecules at greatly divergent release rates. The work resulted in an IVR that gives nearly time-independent vaginal delivery of TFV and LNG for three months.

Design

All clinically-used IVR in the U.S. employ reservoir technologies, however HIV prevention researchers have often investigated simpler matrix IVR designs to reduce manufacturing complexity and cost [26,27,28,29]. Reservoir IVR are more attractive from a pharmacokinetic perspective as they can provide constant drug levels in the reproductive tract over extended durations [25]. Matrix IVR intrinsically provide high initial release rates, followed by continuously attenuated rates over time [17]. This is generally undesirable for PrEP applications, because the maintenance of preventative ARV levels for the intended IVR duration will require an excess of ARV exposure at early times during the release profile, presenting potential safety concerns. Furthermore, design limitations hindering the attainment of sufficient drug release rates can render it impossible to achieve high drug levels throughout the release profile and may result in increased probability of HIV acquisition late in the release profile of a matrix ARV-eluting IVR. These pharmacological limitations drive the investigation of reservoir IVR technologies that have the potential to provide precise and tunable control over the drug release rates for as long as several months.

TFV and LNG exhibit approximately 7-log and 4-log differences in their partition/distribution coefficients and aqueous solubilities, respectively (Figure 1A and 1B), precluding their simultaneous solubilization and controlled release from a single polymeric compartment. To address these differences in molecular properties, we utilized chemically diverse polyether urethanes (PEU) capable of solubilizing and delivering TFV and other ARVs with varying physicochemical properties [30,31,32,33]; an ability not generally afforded by the traditionally used silicone and poly(ethylene-co-vinyl-acetate) elastomers. Poly(ethylene oxide) can be added alongside the poly(tetramethylene oxide) soft segment typically used in PEU to create hydrophilic poly(ether urethanes) (HPEU) that swell in aqueous solution and can solubilize hydrophilic drugs when hydrated. Furthermore, PEU and HPEU are otherwise chemically identical and can be readily melt-welded to form mechanically sound IVR.

In addition to their disparate chemical properties, TFV and LNG also require vastly different release rates for their respective pharmacological effects. Our group designed an HPEU hollow-tube reservoir IVR to release 10 mg TFV per day [25], which we similarly targeted for the TFV/LNG IVR. However, as described above much lower release rates of LNG are employed for topical microdose contraception. We chose targets of 10 and 20 µg LNG per day, similar to the Mirena® intrauterine system and WHO's silicone LNG IVR. To address the challenge of delivering these diverse molecules at divergent release rates we designed a two-segment reservoir IVR system [31] containing an analogous TFV reservoir segment [25] and a PEU reservoir segment containing dissolved LNG. We desired to create a platform technology from which three devices, all with the same overall size (5.5 mm and 55 mm cross-sectional and outer diameters, respectively), could be fabricated to deliver ~10 mg TFV per day with LNG daily doses of either 0 (TFV-only), 10 or 20 µg.

Generally, drug release rates (dM/dt) from end-capped cylindrical reservoir devices, like IVR or IVR segments can be varied by changing the segment length (l), core drug concentration (c_{in}) or the outer, rate controlling membrane (RCM) thickness (represented by the subtraction of outer and inner cross-sectional radii, r_o-r_i). A steady-state description, assuming constant c_{in}, is easily derived from Fick's laws and is ubiquitous in the design of reservoir IVR [34,35]:

$$\frac{dM}{dt} = \frac{2\pi l D c_{in}}{\ln\left(\frac{r_o}{r_i}\right)} \quad (1)$$

where D is the effective diffusivity of the drug in the RCM material. To achieve the membrane-controlled release described in Equation 1, the drug-loaded core must be well-mixed so that the drug concentration remains uniform throughout the core and at the core/membrane boundary. For a solid polymer system, like the LNG segment, this is achieved by choosing a core polymer with much higher drug diffusivity than that of the RCM polymer. Specifically for PEU, drug flux can be hindered by increasing the volume fraction of crystalline hard segments. This is also easily maintained for a hollow-tube system like the TFV segment [25], because of the large differences in diffusivity between the liquid core and the porous membrane of the wall.

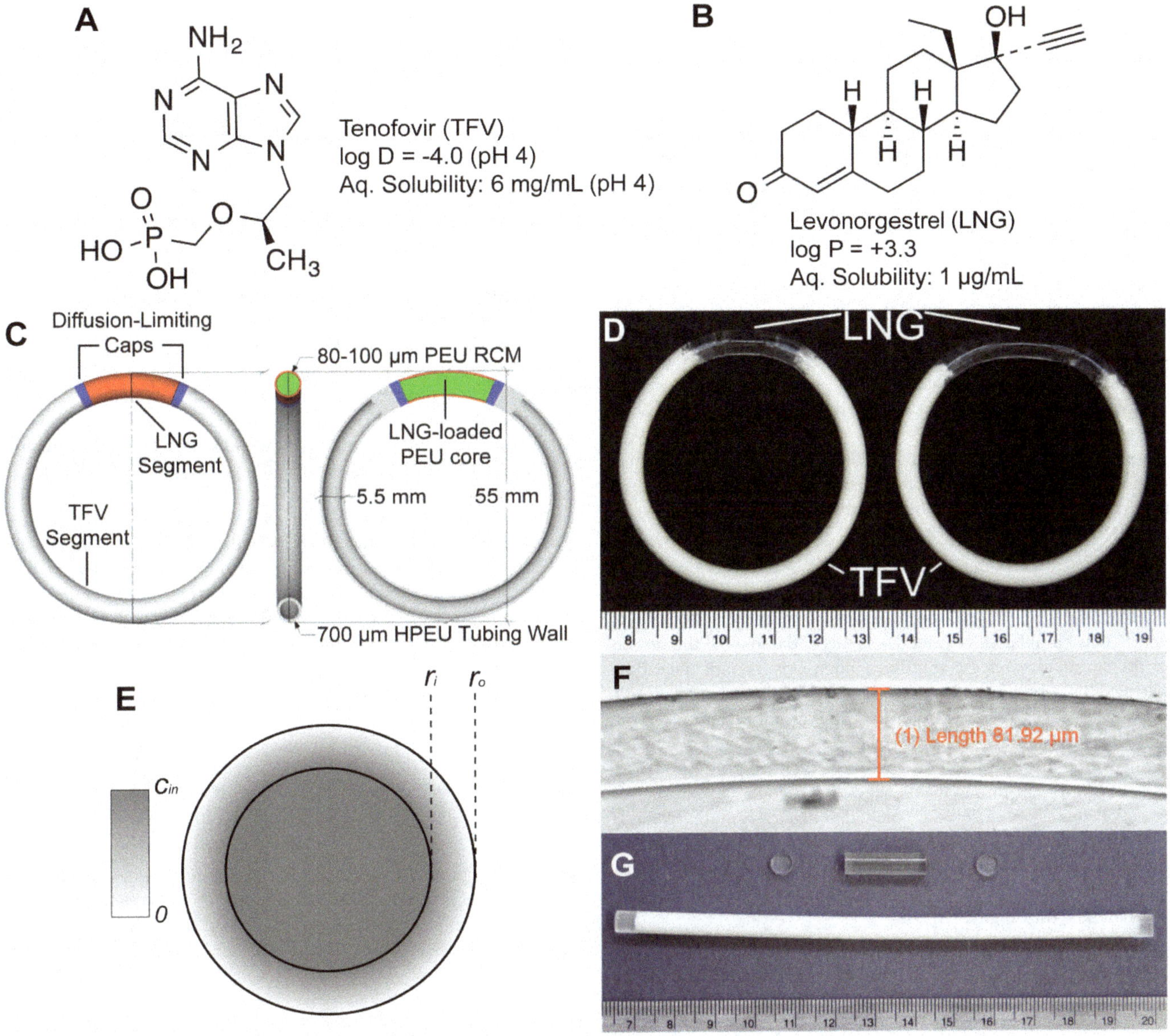

Figure 1. IVR Design Overview. Structural formulae of (A) the HIV-1 nucleotide reverse transcriptase inhibitor tenofovir (TFV) and (B) the progestin contraceptive levonorgestrel (LNG). (C) A design schematic of the full TFV/LNG IVR, shown in the 20 mm LNG segment configuration illustrating the LNG-loaded core (green), the rate-controlling membrane (RCM, red), diffusion-limiting end-caps (blue) and the hollow HPEU tube containing TFV-loaded paste (gray). (D) Photographs of TFV/LNG IVR in the 10 mm (left) and 20 mm (right) LNG segment configurations. (E) Illustration of a reservoir cross-section with outer and inner radii r_o and r_i, and core drug concentration c_{in}. (F) Photomicrograph of the LNG segment cross-section showing microscopic measurement of RCM thickness. (G) Component parts of the TFV/LNG IVR: a TFV paste-filled HPEU tube (bottom), a co-axially extruded LNG-loaded reservoir segment (top) and two diffusion-limiting end-caps (left and right).

We chose to modify LNG release rates by changing the length of the LNG-segment. We desired to minimize LNG segment length to allow for minimal change in TFV dose between devices, but also sought to minimize the core LNG concentration because of potential physical stability issues of supersaturation and re-crystallization on the IVR surface [36]. Thus, we arrived at a target release rate 1 µg/mm/day for the LNG segment, leading to two IVR prototypes with segments of 10 and 20 mm length to deliver 10 µg and 20 µg LNG per day, respectively. A diagram of the 20 mm configuration is shown in Figure 1C, and a photograph showing both IVR configurations (with either 10 mm or 20 mm LNG segments) is shown in Figure 1D. We also added diffusion-limiting end-caps between the two segments (Figure 1C, shown in blue) to prevent circumferential diffusion of LNG from the solid PEU reservoir (green/red) to the HPEU tubing in the TFV-releasing segment (gray). The end-caps are composed of the same PEU used to create the RCM.

Theory

Mathematical models of drug transport can aid the *in silico* design of drug delivery systems [37] including IVR [26,38]. TFV release occurs at a constant rate as predicted by Equation 1, due to an excess of un-dissolved drug which maintains a constant TFV core concentration [25]. For the LNG segment in the TFV/LNG

IVR, two issues confound the simple description of drug release presented in Equation 1. First, if LNG is equally distributed throughout the cross-section (core and membrane) at t = 0, then the device will initially behave as a matrix device, resulting in a period of burst release, which we refer to as the 'burst regime', prior to the onset of steady-state release [34]. Second, as LNG is completely dissolved in the PEU core, the drug source (c_{in}) diminishes with time as drug is released, even after steady-state is achieved. We refer to this pseudo-steady-state (PSS) period as the 'steady state regime'. We derived a comprehensive model which addresses both of these issues. Throughout, we assume the drug is completely dissolved at equal concentration in both the core and outer membrane at t = 0, and that equipartitioning exists between the core and RCM polymer. Axial diffusion is neglected because the loss of LNG to the end-caps occurs on a much longer time-scale than that of drug release.

Radial drug release from cylindrical matrices. Diffusion-limited drug release of a purely dissolved drug from a cylinder with no axial diffusion is presented in the literature [39]. At early times (up to ~20–30% of cumulative release), the following first-term approximation predicts fractional cumulative release:

$$\frac{M(t)}{M_0} = \frac{4}{r_o}\sqrt{\frac{Dt}{\pi}} \qquad (2)$$

where M is cumulative release, M_0 is the initial load of the device (or the cumulative release at infinite time), D is the effective drug-matrix diffusivity, and r_o is the radius of the cylinder. Equation 2 will describe drug release in the burst regime for a solid reservoir with initial homogeneous drug concentration.

Computation of burst duration. We compute the burst regime duration assuming the device will proceed as a matrix until its initial steady state profile is reached. The steady-state profile is then integrated to obtain the mass loss required to complete the burst. First we solve Fick's Second Law in the steady-state form with a $c = c_0$ boundary at $r = r_i$ and a sink outer boundary ($c = 0$ at $r = r_o$) (depicted in Figure 1E):

$$c(r) = \frac{c_0 \ln\left(\frac{r}{r_o}\right)}{\ln\left(\frac{r_i}{r_o}\right)} \qquad (3)$$

We now integrate the right-hand-side of Equation 3 from r_i to r_o and scale appropriately to determine the mass remaining in the RCM at the beginning of the steady-state regime (m_{eq}):

$$m_{eq} = \int_{r_i}^{r_o} c(r)\,dV = 2\pi l \int_{r_i}^{r_o} rc(r)\,dr = \pi l c_0 \left(\frac{r_o^2 - r_i^2}{2\ln\left(\frac{r_o}{r_i}\right)} - r_i^2 \right) \qquad (4)$$

To avoid confusion, in this manuscript a capital "M" will represent to the cumulative drug mass released from the device, while a lower-case "m" will represent the drug mass remaining in various compartments of the device. By subtraction we compute the total burst release (M_b):

$$M_b = m_{RCM,t=0} - m_{eq} = \pi l c_0 \left(r_o^2 - \frac{r_o^2 - r_i^2}{2\ln\left(\frac{r_o}{r_i}\right)} \right) \qquad (5)$$

Combining Equation 5 with Equation 2 and solving for t, we obtain the burst duration or length of the burst regime (t_b):

$$t_b = \frac{\pi r_o^2}{16D}\left(1 - \frac{r_o^2 - r_i^2}{2r_o^2 \ln\left(\frac{r_o}{r_i}\right)} \right) \qquad (6)$$

There is some approximation in the computation of Equation 6, as concentration profiles in a matrix device following release of M_b and in a reservoir system at steady-state are likely not identical. Some time is required for the system to adjust from the matrix to the reservoir profile when the system becomes constrained by the core boundary condition, during which additional drug is depleted from the core. Depending on the relationship between outer boundary flux during this transitional period and the predicted reservoir flux at when $c = c_0$, Equation 11 (below) will over- or underestimate release rates during this period. This phenomenon is discussed further in the Supporting Information (see Table S1 and Figures S1 and S2 in File S1)

Pseudo-steady-state adjustment for variable core concentration. To effectively describe the attenuation of drug release rates in the steady-state regime, we employ a PSS technique which allows c_{in} in Equation 1 to vary with time. First, we must replace c_{in} with an expression which depends on the mass remaining in the device (which we denote as m) and the geometry of the device. However m must represent the total system drug mass (core and membrane):

$$m = M_{core} + M_{eq} = \pi l c_{in}\left(\frac{r_o^2 - r_i^2}{2\ln\left(\frac{r_o}{r_i}\right)} \right) \qquad (7)$$

Solving Equation 7 for c_{in} and substituting into Equation 1 yields a simple ODE, although we must first replace dM/dt, which represents the rate of mass being released from the system, with the rate of mass loss from the system (dm/dt, equal to $-dM/dt$):

$$\frac{dm}{dt} = -am \quad a = \frac{4D}{r_o^2 - r_i^2} \qquad (8)$$

Solving the ODE, applying the initial condition $c = c_0$ at t_b gives an expression for the mass remaining in the steady-state-regime. Taking a time-derivative and applying the negative sign we obtain an expression for attenuated release rates as a function of time in the steady-state regime:

$$\frac{dM}{dt} = \frac{2\pi l D c_0}{\ln\left(\frac{r_o}{r_i}\right)} e^{-a(t-t_b)} \qquad (9)$$

Equation 9 the can be integrated to obtain cumulative release in the steady-state regime:

$$M(t) = M_b + \frac{2\pi l D c_0}{a \ln\left(\frac{r_o}{r_i}\right)}\left(1 - e^{-a(t-t_b)}\right) \qquad (10)$$

We now have a simple exponential time constant ('a') to describe release rate attenuation. A PSS reservoir model was previously described for cylinders [40], but was complicated by consideration of axial release from the device, and did not consider the error in the depletion of drug from the outer membrane.

Complete two stage drug release model. We now have a complete, piece-wise description of cumulative drug release from the LNG segment, depending only on drug-polymer diffusivity in the RCM and device geometry:

$$M(t) = 4r_o l c_0 \sqrt{\pi D t} \quad t < t_b \tag{11a}$$

$$M(t) = M_b + \frac{2\pi l D c_0}{a \ln\left(\frac{r_o}{r_i}\right)} \left(1 - e^{-a(t - t_b)}\right) \quad t \geq t_b \tag{11b}$$

as described previously [26], daily release rates then are readily computed by subtraction. It should be noted that, as Equation 2 is a first-term approximation valid only at early times for a matrix device, Equation 11 will lose accuracy for proportionally thicker RCM (lower values of r_i/r_o). This is further discussed in the Supporting Information (File S1).

Materials and Methods

Materials

Aliphatic polyether urethanes Tecoflex EG-85A, Tecoflex EG-60D, Tecoflex EG-65D, Tecoflex EG-100A and the hydrophilic Tecophilic HP-100A-60 were purchased from Lubrizol Advanced Materials (Wickliffe, Ohio). Additionally, PEU-1 (73A-77A shore hardness), PEU-2 (59D shore hardness) and HPEU-35 (78A shore hardness, 37% equilibrium water absorption) were provided by DSM-PTG (now a subsidiary of DSM Biomedical, Berkeley, California). TFV was provided by Gilead Sciences (Foster City, California), and micronized LNG was obtained from Industriale Chemica (Saronno, Italy) or Haorui Pharma-Chem Inc. (Edison, New Jersey). USP grade glycerol was purchased from Spectrum Chemicals and Laboratory Products (New Brunswick, New Jersey). Solutol HS 15 was obtained from BASF (Florham Park, New Jersey). All water used was either USP grade or double de-ionized (DDI) through an 18 mΩ*cm filtration system. All other solvents were HPLC or ACS grade unless noted.

LNG and TFV quantification by HPLC analysis

TFV and LNG quantification were performed using a 1200 Series HPLC (Agilent Technologies, Santa Clara, California) equipped with a diode array detector. TFV was quantified in *in vitro* release samples by a 15-minute gradient method described previously [25,26]. Various HPLC methods were used to quantify LNG in unknown samples. In all cases a Zorbax ODS 4.6×250 mm, 5 µm column was used and LNG was quantified at 240 nm. For drug extraction samples a 5 minute isocratic run of 20:80 (v/v) DDI H_2O:acetonitrile (ACN) was used, whereas a gradient method was used to quantify LNG in *in vitro* release samples. A longer gradient method was used to quantify LNG in samples containing both TFV and LNG due to interference from TFV elution. Both gradient methods are described in detail in the Supporting Information (see Tables S2 and S3 in File S1).

Dissolution testing of matrix devices to determine LNG-PEU diffusivities

Drug-polymer effective diffusivity was determined using matrix-type PEU segments to aid in the design of the LNG segment and evaluation of RCM polymers. LNG was compounded by roll-coating and hot melt extrusion in each polymer using a Haake Minilab extruder (Thermo Scientific, Tewksbury, Massachusetts) to an approximate final diameter of 5 mm. Next, 2 mm length segments were excised from the extrudate batch and subjected to the extraction method below to determine the LNG loading for each batch. Segments approximately 15 mm in length were then cut and end-capped as described previously [27]. Before capping, the exact length and diameter of each segment were measured with digital calipers and the exact mass of each segment was measured with an analytical balance. Segments were subjected to release testing in sodium acetate buffer (pH 4.2) with 2% Solutol HS 15 [30] for 7 days at either 23°C, 37°C or 50°C. Aliquots of release media were collected daily and analyzed by HPLC. Daily release data were summed sequentially to determine cumulative release, which was normalized to the initial LNG mass in each segment. Linear regressions of cumulative data against the square-root-of-time were performed from day 3 to day 7 (some non-linearity was observed on days 1 and 2).

As discussed above, diffusion-controlled release from a cylindrical matrix device wherein the drug is completely dissolved and axial transport can be neglected can be approximated by a simple relation at early-times (Equation 2). If the expected linearity of fractional cumulative release (M/M_0) against the square-root-of-time is observed experimentally, Equation 1 can be re-arranged to estimate the effective diffusivity:

$$D = \frac{\pi k^2 r_o^2}{16} \tag{12}$$

where r_o is the cross-sectional radius of the device and k is the slope of the linear regression of fractional cumulative release against the square-root-of-time.

LNG Segment and IVR fabrication

A diagram detailing the TFV/LNG IVR manufacturing scheme is shown in the Supporting Information (Figure S3 in File S1). To fabricate LNG reservoir segments, LNG was first dissolved in either PEU-1 or EG-85A by hot-melt extrusion. PEU-1/EG-85A pellets were roll-coated with LNG powder (up to 2% w/w) and flood-fed into a KETSE 12/36 twin-screw extruder (TSE) (C.W. Brabender, South Hackensack, New Jersey) and cut using a Micropelletizer (Randcastle Extrusion Systems Inc., Cedar Grove, New Jersey). The pelletized extrudate was then subjected to extractions and HPLC analysis to determine drug content as described below. In some cases, LNG-loaded pellets were then mixed with placebo pellets to the desired average LNG loading (~1.3% w/w). LNG-containing reservoir strands were then fabricated by co-axial extrusion. The TSE was connected to a 3/4″ single screw extruder (SSE) w/advanced torque rheometer drive (C.W. Brabender) at a 90° angle using a custom-designed mandrel crosshead (Guill Tool, West Warwick, Rhode Island). The LNG-loaded pellet mixture was starve-fed gravimetrically into the TSE using a KCL-24-KQx4 loss-in-weight feeder (K-Tron, Pitman, New Jersey) while PEU-2 or EG-65D pellets were flood fed into the SSE to form an outer rate controlling membrane (RCM) around the LNG-loaded PEU core. In some studies, EG-60D was used as an RCM polymer in place of EG-65D. The coated extrudate was passed through a water trough followed by cold air drying using an Air Wipe cooling ring connected to a Adjustable Spot Cooler vortexing tube (Exair, Cincinnati, Ohio) and fed to a conveyor belt, from which coaxial strands approximately 2–3 feet in length were manually cut. The feed rate of PEU-1, the SSE screw speed and the conveying speed were modulated to form a cylindrical reservoir extrudate with target dimensions of 5.5 mm outer diameter and 5.3 mm inner diameter

(0.1 mm RCM thickness). In some experiments the RCM thickness was varied between 0.05 and 0.15 mm. To facilitate LNG diffusion into the RCM, thus mitigating the lag-times required to achieve steady-state release, strands were treated for 14 days at 40°C/75%RH prior to end-capping. In some cases heat treatment was varied between 4 and 76 days at 40°C/75%RH to assess the kinetic effects on lag/burst behavior during drug release. If segments were fabricated for inclusion in full TFV/LNG IVR, heat treatment was performed on the full IVR instead of the parent co-axial strand as described below. Segments of either 10 or 20 mm length were cut from their parent strands. A process flow diagram for LNG-loading co-axial extrusion is presented in the Supporting Information (Figure S4 in File S1). Exact lengths and diameters of LNG segments were measured by a digital caliper or thickness gage. Exact RCM thicknesses were determined by cutting thin slices of co-axial strand (either throughout the batch or proximal to individual samples) and imaging by bright field microscopy (Figure 1F). Four measurements per cross-section were taken using cellSens Standard software (Olympus, Center Valley, Pennsylvania) and averaged to determine a representative thickness for a given sample or batch. To prevent significant leakage of LNG into the TFV segment, LNG-loaded segments were end-capped with 2 mm length, 5.5 mm diameter EG-65D or PEU-2 caps using an HPS-EM induction welding system (PlasticWeld Systems, Inc., Newfane, NY). End-caps were cut from circular 5.5 mm EG-65D strands extruded using the SSE.

End-sealed TFV segments were fabricated by filling hollow hot-melt extruded HPEU-35 or HP-100A-60 tubes (5.5 mm outer diameter, 4.2 mm inner diameter, 145 or 155 mm length) with 2.1 to 2.3 g TFV/glycerol/water paste (62:36:2 w/w) and end-sealing by induction welding, as described previously [25]. Component parts of the TFV/LNG IVR (filled TFV segments, LNG segments and end-caps) are shown in Figure 1G. To form TFV/LNG IVR, capped LNG segments were welded to sealed TFV segments using a HPS-20 induction welding system with a split-die configuration (PlasticWeld Systems, Inc., Newfane, NY). TFV segments with 131 and 141 mm lengths (post-sealing) were paired with the capped 20 and 10 mm LNG segments, respectively, to form IVR with 55 mm outer ring diameter (Figure 1D). To form a more circular ring shape, IVR were annealed in custom-fabricated aluminum molds for approximately 15 minutes at 65°C. IVR were heat-treated for 14 days at 40°C/75%RH in sealed aluminum pouches prior to *in vitro* release testing.

Prior to any melt processing, all PEU or HPEU resins were dried overnight in a CAFM series compressed air dryer (Dri-Air, East Windsor, Connecticut) to less than 0.05% H_2O (w/w) as determined using a C30 Coulometric Karl Fischer Titrator (Mettler-Toledo, Columbus, Ohio).

Drug extractions to estimate LNG content and in vivo release

LNG was extracted from polymer segments to determine the LNG loading in each batch of co-axial extrudate. Several 2 mm long pieces were cut from various locations throughout the batch. Each piece was placed in a 5 mL volumetric flask, which was filled with 3 mL dichloromethane (DCM). Flasks were agitated on a High Capacity Mixer (Glas-Col, Terre Haute, Indiana) overnight to dissolve the PEU and LNG. Following dissolution, flasks were filled to volume with DCM. Flasks inverted several times to ensure good mixing. To precipitate PEU from the solution, 1.00 mL of the DCM solution was transferred to a 10 mL volumetric flask using a calibrated glass syringe. The 10 mL flask was then filled to volume with acetonitrile (ACN) and vortexed for 5 seconds. Aliquots of the resulting supernatants were then passed through a 0.2 μm PTFE syringe filter into HPLC vials for analysis. The same extraction procedure was also performed on 50 mg samples of LNG-loaded PEU-1/EG-85A pellets to assess the drug loading prior to co-axial extrusion.

The same procedure was also used to determine the average LNG mass loaded per device used in the rabbit PK study (see methods below), except that a 25 mL volumetric flask was used in place of a 5 mL flask for the first dissolution step. When full segments with end-caps were extracted, it was necessary to further cut the segment into 2–3 mm pieces before dissolution. These extractions were also performed after *in vivo* testing to estimate average LNG release rates.

In vitro release testing of LNG segments and TFV/LNG IVR

LNG-containing PEU segments and TFV/LNG IVR were subjected to *in vitro* drug release testing. Samples were immersed in aqueous buffer sink for up to 90 days in 250 mL or 500 mL I-Chem glass jars (Thermo Scientific, Rockwood, Tennessee) in an incubated shaker cabinet set to 37°C and 80 rpm. Media were changed daily and media volumes were adjusted throughout the studies to ensure a sufficient sink for both TFV and LNG. TFV and LNG concentrations were not allowed to exceed 20% of their solubility in the release media. Typically, 25 mM sodium acetate buffer (pH 4.2) was used as the testing media, although Gibco (Life Technologies, Carlsbad California) 1× phosphate buffered saline (pH 7.4) was used for parallel *in vitro* release studies in the rabbit PK study to approximate the neutral vaginal pH typically observed in rabbits. Aliquots of release media were collected 23–25 hours from the previous media change and analyzed by HPLC at several points throughout each study to determine daily TFV and LNG release rates. To assess the validity of the model presented above, release rate profiles were compared to predictions from Equation 11. Some TFV/LNG IVR were also evaluate at an 200 rpm shaking speed to assess the adequacy of the standard 80 rpm in maintaining sink conditions. For *in vitro-in vivo* comparison, numerical integrations of *in vitro* release profiles were performed by trapezoidal approximation to generate time-averaged release rates.

Evaluation of LNG containment by PEU end-caps

To evaluate the potential effectiveness of PEU end-caps in preventing LNG transport into the TFV segment, the full TFV/LNG IVR was rendered in COMSOL Multiphysics 4 and Fickian diffusion simulations were performed using the "Transport of Diluted Species" package. A diffusivity of 7.3×10^{-11} cm^2/s was applied to the RCM and end-cap compartments based on an experimental measurement of LNG diffusivity in PEU-2. An LNG diffusivity of 3.0×10^{-9} cm^2/s was applied to the core compartment and the tubing compartment of the TFV segment representing a typical softer PEU at 37°C (see Table 1), as the exact diffusivity in these compartments should not affect diffusion provided that the value is sufficiently high in the core for LNG to be well-mixed and sufficiently high in the tubing wall so that it acts as a sink. End-cap lengths of 1, 2 and 3 mm were evaluated, while the LNG segment length was fixed at 20 mm and the overall dimensions were fixed at 5.5×55 mm (cross-sectional and outer ring diameters). The RCM thickness was set to 100 μm, and was not loaded with LNG. An initial LNG loading of 42 mol/m^3 (~1.3%w/w, assuming a matrix density of 1.05 g/cm^3), was applied to the core compartment. A free tetrahedral mesh was applied throughout the IVR, with higher node resolution in and near the RCM and near the segment/end-cap interface. Time-dependent effective diffusivity simulations, governed solely by Fick's 2nd Law, were carried out for approximately 5 years.

Table 1. Measured LNG effective diffusivities for various PEUs, calculated using Equation 12. Data represents N between 3 and 8, mean ± SD.

Polymer	LNG Effective Diffusivity ($cm^2/s \times 10^{-10}$)
Tecoflex EG-85A	47±3
Tecoflex EG-100A	2.0±0.1
Tecoflex EG-60D	1.1±0.1
Tecoflex EG-65D	0.51±0.06
PEU-1	17±3
PEU-2	0.78±0.06

Volume integrals of the end-cap and TFV segment compartments were performed every 7 days for the duration of the model and normalized to the initial mass of LNG loaded in the system.

To experimentally validate the model presented above, TFV/LNG IVR (HPEU-35/PEU-1/PEU-2) were stored at 40°C for either 1, 3 or 6 months. IVR stored at −80°C were used as controls. IVR were dissected, and separate LNG extractions, as described above, were performed on the end-caps and TFV plug sections (first ~5 mm of the TFV segment on either side of the LNG segment). As can be seen in Figure 1D, it is difficult to discern where the exact cap/segment interface is on the final IVR. Masses of the dissected LNG segments were compared to the initial segment mass before end-capping, and an adjustment was made to the LNG mass extracted from the end-caps based on the segment mass discrepancy and the initial LNG loading of the co-axial extrudate batch.

Extension testing of TFV/LNG IVR

To assess mechanical robustness of the TFV/LNG IVR before and after 31 day *in vitro* release testing, we performed destructive extension tests to determine the tensile load and resulting extension required to cause joint failure. IVR were tested using an Instron 3342 with 500 N load cell and O-ring testing apparatus with Bluehill Lite software control (Instron, Norwood, Massachusetts). IVR were placed on the testing apparatus with the LNG segment oriented vertically and stretched at a rate of 5 mm/s until failure was observed, at which point the net extension and net load were recorded. The failure type of each IVR was also recorded.

Pharmacokinetic testing of LNG-loaded segments in rabbits

Both 10 mm and 20 mm end-capped LNG-loaded PEU-1/PEU-2 reservoir segments were implanted into New Zealand white female rabbits (age 4–8 months) to assess *in vivo* device performance and LNG pharmacokinetics. This study was carried out in accordance with the U.S. Department of Agriculture's (USDA) Animal Welfare Act (9 CFR Parts 1, 2 and 3) and the Guide for the Care and Use of Laboratory Animals of the National Institutes of Health. The protocol was approved by the Institutional Animal Care and Use Committee of MPI Research (USDA Research License Number: 34-R-0031).

Preoperative and surgical procedures were performed as described previously [41]. Briefly, LNG-loaded segments were placed in the proximal, columnar epithelial region of the vagina, such that the distal end of the segment was approximately 7 to 12 cm from the introitus. Up to three 3-0 or 5-0 Prolene sutures were used to secure the segment to the outer ventral wall. All surgery was performed under analgesia and anesthesia, and all efforts were made to minimize suffering.

Animals weighed between 2.9 and 4.2 kg at implantation. Body weights of test subjects were recorded periodically during implantation. Groups of 6 animals were each administered either 10 or 20 mm segments, for either 28 or 90 days (4 groups total). In the 28-day groups, plasma was collected at 4 hours, 8 hours, and 1, 2, 3, 7, 14, 21 and 28 days post-implantation. In the 90-day groups, plasma was collected at 44, 60, 74 and 90 days post-implantation. Approximately 1 mL blood was drawn from the jugular vein of all animals at each time-point and stored in tubes containing tripotassium EDTA. Tubes were stored on wet ice until centrifuged under refrigeration, at which point samples were aliquoted into cryovials and stored at −50°C to −90°C until analysis could be performed. LNG was quantified in plasma samples by a validated LC-MS/MS method (described in the Supporting Information, see Tables S4 and S5 in File S1). To assess total LNG plasma exposure and device dose dependence, area under the curve (AUC) values were calculated from individual plasma data using WinNonlin Phoenix (Pharsight, St. Louis, Missouri). AUC was calculated from implantation to 28 days post-implantation (AUC_{0-28}) for the 28 day groups and from 44 to 90 days post-implantation for the 90-day groups (AUC_{44-90}).

All test subjects were euthanized at study's end (either day 28 or day 90) by an intravenous overdose of sodium pentobarbital solution followed by exsanguination. Approximately 500 mg of cervical tissue was collected from all animals during necropsy, snap frozen in liquid nitrogen and stored at −50°C to −90°C until LNG extractions could be performed. LNG was extracted from tissue and again quantified by a validated LC-MS/MS method (described in the Supporting Information, see Table S6 in File S1).

LNG segments were recovered post-study during necropsy. Time-averaged *in vivo* LNG release rates were estimated by subtracting the residual LNG mass recovered by extraction (method described above) from the estimated initial LNG mass loaded (batch average LNG loading multiplied by segment mass prior to end-capping), and dividing the net mass by the study duration. In addition, the average cumulative release values from the 28 day and 90 day groups were subtracted to determine the average release rate for the latter portion of the study.

Results and Discussion

LNG Diffusivity in PEUs

We measured effective diffusivities (*D*) for LNG in rate-controlling PEU by analyzing LNG release from cylindrical matrices and applying Equation 12. Figure 2A depicts examples of linear regressions of release against the square-root-of-time for PEU-1 and PEU-2 (R^2>0.998). Diffusivity correlated negatively with manufacturer-reported flexural modulus for Tecoflex PEUs (Figure 2B). The mechanical properties of PEU can be controlled by modulating the molar ratio of the macrodiol (e.g. poly(tetramethylene oxide)) to the chain extender (typically a monomeric diol, e.g. 1,4-butanediol) [42]. Thus, the reduced diffusivity of a dissolved molecule, like LNG, in stiffer PEU, e.g. Tecoflex EG-60D and EG-65D, is likely a result of the lower volume fraction of the amorphous soft segment domains that allow LNG transport [43]. Figure 2C depicts the effect of temperature on LNG diffusivity. Interestingly, diffusivity increased 15-fold in the higher-modulus PEU-2 between 23°C to 50°C, but only 3-fold in PEU-1. This could result from differences in phase transition behavior of the crystalline hard segments between harder and softer PEU. Table 1 contains a summary of LNG diffusivities in various PEU tested. The lower diffusivity in PEU-2 at 23°C vs. 37°C

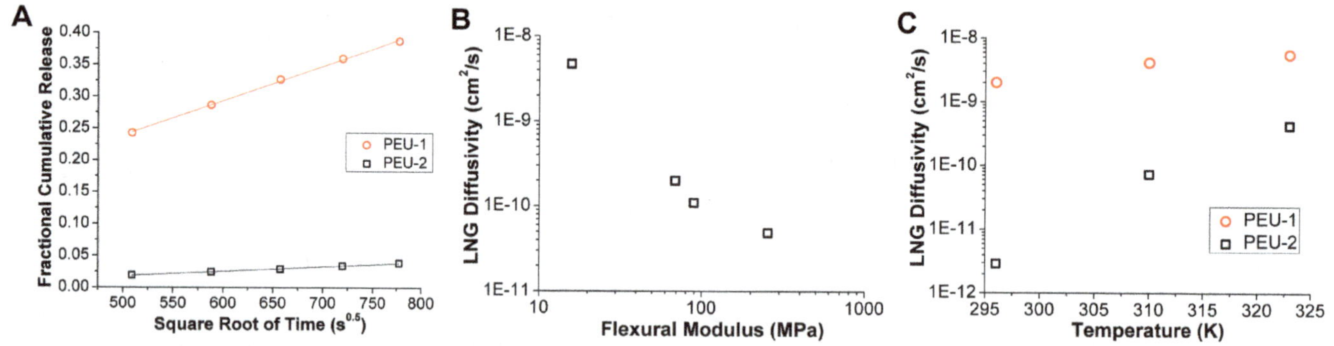

Figure 2. Determination of LNG effective diffusivities in PEU. (A) Example square-root-of-time fitting for PEU-1 and PEU-2 used to estimate LNG-PEU diffusivity values (Eqn. 12). (B) Log-log correlation between LNG diffusivity and reported flexural modulus for Tecoflex PEUs and (C) effect of temperature on LNG diffusivity in PEU-1 and PEU-2.

necessitated heat treatment to allow LNG to load into the RCM, thus eliminating the undesirable lag time required to achieve steady-state release.

Mathematical Modeling of LNG in vitro release

The model for drug release presented in Equation 11 proved useful in the design of the LNG reservoir segment by allowing accurate prediction of 90-day release rate profiles. Figure 3A depicts the full two-stage model (Eqn. 11) result in comparison to LNG release from PEU-1/PEU-2 segments stored at elevated temperature to homogenize LNG concentration across the device (as per the model assumption). The experimental *in vitro* release data agreed with the full two stage model ($R^2 = 0.74$) with a mean prediction error of 17%. This correlation confirmed that our diffusivity measurements in rate-controlling PEU were sufficiently accurate for release rate prediction in the device design process, allowing us to screen potential RCM polymers for LNG diffusivity using simple cylindrical matrices produced on a small-scale batch extruder.

Use of the two-stage model has a practical limitation as the burst regime of the model is only accurate when complete RCM loading is achieved. Therefore, much of the remaining *in vitro* release data presented herein does not demonstrate the full burst predicted by the model. However, as demonstrated below the latter model regime was still useful regardless of the burst magnitude. The burst mass (M_b) is then practically regarded as the maximal burst release that could be achieved from a given system.

Figures 3B and 3C depict the effects of RCM thickness and drug-polymer diffusivity on steady-state regime LNG release, predicted using Equation 11b, from 5.5 mm diameter solid reservoirs. As shown in Equation 8, the release rate time constant (a) varies with the ratio between diffusivity and RCM cross-sectional area. At a fixed diameter, diffusivity or RCM thickness are positively correlated with the magnitude of drug release, but also with the rate of drug release attenuation, as any increase in drug flux results in more rapid depletion of the core drug concentration. The burst duration (t_b, Eqn. 6), is also shown as a function of RCM thickness and diffusivity in Figures 3D and 3E. The burst duration is inversely proportional to diffusivity, while the relationship between burst duration and RCM thickness is not clear from Equation 6 as $r_o - r_i$ is not readily factored. As expected, the RCM thickness also correlates with M_b (Figure 3F). Figures 3B–3F illustrate the complex relationship between burst duration, maximal burst mass and PSS release rate profile encountered when designing reservoir systems.

In vitro release of LNG from end-capped segments

Experimentally, we evaluated the effects of several RCM design inputs on the LNG release profile, including RCM polymer selection, RCM thickness and duration of heat treatment required to load the RCM with LNG. First, effect of heat treatment was performed on segments fabricated from a LNG-loaded PEU-1 core and PEU-2 RCM by storing samples at 40°C for either 4, 14, 21, 28 and 76 days prior to *in vitro* release testing. As depicted in Figure 4A, a 14-day heat treatment mitigated both burst and lag behavior, and was thus incorporated into the manufacturing process. Furthermore, it was necessary to include a 14-day treatment at 40°C of the hydrophilic PEU used in the TFV segment (manuscript in preparation). This allowed us to reduce both procedures to a 14 day annealing of the final TFV/LNG IVR to both stabilize the TFV release rate on subsequent storage and eliminate the lag behavior in the LNG release profile [44].

Almost all reservoir devices will exhibit a drug burst that increases with time as drug is allowed to diffuse into the RCM. This phenomenon is acceptable if the amount of burst release does not result in unsafe drug levels. LNG is given orally as an emergency contraceptive at 1500 μg in a single dose, and our maximum predicted burst (M_b) is over an order of magnitude lower that this dose as shown in Figure 4D. Furthermore, a range of release rates may be acceptable early in the release profile, provided that the eventually PSS release rate in the reservoir-stage is consistent and is consistently efficacious. If highly reproducible burst release profiles are required for other drugs, it may be necessary to manufacture devices with uniform concentration in both compartments to ensure a kinetically stable release profile during storage, either by compounding the drug in both polymers before co-axial extrusion, or by extended heat treatment. This was initially avoided to mitigate the potential for surface re-crystallization. However, in a recent stability study we discovered that LNG does not re-crystallize on the surface of the TFV/LNG IVR (to be reported in an upcoming manuscript).

Next, we evaluated the release of LNG from reservoir segments fabricated with an 1.3% (w/w) LNG-loaded EG-85A core and varying thickness of either EG-65D or EG-60D RCM (Figures 4B and 4C) (all samples heat-treated for 14 days at 40°C). Based on these data and the diffusion model, we selected an 80–85 μm thick EG-65D RCM to target 20 μg/day release on day 45 (the middle of the delivery profile), while also minimizing release rate attenuation throughout the reservoir-stage. The batch with the closest RCM (84 μm EG-65D) was tested for a full 90 days and compared to the model in the steady-state regime (Figure 4D). The reservoir-stage model (Equation 11b) and experimental data

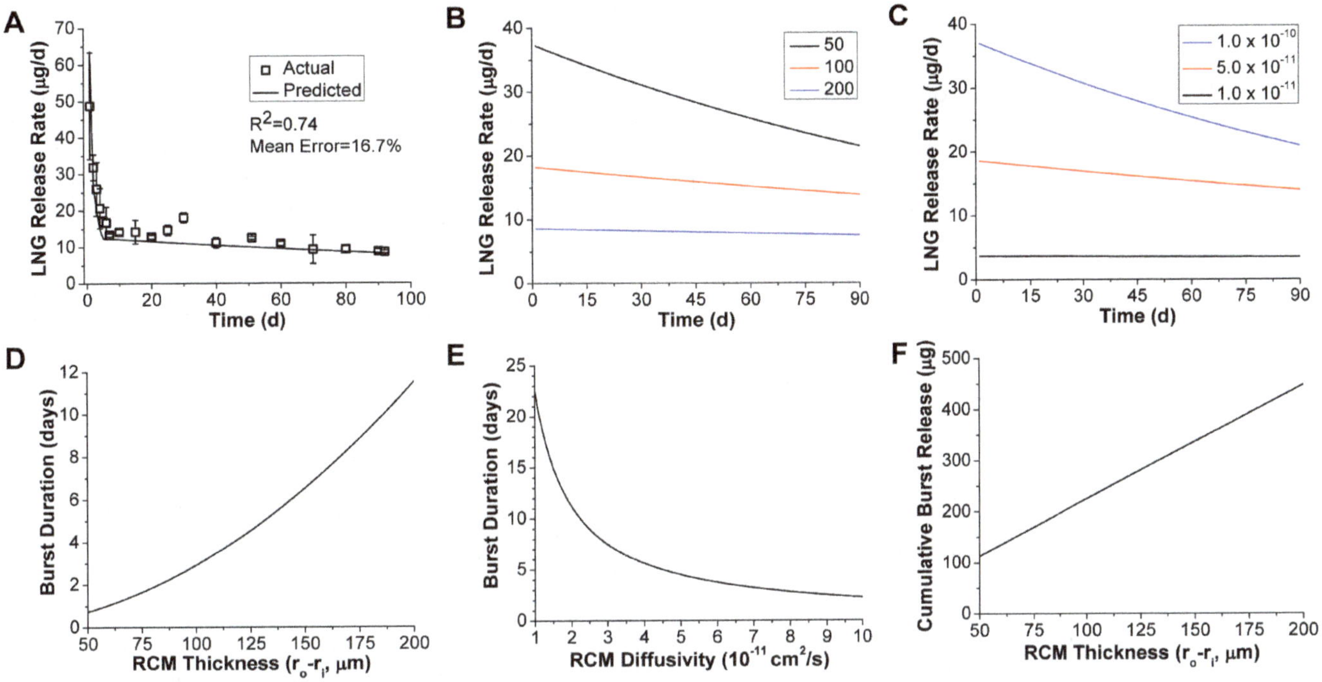

Figure 3. Model for dissolved drug release from cylindrical reservoirs. (A) Accuracy of the two stage drug release model (Eqn. 11) for LNG segments stored 76 days at 40°C to completely equilibrate LNG loading throughout the cross-section. Experimental data represent N = 3, mean ± SD. Effects of (B) EG-65D RCM thickness (in µm) and (C) diffusivity (in cm^2/s) on the reservoir-stage model (Eqn. 11b) for 20 mm length segments with 5.5 mm diameter. Effects of (D) PEU-2 RCM thickness, and (E) diffusivity on the burst duration (t_b) predicted by Equation 6. For panels C and E RCM thickness was fixed at 100 µm. (F) Maximal burst amount (M_b) shown as a function of RCM thickness.

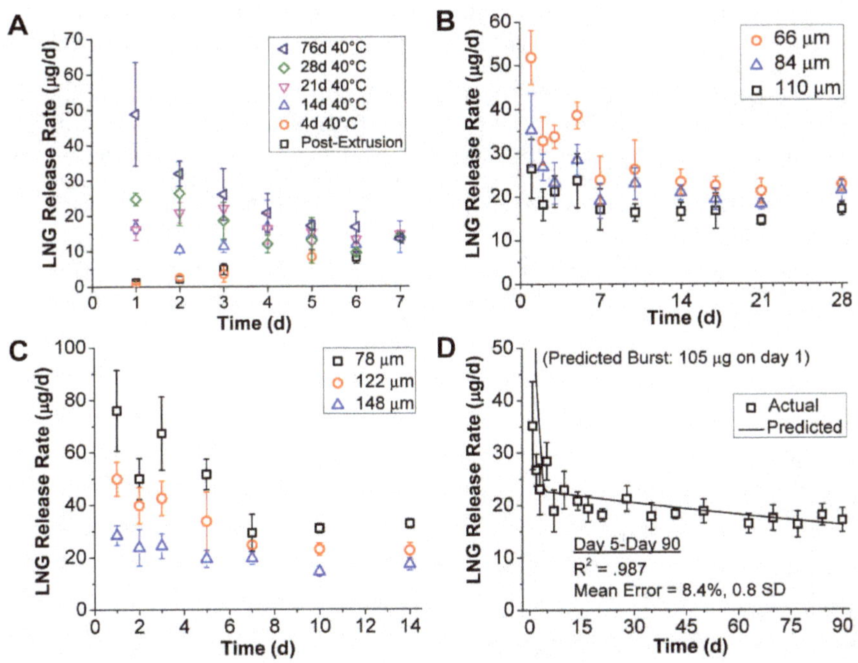

Figure 4. *In vitro* release of LNG from reservoir segments. (A) Effect of partial LNG loadings in the RCM on lag/burst behavior in LNG *in vitro* release kinetics for 10 mm length PEU-1/PEU-2 segments, achieved by 40°C storage for varying duration. *In vitro* LNG release from 20 mm length, 5.5 mm diameter co-axially extruded EG-85A segments with (B) EG-65D or (C) EG-60D RCMs of various thicknesses. (D) Full 90 day *in vitro* release kinetics from the 84 µm EG-65D RCM group with model comparison (Eqn. 11). All data represent N = 5, mean ± SD except panel A (N = 3). Segments in panels B–D were all stored for 14 days at 40°C before testing.

exhibited excellent correlation ($R^2 = 0.987$ from day 5 to day 90), with mean error of 8.4%, or 0.8 experimental standard deviations.

In vitro release of TFV and LNG from full two-segment IVR

In vitro release of TFV and LNG from full IVR for 90 days is shown in Figures 5A and 5B. From day 2 to day 90, IVRs released TFV and LNG at near-constant rates of approximately 7.5±0.1 mg TFV and 21±2 µg LNG per day (N = 5 time-averaged IVRs, mean ± SD), a significant achievement given the disparity in drug properties and release rates.

Based on our recent sheep study comparing pharmacokinetics of the TFV-only IVR (similar *in vitro* release rate) and the TFV 1% gel [25], we hypothesize that a device with this constant TFV dose may protect women against HIV transmission. Also, based on previous data from the WHO silicone LNG IVR [24], we hypothesize that these LNG release rates can provide effective contraception. Given our understanding of how to predict release rates from this system, as well as the adaptability of the segmented IVR design, the release rates of TFV and LNG could be modified should human PK testing suggest different doses are needed.

TFV/LNG IVR evaluated at an increased shaking speed of 200 rpm released 23±1 µg LNG per day over 14 days (N = 3 time-averaged IVRs, mean ± SD), compared to 20±2 µg LNG per day at 80 rpm (N = 5). This comparison suggests that an 80 rpm shake speed sufficiently disrupts the unstirred layer, resulting in sink conditions appropriate for the model presented in Equation 11.

Prevention of LNG diffusion between segments with PEU end-caps

One of the design challenges with developing multi-segment drug delivery systems is the potential for drug diffusion between compartments during storage of the drug product. While diffusion of TFV from the hollow core compartment is hindered by its poor solubility in HPEU [26], LNG diffuses effectively through PEU and thus its "leakage" into the TFV segment is expected. Therefore, we designed end-caps to prevent LNG diffusion into the TFV segment to maintain both LNG release rate magnitude and control in the TFV/LNG IVR following product storage. We evaluated the feasibility of using end-caps made from the same polymers as the LNG-segment RCM (PEU-2 and 65D), but aimed to minimize the end-cap length due to their mechanical rigidity (EG-65D has a flexural modulus of 255 MPa) and the fact that a large cap would eliminate additional length from the TFV segment. We modeled the complex multi-compartment nature of the problem by rendering a full TFV/LNG IVR performing finite-element simulations of Fickian diffusion (Figures 6A–B). Simulations were carried out for 5 years at 37°C, rather than the usual 40°C, due to availability of drug-polymer diffusivities at 37°C from studies presented above. Volume integrals were performed in both the end-cap and TFV segment compartments and normalized to the initial drug load in the 20 mm LNG segment. As depicted in Figures 6C and 6D, the 1 mm, 2 mm and 3 mm end-cap simulations predicted full LNG containment (no LNG in the TFV segment) for 203, 749 and 1484 days at 37°C, respectively. The 2 mm cap configuration ultimately was chosen because complete LNG containment was achieved in the model for 2 years at 37°C, at which time only 6% of the total LNG load had escaped into the end-caps. In Figure 6D, we show that the subsequent leakage into the whole TFV segment, proceeds at a linear but minimal rate (approximately 1% of total LNG load per year for 2 mm caps), suggesting that performance and chemical stability (depending on the quantitative metric used) may be achieved for much longer than 2 years in the 2 mm configuration. The end-caps also function as RCM, where thickness can modulate LNG flux at the TFV/LNG segment interface through the concentration gradient across the segment. Encouragingly, EG-65D (used in our current lead design) exhibits even lower LNG diffusivity than PEU-2 (Table 1), likely lengthening complete containment times from those observed in these simulations.

In an attempt to experimentally approximate the diffusion simulations, TFV/LNG IVR were stored for 6 months at 40°C and the caps and TFV segment plugs were subjected to LNG extractions at various times. The results are shown in Figure 6E. Reasonable agreement was observed between the theoretical and experimental LNG content in the caps, even with the temperature disparity (37°C to 40°C from model to experiment). Trace amounts of LNG (<5 µg total or <0.1% of total load) were detected in the TFV segment plugs, but this likely was not due to leakage through the end-caps as no increase was observed in LNG levels over time.

An "ideal" multi-segment IVR would be thermodynamically stabilized by caps formed from a material miscible with the polymers used and impermeable to all components in the formulation. Here we have demonstrated a practical, kinetically-stabilized system using a material already present in the IVR.

IVR extension testing

Mechanical integrity is an important design consideration for any IVR. In this particular IVR design, we were faced with the

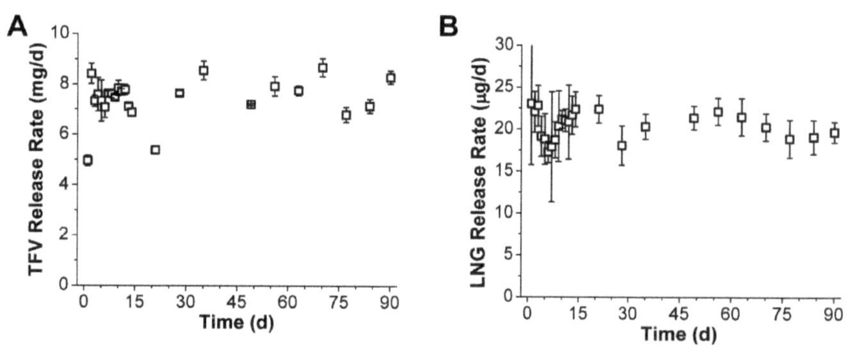

Figure 5. *In vitro* release of TFV and LNG from full two-segment IVR. *In vitro* release of (A) TFV and (B) LNG for 90 days from final TFV/LNG (20 mm) IVR prototypes using Tecophilic and Tecoflex polymers (HP-100A-60 TFV reservoir tube, EG-85A LNG reservoir core and EG-65D LNG reservoir RCM and end-caps). LNG reservoir RCM thicknesses were measured between 74 and 85 µm. All data represent N = 5, mean ± SD.

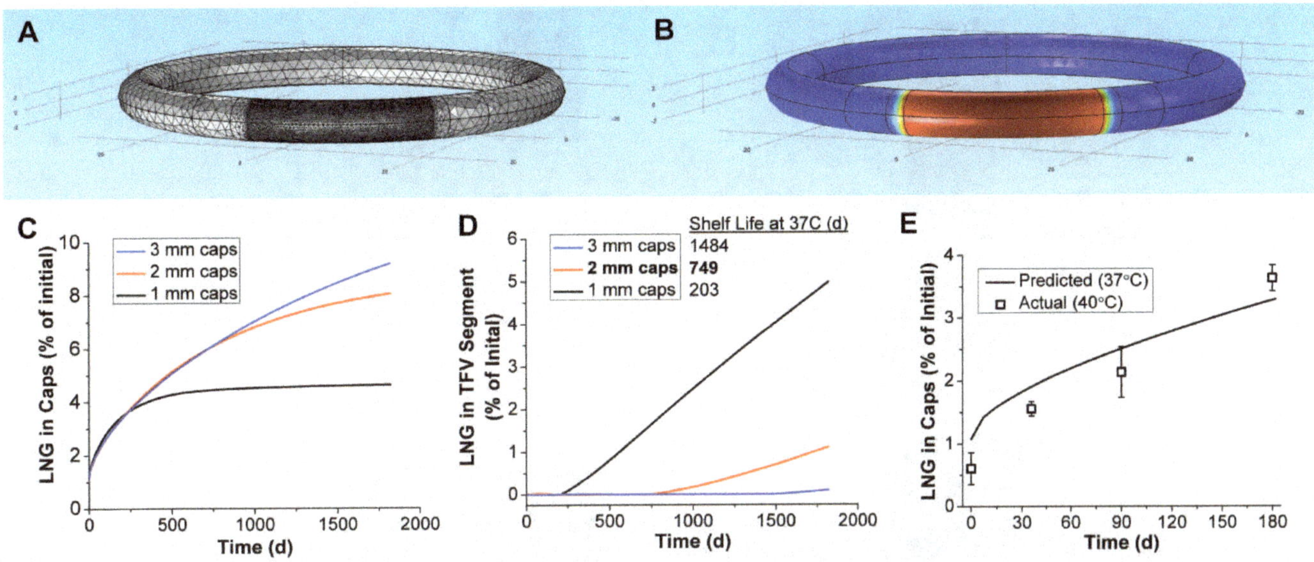

Figure 6. Prevention of LNG diffusion between segments by PEU end-caps. An example (A) finite-element mesh and (B) outer surface model result from the IVR storage diffusion model. The model result represents approximately 2 years storage at 37°C for an IVR with 2 mm length PEU-2 end-caps, where red represents maximum scaled LNG concentration, and blue represents zero LNG. Quantitative results show LNG leakage into the (C) end-caps and (D) entire hollow-tube in the TFV segment during storage by volume integrals of the COMSOL model. Shelf life was determined as the last time-point of complete LNG containment (none detected in the TFV segment). (E) Experimental determination of LNG loss into the caps as a function of TFV/LNG IVR (PEU-1/PEU-2 LNG segments) storage time at 40°C and comparison to the COMSOL result for 37°C storage.

additional challenge of welding swellable HPEU (TFV segment) to rigid, non-swellable PEU (capped LNG segments) while maintaining mechanical integrity both in dry and hydrated ring states. To evaluate this, we performed O-ring extension tests (Figures 7A and 7B) on full IVR after production (dry) and subsequent 31 day *in vitro* release testing (hydrated). As shown in Figures 7C and 7D, all IVR (N = 15) in the dry group endured at least 190 mm extension and 250 N (56.2 lbf) load before failure, and 9 of the 15 rings remained intact following extension to the limit of our instrument (approximately 330 mm deformation). IVR in the wet group exhibited extension and tensile load of 141±47 mm and 239±58 N (N = 15, mean ± SD) at failure, with all IVRs enduring at least 74 mm extension and 152 N (34.2 lbf) tensile load before failure. Thus, a reduction in joint integrity was observed when IVR were soaked in aqueous media, however these data demonstrate that the IVR are still mechanically sound and would require intentional and excessive user-applied stress to separate the segments. In the dry group, all observed failures (6 of 15) occurred between the cap and the LNG segment, whereas, in the hydrated group, an equal number of joint failures occurred between the cap and the LNG solid reservoir versus the cap and the TFV tube plug (7 of each). The remaining hydrated ring experienced a HPEU tubing rupture near the tube seal, but at the highest observed load at failure in the hydrated group (354 N/79.6 lbf). Given the mismatch in the HPEU tube, which exhibits 58% equilibrium swelling by mass, and the non-swellable PEU assembly (caps and LNG reservoir), the mechanical joint integrity observed in dry and hydrated IVR is remarkable and illustrates the utility of the PEU/HPEU platform in sophisticated drug delivery systems.

PK testing of the LNG segment in rabbits

Results from the rabbit pharmacokinetic study are shown in Figure 8. Figure 8A depicts *in vitro* LNG release rates from the same batch used in the rabbit study. On average, 10 and 20 mm segments released 12.6 and 26.4 µg LNG per day *in vitro*, respectively, over the 90 day study. Segments consistently released more LNG *in vivo* than *in vitro* as shown in Figure 8B. Release rates were higher *in vivo* for both the 10 and 20 mm segment groups, however this disparity was diminished in the 90-day group with respect to the 28-day group. In fact, when subtracting the average *in vivo* cumulative LNG release of the 28-day group from the 90-day group, the result was very similar to the time-averaged *in vitro* release rate in both groups (10 mm: 13.5 *in vivo* vs. 12.0 µg/day *in vitro*, 20 mm: 24.0 *in vivo* vs. 25.3 µg/day *in vitro*). This indicates that a higher burst release of LNG occurred *in vivo* than *in vitro*, but that the eventual steady-state regime profile was nearly identical. In all cases, average release rates varied nearly two-fold *in vivo* between the 10 mm and 20 mm segment groups.

LNG plasma results, presented in Figure 8C, strengthened the observation of an additional burst not detected *in vitro*. An approximately 3-fold drop was observed in plasma LNG concentration from the 4 hour to the 7 day time point, while levels remained relatively stable from day 7 to day 28. Plasma levels also dropped markedly from day 28 to day 44 (25% in the 10 mm group and 37% in the 20 mm group), but this may be due to anatomical differences in the two animal groups as plasma was collected from the 28 day group for the first 28 days, and from the 90 day group from day 44 to day 90. Comparatively, plasma levels stabilized from day 44 onward. It is worth noting that test subject body masses increased 14% and 16% over 90 days in the 10 mm and 20 mm test groups, respectively. This may have caused additional attenuation of plasma profiles not expected from the *in vitro* release rate profiles alone. Mean plasma AUC_{0-28} values of 110421 and 218315 pg*hr/mL (ratio: 1.98) and AUC_{44-90} values of 154726 and 261354 pg*hr/mL (ratio: 1.69) were calculated for the 10 mm and 20 mm segment groups, respectively, indicating a dose dependent pharmacokinetic response. This and the agreement of *in vitro* and *in vivo* release rates between day 28 and day 90 suggest that sink conditions exist for LNG *in vivo*, allowing for

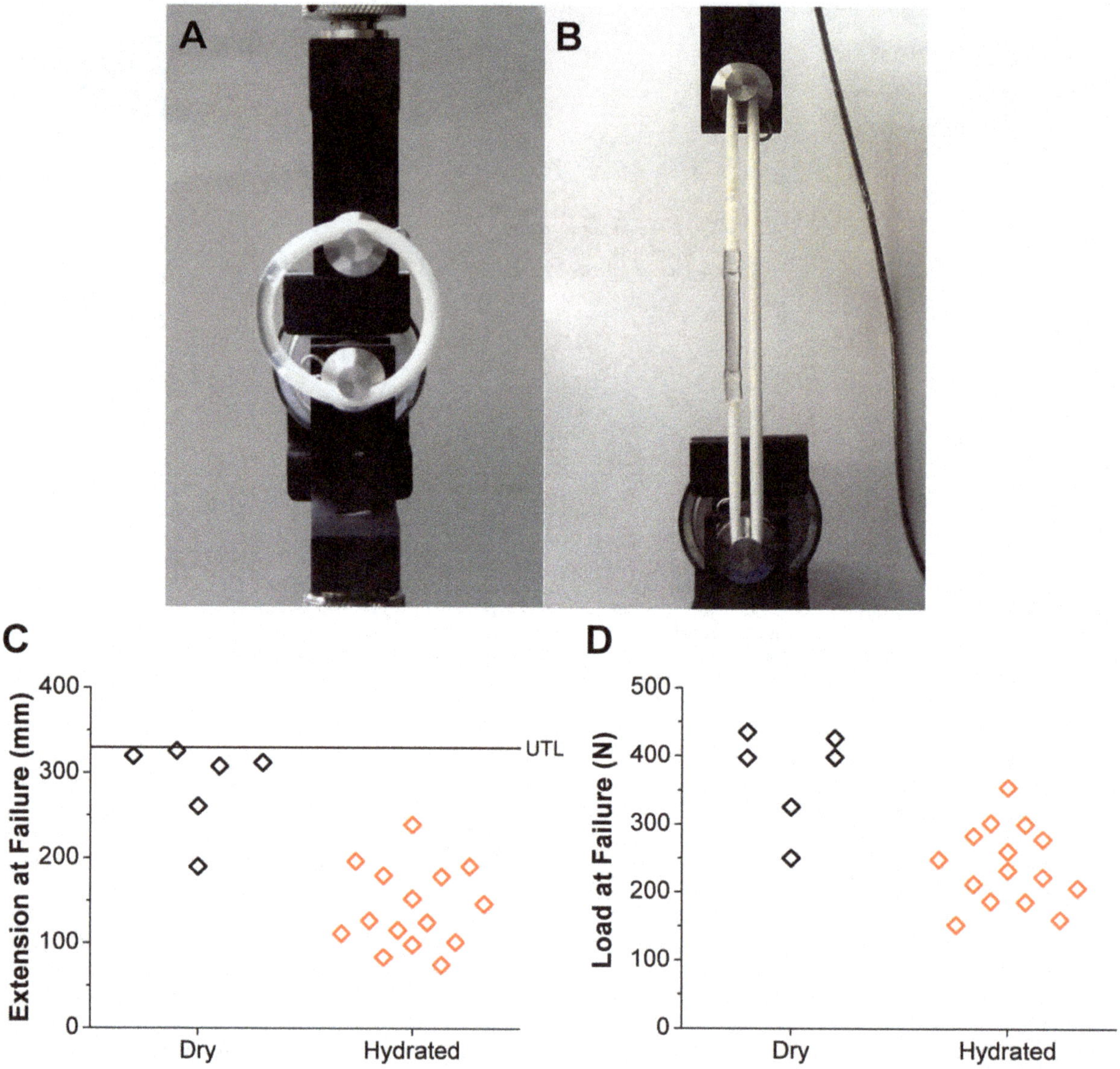

Figure 7. IVR extension testing. (A,B) Extension testing of a full TFV/LNG IVR to 101 mm extension and 145 N (32.6 lbf) load. (C) Extension and (D) load at TFV/LNG IVR both before ("dry") and after ("hydrated") 31 day *in vitro* release testing (N = 15 IVR per group). Nine of the 15 IVR in the dry group did not fail below the upper test limit (UTL, ~330 mm extension).

direct control of LNG pharmacokinetics through polymer selection and device geometry.

Since topical microdose progestin contraception is achieved largely through local effects [45], the pharmacokinetic profile of LNG concentration in the cervical tissue are a potentially more important predictor of eventual device performance. Figure 8D depicts LNG concentrations in cervical tissues collected at day 28 or day 90. Some samples in the 10 mm groups were below the limit of quantification (0.75 ng LNG/g tissue), which hindered a detailed analysis of the data. However, the median value differed two-fold between the 10 and 20 mm groups on day 28 (4.01 vs. 2.02 ng/g), providing further evidence of dose-dependent PK. Also, LNG levels did not differ significantly between tissues taken on day 28 or day 90 ($p = 0.10$, two-tailed, heteroscedastic t-test), confirming near-zero-order LNG release *in vivo* following the burst.

The rabbit model is useful for early *in vivo* testing of vaginal delivery systems [27,41], although rabbit vaginal histology varies greatly from that of the human vaginal vault. Furthermore, the exact magnitude of the plasma profile is likely of little significance as LNG pharmacokinetics will vary between species [46]. However, this study confirmed that near zero-order behavior was achieved *in vivo* following the burst period, and that two biologically distinct LNG doses were in fact achieved from the 10 mm and 20 mm length devices.

Conclusions

Multi-purpose drug delivery systems will need to deliver a physically and chemically diverse set of molecules to target an equally diverse set of indications. Accordingly, there is a need for polymeric materials with a range of properties that are equally chemically diverse. Through successful use of HPEU and PEU in the same device, we have demonstrated that biomedical polyurethanes have potential to fulfill this need for many multi-functional IVR formulations. We have described the design and engineering

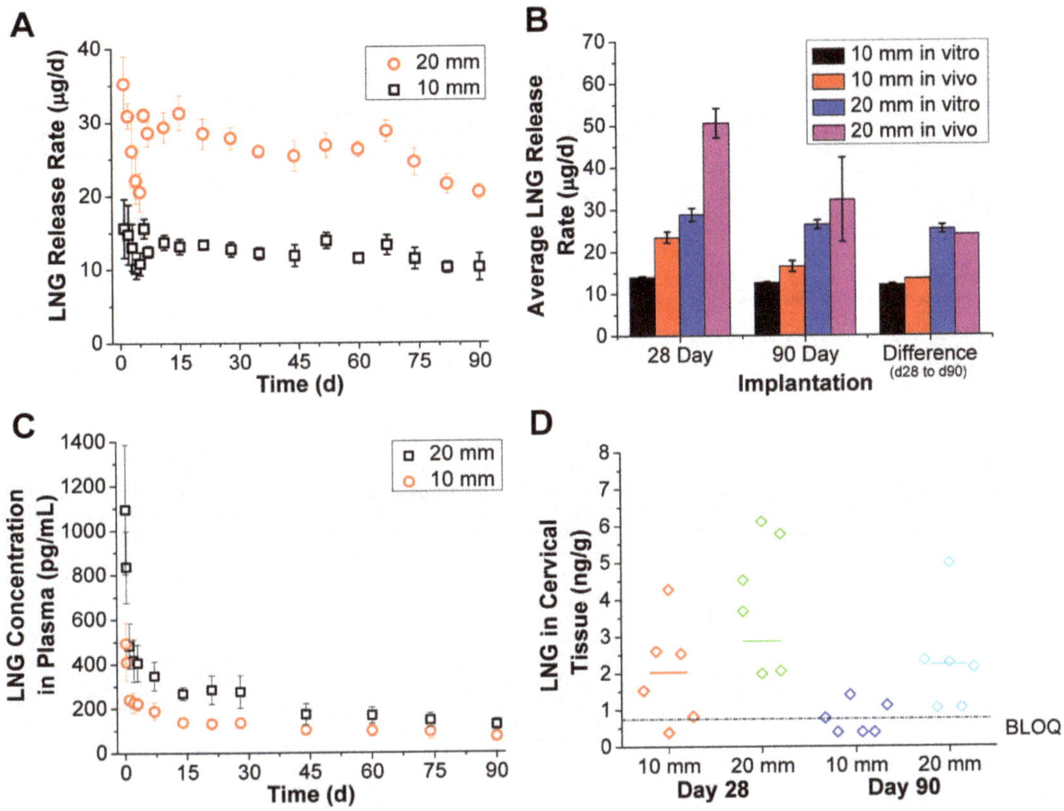

Figure 8. LNG pharmacokinetics in a rabbit model. Pharmacokinetic (PK) testing of end-capped 10 or 20 mm PEU-1/PEU-2 LNG segments in New Zealand white rabbits. (A) Parallel *in vitro* release data for the same LNG segment lot used in the study and (B) comparison with *in vivo* data for the 28 and 90 day study groups. A subtraction of the mean LNG recovery between study groups was performed to directly compare *in vitro* and *in vivo* behavior from day 28 to day 90. (C) Plasma LNG levels measured during the rabbit PK study for 10 and 20 mm LNG segment implantations. (D) Individual and median (bar) LNG levels determined from extractions of cervical tissue. Some samples in the 10 mm study groups were below quantification (BLOQ: <0.750 ng LNG per g tissue). BLOQ data points are graphed as LOQ/2 (0.375 ng/g). *In vitro* data represents N = 5, mean ± SD and *in vivo* data represents N = 6, mean ± SD (except for the *in vivo* "difference" data points, which are subtractions of mean values).

of a two-segment, dual-reservoir TFV/LNG IVR, with focus on the LNG segment, its incorporation into the full device, and the evaluation of its performance using a combination of *in silico*, *in vitro* and *in vivo* methodologies. Our two-stage, mechanistic drug release model provides an improvement to existing models of cylindrical reservoirs with dissolved drug in the literature and enabled the rational design of the long duration LNG segment. We demonstrated the near-zero-order release of LNG at clinically relevant levels both *in vitro* and *in vivo*. We have also presented design challenges specific to this system, including the prevention of drug diffusion between compartments during long-term storage. Through extension testing we have shown the IVR to be mechanically sound in both the dry and hydrated states. This IVR is the first long-acting multifunctional drug delivery system in clinical development and may prove to be an important advancement for women to control their reproductive health. The co-delivery of two drugs as physicochemically diverse as TFV and LNG and at such different release rates, sustained for 90 days, demonstrates the adaptability of this dual-reservoir polyurethane technology. The platform is easily configured to deliver other drugs [12] and a wide range of doses or combinations for other women's heath challenges.

Supporting Information

File S1 Supporting Information.

Acknowledgments

The rabbit PK study and bioanalysis were performed at MPI Research Inc. under the supervision of M. Melissa Peet and Devon Kyle.

Author Contributions

Conceived and designed the experiments: JTC MRC TJJ DRF PFK. Performed the experiments: JTC NBS TJJ EMS AKA JSN JF. Analyzed the data: JTC MRC PFK. Wrote the paper: JTC MRC PFK.

References

1. Folkers GK, Fauci AS (2010) Controlling and ultimately ending the HIV/AIDS pandemic: a feasible goal. JAMA 304: 350–351.
2. Baeten JM, Donnell D, Ndase P, Mugo NR, Campbell JD, et al. (2012) Antiretroviral prophylaxis for HIV prevention in heterosexual men and women. N Engl J Med 367: 399–410.
3. Abdool Karim Q, Abdool Karim SS, Frohlich JA, Grobler AC, Baxter C, et al. (2010) Effectiveness and Safety of Tenofovir Gel, an Antiretroviral Microbicide, for the Prevention of HIV Infection in Women. Science 329: 1168–1174.
4. Marrazzo J, Ramjee G, Nair G, Palanee T, Mkhize B, et al. (2013) Pre-exposure Prophylaxis for HIV in Women: Daily Oral Tenofovir, Oral Tenofovir/

Emtricitabine, or Vaginal Tenofovir Gel in the VOICE Study (MTN 003) (Paper 26LB). 20th Conference on Retroviruses and Opportunistic Infections. Atlanta, Georgia.

5. Heneine W, Kashuba A (2012) HIV prevention by oral preexposure prophylaxis. Cold Spring Harbor Perspect Med 2: a007419/007411-a007419/007413.
6. Shattock RJ, Rosenberg Z (2012) Microbicides: topical prevention against HIV. Cold Spring Harbor Perspect Med 2: a007385/007381-a007385/007317.
7. Friend DR, Kiser PF (2013) Assessment of topical microbicides to prevent HIV-1 transmission: Concepts, testing, lessons learned. Antiviral Res 99: 391–400.
8. Hankins CA, Dybul MR (2013) The promise of pre-exposure prophylaxis with antiretroviral drugs to prevent HIV transmission: a review. Curr Opin HIV AIDS 8: 50–58.
9. van der Straten A, Van Damme L, Haberer JE, Bangsberg DR (2012) Unraveling the divergent results of pre-exposure prophylaxis trials for HIV prevention. AIDS 26: F13–19.
10. Dobard C, Sharma S, Martin A, Pau CP, Holder A, et al. (2012) Durable protection from vaginal simian-human immunodeficiency virus infection in macaques by tenofovir gel and its relationship to drug levels in tissue. J Virol 86: 718–725.
11. Singer R, Mawson P, Derby N, Rodriguez A, Kizima L, et al. (2012) An intravaginal ring that releases the NNRTI MIV-150 reduces SHIV transmission in macaques. Sci Transl Med 4: 150ra123.
12. Smith JM, Rastogi R, Teller RS, Srinivasan P, Mesquita PMM, et al. (2013) An intravaginal ring eluting tenofovir disoproxil fumarate completely protects macaques from multiple vaginal SHIV challenges. Proc Natl Acad Sci 110: 16145–16150.
13. Skoler-Karpoff S, Ramjee G, Ahmed K, Altini L, Plagianos MG, et al. (2008) Efficacy of Carraguard for prevention of HIV infection in women in South Africa: a randomised, double-blind, placebo-controlled trial. Lancet 372: 1977–1987.
14. Iskedjian M, Einarson TR, MacKeigan LD, Shear N, Addis A, et al. (2002) Relationship between daily dose frequency and adherence to antihypertensive pharmacotherapy: evidence from a meta-analysis. Clin Ther 24: 302–316.
15. Kruk ME, Schwalbe N (2006) The relation between intermittent dosing and adherence: preliminary insights. Clin Ther 28: 1989–1995.
16. Andrews C, Gettie A, Russell-Lodrigue K, Moss L, Mohri H, et al. (2013) Long-acting parenteral formulation of GSK1265744 protects macaques against repeated intrarectal challenges with SHIV (Paper 24LB). 20th Conference on Retroviruses and Opportunistic Infections. Atlanta, Georgia.
17. Kiser PF, Johnson TJ, Clark JT (2012) State of the art in intravaginal ring technology for topical prophylaxis of HIV infection. AIDS Rev 14: 62–77.
18. Fetherston SM, Malcolm RK, Woolfson AD (2010) Controlled-release vaginal ring drug-delivery systems: a key strategy for the development of effective HIV miçrobicides. Therapeutic Delivery 1: 785–802.
19. Malcolm RK, Fetherston SM (2013) Delivering on MPTs: addressing the needs, rising to the challenges and making the opportunities. Contraception 88: 321–325.
20. Friend DR (2012) Drug delivery in multiple indication (multipurpose) prevention technologies: systems to prevent HIV-1 transmission and unintended pregnancies or HSV-2 transmission. Expert Opin Drug Delivery 9: 417–427.
21. Friend DR (2011) Intravaginal rings: controlled release systems for contraception and prevention of transmission of sexually transmitted infections. Drug Delivery Transl Res 1: 185–193.
22. Wertheimer AI (2013) The economics of polypharmacology: fixed dose combinations and drug cocktails. Curr Med Chem 20: 1635–1638.
23. Connor J, Rafter N, Rodgers A (2004) Do fixed-dose combination pills or unit-of-use packaging improve adherence? A systematic review. Bull World Health Organ 82: 935–939.
24. Koetsawang S, Ji G, Krishna U, Cuadros A, Dhall GI, et al. (1990) Microdose intravaginal levonorgestrel contraception: a multicentre clinical trial. I. Contraceptive efficacy and side effects. World Health Organization. Task Force on Long-Acting Systemic Agents for Fertility Regulation. Contraception 41: 105–124.
25. Johnson TJ, Clark MR, Albright TH, Nebeker JS, Tuitupou AL, et al. (2012) A 90-day tenofovir reservoir intravaginal ring for mucosal HIV prophylaxis. Antimicrob Agents Chemother 56: 6272–6283.
26. Clark JT, Johnson TJ, Clark MR, Nebeker JS, Fabian J, et al. (2012) Quantitative evaluation of a hydrophilic matrix intravaginal ring for the sustained delivery of tenofovir. J Control Release 163: 240–248.
27. Clark MR, Johnson TJ, McCabe RT, Clark JT, Tuitupou A, et al. (2012) A hot-melt extruded intravaginal ring for the sustained delivery of the antiretroviral microbicide UC781. J Pharm Sci 101: 576–587.
28. Malcolm K, Woolfson D, Russell J, Tallon P, McAuley L, et al. (2003) Influence of silicone elastomer solubility and diffusivity on the in vitro release of drugs from intravaginal rings. Journal of Controlled Release 90: 217–225.
29. Nel A, Smythe S, Young K, Malcolm K, McCoy C, et al. (2009) Safety and pharmacokinetics of dapivirine delivery from matrix and reservoir intravaginal rings to HIV-negative women. Journal of acquired immune deficiency syndromes 51: 416–423.
30. Johnson TJ, Srinivasan P, Albright TH, Watson-Buckheit K, Rabe L, et al. (2012) Safe and sustained vaginal delivery of pyrimidinedione HIV-1 inhibitors from polyurethane intravaginal rings. Antimicrob Agents Chemother 56: 1291–1299.
31. Johnson TJ, Gupta KM, Fabian J, Albright TH, Kiser PF (2010) Segmented polyurethane intravaginal rings for the sustained combined delivery of antiretroviral agents dapivirine and tenofovir. Eur J Pharm Sci 39: 203–212.
32. Mesquita PM, Rastogi R, Segarra TJ, Teller RS, Torres NM, et al. (2012) Intravaginal ring delivery of tenofovir disoproxil fumarate for prevention of HIV and herpes simplex virus infection. J Antimicrob Chemother 67: 1730–1738.
33. Gupta KM, Pearce SM, Poursaid AE, Aliyar HA, Tresco PA, et al. (2008) Polyurethane intravaginal ring for controlled delivery of dapivirine, a nonnucleoside reverse transcriptase inhibitor of HIV-1. J Pharm Sci 97: 4228–4239.
34. van Laarhoven JA, Kruft MA, Vromans H (2002) In vitro release properties of etonogestrel and ethinyl estradiol from a contraceptive vaginal ring. Int J Pharm 232: 163–173.
35. Saltzman WM (2001) Engineering principles for drug therapy. New York: Oxford University Press.
36. van Laarhoven JA, Kruft MA, Vromans H (2002) Effect of supersaturation and crystallization phenomena on the release properties of a controlled release device based on EVA copolymer. J Control Release 82: 309–317.
37. Siepmann J, Siepmann F (2008) Mathematical modeling of drug delivery. Int J Pharm 364: 328–343.
38. Helbling IM, Luna JA, Cabrera MI (2011) Mathematical modeling of drug delivery from torus-shaped single-layer devices. J Control Release 149: 258–263.
39. Vergnaud J (1993) Controlled Drug Release of Oral Dosage Forms. Boca Raton: CRC Press.
40. Siepmann J, Siepmann F (2012) Modeling of diffusion controlled drug delivery. J Control Release 161: 351–362.
41. Clark MR, Kiser PF, Loxley A, McConville C, Malcolm RK, et al. (2011) Pharmacokinetics of UC781-loaded intravaginal ring segments in rabbits: a comparison of polymer matrices. Drug Delivery and Translational Research 1: 238–246.
42. Szycher M (1985) Extrudable Polyurethane for Prothetic Devices Prepared from a Diisocyanate, a Polytetramethylene Ehter Polyol, and 1,4-Butane Diol. United States Patent 4,523,005.
43. Elabd YA, Sloan JM, Tan NB, Barbari TA (2001) Effect of Penetrant–Polymer Interactions on Molecular Diffusion in Conformational Isomers of a Heterogeneous Polymer. Macromolecules 34: 6268–6273.
44. Kiser PF, Johnson TJ, Clark JT, Shelke N, Rastogi R (2013) Intravaginal Devices for Drug Delivery. WO Patent Application PCT/US2012/047649.
45. Rose S, Chaudhari A, Peterson CM (2009) Mirena (Levonorgestrel intrauterine system): a successful novel drug delivery option in contraception. Adv Drug Deliv Rev 61: 808–812.
46. Dusterberg B, Humpel M, Speck U (1981) Terminal half-lives in plasma and bioavailability of norethisterone, levonorgestrel, cyproterone acetate and gestodene in rats, beagles and rhesus monkeys. Contraception 24: 673–683.

17

Bimatoprost-Loaded Ocular Inserts as Sustained Release Drug Delivery Systems for Glaucoma Treatment: *In Vitro* and *In Vivo* Evaluation

Juçara Ribeiro Franca[1], Giselle Foureaux[2], Leonardo Lima Fuscaldi[3], Tatiana Gomes Ribeiro[1], Lívia Bomfim Rodrigues[1], Renata Bravo[1], Rachel Oliveira Castilho[1], Maria Irene Yoshida[4], Valbert Nascimento Cardoso[3], Simone Odília Fernandes[3], Sebastião Cronemberger[5], Anderson José Ferreira[2], André Augusto Gomes Faraco[1]*

1 Department of Pharmaceutical Products, Federal University of Minas Gerais, Belo Horizonte, Minas Gerais, Brazil, **2** Department of Morphology, Federal University of Minas Gerais, Belo Horizonte, Minas Gerais, Brazil, **3** Department of Clinical and Toxicological Analysis, Federal University of Minas Gerais, Belo Horizonte, Minas Gerais, Brazil, **4** Department of Chemistry, Federal University of Minas Gerais, Belo Horizonte, Minas Gerais, Brazil, **5** Department of Ophthalmology and Otolaryngology, Federal University of Minas Gerais, Belo Horizonte, Minas Gerais, Brazil

Abstract

The purpose of the present study was to develop and assess a novel sustained-release drug delivery system of Bimatoprost (BIM). Chitosan polymeric inserts were prepared using the solvent casting method and characterized by swelling studies, infrared spectroscopy, differential scanning calorimetry, drug content, scanning electron microscopy and *in vitro* drug release. Biodistribution of ^{99m}Tc-BIM eye drops and ^{99m}Tc-BIM-loaded inserts, after ocular administration in Wistar rats, was accessed by *ex vivo* radiation counting. The inserts were evaluated for their therapeutic efficacy in glaucomatous Wistar rats. Glaucoma was induced by weekly intracameral injection of hyaluronic acid. BIM-loaded inserts (equivalent to 9.0 µg BIM) were administered once into conjunctival sac, after ocular hypertension confirmation. BIM eye drop was topically instilled in a second group of glaucomatous rats for 15 days days, while placebo inserts were administered once in a third group. An untreated glaucomatous group was used as control. Intraocular pressure (IOP) was monitored for four consecutive weeks after treatment began. At the end of the experiment, retinal ganglion cells and optic nerve head cupping were evaluated in the histological eye sections. Characterization results revealed that the drug physically interacted, but did not chemically react with the polymeric matrix. Inserts sustainedly released BIM *in vitro* during 8 hours. Biodistribution studies showed that the amount of ^{99m}Tc-BIM that remained in the eye was significantly lower after eye drop instillation than after chitosan insert implantation. BIM-loaded inserts lowered IOP for 4 weeks, after one application, while IOP values remained significantly high for the placebo and untreated groups. Eye drops were only effective during the daily treatment period. IOP results were reflected in RGC counting and optic nerve head cupping damage. BIM-loaded inserts provided sustained release of BIM and seem to be a promising system for glaucoma management.

Editor: Thomas Claudepierre, Université de Lorraine, France

Funding: The authors are grateful to PRPq-UFMG, CNPq (for Development Technologic fellowship and financial support), CAPES and FAPEMIG for their financial support. The funders had no role in study design, data collection and analysis, decision to publish, or preparation of the manuscript.

Competing Interests: The authors have declared that no competing interests exist.

* E-mail: andrefaraco@ufmg.br

Introduction

Glaucoma is an ocular disorder with multi-factorial etiology, characterized by a slow progressive degeneration of retinal ganglion cells (RGC) and optic nerve axons [1,2]. The disease is the second leading cause of blindness and, worldwide, it is estimated that about 66.8 million people have contracted some form of visual impairment from glaucoma, with 6.7 million suffering from blindness [3–5]. The most important risk factor for glaucoma is intraocular pressure (IOP) elevation; progressive visual loss is associated with increased IOP, which damages the optic nerve [6–8]. Primary open-angle glaucoma (POAG) is the most common type of glaucoma [9]. In POAG it is not possible to establish a clinical cause to neurodegeneration or to IOP elevation [10,11]. POAG therapy usually begins with medications [3].

Prostaglandin analogs have become the first therapeutic class of choice for medical treatment of POAG because of their improved efficacy and tolerability [12,13]. Prostaglandin analogs are able to control IOP, primarily by increasing uveoscleral outflow via remodeling of the ciliary body [14]. Bimatoprost (BIM) is a prostaglandin analog chemically related to prostamide $F_{2\alpha}$ [15]. The mechanism of IOP lowering induced by BIM is not completely understood. Some authors suggest that BIM is an agonist to "prostamide" receptor [16–18], while another study in human eye tissues has shown that BIM is rapidly hydrolyzed in cornea, iris, sclera, and ciliary muscle to its corresponding 17-phenyl-prostaglandin $F_{2\alpha}$ metabolite (free acid), known to be active at the prostaglandin F receptor [19]. Another recent work also suggested that both BIM and its metabolite promote protective effects on the RCG against oxidative stress [14].

Eye drops are still the mainstay eye disease management, accounting for approximately 90% of all ophthalmic treatments. Nevertheless, only 1% to 7% of the administered drugs actually reach the aqueous humor [20–22]. The inefficiency of this route stems mainly from the precorneal tear clearance mechanism, the highly selective corneal epithelial barrier, and patient compliance, a factor that is quite unpredictable and difficult to control [22]. Clinically, in glaucomatous patients, variable bioavailability of the active ingredients results in diurnal IOP fluctuation [23]. Moreover, patients tend to present inadequate adherence to their daily therapeutic regimen [23]. Altogether, these factors may result in therapeutic inefficacy and progression of the glaucoma damage. Therefore, the development of new vehicles and drug formulations that require less patient effort and enhance the drug bioavailability represent an important aspect in controlling the evolution this disease [22].

Sustained-release drug delivery systems have been developed to overcome eye drops limitations [24]. These systems can achieve prolonged therapeutic drug concentrations in ocular target tissues, while limiting systemic exposure and side effects and improving patient adherence to therapy [25]. Ocular inserts are solid or semi-solid devices meant to be placed in the conjunctival sac (between the lower eyelid and the eye itself) to deliver drugs on the ocular surface [26]. These devices are designed to release the drug at a constant rate for a prolonged time while minimizing systemic absorption through the nasal mucosa and improving patient compliance due to a reduced frequency of administration. Inserts are often matrix based and made of degradable polymers, such as Chitosan (CS) [22,27].

CS is a natural carbohydrate polymer, has number of applications in the field of ophthalmics and has attracted a great deal of attention from the scientific community and environmentalists due to its unique features [28]. CS is a biodegradable, nontoxic, and biocompatible polymer [29], which can enhance the intraocular bioavailability of both hydrophilic and lipophilic drugs [29,30]. Moreover, CS is a promising mucoadhesive material in physiological pH [31–34]. Due to interactions with the mucus layer or the eye tissues, an increase in the precorneal residence time of the preparation can be observed, leading to an increase in the bioavailability of the drug instilled [21]. Thus, mucoadhesive ocular inserts (such as CS-based inserts) could increase the precorneal drug retention (to delay washout), which may result in an enhanced formulation bioavailability.

In this regard, to improve patient compliance by lowering the frequency of administration and to enhance therapeutic effectiveness of glaucoma medical treatment, this research aimed at formulating, physicochemically and *in vivo* evaluating CS-based inserts for a sustained release of BIM, which were able to lower IOP over four weeks after one application, without causing any damage to the animals.

Materials and Methods

Materials

Medium molecular weight CS and Bimatoprost were supplied by Sigma-Aldrich. All other reagents were of analytical grade.

Preparation of BIM-loaded inserts

Inserts were prepared as monolayer films by employing the solvent/casting technique, according to Rodrigues *et al.* [35]. First, 75 μL of acetic acid was added to 5 mL of an aqueous solution containing 1.5 mg of BIM homogeneously dissolved. Next, 250 mg of CS was added in this solution. This viscous dispersion was magnetically stirred overnight to ensure homogeneity of both drug and polymer. Then, it was cast, at room temperature, in circular silicone-molded trays (SMT) containing individual 5 mm×2 mm wells [36] to produce BIM-loaded insert (BI). After casting, inserts were carefully removed from the SMT and stored in receptacles, protected from light and air humidity. Placebo inserts (PI) were produced in a similar manner, by adding 250 mg of CS to 5 mL of a solution containing 75 μL of acetic acid in water.

Characterization studies

Swelling studies. Inserts swelling studies were carried out in a phosphate buffer solution (pH 7.4) (PBS). Each insert was weighed and placed in PBS for predetermined periods of time (5, 10, 20, 40, 60, and 90 min) as described by Eroglu *et al.* [37]. After immersion, the inserts were removed from the medium, the excess surface water was removed by using filter paper, and the pieces were weighed. The degree of swelling was calculated by using the equation: $Swelling index = [(W_t - W_0)/W_0]$. [38].

The weight of the swollen insert after predetermined periods of time (t) is represented by W_t. The original weight of the insert at zero time is represented by W_0. This experiment was performed in triplicate.

ATR-FTIR analysis. Attenuated Total Reflectance Fourier Transformed Infrared spectroscopy (ATR-FTIR) spectra of all the inserts and of the original polymer powders were recorded on a PerkinElmer FTIR Spectrometer, Model Spectrum One (USA).

DSC analysis. Thermal properties of the inserts were also evaluated. Differential Scanning Calorimetry (DSC) measurements were carried out in a Shimadzu DSC50. Samples (inserts, powder CS, and powder HEC) were packed in an aluminum crucible and heated at a rate of 10°C/min. Nitrogen, at the rate of 20 mL/min was used as a purge gas during the role analysis. The specimens were heated from −50°C to 200°C (RUN 1). The specimens were then cooled to −50°C at the same rate of 10°C/min, at which point they were reheated to 400°C at a rate of 10°C/min (RUN 2).

SEM analysis. The inserts morphology was studied using a JEOL scanning electron microscope (SEM), model JSM-6360LV, operating at 15 kV. The samples were prepared by freezing the inserts in liquid nitrogen. Then, the inserts were fractured. Next, the surface and sides of the inserts were analyzed. The devices were analyzed at suitable acceleration voltages using varying magnification for each sample. Representative micrographs were also taken.

Determination of BIM. The high performance liquid chromatography (HPLC) method was chosen to quantify the amount of BIM loaded in the inserts. A Waters HPLC with Pump Control Module (PCM II), a Binary Pump System Waters 515 CLAE Pump, a Waters 717 Plus Autosampler, and a Waters 486 Turnable Absorbance Detector were used. Merck Column Lichro CART 100 (ODS) of 250×4.6 mm, with a particle size of 5 μm, was used for the stationary phase at room temperature. The mobile phase, at a flow rate of 1.0 mL/min, was comprised of methanol/acetonitrile/phosphoric acid at 0.1 vol% (30:30:40), and detection was performed at 210 nm. The solvents were HPLC grade (Tédia Brazil). Samples were dissolved in PBS. After filtration on a 0.45 μm membrane made of regenerated cellulose (Sartorius, Sweden), 20 μL of the samples were automatically injected into the apparatus. The method was validated in accordance with ICH guidelines. BIM, at a concentration of 3.0–15 μg/mL in PBS, was used as a standard solution (phosphate buffer solution, pH 7.4) ($y = 26433.5x + 880.449$, $R^2 = 0.9994$; $n = 3$).

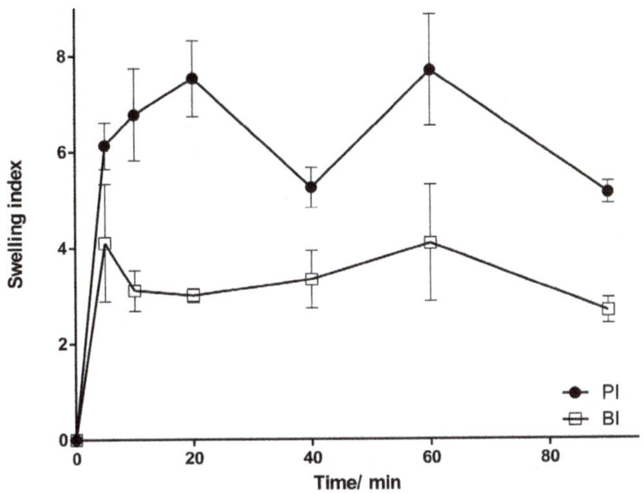

Figure 1. Swelling index of PI and BI in a buffered solution medium (PBS; pH 7.4). Values expressed as mean ± SD.

Drug Content uniformity. Drug Content uniformity was performed according to Brazilian Pharmacopeia [39]. Each ocular insert was hydrated with 100 µL of acetic acid. After 30 minutes, 900 µL of water was added to dissolve the insert. The solution was filtered and suitably diluted. The BIM content was analyzed by HPLC. This test was performed on 10 ocular inserts.

***In vitro* drug release.** *In vitro* drug release was evaluated using the Franz cell system. A cellulose acetate membrane with 0.45 µm pores was used to split the insert compartment from the receptor liquid compartment. PBS was used as a receptor liquid, and the glass cells were incubated at 37±0.5°C. At appropriate time intervals, all the receptor liquid was withdrawn from the glass cells, and an equal volume of the same receptor liquid was added to maintain a constant volume. The amount of drug released was evaluated by HPLC. The experiment was performed in quintuplicate.

In vivo studies

Animals. Male Wistar rats weighing 180 to 220 g were obtained from the animal facility of the Faculty of Pharmacy, Federal University of Minas Gerais. The animals were housed in a temperature-controlled room (22–23 °C) with a 12–12 h light-dark cycle. Water and food were available *ad libitum.* The experimental protocols were performed and approved in accordance with institutional guidelines by the Ethics Committee in Animal Experimentation of the Federal University of Minas Gerais, Brazil (CETEA-UFMG), which are in accordance with the National Institutes of Health (NIH) Guidelines for the Care and Use of Laboratory Animals (protocols n° 251/11 and 211/13). In addition, this study conforms to the Association for Research in Vision and Ophthalmology (ARVO) statement for the use of animals in ophthalmic and vision research.

Biodistribution studies. Biodistribution studies were based on the administration of free and entrapped BIM, radiolabeled with technetium-99m (^{99m}Tc). The method for ^{99m}Tc labeling of BIM was developed in our laboratory, based on the radiolabeling protocols developed by Nunan et al. [40] and de Barros et al. [41], with modifications. BIM was dissolved in 1.0 mL of phosphate buffer (pH 7.4) and radiolabeled with ^{99m}Tc by direct labeling method using stannous chloride as reducing agent. Purification was processed by the addition of 200 mg of G_{60} silica to the radiolabeled solution. After 15 minutes, suspension was centrifuged at 10,000 rpm during 10 minutes and supernatant was

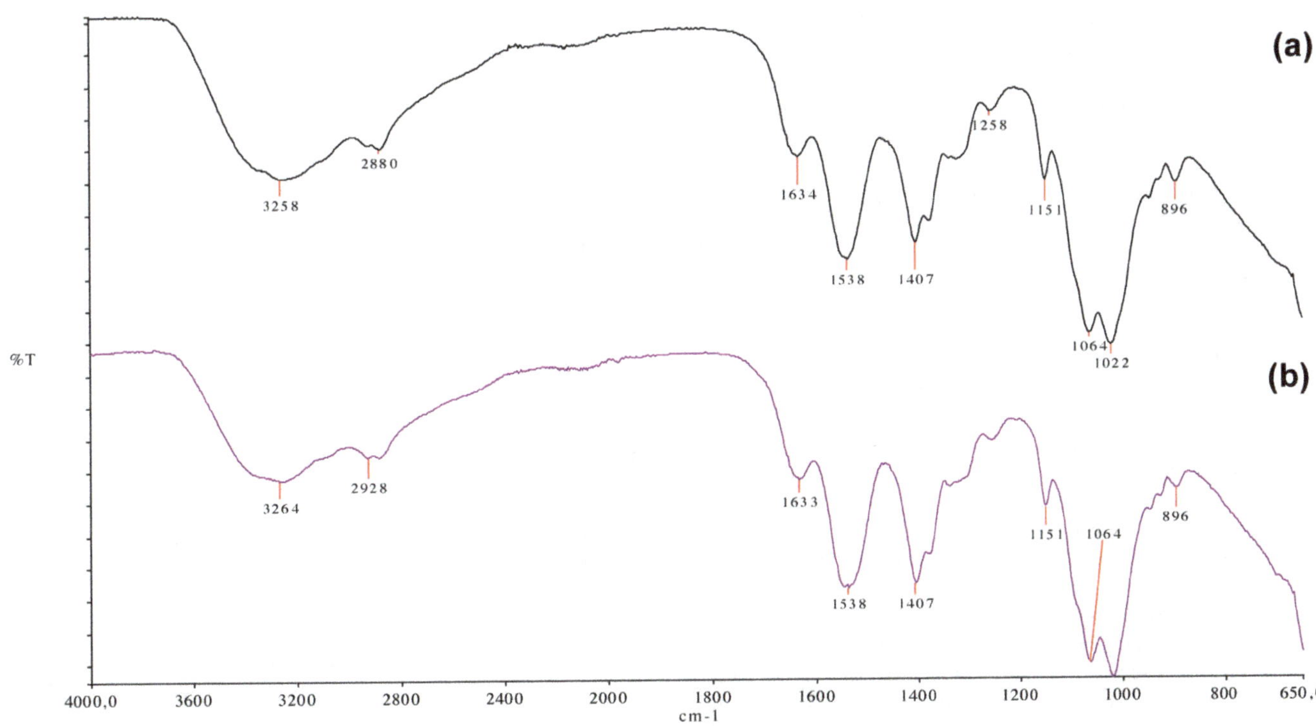

Figure 2. ATR-FTIR spectra of PI (a) and BI (b). BIM shifted first band to a higher frequency (from 3258 to 3264 cm^{-1}) and widened (arrow).

recovered. Radiochemical purity analysis of ^{99m}Tc-BIM was performed by instant thin-layer chromatography on silica gel strips (ITLC-SG, Merck), using a two-solvent system: saline and ethyl acetate/acetone (5:95) to determine the amount of free technetium ($^{99m}TcO_4^-$) and hydrolysed technetium ($^{99m}TcO_2$), respectively. ^{99m}Tc-BIM solution was used to prepare BI as described earlier.

^{99m}Tc-BIM (free and in the insert) was topically administered in the right eye of Wistar rats ($n = 5$), as decribed above. At 8 and 18 hours post-administration, rats were anesthetized intramuscularly with a solution of ketamine (70 mg/Kg) and xylazine (10 mg/Kg) and, then, euthanized. Organs and tissues of interest (spleen, liver, stomach, small and large intestines, kidneys, blood and eyes) were harvested. Then, each organ and tissue was weighed and its associated radioactivity was determined in an automatic gamma counter (Wizard, Finland). The results were expressed as the percentage of radioactivity per gram of tissue (% cpm/g). Data were statistically analyzed by means of unpaired *t test*, using PRISM 5.0 software.

***In vivo* efficacy.** Unilateral glaucoma was induced in the right eye by injection of 30 µL of hyaluronic acid (HA) (10 mg/mL) into the anterior chamber through the clear cornea, near the corneoscleral limbus using an hypodermic needle (22 gauge), once a week, for 6 weeks, on the same calendar day and time, according to Moreno et al. [42]. Rats were anesthetized intramuscularly with ketamine (70 mg/kg) and xylazine (10 mg/kg). In addition, two drops of 0.4% benoxinate hydrochloride were instilled directly on the cornea as a local anesthetic. No procedure was performed in the contralateral eye (control groups). Evaluation of IOP and mean arterial pressure (MAP) were carried out one day before the next HA injection.

BI was placed, once, into the conjunctival sac after the establishment of ocular hypertension (immediately after the second induction). A marketed formulation of BIM eye drops were used as positive control. In this case, animals were treated daily during two weeks. The treatment was also started immediately after the second induction. Untreated animals and PI were used as negative controls. PI was also placed once in the conjunctival sac immediately after the second induction. Five animals were used in each group. Both eyes (sick and healthy) of each animal were submitted to the same treatment. *Inserts* were hydrated with saline for 30 seconds before administration.

IOP measurements were performed using an applanation tonometer TonoPen XL (Mentor, Norwell, MA, USA) which was calibrated before use by an experienced person. A topical anesthetic (benoxinate hydrochloride 0.4%) was applied to each eye prior to the measurement of IOP. To obtain the measures, non-sedated animals (n = 5) were carefully contained with a small cloth and three readings of IOP (with standard error less than 10%) were acquired in each eye. The average of these three measures was considered the corresponding value of IOP. IOP measurements were performed at the same time each day or week (between 11:00 AM and 12:00 PM) to correct diurnal variations in IOP. The tonometrist was masked to the treatment and an assistant performed the randomization process.

Mean arterial pressure (MAP) was evaluated by a tail-cuff method, which is a noninvasive computerized system for measuring blood pressure (Kent Scientific Corporation, Torrington, CT, USA). This tail-cuff blood pressure system utilizes volume pressure recording sensor technology to measure the rat tail blood pressure. The animals (n = 5) were acclimated one day before the beginning of the experiments to restraint and to tail-cuff inflation. The restraint platform was maintained at approximately 32–34°C. For each session the rat was placed in an acrylic box restraint and the tail was inserted into a compression cuff that measured the blood pressure 15 times to calculate the average.

Animals were euthanized and both eye were enucleated for histological analysis. After enucleation, two small sagittal sections were made in each side of the eyes. Then, they were immediately immersed in Bouin's fluid for approximately 24 hours. Thereafter, they were dehydrated in increasing concentrations of ethanol (70, 80, 90, 95 and 100%), diaphanized in xylene, and included and embedded in Paraplast. Semi-serial 6 µm-sections (60 µm of interval) were obtained using a microtome (model HM335E, Microm, Minnesota, USA). For histological analysis and RGC counting, histological sections were stained with hematoxylin-eosin (HE).

Statistical analyses

Data were expressed as mean ± SEM. Comparative results were analyzed using unpaired t test (for Biodistribution) and one-way ANOVA followed by the Tukey post-test (for PIO, MAP and

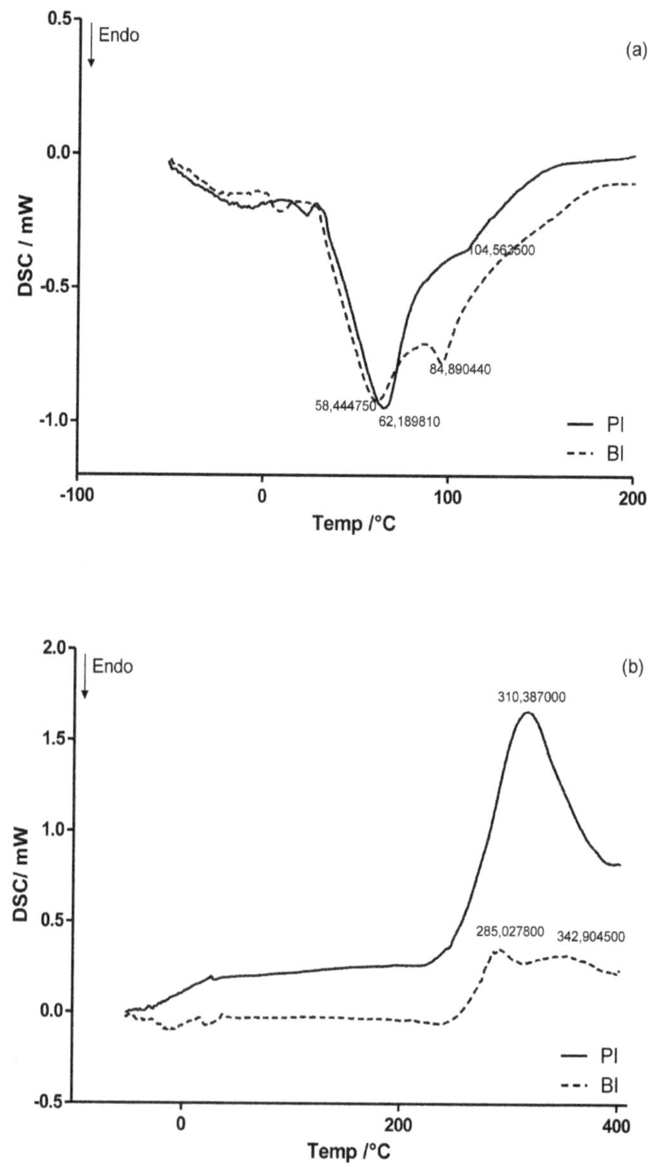

Figure 3. DSC curves of PI and BI. (a) First run; (b) second run.

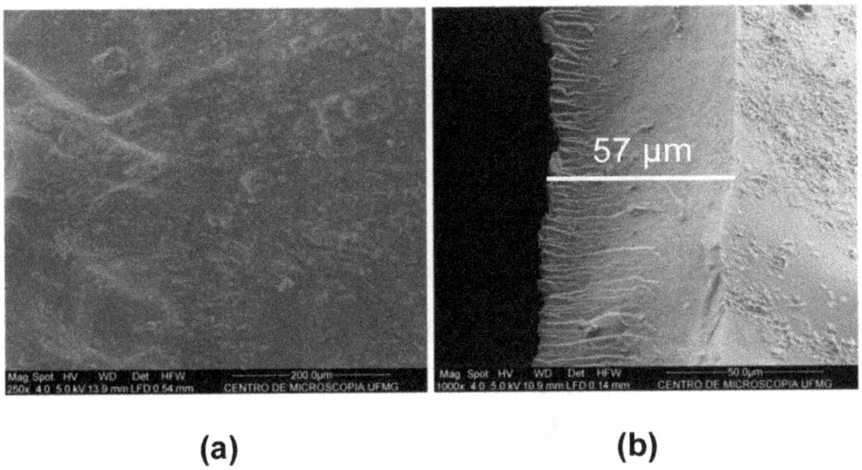

Figure 4. Representative SEM photomicrographs of Bimatoprost-loaded inserts. (a) surface; (b) lateral. Bar indicates the thickness of the insert.

RCG counting). All these tests were performed using the GraphPad Prism 5 software. Results were considered significant at the $p<0.05$ level.

Results

Characterization studies and *in vitro* drug release

Chitosan polymeric inserts were produced as circular flexible films with 5 mm of diameter. Physicochemical interactions between drug and polymeric matrix were evaluated by different techniques. Results of the characterization studies are presented below.

Swelling indexes of inserts are shown in **Fig. 1**. Inserts hydrated very quickly, reaching more than 80% of total hydration in the first 20 min. The effects of BIM on the swelling behavior are also presented in **Fig. 1**. The water soluble drug (BIM) decreased the water uptake of BI, compared to PI. During the accomplishment of the test, the integrity of the tested films was not lost.

Fig. 2 shows the ATR-FTIR spectra PI and BI. In both spectra, two characteristic absorption bands of CS were detected at 1634 and 1538 cm^{-1} and attributed to amide I (C = O stretching) and to N-H (amine) vibration overlapped to amide II (N-H vibration), respectively. In the FTIR spectrum of PI, the wide and overlapped absorption band at 3258 cm^{-1} was due to the stretching vibration of the O-H and N-H bonds [35,43,44]. From the FTIR spectra of BI, it can be seen that the first band shifted to a higher frequency (from 3258 to 3264 cm^{-1}) and widened.

In **Fig. 3** shows the DSC curves of PI and BI. PI presented a broad endothermic peak at 62.19°C, as well as a broad exothermic peak at 310.39°C on the first and second runs, respectively. Both peaks are irregular and can be attributed to an evaporation of residual water and a degradation of the main chain, respectively [35,45,46]. The degradation peak of CS was dismembered and an increase in the degradation temperature from 310.38°C to 342.90°C could be observed when BIM was added to the inserts.

Morphological characterization of inserts was performed by SEM analysis. SEM pictures of PI and BI are shown in **Fig. 4**. From surface images (**Fig. 4 a**), it is possible to notice that inserts showed an irregular surface. However, it is not possible to identify drug crystals in this surface, suggesting the miscibility of the drug in the polymer matrix. Lateral images (**Fig. 4 b**) shows that the insert polymeric matrix is homogeneous, compact, without any kind of crystallized or granular particles and have about 50 µm of thickness.

The drug content in formulations was proved to be uniform. BIM was found at 9.009±0.030 µg/insert. CS inserts reached a controlled-release profile (greater than 4 hours). The **Fig. 5** showed the biphasic kinetic from release to BI. In the first stage it can be observed a burst release and subsequently an extended release of the drug. BI released 100% of the drug in 8 hours.

Biodistribution studies

BIM was radiolabeled with radionuclide Tc-99m for biodistribution studies. The latter was chosen as it emits low-energy gamma rays that do not lead to serious health hazards. BIM was instantaneously labeled with ^{99m}Tc. Radiolabeling procedure can

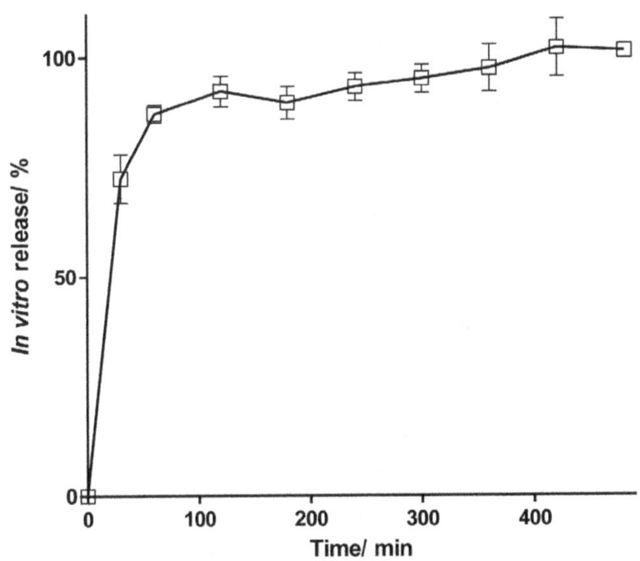

Figure 5. ***In vitro* release profile of BIM from BI.** Values expressed as mean ± SD.

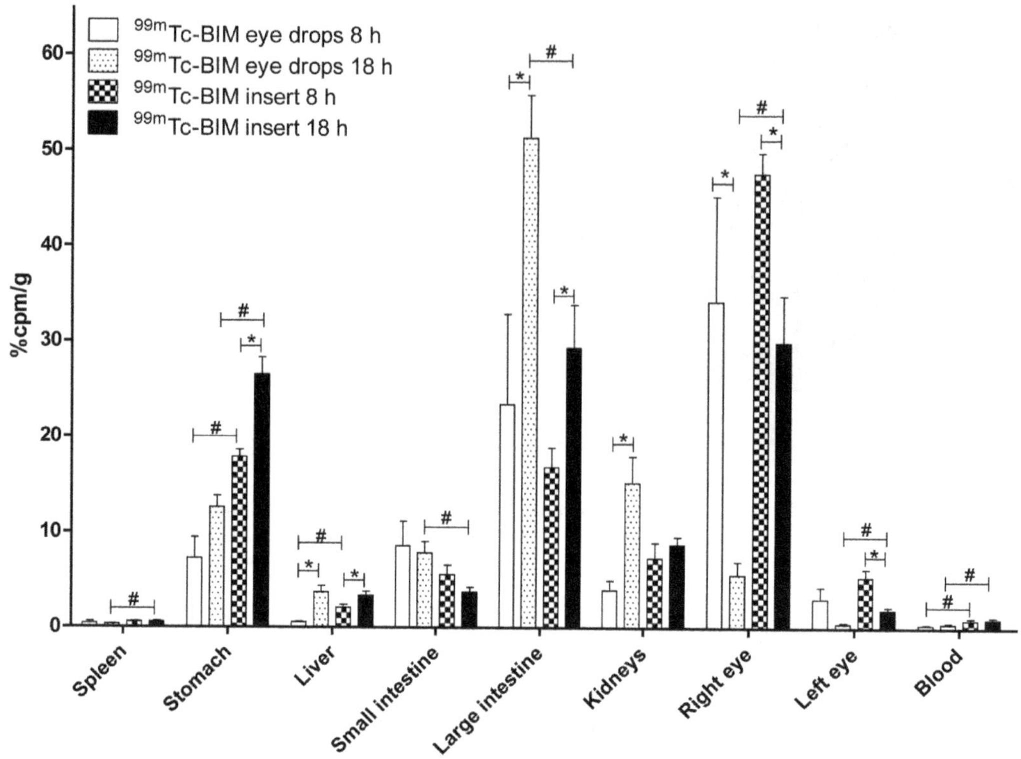

Figure 6. ^{99m}Tc-BIM biodistribution profile after eye drops instillation and chitosan inserts implantation. Values are expressed as 'mean ± SD' ($n = 5$). (*$p<0.05$ for 8 h vs. 18 h and $^{\#}p<0.05$ for eye drops vs. inserts). Unpaired *Student t test.*

yield two mainly radiochemical impurities, free technetium ($^{99m}TcO_4^-$) and hydrolysed technetium ($^{99m}TcO_2$). In both mobile phases, $^{99m}TcO_4^-$ reaches to the top of the ITLC strip ($R_f = 0.9$–1.0), whereas $^{99m}TcO_2$ cannot travel much due to the difference in molecular weight and is retained at the base of the ITLC strip ($R_f = 0.0$). ^{99m}Tc-BIM is a hydrophilic compound, which, similarly to $^{99m}TcO_4^-$,migrates to the top of the ITLC strip with saline and remains at the point of application when ethyl acetate/acetone (5/95) is used as eluent, like $^{99m}TcO_2$. Then, saline was used to determine the amount of $^{99m}TcO_2$, whereas ethyl acetate/acetone (5/95) was used to quantify $^{99m}TcO_4^-$. After preliminary BIM radiolabeling studies, which included the adjustment of labeling parameters, such as the amount of stannous chloride and pH, labeling procedure were optimized and an amount of 20 μg of stannous chloride and a pH of 7.0 were found to give the maximum labeling efficiency (89.38%), after purification.The results showed low levels of radiochemical impurities, allowing for images of better quality.

Results of biodistribution studies are presented in **Fig. 6**. At 8 h post-administration, 34.2±24.8% of ^{99m}Tc-BIM from eye drops and 47.7±4.4% of ^{99m}Tc-BIM from the inserts remained in the right eye. On the other hand, at 18 h, only 5.6±3.1% of ^{99m}Tc-BIM from eye drops persisted in the right eye, whereas 29,9±10,9% of ^{99m}Tc-BIM from the inserts was still present in the application site. In other words, the inserts prolonged retention of ^{99m}Tc-BIM at the corneal site and reduced the extent of nasolacrimal drainage. The ^{99m}Tc-BIM cleaned from the eye after eye drop instillation accumulated preferentially in the large intestine and in the kidneys, while ^{99m}Tc-BIM cleaned from the eye after insert application accumulated preferentially in the stomach and in the large intestine.

In vivo efficacy

The ability of the inserts to controlled release BIM *in vivo* was tested in an experimental model of glaucoma induced by intraocular injection of HA. **Fig. 7** shows the IOP of all experimental groups during the period of 6 weeks (a, glaucomatous eye; b, normal eye). Before the first induction, the IOP of all the groups was at normal levels. After first induction, a significant increase in the IOP of all glaucomatous groups was observed. There was no difference between the groups ($p = 0.2024$). At this point, the treatment started. For the following four weeks after the treatment, it was observed that, while the IOP of non-treated glaucomatous animals and of glaucomatous animals treated with PI remained significantly high, the IOP of glaucomatous animals treated with BI was significantly lowered. The marketed formulation containing BIM reduced IOP for two weeks (period of eye drop instillation) but, when the treatment was interrupted, the IOP increased again. No significant changes in the IOP were induced by treatment of non-glaucomatous animals with BI or with marketed formulation (**Fig. 7 b**). The anti-glaucomatous effects of the BI did not change the Mean Arterial Pressure (**Fig. 8**).

The IOP lowering effects of BI were followed by preservation of the RGC. As viewed in **Fig. 8 a**, we found that non-treated glaucomatous animals and glaucomatous animals treated with PI showed a large reduction in the number of RGC (glaucomatous non-treated group: 393.2±31.5 cells; glaucomatous PI group 408.2±43.4 cells). Similar reduction was not noticed in glaucomatous animals treated either with marketed formulation containing BIM or with BI (473.5±27,9 cells in control group; 502.0±23,2 cells in the glaucomatous BIM eye drops group; 502.8±18,6 in glaucomatous BI group). Again, no significant changes were induced by BI in non-glaucomatous animals (**Fig 8**

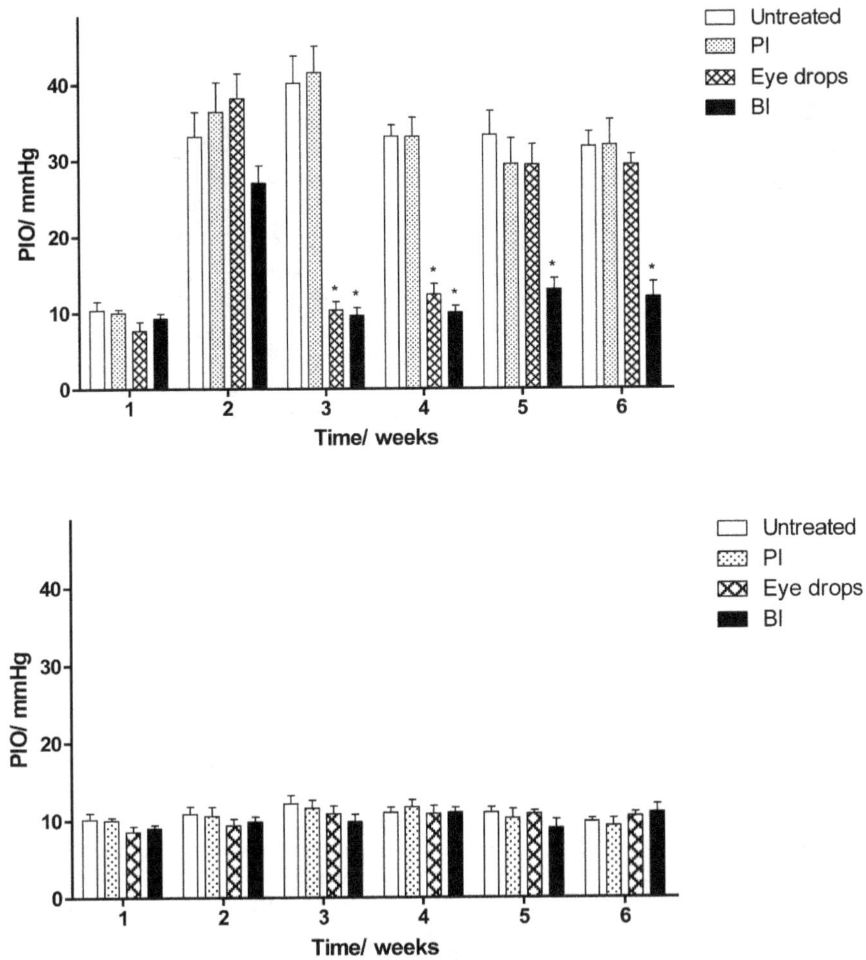

Figure 7. Effects of administration of BI on IOP. (a) Glaucomatous groups; (b) non-glaucomatous groups. Treatments initiated after confirmation of the elevated IOP, i.e. after second week. Values expressed as mean ± SD. *p<0.01 vs. untreated. One-way ANOVA followed by the Tukey post test.

b). Representative histological images of retina showing RGC loss in glaucomatous groups are presented in **Fig. 9**. Additionally, the reduction in the number of RGC caused by elevated IOP led to a severe loss of neural fibers with consequent increase in the optic nerve head cupping (**Fig. 10**). These effects were abolished by the treatment with BI. Altogether, these data indicated that controlled release of BIM induced a neuroprotection by decreasing the loss of RGC and neural fibers.

During *in vivo* efficacy test, eventual eye irritation caused by the insert was evaluated. In all experiments, the inserts were well tolerated. No symptoms of ocular lesions, such as tearing, redness, edema, and inflammation, could be observed during the experimental assays. No anterior chamber inflammation or corneal changes were observed. Ocular surface structures and intraocular tissues proved to be normal. Furthermore, fluorescein staining did not indicate corneal or conjunctival ulcerations.

Discussion

Ocular drug delivery has been a major challenge to pharmacologists and drug delivery scientists due to its unique anatomy and physiology [47]. An ideal therapy for chronic diseases, such as glaucoma, should maintain effective levels of drug for the longer duration following a single application [48]. Novel drug delivery strategies that provide controlled release for the treatment of such diseases and increase the patient's and doctor's convenience to reduce the dosing frequency and invasive treatment have been developed to sustain drug levels at the target site [47,49]. Likewise, a great deal of attention is paid to develop non-invasive sustained drug release for eye disorders [48].

Within this context, we developed CS-based ocular inserts for sustained release of BIM, a highly efficacious ocular hypotensive agent [17]. CS, as well, seemed to be an adequate polymeric matrix due its biodegradable, nontoxic, biocompatible and mucoadhesive proprieties [29,31–34]. Inserts were prepared as circular flexible membranes with 5 mm of diameter and about 50 μm of thickness (**Fig. 4**). Ocular insert used in animal or human clinical trial showed a thickness of 70 to 500 μm [50] suggesting that the inserts developed in our work have a suited breadth for clinical use.

Inserts hydrated very quickly (**Fig. 1**). BIM (hydrophilic drug) decrease the swelling index of BI, compared to PI. This fact, suggesting that there are intermolecular interactions between the drug and the polymeric matrix, is in agreement with the findings of Panomsuk *et al.* [51], in which the addition of mannitol to methylcellulose matrix also reduced the swelling index of the

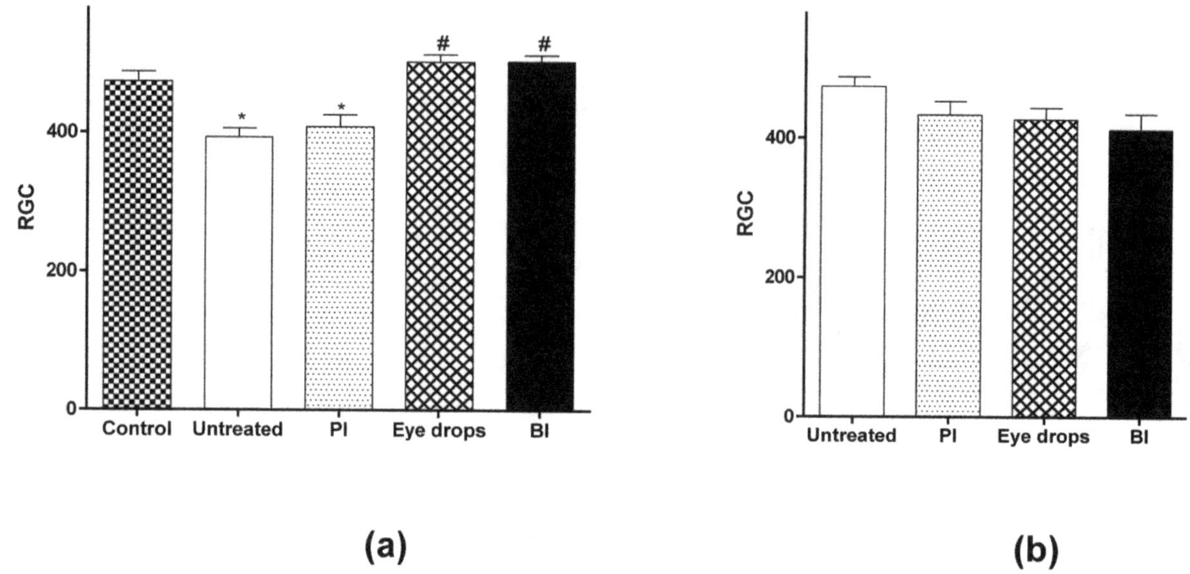

Figure 8. Effects of administration of BI on RGC counting. Quantification of RCG in retinas of (a) glaucomatous groups, compared to control (* $p<0.05$ vs. control and # $p<0.05$ vs. untreated glaucoma) and (b) non-glaucomatous groups. Values expressed as mean ± SD. One-way ANOVA followed by the Tukey post test.

membranes. This result indicates the formation of hydrogen bonding between the drugs and the polymeric matrix. Therefore, the greater the number and strength of hydrogen bonding sites, the slower the diffusion of the water molecules in the hydrated matrix [51]. The presence of hydrogen bonding was further confirmed by ATR-FTIR spectra of BI (**Fig. 2**), in which O-H stretching bands were shifted to higher wave number. In this case, those changes provide evidence of the intermolecular interaction between the hydrophilic drug and polymeric matrix.

In DSC curves (**Fig. 3 b**), it was observed that BIM addition dismembered the degradation peak of CS in two other peaks and increased the degradation temperature of the main chain of CS [45,46]. This data indicates that the drug interacted with the matrix, in turn hampering the degradation of the matrix. Moreover, this finding corroborates those of ATR-FTIR spectra and swelling studies. These results suggest that the polymer and the drug interacted through hydrogen bonding.

Apart from the increase in O-H stretching wave number, no other changes in CS infrared spectrum were detected due the addition of BIM (**Fig. 2**), leading to the conclusion that there was no obvious chemical reaction between the drug and the matrix, in turn suggesting that the drug did not lose its activity in the drug-loaded inserts.

From morphological characterization (**Fig. 4**), it was not possible to identify crystallized particles in the middle or on the surface of the inserts containing BIM that could be attributed to drug crystals, suggesting that the drug was molecularly dispersed within the polymeric matrix. Both surface and lateral areas of inserts were homogeneous. The standard error of measurement (SEM) of drug content uniformity was very low (0,33%). It could be concluded that the drug dispersed uniformly throughout the inserts [52], as predicted by SEM analysis.

In vitro drug release studies (**Fig. 5**) indicated that there is a biphasic kinetic of BI release. This fact can be explained based on the effect of drug solubility and inserts hydratation. In this case, the drug used is highly soluble in aqueous and can pass through the porous structure of inserts. PBS was used as receptor fluid in the Franz cell and hydration of the inserts was very fast, as described above (80% in the first 20 min). These two factors together may have contributed to the burst effect observed.

On the other hand, *in vitro* drug release studies (**Fig. 5**) indicated that inserts were able to sustainedly release BIM. Although the drug is hydrophilic, the *in vitro* release data demonstrate that there is a certain time to release the drug content of the inner polymer matrix. As described above, this difficulty is associated with greater interpenetration of the polymer matrix in the main chain caused by greater interaction between the drug and the matrix itself, reducing the inflow of water into the matrix (after initial hydration) and consequently decreasing the release time of the drug.

Biodistribution studies were performed in order to evaluate the difference between ^{99m}Tc-BIM and ^{99m}Tc-BIM inserts drainage extension, at 8 and 18 hours post-ocular administration. Since the main route of drug elimination from the eye is nasolacrimal drainage, the gastrointestinal organs (stomach and intestines) were collected. Moreover, in order to evaluate possible absorption, blood and common organs of drug elimination (liver, spleen and kidneys) were also harvested. It was evidenced that CS was able to enhance precorneal retention time of BIM, which is probable due to the mucoadhesive proprieties of the polymeric matrix. It has already been proved that CS shows a prolonged precorneal residence time when delivered in the eye [53,54]. Here, we demonstrated that CS was able to confer this property to BIM, most likely because of the physicochemical interaction between the drug and the polymeric matrix. An increment on the precorneal retention time of the drugs associated with polymeric matrix was reported by Gupta et al., when evaluated PLGA nanoparticles entrapping ^{99m}Tc-sparfloxacin [55] or ^{99m}Tc-levofloxacin [56] and PVA inserts entrapping ^{99m}Tc-DTPA[57]. Preferable sites of ^{99m}Tc-BIM accumulation were kidney and gastrointestinal tract (stomach, small intestine and large intestine), which are the two most important ways of elimination of BIM [58].

Reduction of IOP has long been the standard treatment for glaucoma [59]. Thereby, the effectiveness of the inserts was first evaluated by measuring the changes in IOP of glaucomatous rats

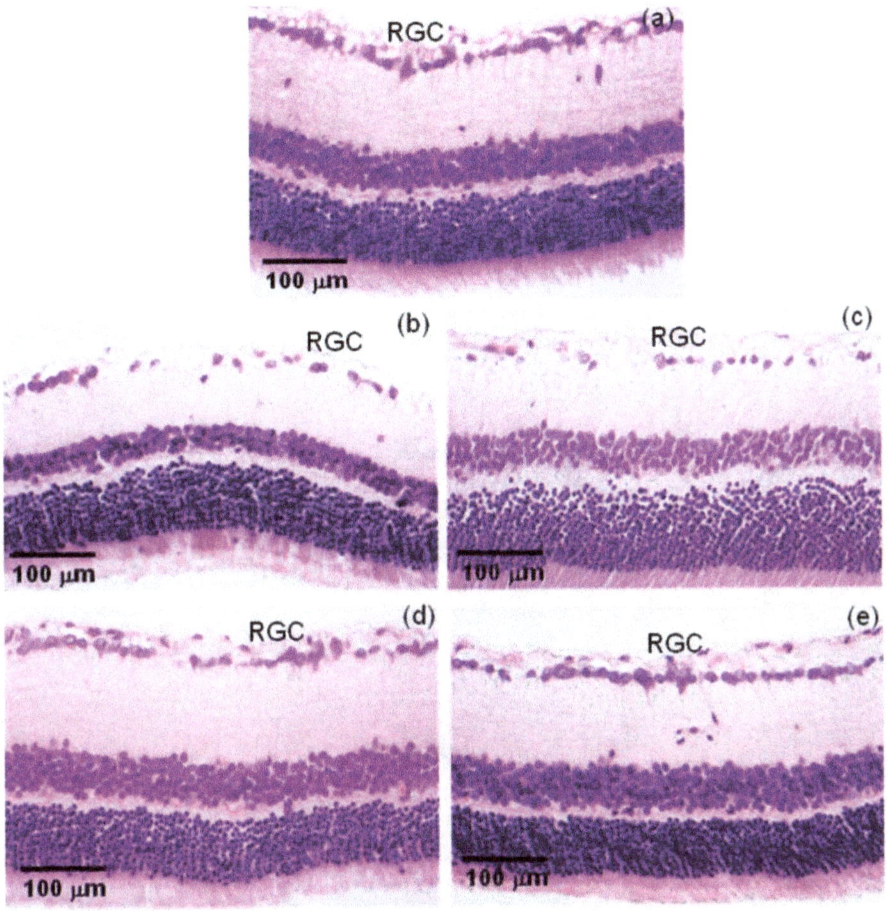

Figure 9. Histological analysis of retinal ganglion cells (RGC). Representative photomicrographs of retinas showing the smaller number of RCG in non-treated and PI-treated glaucomatous rats and the beneficial effect of BIM in this parameter. (a) Non-glaucomatous animals; (b) untreated glaucomatous animals; (c) PI glaucomatous animals; (d) BIM eye drops glaucomatous animals; (e) BI glaucomatous animals.

caused by the inserts application. As expected, IOP lowering with conventional eye drop was only maintained during the daily treatment. As soon as the treatment was interrupted, IOP increased again. BI, on the other hand, were able to reduce IOP for four week after one application. These results showed a different drug delivery profile when comparing the in vitro and the in vivo experiments. It can be due to the fast in vitro drug release in the Franz cell system. So, the drug will be released constantly and fast, as described above. In the eye, such condition does not happen because the present liquid is the small and limited volume of the tears. Then, in this case, the drug will be released more slowly than in vitro In other words, our results suggest that therapeutic regimen of BIM could be reduced from daily to monthly.

If, on the one side, reduction of IOP is essential on treatment for glaucoma [59], by other, RGC damage is responsible for the loss of vision [14]. So, at the end of the treatment, we also evaluated histological sections of retina in optic nerve area in order to determine RGC loss and optic nerve head cupping. As predicted, both non-treated groups have showed significant RGC loss, while in both treated groups (eye drops or inserts), the RGC number was statistically equal to the number of non-glaucomatous animals, indicating that treatment with BIM also promoted neuroprotection [14]. It is important to underline that the same neuroprotection effect was obtained when BI was administered once or when BIM eye drops were administered daily for two weeks. The amount of BIM in one insert is equivalent to the amount of BIM in one drop.

In 2011, Robinson *et al.* developed polymeric systems for the sustained release of BIM [60,61]. The main innovation of the present system, as compared with that developed by Robinson *et al.*, is that, while their system must be implanted in the anterior chamber of the eye, requiring a surgical procedure, the present system can simply be applied topically on the conjunctival sac, a non-invasive procedure. In 2013, Shafiee *et al.* proposed a DuraSite system to reduce the dosing frequency of BIM administration. BIM formulated in DuraSite system had ocular bioavailability superior to that of the conventional eye drops. Commercial DuraSite systems (AzaSite and Besivance) are still administered daily [62].

Natarajan *et al.*, developed liposomes for sustained release of Latanoprost, a prostaglandin analog similar to BIM [61]. The sustained release of Latanoprost was achieved; however, the process for the production of liposomes still involves the use of organic solvents, which is undesirable in the pharmaceuticals industry. In 2013, Giarmoukakis *et al.* also developed biodegradable nanoparticles for sustained release of Latanoprot [23]. Unfortunately, invasive procedures were needed for periocular implantation of the developed formulation.

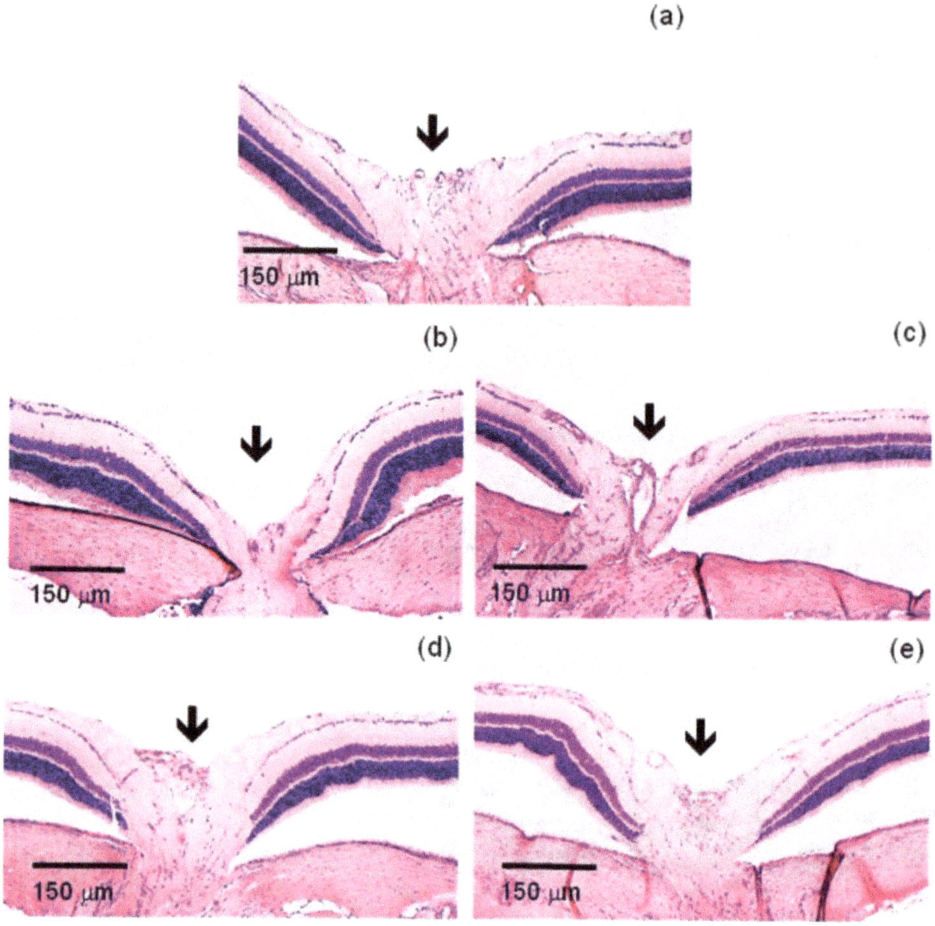

Figure 10. BIM induced neuroprotection in retinas of glaucomatous rats. Representative photomicrographs of excavation of the optic nerve (arrows). (a) Non-glaucomatous animals; (b) untreated glaucomatous animals; (c) PI glaucomatous animals; (d) BIM eye drops glaucomatous animals; (e) BI glaucomatous animals. Note an exacerbation of the excavation in untreated and PI glaucomatous animals (b and c) when compared with all other groups. This effect is reverted by BIM.

Conclusions

The findings of this study revealed that CS-based ocular insert for the sustained release of BIM were successfully produced. A strong interaction between the drug and the polymer was achieved. The formulation enhanced precorneal residence time of the BIM, compared to conventional eye drops. The sustained release of BIM was proven by pharmacodinamic effects (IOP lowering and neuroprotection) and biodistribution studies. Consequently, after the data analysis, BI was able to sustain the release of BIM for over a month with only one dose applied. These results may reveal a potential application of this new formulation in glaucoma management, in order to improve patient compliance by lowering the frequency of administration and to enhance therapeutic effectiveness of glaucoma medical treatment.

Acknowledgments

The authors are grateful to PRPq-UFMG, CNPq (for Development Technologic fellowship and financial support), CAPES and FAPEMIG for their financial support. The authors would like to acknowledge the Center of Microscopy at the Universidade Federal de Minas Gerais (?http://www.microscopia.ufmg.br) for providing the equipment and technical support for experiments involving scanning electron microscopy.

Author Contributions

Conceived and designed the experiments: JRF GF ROC VNC SOF SC AJF AAGF. Performed the experiments: JRF GF LLF TGR LBR RB ROC MIY VNC SOF SC AJF AAGF. Analyzed the data: JRF GF LLF TGR LBR RB ROC MIY VNC SOF SC AJF AAGF. Contributed reagents/materials/analysis tools: JRF GF LLF TGR LBR RB ROC MIY VNC SOF SC AJF AAGF. Wrote the paper: JRF GF ROC SC AJF AAGF.

References

1. Weinreb RN, Khaw PT (2004) Primary open-angle glaucoma. The Lancet 363: 1711–1720.
2. McKinnon SJ, Goldberg LD, Peeples P, Walt JG, Bramley TJ (2008) Current management of glaucoma and the need for complete therapy. Am J Manag Care 14: S20–27.
3. Gupta SK, Niranjan G, Agrawal SS, Srivastava S, Saxena R (2008) Recent advances in pharmacotherapy of glaucoma. Indian Journal of Pharmacology 40: 197–208.
4. Salomao SR, Mitsuhiro MRKH, Belfort RJr (2009) Visual impairment and blindness: an overview of prevalence and causes in Brazil. Anais Da Academia Brasileira De Ciencias 81: 539–549.

5. Resnikoff S, Pascolini D, Etya'ale D, Kocur I, Pararajasegaram R, et al. (2004) Global data on visual impairment in the year 2002. Bulletin of the World Health Organization 82: 844–851.
6. Boland MV, Quigley HA (2007) Risk factors and open-angle glaucoma: Classification and application. Journal of Glaucoma 16: 406–418.
7. Coleman AL, Miglior S (2008) Risk Factors for Glaucoma Onset and Progression. Survey of Ophthalmology 53: S3–S10.
8. Natu MV, Gaspar MN, Fontes Ribeiro CA, Cabrita AM, de Sousa HC, et al. (2011) In vitro and in vivo evaluation of an intraocular implant for glaucoma treatment. International Journal of Pharmaceutics 415: 73–82.
9. Bouhenni RA, Dunmire J, Sewell A, Edward DP (2012) Animal Models of Glaucoma. Journal of Biomedicine and Biotechnology.
10. Casson RJ, Chidlow G, Wood JPM, Crowston JG, Goldberg I (2012) Definition of glaucoma: clinical and experimental concepts. Clinical and Experimental Ophthalmology 40: 341–349.
11. Cook C, Foster P (2012) Epidemiology of glaucoma: what's new? Canadian Journal of Ophthalmology-Journal Canadien D Ophtalmologie 47: 223–226.
12. Rafuse PE, Buys YM, Damji KE, Harasymowycz P, Lajoie C, et al. (2009) Canadian Ophthalmological Society evidence-based clinical practice guidelines for the management of glaucoma in the adult eye Canadian Ophthalmological Society Glaucoma Clinical Practice Guideline Expert Committee. Canadian Journal of Ophthalmology-Journal Canadien D Ophtalmologie 44: S7–S54.
13. Bean GW, Camras CB (2008) Commercially Available Prostaglandin Analogs for the Reduction of Intraocular Pressure: Similarities and Differences. Survey of Ophthalmology 53: S69–S84.
14. Takano N, Tsuruma K, Ohno Y, Shimazawa M, Hara H (2013) Bimatoprost protects retinal neuronal damage via Akt pathway. European Journal of Pharmacology 702: 56–61.
15. Brubaker RF (2001) Mechanism of action of bimatoprost (Luminan (TM)). Survey of Ophthalmology 45: S347–S351.
16. Burk RM, Woodward DF (2007) A historical perspective and recent advances in prostamide research and therapeutics. Current Opinion in Drug Discovery & Development 10: 413–421.
17. Woodward DF, Krauss AHP, Chen J, Lai RK, Spada CS, et al. (2001) The pharmacology of bimatoprost (Lumigan (TM)). Survey of Ophthalmology 45: S337–S345.
18. Liang Y, Woodward DF, Guzman VM, Li C, Scott DF, et al. (2008) Identification and pharmacological characterization of the prostaglandin FP receptor and FP receptor variant complexes. British Journal of Pharmacology 154: 1079–1093.
19. Davies SS, Ju WK, Neufeld AH, Abran D, Chemtob S, et al. (2003) Hydrolysis of bimatoprost (Lumigan) to its free acid by ocular tissue in vitro. Journal of Ocular Pharmacology and Therapeutics 19: 45–54.
20. Gulsen D, Chauhan A (2005) Dispersion of microemulsion drops in HEMA hydrogel: a potential ophthalmic drug delivery vehicle. International Journal of Pharmaceutics 292: 95–117.
21. Ludwig A (2005) The use of mucoadhesive polymers in ocular drug delivery. Advanced Drug Delivery Reviews 57: 1595–1639.
22. Ghate D, Edelhauser HF (2008) Barriers to glaucoma drug delivery. Journal of Glaucoma 17: 147–156.
23. Giarmoukakis A, Labiris G, Sideroudi H, Tsimali Z, Koutsospyrou N, et al. (2013) Biodegradable nanoparticles for controlled subconjunctival delivery of latanoprost acid: In vitro and in vivo evaluation. Preliminary results. Experimental Eye Research 112: 29–36.
24. Aggarwal D, Kaur IP (2005) Improved pharmacodynamics of timolol maleate from a mucoadhesive niosomal ophthalmic drug delivery system. International Journal of Pharmaceutics 290: 155–159.
25. Lee SS, Hughes P, Ross AD, Robinson MR (2010) Biodegradable Implants for Sustained Drug Release in the Eye. Pharmaceutical Research 27: 2043–2053.
26. Aburahma MH, Mahmoud AA (2011) Biodegradable Ocular Inserts for Sustained Delivery of Brimonidine Tartarate: Preparation and In Vitro/In Vivo Evaluation. Aaps Pharmscitech 12: 1335–1347.
27. Kearns VR, Williams RL (2009) Drug delivery systems for the eye. Expert Review of Medical Devices 6: 277–290.
28. Wadhwa S, Paliwal R, Paliwal SR, Vyas SP (2009) Chitosan and its Role in Ocular Therapeutics. Mini-Reviews in Medicinal Chemistry 9: 1639–1647.
29. Zambito Y, Di Colo G (2010) Chitosan and its derivatives as intraocular penetration enhancers. Journal of Drug Delivery Science and Technology 20: 45–52.
30. Chen RH, Lin JH, Yang MH (1994) RELATIONSHIPS BETWEEN THE CHAIN FLEXIBILITIES OF CHITOSAN MOLECULES AND THE PHYSICAL-PROPERTIES OF THEIR CASTED FILMS. Carbohydrate Polymers 24: 41–46.
31. Felt O, Furrer P, Mayer JM, Plazonnet B, Buri P, et al. (1999) Topical use of chitosan in ophthalmology: tolerance assessment and evaluation of precorneal retention. International Journal of Pharmaceutics 180: 185–193.
32. Gaserod O, Jolliffe IG, Hampson FC, Dettmar PW, Skjak-Braek G (1998) The enhancement of the bioadhesive properties of calcium alginate gel beads by coating with chitosan. International Journal of Pharmaceutics 175: 237–246.
33. George M, Abraham TE (2006) Polyionic hydrocolloids for the intestinal delivery of protein drugs: Alginate and chitosan - a review. Journal of Controlled Release 114: 1–14.
34. Valenta C (2005) The use of mucoadhesive polymers in vaginal delivery. Advanced Drug Delivery Reviews 57: 1692–1712.
35. Rodrigues LB, Leite HF, Yoshida MI, Saliba JB, Cunha AS, et al. (2009) In vitro release and characterization of chitosan films as dexamethasone carrier. International Journal of Pharmaceutics 368: 1–6.
36. Perumal VA, Lutchman D, Mackraj I, Govender T (2008) Formulation of monolayered films with drug and polymers of opposing solubilities. International Journal of Pharmaceutics 358: 184–191.
37. Eroglu H, Sargon MF, Oener L (2007) Chitosan formulations for steroid delivery: Effect of formulation variables on in vitro characteristics. Drug Development and Industrial Pharmacy 33: 265–271.
38. Dobaria NB, Badhan AC, Mashru RC (2009) A Novel Itraconazole Bioadhesive Film for Vaginal Delivery: Design, Optimization, and Physicodynamic Characterization. Aaps Pharmscitech 10: 951–959.
39. (BRASIL) ANDVS, CRUZ FO (2010) Farmacopeia brasileira. Brasília: ANVISA: FIOCRUZ.
40. Nunan EA, Cardoso VN, Moraes-Santos T (2002) Technetium-99m labeling of tityustoxin and venom from the scorpion Tityus serrulatus. Applied Radiation and Isotopes 57: 849–852.
41. de Barros ALB, Mota LdG, Ferreira CdA, Cardoso VN (2012) Kit formulation for 99mTc-labeling of HYNIC-βAla-Bombesin(7–14). Applied Radiation and Isotopes 70: 2440–2445.
42. Moreno MC, Marcos HJA, Croxatto JO, Sande PH, Campanelli J, et al. (2005) A new experimental model of glaucoma in rats through intracameral injections of hyaluronic acid. Experimental Eye Research 81: 71–80.
43. Kumirska J, Czerwicka M, Kaczynski Z, Bychowska A, Brzozowski K, et al. (2010) Application of Spectroscopic Methods for Structural Analysis of Chitin and Chitosan. Marine Drugs 8: 1567–1636.
44. Lawrie G, Keen I, Drew B, Chandler-Temple A, Rintoul L, et al. (2007) Interactions between alginate and chitosan biopolymers characterized using FTIR and XPS. Biomacromolecules 8: 2533–2541.
45. Mucha M, Pawlak A (2005) Thermal analysis of chitosan and its blends. Thermochimica Acta 427: 69–76.
46. Neto CGT, Giacometti JA, Job AE, Ferreira FC, Fonseca JLC, et al. (2005) Thermal analysis of chitosan based networks. Carbohydrate Polymers 62: 97–103.
47. Gaudana R, Ananthula HK, Parenky A, Mitra AK (2010) Ocular Drug Delivery. Aaps Journal 12: 348–360.
48. Gaudana R, Jwala J, Boddu SHS, Mitra AK (2009) Recent Perspectives in Ocular Drug Delivery. Pharmaceutical Research 26: 1197–1216.
49. Kuno N, Fujii S (2011) Recent Advances in Ocular Drug Delivery Systems. Polymers 3: 193–221.
50. Lisa Land D, Benjamin WJ (1994) Sizes and shapes of conjunctival inserts. International Contact Lens Clinic 21: 212–217.
51. Panomsuk SP, Hatanaka T, Aiba T, Katayama K, Koizumi T (1996) A study of the hydrophilic cellulose matrix: Effect of drugs on swelling properties. Chemical & Pharmaceutical Bulletin 44: 1039–1042.
52. Semalty M, Semalty A, Kumar G (2008) Formulation and Characterization of Mucoadhesive Buccal Films of Glipizide. Indian Journal of Pharmaceutical Sciences 70: 43–48.
53. Yuan X-B, Li H, Yuan Y-B (2006) Preparation of cholesterol-modified chitosan self-aggregated nanoparticles for delivery of drugs to ocular surface. Carbohydrate Polymers 65.
54. Kuntner C, Wanek T, Hoffer M, Dangl D, Hornof M, et al. (2011) Radiosynthesis and Assessment of Ocular Pharmacokinetics of I-124-Labeled Chitosan in Rabbits Using Small-Animal PET. Molecular Imaging and Biology 13.
55. Gupta H, Aqil M, Khar RK, Ali A, Bhatnagar A, et al. (2010) Sparfloxacin-loaded PLGA nanoparticles for sustained ocular drug delivery. Nanomedicine-Nanotechnology Biology and Medicine 6.
56. Gupta H, Aqil M, Khar RK, Ali A, Bhatnagar A, et al. (2011) Biodegradable levofloxacin nanoparticles for sustained ocular drug delivery. Journal of drug targeting 19: 409–417.
57. Wilson CG, Zhu YP, Frier M, Rao LS, Gilchrist P, et al. (1998) Ocular contact time of a carbomer gel (GelTears) in humans. British Journal of Ophthalmology 82.
58. Curran MP (2009) Bimatoprost A Review of its Use in Open-Angle Glaucoma and Ocular Hypertension. Drugs & Aging 26: 1049–1071.
59. Lavik E, Kuehn MH, Kwon YH (2011) Novel drug delivery systems for glaucoma. Eye 25: 578–586.
60. Robinson MR, Burke J, Schiffman R Treating ocular condition e.g. glaucoma, comprises providing biodegradable sustained release implants containing therapeutic agent e.g. bimatoprost and latanoprost and implanting the implants into the anterior chamber of an eye. Allergan Inc.
61. Natarajan JV, Ang M, Darwitan A, Chattopadhyay S, Wong TT, et al. (2012) Nanomedicine for glaucoma: liposomes provide sustained release of latanoprost in the eye. International Journal of Nanomedicine 7: 123.
62. Shafiee A, Bowman LM, Hou E, Hosseini K (2013) Ocular pharmacokinetics of bimatoprost formulated in DuraSite compared to bimatoprost 0.03% ophthalmic solution in pigmented rabbit eyes. Clinical Ophthalmology 7: 1549–1556.

18

Cellular Uptake and Antitumor Activity of DOX-hyd-PEG-FA Nanoparticles

Wei-liang Ye[1⁹], Jiang-bo Du[1⁹], Bang-le Zhang[1⁹], Ren Na[3], Yan-feng Song[1], Qi-bing Mei[2], Ming-gao Zhao[2], Si-yuan Zhou[1]*

1 Department of Pharmaceutics, School of Pharmacy, Fourth Military Medical University, Xi'an, China, **2** Department of Pharmacology, School of Pharmacy, Fourth Military Medical University, Xi'an, China, **3** West Changle Sanatorium for Xi'an Army Retired Cadres of Fourth Military Medical University, Xi'an, China

Abstract

A PEG-based, folate mediated, active tumor targeting drug delivery system using DOX-hyd-PEG-FA nanoparticles (NPs) were prepared. DOX-hyd-PEG-FA NPs showed a significantly faster DOX release in pH 5.0 medium than in pH 7.4 medium. Compared with DOX-hyd-PEG NPs, DOX-hyd-PEG-FA NPs increased the intracellular accumulation of DOX and showed a DOX translocation from lysosomes to nucleus. The cytotoxicity of DOX-hyd-PEG-FA NPs on KB cells was much higher than that of free DOX, DOX-ami-PEG-FA NPs and DOX-hyd-PEG NPs. The cytotoxicity of DOX-hyd-PEG-FA NPs on KB cells was attenuated in the presence of exogenous folic acid. The IC_{50} of DOX-hyd-PEG-FA NPs and DOX-hyd-PEG NPs on A549 cells showed no significant difference. After DOX-hyd-PEG-FA NPs were intravenously administered, the amount of DOX distributed in tumor tissue was significantly increased, while the amount of DOX distributed in heart was greatly decreased as compared with free DOX. Compared with free DOX, NPs yielded improved survival rate, prolonged life span, delayed tumor growth and reduced the cardiotoxicity in tumor bearing mice model. These results indicated that the acid sensitivity, passive and active tumor targeting abilities were likely to act synergistically to enhance the drug delivery efficiency of DOX-hyd-PEG-FA NPs. Therefore, DOX-hyd-PEG-FA NPs are a promising drug delivery system for targeted cancer therapy.

Editor: Gianfranco Pintus, University of Sassari, Italy

Funding: This research was supported by the Shaanxi Science and Technology Innovation Project (2012KTCL03-18). The funders had no role in study design, data collection and analysis, decision to publish, or preparation of the manuscript.

Competing Interests: The authors have declared that no competing interests exist.

* E-mail: zhousy@fmmu.edu.cn

⁹ These authors contributed equally to this work.

Introduction

Doxorubicin is a widely used anticancer agent, but its toxicity to normal tissue and inherent multidrug resistance effect remain as major problems to be solved [1,2]. Tumor specific nanoparticles are a promising and reliable approach to deliver antitumor drug to the site of action to get the maximum therapy index with the minimum side effects [3–7]. Moreover, it is suggested that nanoparticles may be able to bypass p-glycoprotein mediated drug resistance and result in high intracellular drug concentrations [8–10]. Thus, various nanoparticles are utilized to selectively deliver anticancer agents to the tumor sites. Some of them, such as Doxil (doxorubicin liposomal) and SMANCS (Zinostatin Stimalamer) [11,12], have been successfully used in the clinic. Although passive targeting drug delivery systems form the basis of clinical therapy, a number of them can not efficiently diffuse into the tumor tissue [13]. Therefore, a targeting system with high drug delivery efficiency is needed.

The folate receptor is significantly upregulated in many cancer cells and is lowly expressed in normal tissues [14]. Folic acid (FA) has a very high affinity for folate receptor (Kd = 0.1 nmol/L), even after conjugation with therapeutic drugs. Thus, folic acid is an attractive ligand for receptor targeted therapeutics [15,16]. EC-145 is a conjugate composed of desacetylvinblastine monohydrazide linked through a peptide spacer to folic acid, for the potential treatment of folate receptor overexpressing tumors, in particular ovarian and lung cancers. The *in vitro* studies demonstrated that EC-145 selectively bonded to cells that overexpressed the folate receptor, resulting in dose-dependent cytotoxicity. At present, EC-145 is ongoing phase III clinical trials [17]. In our lab, we synthesized a small molecular FA-mediated targeted delivery system for DOX (FA-AMA-DOX), using aminocaproic acid (AMA) as the linker. AMA was conjugated to the targeting moiety FA via an amide bond, and to the antitumor drug DOX via a hydrazone bond. Although FA-AMA-DOX can deliver DOX to folate over-expressed tumor cells, it is a small molecular conjugate and its drug delivery efficiency *in vivo* needs further evaluation [18].

Polyethylene glycol (PEG) is most frequently used polymeric carrier because of its good biocompatibility, high solubility, low immunogenicity and FDA approval for systemic human use [19]. We conjugated DOX with PEG by hydrazone bond (PEG-hyd-DOX) and amide bond (PEG-ami-DOX) to improve the therapeutic index of DOX. The *in vivo* results indicated that pH-triggered PEG-hyd-DOX conjugate delivered DOX to tumor tissue and released free DOX in acidic tumor environment, and anti tumor efficacy of DOX was improved by using PEG-hyd-DOX conjugate [20].

In this paper, a pH sensitive polymer DOX-hyd-PEG-FA was synthesized. FA was used as targeting moiety, PEG was used as drug carrier, and DOX was conjugated with PEG through hydrazone bond. In theory, for each DOX-hyd-PEG-FA molecule, only one DOX molecule can enter the cell by one FA receptor mediated endocytosis. When the concentration of DOX-hyd-PEG-FA is increased, the FA receptor will be rapidly saturated. Consequently, the internalization of DOX-hyd-PEG-FA is limited. In order to increase the drug delivery efficiency and antitumor efficacy of DOX-hyd-PEG-FA, DOX-hyd-PEG-FA nanoparticles (NPs) were prepared by using DOX-hyd-PEG-FA as an amphiphilic polymer, and free DOX was encapsulated in DOX-hyd-PEG-FA nanoparticles (as shown in figure 1). In general, after being taken up by tumor cells, DOX-hyd-PEG-FA NPs localized in the lysosome, where pH value is approximately 4.0-6.0 [21], the DOX-hyd-PEG-FA NPs became unstable and were depolymerized [19,22]. Subsequently, not only DOX encapsulated in the NPs was released in tumor cells, but also large amount of DOX conjugated with PEG also released in tumor cells. Hence, the drug delivery efficiency was greatly enhanced, and the antitumor efficacy of DOX-hyd-PEG-FA NPs was significantly improved.

Materials and Methods

2.1 Materials

Folic acid (FA), N-hydroxysuccinimide (NHS), dicyclohexylcarbodiimde (DCC), trifluoroacetic acid (TFA), and 3-(4,5-dimethylthiaol-2-yl)-2,5- diphenyl-tetrazolium bromide (MTT) were purchased from Sigma-Aldrich (St. Louis, USA). α-Carboxyl-ω-amino poly (ethylene glycol) ($HOOC\text{-}PEG\text{-}NH_2$, average molecular weight is 5000 Da) was purchased from Shanghai Yare Biotech Inc.(Shanghai, China). Doxorubicin was purchased from Hisun Pharmaceutical Co. (Zhejiang, China). All other chemicals were analytical grade and obtained from commercial suppliers without further purification. RPMI1640 medium without folic acid, lysotracker green and 4′,6-diamidino-2-phenylindole (DAPI) were bought from Invitrogen Technologies Company (Carlsbad, USA). KB cells are human epidermal carcinoma cell line from oral cavity on which folate receptor is over-expressed [23–25]. A549 cells are human lung adenocarcinoma epithelial cell line on which folate receptor is deficient [23,24,26]. HepG2 cells are human liver tumor cell line [27,28]. KB cell, A549 cell and HepG2 cell were purchased from Institute of Biochemistry and Cell Biology, Chinese Academy of Science, Shanghai, China.

Female athymic nude mice (six weeks old, body weight = 20–23 g) were bought from Experimental Animal Center of Fourth Military Medical University and were allowed water and laboratory chow ad libitum (without folate). A 12-hour light-dark cycle was used. All animal procedures were performed in according with protocols approved by the Animal Care and Use Committee of Fourth Military Medical University (approval date: 18/12/2011, number: 11317).

2.2 Preparation of DOX-ami-PEG-FA conjugate

The synthetic scheme for DOX-ami-PEG-FA is shown in figure 2. HOOC-PEG-FA was synthesized as described in the previous study [23]. Briefly, 65 mg of folate (0.15 mmol) dissolved in anhydrous dimethyl sulfoxide (DMSO), and then it was activated by adding dicyclohexyl carbodiimide (DCC, 30.3 mg, 0.15 mmol) and N-hydroxy succinimide (NHS, 16.9 mg, 0.15 mmol) under nitrogen and stired at room temperature for 30 min [29,30]. The $HOOC\text{-}PEG\text{-}NH_2$ (350 mg, 0.07 mmol) was dissolved in DMSO and added to the folate solution. The reaction was carried out in the presence of triethylamine (TEA) (290 mg, 3.68 mmol) under nitrogen at room temperature for 2 h. Then 5 mL of water and 5 mL of dimethyl formamide (DMF) was added. The compound HOOC-PEG-FA was extracted by chloroform. The organic phase was dried over Na_2SO_4 and evaporated. The resulting conjugate was dissolved in water and filtered. The filtered solution was dialyzed against deionized water

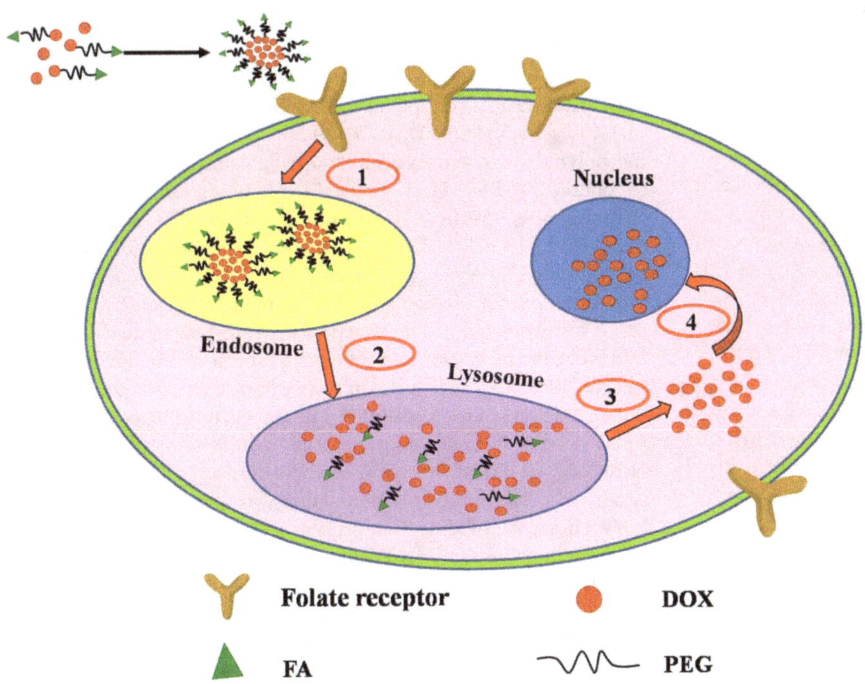

Figure 1. Design of DOX loading DOX-hyd-PEG-FA NPs as an active targeting drug delivery system. (1) FA receptor mediated endocytosis; (2) NPs depolymerization in lysosome; (3) DOX escape from the lysosome; (4) DOX diffuse to nucleus.

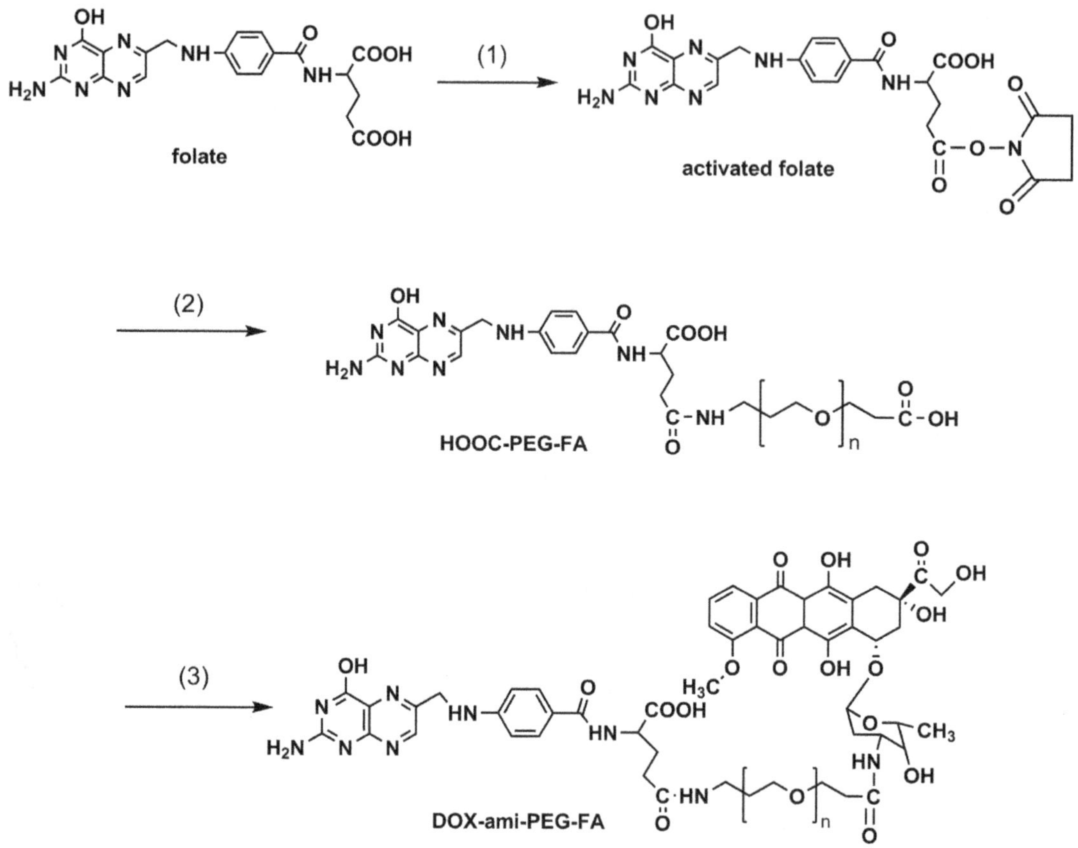

Figure 2. Reaction scheme for the synthesis of DOX-ami-PEG-FA conjugate. (1) NHS, DCC, DMSO; (2) H_2N-PEG-COOH, TEA, DMSO; (3) NHS, DCC, CH_2Cl_2, TEA.

and lyophilized. Finally, the product was purified by using a Sephadex LH20 column (Pharmacia, Uppsala, Sweden).

350 mg of HOOC-PEG-FA was dissolved in CH_2Cl_2, and was reacted with 53 mg of DOX in the presence of 23 mg of NHS, 13 mg of DCC, and 11 mg of TEA. The reaction was performed under nitrogen at room temperature for 4 h. The organic phase was evaporated and the residue was dissolved in water and filtered. The filtered solution was extensively dialyzed against deionized water and lyophilized to obtain DOX-ami-PEG-FA conjugate. The red wine color product was evaluated by HPLC to confirm the absence of unbound free DOX. The productive rate of this step was calculated as the ration between actual yield and theoretical yield of DOX-ami-PEG-FA. In order to synthesize DOX-ami-PEG conjugate without folate, methoxy-PEG-COOH was used instead of HOOC-PEG-FA.

To determine the drug loading of DOX-ami-PEG-FA conjugate, DOX-ami-PEG-FA conjugate was dissolved in 1 mL of 1 mol/L HCl and incubated in a water bath at 50°C for 3 h to yield DOX [31]. The amount of released DOX was analyzed by HPLC with a 2996 photodiode array detector and 2695 pump (Waters Corporation, Milford, MA). A Symmetry C_{18} column (4.6×250 mm, 5 μm; Waters Corporation, Milford, MA) was used. The mobile phase consisted of 70% acetonitrile and 30% H_2O at a flow rate of 1 mL/min. The wavelength was set to 235 nm. Injection volume was 20 μL. The column temperature was maintained at 25°C. Under this HPLC condition, the free DOX was clearly separated from interference.

2.3 Preparation of DOX-hyd-PEG-FA conjugate

Conjugation of DOX with HOOC-PEG-FA through pH sensitive hydrazone bond was achieved as figure 3 shown [32]. First, Boc-protected hydrazine (Boc-Hyd) was conjugated to HOOC-PEG-FA producing FA-PEG-Hyd-Boc in the presence of DCC and NHS in DMSO [29,30]. Second, the Boc group in the polymer was removed in 10% trifluoroacetic acid for 20 min to obtain FA-PEG-Hyd. For DOX conjugation, FA-PEG-Hyd (100 mg) was dissolved in 40 mL of DMSO, 20 mg of DOX dissolved in 10 mL of DMSO was then added with trifluoroacetic acid (0.1 mL TFA) as an acid catalyst [18]. The reaction mixture was stirred under nitrogen at room temperature for 48 h and was protected from light. The reaction mixture was diluted with 100 fold volume of water and filtered to protect the formation of micelle. The filtered solution was extensively dialyzed against deionized water and freeze-dried under vacuum to obtain DOX-hyd-PEG-FA conjugate. The red wine color product was evaluated by HPLC to confirm the absence of free DOX. The productive rate of last step of reaction was calculated as the ration between actual yield and theoretical yield of DOX-hyd-PEG-FA. In order to synthesize DOX-hyd-PEG conjugate, methoxy-PEG-COOH was used instead of HOOC-PEG-FA.

To determine the drug loading of DOX-hyd-PEG-FA conjugate, DOX-hyd-PEG-FA conjugate was dissolved in 1 mL of 1 mol/L HCl and incubated in a water bath at 50°C for 3 h to yield DOX. The amount of released DOX was analyzed by HPLC as described above.

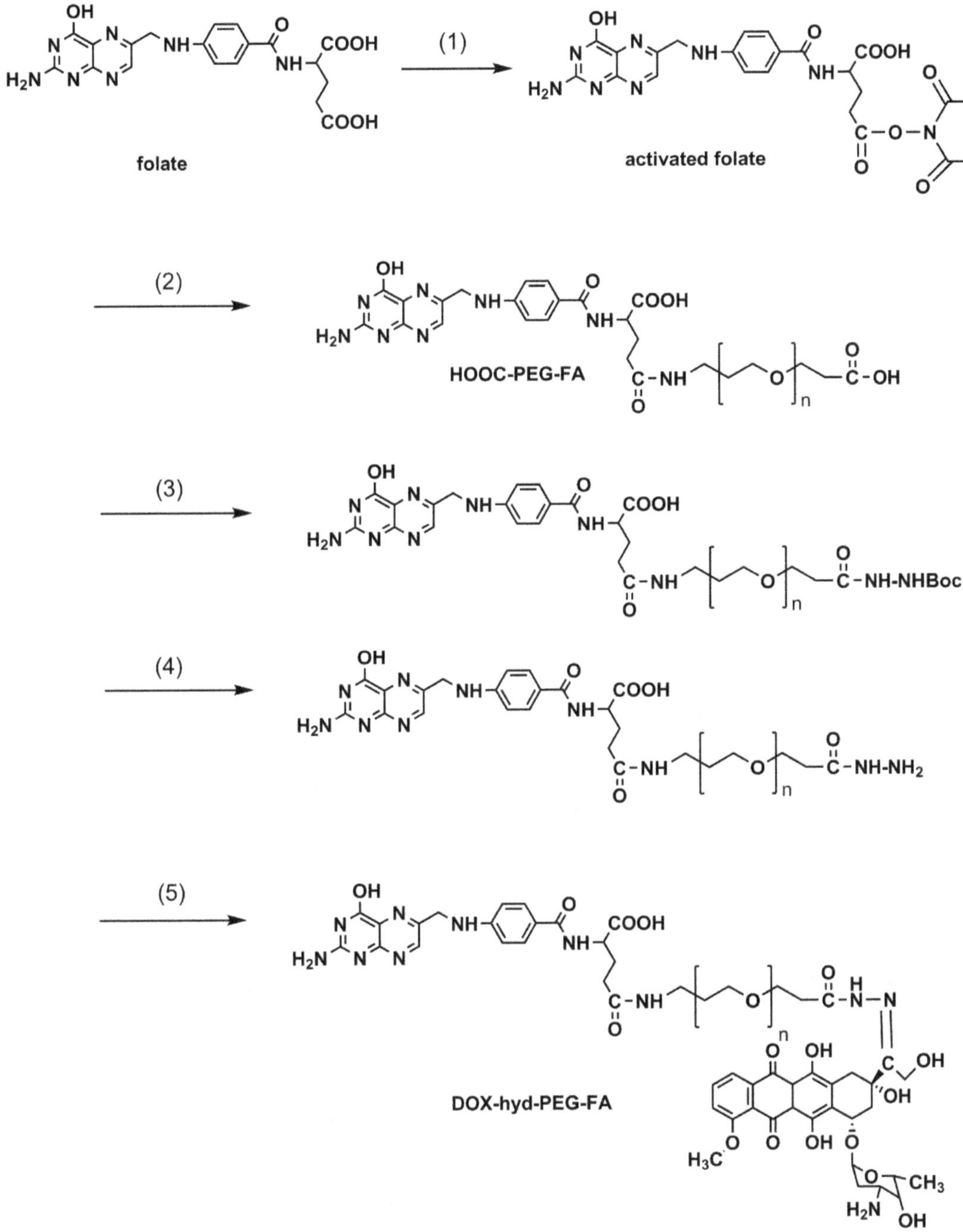

Figure 3. Reaction scheme for the synthesis of DOX-hyd-PEG-FA conjugate. (1) NHS, DCC, DMSO; (2) H_2N-PEG-COOH, TEA, DMSO; (3) NHS, DCC, $BOCNHNH_2$, DMSO, TEA; (4) TFA, DMSO; (5) DOX, TFA, DMSO.

2.4 Preparation of nanopaticles

The nanopaticles were prepared as previously reported method [33]. Five milligram of DOX-hyd-PEG-FA (or DOX-hyd-PEG,DOX-ami-PEG-FA,DOX-ami-PEG) and 2 mg of free doxorubicin were dissolved in 2 ml of CH_2Cl_2, and the mixture solution was added dropwise into 10 ml of deionized water under vigorous stirring. The organic phase was completely evaporated, then centrifuged at 15,000 g for 20 min using CR 21F centrifuge (HITACHI, Japan). After the supernatant was discarded, the nanoparticles were dispersed in water, lyophilized and stored at 4°C until further use. The size, polydispersity index, and zeta potential of nanopaticles were measured by dynamic light scattering (DLS) using a Particle Analyzer (Delsa Nano C, Beckman Coulter).

The drug loading was examined in two methods. (1) Nanoparticles were dispersed in DMSO solution, and the solution was stired for 24 h. The DOX concentration in DMSO solution was detected by HPLC. By this way, the physical drug loading of nanoparticles was calculated. (2) Nanoparticles were dispersed in acetate buffer (pH = 4.0), and the solution was stired for 24 h. The DOX concentration in acetate buffer was detected by HPLC. By this way, the total effective drug loading of nanoparticles was calculated.

2.5 Drug release *in vitro*

The *in vitro* drug release study was performed in phosphate buffer solution (pH 5.0, pH 6.5 and pH 7.4). First, 50 mg of NPs was dispersed in 5 mL of release medium and placed in a dialysis bag with a molecular weight cut off of 1 kDa. The dialysis bag was then immersed in 95 mL of the release medium and incubated in a horizontal laboratory shaker at 37°C. Sample (0.5 mL) was periodically collected and the same volume of fresh blank medium was added into the incubation medium. The amount of released DOX was analyzed by HPLC as described above.

2.6 Cell culture condition

KB cell, which is a human epidermal carcinoma cell from oral cavity, was maintained in a folate-free RPMI 1640 medium. A549 cell, which is a human lung carcinoma cell, was maintained in a RPMI 1640 medium. HepG2 cell, which is human liver tumor cell line, was maintained in a RPMI 1640 medium. All cell lines were supplemented with 100 units/mL penicillin, 100 units/mL streptomycin, and 10% fetal bovine serum. The cells were cultured as a monolayer in a humidified atmosphere containing 5% CO_2 at 37°C.

2.7 Evaluation of cellular uptake of NPs

DOX itself has fluorescence, it is used directly to measure cellular uptake without additional markers. KB cells (or A549 cells) were seeded into coverglass-containing 24-well plates at density of 100,000 cells/well, incubated at 37°C and grown overnight. DOX or NPs at a concentration of 10 μg/mL equivalent DOX was added and incubated for 4 h at 37°C. Then, the cells were washed with PBS three times and fixed with 1.5% formaldehyde. Coverslip was placed onto glass microscope slide and DOX uptake was analyzed by using a confocal laser scanning microscope (CLSM, Leica, Wetzler, Germany). Digital monochromatic images were acquired using Leica Confocal Software (Version 2.61). To determine the DOX distribution in the nucleus and cytoplasm, the DOX mean fluorescence intensity (MFI) in the CLSM images was measured in a 4 μM^2 area located in the nucleus or cytoplasm (n = 10 cells) for each sample using ImageJ software.

Cellular uptake of NPs was also monitored semi-quantitatively by using flow cytometry (Coulter XL, Beckman USA). Briefly, KB cells (or A549 cells) were seeded into 6-well plates at a cell density of 1×10^7 cells/mL in folic acid free medium. After 24 h, the medium was removed, and fresh medium containing 10 μg/mL free DOX or NPs was added (2 mL each well) and incubated with the cells at 37°C for 30 min or 2 h. After incubation for the indicated time, the medium was removed, and cells were washed three times with PBS, then the cells were detached from the plates using trypsin, suspended in PBS and centrifuged for 2 min at $1000\times g$ to remove the supernatant, and then the cells were resuspended in 0.2 mL PBS. Cells were finally analyzed by flow cytometry.

2.8 Subcellular distribution of DOX

A confocal laser scanning microscopy was used to investigate subcellular distribution of DOX in KB cells after it was incubated with different NPs [34]. Toward this, cells were grown on coverslip to 50% confluence and incubated with NPs (containing 5 μg equivalent/mL DOX) dispersed in culture medium at 37°C for 30 min and 4 h, separately. The cells were then washed five times with PBS and incubated with lysotracker green (50 nmol/L) for 0.5 h. The cells then washed five times with PBS and treated with DAPI (10 μg/mL) for 15 min for nucleus staining. The cells were then washed five times with PBS, fixed with paraformaldehyde for 15 min and stored at 4°C. The cells were imaged by a Zeiss 510 LSMNLO confocal microscope (Carl Zeiss Microscope systems, Jena, Germany) with identical settings for each confocal study.

2.9 Cytotoxicity of NPs

The cytotoxicity of NPs against KB cells, A549 cells and HepG2 cells was assessed by using MTT assay. The cells were seeded into 96-well plates and incubated for 24 h. The medium then was replaced with fresh medium containing a series of concentration of NPs and incubated for 48 h. Thereafter, the wells were washed three times with warm PBS and incubated again for another 4 h with FA-free RPMI 1640 containing 5 mg/mL of MTT. After removing the culture medium, 150 μL of DMSO was added to dissolve the precipitate and the resulting solution was measured for absorbance at 490 nm by using a CODA Automated EIA Analyzer (Bio-Rad Laboratories, Hercules, CA).

2.10 Animal experiment

Female athymic nude mice (six weeks old, body weight = 20–23 g) were subcutaneously implanted with KB cells (1×10^7 cells/0.1 mL/animal) in rear right flank. There were 6 mice in each group. Treatment was commenced on day 10 post inoculation when tumor size was approximately 80 mm^3. These tumor-bearing mice were treated with free DOX (5 mg/kg) or NPs (equivalent dose of doxorubicin: 2.5, 5 and 10 mg/kg) by tail vein injection every 7th day (days 1, 7, and 14). Mice were observed daily, and body weight was detected as possible signs of toxicity. Tumor size was measured every 3 days with a caliper in two dimensions and calculated using the formula: volume = $LW^2/2$ (L is the long diameter and W is the short diameter of a tumor). On day 42, all surviving mice were euthanized. The heart were removed and fixed in 10% formaldehyde. Formaldehyde-fixed, paraffin-embedded sections were stained with H&E for further histology study.

For distribution study *in vivo*, free DOX and DOX-hyd-PEG-FA NPs were administered to the tumor bearing nude mice via the tail vein with a dosage of 5 mg DOX/kg. Mice were sacrificed at selected time intervals to collect the plasma, organs and tumors, the tissues were rinsed in buffer, weighed and frozen at −20°C until analysis. The amount of DOX in plasma and tissue was measured by HPLC as described above.

2.11 Statistical analysis

All data were processed and analyzed by Sigma-Plot 8.0 software. The normality test was done before t-test. The statistical significance was evaluated by t-test and $p<0.05$ was considered significant.

Results

3.1 Synthesis of DOX-conjugated polymer

After the product was purified, the yield of DOX-hyd-PEG-FA, DOX-ami-PEG-FA, DOX-hyd-PEG and DOX-ami-PEG was 92%, 89%, 90% and 92% respectively. The DOX conjugated in DOX-ami-PEG, DOX-ami-PEG-FA, DOX-hyd-PEG and DOX-hyd-PEG-FA was 12.8%, 13.2%, 11.7% and 13.6% (w/w) respectively. The ^1H NMR spectrum of DOX-hyd-PEG-FA and DOX-ami-PEG-FA are shown in figure 4. The presence of FA in DOX-hyd-PEG-FA and DOX-ami-PEG-FA was confirmed by the appearance of signals at 6.7–8.7 ppm in ^1H NMR spectrum, which corresponded with the aromatic protons of FA. Moreover, the conjugation of DOX was confirmed by the presence of characteristic DOX peaks at 5.4, 4.0 and 2.5 ppm [35]. The PEG backbone was confirmed by the signal at 3.6 ppm [36]. The purity of DOX-hyd-PEG-FA and DOX-ami-PEG-FA was analyzed by HPLC, and typical chromatograms are shown in figure 5, which exhibited single sharp peak at 12.125 min for DOX-hyd-PEG-FA and 11.326 min for DOX-ami-PEG-FA, suggesting that the conjugates were homogeneous without any free DOX.

3.2. Characterization of nanoparticles

The size, polydispersity index, zeta potential, drug loading and drug encapsulation efficiency of nanoparticles are shown in table 1. There were no significant differences in zeta potential, particle size polydispersity index, and drug encapsulation efficiency between different NPs. The results also showed that there was not significant difference in the physical drug loading between different nanoparticles. But the total effective drug loading of DOX-hyd-PEG-FA NPs and DOX-hyd-PEG NPs were significant higher than that of DOX-ami-PEG-FA NPs and DOX-ami-PEG NPs.

The size stability of DOX-hyd-PEG-FA NPs and DOX-ami-PEG-FA NPs in PBS (pH = 7.4) at 37°C is shown in figure 6. The results indicated that DOX-hyd-PEG-FA NPs and DOX-ami-PEG-FA NPs were stable in five days in PBS (pH = 7.4) at 37°C.

3.3 Drug release characteristics *in vitro*

The drug release characteristics of the DOX-hyd-PEG-FA NPs and DOX-ami-PEG-FA NPs were investigated in a neutral environment (pH 7.4) and in an acidic environment (pH 5.0 and 6.5) at 37°C to assess the feasibility of using DOX-hyd-PEG-FA NPs and DOX-ami-PEG-FA NPs as anticancer drug delivery carriers. The results are shown in figure 7. The rate and amount of DOX released from the DOX-hyd-PEG-FA NPs were dependent on the pH of the medium. DOX-hyd-PEG-FA NPs showed a much faster DOX release in pH 5.0 medium than in pH 7.4 medium. In pH 5.0 medium, DOX-hyd-PEG-FA NPs released out 80% of loaded DOX in 10 h, and liberated 94% of loaded DOX in 58 h. However, in pH 7.4 medium, the DOX-hyd-PEG-FA NPs released only 5% of loaded DOX in 10 h and less than 12% in 58 h. The rate and amount of DOX released from the DOX-ami-PEG-FA NPs were independent on the pH of the medium. DOX-ami-PEG-FA NPs released out 5% of loaded DOX in 58 h in pH 7.4 medium, and released out 11% of loaded DOX in 58 h in pH 5.0 medium.

3.4 Cellular uptake of NPs

After KB cells and A549 cells were incubated with free DOX for 4 h, DOX was predominantly accumulated in the nucleus, which is shown in figure 8A and figure 9A respectively. When KB cells were incubated with DOX-hyd-PEG-FA NPs, large amount of DOX was distributed in the nucleus (figure 8B). Little amount of DOX was distributed in the nucleus after DOX-hyd-PEG NPs were incubated with KB cells (figure 8C). When A549 cells were incubated with DOX-hyd-PEG-FA NPs and DOX-hyd-PEG NPs, little amount of DOX was distributed in the nucleus (figure 9B and figure 9C).

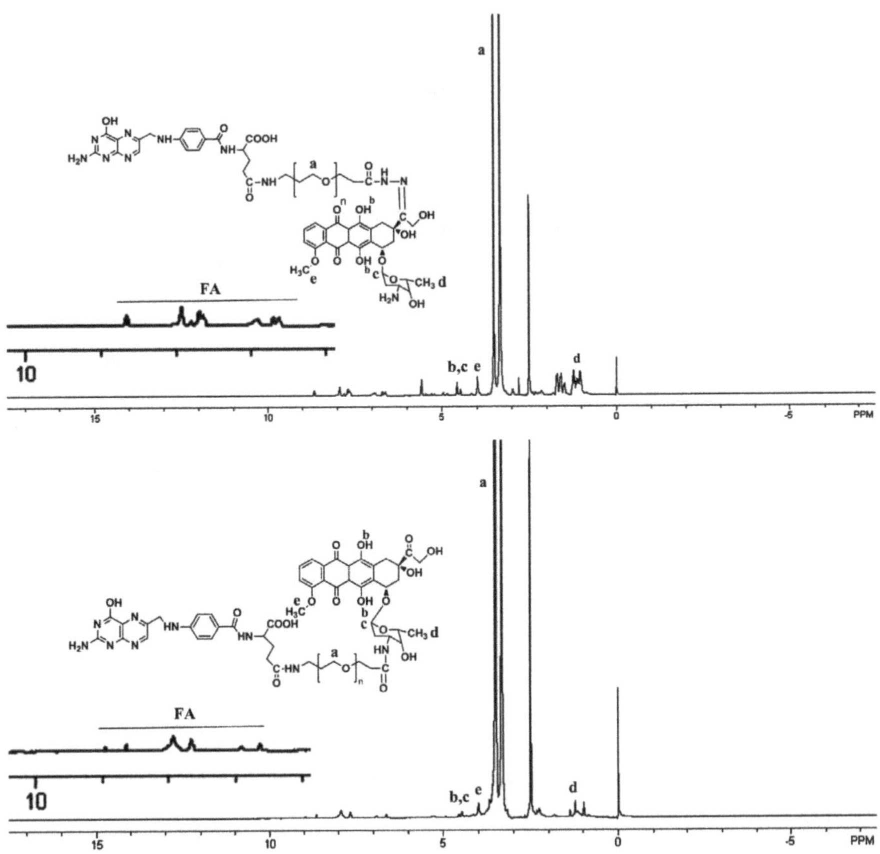

Figure 4. ^{1}H NMR spectrum of DOX-hyd-PEG-FA (upper panel) and DOX-ami-PEG-FA (lower panel).

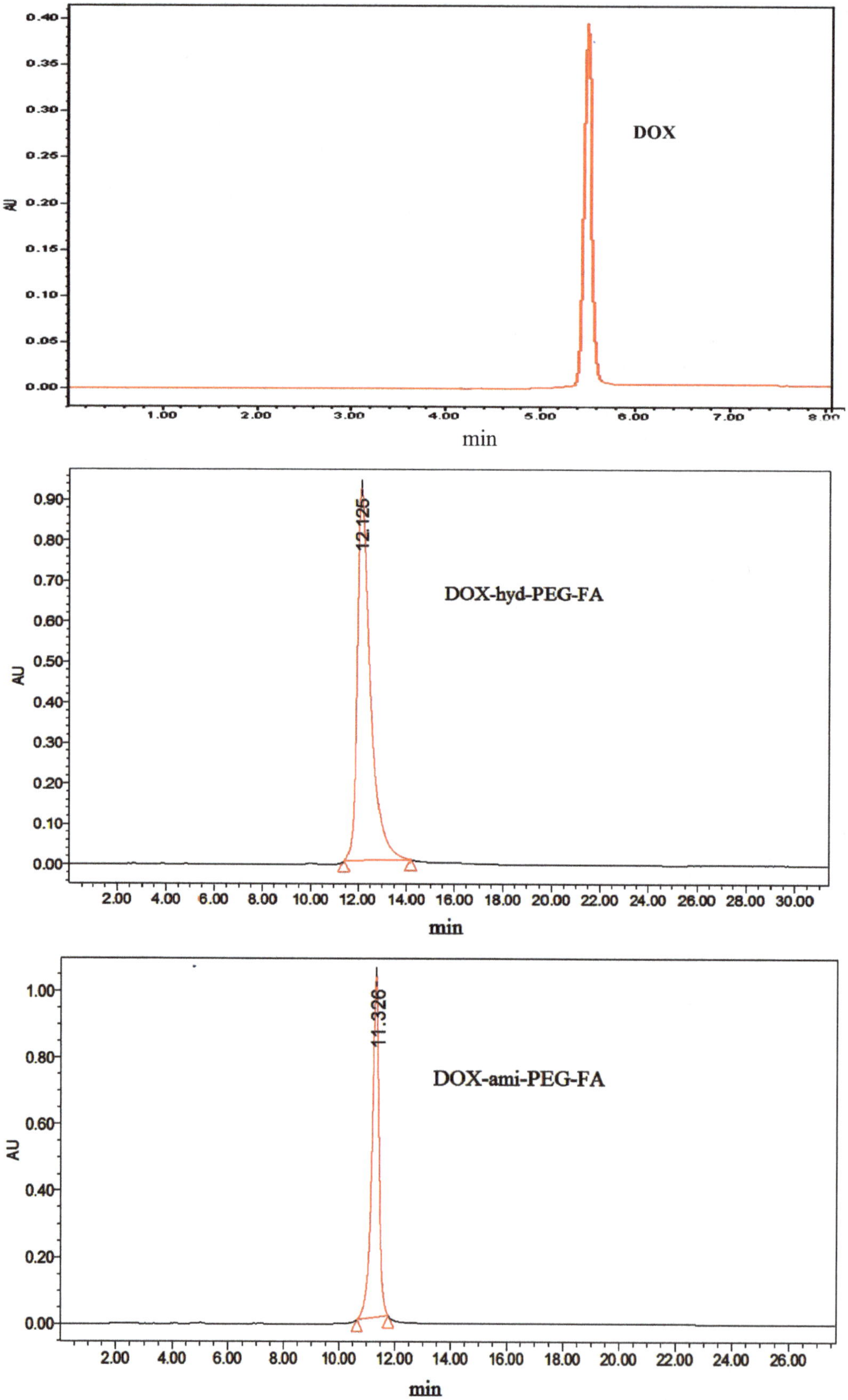

Figure 5. Typical chromatograms of free DOX (upper panel), DOX-hyd-PEG-FA (middle panel) and DOX-ami-PEG-FA (lower panel).

Table 1. Characterization of nanoparticles. Data represented mean±SD (n = 3).

	Particle size (nm)	Zeta potential (mV)	Polydispersity Index	Total effective drug loading[a] (%)	Physical drug loading[b](%)	Physical encapsulation efficiency (%)
DOX-hyd-PEG-FA NPs	186±27	−27.6±4.7	0.102±0.028	29.3±3.7**	15.1±1.7	74.3±8.9
DOX-hyd-PEG NPs	188±20	−22.6±3.5	0.181±0.055	27.5±2.5##	14.3±1.8	65.6±6.6
DOX-ami-PEG-FA NPs	213±28	−26.5±5.3	0.167±0.042	14.7±2.1	14.5±1.9	69.4±8.1
DOX-ami-PEG NPs	221±32	−24.6±4.1	0.201±0.053	15.6±2.7	15.2±1.5	64.7±7.7

[a]: NPs were dispersed in the acetate buffer (pH = 4.0);
[b]: NPs were dispersed in the DMSO.
**p<0.01 vs DOX-ami-PEG-FA NPs;
##p<0.01 vs DOX-ami-PEG NPs.

The cellular uptake of DOX and NPs were further semi-quantitatively investigated in KB cells and A549 cells by using flow cytometry. The typical pictures and statistical results are shown in figure 10. Cellular uptake of DOX-hyd-PEG-FA NPs in KB cells was increased in time-dependent manner. The intracellular uptake of DOX-hyd-PEG-FA NPs in KB cells was greater than that of DOX-hyd-PEG NPs. When KB cells were incubated with exogenous folate and DOX-hyd-PEG-FA NPs, the uptake efficiency of DOX-hyd-PEG-FA NPs was attenuated obviously. The exogenous folate almost had no effect on the intracellular uptake of DOX-hyd-PEG-FA NPs in A549 cells.

3.5 The subcellular distribution of DOX delivered by DOX-hyd-PEG-FA NPs and DOX-ami-PEG-FA NPs

Distribution of DOX in the nucleus and endosome/lysosome was investigated by triple-labelling with the nucleus-selective dye (DAPI, blue), the fluorescent conjugates (DOX, red), and dyes selective for acidic endolysosomes (LysoTracker green, green). The imaged cells treated with DOX-ami-PEG-FA NPs and DOX-hyd-PEG-FA NPs is presented in figure 11. Both NPs were localized in endolysosomes at early time points. DOX-hyd-PEG-FA NPs showed a predominant nuclear distribution at 4 h in KB cells. When KB cells were treated with DOX-ami-PEG-FA NPs, less DOX was seen in the nucleus, and main fraction of DOX was still found in endolysosomes at 4 h, indicating DOX-ami-PEG-FA NPs were relative stable in endolysosomes.

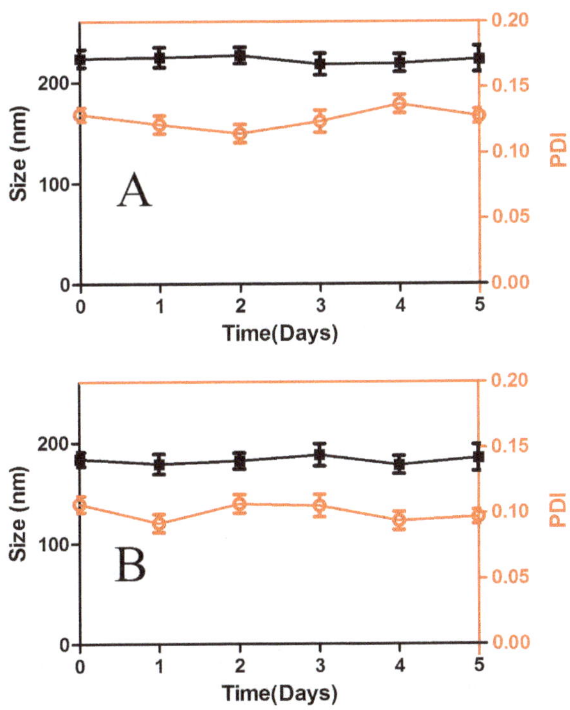

Figure 6. Long-term stability of DOX-ami-PEG-FA NPs (panel A) and DOX-hyd-PEG-FA NPs (panel B) in terms of particle size and polydispersity index (PDI) in PBS at room temperature. n = 3.

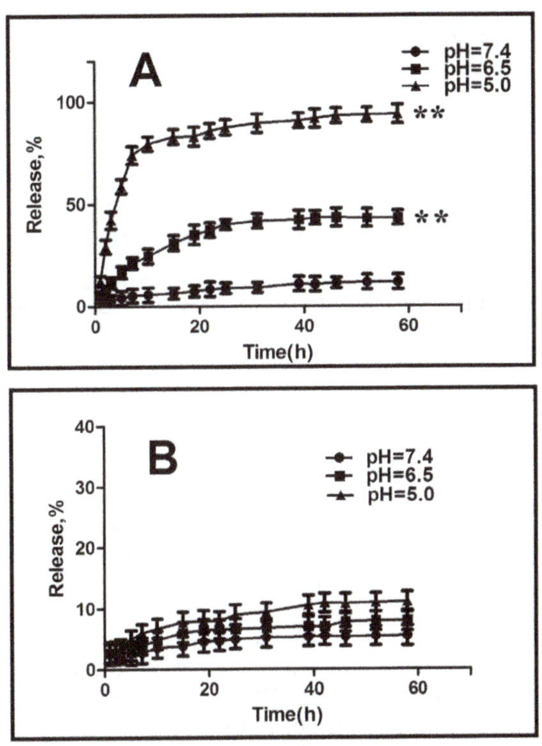

Figure 7. DOX release profiles from the DOX-hyd-PEG-FA NPs (panel A) and DOX-ami-PEG- FA NPs (panel B) in different pH medium. **P<0.01 vs pH 7.4 medium at 58 h, n = 3.

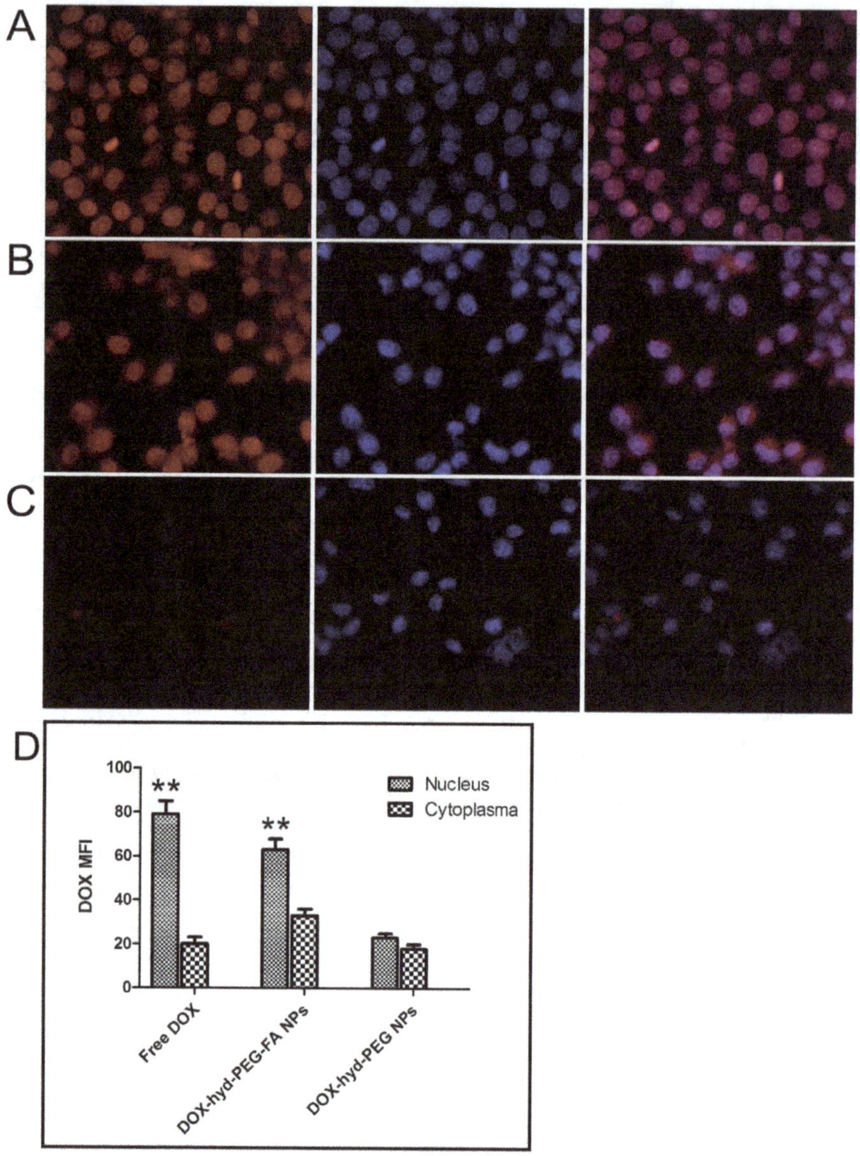

Figure 8. Confocal laser scaning microscopy (CLSM) images of KB cells incubated with DOX (panel A), DOX-hyd-PEG-FA NPs (panel B) and DOX-hyd-PEG NPs (panel C) at 37°C for 4 h. DOX concentration was 10 μg/mL. The pink region shows the localization of DOX (red) in the nucleus (blue). DOX mean fluorescence intensity (MFI) in the nucleus and cytoplasm of the KB cells are shown in panel D. **$P<0.01$ vs cytoplasma with the same treatment, n = 5.

3.6 Cytotoxicity of NPs

The cytotoxic effect of free DOX, DOX-hyd-PEG-FA NPs, DOX-ami-PEG-FA NPs, DOX-hyd-PEG NPs and DOX-ami-PEG NPs against the KB cells, A549 cells and HepG2 cells is shown in table 2. The results showed that the toxicity of DOX-hyd-PEG-FA NPs and DOX-hyd-PEG NPs on A549 cells was much higher than that of DOX-ami-PEG-FA NPs and DOX-ami-PEG NPs respectively. There was no significant difference in the viability when A549 cells were treated with DOX-hyd-PEG-FA NPs and DOX-hyd-PEG NPs. For KB cells, the results showed that the cell viability in the presence of DOX-hyd-PEG-FA NPs was much lower than that of free DOX and DOX-hyd-PEG NPs. HepG2 cells showed the similar results with KB cells. To estimate the effect of free FA on the cytotoxicity of DOX-hyd-PEG-FA NPs, KB cells were incubated with DOX-hyd-PEG-FA NPs and 100 μg/mL FA, and the result is shown in figure 12. The cell viability treated with DOX-hyd-PEG-FA NPs was approximately 29% in FA-free medium, but it was about 52% at the presence of 100 μg/mL FA.

Table 2. Cytotoxicity for A549 cells, KB cells and HepG2 cells treated with DOX, DOX-hyd-PEG-FA NPs, DOX-hyd-PEG NPs, DOX-ami-PEG-FA NPs and DOX-ami-PEG NPs.

3.7 *In vivo* antitumor activity of DOX-hyd-PEG-FA NPs

In order to further elucidate the role of FA and hydrazone bond in NPs *in vivo*, DOX-hyd-PEG-FA NPs, DOX-hyd-PEG NPs and DOX-ami-PEG-FA NPs were used to treat female athymic nude mice xenografted with KB cells. The *in vivo* anti-tumor activities of DOX-hyd-PEG-FA NPs, DOX-hyd-PEG NPs and DOX-ami-PEG-FA NPs are shown in figure 13. The statistic results of

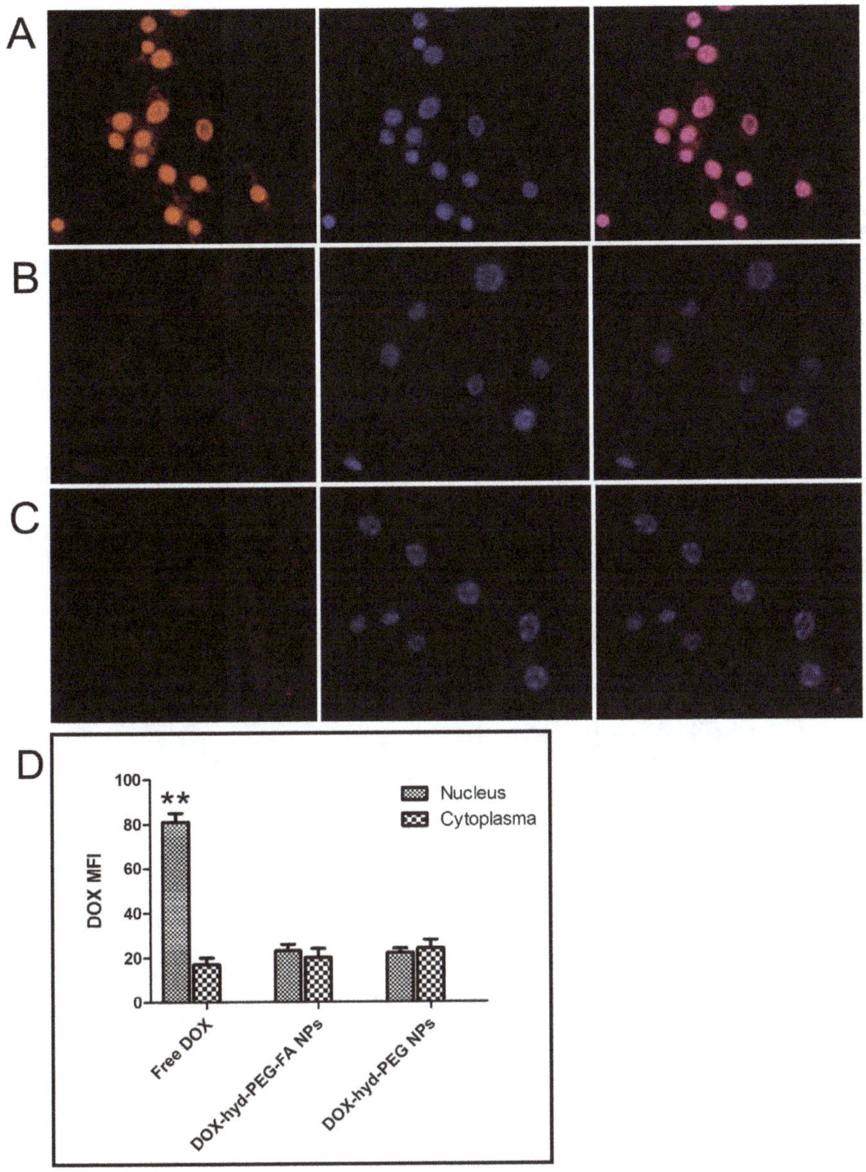

Figure 9. Confocal laser scaning microscopy (CLSM) images of A549 cells incubated with DOX (panel A), DOX-hyd-PEG-FA NPs (panel B) and DOX-hyd-PEG NPs (panel C) at 37°C for 4 h. DOX concentration was 10 μg/mL. The pink region shows the localization of DOX (red) in the nucleus (blue). DOX mean fluorescence intensity (MFI) in the nucleus and cytoplasm of the KB cells are shown in panel D. $^{**}P<0.01$ vs cytoplasma with the same treatment, n = 5.

survival are shown in table 3. Overall, compared with same dose of DOX, DOX-hyd-PEG NPs and DOX-ami-PEG-FA NPs treated group, DOX-hyd-PEG-FA NPs treated group showed an improved therapeutic effect in dose-dependent manner in terms of survival rate and tumor growth inhibition. DOX-hyd-PEG-FA NPs treated mice did not show any obvious side effect. The life span of animals treated with DOX-hyd-PEG-FA NPs was significantly longer than that of the animals treated with DOX.

3.8 Drug biodistribution

The distribution of DOX in tumor bearing nude mice after intravenous injection of free DOX or DOX-hyd-PEG-FA NPs is shown in figure 14. DOX was typically accumulated in liver, heart, spleen, lung, kidneys and tumor after intravenous injection of either free DOX or DOX-hyd-PEG-FA NPs. Compared with free DOX, DOX-hyd-PEG-FA NPs greatly increased the accumulation of DOX in the tumor, and significantly decreased the accumulation of DOX in heart and blood.

3.9 Pathological findings

Representative heart section in the control, doxorubicin treated and DOX-hyd-PEG-FA NPs treated groups are shown in figure 15. Structural abnormalities were not found in tumor bearing mice treated with normal saline. Cardiac tissues from doxorubicin-treated animals showed widespread marked structural abnormalities, including cardiomyocyte necrosis, vacuolization and myofibrillar loss. In contrast, necrotic cardiomyocytes, vacuolization and myofibrillar loss were rare in heart tissue from mice treated with DOX-hyd-PEG-FA NPs.

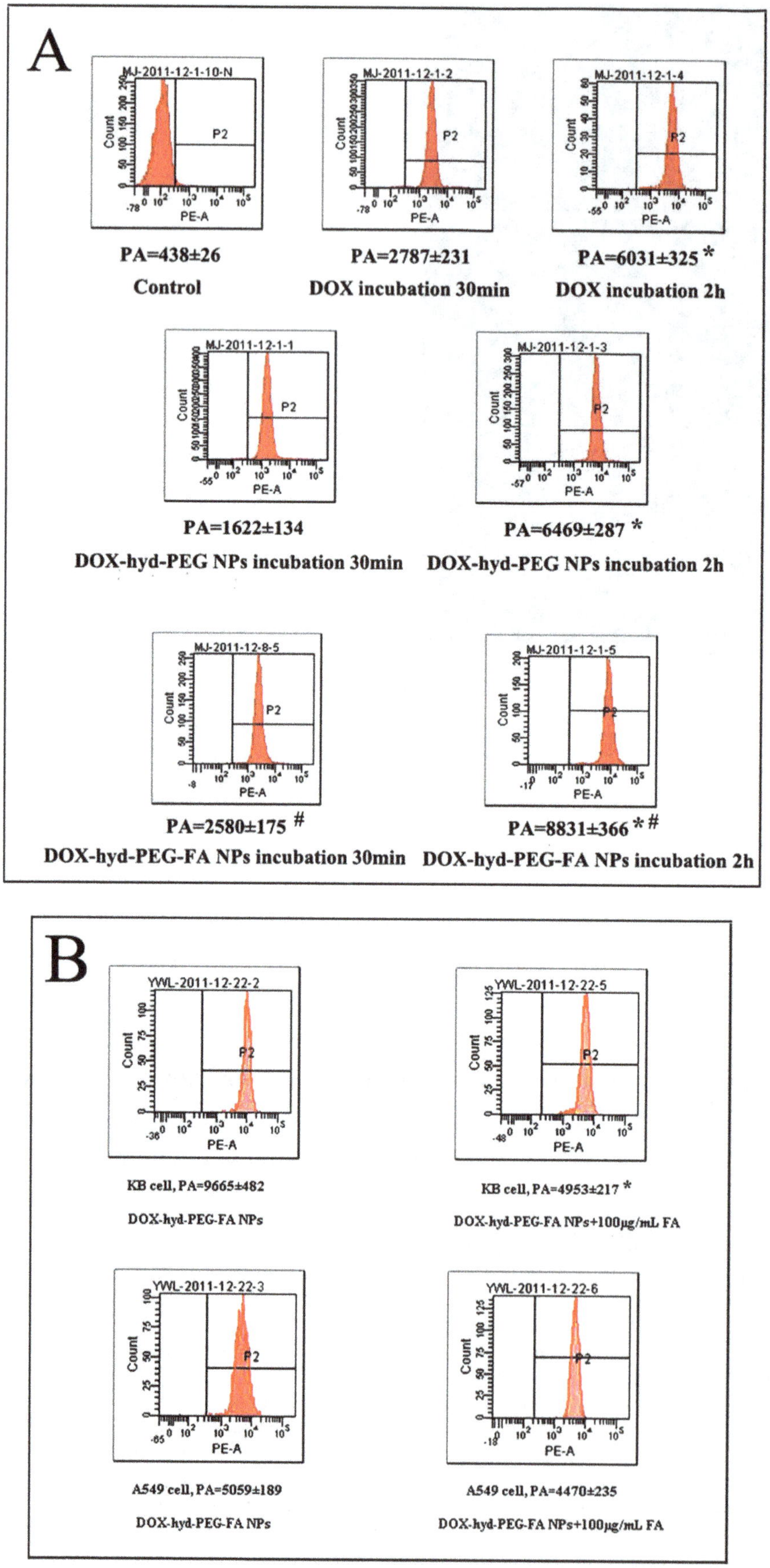
A
MJ-2011-12-1-10-N
PA=438±26
Control
MJ-2011-12-1-2
PA=2787±231
DOX incubation 30min
MJ-2011-12-1-4
PA=6031±325 *
DOX incubation 2h
MJ-2011-12-1-1
PA=1622±134
DOX-hyd-PEG NPs incubation 30min
MJ-2011-12-1-3
PA=6469±287 *
DOX-hyd-PEG NPs incubation 2h
MJ-2011-12-8-5
PA=2580±175 #
DOX-hyd-PEG-FA NPs incubation 30min
MJ-2011-12-1-5
PA=8831±366 * #
DOX-hyd-PEG-FA NPs incubation 2h
B
YWL-2011-12-22-2
KB cell, PA=9665±482
DOX-hyd-PEG-FA NPs
YWL-2011-12-22-5
KB cell, PA=4953±217 *
DOX-hyd-PEG-FA NPs+100μg/mL FA
YWL-2011-12-22-3
A549 cell, PA=5059±189
DOX-hyd-PEG-FA NPs
YWL-2011-12-22-6
A549 cell, PA=4470±235
DOX-hyd-PEG-FA NPs+100μg/mL FA
Count
PE-A
P2

Figure 10. Panel A-Flow cytometry results of KB cells that were incubated with DOX,DOX-hyd-PEG NPs and DOX-hyd-PEG-FA NPs for 30 min and 2 h. DOX concentration was 10 μg/mL. PA-peak area. *$p<0.05$ vs same treatment at 30 min; #$p<0.05$ vs DOX-hyd-PEG NPs at the same time point, n = 5. Panel B-Flow cytometric analysis of KB cells and A549 cells treated with DOX-hyd-PEG-FA NPs when exogenous folate was absent and present in the culture medium. DOX concentration was 10 μg/mL.Incubation time was 2 h. PA-peak area. *$p<0.05$ vs DOX-hyd-PEG-FA NPs on KB cells, n = 5.

Discussion

When polymeric NPs are designed and prepared, there are several parameters that need to be taken into consideration, such as particle size, drug loading, biocompatibility and stability. Particle size decides the distribution of the NPs in the body. Larger NPs tend to be cleared faster in the blood, and more particles were distributed in the liver, lung and spleen. Smaller NPs (10–200 nm) with negative surface charge tend to accumulate in tumor and be cleared from the blood at a slower rate [37]. Drug loading capacity is directly correlated to the drug delivery efficiency. The stability of NPs is another important factor that affects NPs behavior in the blood stream [38]. Biodegradable and environment responsive NPs, whose degradation and subsequent drug release occur in pathological sites, become a subject of interest [39].

In our study, a pH sensitive DOX-hyd-PEG-FA NPs were successfully self-assembled into the core-shell structured micelles in aqueous solution, in which DOX molecules were packed in the core through intermolecular interaction between the anthracycline rings of DOX, while the folic acid ligands were exposed outside of the shell. The particle size and PDI value were stable in 5 days in PBS (pH = 7.4) at 37°C. The zeta potential of DOX-hyd-PEG-FA NPs and DOX-ami-PEG-FA NPs was −27.6 mV and −26.5 mV respectively. It was reported that negatively charged surface nanoparticles showed a reduced plasma protein adsorption and low rate of nonspecific cellular uptake [37,40]. Meanwhile, the charged NPs can repel one another to overcome the natural tendency of aggregation of NPs [41]. Thus, DOX-hyd-PEG-FA NPs and DOX-ami-PEG-FA NPs had enough dispersion stability in the blood and were favorable for accumulation in the tumor tissue the by EPR effect.

It is very important to improve drug loading capacity and drug delivery efficiency for the active environment responsive NPs. The drug loading varied greatly in different drug delivery systems [42]. A tLyp-1-PEG-PLA nanoparticles loaded with paclitaxel was prepared through the emulsion/solvent evaporation technique, the drug loading was (1.43±0.10)%, and drug encapsulation efficiency was (47.5 ±2.4)% [43]. Guo X et al prepared a FA-PEG-PCL-hyd-DOX micelle. The DOX content in micelle was 4.57%. Moreover, it needs 8 steps reaction to synthesize FA-PEG-PCL-hyd-DOX [44]. In order to increase the drug delivery efficiency, DOX-hyd-PEG-FA NPs, DOX-hyd-PEG NPs, DOX-ami-PEG-FA NPs and DOX-ami-PEG NPs were prepared, and free DOX was encapsulated in NPs. There was not significant difference in the physical drug loading between different NPs. However, the total effective drug loading of DOX-hyd-PEG-FA NPs and DOX-hyd-PEG NPs were significant higher than that of DOX-ami-PEG-FA NPs and DOX-ami-PEG NPs. This was because large amount of DOX was released from DOX-hyd-PEG-FA and DOX-hyd-PEG polymer in acidic environment. Furthermore, there was not significant difference in zeta potential and particle size between DOX-hyd-PEG-FA NPs (−27.6±4.7 mV; 186±27 nm) and DOX-ami-PEG-FA NPs (−26.5±5.3 mV; 213±28 nm). Thus, the difference in anti-tumor efficacy between DOX-hyd-PEG-FA NPs and DOX-ami-PEG-FA NPs was resulted from the difference in the total effective drug loading. In a word, higher total effective drug loading was a very important

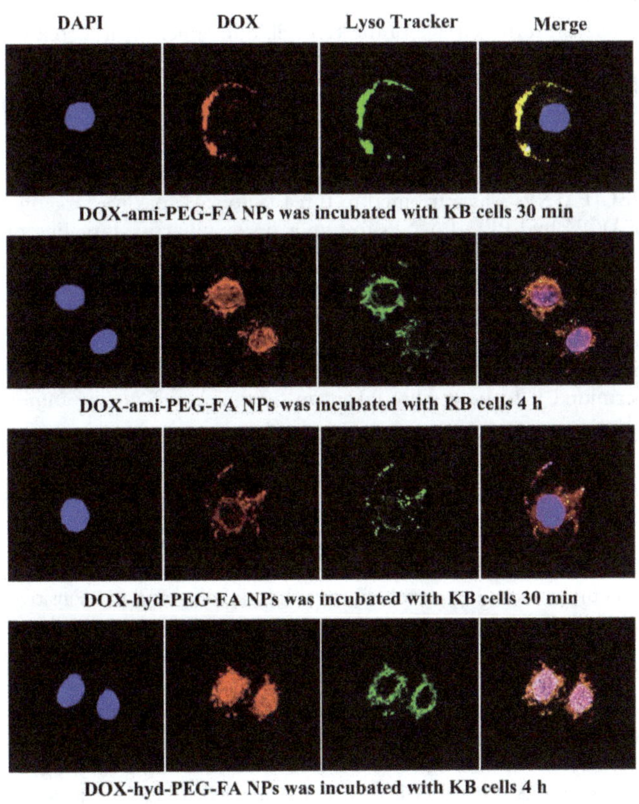

Figure 11. Subcellular localization of DOX in KB cells delivered by DOX-ami-PEG-FA NPs and DOX-hyd-PEG-FA NPs. The pink region shows the localization of DOX (red) in the nucleus (blue), the yellow region shows the localization of DOX (red) in the lysosome/endosome (green).

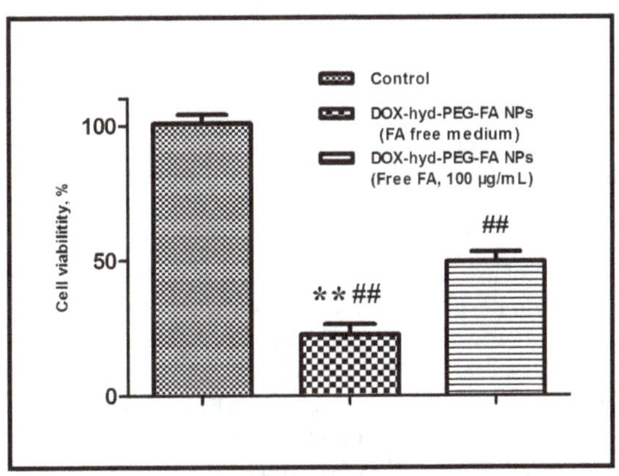

Figure 12. Effect of exogenous free FA on the viability of KB cells incubated with DOX-hyd-PEG-FA NPs for 48 h. DOX concentration was 0.6 μg/mL. **$p<0.01$ vs DOX-hyd-PEG-FA NPs+FA; ##$p<0.01$ vs control, n = 5.

Table 2. Cytotoxicity for A549 cells, KB cells and HepG2 cells treated with DOX, DOX-hyd-PEG-FA NPs, DOX-hyd-PEG NPs, DOX-ami-PEG-FA NPsz and DOX-ami-PEG NPs.

Drugs	IC_{50} (μmol/L)		
	A549 cells	**KB cells**	**HepG2 cells**
DOX	3.3±0.8	2.2±0.6	2.9±0.4
DOX-hyd-PEG-FA NPs	2.7±0.4*	0.8±0.2**## $$	1.5±0.3*# $
DOX-hyd-PEG NPs	3.2±0.7	2.8 ±0.3	3.1±0.6
DOX-ami-PEG-FA NPs	4.9±1.1	3.3±0.9	3.8±1.3
DOX-ami-PEG NPs	4.7±0.9	4.0±1.2	4.3±0.8

*p<0.05,
**p<0.01 vs DOX-ami-PEG-FA NPs.
#p<0.05,
##p<0.01 vs DOX-hyd-PEG NPs.
$p<0.05,
$$p<0.01 vs DOX.

advantage of DOX-hyd-PEG-FA NPs.

The faster release rate of DOX from the DOX-hyd-PEG-FA NPs in pH 5 medium (mimicking the endosomal/lysosomal environment of the tumor cells) was because of the acid-cleavable characteristics of the hydrazone linkage between the DOX and PEG, which resulted in the depolymerization of NPs in acidic medium. The slow DOX release rate of DOX-hyd-PEG-FA NPs observed at pH 7.4, mimicking the physiological conditions of the bloodstream, greatly reduced the chance of premature drug release in the blood circulation. The slow release rate of DOX from DOX-ami-PEG-FA NPs in acidic environment was because the amide bond between DOX and PEG was relative stable. Thus, DOX-ami-PEG-FA NPs were stable in acidic and neutral environment. It was relative difficulty to release DOX from DOX-ami-PEG-FA NPs in acidic and neutral environment.

After KB cells and A549 cells were incubated with free DOX for 4 h, the DOX mainly accumulated in the nucleus. Compared with the KB cells incubated with DOX-hyd-PEG NPs, the cells incubated with DOX-hyd-PEG-FA NPs showed more fluorescence in the nucleus and cytoplasm. Compared with KB cells, A549 cells incubated with DOX-hyd-PEG-FA NPs showed less fluorescence in the nucleus and cytoplasm. These results clearly indicated that the cellular uptake of DOX-hyd-PEG-FA NPs was facilitated by a folate receptor mediated endocytosis process. Furthermore, when DOX-hyd-PEG-FA NPs and DOX-ami-PEG-FA NPs were incubated with KB cells, they were localized in endolysosomes at 30 min. DOX-hyd-PEG-FA NPs showed a predominant nucleus distribution of DOX at 4 h. This was expected due to the dissociation of DOX-hyd-PEG-FA NPs in endolysosomes, subsequently faster release of DOX and led to a similar pattern of cellular distribution of free DOX by proton sponge effect [45]. However, DOX-ami-PEG-FA NPs were still found in endolysosomes after they were incubated with KB cells for 4 h. This was because DOX-ami-PEG-FA NPs were relative stable in acidic lysosomes.

The cytotoxicity of DOX-hyd-PEG-FA NPs and DOX-hyd-PEG NPs on A549 cells was much higher than that of DOX-ami-PEG-FA NPs and DOX-ami-PEG NPs respectively. This was due to the acidic sensitivity of DOX-hyd-PEG-FA NPs and DOX-hyd-PEG NPs, and more DOX was released in A549 cells. There was not significant difference in the viability when A549 cell was cultured with DOX-hyd-PEG-FA NPs and DOX-hyd-PEG NPs. This was because of the lack of FA receptors on A549 cells. For KB cells and HepG2 cells, the results showed that the cell viability in the presence of DOX-hyd-PEG-FA NPs was much lower than that of DOX-hyd-PEG NPs and free DOX, higher drug delivery efficiency of DOX-hyd-PEG-FA NPs was the reason for this observation. Meanwhile, the cytotoxicity of DOX-hyd-PEG-FA NPs against KB cells was inhibited by exogenous free FA. All the above results suggested that FA in DOX-hyd-PEG-FA NPs played an important role in enhancing the cytotoxic effect of DOX-hyd-PEG-FA NPs by binding itself with the overexpressed FA receptor, localized on the surface of the KB cell. Subsequently, it increased the intracellular uptake of DOX-hyd-PEG-FA NPs as a result of the receptor mediated endocytosis.

Compared with DOX, DOX-hyd-PEG NPs and DOX-ami-PEG-FA NPs, DOX-hyd-PEG-FA NPs significantly delayed the tumor growth. The enhanced *in vivo* antitumor effect of DOX-hyd-PEG-FA NPs was attributed to three factors: (1) passive targeting of DOX-hyd-PEG-FA NPs to tumor tissue; (2) active targeting of DOX-hyd-PEG-FA NPs to tumor cell overexpressing FA receptor; (3) high total effective drug loading and pH sensitive characteristics lead to the burst release of DOX from DOX-hyd-PEG-FA NPs in tumor cells. The passive targeting allowed DOX-hyd-PEG-FA NPs to accumulate in the tumor site, while the active targeting permitted it to be readily taken up by tumor cells at the tumor tissue.

The results of distribution experiment indicated that the level of DOX was above 15 μg/ g tissue in tumor tissue and was sustained for 24 h after DOX-hyd-PEG-FA NPs were administered. Longer exposure to DOX with the effective concentration leaded to a greater antitumor efficacy. Thus, the combined passive and active targeting effects, high total effective drug loading and pH sensitive were likely to act synergistically to increase the drug delivery efficiency of DOX-hyd-PEG-FA NPs, subsequently, delayed tumor growth. Finally, treatment with free DOX produced obvious side effects such as reduced activities and weight loss in animals. In contrast, we did not observe obvious side effects in mice treated with DOX-hyd-PEG-FA NPs, indicating that higher dose of DOX-hyd-PEG-FA NPs can be used to achieve a better therapeutic effect without introducing serious toxic effect.

In our lab, we previously synthesized FA-AMA-DOX and DOX-hyd-PEG conjugate to deliver DOX to tumor cell [18,20]. The IC_{50} of FA-AMA-DOX and DOX-hyd-PEG conjugate on HepG2 cells was 5.0±0.8 mol/L and 7.6±0.9 μM respectively. The IC_{50} of DOX-hyd-PEG-FA NPs on HepG2 cells was

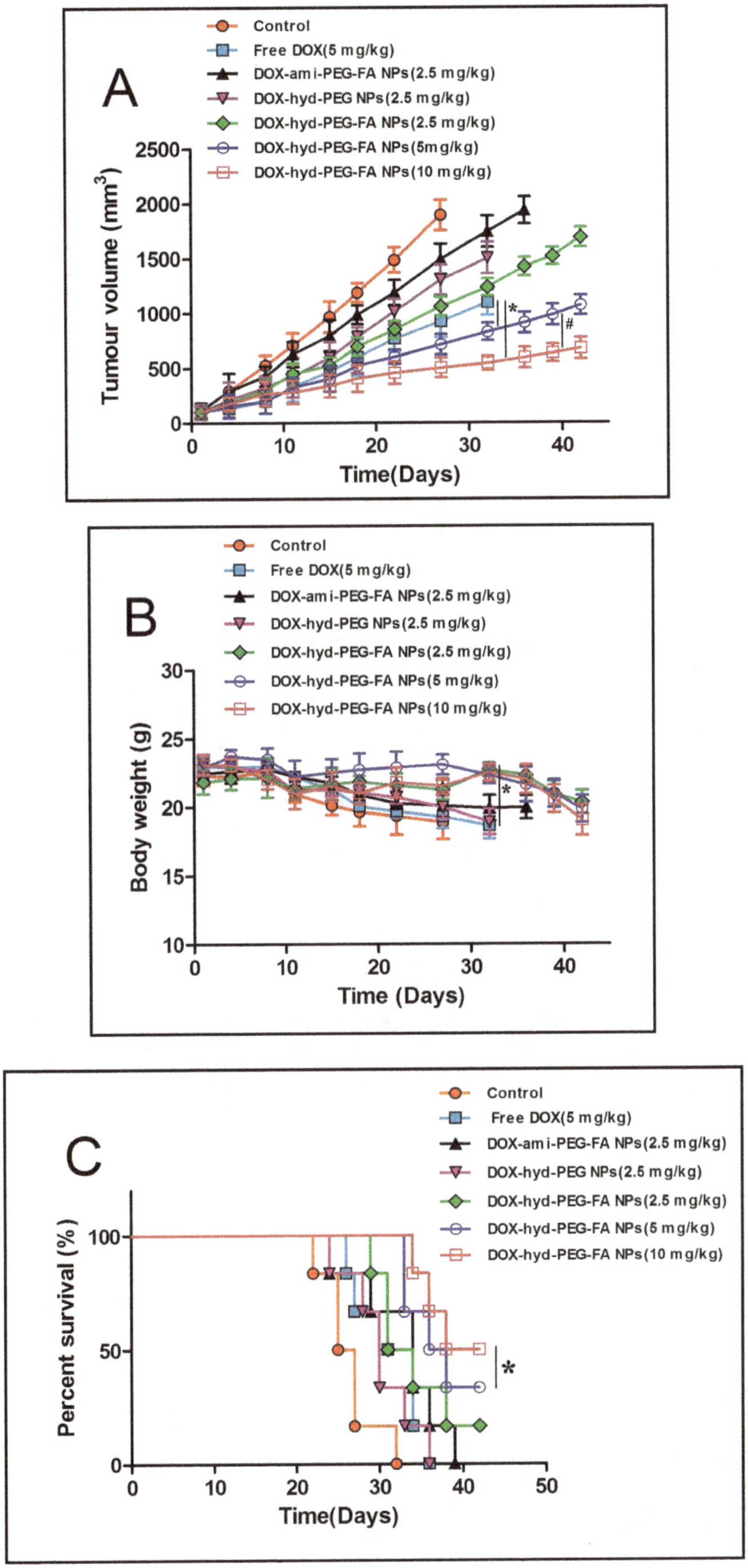
A
Control
Free DOX(5 mg/kg)
DOX-ami-PEG-FA NPs(2.5 mg/kg)
DOX-hyd-PEG NPs(2.5 mg/kg)
DOX-hyd-PEG-FA NPs(2.5 mg/kg)
DOX-hyd-PEG-FA NPs(5mg/kg)
DOX-hyd-PEG-FA NPs(10 mg/kg)
Tumour volume (mm3)
2500
2000
1500
1000
500
0
0
10
20
30
40
Time(Days)
*
#
B
Control
Free DOX(5 mg/kg)
DOX-ami-PEG-FA NPs(2.5 mg/kg)
DOX-hyd-PEG NPs(2.5 mg/kg)
DOX-hyd-PEG-FA NPs(2.5 mg/kg)
DOX-hyd-PEG-FA NPs(5 mg/kg)
DOX-hyd-PEG-FA NPs(10 mg/kg)
Body weight (g)
30
25
20
15
10
0
10
20
30
40
Time (Days)
*
C
Control
Free DOX(5 mg/kg)
DOX-ami-PEG-FA NPs(2.5 mg/kg)
DOX-hyd-PEG NPs(2.5 mg/kg)
DOX-hyd-PEG-FA NPs(2.5 mg/kg)
DOX-hyd-PEG-FA NPs(5 mg/kg)
DOX-hyd-PEG-FA NPs(10 mg/kg)
Percent survival (%)
100
50
0
0
10
20
30
40
50
Time(Days)
*

Figure 13. In vivo antitumor activity of DOX-hyd-PEG-FA NPs. Athymic nude mice xenografted with KB cells were intravenously injected with different doses of DOX-hyd-PEG-FA NPs (2.5, 5 and 10 mg/kg equivalent DOX) and one dose of DOX (5 mg/kg) every 7 day (days 1, 7, and 14). Panel **A**-tumor volume changes of tumor bearing mice, *P<0.05 vs free DOX, #P<0.05 vs 5 mg/kg DOX-hyd-PEG-FA NPs, n = 3. Panel **B**-body weight changes in tumor bearing nude mice, *P<0.05 vs free DOX, n = 3. Panel **C**-survival curve of tumor bearing mice. *P<0.05 vs free DOX, n = 3.

Table 3. Statistic analysis of survival of tumor bearing mice.

Treatment group	Median survival (d)	Mean survival (d)	Maximal survival (d)	*P*
Control	25	26.33±1.63	32	-
Free DOX(5 mg/kg)	31	31.33±1.68	36	0.045[a]
DOX-hyd-PEG-FA NPs (2.5 mg/kg)	31	34.17±1.85	42	0.386[b]
DOX-hyd-PEG-FA NPs (5 mg/kg)	36	37.33±1.52	42	0.049[b]
DOX-hyd-PEG-FA NPs (10 mg/kg)	38	39.00±1.31	42	0.007[b]

a-compared with control, b-compared with free DOX.

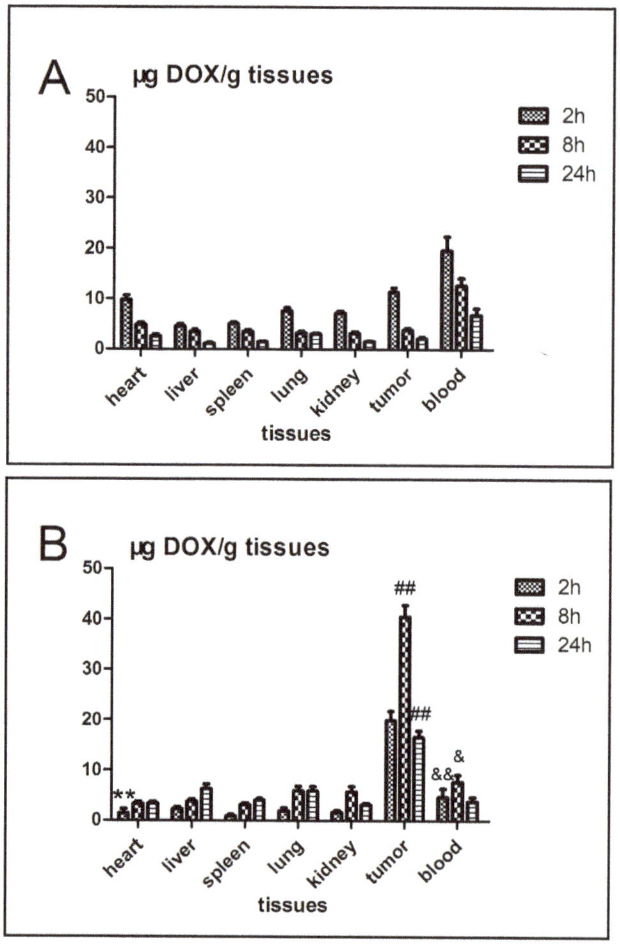

Figure 14. The DOX distribution in tumor bearing nude mice after intravenous injection of either free DOX (panel A) or DOX-hyd-PEG-FA NPs (panel B). **P<0.01 vs free DOX group in heart tissue at the same time point; ##P<0.01 vs free DOX group in tumor tissue at the same time point; &P<0.05, &&P<0.01 vs free DOX group in blood at the same time point. n = 5.

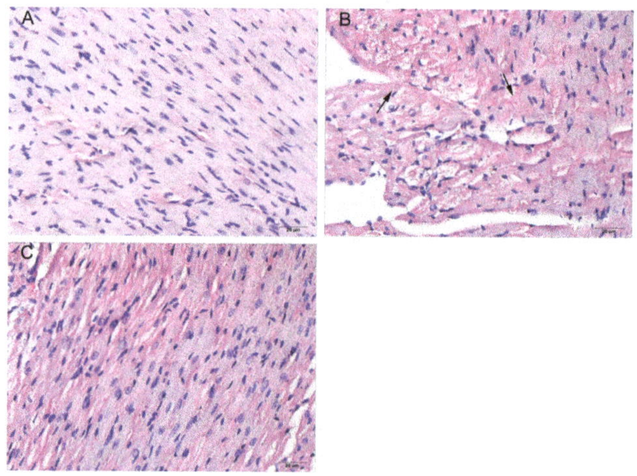

Figure 15. Histological sections of heart from tumor bearing nude mice. Haematoxylin and eosin stain. Panel **A**-negative control mice (tumor bearing mice treated with normal saline). Panel **B**-doxorubicin treated mice (5 mg/kg), degenerative myofibrils (arrows) are seen. Panel **C**-DOX-hyd-PEG-FA NPs treated mice (equivalent dose of doxorubicin:5 mg/kg).

1.5±0.3 μmol/L. Moreover, compared with DOX-hyd-PEG conjugate, DOX-hyd-PEG-FA NPs delivered more DOX in tumor tissue, which resulted in a better antitumor activity in tumor bearing nude mice. The above results implied that DOX-hyd-PEG-FA NPs had more potential in targeted cancer therapy.

Author Contributions

Conceived and designed the experiments: SYZ. Performed the experiments: WLY JBD BLZ RN YFS. Analyzed the data: WLY. Contributed reagents/materials/analysis tools: QBM MGZ SYZ. Wrote the paper: WLY SYZ.

References

1. Minko T, Kopeckova P, Pozharov V, Kopecek J (1998) HPMA copolymer bound adriamycin overcomes MDR1 gene encoded resistance in a human ovarian carcinoma cell line. J Control Release 54: 223–33.

2. Colin DVA, Dubernet C, Nemati F, Poupon MF, Puisieux F, et al. (1994) Uptake of doxorubicin from loaded nanoparticles in multidrug-resistant leukemic murine cells. Cancer Chemother Pharmacol 33: 504–08.
3. Duncan R (2003) The dawning era of polymer therapeutics. Nat Rev Drug Discov 2: 347–60.
4. Maeda H, Matsumura Y (1989) Tumoritropic and lymphotropic principles of macromolecular drugs. Crit Rev Ther Drug Carrier Syst 6: 193–210.
5. Fang J, Nakamura H, Maeda H (2011) The EPR effect: Unique features of tumor blood vessels for drug delivery, factors involved, and limitations and augmentation of the effect. Adv Drug Deliv Rev 63: 136–51.
6. Maeda H (2012) Vascular permeability in cancer and infection as related to macromolecular drug delivery, with emphasis on the EPR effect for tumor-selective drug targeting. Proc Jpn Acad Ser B Phys Biol Sci 88: 53–71.
7. Torchilin V (2011) Tumor delivery of macromolecular drugs based on the EPR effect. Adv Drug Deliv Rev 63: 131–35.
8. Cho K, Wang X, Nie S, Chen ZG, Shin DM (2008) Therapeutic nanoparticles for drug delivery in cancer. Clin Cancer Res 14: 1310–16.
9. Lee ES, Na K, Bae YH (2005) Doxorubicin loaded pH-sensitive polymeric micelles for reversal of resistant MCF-7 tumor. J Control Release 103: 405–18.
10. Sahoo SK, Labhasetwar V (2005) Enhanced antiproliferative activity of transferrin-conjugated paclitaxel-loaded nanoparticles is mediated via sustained intracellular drug retention. Mol Pharm 2: 373–83.
11. Barenholz Y (2012) Doxil®—the first FDA-approved nano-drug: lessons learned. J Control Release 10;160(2):117–34.
12. Koyama J, Honjo S, Morizono R, Goto T, Morita K, et al. (2011) Hepatocellular carcinoma with multiple lung metastasis resulting in long-term disease-free survival by transcatheter arterial infusion chemotherapy of SMANCS. Gan To Kagaku Ryoho 38(3):461–4.
13. Peer D, Karp JM, Hong S, Farokhzad OC, Margalit R, et al. (2007) Nanocarriers as an emerging platform for cancer therapy. Nat Nanotechnol 2: 751–60.
14. Parker N, Turk MJ, Westrick E, Lewis JD, Low PS, et al. (2005) Folate receptor expression in carcinomas and normal tissues determined by a quantitative radioligand binding assay. Anal Biochem 338: 284–93.
15. Low PS, Antony AC (2004) Folate receptor-targeted drugs for cancer and inflammatory diseases. Adv Drug Deliv Rev 56: 1055–58.
16. Dhawan D, Ramos-Vara JA, Naughton JF, Cheng L, Low PS, et al. (2013) Targeting folate receptors to treat invasive urinary bladder cancer. Cancer Res 73: 875–84.
17. Dosio F, Milla P, Cattel L (2010) EC-145, a folate-targeted Vinca alkaloid conjugate for the potential treatment of folate receptor-expressing cancers. Curr Opin Investig Drugs 11: 1424–33.
18. Ye WL, Teng ZH, Liu DZ, Cui H, Liu M, et al. (2013) Synthesis of a new pH-sensitive folate-doxorubicin conjugate and its antitumor activity in vitro. J Pharm Sci 102(2):530–40.
19. Filpula D, Zhao H (2008) Releasable PEGylation of proteins with customized linkers. Adv Drug Deliv Rev 60: 29–49.
20. Huan M, Zhang B, Teng Z, Cui H, Wang J, et al. (2012) In vitro and in vivo antitumor activity of a novel pH-activated polymeric drug delivery system for doxorubicin. PLoS One 7:e44116.
21. Huang L, Liu Y (2011) In vivo delivery of RNAi with lipid-based nanoparticles. Annu Rev Biomed Eng 13: 507–30.
22. Prabaharan M, Grailer JJ, Pilla S, Steeber DA, Gong S (2009) Gold nanoparticles with a monolayer of doxorubicin-conjugated amphiphilic block copolymer for tumor-targeted drug delivery. Biomaterials 30: 6065–75.
23. Yoo HS, Park TG (2004) Folate-receptor-targeted delivery of doxorubicin nano-aggregates stabilized by doxorubicin-PEG-folate conjugate. J Control Release 100: 247–56.
24. Kim SH, Jeong JH, Joe CO, Park TG (2005) Folate receptor mediated intracellular protein delivery using PLL–PEG–FOL conjugate. J Control Release 103: 625–34.
25. Ghaghada KB, Saul J, Natarajan JV, Bellamkonda RV, Annapragada AV (2005) Folate targeting of drug carriers: a mathematical model. J Control Release 104: 113–28.
26. Liu F, Deng D, Chen X, Qian Z, Achilefu S, et al. (2010) Folate-polyethylene glycol conjugated near-infrared fluorescence probe with high targeting affinity and sensitivity for in vivo early tumor diagnosis. Mol Imaging Biol 12: 595–607.
27. Lancon A, Delmas D, Osman H, Thenot JP, Jannin B, et al. (2004) Human hepatic cell uptake of resveratrol: involvement of both passive diffusion and carrier-mediated process. Biochem Biophys Res Commun 316: 1132–37.
28. Lancon A, Hanet N, Jannin B, Delmas D, Heydel JM, et al. (2007) Resveratrol in human hepatoma HepG2 cells: metabolism and inducibility of detoxifying enzymes. Drug Metab Dispos 35: 699–703.
29. Arote RB, Hwang SK, Lim HT, Kim TH, Jere D, et al. (2010) The therapeutic efficiency of FP-PEA/TAM67 gene complexes via folate receptor-mediated endocytosis in a xenograft mice model. Biomaterials 31(8):2435–45.
30. van Steenis JH, van Maarseveen EM, Verbaan FJ, Verrijk R, Crommelin DJ, et al. (2003) Preparation and characterization of folate-targeted PEG-coated pDMAEMA-based polyplexes. J Control Release 87(1–3):167–76.
31. Andersson L, Davies J, Duncan R, Ferruti P, Ford J, et al. (2005) Poly(ethylene glycol)-poly(ester-carbonate) block copolymers carrying PEG-peptidyl-doxorubicin pendant side chains: synthesis and evaluation as anticancer conjugates. Biomacromolecules 6(2):914–26.
32. Leamon CP, Low PS (1991) Delivery of macromolecules into living cells: a method that exploits folate receptor endocytosis. Proc Natl Acad Sci U S A 88: 5572–76.
33. Hu Q, Gao X, Gu G, Kang T, Tu Y, et al. (2013) Glioma therapy using tumor homing and penetrating peptide-functionalized PEG-PLA nanoparticles loaded with paclitaxel. Biomaterials 34: 5640–50.
34. Xiong XB, Ma Z, Lai R, Lavasanifar A (2010) The therapeutic response to multifunctional polymeric nano-conjugates in the targeted cellular and subcellular delivery of doxorubicin. Biomaterials 31: 757–68.
35. Jayant S, Khandare JJ, Wang Y, Singh AP, Vorsa N, et al. (2007) pH-triggered intracellular release from actively targeting polymer micelles. Pharm Res 24(11):2120–30.
36. Ma R, Yang H, Li Z, Liu G, Sun X, et al. (2012) Phenylboronic acid-based complex micelles with enhanced glucose-responsiveness at physiological pH by complexation with glycopolymer. Biomacromolecules 13(10):3409–17.
37. He C, Hu Y, Yin L, Tang C, Yin C (2010) Effects of particle size and surface charge on cellular uptake and biodistribution of polymeric nanoparticles. Biomaterials 31: 3657–66.
38. Yang C, Attia AB, Tan JP, Ke X, Gao S, et al. (2012) The role of non-covalent interactions in anticancer drug loading and kinetic stability of polymeric micelles. Biomaterials 33: 2971–79.
39. Torchilin VP (2007) Micellar nanocarriers: pharmaceutical perspectives. Pharm Res 24: 1–16.
40. Alexis F, Pridgen E, Molnar LK, Farokhzad OC (2008) Factors affecting the clearance and biodistribution of polymeric nanoparticles. Mol Pharm 5: 505–15.
41. Aggarwal P, Hall JB, McLeland CB, Dobrovolskaia MA, McNeil SE (2009) Nanoparticle interaction with plasma proteins as it relates to particle biodistribution, biocompatibility and therapeutic efficacy. Adv Drug Deliv Rev 61(6):428–37.
42. Lalatsa A, Schatzlein AG, Mazza M, Le TB, Uchegbu IF (2012) Amphiphilic poly(L-amino acids) - new materials for drug delivery. J Control Release 161: 523–36.
43. Hu Q, Gao X, Gu G, Kang T, Tu Y, et al. (2013) Glioma therapy using tumor homing and penetrating peptide-functionalized PEG-PLA nanoparticles loaded with paclitaxel. Biomaterials 2013;34: 5640–50.
44. Guo X, Shi C, Wang J, Di S, Zhou S (2013) pH-triggered intracellular release from actively targeting polymer micelles. Biomaterials 34: 4544–54.
45. Midoux P, Pichon C, Yaouanc JJ, Jaffres PA (2009) Chemical vectors for gene delivery: a current review on polymers, peptides and lipids containing histidine or imidazole as nucleic acids carriers. Br J Pharmacol 157: 166–78.

19

Submicron-Bubble-Enhanced Focused Ultrasound for Blood–Brain Barrier Disruption and Improved CNS Drug Delivery

Ching-Hsiang Fan[1], Hao-Li Liu[2], Chien-Yu Ting[1], Ya-Hsuan Lee[1], Chih-Ying Huang[2], Yan-Jung Ma[2], Kuo-Chen Wei[3], Tzu-Chen Yen[4,5]*, Chih-Kuang Yeh[1]*

1 Department of Biomedical Engineering and Environmental Sciences, National Tsing Hua University, Hsinchu, Taiwan, 2 Department of Electrical Engineering, Chang-Gung University, Tao-Yuan, Taiwan, 3 Department of Neurosurgery, Chang Gung University College of Medicine and Memorial Hospital, Tao-Yuan, Taiwan, 4 Department of Nuclear Medicine, Chang Gung University College of Medicine and Memorial Hospital, Tao-Yuan, Taiwan, 5 Molecular Imaging Center, Chang Gung University College of Medicine and Memorial Hospital, Tao-Yuan, Taiwan

Abstract

The use of focused ultrasound (FUS) with microbubbles has been proven to induce transient blood–brain barrier opening (BBB-opening). However, FUS-induced inertial cavitation of microbubbles can also result in erythrocyte extravasations. Here we investigated whether induction of submicron bubbles to oscillate at their resonant frequency would reduce inertial cavitation during BBB-opening and thereby eliminate erythrocyte extravasations in a rat brain model. FUS was delivered with acoustic pressures of 0.1–4.5 MPa using either in-house manufactured submicron bubbles or standard SonoVue microbubbles. Wideband and subharmonic emissions from bubbles were used to quantify inertial and stable cavitation, respectively. Erythrocyte extravasations were evaluated by *in vivo* post-treatment magnetic resonance susceptibility-weighted imaging, and finally by histological confirmation. We found that excitation of submicron bubbles with resonant frequency-matched FUS (10 MHz) can greatly limit inertial cavitation while enhancing stable cavitation. The BBB-opening was mainly caused by stable cavitation, whereas the erythrocyte extravasation was closely correlated with inertial cavitation. Our technique allows extensive reduction of inertial cavitation to induce safe BBB-opening. Furthermore, the safety issue of BBB-opening was not compromised by prolonging FUS exposure time, and the local drug concentrations in the brain tissues were significantly improved to 60 times (BCNU; 18.6 µg versus 0.3 µg) by using chemotherapeutic agent-loaded submicron bubbles with FUS. This study provides important information towards the goal of successfully translating FUS brain drug delivery into clinical use.

Editor: Ralph V. Shohet, University of Hawaii, United States of America

Funding: The authors acknowledge the supports of National Science Council of Taiwan (NSC 99-2218-E-182-002, 100-2218-E-182-001, 101-2221-E-007-035-MY3) and National Tsing Hua University (102N2046E1). The funders had no role in study design, data collection and analysis, decision to publish, or preparation of the manuscript.

Competing Interests: The authors have declared that no competing interests exist.

* E-mail: yentc1110@gmail.com (TCY); ckyeh@mx.nthu.edu.tw (CKY)

These authors contributed equally to this work.

Introduction

The blood–brain barrier (BBB) presents a major obstacle to the entry of therapeutic molecules into the central nervous system (CNS) [1]. Recent experiments have confirmed that the permeability of the BBB can be increased by combining microbubbles with focused ultrasound (FUS) at frequencies ranging from 0.3 to 8.0 MHz [2–5]. The interaction between microbubbles and FUS temporarily deforms endothelial cells and changes the integration of tight junctions [6,7]. This procedure leads to temporarily disruption of the BBB and thereby increases the efficiency of drug delivery locally in the CNS. This technology is ideally suited for the transcranial delivery of water-soluble drugs, and has the potential to deliver macromolecules (e.g. monoclonal antibodies) with up to tens of kilodaltons in size. Off-target effects are thus minimized in contrast to traditional systemic BBB-opening procedures such as osmotic BBB-opening through carotid infusion of a hypertonic solution [8,9]. Furthermore, FUS-induced BBB opening is reversible within several hours, providing a window of opportunity for local delivery of therapeutic agents into the brain [10–15].

Despite the advantages of FUS-induced BBB opening, the interaction of microbubbles with FUS may occasionally be accompanied by side effects [4]. The most common side effect is brain tissue damage, which can be caused by ultrasound overexcitation (including excessive acoustic pressure, and/or duration of sonication) [16], or microbubble overdosing [17]. The presence of microbubbles in an ultrasonic field induces two modes of cavitation, stable and inertial. At low acoustic power levels, microbubbles oscillate within the ultrasound field and enlarge via rectified diffusion. Bubble activity of this type is called stable cavitation, and it induces stable bubble oscillation to emit acoustic harmonic signals (i.e. at harmonic or subharmonic frequencies) [18] and produce mild microstreaming forces in the bloodstream that stimulate surrounding endothelial cells [19].

Bubble activity with rapid growth and violent collapse under ultrasound exposure is referred to as inertial cavitation, which may be responsible for inducing erythrocyte extravasations, or possibly cell apoptosis, and tissue injury that accompanies FUS-induced BBB-opening [20,21]. A number of studies have shown the importance of stable and inertial cavitation during BBB-opening process. For example, McDannold *et al.* have demonstrated that the threshold of BBB-opening was 0.29 MPa with ultrasound frequency of 0.26 MHz, whereas the inertial cavitation was induced exceeding 0.4 MPa [20]. Tung *et al.* have illustrated that the BBB-opening accompanied with harmonic activities which contributed to stable cavitation [21]. Liu *et al.* showed that erythrocyte extravasations occurred at high acoustic pressures (1.9 MPa) during the BBB-opening process [4], and erythrocyte extravasations further limited the permeability of BBB [10]. However, the exact roles of stable and inertial cavitation in BBB-opening and erythrocyte extravasations are not well confirmed, mainly because current micron-sized bubbles are polydispersed and can simultaneously undergo both kinds of cavitation activities under FUS exposure making it hard to characterize individual effects. The possibility of inducing erythrocyte extravasations is a major concern, and would greatly limit the application of repetitive microbubble-assisted FUS procedures aimed at increasing local drug concentration and delivery.

Therefore, the aim of this study is to propose a synergistic use of submicron bubbles (to greatly increase the threshold of inertial cavitation) and on-resonant frequency FUS (to amplify the stable cavitation activity) to maximize the separation of inertial and stable cavitation. Finally, the optimized FUS-enhanced chemotherapeutic agent delivery was performed by characterizing stable and inertial cavitation activities. Concurrence of BBB-opening and chemotherapeutic agents delivery for anti-glioma therapy has been verified by using multi-functional bubbles in our previous study [22]. Thus, another purpose of this study is to verify that a high concentration of chemotherapeutic agent (1,3-bis(2-chloroethyl)-1-nitrosourea, BCNU) can be safely and locally delivered by these submicron-sized drug-loaded bubbles upon FUS sonication. We compared the BBB-opening effect brought about by our in-house designed submicron bubbles to the traditional setup using commercial microbubbles. Cavitation activities were analyzed, and magnetic resonance imaging (MRI) and histological examinations were conducted to assess the occurrence of brain damages. Finally, the efficiency of drug delivery was determined by measuring the amounts of BCNU delivered into brain tissues by high performance liquid chromatography (HPLC).

Materials and Methods

Submicron Bubble Preparation

Submicron bubbles were prepared in-house via thin-film hydration method. Briefly, one milliliter of bubble formulation was prepared from 1,2-distearoyl-sn-glycero-3-phosphocholine (DSPC) (Avanti Polar Lipids, AL, USA) and 1,2-distearoyl-sn-glycero-3-phosphoethanolamine-N-[methoxy(polyethyleneglycol)-2000] (DSPE-PEG-2000) (Avanti Polar Lipids) at a molar ratio of 18:1. The lipid mixture was dissolved in chloroform, which was then removed by evaporation in a rotary evaporator (Rotavapor R-210, Büchi Labortechnik AG, Flawil, Switzerland) so that a thin lipid film remained on the wall of the vial. The vial was lyophilized and stored at −20°C. To prepare the aqueous lipid solution, 1 mL of degassed 5 μL/mL glycerol in phosphate-buffered saline (PBS, pH 7.4) was added to the vial to dissolve the thin film. The lipids were dispersed by sonication for 5 min at room temperature. The sample was degassed in the same airtight vial which was then refilled with perfluoropropane gas (C_3F_8) and was heated to 65°C for 5 min. Submicron bubble suspensions were finally produced by intense shaking using a home-built agitator [23]. The bubbles were counted and sized using a Coulter counter equipped with a 30 μm sensor orifice (Multisizer 3, Beckman Coulter, Miami FL, USA) for a 0.7–20 μm range. Smaller particles (<1 μm) were measured by dynamic light scattering (DLS, Nanosizer-S, Malvern, London, UK). The mean bubble diameter was 1.10±0.07 μm and 0.65±0.01 μm by Coulter counter and DLS, respectively. The mean bubble concentration was $(42.80\pm1.53)\times10^9$ bubbles/mL by Coulter counter measurements (Figure 1A). The stability tests of submicron bubbles were listed in File S1 (Figure S1–S2). The resonance frequency of submicron bubbles were estimated at 10 MHz based on a standard procedure that literature has proposed (see Method S1, Table S1 and Figure S3–S4 in File S1) [24].

Commercially available microbubbles, SonoVue (Bracco Diagnostics Inc., Milan, Italy), had a mean diameter of 2.5 μm (resonance frequency of several megahertz) and were used at a concentration of approximately $(3–5)\times10^8$ bubbles/mL for comparison [25].

Animal Preparation

All animal experiments were approved by the Institutional Animal Care and Use Committee of National Tsing Hua University and adhered to the experimental animal care guideline (IACUC approval number: NTHU10044). A total of 148 adult male Sprague-Dawley (SD) rats weighing about 300–350 g were studied. Animals were anesthetized intraperitoneally with chloral hydrate (400 mg/kg) before experiments. A cranial window of approximately 1×1 cm^2 was fashioned with a high-speed drill before FUS irradiation to reduce distortion of the ultrasound beam. The skull defects were covered with saline-soaked gauze to prevent dehydration until the application of FUS. A catheter (PE50, Intramedic, Clay Adams Inc., NJ, USA) was inserted into the jugular vein to allow intravenous (IV) injection of bubbles, dyes and drugs. During the experiment, body temperature of the animals were maintained at 36±1°C by a heating pad (THM 100, Indus Instruments, Houston, TX, USA).

Experimental Setup

The experimental arrangement is shown in Figure 1B. The FUS transducer and a passive cavitation detector (PCD) were arranged confocally using a self-made holder, with an included angle of approximately 120 degrees which was limited by their focal lengths and physical dimensions [21]. Two single-element FUS transducers with different center frequencies were used to transmit sonication pulses. The first FUS transducer was a single-element spherically-focused 10-MHz transducer (diameter: 25.4 mm, focus length: 52.2 mm, −6 dB bandwidth: 68.9%; V322, Panametrics, Waltham, MA, USA) and the second one was a single-element spherically-focused 1-MHz transducer (diameter: 25.4 mm, focus length: 52.7 mm, −6 dB bandwidth: 70.0%; V302, Panametrics). The PCD was a single-element spherically-focused 5-MHz transducer (diameter: 19.1 mm, focus length: 51.4 mm, −6 dB bandwidth: 57.1%; V308, Panametrics). The holder was mounted on a computer-controlled 2-D motion stage (HR8, Nanomotion, Yokneam, Israel). A waveform generator (model 2041, Tabor Electronics, Tel Hanan, Israel) was used to generate the transmitting pulse. A radio-frequency (RF) power amplifier (150A100B, AR, Souderton, PA, USA) amplified the pulses to drive the 1-MHz/10-MHz FUS transducers. The scattered echoes from bubbles were received by the PCD, and then amplified by a broadband receiver (BR-640, Retec, Warwick, RI, USA). The

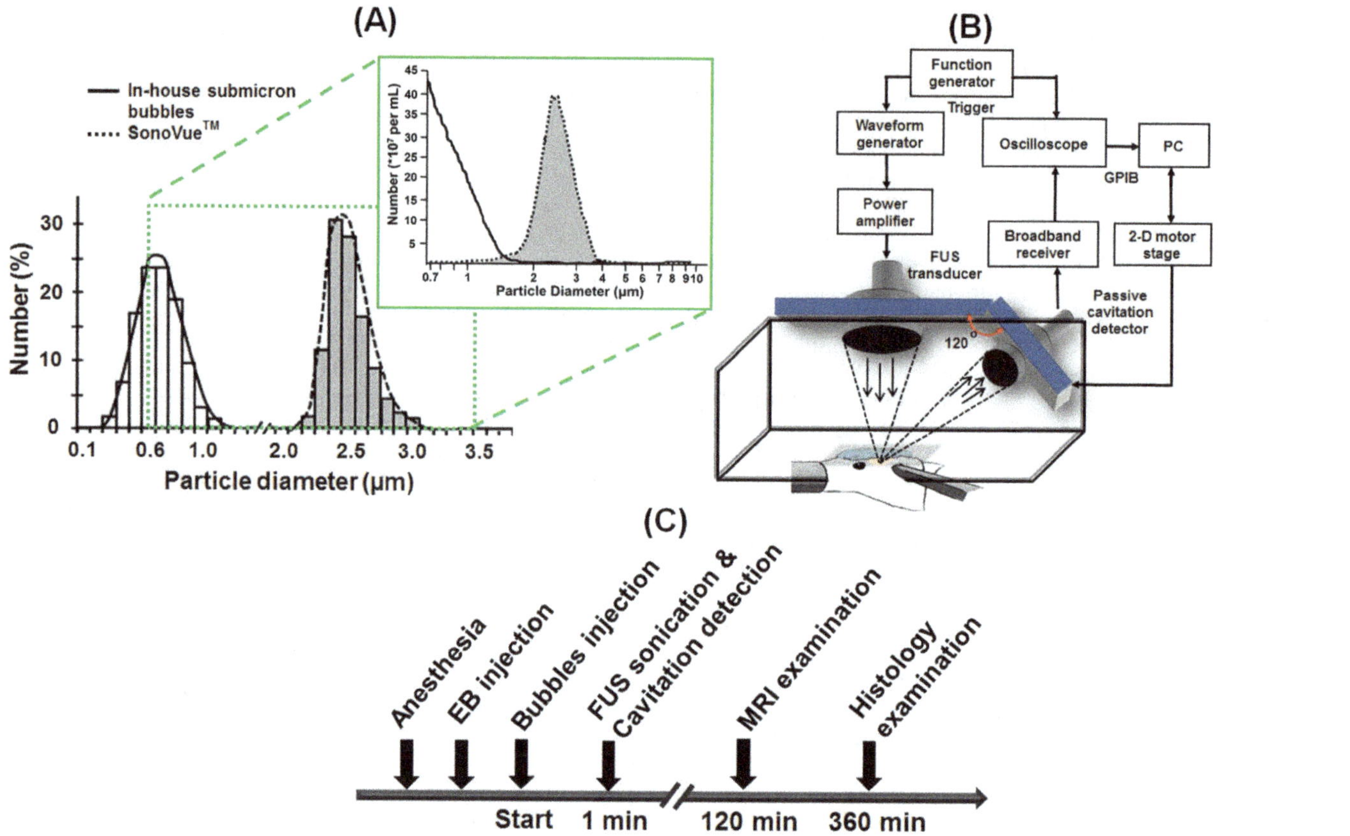

Figure 1. Experimental settings and procedures. A: Size distributions of in-house submicron bubbles and commercial SonoVue bubbles. Left diagram was measured by DLS and right one was determined by Coulter counter, which could provide both size distribution and concentration information. B: Experimental setup. C: Timeline of the *in vivo* experiment.

amplified RF signals were sampled at 25 MHz to accommodate the highest memory limit of the oscilloscope (LT354, LeCory Co., Chestnut Ridge, NY, USA) and then stored on the personal computer for off-line analysis. A function generator (33120A, Hewlett-Packard Co., Palo Alto, CA, USA) transmitted a trigger to synchronize the waveform generator used in sonication and the oscilloscope.

A water reservoir with a 4×4 cm^2 opening at the bottom was used for animal experiments. The opening was sealed by a polyurethane membrane to allow the entry of ultrasound. The rats were laid prone under the water reservoir with their heads tightly attached to the membrane window. Ultrasound coupling gel (Aquasonic 100, Parker laboratories, Fairfield, NJ, USA) was applied between the cranial window and the membrane to maximize the transmission of ultrasound between the transducer and the brain. During the experiment, the animal was secured on the in-house stereotaxic apparatus with ear bars and a bite bar to reduce any undesired motion. The water in the reservoir was kept at 37°C by a heater to assist in maintaining the body temperature of the animals.

FUS Calibration and Sonication

The acoustic pressure maps of the applied FUS transducers were measured in an acrylic water tank by using the FUS transducer attached to a semiautomatic 3-D positioning system. A polyvinylidene difluoride (PVDF) type hydrophone (HNP-0400, Onda, Sunnyvale, CA, USA; calibration range: 1–20 MHz) was used to measure axial and lateral acoustic pressure fields generated by the 10-MHz transducer in the water tank with which filled 25°C distilled/degassed water. The spatial resolution of the measurement was set to 300 μm. The measured half-maximum pressure amplitude of 10-MHz transducer at the focal zone had a diameter of 1.0 mm and length of 3.7 mm. The 1-MHz transducer was calibrated as the same way and the measured half-maximum pressure amplitude at the focal zone had a diameter of 2.9 mm and length of 24.8 mm. The acoustic pressure maps of 1-MHz, 5-MHz, and 10-MHz transduces were shown in File S1, Figure S5.

The resonance frequency of a gas bubble increases as its radius decreases [26]. To investigate the BBB-opening effect caused by different resonance frequencies of bubbles and excitation frequencies of FUS, we comprehensively perform verifications by testing all combinations of the submicron bubbles/SonoVue under the exposure of 1-MHz/10-MHz FUS energy to discriminate the playing roles of inertial cavitation/stable cavitation on BBB-opening/tissue damage. FUS sonication experiments were divided into four groups: (1) in-house submicron bubbles with 10-MHz FUS sonication; (2) SonoVue with 10-MHz FUS sonication; and (3) in-house submicron bubbles with 1-MHz FUS sonication; and (4) SonoVue with 1-MHz FUS sonication. Group 1 was used to verify that matching of the FUS frequency to the resonance frequency of the in-house submicron bubbles would maximize stable cavitation, Group 2 was used to verify that a large mismatch between the FUS frequency and the bubble resonance frequency resulted in no BBB-opening, Group 3 was used to demonstrate the BBB-opening caused by another off-resonant case of 1-MHz FUS excitation with the in-house submicron bubbles, and Group 4 was used to replicate the current common 1-MHz FUS protocol with SonoVue for comparison with Group 1. Detailed sonication conditions are summarized in Table 1. Pulsed-wave FUS was applied for 60 s by the 1-MHz/10-MHz transducer. For 10-MHz FUS sonication, acoustic pressure amplitudes of 0.5, 1.0, 1.5, 2.0, 2.5 and 4.5 MPa were investigated due to the importance of knowing the pressure threshold and minimizing inertial cavitation events. For 1-MHz FUS sonication, the rats were sonicated at 0.1, 0.2, 0.3, 0.5, 1.0 and 1.5 MPa. The cycle number of 1-MHz and 10-MHz FUS sonication experiments were set as a constant since we aimed to maintain the same oscillation number of bubbles during sonication. The center of the FUS focal zone was placed at 3.5 mm posterior and 2.5 mm lateral to the bregma, and 3 mm below the skull surface. The experimental protocol is shown in Figure 1C. A bolus of bubbles was injected 20 s prior to sonication. Each bolus injection contained a similar number of bubbles (1.5×10^7) diluted to 0.2 mL with 0.9% normal saline solution for the two sets of bubbles. The bolus bubble injection was completed within 3 s. During sonication, the PCD setup was used to acquire acoustic-emission signals. About 120 min after sonication, rats were sent to the MRI scanning room to verify the occurrence of erythrocyte extravasations *in vivo*. After the experiments were completed, the brains were removed for histological examination.

Acquisition and Analysis of Passive Cavitation Detection (PCD)

The acoustic-emission signals collected by the PCD setup were used to quantify the subharmonic-frequency component and inertial cavitation dose (ICD) [27]. Note that the subharmonic-frequency component and ICD are indices of stable cavitation and inertial cavitation, respectively. In order to reduce the fragment of in-house submicron bubbles over time and bubble concentration decay during repeated ultrasound exposures, we primarily measured the acoustic-emission from the first excitation bursts. For each experimental group, the changes in the ratio of the acoustic-emission signals to the pressure amplitude were calculated. The acquired RF signals were analyzed to generate frequency spectra via fast Fourier transform with MATLAB (The Mathworks, Natick, MA, USA). The spectra consisted of energy from the scattered FUS signal (fundamental and higher-order harmonics; $n\times f$, $n=1, 2, \ldots$, and f is the fundamental frequency), stable cavitation (sub- and super-harmonics frequency; $n\times f/2$, $n=1, 2, \ldots$) and the radiated pressure from inertial bubble collapses (wideband frequency) [28]. The areas under the peaks of the subharmonic and wideband signals were measured to quantify stable and inertial cavitation dosages, respectively. For 10-MHz FUS sonication, the subharmonic signal area was estimated over the range of 4.85–5.15 MHz and the ICD was calculated as the area within the bandwidth of PCD (2.2–6.8 MHz), but excluded the subharmonic signal area (Figure 2A). For 1-MHz FUS sonication, the subharmonic signal area was estimated over the range of 0.35–0.65 MHz and the ICD was calculated within the area of 2.2–6.8 MHz but excluded the transducer's harmonic and ultraharmonic frequencies (Figure 2B). The change ratio in the acoustic emission signals (AE) was calculated by

$$Acoustic-emissionchangeratio(\%)=\frac{AE_{(post)}-AE_{(pre)}}{AE_{(pre)}}\times100\%$$

where $AE_{(pre)}$ and $AE_{(post)}$ are the areas of the spectrum with FUS exposure before and after bubble injection, respectively. The change ratios of acoustic-emission signals were also compared to the applied acoustic pressure amplitudes.

Evaluation of BBB-opening

The permeability of the BBB was assessed by extravasation of Evans blue dye (EB; Sigma-Aldrich, St. Louis, MO, USA). This dye binds to albumin in the bloodstream, which prevents it from penetrating through the intact BBB. BBB-opening can be visualized as blue staining in brain tissues, and the level of BBB-opening can be estimated by quantitating the amount of EB extravasation into brain [17]. A bolus of EB (100 mg/kg) was injected 5 min prior to FUS sonication. Animals were sacrificed approximately 6 h after sonication and perfused with 0.9% normal saline via the left ventricle until colorless perfusion fluid appeared from the right atrium. Rat brains were then removed and sliced into coronal sections for observation. EB-stained brain samples were also withdrawn to measure the amounts of EB extravasation. The samples were weighed and then soaked in 50% trichloroacetic acid. After homogenization and centrifugation, the extracted dye was diluted with ethanol (1:3) and the fluorescence was measured using a spectrophotometer (Cytofluor 2300, Millipore, Bedford, MA, USA; 620-nm excitation and 680-nm emission). EB extravasation in the brain was quantified by a linear regression standard curve derived from seven concentrations of the dye, and was expressed as nanounits per gram of tissue. All results are

Table 1. Sonication parameters of the four experimental groups.

	Group 1	Group 2	Group 3	Group 4
Number of rats	34	34	30	30
Acoustic pressure (MPa)	0.5–4.5	0.5–4.5	0.1–1.5	0.1–1.5
Pulse repetition frequency (Hz)	10	10	10	10
Number of cycles	10000	10000	10000	10000
Duration of sonication (s)	60	60	60	60
Number of MRI evaluations	18	18	18	18
Number of H&E staining evaluations	18	18	18	18
Number of TUNEL staining evaluations	18	18	18	18
Number of EB staining evaluations	34	34	30	30

Group 1 = in-house submicron bubbles with 10-MHz FUS sonication; Group 2 = SonoVue with 10-MHz FUS sonication; Group 3 = in-house submicron bubbles with 1-MHz FUS sonication; Group 4 = SonoVue with 1-MHz FUS sonication.

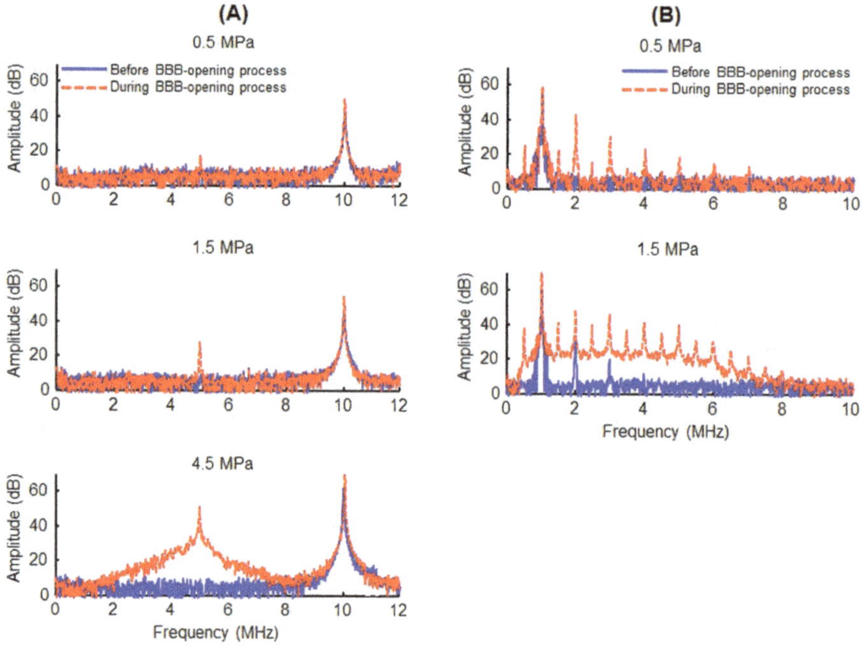

Figure 2. Acoustic-emission signal spectra. A: Frequency spectra acquired from PCD during 10-MHz FUS sonication with (red) or without (blue) in-house submicron bubbles. Top: 0.5 MPa, only the fundamental frequency (10 MHz). Middle: 1.5 MPa, the additional peak appeared at about subharmonic frequency (5 MHz). Bottom: 4.5 MPa, the spectrum was accompanied by wideband acoustic emission, indicated by a bump at approximately 2.2–6.8 MHz. B: Frequency spectra acquired from PCD during 1-MHz FUS sonication with (red) or without (blue) SonoVue. Top: 0.5 MPa. With injecting bubbles, both the fundamental frequency (1 MHz) and subharmonic signal (0.5 MHz) could be measured. Bottom: 1.5 MPa, with injecting bubbles, the frequency spectrum was accompanied by wideband acoustic emission, indicated by a bump at approximately 0.5–8 MHz.

presented as mean and standard error of the mean values. The amount of EB extravasation was compared to the change ratio of acoustic emission signals. The BBB opening pressure threshold is the pressure level at which 100% sonicated animals underwent BBB permeability increase.

MRI Examination

We used two different MRI protocols to verify the occurrence of brain damage *in vivo* by a 3-T MRI system (Trio with Tim, Siemens, Erlangen, Germany) and a standard wrist coil with an inner diameter of 13 cm. The first protocol was a T2-weighted sequence, which was used to confirm the absence of anatomical changes after sonication [4]. The following parameters were used: TR/TE = 3730 ms/115 ms, slice thickness = 1 mm, matrix size = 168×384, field of view (FOV) = 80×170 mm, which gave a voxel size of 0.4×0.4×1 mm^3. The total acquisition time was 6 min and 3 s for six averages. The second protocol was a susceptibility-weighted imaging (SWI) sequence, which was used to determine the distribution of erythrocyte extravasations in the brain. The SWI sequence was modified from a heavy T2*-weighted gradient-recalled 3-D fast low-angle shot sequence with full flow compensation in all three directions. The SWI sequence was acquired with the following parameters: TR/TE/flip angle = 28 ms/20 ms/15°, slice thickness = 0.7 mm, number of slices = 16, matrix size = 256×384 and FOV = 80×130 mm, which gave a voxel size of 0.3×0.3×0.7 mm^3. The acquisition time for single measurement was 2 min 24 s. Ten measurements of the SWI sequence were acquired and averaged to increase the signal-to-noise ratio. During MRI imaging process, animals were anesthetized with a mixture of oxygen (0.8 L min^{-1} at 1.0 Bar, 21°C) and 2% vaporized isoflurane using an anesthesia vaporizer.

Brain Damage Evaluation

The removed brain was fixed in 10% neutrally buffered formalin (Sigma-Aldrich) followed by embedding in optimal cutting temperature compound (Tissue-Tek OCT, Sakura Finetek Inc., Torrance, CA, USA) and storage at −50°C. The brain samples were serially sectioned with a slice thickness of 15 μm. The direction of these slices was the same to FUS sonication direction. The bluest section was identified and subjected to hematoxylin and eosin (H&E) staining to confirm the presence of erythrocyte extravasations. In addition, terminal deoxynucleotidyl transferase biotin-dUTP nick end labeling (TUNEL, ApopTag kit, Intergen Co., Purchase, NY, USA) was used to detect apoptotic neurons [29]. Histology evaluations were performed using light microscopy by a person who was blinded to the ultrasound parameters but was informed of sonication location of the brain.

The extent of brain damage was rated according to a four-point scale as follows [3,4]: grade 0 = no tissue damage or erythrocyte extravasation; grade 1 = presence of few extravasated erythrocytes, but no neuronal loss; grade 2 = presence of extensive erythrocyte extravasations; and grade 3 = extensive erythrocyte extravasations along with apoptotic neuronal death.

Synthesis of Submicron-Sized BCNU-Loaded Bubbles

To synthesize BCNU-loaded bubbles (BCNU-bubbles), dipalmitoyl-phosphatidyl-choline (DPPC) (Avanti Polar Lipids) and DSPC-PEG-2000 at a molar ratio of 19:1 were mixed with 37.6 μL BCNU solution (100 mg BCNU dissolved in 3 mL purified ethanol) (Bristol-Myers Squibb, NY, USA) in chloroform in a vial. The organic solvent was eliminated at 0–4°C under reduced pressure over 24 h using a rotary evaporator. The procedure for preparing BCNU-bubbles was almost the same as that used to prepare submicron bubbles. The mean diameter of

BCNU-bubbles was approximate 0.86±0.18 μm by DLS and 1.16±0.11 μm by Coulter counter, and the concentration was $(19.78\pm4.9)\times10^9$ bubbles/mL by Coulter counter.

BCNU encapsulation efficiency was analyzed using a reverse method by HPLC with a UV detector (L-2400, Hitachi, Tokyo, Japan) [22]. BCNU-bubble formulations were gently centrifuged for 3 min at 6000 rpm (mini-micro centrifuge, Bertec Enterprise Co., Taipei, Taiwan). The underlying liquid phase was carefully separated from the top foam cake with a syringe needle and the residual BCNU after production of BCNU-bubbles (W_{res}) was determined. Drug payload (W_{BCNU-B}) was calculated as the difference between the total amount of BCNU (W_{tot}) and W_{res}. Drug encapsulation efficiency was then calculated by the equation:

$$Encapsulation\ efficiency(\%) = \frac{W_{BCNU-B}}{W_{tot}} \times 100\%$$

The mobile phase solution consisted of 60 vol% HPLC-grade methanol in deionized water. A column packed with mightysil RP-18 GP 250-4.6 (Kanto Chemicals, Tokyo, Japan) was used with a flow rate of 2.0 mL/min and a detection wavelength of 237 nm. The amount of BCNU was quantified by the area under its characteristic peak at a retention time of 3.2 min.

Quantitative Determination of BCNU Accumulation in Brain Tissue

The feasibility of enhanced local BCNU delivery by BCNU-bubbles and repetitive sonication was investigated by delivery of 10-MHz FUS transcranially in the presence of BCNU-bubbles. Experiments with four different FUS exposure conditions were conducted: (1) 1.5-MPa exposure (60 s) with BCNU-bubbles; (2) 2.5-MPa exposure (60 s) with BCNU-bubbles; and (3) 2.5-MPa exposure (240 s) with BCNU-bubbles; and (4) 4.5-MPa exposure (240 s) with BCNU-bubbles. Besides, two experiments including BCNU administration-only (without FUS exposure) as well as BCNU-bubbles administration only (without FUS exposure) were also conducted to serve as the reference groups. The detailed sonication parameters are described in Table 2. Twenty-four skull-intact SD rats were used. Before sonication, the fur on the top of the head was completely removed using an electric trimmer. Rats were IV injected with 0.5 mL of BCNU-bubbles diluted to 1 mL with 0.9% normal saline. Sonication started 20 s after injection of BCNU-bubbles at the left hemisphere brain and the untargeted right hemisphere brain was used as a control.

Quantitation of BCNU Accumulation in Brain Tissue

Animals were sacrificed after FUS exposure, and the concentration of local BCNU deposited in the brain hemisphere was measured. To minimize the loss of BCNU caused by hydrolysis *in vivo*, rat brains were perfused with saline and removed within 10 min after FUS sonication. Procedures were performed at 0–4°C to reduce BCNU degradation. Each brain sample was homogenized in a 15 mL centrifuge tube with 0.5 mL methanol, and BCNU was extracted in 2 mL methanol with a sonicator (model 2510, Branson Co., Danbury, CT, USA). After BCNU extraction, the samples were centrifuged at 13500 rpm for 10 min. The clear supernatants were collected and the precipitates were re-extracted twice. The final supernatants were filtered through a 0.2 mm filter before quantitative analysis and were finally analyzed by HPLC with UV detection. BCNU deposition was quantified using a linear regression standard curve derived from BCNU standard solutions (0.25–25 μg/mL).

Statistical Analysis

Results are presented as the mean and standard error of the mean of at least three independent measurements. All statistical evaluations including the change ratio of acoustic-emission signals, the amount of EB extravasation, and BCNU uptake at the sonicated side of the brain were carried out with unpaired two-tailed Student's *t*-tests. A *p*-value of less than 0.05 ($p<0.05$) was considered significant. Statistical analysis was performed using Microsoft Excel 2010 (Microsoft, NY, USA).

Results

In Vivo Cavitation Detection

In Group 1, BBB-opening was successfully induced with acoustic pressures above 1.0 MPa. No erythrocyte extravasations were observed in the gross histological sections. Stable cavitation activity increased profoundly when the acoustic pressure was increased to 1.0 MPa, whereas inertial cavitation activity remained reduced. By comparison, the results of Group 2 demonstrated that stable cavitation activity could be induced with mismatched the frequency of FUS, and therefore BBB-opening occurred at pressure of 2.0 MPa (Figure 3A and 3B). From the observation of brain section, the combined use of 10-MHz FUS and submicron bubbles has the most profound BBB-opening effect. However, SonoVue excited at 10-MHz with 4.5 MPa did not reproduce the BBB-opening. It should be noted that the PCD measurements indicated that the activity of stable cavitation increased significantly from 0.5 to 2.5 MPa, but decreased at 4.5 MPa (Figure 3B). The possible reason is that the micrometer-sized bubbles could not sustain under the high pressure and gas bubbles diffused quickly [30]. The gas-diffused bubbles could not vibrate and expand effectively, and thus did not induce enough cavitation dosage to stimulate surrounding vessels.

In Group 3, the occurrence of BBB-opening and stable cavitation started from at 0.3 MPa. Because inertial cavitation

Table 2. Summary of 10-MHz FUS with BCNU-bubbles for enhanced BCNU delivery.

	BCNU	BCNU-bubble w/o FUS	Case 1	Case 2	Case 3	Case 4
Number of rats	4	4	4	4	4	4
Acoustic pressure (MPa)	-	-	1.5	2.5	2.5	4.5
Pulse repetition frequency (Hz)	-	-	10	10	10	10
Number of cycles	-	-	10,000	10,000	10,000	10,000
Number of sonication sites	-	-	1	1	1	1
Duration of sonication per site (s)	-	-	60	60	240	240

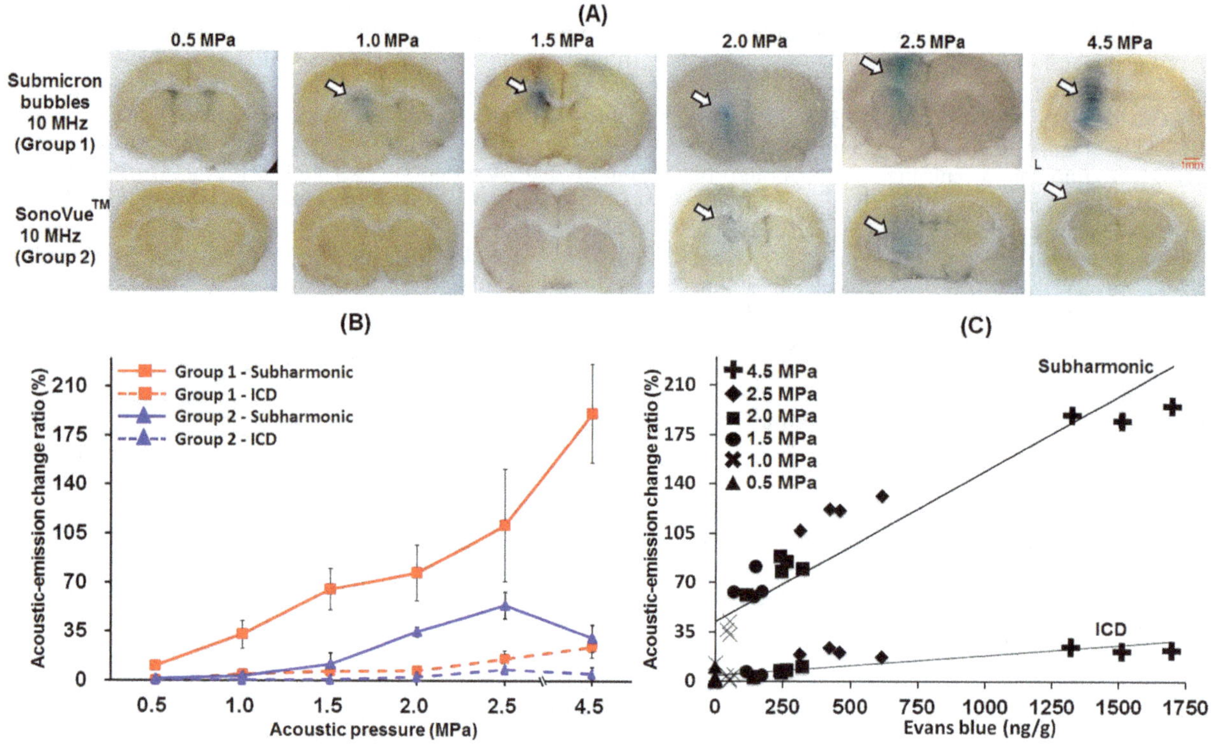

Figure 3. Relations between levels of BBB-opening and acoustic-emission signals under 10-MHz sonication. A: EB extravasation into brain tissue. (white arrows: the BBB-opening region; red arrows: areas of erythrocyte extravasations). B: Acoustic-emission change ratio (red line: in-house submicron bubbles with 10-MHz FUS sonication; blue line: SonoVue with 10-MHz FUS sonication; solid line: subharmonic-frequency signal; dotted line: ICD. C: Correlation between acoustic-emission signals and amount of EB extravasation for in-house submicron bubbles with 10-MHz FUS sonication.

activity increased along with stable cavitation activity at 0.5 MPa, BBB-opening was accompanied by erythrocyte extravasations. In contrast, Group 4 showed that the appearance of BBB-opening and stable cavitation started from 0.2 MPa. However, since the inertial cavitation was not reduced while increasing the acoustic pressure, BBB-opening was produced and accompanied with mild erythrocyte extravasations at 0.3 MPa. Another noteworthy point was that in Group 4, increasing pressure from 1 to 1.5 MPa induced a dramatic increase in inertial cavitation (from 50% to 110%), which caused erythrocyte extravasations to become the dominant effect (Figure 4A and 4B).

Group 1-2 showed a smaller BBB-opening area than Group 3–4 due to the smaller sample volume of the 10-MHz FUS beam compared to the 1-MHz FUS beam (at 1.5 MPa, the width of the BBB-opening area was 1 mm for 10-MHz FUS and 5 mm for 1-MHz FUS). This finding suggested that 10-MHz FUS introduced more local and precise BBB-opening. The change in EB extravasation due to the activity of in-house submicron bubbles was highly correlated with the subharmonic-frequency signal increase but not with ICD. There was almost no change in ICD despite a profound increase in EB extravasation, indicating that inertial cavitation was only weakly correlated with BBB-opening (Figure 3C). In addition, at the BBB-opening threshold of Group 3 and Group 4 (0.3 and 0.2 MPa), there were only subharmonic-frequency signal be detected. Therefore, our data provided convincing evidence that the occurrence of stable cavitation was responsible for BBB-opening, whereas erythrocyte extravasations were mainly caused by inertial cavitation.

Safety Assessment

We did not detect any alterations in SWI and T2-weighted imaging at the BBB-opening location in Group 1 (Figure 5A), indicating the absence of erythrocyte extravasations and brain anatomical changes at all acoustic pressure levels. In Group 2 (Figure 5B), the mismatch between the FUS frequency and the bubble resonance frequency resulted in BBB-opening occurring at 2.0, 2.5 and 4.5 MPa, and the MRI results therefore did not change with the acoustic pressure level. This finding indicated that 10-MHz FUS was safe because it only produced bubble cavitation activity when the frequencies were matched, and no side effects were observed when the frequencies were mismatched, even at high pressures of up to 4.5 MPa. In contrast, in Group 3, we observed erythrocyte extravasations and brain edema occurrence (using 1.5 MPa as an example) in SWI images (black spots) and T2-weighted images (positive signal changes for edema) respectively. (Figure 5C) In Group 4, severe erythrocyte extravasations and edema were also detected in SWI images and T2-weighted images, individually (Figure 5D).

H&E staining and TUNEL assays were used to reveal the extent of erythrocyte extravasations and neuronal apoptosis, respectively. Only mild erythrocyte extravasations were found in Group 1 (Figure 6) at pressures from 2.0 to 4.5 MPa, indicating that the in-house submicron bubbles resonated at 10 MHz indeed did not produce server brain damage or cell apoptosis after FUS sonication.

We then plotted the occurrence and severity of erythrocyte extravasations according to increasing acoustic pressure (Figure 7). In Group 1, the prevalence of grade 0 lesions (intact brain)

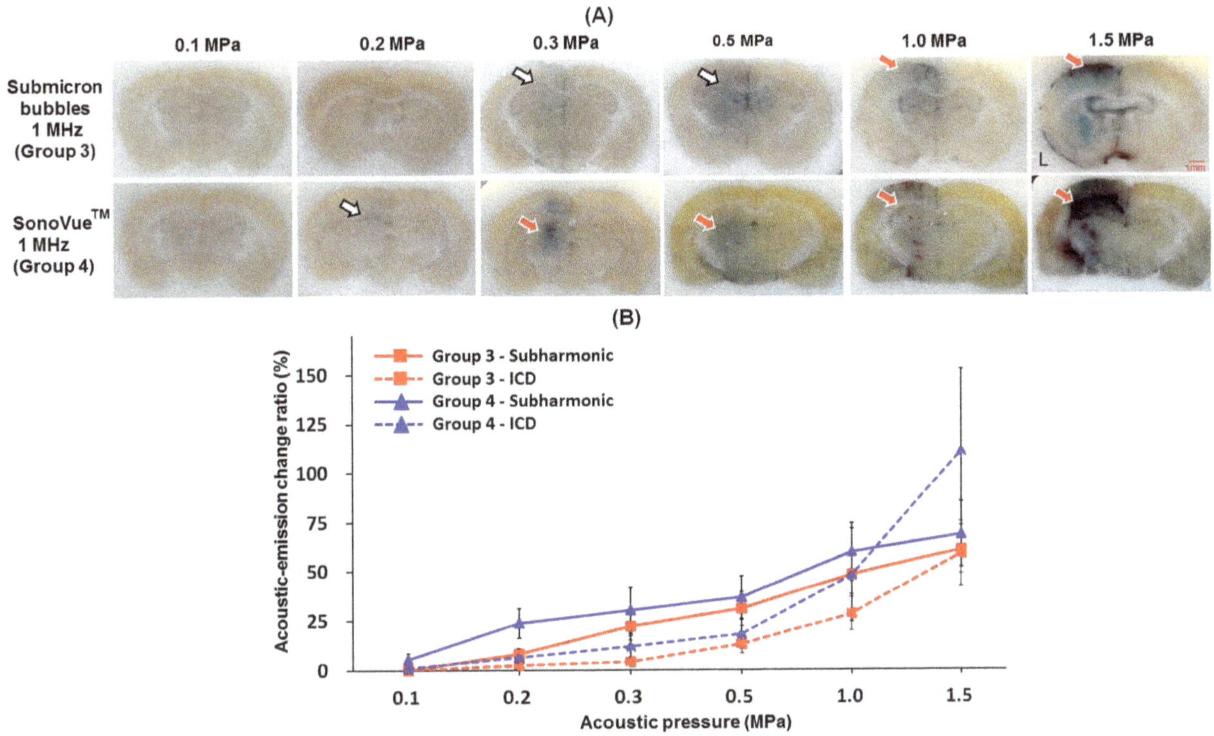

Figure 4. Relations between levels of BBB-opening and acoustic-emission signals under 1-MHz sonication. A: EB extravasation into brain tissue. (white arrows: the BBB-opening region; red arrows: areas of erythrocyte extravasations). B: Acoustic-emission change ratio (red line: in-house submicron bubbles with 1-MHz FUS sonication; blue line: SonoVue with 1-MHz FUS sonication; solid line: subharmonic-frequency signal; dotted line: ICD.

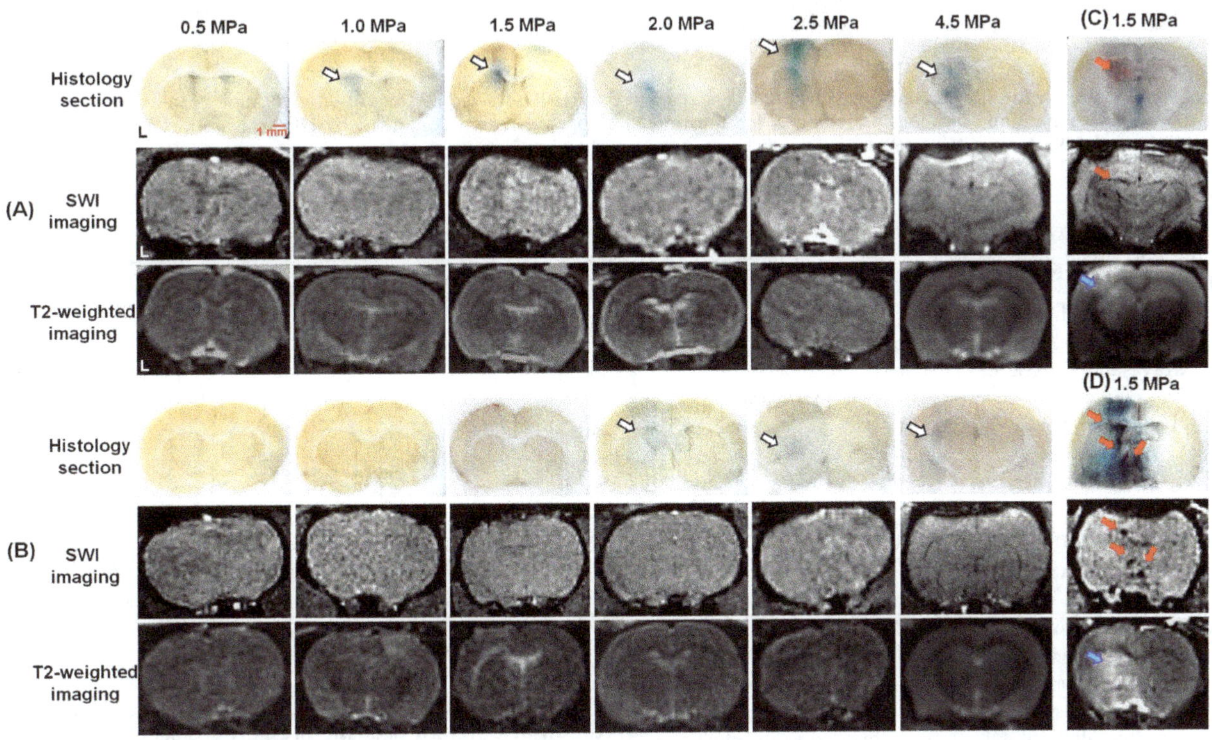

Figure 5. MRI results after FUS sonication. A: In-house submicron bubbles with 10-MHz FUS sonication. B: SonoVue with 10-MHz FUS sonication. C: In-house submicron bubbles with 1-MHz FUS sonication. D: SonoVue with 1-MHz FUS sonication. (white arrows: the BBB-opening region; red arrows: areas of erythrocyte extravasations; blue arrows: brain edema).

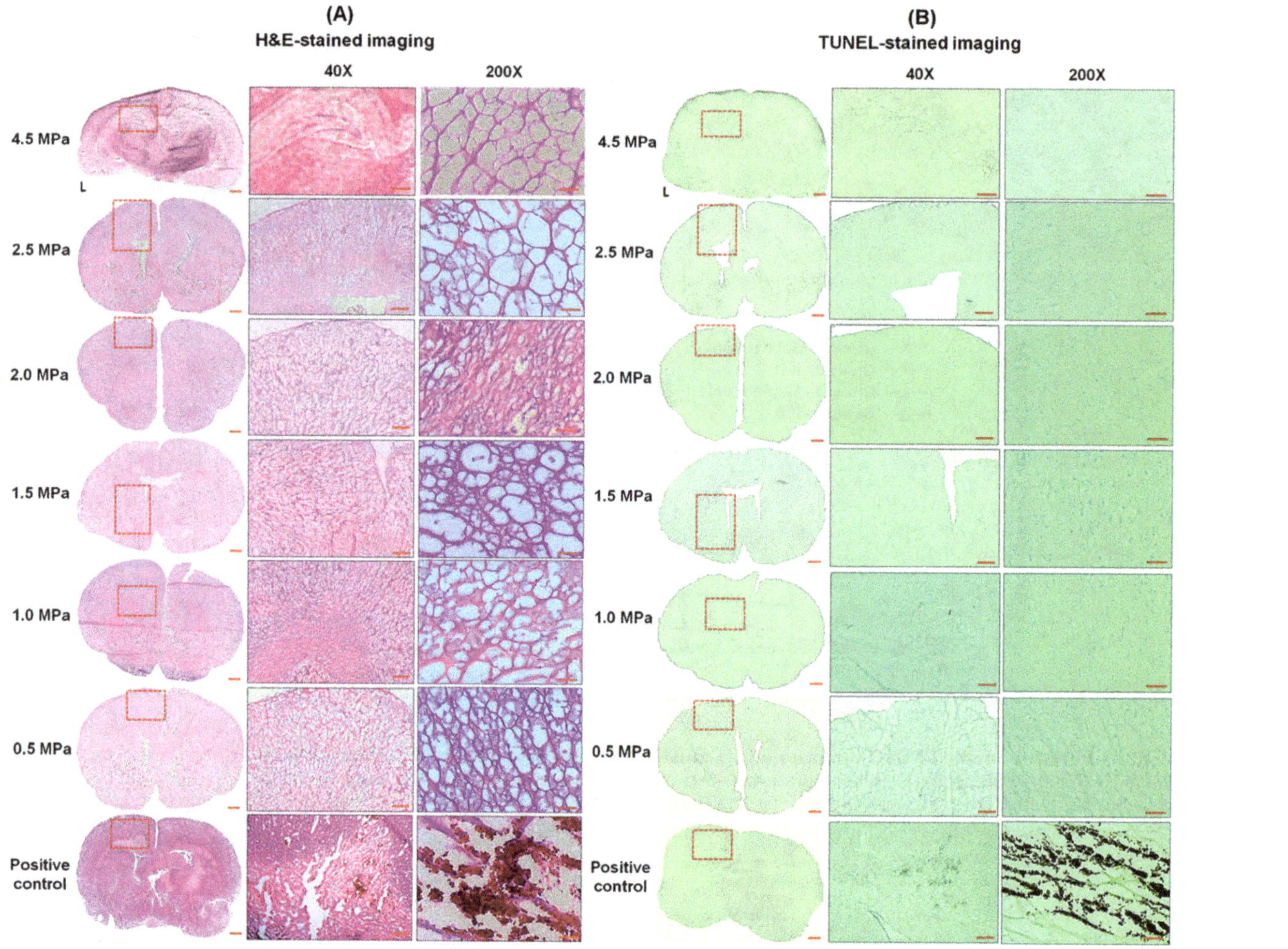

Figure 6. Histological evaluations after BBB-opening. A: H&E-stained and B: TUNEL-stained sections after application of in-house submicron bubbles with 10-MHz FUS sonication. The dotted rectangles indicate the BBB-opening region confirmed by EB extravasation. Positive control: hemorrhage and apoptotic cells (group 4, 1.5 MPa). Scale bars: 1 mm, 1 mm, and 50 μm.

decreased linearly with increasing acoustic pressure levels. On the other hand, the percentage of mild lesions (grade = 1) increased proportionally to the acoustic pressure level, despite the continued absence of severe hemorrhage (grade = 2 or 3) at the highest applied acoustic pressure (4.5 MPa). In contrast, in Group 4, mild erythrocyte extravasations (grade = 1) could be detected at 0.3 MPa, whereas moderate or severe erythrocyte extravasations (grade = 2 or 3) became apparent with acoustic pressure exceeding 1.0–1.5 MPa. Neuronal apoptosis as detected by TUNEL staining was evident with an acoustic pressure exceeding 1.5 MPa.

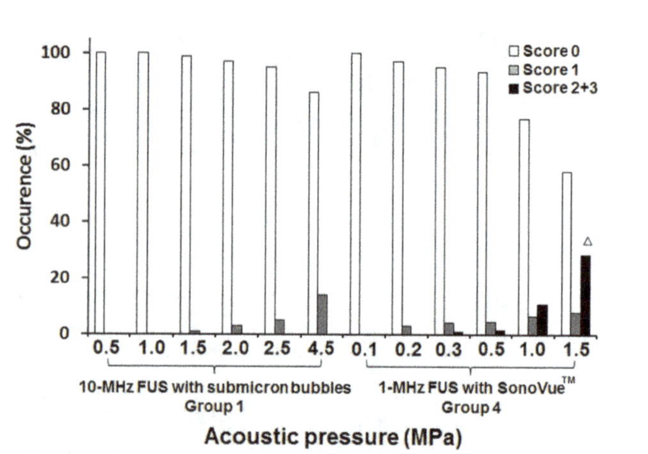

Figure 7. Occurrence of brain hemorrhage according to sonication at different acoustic pressures. Grade 0 indicates no detectable damage, whereas grade 1 denotes erythrocyte extravasations that are considered to be safe. Grades 2 or 3 show hemorrhage regarded as severe. [Δ]Detected cell apoptosis as assessed by the TUNEL assay.

Repetitive and Transcranial FUS Treatment for Enhancing Delivery of Encapsulated Drugs

One possible application of FUS-mediated BBB-opening is the safe and enhanced delivery of drugs such as BCNU to brain tissue. BCNU is a clinically approved chemotherapeutic alkylation agent for treatment of brain tumors, but its efficacy is limited by the inability of delivering a sufficient drug dose to tumors. Its hydrophobic properties allow BCNU to be embedded in the shell of the bubbles and can be attached to the phospholipid shell of bubbles by both electrostatic and hydrophobic interactions without affecting the physical characteristics of the submicron bubbles [22]. BCNU was expected to be locally released by bubble-disruption at a higher pressure level, triggered by 10-MHz FUS exposure. To investigate the feasibility of local drug release by repetitive 10-MHz FUS-triggered bubble oscillations, we therefore synthesized BCNU-loaded submicron-sized bubbles. The safety and efficacy of transcranial and repetitive FUS sonication at the same location was then investigated, with concomitant quantification of drug release by the BCNU-bubbles.

We found that the BCNU encapsulated in bubbles was not released into brain tissues unless its release was triggered by 10-MHz FUS sonication (Figure 8A). The intact BBB of rat brains blocked any noticeable drug accumulation when BCNU was delivered as BCNU-bubble alone (0.31±0.04 μg). Both properties of lipid-soluble and relative small molecular weight (214.1) of BCNU bring it to partially pass through the BBB, depositing in brain tissue (4.61±0.33 μg). Delivery of BCNU to brain tissues could be enhanced by both higher acoustic pressure and a longer time of sonication. Importantly, BCNU release could be improved up to 60 times in comparison to control non-sonicated brains (18.6 μg versus 0.3 μg), and could be enhanced at least 100% comparing to a one-time exposure using the same acoustic pressure. Most notably, the repetitive FUS sonication process significantly enhanced BCNU deposition without causing hemorrhagic damage to the brain. This BBB-opening effect was guaranteed for a total sonication time up to 4 min (Figure 8B and 8C). Thus it is feasible that local drug concentration can be increased without damaging the brain tissue by prolonging FUS irradiation time with drug-loaded bubbles.

Discussion

The investigation of the bubble activity type (such as stable or inertial cavitation) that leads to different brain effects (such as BBB-opening or erythrocyte extravasations) has been an important issue, since the real use of the FUS-mediated BBB-opening technique for brain drug delivery can be realized only if this mechanism can be fully understood and predictable. It has been shown in several cases that bubbles (2–3 microns in size) can be used to disrupt the BBB at acoustic pressures as low as 0.25–0.3 MPa without evidence of tissue damage or erythrocyte extravasations [31–33]. McDannold *et al.* revealed that BBB-opening occurs without inertial cavitation appearance in rabbits [20]. Tung *et al.* discovered that the cavitation activity could be detected in mice and nonhuman primate, and inertial cavitation may not be required for BBB-opening [21,33]. Wang *et al.* noted that the type and distribution of microbubble might affect the BBB-opening at lower acoustic pressures [34]. Previous reports all pointed out the induction the bubbles on-resonance (or so-called stable cavitation) should play the dominant role of BBB-opening. When further increasing the FUS pressure, erythrocyte extravasations may be accompanied in the BBB-opening process and this should contribute to inertial cavitation. However, a confirmation may not easily be made since two of these bubble activities is usually coupled and mixed in the observation, and is difficult to exclude one from another during the experimental design. One possibility is that the use of about 0.5–1 MHz transducer contains a low inertial cavitation threshold (about 0.066–0.48 MPa) [35,36]. Also, since the bubbles is nearly impossible to be monodispersed, that magnifies the possibility to have stable and inertial cavitation to be mixed during the FUS exposure. All these causing previous studies have difficulty in making solid and confirmed claims of the playing roles of inertial and stable cavitation.

To characterize the individual role of the inertial and stable cavitation activities, first, we proposed the use of submicron bubbles that fabricated with an improved process to have low size-dispersed distribution to majorly with 350 nm and also the submicron bubbles having the on-resonance frequency close to 10 MHz; second, we employed the 10-MHz FUS so that the pressure threshold of intrinsic inertial cavitation was significantly increased (about 0.62 MPa) [36]. This synergistic approach provided a more reliable evidence to demonstrate that the BBB-opening is dominated by stable cavitation, whereas the erythrocyte extravasation is mainly contributed to inertial cavitation activity.

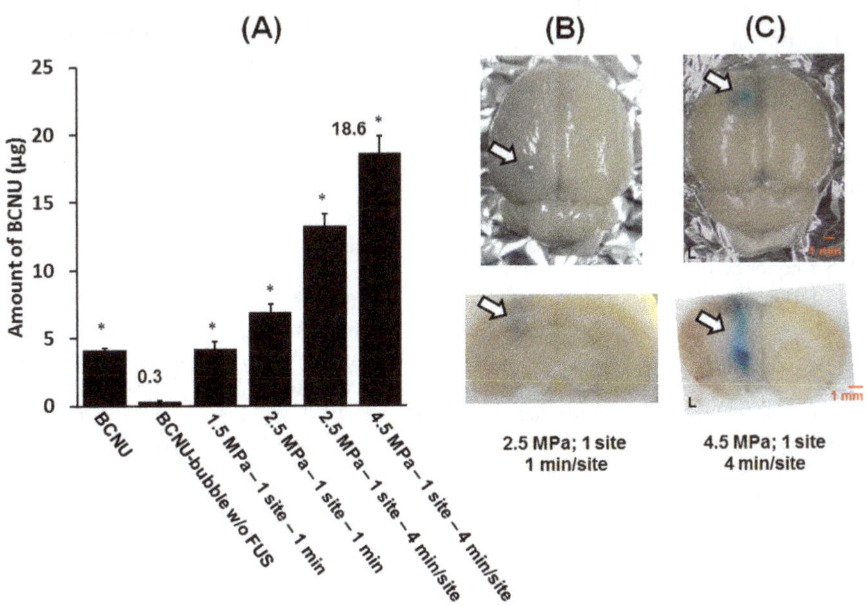

Figure 8. Repetitive and transcranial FUS treatment for enhancing delivery of encapsulated drugs. A: Quantitative evaluation of BCNU release into brain tissue associated with transcranial FUS-triggered destruction of BCNU-bubbles (Single asterisk, $P<0.05$). The corresponding brain sections: B: 2.5 MPa; 1 site; 1 min/site, and C: 4.5 MPa; 1 site; 4 min/site. The treated hemisphere brain was the left brain.

Our data have demonstrated that the commercial microbubbles with the 1-MHz FUS provided the chance to induce erythrocyte extravasations-accompanied BBB-opening as the pressure was high enough to excite sufficient high inertial cavitation activities (Group 4). On the other hand, exciting FUS with an off-resonant microbubbles did not provide benefits as the pressure required to induce BBB-opening was increased (Groups 2) due to the inefficient induction of bubbles cavitation activities (either stable or inertial cavitation). Of note, the combined use of submicron bubbles and the on-resonance FUS excitation provided merits of selectively triggering stable cavitation (i.e., subharmonics activities) but not inertial cavitation (Group 1; Figure 3B). This is considered to be the optimized FUS-induced BBB-opening conditions since the erythrocyte extravasations can be completely avoid so that the safety can be guaranteed (Figure 3A). On the other hand, the pressure threshold for inertial cavitation of our proposed method is very high, thereby minimizing the risk of inertial cavitation and damage occurring BBB-opening. The wide range of pressures at which BBB-opening can be achieved in the absence of inertial cavitation improves the safety of the procedure.

We also observed that in Group 1 and Group 2, the BBB-opening occurred at pressures of 1.0 and 2.0 MPa, respectively. The reason for this difference of pressure thresholds is not clear. If the major mechanism of BBB-opening was the mechanical stress to the vascular wall caused by steady acoustic-driven bubbles oscillation (stable cavitation), then the matched resonance frequency would be effectively to induce this effect for the submicron bubbles than for the SonoVue bubbles. However, the lowest acoustic pressures inducing BBB-opening in Group 3 and Group 4 were 0.3 and 0.2 MPa, individually. The possible reason for this difference is owing to that the larger bubbles are easier to expand sufficient sizes that could stimulate the vessel walls, and thereby BBB-opening can be achieved at lower acoustic pressures in SonoVue bubbles. In other words, Group 3 showed the erythrocyte extravasations appearance threshold higher than Group 4. The most likely explanation is the smaller size (less than 1 μm) of the in-house submicron bubbles compared to SonoVue bubbles. Bubbles smaller than 2 μm would be likely to fragment at some distance from the endothelial wall when they collapse inside a blood vessel, whereas larger bubbles will expand and fragment while in contact with the endothelial wall. These results pointed out that small size bubbles maybe more safe in low frequency FUS induced BBB-opening process [37,38].

With submicron bubbles, the BBB-opening threshold of 10-MHz and 1-MHz FUS are 1.0 and 0.3 MPa, respectively. By the contrast, with SonoVue bubbles, the BBB-opening threshold of 10-MHz and 1-MHz FUS are 2.0 and 0.2 MPa, individually. Both two kinds of bubbles show that increasing the FUS frequency of sonication just increases the acoustic pressure required to get BBB-opening. Mcdannold *et al.* found that BBB-opening threshold was the mechanical index (MI) = 0.46 (defined as $\frac{P_r}{\sqrt{f_c}}$, the peak rarefactional pressure (P_r) divided by the square root of the center frequency (f_c)) [39]. Therefore, it is reasonable that increasing sonication FUS frequency would increase BBB-opening threshold. On the other hand, the results of this study also indicated that applying higher frequency FUS increases the safety of BBB-opening due to the MI decrease (Figure 3A; Figure 4A). Thus, the safety of FUS-induced BBB-opening can be improved by manipulating the frequency of FUS.

In Group 2, SonoVue excited at 10-MHz FUS with 4.5 MPa did not reproduce the BBB-opening probably due to the FUS-driving bubble diffusion. Therefore, SonoVue bubbles may be safer than the submicron bubbles since SonoVue bubbles would diffuse before they cause damage. However, the submicron bubbles can produce higher BBB permeability than SonoVue bubbles under all acoustic pressures (Figure 3A). Furthermore, we did not discover the occurrence of brain damage in the submicron bubbles case between 0.1–4.5 MPa (Figure 5A; Figure 6). Taken together, these data suggest that the submicron bubbles still have the potential for effective FUS-induced BBB-opening.

Previous studies have suggested that acoustic-emission signals including harmonics or ultraharmonics could be used to predict the occurrence of BBB-opening [20,21,34,40,41]. In this study, subharmonic-frequency signals were detected only when BBB-opening occurred. Furthermore, the intensity of the signal was strongly correlated with the quantity of EB extravasation as a function of BBB permeability. The subharmonic content is only produced by bubble oscillations and thus provides a more direct index of stable cavitation. The intensities of these signals might be used to estimate the level of BBB-opening and the location of their occurrence. Therefore, the subharmonic nonlinear component has the potential as a real-time index of BBB-opening.

It was observed that brain regions stained with EB leakage co-localized with the FUS exposure positions (Figure 3, 4, 5, and 6) and with wider distributions than the focal dimension of FUS transducer, which may be possibly due to EB dye leak and diffuse into brain tissue after BBB-opening. Also, the inconsistence of the EB stained positions among animals was due to the small dimension of focal spot induced by the 10-MHz transducer but with a rather wide tissue slicer gap (typically about 1 mm).

The major limitation of this research is the difficulty of applying our results to human brain in current clinical settings, due to the penetration capability of ultrasound frequencies currently in use (i.e., 10-MHz). Indeed the frequency of ultrasound used in this study (10 MHz) is higher than the clinical used 5-MHz ultrasound [42], however, the 7–8 MHz probe has been clinically applied for white matter injury [43] and cerebral palsy [44] diagnostic application, implying the using of 10-MHz therapeutic ultrasound is also possible. On the other hand, the concept of this study may translate to lower resonance frequency of bubble (mono-disperse micron-sized bubbles) and requirement of lower frequency FUS (e.g., 1–5 MHz) which are more relevant for application in human brain. Thereby improve the safety of novel low frequency FUS induced BBB-opening process in the future.

Conclusions

In this study, the roles of both cavitation activities within FUS-induced BBB-opening process and the feasibility of enhancing local drug release to brain tissue have been confirmed by our designed submicron bubbles and matched the frequency FUS sonication. This study confirmed that inertial cavitation is responsible for brain hemorrhagic damage, and that pure stable cavitation results in BBB-opening. When submicron bubbles are exposed to resonant-frequency matched FUS, inertial cavitation can be reduced, ensuring safe BBB-opening. We also successfully demonstrated that repetitive FUS exposure in combination with drug-loaded submicron bubbles can significantly enhance local chemotherapeutic agent delivery in the brain without the risk of erythrocyte extravasations. These findings are particularly important for increasing the local delivery of high concentrations of drugs to treat CNS diseases, and simultaneously limiting their systemic toxicity. Compared with low frequency FUS (1 MHz), our higher-frequency technique (10 MHz) could provide more precise BBB-opening in brain tissues, suggesting that its potential applications could include local drug delivery in small animals model. This study provides important information towards the goal of successfully translating FUS brain drug delivery into clinical use.

Supporting Information

File S1 File includes Method S1, Table S1, and Figures S1-S5. Table S1: Transducer characteristics and operating frequency ranges. Figure S1: The size distribution of submicron bubble measured by (A) Coulter counter and (B) dynamic light scattering at 4°C or 37°C at different time point (post bubble preparation 0 min, 30 min, 1 h, 2 h and 4 h). Figure S2: The concentration of submicron bubble measured by Coulter counter and at 4°C or 37°C at different time point (post bubble preparation 0 min, 30 min, 1 h, 2 h and 4 h). Figure S3: The experimental setup for measuring the acoustic attenuation of the submicron bubbles. Figure S4: The Attenuation measurement results of submicron bubbles. Figure S5: The acoustic pressure maps of (A) 10-MHz, (B) 5-MHz and (C) 1-MHz transducers, respectively.

Acknowledgments

The authors acknowledge the supports of Professors R.-A. Doong, C.-S. Chiang, and Y.-F. Huang for their help with experiments.

Author Contributions

Conceived and designed the experiments: CHF HLL CKY. Performed the experiments: CHF CYT YHL CYH YJM. Analyzed the data: CHF CYT. Contributed reagents/materials/analysis tools: KCW TCY. Wrote the paper: CHF HLL CYT CKY.

References

1. Bickel U, Pardridge WM (1995) Vector-mediated delivery of opioid peptides to the brain. NIDA Res Monogr 154: 28–46.
2. Hynynen K, McDannold N, Vykhodtseva N, Jolesz FA (2001) Noninvasive MR imaging-guided focal opening of the blood-brain barrier in rabbits. Radiology 154: 640–646.
3. Hynynen K, McDannold N, Sheikov NA, Jolesz FA, Vykhodtseva N (2005) Local and reversible blood–brain barrier disruption by noninvasive focused ultrasound at frequencies suitable for trans-skull sonications. Neuroimage 24: 12–20.
4. Liu HL, Wai YY, Chen WS, Chen JC, Hsu PH, et al. (2008) Hemorrhage detection during focused-ultrasound induced blood–brain-barrier opening by using susceptibility-weighted magnetic resonance imaging. Ultrasound Med Biol 34: 598–606.
5. Bing KF, Howles GP, Qi Y, Palmeri ML, Nightingale KR (2009) Blood–brain barrier (BBB) disruption using a diagnostic ultrasound scanner and Definity in mice. Ultrasound Med Biol; 35: 1298–1308.
6. Sheikov N, McDannold N, Vykhodtseva N, Jolesz F, Hynynen K (2004) Cellular mechanisms of the blood-brain barrier opening induced by ultrasound in presence of microbubbles. Ultrasound Med Biol 30: 979–989.
7. Deng J, Huang Q, Wang F, Liu Y, Wang Z, et al. (2012) The role of caveolin-1 in blood–brain barrier disruption induced by focused ultrasound combined with microbubbles. J Mol Neurosci 46: 677–687.
8. Doolittle ND, Miner ME, Hall WA, Siegal T, Jerome E, et al. (2000) Safety and efficacy of a multicenter study using intraarterial chemotherapy in conjunction with osmotic opening of the blood-brain barrier for the treatment of patients with malignant brain tumors. Cancer 88: 637–647.
9. Emerich DF, Winn SR (2001) Immunoisolation cell therapy for CNS diseases. Crit Rev Ther Drug Carr Syst 18: 265–298.
10. Liu HL, Hua MY, Chen PY, Chu PC, Pan CH, et al. (2010) Blood-brain barrier disruption with focused ultrasound enhances delivery of chemotherapeutic drugs for glioblastoma treatment. Radiology 255: 415–425.
11. Jordão JF, Ayala-Grosso CA, Markham K, Huang Y, Chopra R, et al. (2010) Antibodies targeted to the brain with image-guided focused ultrasound reduces amyloid-beta plaque load in the TgCRND8 mouse model of Alzheimer's disease. PLoS One 5: e10549.
12. Sheikov N, McDannold N, Sharma S, Hynynen K (2008) Effect of focused ultrasound applied with an ultrasound contrast agent on the tight junctional integrity of the brain microvascular endothelium. Ultrasound Med Biol 34: 1093–1104.
13. Hynynen K, McDannold N, Sheikov NA, Jolesz FA, Vykhodtseva N (2005) Local and reversible blood-brain barrier disruption by noninvasive focused ultrasound at frequencies suitable for trans-skull sonications. Neuroimage 24: 12–20.
14. Yang FY, Lin YS, Kang KH, Chao TK (2011) Reversible blood-brain barrier disruption by repeated transcranial focused ultrasound allows enhanced extravasation. J Control Release 150: 111–116.
15. Samiotaki G, Vlachos F, Tung YS, Konofagou EE (2012) A quantitative pressure and microbubble-size dependence study of focused ultrasound-induced blood-brain barrier opening reversibility in vivo using MRI. Magn Reson Med 67: 769–777.
16. Chopra R, Vykhodtseva N, Hynynen K (2010) Influence of exposure time and pressure amplitude on blood–brain barrier opening using transcranial ultrasound exposures. ACS Chem Neurosci 1: 391–398.
17. Yang FY, Fu WM, Yang RS, Liou HC, Kang KH, et al. (2007) Quantitative evaluation of focused ultrasound with a contrast agent on blood–brain barrier disruption. Ultrasound Med Biol 33: 1421–1427.
18. Shi WT, Forsberg F, Raichlen JS, Needleman L, Goldberg BB (1999) Pressure dependence of subharmonic signals from contrast microbubbles. Ultrasound Med Biol 25: 275–283.
19. Miller DL (1987) A review of the ultrasonic bioeffects of microsonation, gas-body activation, and related cavitation-like phenomena. Ultrasound Med Biol 13: 443–470.
20. McDannold N, Vykhodtseva N, Hynynen K (2006) Targeted disruption of the blood-brain barrier with focused ultrasound: association with cavitation activity. Phys Med Biol 51: 793–807.
21. Tung YS, Vlachos F, Choi JJ, Deffieux T, Selert K, et al. (2010) In vivo transcranial cavitation threshold detection during ultrasound-induced blood-brain barrier opening in mice. Phys Med Biol 55: 6141–6155.
22. Ting CY, Fan CH, Liu HL, Huang CY, Hsieh HY, et al. (2012) Concurrent blood-brain barrier opening and local drug delivery using drug-carrying microbubbles and focused ultrasound for brain glioma treatment. Biomaterials 33: 704–712.
23. Kang ST, Yeh CK (2011) A maleimide-based in-vitro model for ultrasound targeted imaging. Ultrason Sonochem 18: 327–333.
24. Sun Y, Kruse DE, Dayton PA, Ferrara KW (2005) High-Frequency Dynamics of ultrasound contrast agents. IEEE Trans Ultrason Ferroelectr Freq Control 52: 1981–1991.
25. Van der Meer SM, Versluis M, Lohse D, Chin CT, Bouakaz A (2004) The resonance frequency of SonoVue as observed by high-speed optical imaging. Proc IEEE Ultrason Symp 1: 343–345.
26. Goertz DE, Needles A, Burns PN, Foster FS (2005) High-frequency, nonlinear flow imaging of microbubble contrast agents. IEEE Trans Ultrason Ferroelectr Freq Control 52: 495–502.
27. Chen WS, Brayman AA, Matula TJ, Crum LA, Miller MW (2003) The pulse length-dependence of inertial cavitation dose and hemolysis. Ultrasound Med Biol 29: 739–748.
28. Farny CH, Holt RG, Roy RA (2009) Temporal and spatial detection of HIFU induced inertial and hot-vapor cavitation with a diagnostic ultrasound system. Ultrasound Med Biol 35: 603–615.
29. Gavrieli Y, Sherman Y, Ben-Sasson SA (1992) Identification of programmed cell death in situ via specific labeling of nuclear DNA fragmentation. J Cell Biol 119: 493–501.
30. Jalali S, Huang Y, Dumont DJ, Hynynen K (2010) Focused ultrasound-mediated BBB disruption is associated with an increase in activation of AKT: experimental study in rats. BMC Neurol 10: 114.
31. Baseri B, Choi JJ, Tung YS (2010) Multi-modality safety assessment of blood-brain barrier opening using focused ultrasound and definity microbubbles: a short-term study. Ultrasound Med Biol 36: 1445–1459.
32. Tung YS, Marquet F, Teichert T, Konofagou EE (2011) Feasibility of noninvasive cavitation-guided blood-brain barrier opening using focused ultrasound and microbubbles in nonhuman primates. Appl Phys Lett 98: 163704.
33. Tung YS, Choi JJ, Baseri B, Konofagou EE (2010) Identifying the inertial cavitation threshold and skull effects in a vessel phantom using focused ultrasound and microbubbles. Ultrasound Med Biol 36: 840–852.
34. Wang S, Samiotaki G, Olumolade O, Feshitan JA, Konofagou EE (2014) Microbubble type and distribution dependence of focused ultrasound-induced blood-brain barrier opening Ultrasound Med Biol 40: 130–137.
35. Lai CY, Wu CH, Chen CC, Li PC (2006) Quantitative relations of acoustic inertial cavitation with sonoporation and cell viability. Ultrasound Med Biol 32: 1931–1941.
36. Miller DL, Dou C (2004) Membrane damage thresholds for 1- to 10-MHz pulsed ultrasound exposure of phagocytic cells loaded with contrast agent gas bodies in vitro. Ultrasound Med Biol 30: 973–977.
37. Choi JJ, Feshitan JA, Baseri B, Wang S, Tung YS, et al. (2010) Microbubble-size dependence of focused ultrasound-induced blood-brain barrier opening in mice in vivo. IEEE Trans Biomed Eng 57: 145–154.
38. Samiotaki G, Vlachos F, Tung YS, Konofagou EE (2012) A quantitative pressure and microbubble-size dependence study of focused ultrasound-induced

blood-brain barrier opening reversibility in vivo using MRI. Magn Reson Med 67: 769–777.
39. McDannold N, Vykhodtseva N, Hynynen K (2008) Blood-brain barrier disruption induced by focused ultrasound and circulating preformed microbubbles appears to be characterized by the mechanical index. Ultrasound Med Biol 34: 834–840.
40. O'Reilly MA, Hynynen K (2012) Blood-brain barrier: real-time feedback-controlled focused ultrasound disruption by using an acoustic emissions-based controller. Radiology 26: 96–106.
41. Arvanitis CD, Livingstone MS, Vykhodtseva N, McDannold N (2012) Controlled ultrasound-induced blood-brain barrier disruption using passive acoustic emissions monitoring. PLoS One 7: e45783.
42. Fukuda S, Kato T, Kakita H, Yamada Y, Hussein MH, et al. (2006) Hemodynamics of the cerebral arteries of infants with periventricular leukomalacia. Pediatrics 117: 1–8.
43. Inder T, Anderson NJ, Spencer C (2003) White matter injury in the premature infant: a comparison between serial cranial sonographic and MR findings at term. AJNR Am J Neuroradiol 24: 805–809.
44. De Vries LS, Van Haastert IL, Rademaker KJ, Wells S, Volpe JJ (2004) Ultrasound abnormalities preceding cerebral palsy in high-risk preterm infants. J Pediatr 144: 815–820.

20

Efficacy of a Metalloproteinase Inhibitor in Spinal Cord Injured Dogs

Jonathan M. Levine[1]*, Noah D. Cohen[2], Michael Heller[3], Virginia R. Fajt[4], Gwendolyn J. Levine[5], Sharon C. Kerwin[1], Alpa A. Trivedi[6], Thomas M. Fandel[6], Zena Werb[7], Augusta Modestino[3], Linda J. Noble-Haeusslein[6,8]

1 Department of Small Animal Clinical Sciences, College of Veterinary Medicine and Biomedical Sciences, Texas A&M University, College Station, Texas, United States of America, **2** Department of Large Animal Clinical Sciences, College of Veterinary Medicine and Biomedical Sciences, Texas A&M University, College Station, Texas, United States of America, **3** Department of Bioengineering, University of California San Diego, San Diego, California, United States of America, **4** Department of Veterinary Physiology and Pharmacology, College of Veterinary Medicine and Biomedical Sciences, Texas A&M University, College Station, Texas, United States of America, **5** Department of Veterinary Pathobiology, College of Veterinary Medicine and Biomedical Sciences, Texas A&M University, College Station, Texas, United States of America, **6** Department of Neurological Surgery, University of California San Francisco, San Francisco, California, United States of America, **7** Department of Anatomy, University of California San Francisco, San Francisco, California, United States of America, **8** Department of Physical Therapy and Rehabilitation, University of California San Francisco, San Francisco, California, United States of America

Abstract

Matrix metalloproteinase-9 is elevated within the acutely injured murine spinal cord and blockade of this early proteolytic activity with GM6001, a broad-spectrum matrix metalloproteinase inhibitor, results in improved recovery after spinal cord injury. As matrix metalloproteinase-9 is likewise acutely elevated in dogs with naturally occurring spinal cord injuries, we evaluated efficacy of GM6001 solubilized in dimethyl sulfoxide in this second species. Safety and pharmacokinetic studies were conducted in naïve dogs. After confirming safety, subsequent pharmacokinetic analyses demonstrated that a 100 mg/kg subcutaneous dose of GM6001 resulted in plasma concentrations that peaked shortly after administration and were sustained for at least 4 days at levels that produced robust *in vitro* inhibition of matrix metalloproteinase-9. A randomized, blinded, placebo-controlled study was then conducted to assess efficacy of GM6001 given within 48 hours of spinal cord injury. Dogs were enrolled in 3 groups: GM6001 dissolved in dimethyl sulfoxide (n = 35), dimethyl sulfoxide (n = 37), or saline (n = 41). Matrix metalloproteinase activity was increased in the serum of injured dogs and GM6001 reduced this serum protease activity compared to the other two groups. To assess recovery, dogs were *a priori* stratified into a severely injured group and a mild-to-moderate injured group, using a Modified Frankel Scale. The Texas Spinal Cord Injury Score was then used to assess long-term motor/sensory function. In dogs with severe spinal cord injuries, those treated with saline had a mean motor score of 2 (95% CI 0–4.0) that was significantly ($P < 0.05$; generalized linear model) less than the estimated mean motor score for dogs receiving dimethyl sulfoxide (mean, 5; 95% CI 2.0–8.0) or GM6001 (mean, 5; 95% CI 2.0–8.0). As there was no independent effect of GM6001, we attribute improved neurological outcomes to dimethyl sulfoxide, a pleotropic agent that may target diverse secondary pathogenic events that emerge in the acutely injured cord.

Editor: Hatem E. Sabaawy, Rutgers-Robert wood Johnson Medical School, United States of America

Funding: This study was supported by funds from National Institutes of Health R01NS039278 (Supp)(www.nih.gov) and US Department of Defense SC100140 (http://cdmrp.army.mil/funding/_. Dr. Cohen was supported in part by the Link Equine Research Endowment at Texas A&M University. The funders had no role in study design, data collection and analysis, decision to publish, or preparation of this manuscript.

Competing Interests: The authors have declared that no competing interests exist.

* E-mail: jlevine@cvm.tamu.edu

Introduction

Matrix metalloproteinases (MMPs) are endopeptidases that degrade the extracellular matrix [1]. Several members of the MMP family, including MMP-9 (gelatinase B) and MMP-12, have been implicated in early secondary pathogenesis after spinal cord injury (SCI) [2–4]. These MMPs are released by local cells as well as by infiltrating leukocytes and result in reduced cell-cell adhesion, disruption of the blood-spinal cord barrier, up-regulation of pro-inflammatory cytokines, and demyelination [1,4,5].

Early blockade of MMPs confers neuroprotection after SCI [2,6,7]. Short-term administration of the broad-spectrum MMP inhibitor, GM6001, results in sparing of white matter and improves locomotor function when the drug is given over the first 3 days post-injury [2]. Several lines of evidence suggest that one likely target of GM6001 is MMP-9. This protease is not actively expressed in the uninjured spinal cord and is up-regulated over the first 3 days post-injury, corresponding to the time-course for infiltration of neutrophils [8]. While there are local sources of MMP-9, including glia and endothelial cells, neutrophil depletion studies confirm that these leukocytes are the major source of MMP-9 in the acutely injured cord [7]. As this protease is not complexed with tissue inhibitor of MMP-1, degranulation of neutrophils results in release of activated MMP-9 [9], which then may disrupt the barrier and facilitate transmigration of leukocytes into the injured spinal cord. It thus is not surprising that early administration of GM6001 attenuates the trafficking of neutrophils into the injured spinal cord and stabilizes the blood-spinal cord barrier [2]. There are other members of the MMP family that are also determinants of recovery after SCI including MMP-12 and ADAM-8 (a disintegrin and metalloprotease domain) [3]. Thus, broad inhibitors of MMPs may offer greater benefit than specific inhibitors of these proteases.

In this study, we have used dimethyl sulfoxide (DMSO) in combination with GM6001 [10,11]. While DMSO is commonly used as a vehicle to increase solubility of a drug, it has been reported to have neuroprotective properties in traumatic brain injury and SCI [12,13]. The putative neuroprotective activity of DMSO is thought to arise from its ability to block voltage-sensitive sodium channels and calcium influx into cells, and mitigate opening of ionotropic channels that are activated by glutamate [14].

Few studies have considered a pre-clinical platform involving dogs with naturally occurring SCIs resulting from intervertebral disk herniation (IVDH) [15–17]. This approach mimics pathologic aspects of human SCI including compressive/contusive injuries and a pro-inflammatory response that includes the infiltration of neutrophils and up-regulation of MMP-9 [18–20]. Moreover, these naturally-occurring injuries provide a means for studying therapeutics in the challenging context of varying degrees of injury severity, common in human SCI, but without confounding factors such as anesthetics that are necessary during creation of injury in experimental models.

Here we evaluate the efficacy of GM6001 in dogs with IVDH. Based on a double-blind, randomized, placebo-controlled trial, consisting of 3 groups (GM6001 in DMSO, DMSO alone, or saline) we show enhanced neurological recovery in dogs sustaining severe SCIs when treated acutely with GM6001 solubilized in DMSO or DMSO alone, relative to the saline group. Such findings implicate DMSO in improving neurological recovery, which is consistent with its reported ability to attenuate secondary pathogenic events in various models of neurotrauma [14].

Materials and Methods

Study Design and Inclusion Criteria

A preliminary drug tolerance study was constructed based on Food and Drug Administration guidelines (http://www.fda.gov/AnimalVeterinary/default.htm) and performed in 4 healthy, purpose-bred Beagles. Ten healthy, purpose-bred Beagles were obtained to evaluate pharmacokinetics (PK); this sample size was based on similar animal studies and general recommendations for canine PK investigations [21].

Guidelines for the conduct of SCI trials developed by the International Campaign for Cures of Spinal Cord Injury Paralysis were utilized to assist with the design of a randomized, double-blinded (clinicians and clients were unaware of treatment group), placebo-controlled canine trial including inclusion/exclusion criteria, randomization protocol, data handling, and the *a priori* definition of outcome metrics and statistical approaches.[22]. Consolidated Standards of Reporting Trials (CONSORT) Statement Guidelines were used to assist with trial performance and data reporting [23,24]. Client-owned dogs with IVDH-associated SCI, admitted to the Texas A&M University Veterinary Medical Teaching Hospital between September 2008 and February 2012, were recruited. The study interval was selected to generate a sample size of >100 dogs, which was considered robust based on previous human phase II and III SCI studies [25,26], animal model studies of SCI using MMP blockers [2], and completed canine SCI studies [27,28]. A formal power calculation was not performed due to the absence of a phase I canine study examining the effects of GM6001.

Dogs had to meet the following criteria to be included in the clinical trial population: 1) duration of SCI was required to be ≤48 hours; 2) IVDH-associated SCI had to result in non-ambulatory paraparesis or paraplegia at enrollment; 3) IVDH-associated SCI had to be identified between the T8-L6 vertebral articulations and treated via surgical decompression. The exclusion criteria were: 1) concurrent disseminated neoplasia or systemic inflammation; 2) a history of recent breeding/pregnancy; and, 3) glucocorticoid treatment within 7 days of SCI.

The primary outcome of the clinical trial was a validated ordinal SCI score (the Texas Spinal Cord Injury Score [TSCIS]) conducted at 42 days post-injury [29]. The secondary outcome was TSCIS at 3 days after SCI. Dogs were stratified into those with behaviorally severe SCI (absent pelvic limb movement and deep nociception) and those with mild-to-moderate SCI (intact pelvic limb deep nociception with or without movement) at study entry to examine primary and secondary outcomes. This *a priori* stratification was utilized because a substantially lower proportion of dogs with severe SCI recover independent ambulation at long-term follow-up time-points (approximately 50–60%) in comparison to dogs with mild-to-moderate SCI (approximately 85 to 95%); thus, injury severity might influence the ability to detect treatment-related effects [30–33].

Ethics Statement

All animal procedures were approved by the Texas A&M University Institutional Animal Care and Use Committee (AUP 2007–115; AUP 2011–057; AUP-2011–145) and in the case of client-owned dogs were performed with signed consent. All studies adhered to the National Institutes of Health Guide for the Care and Use of Laboratory Animals.

Drug Preparation, Drug Tolerance, and Pharmacokinetic Procedures

For all canine studies, GM6001 (SAI Advantium, Hyderabad, India) was dissolved in 90% DMSO (Domoso, Fort Dodge Corp, Fort Dodge, IA) at a concentration of 250 mg/mL. The solution was sterilized using a 25-mm syringe filter with 0.22-μm HT Tuffryn membrane (Pall Corporation, East Hills, NY).

Dogs, participating in the drug tolerance study, were acclimatized for 14 days and then randomized as follows: DMSO (at a volume equivalent to that present in a 100 mg/kg GM6001 treatment), 100 mg/kg GM6001, 150 mg/kg GM6001, or 300 mg/kg GM6001 subcutaneously (SC) every 12 hours for 3 days. The doses of GM6001 were selected to exceed those reported previously in a murine model of SCI [2]. A SC route of administration was selected as 1) GM6001 does not remain solubilized in DMSO when exposed to hydrophilic solutions such as blood, prohibiting intravenous delivery and 2) intraperitoneal drug administration is not generally permitted in client-owned dogs at our institution, due to challenges in managing any local drug reactions. Adverse event monitoring was performed for 7 days following the completion of drug administration. All dogs had physical examinations, injection site evaluations, and assessment of food and water intake twice daily. A complete blood count, serum biochemistry profile, urinalysis, and coagulation profile were performed 3 and 7 days following the completion of drug administration. Following the completion of this study, the vehicle and 300 mg/kg GM6001 dogs were euthanized via intravenous administration of 120 mg/kg pentobarbital (Fatal Plus, Vortech Pharmaceuticals, Dearborn, MI). The brain, heart, liver, kidney, lung, intestine, and injection sites were evaluated.

For PK assessments, a single 100 mg/kg SC administration of GM6001 was delivered in 5 dogs with 5 additional dogs receiving a second 100 mg/kg SC of GM6001, 12 hours following the first dose. In dogs with single dosing, serial plasma samples were obtained at 5, 15, and 30 minutes and 1, 2, 3, 6, 12, 24, 36, 48, and 96 hours after GM6001 delivery. In dogs with multiple dosing, blood samples were collected shortly after the second dose, and then at 24, 48, 72, and 96 hours. All samples were stored in a −80°C freezer until analyzed by high performance chromatography (Thermo Electron Co., Waltham, MA) and tandem mass spectroscopy (MDS-Sciex/Applied Biosystems API3000, Concord, ONT) (LC-MS/MS). Concentrations of GM6001 (m/z 389.0→356.0) were determined, using MMP Inhibitor III (m/z 364.0→356.0, Calbiochem, Billerica, MA) as the internal standard. A standard curve was created with blank dog plasma at concentrations 10.0 to 10,204.0 ng/mL, with linear regression and weighting of concentrations ($1/x^2$). After thawing and addition of internal standard (300 µL of 100 ng/mL in 0.5% acetic acid in methanol), plasma samples or standards (100 µL) were centrifuged and reconstituted with 30/70 methanol/10 mM ammonium formate buffer, pH 3.0, for protein precipitation. Supernatant (100 µL) was collected, vortexed, and refrigerated until injection on LC-MS/MS. The mobile phase consisted of 0.1% formic acid in deionized water (A) and acetonitrile/methanol/formic acid (40:60:0.1, v/v/v) (B) with a flow rate of 0.30 mL/minute using a linear gradient starting at 40% B from 0 to 0.01 minutes, to 80% B at 1.5 minutes, to 90% B at 3.5 minutes, to 40% B at 3.6 minutes, with a total run time of 5 minutes.

Randomized, Placebo Controlled Study in Dogs with IVDH-associated SCI

Dogs, enrolled in the clinical trial, had physical and neurological examinations, complete blood count and serum biochemistry profile. Anesthesia was induced with propofol (Rapinovet, Schering-Plough Animal Health Corp, Union, NJ) and maintained with inhalant sevoflurane (SevoFlo, Abbott Laboratories, North Chicago, IL). Diagnostic imaging consisting of myelography, computed tomography (CT), or MRI was performed to identify IVDH. Cerebrospinal fluid (CSF) was collected from the cisterna magna for routine analysis and a 200-µL aliquot was stored at −80°C for determination of MMP-2/MMP-9 activity. Six mL of whole blood were obtained at the time of CSF collection and 3 days following treatment delivery; serum was isolated and frozen at −80°C.

Immediately after collection of CSF and blood, dogs were randomized to receive 100 mg/kg GM6001+ DMSO, DMSO, or saline placebo. The dose of both DMSO and saline was 0.4 mL/kg, a volume equivalent to that of 100 mg/kg GM6001+DMSO; this approach was taken to maintain blinding. A randomization sequence was developed prior to the initiation of this trial and randomization was accomplished by blocking the dogs by gender status in a 1:1:1 ratio to each of the treatment groups. Sealed envelopes contained treatment allocations and were delivered to a central location where treatments were formulated by individuals not involved in the assessment of animals. Treatments were covered and marked only with animal identifiers to ensure blinding.

Following surgical decompression, all dogs were recovered in an intensive care unit for 24 hours and during that time were provided post-operative opioid analgesia and bladder evacuation. Physical rehabilitation protocols were standardized for dogs participating in this study. Dogs received thoracic limb and pelvic limb passive range of motion exercises beginning 24 hours post-operatively and until dogs could independently ambulate. Each limb was gently flexed and extended at the carpal, elbow, and hip joints in 3 sets of 10 repetitions, 2 times daily. Supported standing exercises were performed twice daily for 5 minutes by placing a sling immediately cranial to the pelvic limbs and continued until dogs could independently ambulate. Dogs that were non-ambulatory were walked using a sling placed immediately cranial to the pelvic limbs for 5 minutes twice daily. Independently ambulatory dogs were permitted to walk on a leash for 5 minutes 3–4 times per day during hospitalization and were allowed to continue this activity until 42-day re-check. Participating dogs were housed in cages that permitted limited additional activity until 42-day re-check evaluation.

Neurological Assessments

Clinicians responsible for neurologic scoring were blinded to treatment assignments. Two ordinal SCI scores were used to address injury severity at study entry, day 3 post-treatment, and day 42 post-treatment. In both scoring systems, dogs were considered ambulatory if they could spontaneously rise, bear weight, and take at least 10 steps without falling. Dogs that were non-ambulatory had pelvic limb movement evaluated using tail support. Postural responses were evaluated by placing the dorsum of the pes on a non-slick surface while manually supporting the animal and waiting for limb correction. Pelvic limb deep and superficial nociception were evaluated by applying hemostats to a nail-bed or interdigital webbing, respectively and evaluating for the presence of a behavioral or physiological response.

A modified Frankel scale (MFS) was developed to broadly parallel the American Spinal Cord Injury Association Impairment Scale (AIS) [15,29]. Dogs were scored as paraplegic with absent deep nociception (0; equivalent to AIS A), paraplegic with absent superficial nociception (1; equivalent to AIS B), paraplegic with intact nociception (2; equivalent to AIS B), or non-ambulatory with identifiable pelvic limb movement (3; equivalent to AIS C). The MFS was not a primary trial outcome, but instead was used to describe the baseline population (overall and by treatment group) and to stratify the study population for analysis.

The Texas Spinal Cord Injury Score (TSCIS) was used to assess pelvic limb gait, posture and nociception. This is a more refined scale than the MFS [15] with a larger array of sub-categories, including gait assessment that parallels the Basso, Beattie, Bresnahan Scale [34]. The TSCIS gait score ranges from 0 to 6 in each pelvic limb and correlates to the degree of limb protraction and weight bearing. The gait classifications include: no voluntary movement seen when the dog is supported (score = 0); intact limb protraction with no ground clearance (1); intact limb protraction with inconsistent ground clearance (2); intact protraction with ground clearance >75% of steps (3); ambulatory with consistent ground clearance and significant paresis-ataxia that results in occasional falling (4); ambulatory with consistent ground clearance and mild paresis-ataxia that does not result in falling (5); and normal gait (6). Pelvic limb postural responses using the TSCIS were scored in each limb as absent (0), delayed (1, correction occurred >1 second after positioning), and present (2). Nociception was scored in each limb as absent (0), deep nociception only present (1), or both deep and superficial nociception present (2).

Magnetic Resonance Imaging (MRI)

Vertebral column MRI was performed on enrolled dogs, except in cases where animals were evaluated outside of normal operating hours or the scanner was unavailable due to mechanical failure. Between September 2008 and July 2011, a 1.0 T system (Siemens Magnetom, Malvern, PA) was utilized to acquire images; for the remainder of the trial images were generated using a 3.0 T MRI

(Simens Verio, Malvern, PA). Dogs that received MRI had sagittal T2-weighted (T2W) images reviewed by 1 investigator (JML) using commercially available software (eFILM, Merge Healthcare, Chicago, IL) prior to un-blinding. The acquisition parameters for sagittal T2W images generated at 1T and 3T included a repetition time of 3500 ms, echo time of 90 ms, and slice thickness of 2.0 mm. The presence of spinal cord T2W hyperintensity was determined by visually comparing injured parenchyma to surrounding spinal cord. This technique has been used extensively in human and canine MRI studies and produces repeatable results that correlate with behavioral measures of SCI severity and recovery [35,36].

MMP-2/MMP-9 Activity in CSF and Serum

CSF and serum samples (n = 16/treatment group) were randomly selected at the end of the trial by computerized sorting on random numbers. Purpose-bred Beagle dogs (n = 5) were sampled as controls. Serum samples with overt hemolysis were excluded from analysis.

Activity of MMP-2 and MMP-9 in serum and CSF samples was assessed in a blinded manner using a previously developed electrophoretic method [37–39] that included a synthetic peptide (AAPPtec, Louisville, KY) (sequence: Ac-NGDPVGLTAGAGK-NH2), tagged with a fluorophore BODIPY-FL-SE (Invitrogen, Carlsbad, CA). The substrate was mixed with either serum or CSF, with phosphate buffered saline as the negative control. After reacting for 1 hour, aliquots were loaded onto 20% polyacrylamide gels and the samples were electrophoresed. Gels were imaged using a BioDoc-It M-26 transilluminator (UVP, Upland, CA, USA). The image was scanned in a Storm 840 workstation (Molecular Dynamics, Sunnyvale, CA, USA) with ImageQuant v5.2 software and fluorescent signal was quantified using ImageJ (1.440, National Institutes of Health, Bethesda, MD).

To assess ability of GM6001 to inhibit MMP-9, activity (described above) was determined using human recombinant MMP-9 (Sigma, St. Louis, MO) that was serially diluted in DMSO to final concentrations of 0.01 μM to 200 μM. Controls consisted of enzyme and substrate only and substrate and GM6001 only.

Statistical Analyses

Noncompartmental pharmacokinetic analysis was performed (Phoenix WinNonLin 6.3, Pharsight, St. Louis, MO), and estimates of the parameters of T_{max}, C_{max}, $T_{1/2}$, and area $AUC_{0\text{-obs}}$ and $AUC_{0\text{-}\infty}$ were calculated for the single dose.

Activities of MMP-2/MMP-9 in CSF and serum were compared between healthy control dogs and the dogs with SCI using the Wilcoxon rank-sum test. The Wilcoxon rank-sum test was also used to compare CSF and serum MMP-2/MMP-9 activities between dogs with and without selected characteristics that were potential modifiers of MMP-2/MMP-9 (i.e., age, breed, sex, and markers of disease duration or severity). To compare serum MMP-2/MMP-9 values among treatment groups, the serum MMP-2/MMP-9 activities were converted to ranks, and the ranks were compared using a generalized linear model; multiple pair-wise comparisons between treatments were made using the method of Sidak. Model fit was assessed graphically using diagnostic plots of residuals.

For the clinical trial data, a strategy for analysis of data was developed *a priori*, including our decision to stratify the population based on SCI severity at admission. Baseline characteristics were compared among the 3 treatment groups to determine whether there was any evidence of differences among groups. Categorical variables were compared using chi-squared analysis and continuous or ordinal variables were compared using Kruskal-Wallis tests. The primary outcome for the trial was the TSCIS score on day 42. The TSCIS on day 3 was considered a secondary outcome. The association of TSCIS with treatment group and other individual variables was assessed using generalized linear modeling. Individual variables significantly associated with TSCIS were analyzed using multivariable generalized linear modeling using maximum likelihood estimating methods. Multiple comparisons among groups were adjusted using the method of Sidak. Model fit was assessed graphically using diagnostic plots of residuals. Comparisons of proportions among treatments groups (e.g., frequency of adverse events) were made using chi-squared or, when appropriate, Fisher's exact tests. Significance was set at $P < 0.05$ for all analyses. Analyses were performed using S-PLUS statistical software (Version 8.2, TIBCO, Inc., Seattle, WA).

Results

GM6001 is Well Tolerated in Naive Dogs

We first addressed the safety of GM6001 using a dose tolerance study. Four healthy dogs were randomized to receive DMSO vehicle, 100 mg/kg GM6001, 150 mg/kg GM6001, or 300 mg/kg GM6001 SC every 12 hours for 3 days. Following drug delivery, all studied parameters were within normal limits, with the following exceptions: 1) increase in body temperature in all GM6001-treated dogs which peaked 6 days after treatment was completed (Fig. S1); 2) transient decrease in food consumption during the 3 days of drug delivery (mean percentage of food consumed, 64.5% ±12.9%) in comparison to the 3 days following delivery (mean percentage of food consumed, 91.7% ±16.3%); and 3) the presence of subcutaneous nodules at the drug delivery sites that regressed in size following delivery in all animals (Fig. S2). No lesions were detected via necropsy or histopathology in the dog that received vehicle. In the dog receiving 300 mg/kg GM6001 twice daily for 3 days, sites of subcutaneous drug deposition were surrounded by a connective tissue capsule with minimal inflammation; additionally, there was mild bile duct hyperplasia. The absence of substantial adverse events in this tolerance study suggested that GM6001 would have an acceptable safety profile in injured dogs.

GM6001 is Rapidly Detected in Plasma After Subcutaneous Administration

As the PK of GM6001 might differ from that in rodent [40], we determined the PK in normal dogs. GM6001, administered once at 100 mg/kg SC, was detected in plasma at 5 minutes in all dogs, with a mean time to peak concentration (T_{max}) of 0.7 hours (S.D. ±1.3 hours) (Fig. 1). The mean peak concentration (C_{max}) was 1370 ng/mL (S.D. ±361 ng/mL), mean apparent elimination half-life ($T_{1/2}$) was 524 hours (S.D. ±428 hours), and the mean plasma concentration of GM6001 at 96 hours was 80 ng/mL (S.D. ±20 ng/mL). Mean area under the curve (AUC) from time 0 to last observed concentration ($AUC_{0\text{-obs}}$) (16,100 hr*ng/mL ±2981) and mean AUC from time 0 to infinity ($AUC_{0\text{-}\infty}$) (58,225 hr*ng/mL ±37,054) resulted in an extrapolated percentage of AUC of 65%. The only notable adverse event was the presence of focal subcutaneous nodules that regressed with time. The GM6001 utilized in the clinical trial had marked *in vitro* MMP-9 inhibition at concentrations approximating those achieved in dog plasma 96 hours post-drug delivery (Fig. 2). As the objective was to target the acutely injured cord, we selected a single 100 mg/kg SC dose of GM6001 in dogs to achieve plasma drug concentrations which would peak almost immediately after delivery and be sustained at levels sufficient to inhibit MMPs *in vitro* for at least 96 hours following delivery.

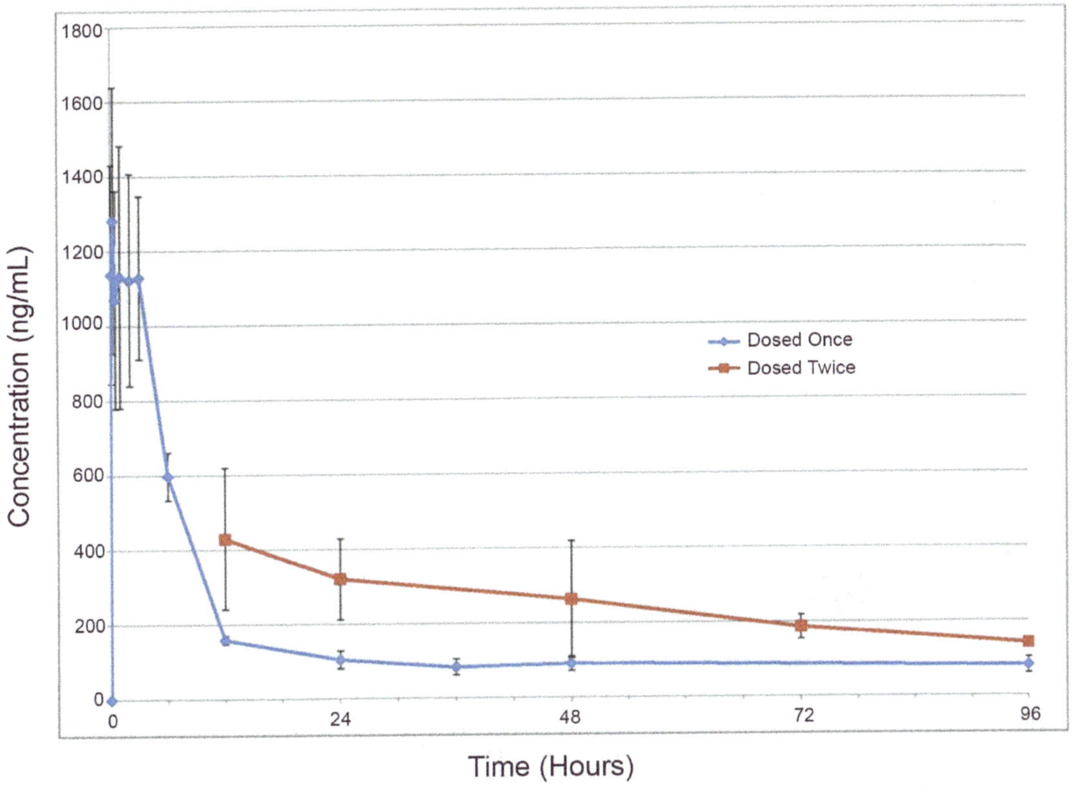

Figure 1. Pharmacokinetics of GM6001 in dogs. Administration of a single 100 mg/kg subcutaneous dose of GM6001 to dogs resulted in the rapid development of peak plasma drug concentrations with drug still detectable 96 hours post-delivery. Administration of a second dose of GM6001 to a sub-group of dogs 12 hours following initial drug delivery resulted in increased plasma drug concentrations at all assessed time points.

Clinical Trial Enrollment

Enrolled dogs were randomized to a saline placebo group (n = 38 dogs), a DMSO group (n = 37), and a GM6001 group (n = 33) (Fig. 3). Three dogs were euthanized prior to discharge from the hospital due to neurologic deterioration and 17 dogs did not return for 42-day follow-up examination. Of critical importance, there were no differences in baseline population characteristics such as breed, gender, or injury level among treatment groups, indicating that confounding based on these parameters was unlikely (Table 1).

Adverse Events in Spinal Cord Injured Dogs

Adverse events were recorded during hospitalization and were classified as fever, gastrointestinal, injection site, urinary, or other (Table S1). A significantly greater number of dogs in the GM6001 group had injection site reactions (45%; 15/33) relative to either the saline control dogs (5%; 2/38) or DMSO dogs (0%; 0/36) ($P < 0.0001$; Kruskal-Wallis test). These reactions were transient and consisted of focal dermal and subcutaneous swelling.

Increased MRI T2W Signal within the Spinal Cord is Associated with Poor Recovery

Vertebral column MRI was performed on 76/107 dogs enrolled in the clinical trial. In all cases, spinal cord compression associated with IVDH was identified with variable presence of increased T2W signal (27/76 dogs) within the spinal cord (Fig. 4). High spinal cord T2 signal, suggestive of contusion, was significantly more common in dogs with severe SCIs (MFS = 0; 11/13) compared with those with mild-to-moderate SCIs (MFS>0; 16/63) ($P = 0.0001$; Fisher's exact test). Dogs with increased T2W spinal cord also had significantly ($P < 0.0001$; generalized linear model) poorer recovery of function 42 days following SCI (estimated TSCIS 9, 95% CI 7–12) compared to dogs with normal spinal cord T2W signal (estimated TSCIS 15, 95% CI 14–17). The presence of compressive SCI with variable presence of T2W hyperintensity in the spinal cord parallels what is found on MRI in humans with traumatic myelopathy, including relationships between function and spinal cord T2 signal [36].

Characterization of Cells in CSF Following Spinal Cord Injury

CSF was acquired immediately prior to drug or placebo delivery in 102/107 (95%) clinical trial dogs; all 5 un-injured control animals also had CSF collected. Total nucleated cell count was significantly ($P = 0.0034$, Wilcoxon rank-sum test) higher in SCI dogs (median = 3 cells/μL, range 0–71) compared with control dogs (median = 0 cells/μL, range 0–1). Amongst dogs with CSF pleocytosis (total nucleated cell count >5 cells/μL), neutrophils were most frequently identified (median 43%, range 2–89%), followed by mononuclear cells (median 25%, range 6–95%) and lymphocytes (median 18%, range 4–70%). CSF red blood cell count was likewise significantly ($P = 0.0022$, Wilcoxon rank-sum test) increased in dogs with SCI (median 48 cells/μL, range 0–15,040). Together, these findings support a pro-inflammatory state in the acutely injured canine spinal cord.

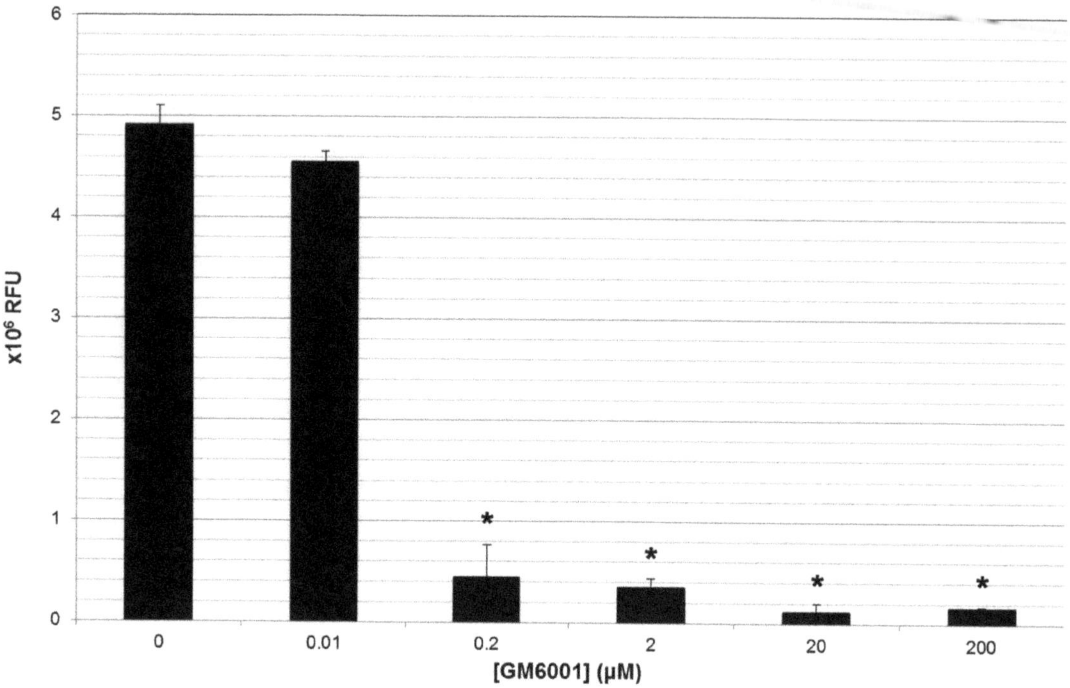

Figure 2. ***In vitro*** **inhibition of MMP-9 by GM6001.** Calibrated MMP-9 activity (Log 10^6), as measured by a fluorescent electrophoretic technique, was dramatically attenuated by GM6001 *in vitro* at various concentrations. Plasma concentrations of GM6001, measured 96 hours following a single 100 mg/kg subcutaenous dose (range 0.16–.26 µM or 60–100 ng/mL), approximated those needed *in vitro* to robustly inhibit MMP-9 (0.2 µM or 77 ng/mL). Groups marked with an asterisk (*) had significantly ($P<0.05$) different calibrated MMP-9 activity from reference (no GM6001) using a one tailed Student's t-test.

GM6001 Reduces Gelatinase Activity in Serum of Spinal Cord Injured Dogs

We utilized a fluorescent electrophoretic technique to determine if MMP-2/MMP-9 activity increases in CSF and serum in dogs with SCI and whether activity is reduced after treatment [37–39]. MMP-2/MMP-9 activity in the CSF did not differ between dogs with SCI and control dogs ($P = 0.5011$; Wilcoxon rank-sum test) (Table S2, Fig. S3). Dogs with SCI had significantly ($P = 0.0128$; Wilcoxon rank-sum test) higher serum MMP-2/MMP-9 activity prior to treatment compared with control dogs, but activity did not vary based on clinical factors or MRI features of SCI (Table 2, Fig. 5). Serum MMP-2/MMP-9 activity was significantly ($P<0.05$; generalized linear model) lower in dogs receiving GM6001 3 days following treatment compared to dogs receiving either DSMO or saline (Fig. 6). Thus, these findings confirm the effectiveness of GM6001 in reducing the abnormal elevation of MMP-2/MMP-9 in serum of spinal cord injured dogs.

DMSO Enhances Recovery in Dogs with Severe Spinal Cord Injuries

In dogs with mild-to-moderate SCI (i.e., MFS >0), there was robust recovery of function by 42 days with 64 of 71 (90%) dogs independently walking and 69 of 71 (97%) having intact pelvic limb nociception. Treatment group did not influence 3 or 42 day TSCIS (Fig. 7, Fig. S4). Dogs with mild-to-moderate SCI had significantly higher 42-day TSCIS (mean 15; 95% CI 12–18) compared to those with severe SCI (mean 7; 95% CI 4–9) ($P<0.0010$; generalized linear model).

In dogs with severe SCI (i.e., MFS = 0), those receiving either DMSO or GM6001 had significantly ($P<0.05$; generalized linear model) more robust functional recovery compared with those receiving saline placebo (Fig. 7) at 42 days. Sub-components of the 42-day TSCIS were examined in dogs with severe SCI to better capture the influence of treatment on motor, sensory, and postural recovery. Sensory and postural scores did not differ significantly between treatment groups. Dogs receiving saline had an estimated mean motor score of 2 (95% CI 0–4.0) (suggesting absent to minimal pelvic limb movement with tail support) that was significantly ($P<0.05$; generalized linear model) less than the estimated mean motor score for dogs receiving DMSO (mean, 5; 95% CI 2.0–8.0) or GM6001 (mean, 5; 95% CI 2.0–8.0) (Fig. 8). The distribution of motor scores for both the DMSO and GM6001 treated dogs indicated that the majority of animals in these groups developed coordinated stepping movements with tail support and of those regaining movement many (6 of 12; 50%) walked without any support. Dogs that were treated with DMSO or GM6001 that regained pelvic limb movement typically (10 of 12; 83%) also recovered limb nociception. The extent of neurological recovery at 42 days post-injury was not significantly different in DMSO- and GM6001 (dissolved in DMSO)-treated groups. Such findings suggest that DMSO, rather than GM6001 contributed to enhanced recovery in these treatment groups.

Discussion

This study was designed as a large-scale clinical trial to evaluate MMP inhibition in a clinically relevant, naturally occurring canine SCI model. Using advanced technology to measure activity of MMP-2/MMP-9, we show that these proteases are elevated in serum of dogs across all levels of injury severity and that GM001, given as a single bolus subcutaneously, significantly reduced this activity. Despite the effectiveness of GM6001 in targeting early MMP activity, both GM6001, solubilized in DMSO, and DMSO

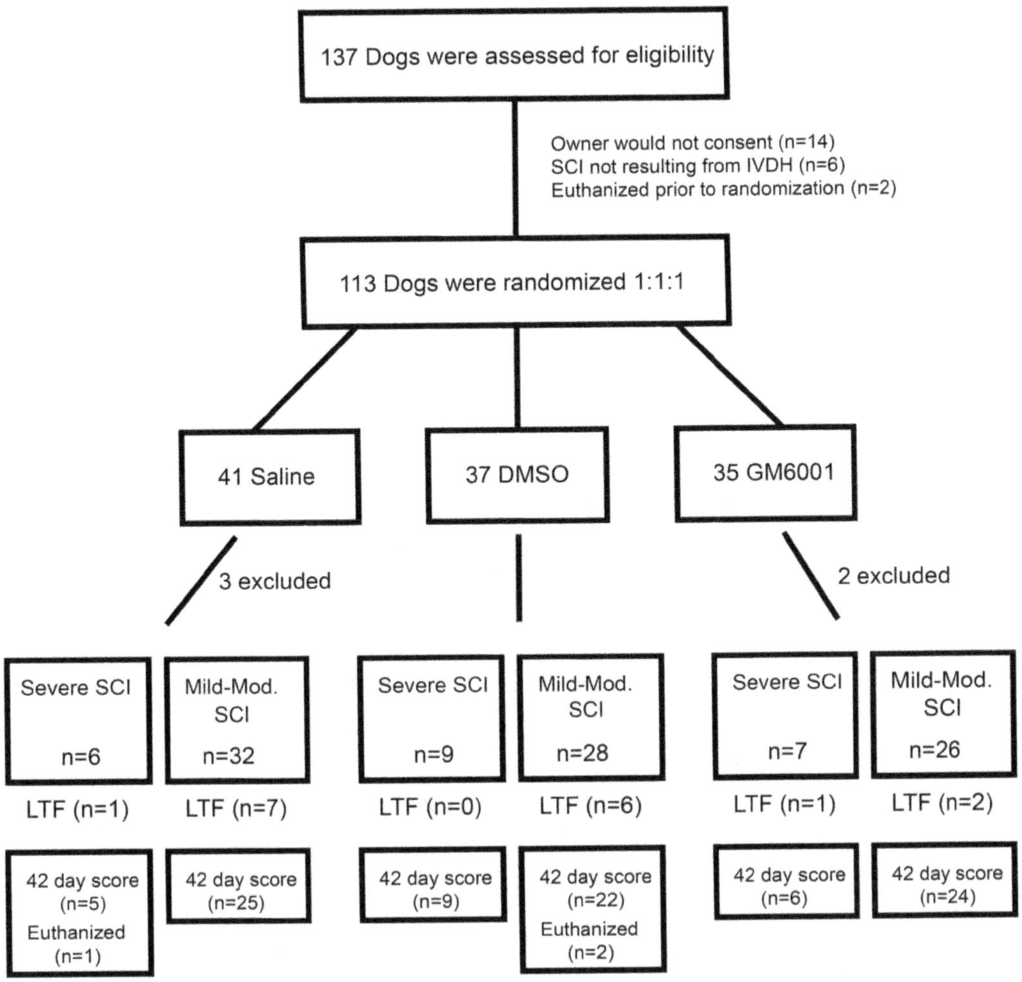

* Dogs were excluded from data analysis due to the fact that they were ambulatory when randomized, which was not permitted according to inclusion criteria (n= 4) or due to herniation of an adjacent disk during the course of the trial (n=1). Abbreviations: IVDH = intervertebral disk herniation; LTF = lost to follow-up; SCI = spinal cord injury.

Figure 3. Consolidated Standards of Reporting Trials (CONSORT) Diagram. Flow diagram depicting progress through different phases of the clinical trial including enrollment, group allocation, and follow-up.

alone produced similar levels of neurological improvement in dogs with severe SCIs, relative to saline controls. At 42 days post-injury, these dogs showed robust stepping movements that were visible with tail support and many independently ambulated; saline-treated dogs either showed no movement or had minimal limb advancement without stepping. Together, these findings demonstrate that early blockade of MMPs did not improve long-term neurological recovery. Rather, DMSO alone was responsible for the beneficial outcomes in dogs with severe SCIs.

The clinical trial described here was designed to include dogs with both severe (paraplegia and absent nociception) and mild-to-moderate SCIs (non-ambulatory with intact nociception) for several reasons. First, there is an abnormal elevation of MMP-9 in serum [20], CSF [20,41] and spinal cords of dogs [42] with IVDH across a spectrum of injury severities. Second, while long-term recovery of ambulation is common (64 of 71 dogs in this trial walked independently) in the mild-to-moderate injury group, few animals normalize with reference to motor or postural scores [43]. Thus, there is an opportunity, even within animals that are likely to show marked recovery, to examine the effect of therapeutics. We chose to stratify our population based on SCI severity to examine the effect of treatment on neurologic recovery. This approach was necessary given the well-known difference in outcome between these populations (approximately 85–95% of mildly-to-moderately and 50–60% of severely injured dogs recover independent ambulation) and the potential for differential activation of secondary injury pathways based on SCI severity [30–33]. Stratification based on SCI severity is common and accepted in human clinical trials because of expected differences in recovery between injury groups and the potential impact of this difference on evaluation of effectiveness of therapies [44,45].

GM6001 is a broad-spectrum MMP inhibitor that has been shown to exert neuroprotection in rodent models of brain and SCIs, primarily via antagonism of MMP-9 associated with neutrophils [1]. Evidence supporting this position includes a temporal association between neutrophil trafficking and MMP-9

Table 1. Baseline characteristics did not differ significantly among treatment groups.

A. Continuous variables: Medians (range); P values from Kruskal-Wallis testing

Variable	Saline Controls	DMSO	Drug+DMSO	P value
	(N=38)	*(N=33)*	*(N=33)*	
Age (years)	5 (2 to 13)	5 (3 to 13)	5 (2 to 14)	0.9833
Duration of signs prior to admission (hours)	24 (1 to 48)	18 (4 to 36)	12 (2 to 48)	0.2246
*MFS**	2 (0 to 3)	2 (0 to 3)	2 (0 to 3)	0.7409
TSCIS#	4 (0 to 10)	4 (0 to 11)	4 (0 to 10)	0.5907

B. Categorical variables: P values from chi-squared testing

Variable			DMSO	Drug+DMSO	P value
		(N=38)	*(N=37)*	*(N=33)*	
Sex	**Female**	61% (23/38)	53% (19/36)	39% (13/33)	0.3039
	Male	39% (15/38)	47% (17/36)	61% (20/33)	
Neutered	**No**	16% (6/38)	22% (8/36)	18% (6/33)	0.9078
	Yes	84% (32/38)	78% (28/36)	82% (27/33)	
Breed	**Dachshund**	71% (27/35)	61% (22/36)	85% (28/33)	0.1560
	Other	29% (8/35)	39% (14/36)	15% (5/33)	
Chondrodystrophoid	**Yes**	89% (34/38)	86% (31/36)	88% (29/33)	0.9628
	Other	11% (4/38)	14% (5/36)	12% (4/33)	
Level of Spinal Cord Injury	**T12-T13**	34% (13/38)	36% (13/36)	24% (8/33)	0.6986
	T13-L1	29% (11/38)	25% (9/36)	33% (11/33)	0.8705
	L1-L2, L2-L3, or L3-L4	29% (11/38)	33% (12/36)	24% (8/33)	0.8390
T2-Weighted Hyperintensity (only available for 76 dogs)	**Absent**	62% (18/29)	76% (22/29)	50% (9/18)	0.3225
	Present	38% (11/29)	24% (7/29)	50% (9/18)	

Panel A summarizes continuous variables using medians (ranges) by group, with P values from Kruskal-Wallis tests; panel B describes categorical variables using proportions by group with P values from chi-squared testing.
* MFS = Modified Frankel Score; # TSCIS = Texas Spinal Cord Injury Score.

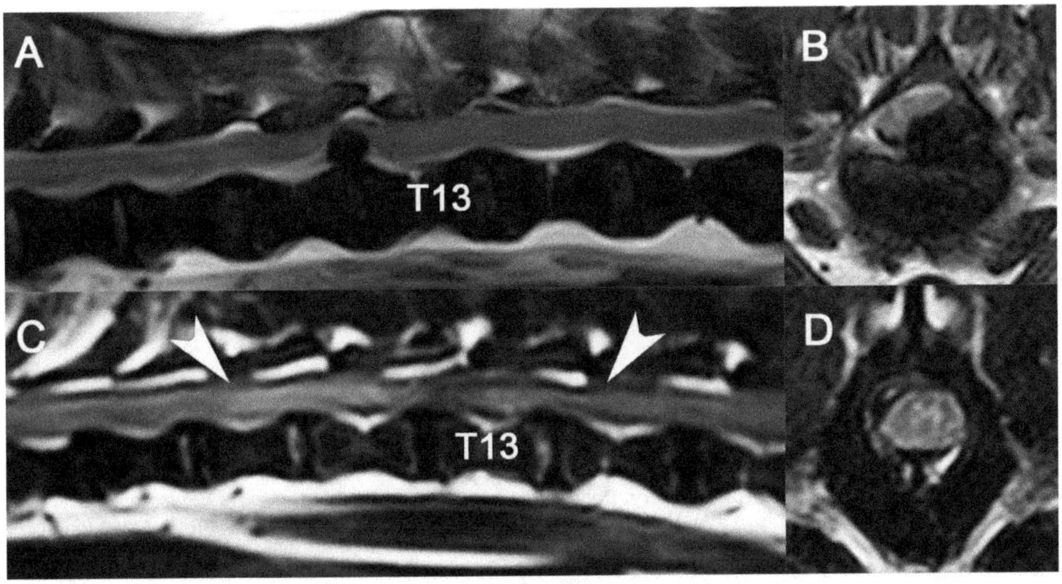

Figure 4. T2-weighted magnetic resonance images in dogs with spinal cord injuries from intervertebral disk herniation. In 1 dog (A, B) that was non-ambulatory with intact pelvic limb movement and sensation, there was focal ventrolateral spinal cord compression at the T12-T13 vertebral articulation without spinal cord signal change. A second dog (C, D) with paraplegia and absent pelvic limb deep nociception had compression at the T12-T13 vertebral articulation. There was extensive spinal cord T2-weighted hyperintensity (white arrows) visible on the sagittal image (C), suggestive of processes seen in contusion injuries such as edema, necrosis, hemorrhage, or cellular infiltrates. The transverse image (D, level of T13 vertebral body) indicated that T2-weighted hyperintensity was predominantly localized to the gray matter.

expression, reduced expression of MMP-9 in spinal cord injured mice that are neutrophil-depleted, and reduced neutrophil content within injured spinal cords of MMP-9 null mice [2,8,46]. In this study, GM6001 was delivered SC using DMSO as a vehicle. While the high prevalence of injection site reactions and route of administration may have altered drug absorption in comparison to

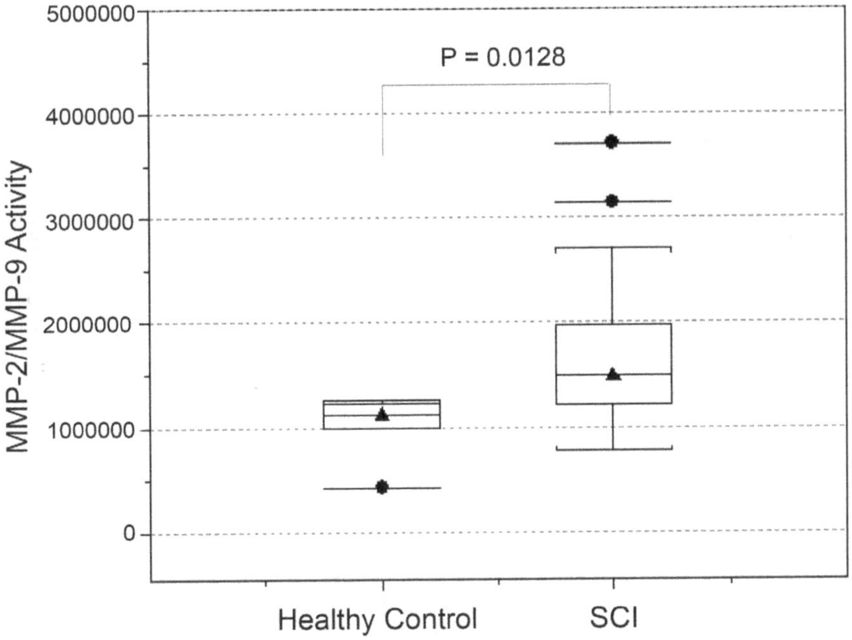

Figure 5. Serum MMP-2/MMP-9 activity in healthy and injured dogs. Box-and-whisker plots summarizing the distribution of MMP 2/9 activity for healthy control dogs (N = 5) and dogs with spinal cord injury (SCI; N = 42) that had serum collected. Values of serum MMP 2/9 activities were significantly (P = 0.0128) greater for dogs with SCI included in the trial than control dogs. The horizontal lines with triangles represent the median value; the horizontal lines at the bottom and top of the boxes represent the 25th and 75th percentiles of the data, respectively. The thin vertical lines extending up or down from the boxes to horizontal lines (so-called whiskers) extend to a multiple of 1.75 × the distance of the upper and lower quartile, respectively. Horizontal lines with circles represent values outside the limits of the whiskers.

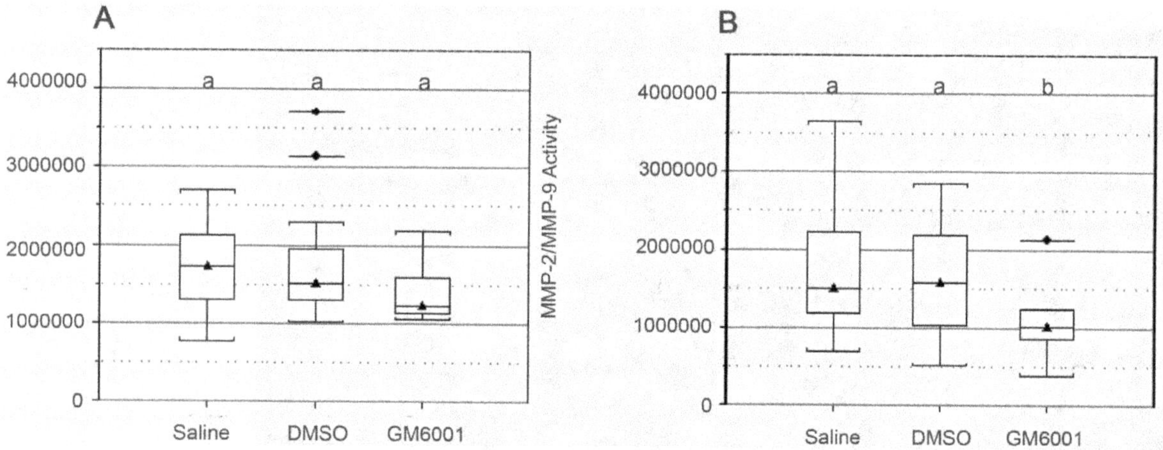

Figure 6. Serum MMP-2/MMP-9 activity pre- and post-drug delivery. Dogs were first randomized into 3 treatment groups, and serum was obtained prior to administration of saline, DMSO, or GM6001 (panel A). There were no differences in serum MMP-2/MMP-9 activity among treatment groups at the time of admission (panel A); however, at day 3, there was a significant ($P = 0.0482$) difference in serum activity between GM6001-treated dogs and the other treatment groups (panel B). See Figure 5 for a description of box-and-whisker plots. Groups marked with different letters differ significantly ($P<0.05$).

studies in other species, our data support favorable PK via SC administration of GM6001. Furthermore, relatively small plasma concentrations of GM6001 present 3 days post-delivery appear capable of modulating MMP-2/MMP-9 activity in study dogs.

Here we studied the effects of GM6001 on MMP-2/MMP-9 activity in serum. While there was no relationship between injury severity and level of MMP-2/9 activity in serum, spinal cord injured dogs showed an increase in these proteases relative to healthy controls. Moreover, the early elevation of serum MMP-2/MMP-9 activity was significantly reduced following treatment with GM6001, a finding which serves to confirm the effectiveness of the drug in reducing proteolytic activity.

While MMP-2/MMP-9 activity was detected in the CSF of injured dogs, activity did not differ between healthy control dogs and those with SCI. The lack of a demonstrable difference in CSF MMP-2/MMP-9 between SCI and control groups may reflect the inability of this assay to distinguish between the 2 proteases. Based upon an earlier study using gelatin zymography [20], MMP-2 was found to be expressed in the CSF of normal dogs and remained unchanged after SCI. In contrast, MMP-9 was only detected in

Table 2. Values of serum MMP-2/MMP-9 activity were not significantly associated with various clinical variables.

Variable	Median (Range) of MMP-2/MMP-9 Activity in Serum		P value
Age	*≤5 Years (N = 28)*	*>5 Years (N = 12)*	
	1,519,998 (1,009,205–3,708,449)	1,315,180 (769,191–2,700,981	0.1458
Sex	*Male (N = 22)*	*Female (N = 18)*	
	1,504,968 (1,009,205–3,708,449)	1,455,587 (769,191–2,700,981)	0.2625
Neutered	*Not neutered (N = 9)*	*Neutered (N = 31)*	
	1,492,947 (1,009,205–2,266,638)	1,479,017 (769,191–3,708,449)	0.5881
Breed	*Dachshund (N = 28)*	*Other (N = 12)*	
	1,411,546 (769,191 - 3,144,395)	1,528,755 (941,766 - 3,708,449)	0.4932
Chondrodysplastic	*Yes (N = 38)*	*Other (N = 2)*	
	1,474,618 (769,191–3,708,449)	1,983,362 (1,975,379–1,991,345)	0.2564
Duration of clinical signs prior to admission	*≤12 hours (N = 12)*	*>12 hours (N = 28)*	
	1,453,961 (1,009,205 - 3,708,449)	1,485,982 (769,191–3,144,395)	0.9189
	≤24 hours (N = 35)	*>24 hours (N = 5)*	
	1,492,947 (941,766–3,708,449)	1,310,144 (769,191–2,306,259)	0.5243
T2-weighted hyperintensity	*Absent (N = 20)*	*Present (N = 11)*	
	1,507,977 (769,191–3,708,449)	1,523,790 (1,062,500–3,144,395)	0.6995
MFS at admission	*≤2 (N = 22)*	*>2 (N = 18)*	
	1,455,587 (1,009,205 - 2,292,539)	1,504,968 (769,191–3,708,449)	0.4924

Medians (and ranges) and P values derived from Wilcoxon-rank sum tests are reported for the categorical variables listed above. MMP = matrix metalloproteinase; MFS = Modified Frankel Score.

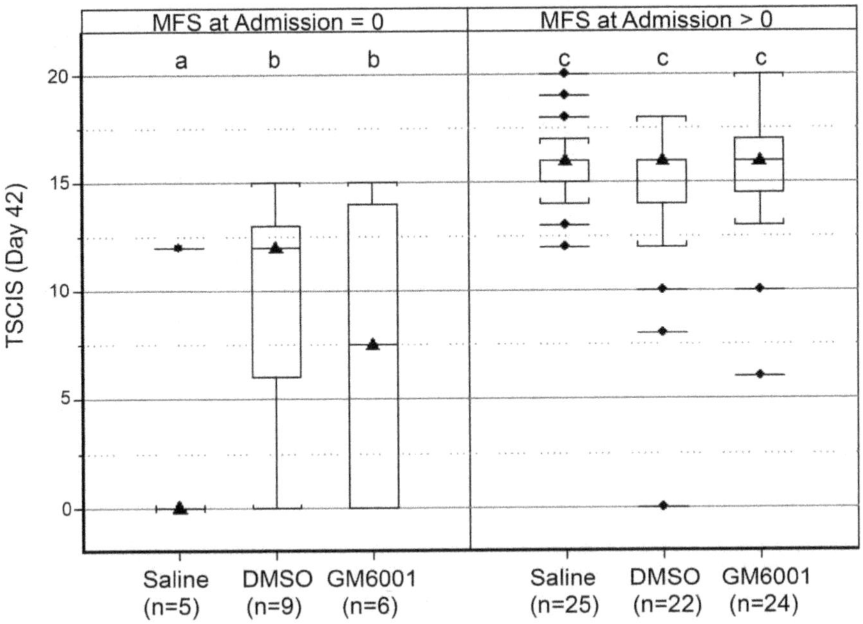

Figure 7. Evaluation of primary outcome in dogs with SCI. Box-and-whisker plots of TSCIS on day 42 by treatment group, stratified by MFS at admission (MFS = 0, left panel; or MFS >0, right panel). There were no significant differences in TSCIS among dogs with MFS score >0 (right panel), but TSCIS was significantly ($P<0.05$) greater for the GM6001 and the DMSO group than saline treated dogs with MFS = 0 (left panel). See Figure 5 for a description of box-and-whisker plots. Groups marked with different letters differ significantly ($P<0.05$).

spinal cord injured dogs [20,41]. Thus, in the current study, the absence of any differences between injured and control dogs may have been confounded by the constitutive activity of MMP-2 in CSF that may have masked any increase in MMP-9.

There are likely a number of possible explanations for why GM6001 failed to improve neurological recovery in spinal cord injured dogs. First, while GM6001 has been shown to improve neurological outcomes in various rodent models of brain and spinal cord injury [2,47,48], no studies to date have evaluated efficacy in dogs. Thus, there may be species differences in responsiveness to GM6001 and/or MMP-directed pathogenesis. Additionally, effects of GM6001 demonstrated in rodents may not

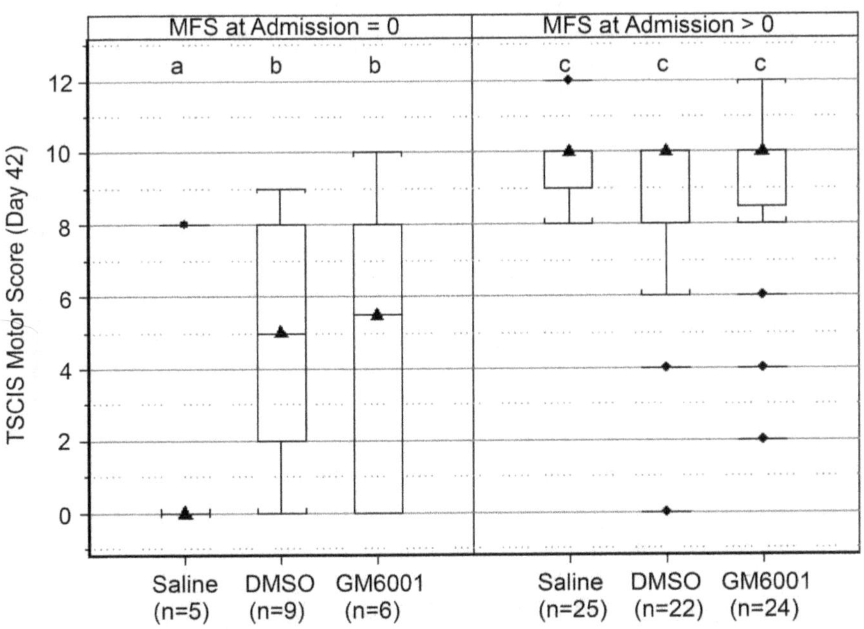

Figure 8. Evaluation of TSCIS motor score at day 42 following SCI. Box-and-whisker plots of TSCIS motor score on day 42 by treatment group, stratified by MFS at admission (MFS = 0, left panel; or MFS >0, right panel). There were no significant differences in motor score among dogs with MFS >0 (right panel), but motor score was significantly ($P<0.05$) greater for the GM6001 and the DMSO group than saline treated dogs with MFS = 0 (left panel). See Figure 5 for a description of box-and-whisker plots. Groups marked with different letters differ significantly ($P<0.05$).

be sufficiently robust to positively influence outcome under the clinical conditions of this study [49,50]. Second, the drug was active beyond the first several days post-injury and as such could have interfered with mechanisms underlying recovery in SCI. Pharmacokinetics in healthy dogs demonstrated that plasma concentration of GM6001, present at even the 96-hour time-point, approximated or exceeded that necessary to block MMP-9 *in vitro*. As some MMPs modulate the formation of a glial scar and axonal plasticity [4], their subacute/chronic blockade may result in adverse neurological outcomes. Third, the timing between SCI and administration of GM6001 may not have been optimal. The strong association between MMP-9 expression and neutrophils suggests that an optimal therapeutic window for GM6001 is defined by the early trafficking of neutrophils into the injured cord. Such a position is supported by evidence of pronounced neurological recovery when the drug was given beginning 3 hours post-injury in a murine model of SCI [2]. In dogs treated with GM6001, median delay between injury and enrollment was 12 hours, which may have exceeded the window of efficacy for GM6001. Finally, while the use of dogs with thoracic and lumbar spinal cord lesions could have influenced our ability to detect drug-related effects [51], the proportion of dogs with lumbar lesions was similar amongst treatment groups (Table 1). Additionally, the inclusion of lesion location (lumbar versus thoracic) in multivariable generalized linear modeling did not alter the significance or magnitude of observed treatment effects (data not shown).

We found that DMSO improved motor recovery in dogs with severe SCIs. This finding is perhaps not too surprising as DMSO, under defined dosing conditions, has the ability to function as a neuroprotectant [14] and in some cases when used as a vehicle, may be synergistic. In the setting of neurotrauma, neuroprotection is exemplified in a study by Di Giorgio et al [52] which compared the antioxidant curcumin, α-tocopherol, DMSO and saline in a model of traumatic brain injury. These authors reported similar levels of early neuroprotection across all agents relative to the saline control group. Beneficial effects of DMSO might also be indicated in studies where DMSO is used as a vehicle without any additional negative control group. For example, in a recent study the efficacy of an epidermal growth factor receptor inhibitor was assessed in a rodent model of SCI [53]. This inhibitor was compared against its vehicle, DMSO. Recovery of motor and bladder function was significantly greater in rats that received DMSO relative to the inhibitor. The authors concluded that the receptor inhibitor showed no efficacy relative to the "baseline" values as defined by DMSO. Based upon our study, an alternative explanation is that DMSO did not serve as the "baseline" but rather may have exerted a beneficial effect. Finally, DMSO, when co-administered with a candidate therapeutic, offers potential for synergism, by acting through separate and/or overlapping pathways. While we found no evidence of this in the current study, others have reported synergism in a model of brain ischemia where DMSO was either combined with fructose 1,6-disphosphate, an intermediate of anaerobic metabolism, or prostacyclin (PG_{I2}) which blocks aggregation of platelets and functions as a vasodilator [12,54].

The mechanisms underlying DMSO-mediated neuroprotection have been attributed to its ability to function as a free radical scavenger and suppress a variety of pathobiologic events including inflammation, calcium influx, and glutamate excitoxicity [14]. Such broad-based, temporally-defined targets may account for the extended window of efficacy (within 48 hours of injury) in spinal cord-injured dogs.

Dogs with severe SCIs and treated with either DMSO or GM6001 in DMSO showed a consistent (>80%), improvement in pelvic limb stepping. A critical question is whether this stepping was voluntary or mediated through the central pattern generator (i.e., spinal stepping). The vast majority of these dogs with motor recovery also regained pelvic limb nociception (10 of 12; 83%) and 50% walked independently (without tail support) when evaluated at 42 days post injury. These data would argue that pelvic limb movement was indeed voluntary in the majority of dogs with severe SCIs treated with either DMSO or GM6001.

In summary, while this study and others [12,13,52,54] underscore the potential utility of DMSO for the treatment of brain and SCI, there remain conflicting reports about the efficacy of DMSO. This is illustrated in recent studies reporting either no effects or reduced performance on behavioral tests after traumatic brain injury [55] and others suggesting improved learning ability in cerebellar mutant Lurcher mice [56]. As it is shrouded in controversy as a therapeutic yet commonly used as a vehicle, there is a need to rigorously evaluate DMSO from the standpoint of safety, dosing, and efficacy. Given that it is a common vehicle for drug delivery, there is opportunity to evaluate its synergistic properties. Such logic has been successfully applied to the treatment of human interstitial cystitis, where DMSO is given as part of multimodal regimen [57]. With FDA approval for the treatment of interstitial cystitis, there is potential for the repurposing of DMSO, capitalizing on its favorable properties as a solvent, in developing combinatorial therapies for SCI. The current study suggests that DMSO has an extended therapeutic window (up to 48 hours). As time to treatment for human SCI may be delayed for up to 1 to 3 days post-injury [58], a broader therapeutic window could potentially expand the population of spinal cord injured patients that would otherwise not qualify for treatments with more restricted windows of intervention.

Supporting Information

Figure S1 Rectal body temperature in healthy dogs delivered DMSO or GM6001. All dogs delivered GM6001 at 6–18 times the cumulative clinical trial dose (100–300 mg/kg six times) experienced body temperature elevations beyond normal. The elevation in body temperature qualitatively appeared greatest in dogs receiving higher doses of GM6001.

Figure S2 Drug delivery site diameters in healthy dogs receiving GM6001. Delivery site diameter appeared greatest one day after administration (panel A) and diminished by day 8 post-administration (panel B) in dogs receiving 6–18 times the cumulative clinical trial dose of GM6001.

Figure S3 Cerebrospinal fluid MMP-2/MMP-9 activity in healthy and spinal cord injured dogs. Although MMP-2/MMP-9 activity tended to be higher in dogs with spinal cord injuries ($n = 40$) than healthy controls ($n = 5$), the difference was not significant ($P = 0.5011$; Wilcoxon rank-sum test).

Figure S4 Texas Spinal Cord Injury Score (TSCIS) on day 3 following spinal cord injury. There were no significant differences in TSCIS based on treatment group for dogs with severe ($MFS = 0$) and mild-to-moderate ($MFS > 0$) spinal cord injuries. Box-and-Whiskers with different letters differ significantly ($P < 0.05$).

Table S1 Frequency of adverse events and survival (died or euthanized) by treatment group. Injection site reactions were significantly associated with GM6001 delivery, but no other adverse events were significantly associated with treatments.

Table S2 Cerebrospinal MMP-2/MMP-9 activity in dogs with spinal cord injury. Cerebrospinal fluid MMP-2/MMP-9 activity in dogs with spinal cord injury was not significantly associated with signalment, duration of clinical signs, or MFS at the time of admission. Medians (and ranges) and P values derived from Wilcoxon-rank sum tests were reported for the categorical variables.

Acknowledgments

We thank Ms. Alisha Selix for coordinating canine trial enrollment and providing technical support for canine studies. We also thank Dr. George Lemieux for advice on the inhibitor. Finally, we would like to thank Matthew Tyndall for his assistance in developing the fluorescent electrophoretic assay to detect MMP-2/MMP-9 activity.

Author Contributions

Conceived and designed the experiments: JML NDC MH VRF GJL AAT AM ZW LJN. Performed the experiments: JML GJL SCK AM LJN. Analyzed the data: NDC VRF. Contributed reagents/materials/analysis tools: JML MH AM. Wrote the paper: JML NDC MH VRF GJL SCK AAT TMF ZW AM LJN.

References

1. Zhang H, Adwanikar H, Werb Z, Noble-Haeusslein LJ (2010) Matrix metalloproteinases and neurotrauma: evolving roles in injury and reparative processes. Neuroscientist 16: 156–170.
2. Noble LJ, Donovan F, Igarashi T, Goussev S, Werb Z (2002) Matrix metalloproteinases limit functional recovery after spinal cord injury by modulation of early vascular events. J Neurosci 22: 7526–7535.
3. Wells JE, Rice TK, Nuttall RK, Edwards DR, Zekki H, et al. (2003) An adverse role for matrix metalloproteinase 12 after spinal cord injury in mice. J Neurosci 23: 10107–10115.
4. Zhang H, Trivedi A, Lee JU, Lohela M, Lee SM, et al. (2011) Matrix metalloproteinase-9 and stromal cell-derived factor-1 act synergistically to support migration of blood-borne monocytes into the injured spinal cord. J Neurosci 31: 15894–15903.
5. Shigemori Y, Katayama Y, Mori T, Maeda T, Kawamata T (2006) Matrix metalloproteinase-9 is associated with blood-brain barrier opening and brain edema formation after cortical contusion in rats. Acta Neurochir Suppl 96: 130–133.
6. Lee JY, Kim HS, Choi HY, Oh TH, Yune TY (2012) Fluoxetine inhibits matrix metalloprotease activation and prevents disruption of blood-spinal cord barrier after spinal cord injury. Brain 135: 2375–2389.
7. Lee JY, Kim HS, Choi HY, Oh TH, Ju BG, et al. (2012) Valproic acid attenuates blood-spinal cord barrier disruption by inhibiting matrix metalloprotease-9 activity and improves functional recovery after spinal cord injury. Journal of neurochemistry 121: 818–829.
8. Stirling DP, Yong VW (2008) Dynamics of the inflammatory response after murine spinal cord injury revealed by flow cytometry. J Neurosci Res 86: 1944–1958.
9. Opdenakker G, Van den Steen PE, Dubois B, Nelissen I, Van Coillie E, et al. (2001) Gelatinase B functions as regulator and effector in leukocyte biology. J Leukoc Biol 69: 851–859.
10. Kobayashi H, Chattopadhyay S, Kato K, Dolkas J, Kikuchi S, et al. (2008) MMPs initiate Schwann cell-mediated MBP degradation and mechanical nociception after nerve damage. Mol Cell Neurosci 39: 619–627.
11. Sifringer M, Stefovska V, Zentner I, Hansen B, Stepulak A, et al. (2007) The role of matrix metalloproteinases in infant traumatic brain injury. Neurobiol Dis 25: 526–535.
12. De La Torre JC (1995) Treatment of head injury in mice, using a fructose 1,6-diphosphate and dimethyl sulfoxide combination. Neurosurgery 37: 273–279.
13. De La Torre JC, Johnson CM, Goode DJ, Mullan S (1975) Pharmacologic treatment and evaluation of permanent experimental spinal cord trauma. Neurology 25: 508–514.
14. Jacob SW, de la Torre JC (2009) Pharmacology of dimethyl sulfoxide in cardiac and CNS damage. Pharmacological reports : PR 61: 225–235.
15. Levine JM, Levine GJ, Porter BF, Topp K, Noble-Haeusslein LJ (2011) Naturally occurring disk herniation in dogs: an opportunity for pre-clinical spinal cord injury research. J Neurotrauma 28: 675–688.
16. Jeffery ND, Hamilton L, Granger N (2011) Designing clinical trials in canine spinal cord injury as a model to translate successful laboratory interventions into clinical practice. Vet Rec 168: 102–107.
17. Jeffery ND, Smith PM, Lakatos A, Ibanez C, Ito D, et al. (2006) Clinical canine spinal cord injury provides an opportunity to examine the issues in translating laboratory techniques into practical therapy. Spinal Cord 44: 1–10.
18. Griffiths IR (1972) Some aspects of the pathology and pathogenesis of the myelopathy caused by disc protrusions in dogs. J Neurol Neurosurg Psychiatry 35: 403–413.
19. Smith PM, Jeffery ND (2006) Histological and ultrastructural analysis of white matter damage after naturally-occurring spinal cord injury. Brain Pathol 16: 99–109.
20. Levine JM, Ruaux CG, Bergman RL, Coates JR, Steiner JM, et al. (2006) Matrix metalloproteinase-9 activity in the cerebrospinal fluid and serum of dogs with acute spinal cord trauma from intervertebral disk disease. Am J Vet Res 67: 283–287.
21. Riviere JE (1999) Study Design and Data Analysis. Comparative Pharmacokinetics: Principles, Techniques, and Applications. Ames, Iowa: Iowa State University Press. 239–258.
22. Lammertse D, Tuszynski MH, Steeves JD, Curt A, Fawcett JW, et al. (2007) Guidelines for the conduct of clinical trials for spinal cord injury as developed by the ICCP panel: clinical trial design. Spinal Cord 45: 232–242.
23. Moher D, Hopewell S, Schulz KF, Montori V, Gotzsche PC, et al. (2010) CONSORT 2010 explanation and elaboration: updated guidelines for reporting parallel group randomised trials. BMJ 340: c869.
24. Schulz KF, Altman DG, Moher D (2010) CONSORT 2010 statement: updated guidelines for reporting parallel group randomised trials. BMJ 340: c332.
25. Dobkin B, Barbeau H, Deforge D, Ditunno J, Elashoff R, et al. (2007) The evolution of walking-related outcomes over the first 12 weeks of rehabilitation for incomplete traumatic spinal cord injury: the multicenter randomized Spinal Cord Injury Locomotor Trial. Neurorehabil Neural Repair 21: 25–35.
26. Geisler FH, Dorsey FC, Coleman WP (1991) Recovery of motor function after spinal-cord injury–a randomized, placebo-controlled trial with GM-1 ganglioside. N Engl J Med 324: 1829–1838.
27. Blight AR, Toombs JP, Bauer MS, Widmer WR (1991) The effects of 4-aminopyridine on neurological deficits in chronic cases of traumatic spinal cord injury in dogs: a phase I clinical trial. J Neurotrauma 8: 103–119.
28. Laverty PH, Leskovar A, Breur GJ, Coates JR, Bergman RL, et al. (2004) A preliminary study of intravenous surfactants in paraplegic dogs: polymer therapy in canine clinical SCI. J Neurotrauma 21: 1767–1777.
29. Levine GJ, Levine JM, Budke CM, Kerwin SC, Au J, et al. (2009) Description and repeatability of a newly developed spinal cord injury scale for dogs. Prev Vet Med 89: 121–127.
30. Ferreira AJ, Correia JH, Jaggy A (2002) Thoracolumbar disc disease in 71 paraplegic dogs: influence of rate of onset and duration of clinical signs on treatment results. J Small Anim Pract 43: 158–163.
31. Ito D, Matsunaga S, Jeffery ND, Sasaki N, Nishimura R, et al. (2005) Prognostic value of magnetic resonance imaging in dogs with paraplegia caused by thoracolumbar intervertebral disk extrusion: 77 cases (2000–2003). J Am Vet Med Assoc 227: 1454–1460.
32. Olby N, Levine J, Harris T, Munana K, Skeen T, et al. (2003) Long-term functional outcome of dogs with severe injuries of the thoracolumbar spinal cord: 87 cases (1996–2001). J Am Vet Med Assoc 222: 762–769.
33. Ruddle TL, Allen DA, Schertel ER, Barnhart MD, Wilson ER, et al. (2006) Outcome and prognostic factors in non-ambulatory Hansen type I intervertebral disc extrusions: 308 cases. Vet Comp Orthop Traumatol 19: 29–34.
34. Basso DM, Beattie MS, Bresnahan JC (1995) A sensitive and reliable locomotor rating scale for open field testing in rats. J Neurotrauma 12: 1–21.
35. Levine JM, Fosgate GT, Rushing R, Nghiem PP, Platt SR, et al. (2009) Magnetic resonance imaging in dogs with neurologic impairment due to acute thoracic and lumbar intervertebral disk herniation. J Vet Intern Med 23: 1220–1226.
36. Miyanji F, Furlan JC, Aarabi B, Arnold PM, Fehlings MG (2007) Acute cervical traumatic spinal cord injury: MR imaging findings correlated with neurologic outcome - prospective study with 100 consecutive patients. Radiology 243: 820–827.
37. Lefkowitz RB, Schmid-Schonbein GW, Heller MJ (2010) Whole blood assay for elastase, chymotrypsin, matrix metalloproteinase-2, and matrix metalloproteinase-9 activity. Anal Chem 82: 8251–8258.
38. Lefkowitz RB, Schmid-Schonbein GW, Heller MJ (2010) Whole blood assay for trypsin activity using polyanionic focusing gel electrophoresis. Electrophoresis 31: 2442–2451.
39. Lefkowitz RB, Marciniak JY, Hu CM, Schmid-Schonbein GW, Heller MJ (2010) An electrophoretic method for the detection of chymotrypsin and trypsin activity directly in whole blood. Electrophoresis 31: 403–410.
40. Mahmood I (2010) Theoretical versus empirical allometry: Facts behind theories and application to pharmacokinetics. J Pharm Sci 99: 2927–2933.

41. Nagano S, Kim SH, Tokunaga S, Arai K, Fujiki M, et al. (2011) Matrix metalloprotease-9 activity in the cerebrospinal fluid and spinal injury severity in dogs with intervertebral disc herniation. Res Vet Sci 91: 482–485.
42. Bock P, Spitzbarth I, Haist V, Stein VM, Tipold A, et al. (2013) Spatio-temporal development of axonopathy in canine intervertebral disc disease as a translational large animal model for nonexperimental spinal cord injury. Brain Pathol 23: 82–99.
43. Olby N, Harris T, Burr J, Munana K, Sharp N, et al. (2004) Recovery of pelvic limb function in dogs following acute intervertebral disc herniations. J Neurotrauma 21: 49–59.
44. Lammertse DP (2013) Clinical trials in spinal cord injury: lessons learned on the path to translation. The 2011 International Spinal Cord Society Sir Ludwig Guttmann Lecture. Spinal Cord 51: 2–9.
45. Geisler FH, Coleman WP, Grieco G, Poonian D, Group SS (2001) Measurements and recovery patterns in a multicenter study of acute spinal cord injury. Spine 24S: S68–S86.
46. Zhang H, Chang M, Hansen CN, Basso DM, Noble-Haeusslein LJ (2011) Role of matrix metalloproteinases and therapeutic benefits of their inhibition in spinal cord injury. Neurotherapeutics 8: 206–220.
47. Wang J, Tsirka SE (2005) Neuroprotection by inhibition of matrix metalloproteinases in a mouse model of intracerebral haemorrhage. Brain 128: 1622–1633.
48. Gursoy-Ozdemir Y, Qiu J, Matsuoka N, Bolay H, Bermpohl D, et al. (2004) Cortical spreading depression activates and upregulates MMP-9. J Clin Invest 113: 1447–1455.
49. Kwon BK, Okon E, Hillyer J, Mann C, Baptiste D, et al. (2011) A systematic review of non-invasive pharmacologic neuroprotective treatments for acute spinal cord injury. J Neurotrauma 28: 1545–1588.
50. Kwon BK, Okon EB, Tsai E, Beattie MS, Bresnahan J, et al. (2010) A Grading System to Objectively Evaluate the Strength of Preclinical Data of Acute Neuroprotective Therapies for Clinical Translation in Spinal Cord Injury. J Neurotrauma 28: 1525–1543.
51. Magnuson DS, Lovett R, Coffee C, Gray R, Han Y, et al. (2005) Functional consequences of lumbar spinal cord contusion injuries in the adult rat. J Neurotrauma 22: 529–543.
52. Di Giorgio AM, Hou Y, Zhao X, Zhang B, Lyeth BG, et al. (2008) Dimethyl sulfoxide provides neuroprotection in a traumatic brain injury model. Restor Neurol Neurosci 26: 501–507.
53. Sharp K, Yee KM, Steward O (2012) A re-assessment of the effects of treatment with an epidermal growth factor receptor (EGFR) inhibitor on recovery of bladder and locomotor function following thoracic spinal cord injury in rats. Exp Neurol 233: 649–659.
54. de la Torre JC (1991) Synergic activity of combined prostacyclin: dimethyl sulfoxide in experimental brain ischemia. Can J Physiol Pharmacol 69: 191–198.
55. Budinich CS, Tucker LB, Lowe D, Rosenberger JG, McCabe JT (2013) Short and long-term motor and behavioral effects of diazoxide and dimethyl sulfoxide administration in the mouse after traumatic brain injury. Pharmacol Biochem Behav 108: 66–73.
56. Markvartova V, Cendelin J, Vozeh F (2013) Effect of dimethyl sulfoxide in cerebellar mutant Lurcher mice. Neurosci Lett 543: 142–145.
57. Stav K, Beberashvili I, Lindner A, Leibovici D (2012) Predictors of response to intravesical dimethyl-sulfoxide cocktail in patients with interstitial cystitis. Urology 80: 61–65.
58. Furlan JC, Tung K, Fehlings M (2013) Process Benchmarking Appraisal of Early Surgical Decompression of Spinal Cord following Traumatic Cervical Spinal Cord Injury: Opportunities to Enhance the Time to Definitive Treatment. J Neurotrauma 30: 487–491.

Permissions

All chapters in this book were first published in PLOS ONE, by The Public Library of Science; hereby published with permission under the Creative Commons Attribution License or equivalent. Every chapter published in this book has been scrutinized by our experts. Their significance has been extensively debated. The topics covered herein carry significant findings which will fuel the growth of the discipline. They may even be implemented as practical applications or may be referred to as a beginning point for another development.

The contributors of this book come from diverse backgrounds, making this book a truly international effort. This book will bring forth new frontiers with its revolutionizing research information and detailed analysis of the nascent developments around the world.

We would like to thank all the contributing authors for lending their expertise to make the book truly unique. They have played a crucial role in the development of this book. Without their invaluable contributions this book wouldn't have been possible. They have made vital efforts to compile up to date information on the varied aspects of this subject to make this book a valuable addition to the collection of many professionals and students.

This book was conceptualized with the vision of imparting up-to-date information and advanced data in this field. To ensure the same, a matchless editorial board was set up. Every individual on the board went through rigorous rounds of assessment to prove their worth. After which they invested a large part of their time researching and compiling the most relevant data for our readers.

The editorial board has been involved in producing this book since its inception. They have spent rigorous hours researching and exploring the diverse topics which have resulted in the successful publishing of this book. They have passed on their knowledge of decades through this book. To expedite this challenging task, the publisher supported the team at every step. A small team of assistant editors was also appointed to further simplify the editing procedure and attain best results for the readers.

Apart from the editorial board, the designing team has also invested a significant amount of their time in understanding the subject and creating the most relevant covers. They scrutinized every image to scout for the most suitable representation of the subject and create an appropriate cover for the book.

The publishing team has been an ardent support to the editorial, designing and production team. Their endless efforts to recruit the best for this project, has resulted in the accomplishment of this book. They are a veteran in the field of academics and their pool of knowledge is as vast as their experience in printing. Their expertise and guidance has proved useful at every step. Their uncompromising quality standards have made this book an exceptional effort. Their encouragement from time to time has been an inspiration for everyone.

The publisher and the editorial board hope that this book will prove to be a valuable piece of knowledge for researchers, students, practitioners and scholars across the globe.

List of Contributors

Gobinda Sarkar and Robert B. Jenkins
Department of Experimental Pathology, Mayo Clinic and Foundation, Rochester, Minnesota, United States of America

Geoffry L. Curran
Department of Neurology, Mayo Clinic and Foundation, Rochester, Minnesota, United States of America

Jann N. Sarkaria
Department of Radiation Oncology, Mayo Clinic and Foundation, Rochester, Minnesota, United States of America

Val J. Lowe
Department of Nuclear Medicine, Mayo Clinic and Foundation, Rochester, Minnesota, United States of America

Feng-Yi Yang
Department of Biomedical Imaging and Radiological Sciences, National Yang-Ming University, Taipei, Taiwan
Biophotonics and Molecular Imaging Research Center, National Yang-Ming University, Taipei, Taiwan

Chia-En Ko
Department of Biomedical Imaging and Radiological Sciences, National Yang-Ming University, Taipei, Taiwan

Sheng-Yao Huang and I-Fang Chung
Institute of Biomedical Informatics, National Yang-Ming University, Taipei, Taiwan

Gin-Shin Chen
Division of Medical Engineering Research, National Health Research Institutes, Miaoli County, Taiwan

Xudong Shi, Lian-Wang Guo, Yi Si, K. Craig Kent and Bo Liu1
Department of Surgery, University of Wisconsin Hospital and Clinics, Madison, Wisconsin, United States of America

Guojun Chen, Men Zhu and Srikanth Pilla
Wisconsin Institutes for Discovery, University of Wisconsin, Madison, Wisconsin, United States of America
Materials Science Program, University of Wisconsin, Madison, Wisconsin, United States of America

Shaoqin Gong
Wisconsin Institutes for Discovery, University of Wisconsin, Madison, Wisconsin, United States of America
Materials Science Program, University of Wisconsin, Madison, Wisconsin, United States of America
Department of Biomedical Engineering, University of Wisconsin, Madison, Wisconsin, United States of America

Wenlong Gou, Xin Wang, Jiang Peng, Qiang Lu, Yu Wang, Aiyuan Wang, Quanyi Guo, Xupeng Gao, Wenjing Xu and Shibi Lu
Insistute of Orthopaedics, Chinese PLA General Hospital, Haidian District, Beijing, P.R. China

Wen-Hsuan Chiang, Wen-Chia Huang, Che-Hsu Wang and Hsin-Cheng Chiu
Department of Biomedical Engineering and Environmental Sciences, National Tsing Hua University, Hsinchu, Taiwan

Ming-Yin Shen1
Department of Biomedical Engineering and Environmental Sciences, National Tsing Hua University, Hsinchu, Taiwan
Department of Surgery, National Taiwan University Hospital-Hsinchu Branch, Hsinchu, Taiwan

Yi-Fong Huang and Sung-Chyr Lin
Department of Chemical Engineering, National Chung Hsing University, Taichung, Taiwan

Chorng-Shyan Chern
Department of Chemical Engineering, National Taiwan University of Science and Technology, Taipei, Taiwan

Gavin Dreyer and Muhammad M. Yaqoob
Department of Renal Medicine, Barts Health NHS Trust, London, United Kingdom
Department of Translational Medicine and Therapeutics, Queen Mary University of London, London, United Kingdom

Arthur T. Tucker
Ernest Cooke Microvascular Unit, Barts Health NHS Trust, London, United Kingdom

Steven M. Harwood
Department of Translational Medicine and Therapeutics, Queen Mary University of London, London, United Kingdom

Rupert M. Pearse
Department of Critical Care Medicine, Barts Health NHS Trust, London, United Kingdom

Martin J. Raftery
Department of Renal Medicine, Barts Health NHS Trust, London, United Kingdom

Renee R. Hood
Fischell Department of Bioengineering, University of Maryland, College Park, Maryland, United States of America

Eric L. Kendall
Department of Mechanical Engineering, University of Maryland, College Park, Maryland, United States of America

Mariana Junqueira, Zenaide Quezado and Julia C. Finkel
Department of Anesthesiology, Sedation, and Perioperative Medicine, Children's National Medical Center, Washington, DC, United States of America

Wyatt N. Vreeland
Biomolecular Measurement Division, National Institute of Standards and Technology, Gaithersburg, Maryland, United States of America

Don L. DeVoe
Fischell Department of Bioengineering, University of Maryland, College Park, Maryland, United States of America
Department of Mechanical Engineering, University of Maryland, College Park, Maryland, United States of America

Seungmoon Jung, Minji Bang, Byung Sun Kim and Daejong Jeon
Department of Bio and Brain Engineering, Korea Advanced Institute of Science and Technology (KAIST), Daejeon, Republic of Korea

Sungmun Lee
Department of Biomedical Engineering, Khalifa University of Science, Technology, and Research, Abu Dhabi, United Arab Emirates

Nicholas A. Kotov
Department of Chemical Engineering, University of Michigan, Ann Arbor, Michigan, United States of America

Bongsoo Kim
Department of Chemistry, Korea Advanced Institute of Science and Technology (KAIST), Daejeon, Republic of Korea

Paul R. Carney
Department of Pediatrics, Neurology, Neuroscience, and J. Crayton Pruitt Family Department of Biomedical Engineering, Wilder Center of Excellence for Epilepsy Research, Gainesville, Florida, United States of America

Malisa Sarntinoranont
Department of Mechanical & Aerospace Engineering, University of Florida, Gainesville, Florida, United States of America

Fernando Casanova
Department of Mechanical & Aerospace Engineering, University of Florida, Gainesville, Florida, United States of America
Escuela de Ingeniería Mecánica, Universidad del Valle, Cali, Colombia

Kulam Najmudeen Magdoom, Gregory L. Pishko and Malisa Sarntinoranont
Department of Mechanical and Aerospace Engineering, University of Florida, Gainesville, Florida, United States of America

Lori Rice, Chris Pampo and Dietmar W. Siemann
Department of Radiation Oncology, University of Florida, Gainesville, Florida, United States of America

Ilaria Naldi, Monia Taranta, Lisa Gherardini and Caterina Cinti
Institute of Clinical Physiology, Consiglio Nazionale delle Ricerche (CNR), Experimental Oncology Unit, Siena, Italy

Gualtiero Pelosi and Federica Viglione
Institute of Clinical Physiology, Consiglio Nazionale delle Ricerche (CNR), Pisa, Italy

Settimio Grimaldi
Institute of Translational Pharmacology, Consiglio Nazionale delle Ricerche (CNR), Rome, Italy

Luca Pani
Institute of Translational Pharmacology, Consiglio Nazionale delle Ricerche (CNR), Cagliari, Italy

Matthew Rinehart and Adam Wax
Department of Biomedical Engineering, Duke University, Durham, North Carolina, United States of America

Sheila Grab and Lisa Rohan
University of Pittsburgh, School of Pharmacy, Magee Womens Research Institute, Pittsburgh, Pennsylvania, United States of America

David Katz
Department of Biomedical Engineering, Duke University, Durham, North Carolina, United States of America
Department of Obstetrics and Gynecology, Duke University, Durham, North Carolina, United States of America

Vlad Oncescu, Seoho Lee and David Erickson
Sibley School of Mechanical and Aerospace Engineering, Cornell University, Ithaca, New York, United States of America

Abdurrahman Gumus and Kolbeinn Karlsson
Electrical and Computer Engineering, Cornell University, Ithaca, New York, United States of America

M. Carme Coll Ferrer
Department of Anesthesiology and Critical Care, University of Pennsylvania, Philadelphia, Pennsylvania, United States of America
Materials Science and Engineering, University of Pennsylvania, Philadelphia, Pennsylvania, United States of America

Vladimir V. Shuvaev, Blaine J. Zern and Vladimir R. Muzykantov
Department of Pharmacology and Center for Targeted Therapeutics and Translational Nanomedicine, University of Pennsylvania, Philadelphia, Pennsylvania, United States of America

Russell J. Composto
Materials Science and Engineering, University of Pennsylvania, Philadelphia, Pennsylvania, United States of America

David M. Eckmann
Department of Anesthesiology and Critical Care, University of Pennsylvania, Philadelphia, Pennsylvania, United States of America

Alexander V. Andriyanov, Erez Koren and Yechezkel Barenholz
Laboratory of Membrane and Liposome Research, Department of Biochemistry, Institute for Medical Research Israel-Canada, Hebrew University-Hadassah Medical School, Jerusalem, Israel

S. Nahum Goldberg
Radiology Department, Hadassah Hebrew University Medical Center, Ein Kerem, Jerusalem, Israel and Beth Israel Deaconess Medical Center, Boston, Massachusetts, United States of America

Justin T. Clark, Namdev B. Shelke, Todd J. Johnson, Eric M. Smith, Andrew K. Andreasen, Joel S. Nebeker and Judit Fabian1
Department of Bioengineering, University of Utah, Salt Lake City, Utah, United States of America

Meredith R. Clark and David R. Friend
CONRAD, Department of Obstetrics and Gynecology, Eastern Virginia Medical School, Arlington, Virginia, United States of America

Patrick F. Kiser
Department of Biomedical Engineering, Northwestern University, Evanston IL, United States of America

Juçara Ribeiro Franca, Tatiana Gomes Ribeiro, Lívia Bomfim Rodrigues, Renata Bravo, Rachel Oliveira Castilho and André Augusto Gomes Faraco
Department of Pharmaceutical Products, Federal University of Minas Gerais, Belo Horizonte, Minas Gerais, Brazil

Giselle Foureaux and Anderson José Ferreira
Department of Morphology, Federal University of Minas Gerais, Belo Horizonte, Minas Gerais, Brazil

Leonardo Lima Fuscaldi, Valbert Nascimento Cardoso and Simone Odília Fernandes
Department of Clinical and Toxicological Analysis, Federal University of Minas Gerais, Belo Horizonte, Minas Gerais, Brazil

Maria Irene Yoshida
Department of Chemistry, Federal University of Minas Gerais, Belo Horizonte, Minas Gerais, Brazil

Sebastião Cronemberger
Department of Ophthalmology and Otolaryngology, Federal University of Minas Gerais, Belo Horizonte, Minas Gerais, Brazil

Wei-liang Ye, Jiang-bo Du, Bang-le Zhang, Yan-feng Song and Si-yuan Zhou
Department of Pharmaceutics, School of Pharmacy, Fourth Military Medical University, Xi'an, China

Ren Na
West Changle Sanatorium for Xi'an Army Retired Cadres of Fourth Military Medical University, Xi'an, China

Qi-bing Mei and Ming-gao Zhao
Department of Pharmacology, School of Pharmacy, Fourth Military Medical University, Xi'an, China

Ching-Hsiang Fan, Chien-Yu Ting, Ya-Hsuan Lee and Chih-Kuang Yeh
Department of Biomedical Engineering and Environmental Sciences, National Tsing Hua University, Hsinchu, Taiwan

Tzu-Chen Yen
Department of Nuclear Medicine, Chang Gung University College of Medicine and Memorial Hospital, Tao-Yuan, Taiwan
Molecular Imaging Center, Chang Gung University College of Medicine and Memorial Hospital, Tao-Yuan, Taiwan

Hao-Li Liu, Chih-Ying Huang and Yan-Jung Ma
Department of Electrical Engineering, Chang- Gung University, Tao-Yuan, Taiwan

Kuo-Chen Wei
Department of Neurosurgery, Chang Gung University College of Medicine and Memorial Hospital, Tao-Yuan, Taiwan

Jonathan M. Levine and Sharon C. Kerwin
Department of Small Animal Clinical Sciences, College of Veterinary Medicine and Biomedical Sciences, Texas A&M University, College Station, Texas, United States of America

Noah D. Cohen
Department of Large Animal Clinical Sciences, College of Veterinary Medicine and Biomedical Sciences, Texas A&M University, College Station, Texas, United States of America

Michael Heller and Augusta Modestino
Department of Bioengineering, University of California San Diego, San Diego, California, United States of America

Virginia R. Fajt
Department of Veterinary Physiology and Pharmacology, College of Veterinary Medicine and Biomedical Sciences, Texas A&M University, College Station, Texas, United States of America

Gwendolyn J. Levine
Department of Veterinary Pathobiology, College of Veterinary Medicine and Biomedical Sciences, Texas A&M University, College Station, Texas, United States of America

Alpa A. Trivedi and Thomas M. Fandel
Department of Neurological Surgery, University of California San Francisco, San Francisco, California, United States of America

Zena Werb
Department of Anatomy, University of California San Francisco, San Francisco, California, United States of America

Linda J. Noble-Haeusslein
Department of Neurological Surgery, University of California San Francisco, San Francisco, California, United States of America
Department of Physical Therapy and Rehabilitation, University of California San Francisco, San Francisco, California, United States of America

Index

A

Acetylcholine, 51-52, 61, 75-76
Adenocarcinoma, 92, 104, 115, 146, 177
Ambulatory, 131, 206-207, 211, 213, 217
Aminolysis, 41, 43, 45-46
Analgesia, 56, 138, 157, 207
Anatomical, 15, 92-93, 101, 136, 161, 196, 198
Anesthesia, 2, 20-21, 32, 67, 78, 105, 134, 138, 141, 157, 196, 207
Angioplasty, 19-21, 25, 28, 30
Anticancer, 10, 30, 40, 46, 49-50, 103-104, 108, 110-115, 139-140, 147-149, 176, 181, 191
Antiretroviral, 116, 124, 151, 163-164
Atherosclerosis, 61, 137

B

Bandwidth, 124, 193, 195
Bimatoprost, 165-166, 169, 175
Bioadhesive, 124, 175
Bioavailability, 25, 40, 66, 103, 113, 164, 166, 173
Bioelectrical, 69-70, 72, 75
Biomacromolecules, 50, 175, 191
Biomedical, 11, 19, 30, 40, 69-70, 77, 90-91, 102, 116, 128, 138, 151-152, 155, 162, 192, 205
Biosensor, 126-129, 131
Bloodstream, 62, 65, 77, 125, 128, 132, 192, 195

C

Carbodiimide, 32, 126, 177
Carboxymethylcellulose, 119
Cardiovascular, 19, 51-52, 61, 132
Cavitation, 192-195, 197-198, 201-203
Cellulose, 39, 44, 50, 119, 124, 166-167, 175
Chemotherapeutic, 1, 4, 9, 140, 192-193, 200, 202-203
Chemotherapy, 10-11, 18, 92, 101, 113-114, 139, 149-150, 191, 203
Chondrodystrophoid, 212
Chromatograms, 107, 181-182
Cytokines, 132, 137, 205
Cytoplasm, 22, 49, 106, 108, 180, 184-185, 188

D

Decitabine, 103-104, 111-115
Defibrillators, 125, 130
Deionized, 20, 41, 118, 133, 177-179, 197, 207
Demyelination, 205
Deoxycytidine, 103, 115
Depolymerization, 177, 188
Dexamethasone, 132-133, 137-138, 175
Diagnostic, 38, 80, 113, 115, 202-203, 207-208
Dichloromethane, 156
Diethylenetriamine, 11, 15
Dimethylaminopropyl, 32, 126

E

Electrophoretic, 208, 210, 217
Electrostatic, 41-42, 46-47, 49, 135, 200
Endarterectomy, 19, 25, 28
Endothelial, 7, 9, 19-20, 25, 27-30, 50-53, 56-57, 59-61, 132-138, 192, 202, 205
Endotoxemia, 134-135, 137
Epigenetic, 103-104, 111, 113-115
Evaporation, 119, 169, 187, 193
Exogenous, 176, 183, 187-188

G

Gasselhuber, 147, 149-150
Glaucomatous, 165-166, 170-174
Glomerulonephritis, 55, 60, 137
Glycoprotein, 10, 76, 104, 132, 176

H

Haemodialysis, 59, 61
Hemorrhagic, 125, 127, 129, 131, 202
Heterogeneous, 52, 92-97, 99, 101-102
Hyaluronic, 41, 50, 165, 168, 175
Hydrochloride, 32, 41, 141, 168
Hyperplasia, 19, 23, 25-26, 28, 30, 208

I

Immersion, 119, 166
Immunodeficiency, 124, 164
Immunogenicity, 69, 176
Incubarapamycin, 21
Instillation, 149, 165, 170
Intraperitoneal, 15, 32, 141, 206
Iontophoresis, 51-53, 55, 57, 59-61

L

Lipophilic, 10, 63-67, 166

Liposomal, 18, 41, 49, 65-66, 139-144, 146-150, 176

Lysosomes, 40, 49, 133, 176, 188

M

Macrocirculatory, 53, 55

Macromolecules, 50, 77, 90-92, 101-102, 137-138, 164, 191-192

Macrovascular, 51-52, 58

Malignant, 9, 90, 102, 149, 203

Medulloblastoma, 140-141, 146, 149

Membranes, 21, 29, 41, 49, 62, 76, 78, 104, 134, 149, 171-172

Metalloproteinase, 205, 214, 217

Methyltransferases, 103, 114

Microbicide, 116, 123-124, 163-164

Microcirculation, 52-53, 55, 58-59, 61, 101

Monolayer, 132, 166, 180, 191

Mononuclear, 133, 135-137, 209

Morphology, 20, 35, 44-46, 50, 67, 133, 135, 165-166

Mucoadhesive, 166, 171-172, 175

N

Nanovehicles, 40, 46, 48

Neurodegenerative, 9-10

Neurological, 1, 69-70, 73, 77, 132, 205-207, 210-211, 215-217

Neuroprotection, 171, 174, 205, 211, 216, 218

Neutrophils, 205, 209, 211, 216

O

Oligonucleotide, 70

Ophthalmology, 165, 167, 175

Oscillation, 192, 195, 202

Osteoclasts, 31, 35, 37, 39

P

Parenchyma, 52, 77, 102, 208

Pathogenesis, 9, 31, 103, 132, 205, 215, 217

Pegylated, 63-68, 115, 139-141, 146, 149-150

Pennsylvania, 116, 132, 134, 156

Phosphoethanolamine, 141, 193

Physiological, 9, 11, 40, 69-70, 74, 76, 90, 93, 113, 125, 127-128, 130, 133, 142, 166, 188, 191, 207

Pyrimidinedione, 124, 164

R

Radiolabeling, 167, 169-170

Rapamycin, 19-23, 25-30

Reendothelialization, 20, 22, 25, 28

S

Sonoporation, 203

Spatiotemporal, 123

Spectrometer, 42, 104-105, 166

Spherical, 45, 47, 70, 93, 99, 135

Subcutaneous, 66, 141, 150, 205, 208-209

Supersaturation, 153, 164

T

Tenofovir, 116, 118-119, 123-124, 151-153, 163-164

Testicular, 102-103, 114-115

Therapeutic, 1-4, 7, 9-13, 18-20, 37-38, 40, 46, 48-49, 52, 65, 68-69, 75, 77, 90-92, 102-104, 109-115, 125, 132, 135-137, 139-140, 142-150, 164-166, 173-176, 185, 188, 191-193, 202, 216, 218

Thermodox, 140-141, 147, 149

Transducer, 15, 80, 193-195, 201-203

Traumatic, 90, 125, 131, 206, 209, 216-218

Triarylmethane, 10

Trifluoroacetic, 177-178

Triphosphate, 104-105, 108

Tuberculosis, 20, 76

U

Ultrasonic, 192, 203

Unwrapping, 117, 124

Urethanes, 151-152, 155

V

Vasculature, 1, 7, 12, 14, 93, 99, 101-102, 132, 134-135

Ventricular, 51-52, 55, 58

Vincristine, 140, 149

Viscoelastic, 80, 88, 90

Volumetric, 67, 77-78, 88-89, 131, 156

Vykhodtseva, 10, 18, 203-204

X

Xenograft, 103-105, 107, 110-114, 146, 149, 191

Z

Zetasizer, 20, 44, 67, 141

Zoledronate, 31-32, 38-39

www.ingramcontent.com/pod-product-compliance
Lightning Source LLC
LaVergne TN
LVHW080702210926
848485LV00003B/405